# China in War and Revolution, 1895–1949

In 1895 the military forces of the Great Qing empire were defeated by Japan. The stakes seemed modest – a struggle for supremacy in peripheral Korea – but the defeat prompted an explosion of radical reform proposals in China and the beginning of elite Chinese disillusionment with the Qing government. In a larger sense, it also prompted five decades of struggles for power and efforts to strengthen the state and the nation, to democratize the political system, and to build a fairer, more cohesive and unified society.

This book weaves narrative together with thematic chapters that pause to address in depth central themes of China's transformation. While the book proceeds chronologically, the chapters in each part examine particular aspects of these decades in a more focused way, using the social sciences and cultural studies as well as providing a narrative history. *China in War and Revolution* draws a picture of the personalities, ideas, and processes by which a modern state was created out of the violence and trauma of these decades.

**Peter Zarrow** is Associate Research Fellow at the Institute of Modern History, Academia Sinica, Taipei, Taiwan.

## Asia's transformations
Edited by Mark Selden
*Binghamton and Cornell Universities, USA*

The books in this series explore the political, social, economic, and cultural consequences of Asia's transformations in the twentieth and twenty-first centuries. The series emphasizes the tumultuous interplay of local, national, regional, and global forces as Asia bids to become the hub of the world economy. While focusing on the contemporary, it also looks back to analyse the antecedents of Asia's contested rise.

This series comprises several strands:

*Asia's transformations* aims to address the needs of students and teachers, and the titles will be published in hardback and paperback.
Titles include:

**Debating Human Rights**
Critical essays from the United
States and Asia
*Edited by Peter Van Ness*

**Hong Kong's History**
State and society under colonial rule
*Edited by Tak-Wing Ngo*

**Japan's Comfort Women**
Sexual slavery and prostitution
during World War II and the US
occupation
*Yuki Tanaka*

**Opium, Empire and the Global
Political Economy**
*Carl A Trocki*

**Chinese Society**
Change, conflict and resistance
*Edited by Elizabeth J Perry and
Mark Selden*

**Mao's Children in the New China**
Voices from the Red Guard
generation
*Yarong Jiang and David Ashley*

**Remaking the Chinese State**
Strategies, society and security
*Edited by Chien-min Chao and
Bruce J Dickson*

**Korean Society**
Civil society, democracy and the state
*Edited by Charles K Armstrong*

**The Making of Modern Korea**
*Adrian Buzo*

**The Resurgence of East Asia**
500, 150 and 50 year perspectives
*Edited by Giovanni Arrighi,*
*Takeshi Hamashita and*
*Mark Selden*

**Chinese Society, 2nd edition**
Change, conflict and resistance
*Edited by Elizabeth J Perry and*
*Mark Selden*

**Ethnicity in Asia**
*Edited by Colin Mackerras*

**The Battle for Asia**
From decolonization to globalization
Mark T. Berger

**State and Society in 21st Century China**
*Edited by Peter Hays Gries and*
*Stanley Rosen*

**Japan's Quiet Transformation**
Social change and civil society in the
21st century
*Jeff Kingston*

**Confronting the Bush Doctrine**
Critical views from the Asia-Pacific
*Edited by Mel Gurtov and*
*Peter Van Ness*

**China in War and Revolution, 1895–1949**
*Peter Zarrow*

*Asia's Great Cities*

Each volume aims to capture the heartbeat of the contemporary city from multiple perspectives emblematic of the authors own deep familiarity with the distinctive faces of the city, its history, society, culture, politics and economics, and its evolving position in national, regional and global frameworks. While most volumes emphasize urban developments since the Second World War, some pay close attention to the legacy of the longue durée in shaping the contemporary. Thematic and comparative volumes address such themes as urbanization, economic and financial linkages, architecture and space, wealth and power, gendered relationships, planning and anarchy, and ethnographies in national and regional perspective.

Titles include:

**Bangkok**
Place, practice and representation
*Marc Askew*

**Beijing in the Modern World**
*David Strand and Madeline*
*Yue Dong*

**Shanghai**
Global city
*Jeff Wasserstrom*

**Hong Kong**
Global city
*Stephen Chiu and Tai-Lok Lui*

**Representing Calcutta**
Modernity, nationalism and the
colonial uncanny
*Swati Chattopadhyay*

**Singapore**
Wealth, power and the culture of
control
*Carl A. Trocki*

*Asia.com* is a series which focuses on the ways in which new information and
communication technologies are influencing politics, society, and culture in
Asia. Titles include:

**Japanese Cybercultures**
*Edited by Mark McLelland and*
*Nanette Gottlieb*

**The Internet in Indonesia's New**
**Democracy**
*David T. Hill & Krishna Sen*

**Asia.com**
Asia encounters the internet
*Edited by K. C. Ho, Randolph Kluver*
*and Kenneth C. C. Yang*

*Literature and Society* is a series that seeks to demonstrate the ways in which
Asian Literature is influenced by the politics, society and culture in which it
is produced. Titles include:

**The Body in Postwar Japanese**
**Fiction**
*Edited by Douglas N Slaymaker*

**Chinese Women Writers and the**
**Feminist Imagination, 1905–1948**
*Haiping Yan*

*Routledge Studies in Asia's Transformations* is a forum for innovative new
research intended for a high-level specialist readership, and the titles will
normally be available in hardback only. Titles include:

1. **The American Occupation of**
   **Japan and Okinawa***
   Literature and memory
   *Michael Molasky*

2. **Koreans in Japan***
   Critical voices from the margin
   *Edited by Sonia Ryang*

3. **Internationalizing the Pacific**
   The United States, Japan and the
   Institute of Pacific Relations in
   War and Peace, 1919–1945
   *Tomoko Akami*

\* Now available in paperback

*Critical Asian Scholarship* is a series intended to showcase the most important individual contributions to scholarship in Asian Studies. Each of the volumes presents a leading Asian scholar addressing themes that are central to his or her most significant and lasting contribution to Asian studies. The series is committed to the rich variety of research and writing on Asia, and is not restricted to any particular discipline, theoretical approach or geographical expertise. Titles include:

# China in War and
# Revolution, 1895–1949

**Peter Zarrow**

Routledge
Taylor & Francis Group

LONDON AND NEW YORK

First published 2005
by Routledge
2 Park Square, Milton Park, Abingdon, Oxon OX14 4RN

Simultaneously published in the USA. and Canada
by Routledge
270 Madison Ave, New York, NY 10016

*Routledge is an imprint of the Taylor & Francis Group*

Typeset in Times New Roman by Taylor & Francis Books
Printed and bound in Great Britain by Antony Rowe Ltd,
Chippenham, Wiltshire

*British Library Cataloguing in Publication Data*
A catalogue record for this book is available from the British Library

*Library of Congress Cataloging in Publication Data*
Zarrow, Peter Gue
  China in war and revolution, 1895–1949 / Peter Zarrow. – 1st ed.
  p. cm. – (Asia's transformations ; 1)
    1. China–History–1861-1912. 2. China–History–Republic, 1912-
1949. I. Title. II. Series.
  DS761.Z37 2005
  951.04–dc22
                        2004023492

ISBN 0–415–36447–7 (hbk)
ISBN 0–415–36448–5 (pbk)

T&F informa
*Taylor & Francis Group is the Academic Division of T&F Informa plc.*

# Contents

# Illustrations

## Maps

## Tables

## Figures

# Preface

Over the first half of the twentieth century China experienced profound changes, some violent, many slow and unobtrusive. This book explores the meaning of these changes for the Chinese people in the context of efforts to create a strong and modern nation-state. I hope to illuminate the dynamic and often conflictual interplay between authority and liberty, locality and center, society and state, revolution and stability, and utopianism and pragmatism in modern China.

This book approaches the understanding of Republican China not as a straightforward narrative but as a synthesis that weaves narrative together with thematic chapters that pause to address in depth central themes of China's transformation. While the book proceeds chronologically, the chapters in each part examine particular aspects of those decades in a more focused way: chapters shift back and forth among politics, social relations, thought, foreign affairs, economics, and other topics. This work, then, is a kind of anti-textbook, avoiding a single storyline. What holds it together is a series of recurring motifs that span the epoch and beyond. By examining the different-colored threads, we can see how the coat was put together.

In the final decades of the nineteenth and the early decades of the twentieth century, China's ancient dynastic political system and the social structure that supported it collapsed amid foreign intervention, war, and economic dislocation. Millions of Chinese struggled for survival – for dignity for themselves and their families, and sometimes for their nation. This nation itself had to be created. Although, as we will see, various versions of Chinese identity had long existed, it was in the beginning of the twentieth century that intellectuals and activists first attempted to define a Chinese nation through a mix of ideas about race, culture, and history. These exciting ideas struck a chord among the educated classes and urban groups; eventually they spread among the peasantry as well. Meanwhile, the Revolution of 1911 overthrew the Manchu Qing dynasty, spelling the end to the dynastic system, and attempts to found a republican state followed. The Qing was overthrown in the name of Chinese nationalism, as its Manchu rulers came to be seen as foreign invaders who had swooped out of the northeast forests to conquer China two-and-a-half centuries earlier. For most Chinese before 1911, the Qing dynasty was simply the latest in a series of some twenty-plus royal houses that could be traced back in "orthodox succession" for over two thousand years. Like all the dynasties before it, the Qing ruled not in the name of the people but in its own name.

This proved intolerable to increasing numbers of people in the last years of the dynasty. They wanted a strong government that would represent the interests of the Chinese. The Republic founded in 1912 thus linked nationalism to democracy. For educated groups – such as the growing numbers of students, military men, professionals, and merchants – these were ideas to be fought over as much as fought for. And by the 1920s urban workers and many rural communities had become significant political actors as well, and they too pressed for their own ideas of community and justice. Nationalism redefined those who counted, or who should count, as members of the political community. It called attention to the question of how a weak and fragmented China was to defend itself against foreign threats that had menaced it since the nineteenth century. And it inevitably became intertwined with the question of social justice – how power and wealth were to be generated and distributed within China.

Struggles over building a new kind of government were thus concerned with *how* the members of the political community were to behave – which members should have what rights and duties. This was contested against the pressing need for a strong state to resist foreign threats and outright invasion. War stalked these decades, leaving no city, village, or family untouched, and with enormous implications for the new sources of power – and resistance – that emerged. Foreign imperialism and outright invasion, civil war, regional and clan violence, and banditry all played roles in destroying the old social structure and opening the way for new contenders for power to emerge. China was also drawn further into the world economy during these decades, which encouraged urbanization, especially along the eastern coast, and opened the way to new cultural interactions and social change.

Almost all the political movements of these decades spoke in the name of democracy, which naturally meant different things to different groups at different times. Democracy sometimes referred to electoral systems or the promise of elections (in the manner most familiar to Westerners), but it also referred to all sorts of mass mobilization and various rights regimes from civic rights to economic security. In the early decades of the twentieth century new social groups – for example, women, workers, merchants, minority peoples, and "patriots" of all kinds – demanded a political voice. Urban elites used both nationalism and democracy to justify their challenges to dynastic power and later against would-be state-builders. Democracy, social justice, and nationalism became powerful currents among workers and peasants as well, shaping the course of a long revolutionary struggle. China's revolutionaries fought against the heavy weight of traditional habits and morals and against the new power-holders that emerged in the course of the Republican era.

Concepts of "nation" and "democracy" were thus arenas of struggle between competing social and political groups. At the same time, the state-building efforts and experiments that marked the first half of China's twentieth century claimed to be strengthening the nation and creating democracy: indeed, usually strengthening the nation *by* creating democracy. However, the liberatory and utopian impulses seen in social movements like communism, anarchism, feminism, and, for that matter, democracy could also be restricted by the claims of national unity and the suppression of resistance to state or corporate power. Chinese nationalism was shaped by a sense of humiliation in the face of repeated foreign intrusions and invasions. Leaders and people were also acting to *restore* historic greatness. They understood China as a land of ancient glory. To survive and prosper, however, it needed new institutions. Above all it needed new citizens, to be shaped into a cohesive whole by common institutions like schools, the law, military service, and state propaganda. Much of this book, then, traces in theory and practice attempts to universalize schooling, standardize the language, remake the legal system, and generally strengthen government.

Nationalism and democracy could work at cross purposes. Leaders criticized democracy as an invitation to disunity and inefficiency. Critics of the government had to defend their patriotism – though they might also attack the government precisely for not protecting the nation's interests. The conflictual elements among and between nationalism and democracy cannot be denied; however, at the same time, the link between them was not merely hypocrisy or pipe dream. The entire logic of the nation-state in a system of competing nation-states rested on the mobilization of the people. While the old dynastic state had been largely content to leave the people to their own devices as long as they paid their taxes, the new nation-state needed their enthusiastic cooperation. This book examines China's struggles to create citizens. Citizenship, then, understood as a combination of rights and duties, also combined nationalism and democracy. Nationalism demanded the creation of citizens: people who identified themselves with the political community. And so to be a citizen was to have a stake in that community. In addition to such political questions, this book also examines changing attitudes toward the family, desire, sexual relations, leisure, and the body itself (how it was carried and clothed for example), which bear upon the issue of citizenship and much else besides.

Centered on these motifs, this book promiscuously borrows from the methodologies of the social sciences, cultural studies, and empirical historicism. The reader I have in mind does not necessarily know anything about China but is willing to splash around in a few well-known events and at times to swim in deeper waters, considering the whys, hows, and potential alternatives of those events.

A note on romanization: I use the Hanyu pinyin system of romanization throughout this text with two exceptions: in some references to Taiwan, where the Wade–Giles system is in general use; and in retaining the better-known non-Mandarin versions of names of such individuals as Sun Yat-sen (in Mandarin, Sun Yixian or Sun Zhongshan) and Chiang Kai-shek (Jiang Jieshi). I follow the Chinese practice of giving the surname (family name) first.

Recommended readings, chapter questions, and other resources related to this book can be found at: http://www.routledge.com/textbooks/isbn0415364485

# Acknowledgements

This book has taken over a decade to write. I am grateful to people who have read various drafts, some of them so long ago they probably don't remember (but I hope I do). Political scientists, sociologists, historians, and civilians have all been generous with their time. I thank Pamela Crossley, Bruce R. Dickson, Li Hsiao-t'i, Richard Lufrano, Pan Kwang-che, Thomas Allen Schwartz, David Shillieto, and Young-tsu Wong for reading all or parts of the manuscript at various stages. The detailed comments of David Buck and John Fitzgerald on the penultimate draft have improved the final text immeasurably. Ellen Neskar and Ari Borrell also gave me emotional support as well as the use of a printer in Taipei at an embryonic stage. Institutions that have aided this project while I was supposed to be conducting other research include the Foundation for Scholarly Exchange (Fulbright–Hays program) of Taipei; the University Research Council of Vanderbilt University; the Center for Chinese Studies, Taipei; the Institute for Advanced Study, Princeton, and the Institute of Modern History, Academia Sinica. In the final stages the sensitive copy-editing of Rosemary Carstens was invaluable, and the ever-organized and accurate aid of my assistant, Ching-yi Jodie Hung, saved me months of labor. Above all, I am grateful for the careful, critical readings of Mark Selden, whose editor's pen has greatly strengthened my language and arguments. I of course remain responsible for remaining errors and prejudices.

# Part I

# The road to revolution, 1895–1919

Telling time is a matter of politics, religion, and worldview. When Christian Europeans started to date events from the birth of Christ about 1,200 years ago, they began thinking in units of 100 and even 1,000 – hence the importance of millennia to the Western imagination. Chinese, however, demarcated time in terms of a 60-year cycle and also in terms of imperial reigns. When the Boxer rebels invaded Beijing, therefore, to Westerners the year was 1900 but to Chinese it was Guangxu 28 (the 28th year of the reign of the Guangxu emperor) or the gengzi year of the 60-year cycle scheme. Few Chinese thought of 1900 as a turning point – the end of one century and the beginning of another – but many educated Chinese felt their society and culture had already entered a fateful decline. Japan's shocking defeat of Chinese troops in Korea, and of the Chinese navy in 1895 (or the jiawu year), had provoked furious self-reflection. It prompted a movement of radical reform that was, however, defeated by conservative court officials in 1898. Indeed, looking back, we might say most of China's nineteenth century saw conflicts between reformism and conservatism.

Massive peasant rebellions that broke out at the end of the great emperor Qianlong's reign were finally suppressed in the early 1800s. But the treasury was empty and foreign incursions were becoming more menacing. Opium, imported to China by the British, was spreading, and wars and peasant rebellion were to mark the century. Historians see the nineteenth century – or in Chinese terms, the period after Qianlong – as a time of dynastic decline and a failure to confront problems. Yet the cultural confidence of China's elites was so great that these problems, though recognized, did not prompt a truly fundamental reappraisal of the culture until Japan's military victory in 1895. And most conservatives were not forced to agree to reforms until the disaster of the Boxer Uprising five years later. The Western year of 1900 began with the usual patterns of life proceeding as pretty much normal in most of the country. The spring planting gave every reason to expect good harvests, and regional and international trade continued to give employment to hundreds of thousands, even millions.

As "normal" as 1900 may have seemed on the surface, a popular anti-foreign movement in the northern countryside was rapidly spreading out of control. Unlike the rest of the country, the north was experiencing a prolonged drought. Calling themselves "Boxers United in Righteousness," thousands of peasants joined armies of men (and not a few women), who attacked local missionaries and Chinese Christians and unsteadily made their way to the capital, Beijing.[1] Why did they object to Christians? And why was the event to prove a milestone for Chinese political elites who lived in a different world from the Boxers?

## A prologue: The Boxers

Angry and scared, the Boxers spread out of northwestern Shandong Province into adjoining Zhili, the capital province, as well as Henan, Shanxi, and even Inner Mongolia and Manchuria. Rooted in north Chinese popular culture and without central organization, the Boxers produced hundreds of local bands rather than a centralized army. In the winter of 1899–1900, these community-based bands began to go on the move. By the spring, the Boxers were burning down Christian churches and looting convents, and they collected money and grain from local elites who either supported or feared them. Soon all foreigners, and foreign things such as railway tracks, became targets. A good many Boxers ended up in Beijing and Tianjin by June, and they virtually occupied these cities, though, again, in such an unorganized fashion that in Beijing the foreign legation quarter was able to withstand a siege until help arrived in August. Meanwhile, the Qing imperial court, after much indecision, decided to support the Boxers and declared war on the foreigners in June – but basically it had lost control of the situation.

It was the decision of the Empress Dowager Cixi to support the Boxers, but in fact the government remained divided. A number of powerful officials understood that success against Westerners would be worse than failure – that is, it would invite certain retaliation. Still, faced with the murders of missionaries in several provinces and the siege of the foreign legations in Beijing, the Western Powers and Japan put together an army that handily defeated both Boxers and Qing forces. Most Boxers then slipped back into the anonymous population. The Qing court, including the Empress Dowager and the Emperor, put on ordinary commoners' blue cotton clothing and, so disguised, fled Beijing in a donkey cart as the foreign invaders arrived.

In the end, over 200 foreign missionaries and many thousands of Chinese Christians were killed in the initial Boxer attacks across north China; in the fighting between June and August nearly 800 foreigners and countless thousands of Boxers and Qing troops were killed. Many Chinese died as the foreign troops moved through hundreds of villages between the coast and Beijing, looting, raping, and burning along their route. The conquest of Beijing was followed by mopping-up operations carried out by Japanese and Western troops, who punished whole communities for former Boxer activities.

How could all this happen? The practices and beliefs of the Boxers were rooted in the popular culture of North China, and the long-simmering disputes between those Chinese following the traditional gods and the new Christians created flashpoints. As drought devastated the countryside in the late 1890s, thousands of farm boys with no crops to take care of learned the Boxer rituals that they believed would make them invulnerable to swords and bullets. Meanwhile, although missionaries and Chinese Christians had their own prayers for rain, the prayers to the traditional gods were going unheeded, it was said, because of the pollution of the Christians. Many Chinese Christians refused to join their neighbors in what had traditionally been community rituals. The crops continued to whither. Rumors told of Christians poisoning village wells. Moreover, stories spread about foreign missionaries and their traitorous Chinese followers. They were said to be devils who practiced incest, raped at random, and tore out the eyes and organs of Chinese for their evil magic: in other words, the embodiment of all that the people feared.

> No rain comes from Heaven.
> The earth is parched and dry.
> And all because the churches
> Have bottled up the sky.[2]

During the more than four decades of Christian proselytizing in the countryside, tensions between Chinese villagers and Western missionaries had often erupted. Missionaries were known to interfere in disputes over land or water rights, thus challenging one of the traditional prerogatives of local elites as well as upsetting villagers. If a Christian and a non-Christian argued about straying pigs, the missionary could pressure officials to find in favor of the Christian. Missionaries took complaints to their embassies, which in turn directly pressured the Qing government to force the hands of those local officials. It is probably not an accident that the origins of the Boxers can be traced to western Shandong, where a particularly aggressive order of German Catholics had alienated the local population. When two missionaries were murdered at the end of 1897, Germany's Kaiser Wilhelm was glad to have such a splendid excuse for seizing the port of Jiaozhou to further build up the German presence in Shandong.[3] Meanwhile, more and more young men banded together under religious and martial arts masters to learn the rituals that would make them invulnerable. In a word, these consisted of ways to call upon the gods to take possession of one's body, turning it into an indestructible fighting machine. It is in this sense we can say that the Boxers were rooted in popular culture. Normally, god-possession was reserved for a few professional healers, fortune-tellers, or mystics, and ordinary Chinese could be as skeptical of charlatans as anyone. But that it was possible for the gods to play a role in the lives of humans no one doubted.

The Qing court, like all imperial governments, would have normally cracked down on a mass movement that made unsanctioned use of the gods. But the Qing's best forces had recently been mauled in the Sino-Japanese war of 1895, and at first the early Boxer groups seemed to offer a way for communities to protect themselves in ways the Chinese imperial system had long countenanced. Boxer-type groups began as inward-looking village defense militia rather than outward-moving aggressors. And the Boxers themselves claimed that they were loyal to the Qing. Some high officials in the Qing court, including probably Cixi herself, wondered if there might not be something to the Boxers' magic, or at least to their determination, morale, and enthusiasm.

The Allied Expedition of Western and Japanese troops that captured Tianjin and Beijing was determined simultaneously to "punish" the Qing while leaving it in power. Severity was measured. The British, for example, targeted the Summer Palace on the grounds that it belonged to the emperor and its destruction and plunder would not hurt ordinary people. On the other hand, discussing the need to avenge the murder of the German minister to the Qing court, Kaiser Wilhelm commented, "Just as the Huns, a thousand years ago, under the leadership of Attila, gained a reputation by virtue of which they still live in historical tradition, so may the name of Germany become known in such a manner in China that no Chinese will ever again even dare to look askance at a German."[4] Pro-Boxer officials were executed – like the governor of Shanxi, who had offered forty-four missionaries and their families refuge from the Boxers and then had his troops kill them. But Cixi was spared to return to Beijing and lead the government.

The "Boxer Protocol" imposed on the Qing in 1901 fined the government 450 million taels of silver (just under US$334 million) to be paid over thirty-nine years at an interest rate of 4 percent (bringing the grand total to almost 1 billion taels).[5] This was real money. Annual Qing revenues were only about 250 million taels. It meant that the Qing had to turn over to direct foreign control the last remaining revenue sources of any significance: maritime customs, native customs (i.e. internal transit taxes), and the salt tax.[6] The Qing also promised to build monuments to the dead missionaries and to the German minister killed in Beijing. Military restrictions were imposed on the Qing, and the foreign military presence was increased. The Boxer Protocol thus had a lasting significance, further weakening the Qing state and increasing the powers of foreigners in China. The Boxers also marked a critical point in Chinese history; only after the humiliation of the Qing's defeat did the imperial court turn to reform in earnest. Its reform policies, put into place once Cixi was back in Beijing, began the modern state-building and nation-building enterprises that marked China's twentieth century.

Much of the Boxers' importance lay in the images they left. While the conflagration they lit burned hotly, it was soon enough put out, leaving a few hundred foreigners and thousands of Chinese dead. Life on the north China plains soon returned to normal, but for Londoners, New Yorkers, and Berliners reading about the fate of their brave missionaries and soldiers in faraway benighted China, the Boxers represented everything fearful, evil, and dark in the world: that is to say, the mirror image of the Boxers' views of the foreigners. The Boxers, then, unknowingly contributed to the age of the "yellow peril" that did so much to sell newspapers at the turn of the century. In the Hollywood version, the role of imperialism and drought in creating the Boxers is scarcely shown. In *55 Days At Peking*, a 1963 color epic lasting some two-and-a-half hours, a ruggedly handsome Charlton Heston and an intrepid David Niven lead the besieged Westerners – including a stunningly beautiful and self-sacrificing Ava Gardner – until help arrives. Although the Empress Dowager makes an appearance in the cast of thousands, the audience does not see much of the Boxers themselves. The Boxers are a mere social force, a "wind" destined to pass destructively but quickly.

For the Chinese, the Boxers became something of a mirror in which what you saw depended mostly on who you were. The historian Paul A. Cohen has elegantly pointed to the ways the Boxers were "mythologized" by later generations.[7] The Boxers could be read forward or backward. Forward, they patriotically stood for Chinese resistance against the forces of imperialism. They showed peasants standing up for themselves: they foreshadowed the revolution to come. Backward, they displayed ignorance and superstition. Supporters of the feudal dynasty of the Qing: they represented reactionary impulses. Modern-looking Chinese elites were convinced of the Boxers' backwardness and took them as proof for the need for a complete national regeneration. It is worth noting, however, that these same elites agreed that if the masses were educated and properly mobilized they could become fit citizens of a modern state. This education in citizenship became a central task of the Chinese elite.

For some Chinese, on the other hand, the Boxers showed what could be done through hope, faith, and organization. As anti-imperialist nationalism strengthened in the 1920s, the Boxers were reclassified as patriots. In this view, the central problem facing China was not the ignorant masses or their superstitions; the problem was the forces of imperialism pressing down on the whole country. One way to think about this is to ask: what is worth remembering? The "superstitions" of the Boxers or the gross injustice of the Boxer Protocol? Chinese patriots accused British soldiers of greater barbarism than the Boxers ever displayed. Communists even tended to romanticize the Boxers as patriotic Robin Hoods.

Of course, the Boxers cannot be summed up as either (simply) superstitious and feudal or as (simply) progressive and patriotic. They show us much that was important in twentieth-century China. Consider these elements: the missionary presence in rural areas, which disrupted traditional power relations; the political economy of acute scarcity in the north China plains; the direct interference of the foreign powers (gunboat diplomacy, "unequal treaties"); the complex political pressures on the Qing court and on local officials; the vulnerability of the peasant economy to flood and drought; the hopefulness and resolution of reforming elites; a culture with the capacity to turn toward violence; and popular resources of resistance. Above all, the Boxers foreshadowed the politicization of the Chinese masses. Looking backward, they resembled the vast peasant armies of bandits and warlords (and occasionally future emperors) that passed like massive storms but with no way to reshape the political or social structure. But looking forward, they offered a glimpse of how ordinary people – under the right circumstances – could not only affect historical trends but also consciously join political movements.

## The state of China at the dawn of the twentieth century

The Boxers thus offer a way into China's twentieth century. In 1900 some 80 percent of a population of about 400 million tilled the land. On the surface the rhythms of rural China scarcely seem to have changed even today. The rice paddies of the south and the wheat and barley fields of the north are tilled so intensively that to Westerners Chinese agriculture looked more like gardening than farming. Until about 1750 or 1800, China's "average" standard of living was probably slightly superior to Europe's; it declined slightly but steadily over the course of the nineteenth century. *Relatively speaking*, however, compared to per capita growth rates in Europe and North America, the Chinese economy, like that of most of the rest of the world, declined dramatically in the nineteenth century. The peace that the Qing rulers had made in the seventeenth century, the development of agricultural techniques, and China's advantageous participation in world trade had encouraged the population to increase from about 100 million in the late 1600s to well over 300 million in 1800. By that point, severe pressures were building as, essentially, too many people tried to divide up too little land. Landlord–tenant relations worsened, and an ecologically disastrous cycle of over-planting and soil erosion occurred.

At the same time, silver began to flow out of China: nine million taels annually by the 1830s to pay for opium imports from British India. The result was especially hard on farmers, whose rents and taxes increased (these were paid in silver, which farmers had to buy with the currency of daily life, copper). British troops defeated Qing defenders in the on-again, off-again series of battles known as the Opium War (1839–42): beginning the process by which China would be forced to accommodate foreign demands for more open trade, diplomatic exchanges, missionaries, foreign troops, indemnities, and after 1895 direct foreign investment. The Qing rulers thus lost control of an economy tied to international trade and capital flows. The first two decades of the twentieth century did not see economic crisis in overall national terms, though local crises were destabilizing. But neither did they see the accumulation of capital necessary for a qualitative leap into industrialization. Per capita GNP was still only 60 yuan (US$200–250).

The role of imperialism on the Chinese economy has been subject to considerable dispute, the terms of the debate ranging from the view that imperialism caused Chinese backwardness by preventing the natural development of the economy, to the view that it stimulated economic growth and progress. Analytically, foreign economic penetration (trade and investment) should be distinguished from the economic impact of essentially political decisions like imposing indemnities on China or taking over customs collection. These actions, whatever their economic impact, also weakened the Qing and Republican governments. Such political consequences also affected the economy as physical, legal, and even moral infrastructure was destroyed. It thus seems fair to conclude that, whether international trade disrupted or improved the Chinese economy (or both), the overall impact of imperialism was disastrous. Running a favorable balance of trade into the early nineteenth century, and with the government virtually debt-free before the Sino-Japanese War of 1894, by the time of the 1911 Revolution, China's foreign debt was a staggering 900 million taels. Anywhere from a quarter to a third of government revenue went to repay foreign debts and indemnities.

At the level of perceptions, the Chinese at the turn of the century were beginning to understand imperialism as a growing web that threatened to smother them. The foreign missionary, the foreign businessman, the foreign diplomat, and the foreign soldier were parts of a single enterprise dedicated to the exploitation of China. And laws preventing immigration by Chinese to America and Australia were even more widely resented. It is significant that railroads – that great nineteenth-century symbol of progress, domination over nature, and opening the land – were seen by some Chinese as symbols of foreign aggression: pushing China into debt, as the government borrowed foreign funds to build them; giving foreign goods and foreign troops easy access to the interior; throwing people out of work; and allowing foreign troops to move quickly across the nation. No wonder the Boxers tore up railroad tracks.

The forms of imperialism were many and various. After Britain's victory in the Opium War, *extraterritoriality* protected foreigners from Chinese law everywhere, and *treaty ports* fell under foreign administration.[8] By 1890 thirty-three cities were open to foreign trade and residence, and between 1894 and 1917, 59 more were added to the list (missionaries could legally set up missions anywhere after the 1860s, while businessmen were supposed to get a passport to travel inland). Not all the treaty ports housed sizeable foreign populations, but sixteen cities contained *concessions* which foreigners and their home governments directly administered: mini-colonies in effect beyond the jurisdiction of the Chinese government. The largest concessions were in Shanghai. In 1898 China granted five *leaseholds* or more extensive territories:

- to Germany, Jiaozhou Bay in Shandong and over 500 square kilometers of the surrounding region, plus the right to build railroad lines and quarry mines, for 99 years;
- to Russia, the Liaodong peninsula in southern Manchuria, for 25 years, plus the right to build a railroad line from Port Arthur to Harbin and exploit timber and mines along it;
- to France, Guangzhouwan port in the southeast, for 99 years;

- to Britain, the New Territories opposite Hong Kong (already made a supposedly permanent British colony after the Opium War), for 99 years; and also
- to Britain, Weihaiwei port, "for as long a period as Port Arthur shall remain in the occupation of Russia."

The role of great power rivalry is obvious here. This rivalry ensured that no single Power would colonize China. Naturally enough, Chinese grew afraid that foreigners would simply carve up their land. The Powers also lay looser claim to *spheres of influence*: areas dominated by one of the Powers through a combination of treaty rights and de facto military presence. Spheres of influence coincided with economic penetration: Britain dominated the lower and central Yangzi River valley and the Guangzhou area (from Hong Kong); France, from its colonial base in Vietnam and Cambodia, claimed influence across southern China in the provinces of Yunnan, Guizhou, and Guangxi; and Germany, Russia, and Japan vied to control the north, until Japan defeated Russia in 1905 and Germany lost World War I. Japan dominated Manchuria and much of Inner Mongolia as well, officially turning Korea into its colony in 1910 and taking Shandong from Germany in 1914. The following year the Chinese government gave Japan a 99-year lease to the Liaodong Peninsula and railroad concessions. The United States, demanding an "open door" through which all the Powers could trade with China on equal terms, maintained a significant naval presence on the rivers as well as along the coast. It was Britain, however, that held the system together, at least until World War I. British domination of the lower Yangzi gave it the key to inland China, and Britain's economic confidence was the basis of a policy that tolerated the presence of the other Powers in China. In other words, Britain opposed any nation claiming exclusive economic rights in a given part of China and supported a unified Chinese state.

Some tens of thousands of foreigners were living in China by 1900; over 400,000 by 1920, including Japanese, Korean, and Russian civilians moving into Manchuria to mine, log, and farm. Missionaries made their way into most of China's counties. In the wake of the Boxer Uprising, the numbers of foreign and Chinese Roman Catholic priests and nuns climbed to over 5,000, and the total number of Catholics rose from 721,000 at the turn of the century to 2 million by 1920. The number of Protestant missionaries also climbed, to over 6,600, claiming 345,853 followers. Various Protestant denominations maintained over 1,000 mission stations; both Catholics and Protestant founded schools. At the turn of the century, the French dominated the Catholic missions and the British the Protestant, though by 1920 Americans had come to dominate Protestant missions. By this time many Protestant missions were paying less attention to saving the heathen from Hell and were more concerned with the "social gospel" of improving people's lives on earth: medical work, famine relief, recreational programs, and schools and literacy work.

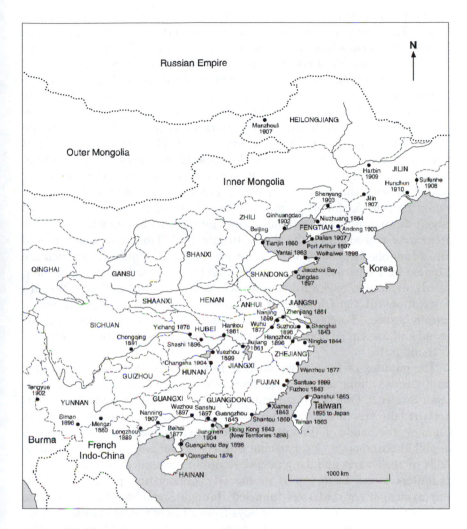

*Map 1* China's treaty ports

The post-Opium War treaties of the 1840s first opened five ports to foreign merchants and diplomats. Over the following decades, more coastal and riverine cities were opened. In some of these cities, "concessions" were established where foreigners were essentially self-governing beyond the laws of the Qing and the later Republic of China. As well, less formal but much broader "spheres of influence" were guaranteed by the right to send warships and armies into the interior. The most important spheres of influence were those of Britain in Hong Kong and Guangzhou (Canton), and especially Shanghai, Hankou, and the Yangzi Valley; France in Guangzhou Bay and Fujian; Russia and Japan in the northeast; and Germany and Japan in Shandong.

*Source*: Courtesy of Geospatial Information Science Team, Computing Center, Academia Sinica.

The Chinese Marxist category of "semi-colony" for China is therefore fitting. The foreign presence was limited, and China was not anybody's full colony – but so much of it was under the partial control of so many of the Powers, it became like a colony. Chinese felt they were being colonized, and the foreigners felt like colonizers. Foreign nationals carried their extraterritoriality with them wherever they went – they were literally beyond Chinese law, civil as well as criminal. Foreign firms were freed from Chinese taxes, and foreign banks issued their own currencies. Foreign military forces and missionaries could and did move around at will. The Chinese governments were often not even consulted about the disposition of a variety of problems. Bilateral agreements between the Powers could determine where railroads would go and who would own them, and how the spheres of influence would be run. As for those parts of the old Qing Empire that remained largely autonomous and culturally non-Chinese, vast but mostly non-arable areas were picked up on the cheap: Britain took Tibet and Russia moved into Mongolia. At the same time, for all the racist contempt in which the Chinese were regarded – the usual colonial litany of such adjectives as lazy, greedy, dishonest, backward, and malicious are not hard to find in Western descriptions of the Chinese – the nation and its peoples still aroused a certain respect. Foreigners noted its huge size and large population, its proud and ancient civilization, and they wondered about its future potential as friend or foe.

The paradox of the foreign presence in China was that it was simultaneously overwhelming and inconspicuous. The vast majority of Chinese never saw a foreigner. Only a tiny percentage of Chinese converted to Christianity. Yet virtually everyone felt the impact of the economic changes coming to China at the hands of the foreigners. Jobs were gained and lost according to global economic cycles. Farming households suffered when the spinning skills of their wives and daughters were no longer needed, but gained when daughters found factory jobs in the city. Guangzhou porters lost their employment when trade was funneled through Shanghai after the Opium War, but there were more jobs for boys from Zhejiang. And gradually thousands of Chinese learned how to manage modern banks and hospitals, build new industrial enterprises and financial institutions, run newspapers and publishing houses, and, in sum, build a modern economy.

Under the combination of internal and external strains, then, the dynastic system began to fall apart. The Revolution of 1911 can only be understood in the context of foreign imperialism. But it had deep domestic roots as well, and its centrality to modern Chinese history cannot be exaggerated. The first part of this book, Chapters 1 through 7, deals with the causes and effects of the revolution. Although later generations of Chinese saw the revolution as incomplete, it was the pivotal event in breaking a whole set of assumptions and prejudices: the sacrality of the emperor, the pre-eminence of the gentry class, and the importance of classical learning for elites. The entire cultural and religious symbolism of power was severely disrupted.[9] Intellectual radicalism played a defining role in the revolution and, indeed, throughout the century. Our story thus begins with the Sino-Japanese War of 1894–5 and the 1895–1911 period of ferment. It continues through the revolution and the attempts through the 1910s to build a new government, a new society, and even a new culture. Time itself was restarted in 1912 – which became Year One of the Republic.

# 1 The rise of Confucian radicalism

At the end of April, 1895, Kang Youwei, a 37-year-old aspiring candidate to high government, drafted a petition to the emperor demanding that the Qing refuse to surrender to Japan and that it immediately undertake a series of fundamental reforms. Shocked equally by China's defeat at the hands of the Japanese in Korea and by the harshness of the Treaty of Shimonoseki, about 1,200 of the candidates who had come along with Kang to Beijing for the highest-level civil service examinations (*jinshi*) signed the petition. This was equivalent to a mass protest. The signers risked the wrath of the Qing court, which had, after all, committed itself to the treaty and did not countenance criticism.

According to the treaty, the Qing would pay 200 million taels in indemnities; recognize Japan's pre-eminence in Korea; cede Taiwan and the Pescadores to Japan; open four more treaty ports; and grant Japan the right to build factories around any treaty port. Through most-favored-nation clauses in earlier treaties, the other Powers automatically received the same rights. Looking forward, we can see that the war thus opened China to direct foreign investment: this became a major route for modern technology to reach China. As foreign investments grew – almost $800 million in 1902 and well over $1.5 billion by 1914 – the Powers found themselves with a stake in China's economic stability. The war also marked Japan's rise as a Pacific power in its own right. Looking back, we can see it as one of a string of defeats China had suffered since the 1840s, each defeat giving the foreign powers greater commercial, religious, diplomatic, and even territorial rights. But this particular defeat was especially shocking since China – after several decades of "self-strengthening" modeled on Western technology – had expected to win the war. It was even more shocking because Chinese officials had long perceived Japan as an insignificant island on the periphery of Chinese civilization.

In this chapter I outline the basis of the 1895 protest movement and the political typhoon it provoked, and I try to show why this period marks the origins of modern politics and culture in China. What "modern" suggests here is the first of a series of calls to enlarge political participation, a process that involved rethinking how the Chinese state should be structured. In addition, as Kang Youwei (1858–1927) was aware, the older generation of political leaders had little sense of the enormous economic, technological, and cultural dynamism of Western civilization, the cut-throat rivalries of the nation-state system, the relentless nature of progress, or the need to reform China's most fundamental institutions to employ national energies more efficiently. The movement Kang spearheaded looked backward to Chinese tradition for sources of inspiration, sideways to Europe and Japan for models that could be utilized, and forward, against its own original intentions, to the overthrow of a dynasty that proved unable to reform quickly enough.[1] Kang and his generation of Confucian radicals wished to combine loyalty to the Confucian values and worldview that they had been raised on with loyalty to the emperor; loyalty to the emperor with loyalty to a reformed Qing system; and loyalty to the Qing with loyalty to the nation, the Chinese people as a whole. They began to ask new questions: Who was the nation? How were the Chinese people to be defined? Did loyalty to the nation mean support for strong government? What kind of government?

"Confucian radicalism" – though it may sound like an oxymoron – signifies strident calls for thorough-going reform based on readings of the Confucian classics and made by men (women had not yet found a political voice) educated in the Confucian tradition. If these men called for a measure of Westernization, it was a program none the less rooted in a Confucian view of the world. They wanted China to become strong, standing unchallenged among the sovereign powers. They wanted, in other words, to be able to pick and choose what foreign ideas they would adopt. However, in the rapid expansion of imperialist threats against China after 1895 the fear was that these foreign powers would "carve up China like a melon" and even that the Chinese people might perish. Hopes and fears thus meshed to produce an atmosphere of unimaginable tension. In 1895, though, even the younger generation of educated Chinese gentlemen still had few doubts about the fundamental legitimacy of their culture.

Their immediate political challenge was that mere examination candidates, even experienced, mature men like themselves, did not have the right to petition the emperor. Neither the emperor nor the Empress Dowager, Cixi, who actually controlled the court, saw Kang's petition, since Beijing officials confiscated it. It was lengthy (nicknamed the "ten-thousand-word memorial"), and its real point went beyond the demand for continued resistance against Japan, significant as that was. Kang and his cohorts were demanding a fundamental reordering of the entire political system. A few of the most insightful of the younger gentry understood something of the power of national unity. Tang Caichang, soon to become one of Kang's followers, wrote his brother in 1895: "You cannot stand alone as a scholar and despise them [the peasants] as the ignorant masses. If you first gain their hearts, in the future when war comes, you will have help in the midst of confusion."[2] Kang's petition called upon the government to promote industry; modernize the army; build railroads, a postal system, and a merchant marine; employ "good men," even using the talents of the Overseas Chinese (mostly lower-class merchants but technically and commercially skilled); and improve agriculture through training schools. Today, such reforms may not sound particularly radical, but they envisioned a much more active government than any China had seen before. The petition did not shrink from calling on the government to raise taxes. More tellingly, the reformers envisioned an active citizenry: people not just dedicated to their families and local community good but to fueling China's growth and progress.

Kang Youwei was from Guangdong Province, near Guangzhou (Canton), the city where the modern Western presence had been felt for the longest time. His background is described by the historian Jerome Grieder: "born into a solid gentry family, an heir to the great culture … he set out at an early age to become what in fact he became, in his own estimate at least: a Confucian Sage."[3] From an early age, Kang appointed himself to save humankind, and although he studied the Confucian classics and Buddhism and read many Western works in translation, he can only be understood as a religious leader, not a scholar. After a period of intense study in 1878, when he was twenty-one, he experienced a breakdown, followed by an awakening. As Kang later recollected:

> While sitting in meditation, I suddenly saw that the ten thousand creatures of Heaven and Earth and I were all of the same body; a great light dawned, and I believed I was a sage: then I laughed with joy. Suddenly I thought of the sufferings of life: then I cried with melancholy. Suddenly I thought of the parent I was not serving – how could I be studying? – then forthwith I packed up and went back to dwell by his grave.[4]

Kang succeeded in passing the 1895 *jinshi* exams. Leaving Beijing that autumn, Kang and his disciples, most notably Liang Qichao (1873–1929), quickly went on to establish new "study societies" designed to turn young, educated Chinese into a potent political force. With revealing names like the "Society for the Study of National Strength" a number of similar groups formed libraries, schools, and publishing projects, sometimes under the auspices of sympathetic provincial governors. Their journals called for ever more radical reforms: notions of parliamentary democracy, "popular power," and equality began to be aired.

The radical Confucians' main goal was to "unify" the emperor and the people. Thus parliaments were not thought of as bodies representing diverse interests, much less conflicting wills, but as locations where "communication between top and bottom" would be established and consensus reached. The old Confucian faith in community solidarity was thus given fresh institutional guise. But the sense that non-officials, even commoners, should *participate* in the affairs of state was a sign of the radicalism of the day. The "people" were emerging into Chinese public consciousness as a force in their own right. Who the people were exactly remained to be determined, but the Confucian radicals looked to them with hope. The Confucian classics spoke of *minben* – the people as the basis of the state – saying that the duty of the ruler was to feed and clothe his people, since the kingdom would collapse without them. *Minben* was thus a rather paternalistic morality of the elite and also a practical tool. Although the reformers saw *minben* as the cultural basis on which real democracy might be built, the Confucian *minben* had never allowed for the people's active political participation. In other words, it represented an ideal of rulership *for* the people, but not *of* or *by* the people. The Confucian radicals did not regard themselves as mere commoners and, in their calls for the court to expand the political processes, they had themselves mostly in mind. Still, the reformers understood that in the new world of imperialism and competing nation-states, the people had to be incorporated into the political life of the community. The first to preach this doctrine was Liang Qichao.

## Calls for institutional reform

Liang was a precocious student of Kang who went on to become the leading spokesman for reform in the decade leading up to the 1911 Revolution. Liang was more sober-minded than Kang, and he emerged as a reform leader when he was still in his twenties. His "General Discussion of Reform," published serially in 1896 and 1897, called for the government to encourage ideas from below and to expand the educational system – including girls' schools – rapidly. These ideas amounted to calling for the restructuring of Chinese society. For example, Liang foresaw the replacement of the hoary examination system, one of the most fundamental institutions of imperial China, with a system of mass education. He praised the reforms of Meiji Japan that had established a school system based largely on a Westernized curriculum. Liang thought the Chinese people too "ignorant" and "aimless" to immediately be given power, so he supported top-down reforms, but there should be no mistaking his ultimate intentions. In calling for a kind of gentry democracy, Liang was challenging the political monopolies of the court and the bureaucracy. Furthermore, Liang's published criticisms of the "despotism" of the monarchical system were pointed if indirect. He criticised emperors who had isolated themselves from the people and selfishly refused to take care of them. In a private letter he frankly explained his views:

> The strength of a nation stems ultimately from democracy. This is the nature of democracy. Monarchism is simply selfishness while democracy is simply public-mindedness. "Public-mindedness" is the ultimate standard of governance while "selfishness" is rooted in humanity.[5]

And privately, to his students, Liang raised the treasonous question of whether the Qing rulers, as foreign Manchus, could lead the necessary reforms.

By the summer of 1898 Cixi was in semi-retirement and the reformers finally won the ear of the Guangxu emperor, her nephew. They fought to streamline the bureaucracy and to strengthen the powers of the emperor so he could push through reforms – ideas that aroused enormous opposition from vested interests. The emperor announced his intention to listen to all good ideas, but the reform proposals stopped well short of a parliament, a constitution, or other democratic institution-building. Still, the specter of outside challenges to the intertwined interests of the Manchus, the court, and the bureaucracy had suddenly emerged from the shadows.

Many historians feel this was China's last chance to "enter the modern era without revolution."[6] Others think this view vastly overblown, a reflection of the propaganda spread by the reformers after their defeat. At any rate, the Guangxu emperor did issue a stream of decrees and edicts over the summer of 1898. He reformed the examination system to emphasize current affairs over the classics, he converted Buddhist monasteries to public schools, he abolished Manchu sinecures and many government positions, and he established new bureaus of commerce, industry, and agriculture. The army and navy were to be modernized. And, in a kind of vindication of Kang's temerity of 1895, low-level officials and even ordinary literati were encouraged to send memorials directly to the emperor.

The reforms challenged not only officeholders but the great majority of educated Chinese whose livelihoods, educations, and cultural assumptions were all threatened. Some officials and Manchu aristocrats felt the dynasty itself was in jeopardy. And the vast bureaucracy took no steps to carry out Guangxu's wishes, instead waiting inert for the reaction of his aunt, Cixi. Guangxu's remaking of the Chinese state was only a revolution on paper.

Cixi had been the dominant political figure in China since the 1870s, balancing reformist and conservative officials without ever committing the court fully to either side. Originally a minor concubine of the Xianfeng emperor, Cixi had provided him with his only son. After Xianfeng's death in 1861 in the wake of the first British invasion of Beijing, with the help of some powerful royal allies, she was able to gain a share of power as de facto regent for her son. Cixi cemented her powers in 1875 when her young nephew was named the Guangxu emperor after her son's death. None the less, as Guangxu entered his twenties, Cixi began to step into the background. She was apparently content with the new reformist agenda, at least when it first began in 1898.

However, by the end of the summer, after Guangxu had begun firing important officials and promoting his own men, fearing for her own position and perhaps believing court rumors that the reformers were plotting to overthrow the Manchus, Cixi acted. Indeed, by this time the reformers were looking for a way to eliminate her, asking the reforming military leader Yuan Shikai to help them. He, however, reported the plot, and on 21 September she announced her resumption of power. Cixi in effect staged a coup, putting the emperor under house arrest. She had Guangxu's supporters cashiered and six reformers executed without trial – a rare event that shows how frightened the court was. She even ordered Kang Youwei's family graves destroyed. There would have been more deaths, but Kang Youwei and Liang Qichao, among others, managed to escape with help from foreign legations. Guangxu was kept under a kind of house arrest for the rest of his life, living on a small island in the Forbidden City's lakes. By the end of the week, virtually all the emperor's reforms were revoked. A new era of reaction was instituted as, after the coup, the court fell more firmly than ever into the hands of conservatives who were to prove sympathetic to the Boxers.

The crisscrossing lines of historians' debates have divided those sympathetic to Guangxu and the radical reform effort from those sympathetic, if not to Cixi and reaction, at least to a better-planned reform program; those who feel Kang was a strong influence on Guangxu and the reform from those who think his role was smaller; those who blame Kang for causing disorder from those who think he was trying to shore up the failing dynasty; those who see the events of 1898 as political infighting between court supporters of Cixi and Guangxu from those who see 1898 as about more significant issues; and those who see in 1898 a real break with the past from those who see more continuity with the "self-strengthening" program of the earlier generation. Generally, most historians agree that Kang's influence on the emperor and the imperial camp was crucial to giving the reforms their thoroughgoing edge, and that while the reforms were not well planned, they were in historical fact defeated by the coup led by Cixi, a woman skilled in court intrigue but ignorant of the world. In other words, an old story: goodguy reformers versus evil reactionaries.

Revisionists have struck at this view from a variety of perspectives. One issue they all raise is the problems in the accounts of the events of 1898, written by Kang and Liang as part of their attacks on the Qing.[7] However, to pick holes in the Kang–Liang story of good versus evil is not the same as proving that an essentially different chain of events transpired. Even if not true in every detail, the standard version of 1898 influenced the attitudes of contemporaries and later generations alike. How Liang Qichao's interpretation of events became mainstream history and how it played to existing prejudices (that women should not hold power, for example) is a fascinating story in its own right.[8] But the immediate point is that even the most sympathetic approach to Cixi cannot make her into a great reformer in an era when reforms were plainly necessary. If she was not the monster of traditional image, neither was she capable of providing China dynamic leadership.

Cixi was wrong to think that Kang Youwei was trying to subvert the dynasty, but he did want – eventually – to turn the Qing into a constitutional monarchy. At the same time, Kang urged Guangxu to act as forcefully as Japan's Meiji Emperor or Russia's Peter the Great. The problem was that, although Cixi was not entirely opposed to reform, her political career was based on balancing reformist and conservative impulses in the court and among the military. Reforms had thus been left largely to individual provincial governors, some of whom built new schools and military arsenals, developed mines and railroads, and streamlined administration – and some of whom did not. Yuan Shikai was himself a proponent of reform, but that did not mean he was willing to risk turning the government over to inexperienced and untried men. In 1898 Guangxu was willing to go beyond the leisurely and piece-meal reforms of the previous two generations, no doubt in part because this provided an avenue for advancing his power, and Kang Youwei provided the intellectual inspiration for policy reforms. However, when it came to the diffi-cult question of implementing reforms, neither Kang nor Guangxu had much political experience. Kang's arrogance and self-righteousness discouraged strategic alliances. The Beijing bureaucracy was strongly conservative, and by September leading officials apparently convinced Cixi that Guangxu's actions were threatening the dynasty. Both sides mobilized their forces, and both appealed to Yuan Shikai. Thus did the reform movement come to a literally bloody end.

Kang Youwei had offered Guangxu a new kind of monarchy. Ultimately, through a constitution and a parliament, Guangxu could achieve the ideals established by the ancient sage-kings. The emperor was to form "one body" with the people, as a sacred symbol but not possessing many real political powers. Kang explained that in a parliamentary system "the ruler and the citizens discuss the nation's politics and laws together."[9] The parliament made the laws, legal officials adjudicated them, and the government admin-istered them. "The ruler remains in general charge." But apparently has little to do. Perhaps, then, Cixi was right to see the reformers as a direct threat, but the Confucian sage-ruler (and his sage-adviser) appear alive and well in Kang's vision.

The reason why Chinese still remember the hundred days of reform – as witnessed by public discussions held around China on its hundredth anniver-sary in 1998 – is precisely because Kang and Liang made it the opening chapter of an ongoing drama of change and redemption for the Chinese nation. The "hundred days" suggested that China might adopt a fast, top-down route to modernity. This dream scarcely died with the martyrs of 1898.

The defeat of the reforms in September 1898 led directly to the Boxer Uprising. The Boxers, of course, had their own pressing concerns, having nothing to do with court politics or gentry intellectuals. But they achieved importance on the national – and international – stage solely because of the court's toleration. Like modern historians, conservative court officials inter-preted the 1898 reform movement in terms of foreign influences. The Boxers seemed, just possibly, the answer to this problem. Ironically, however, the convincing defeat of the unorganized Qing forces, Cixi's humiliating escape from Beijing, and the general failure of the conservatives' response to the reformers, resulted in a real reform program after 1901.

The Qing's "New Policy" reforms differed little from the proposals of 1898, now no longer seen as so radical. The bureaucracy was to be stream-lined, new schools built, a modern infrastructure developed; within a few years, the old examination system was to be abolished and a constitution put into place. By this time, the Qing faced continuous pressure to do more, faster. Impatient reformers like Liang Qichao still castigated the Qing for not moving fast enough; and in many towns and cities across China local elites, often reading Liang and other "radicals," were pressing for their own rights to political participation. Outright revolutionaries were claiming that the Qing reforms were merely a trap designed to fool the Chinese into accepting a foreign, Manchu court's continued misrule. Before we turn to these struggles in Chapter 2, the rest of this chapter will examine the political and cultural background of the reform movement.

## Confucian radicalism in political context

As political activists demanding to be heard, Kang Youwei and Liang Qichao pointed forward to the twentieth century. They demanded that the political realm be expanded to all educated men. But to understand them, we must also look at the milieu from which they emerged. The traditional literati expected respect and power to accrue to themselves, first on the basis of their participation in Confucian culture – their mastery of sacred classic texts – and second, more clearly, on the basis of their examination success. For the successful individual, schooling led to taking a series of exams, often over twenty years or more, and eventually to degree status, prestige, and office. This is one of the dreams Kang Youwei had for himself. There were essentially three sets of exams of increasing difficulty. First, the county-level exams produced a relatively large number of *xiucai*, "budding scholars"; then the provincial-level exams produced a much smaller number of *juren*, "raised candidates"; and finally the metropolitan exams (held every three years in Beijing) produced a few dozen *jinshi*, or "literati presented" to the emperor for appointment. In 1895 Kang Youwei and Liang Qichao were *juren* come to Beijing to try to become *jinshi*. That the student (Liang) had begun passing the exams at a much younger age than his teacher (Kang) denoted his precocious brilliance, but did not affect their master–disciple relationship, if only because everybody understood that the exams were in part a lottery. Even though the quotas were kept low, by the late Qing there were too many educated men passing the exams for the government to employ them all. Many became teachers (like Kang), or secretaries to high officials, or went into business, managed their family's properties, wrote books, pursued antiquarian researches, retired to genteel poverty, or perhaps even joined the revolution. Yet whatever their careers, all such men were members of an elite culture that revolved around classical learning.

Moreover, all the members of this culture learned the dictates of Confucian morality. Morality was based on a hierarchical vision of society and emphasized ritual conduct. Inequality was natural: as Heaven stands above the earth, so men above women, fathers above sons, and emperors above their subjects. There were obligations on both sides: essentially, the lower owed loyalty and obedience to the higher, the higher were to take care of and love the lower. The gentry who studied the classics and took the exams that the government organized assumed they were responsible for the social order. For one, the imperial government did not have enough officials to take care of all the tasks that governments now perform. The scholars thus became natural community leaders in the villages and towns across all China. This role was confirmed by the Confucian classics, which called on men of "virtue" to lead, and by history, which repeatedly proved their indispensability in resolving disputes between neighbors, in raising funds to build dikes or raise militia, in teaching the masses how to behave. A deep-seated sense of social responsibility was something that shaped even the most anti-traditional Chinese intellectuals.

It must be stressed that Confucian morality was by no means restricted to a small minority. Rather, since basic literacy was fairly widespread, various popularized versions of Confucianism dominated most levels of Chinese society. For example, although Confucius himself condemned "profit" and valued the peasantry, in a way often found among elites in agrarian societies, merchants still found much of value in the Confucian tradition. Guides on how to morally achieve commercial success proliferated during the Qing.[10] They even promised that the ambitious businessman could make money and be a gentleman at the same time. Many of the most basic values associated with Confucianism like filial piety – the duties owed by children to their parents – might simply be called Chinese. It is also worth noting that the high Confucian world was not restricted by birth; nearly all male subjects of the Empire could legally take the exams. Where boys had to work from an early age, they had no time for the necessary training, but economic mobility could eventually lead a family's descendants to exam success. Only a few despised castes and professional groups such as boatmen and actors were banned from the exams; lower-level government workers such as constables, tax prompters, and office clerks were banned as well, presumably in order to keep such a potentially powerful but non-classically trained group in order.

A man *might*, if he were talented and lucky, pass the county exams in his early twenties; the provincial in his late twenties or early thirties, thus perhaps qualifying for office after a period; and the metropolitan exams any time between thirty and death, which might lead to immediate appointment in the Outer Court. By 1850, of the men qualified to take them, only 0.05 percent would pass the provincial exams. Memorization of the standard texts began by the age of five. Of course, the vast majority of such men came from quite privileged backgrounds or had wealthy relatives who could sponsor the long years of schooling that were required. A few prominent families managed to produce exam successes across five centuries, which also suggests the social stability of late imperial China. This was in some ways a grim world of arid pedantry, whole lives blighted in futile attempts to please the examiners year after year. But it could also be an exciting world: intellectually dynamic, open to sensuous and literary experience, and with the promise of prestige, wealth, and power.[11]

The group of exam-aspirants comprised at least several million men. Highly acculturated "Confucians" represented about 5 percent of the population.[12] Their world was marked by mastery of a difficult literary language, and its members shared a refined manner and etiquette. Even the low-ranking "budding scholars" were allowed to wear clothing that set them off from the masses. They won certain legal privileges, including immunity from judicial torture and some tax exemptions. But official status was no guarantee of morality, honesty, or even much capacity to earn a living. Higher officials wore minutely graded marks of their status, earned generous salaries, and could usually count on receiving even more generous gifts from supplicants. All were "gentry," a term that refers to two overlapping categories in the English-language literature on China. First, it is a translation of the Chinese *shenshi*, which was essentially a legal category denoting precisely those who had passed the exams; second, it refers in a broader way not only to these men but also their families, perhaps even down to a third generation, and even more broadly to families with simply the wealth, education, and manners necessary to adopt the gentry lifestyle.

Kang and Liang sought in 1895 to take these individuals who loosely shared a culture and organize them into a community, a kind of lobbying group, through "study societies" and journals. They found a ready audience precisely because of the changes China had already produced. After the great Taiping Rebellion of the 1860s, the Qing began to include modern specializations like mathematics in some of the exams. Examiners began to ask about the history of Western institutions and politics. The purely classical education was being nudged in new directions. Moreover, the schools, arsenals, and shipyards created by the self-strengthening movement had produced new career paths like military technicians and Western experts. They lacked the prestige of the regular civil service, but the two groups were not isolated from one another. Missionary schools had even produced Western-style doctors and nurses. Thus a broad and socially diverse constituency for reform emerged.

The actions taken by Kang and his co-conspirators were illegal but not entirely unprecedented. Kang had presented his first illegal demand for reforms directly to the Throne in 1888. The Qing was particularly allergic to "factions." Officials were to serve as individuals: not exactly as cogs in the bureaucratic machine, but as disinterestedly loyal to the emperor alone. Yet the political reality had long been one of political groupings, often in the guise of scholarly and literary affiliations. Officials, powerful provincial gentry families, and lowly secretaries all had ways of finding each other. These collaborations became widespread in the disturbed decades leading up to the Opium War of 1840.[13] There were earlier examples as well. In the histories written by the gentry, exemplary officials risked all to remonstrate with their emperor. During the Southern Song (1127–1279), a "war party" repeatedly demanded that the North be won back from the barbarians. An example closer to home was the "Donglin movement" that had emerged in the late Ming (1368–1644) as a response to corruption and disorder.[14] Proclaiming its adherence to orthodox Confucian virtue, the Donglin movement criticized court morality and demanded that "good men" be appointed to office. These were not mere platitudes; they were weapons in a factional struggle encouraged by the emperor's blatant disregard of all governmental affairs. Unlike the late Qing reformers, the Donglin movement lacked a specific political program, but its leaders provided some inspiration for the later generation.

More immediately, Kang Youwei was heir to the *qingliu* (disinterested scholars) movement. This had been a self-consciously orthodox reaction to the Opium War and the Taiping Rebellion, and originally earned a hawkish, "conservative" reputation for its anti-Westernism. But a sharp rhetoric of protest and critique, under conditions of growing foreign pressure, led to surprising shifts. Although *qingliu* adherents tended to come from the lower ranks of the bureaucracy, they were involved in court politics and had a few high-ranking sponsors. They were less a specific political faction, however, than networks of associates based on scholarly interests, political concerns, and ties of patronage and friendship. Their *qingyi* (pure opinions) provided a context for exchanges over the relationship between morality and policy. A call for the promotion of talent and broadening of discussion was hardly unorthodox, but implied a challenge to autocracy. By the 1890s *qingliu* adherents formed the basis of the "Emperor's party" as young Guangxu began to emerge from Cixi's shadow. They called for "public discussion": that is, for the government to listen to the lower officials. And so Kang was hardly alone in demanding that imperialist pressures be resisted. Not modern military technology but rousing the people to fight for their country would defeat the foreigners. Distrust of the people was the mark of a corrupt and flaccid regime. The *qingyi* movement of the 1890s thus sought to reform government and the economy in order to mobilize the population – under local gentry, in turn cooperating with the bureaucracy.

In this way a new political force – public opinion – was being created. Kang Youwei's role was to break out of the bureaucratic embrace to mobilize a general literati protest. Most *qingliu* officials were shocked by Kang's views of "Confucius as a reformer" and his "wild" interpretations of the classics. None the less, they had done much to prepare the way for Kang. Following the Sino-Japanese War, Kang's writings began to appear openly in the newspapers that had become essential reading for gentry and students in the cities. Kang was not the only man demanding to be heard during the never-ending national and local crises of the late Qing. He was a singular example of larger trends, trends that culminated in the 1911 Revolution.

## Confucian radicalism in cultural context

To gauge the full extent of Kang's radicalism, it is not enough merely to look at his political views. His attempt to reinvent Confucianism as a philosophy of social change was even more radical since it challenged not just the policies of the government but its cultural basis. And in the *failure* to rein-vent Confucianism lay the future destruction of the entire cultural edifice of the imperial system: the emperor and his court, the recruitment of the bureaucracy through the exam system, and the very enterprise of classical learning – the worldview that had not only socialized generation after gener-ation of gentry, but also provided the glue that held together the various regions and the diverse classes. To understand the significance of this, it is necessary to review such esoteric debates of the eighteenth century as "Song Learning" versus "Han Learning," "New Text" versus "Old Text," and the rise of "evidential studies" (*kaozhengxue*). To the scholars of the eighteenth century, of course, these were not esoteric: they were the stuff of academic careers, social commentary, and even political snakes-and-ladders.

The academic trends of the Qing period led eventually to the de-canon-ization of classical learning. Qing scholars proved that various parts of the sacred classics (supposedly written before Confucius, or before the sixth century BC) were in fact later forgeries of the Han dynasty (209 BC–AD 206). Having noted this problem, however, Qing scholars did *not* immediately suffer a crisis of faith but, rather, found ways to continue believing in the essential truths of the classics. Well into the nineteenth century, there seemed no pressing reason to doubt them. But after the political catastrophes of foreign invasion and domestic rebellions, the cosmological kingship could no longer stand. Before discussing its collapse, let us examine the roots of a political ideology of enormous persuasive power, linking the emperor to the very nature of the cosmos.

The ideology that proclaimed the emperor to be the Son of Heaven had possessed about the same propaganda functions as "divine right" in the West, but it rested on a completely different base. "Heaven" to Chinese literati was not an anthropomorphic, omnipotent, intentional force but rather more like the balance of the cosmos or a kind of natural law. The Chinese emperor was given a "mandate" due to the sacred qualities of virtue and ritual propriety that he embodied. Real emperors of course were known to make mistakes, act at whim, and even commit crimes. Moreover, the principle of inheritance of the Throne by sons from their fathers was at odds with Confucian ideals. One of the fundamental tensions of the traditional Chinese polity thus lay between the emperor as the Son of Heaven on the one hand and as the mere son of his father on the other. Another tension – institutional as well as ideo-logical – lay between the emperor on the one hand and the gentry as the masters of the tradition, of the sacred texts, on the other. Individually, gentry and even officials were politically powerless before the Throne, but collec-tively they maintained a certain moral autonomy. Most Sons of Heaven acknowledged their need to practice self-cultivation and engaged in self-criti-cisms when disaster struck. An earthquake or even a peasant uprising, for example, were seen to reflect the personal morality of the emperor. And though it would have been impolitic to dwell on it, everyone knew that in the end all dynasties were subject to Heaven's change of the Mandate.

The political order and the moral order were both related to a cosmological symbolism that represented change within a larger harmony. On the popular level as well as in the sometimes cabalistic musings of philosophers, ideas about the five agents, yin–yang, and the hexagrams of the *Classic of Changes* (*Yijing*) presented an organic vision of the universe all of whose parts were interrelated. In the Song dynasty (960–1279) Confucian thinking developed a cosmology that both rationalized these elements in terms of a sophisticated metaphysics and emphasized the moral nature of the cosmos. The interpretations of the Cheng-Zhu school (named after its leading spokesmen) eventually became orthodoxy and were enshrined as the basis of the examination system until nearly the end of the Qing dynasty. Although Cheng-Zhu emphasized that social hierarchies were embedded in the nature of the cosmos, it also spoke of the obligations of parents, elders, and rulers. This is why the Son of Heaven himself would engage in self-criticism. Not merely outright rebellion, but unusual natural occurrences might call forth rituals of humility. An earthquake, say, might be interpreted by the court as a sign of Heaven's warning that the emperor had neglected his duties or that the people were suffering. This did not diminish the emperor's real powers in the least, but clearly shows how nature, morality, and the political and social orders were placed in the same conceptual net.

Some of the premises of this worldview fell under attack in the eighteenth century.[15] Qing "evidential studies" and Han Learning began as rebellions against trends of the Ming dynasty that were considered decadent. Qing scholars blamed a subjective approach to the classics for resulting in a kind of individualism that was destructive of good order and ultimately the fall of the Ming. Intuitive moral reasoning was condemned; instead, Qing scholars turned back to the original classics, using techniques of philology and astronomical dating to authenticate what were Confucius's real words. This more empirical approach was thus "evidential" and compared different texts in great detail; it was also called "Han Learning" because it relied on Han dynasty commentaries as being closer to the original texts, as opposed to the more intuitive Song Learning.

This fundamental philosophical shift dominated most of the intellectual life of the Qing, much as the European Enlightenment challenged Christian orthodoxy in the eighteenth century or the "postmodern" rebellion challenged the received epistemology of the Enlightenment in the last decades of the twentieth century. As in the West, orthodoxy in China had its defenders. But so many of the best minds of the period were influenced by the new trends that they altered the perspectives of all. The historical irony is that rebellion against Song and Ming Confucianism began in a conservative and fundamentalist spirit – to recover the original meaning of the Classics. Indeed, this intellectual rebellion was entirely orthodox politically, seeking to put the new Qing dynasty on sounder footing by correcting the excesses of the Ming.

Yet in practice the evidential studies movement was literally deconstructive. Philological proofs showed how Song–Ming metaphysics were "contaminated" by Daoist and Buddhist influences. That the classics, such as the seminal *Documents* or *History* (*Shangshu*) cited by Confucius, contained forgeries inserted into them later was demonstrated beyond refutation. Such questioning spread to other classics. The Han Learning scholars of the Qing tended to be professionally skeptical and rationalist, and the process of pruning away the historical accumulation of misinterpretation was potentially subversive. Where would it end? Indeed, the intellectual historian Benjamin Elman has suggested, "Han Learning represented more than just an antiquarian quest. Its advocates cast doubt on the Confucian ideology enshrined by Manchu rulers when they legitimated imperial power."[16] Above all, Han Learning historicized what had previously been the transcendental sacred. In showing that certain texts important to the broadly defined Confucian tradition – and central to imperial Confucianism specifically – contained forgeries, Han Learning raised doubts about the entire corpus. Moreover, in making philology something of a scientific method, the movement raised questions about objective standpoint. Confucianism had not faced such a serious challenge since the outside threat of Buddhism a thousand years earlier, even though the Han Learning scholars considered themselves true followers of Confucius.

In spite of its findings, the subversive potential of Han Learning mostly remained latent. One reason was that the majority of its adepts deliberately ignored the broader implications of their scholarship. Han Learning thus tended to bog down in philological trivia. Han Learning shared with the Cheng-Zhu mainstream both a respect for scholarship and a skepticism of utopian thinking. As a fairly technical art requiring years of specialized training, it encouraged skeptical more than speculative habits of mind. It abjured questions of morality and cosmology for more narrowly focused research concerns.

Eventually the pendulum swung back – but not exactly to the previous status quo. By the beginning of the nineteenth century, a feeling that thoughtful people had better consider questions of morality and even metaphysics had become fairly widespread. In attacking the philosophy of the Song and Ming periods, the Qing's Han Learning had not really tried to replace it. The answers were still supposed to lie in the classics, as now better understood. But in fact the answers still had to come from *interpretation*, the kind of approach evidential studies by itself simply could not handle. One new approach was self-consciously synthetic: to combine the precise scholarship of Han Learning for textual questions but then to go on to use Song Learning as a guide to basic principles, especially in ethics. Precisely to the extent Han Learning had succeeded in rediscovering the words of the sages, the problem of how to make them relevant was accentuated.

In order to understand the real intellectual revolution of the late Qing, one other feature of evidential studies must be mentioned. The Han Learning scholars, in their pursuit of all the evidence from the most ancient times, rediscovered the philosophical debates of the Warring States era (fourth to third centuries BC). This was the period, of the generations following

Confucius, when competing schools against and within Confucianism were elaborated – some of which had been lost. Qing scholars discovered how to tease them out from the very partial documentary evidence available. In turn, some of these ideas from Mohist, Daoist, and Legalist traditions provided important resources for late Qing intellectuals. These new resources enriched the philosophical vocabulary. Suddenly, Chinese culture became more than Confucian orthodoxy.

Finally, the direct antecedent to Kang Youwei's philosophy, the "New Text" school, also arose out of Han Learning. The "New Text" versus "Old Text" controversy was originally an ancient one. Somewhat different versions of the classics – in two different writing styles – appeared in the Han dynasty when Confucianism was revived after the attempt of the Qin dynasty (221–6 BC) to eradicate it. "New Texts" referred to writings in the contemporary epigraphical style, written by contemporary scholars from memory, while "Old Text" versions written in pre-Han styles were allegedly discovered hidden in the walls of Confucius's old house. The Former Han (206 BC–AD 8) had favored New Text while Later Han (AD 25–220) scholars, after some debate, favored the Old Text versions (they had much in common but differed in a few features). By the Qing, the New Text school was long forgotten. The Han Learning school of the Qing had rediscovered this controversy and by the eighteenth century some, though by no means all, evidential studies scholars were denouncing the Old Text tradition as based on fabrication. Certainly, portions of Old Text classics were Han period forgeries, but the main point was not relatively small textual differences.

The substantive issue at stake was the image of Confucius. Confucius allegedly wrote or at least edited all of the classics. One of the briefest of these was the *Spring and Autumn Annals*, sparse court annals of Confucius's own small state of Lu. Various commentaries were attached to explain these annals, and of these the New Text school paid special attention to the *Gongyang* commentary. While Old Text commentaries pictured Confucius as a teacher whose greatness resided in his revival of ancient traditions, the *Gongyang* treated Confucius as the "uncrowned king" whose greatness lay in founding new institutions. The *Gongyang* Confucius was a charismatic, even mystical leader. The political point was that in orthodox Confucianism Confucius himself was safely dead: gentry might claim to be masters of sacred texts but they were bound to the status quo. But in New Text thinking Confucius became a living, disturbing presence: though never a king or even a prime minister, he had understood how to preserve Chinese culture in a time of turmoil, laid the foundation of the unitary empire, and even foreseen the future. Anyone who could speak in the name of this magical Confucius became a prophet or "sage" himself, and might in turn challenge the established order. New Text scholars found Han dynasty references to an evolutionary scheme of "three ages" – from "Chaos" to "Lesser Peace" to finally a "Great Peace" and unity. Such progressivism, however vague, supported a basically optimistic worldview and justified Kang Youwei's radical Confucianism.

## Ideological revolution

Such esoteric debates about the nature of Confucius became politically important when the Qing's institutions began to fail. Late Qing political discourse
was created as the cosmological kingship declined. With this background,
then, we can see more precisely how Kang's ideas were truly radical and yet
how they also had deep roots in Chinese culture. Kang saw himself not as
a politician but as a charismatically endowed sage. His ultimate goal was a
Confucian one influenced by Buddhist ethics: to lead all humankind to moral
perfection. The scheme of the "three ages," made explicitly evolutionary in his
thought, formed the pivot of that goal; ultimately, not just China but all
humankind – indeed the entire natural world – would reach perfection.

Kang read widely in his youth, including translations of Western works,
and was impressed by what he saw on a trip to the British colony of Hong
Kong. Not personally tempted to become a Christian, he understood that
Christianity was a great social force in the West. It therefore constituted
both a threat to Chinese culture and a model for what Confucianism should
be. By the 1880s he was urging the emperor (in those unread memorials)
to make Confucianism into an established Church, like the Church of
England. In itself, this was an extraordinary suggestion. Confucianism was a
"Teaching" and, although surrounded by ritual and awe, it had never
possessed a clergy or an ecclesiastic apparatus. But Kang thought a
Confucian state Church could provide the common people with spiritual
comfort and a value system. Kang thus saw a spiritual vacuum as the
greatest threat to China. He often commented that the Jews had long ago
lost their nation but kept their identity because of their religion, but a
people that lost its identity had lost everything. Yet Kang himself
contributed to the destruction of the sacred texts on which Han Learning
had been dripping corrosive criticism for two hundred years.[17] Kang never
quit trying to turn China into a Confucian state. Nor did he ever quit trying
to make China into a constitutional or titular monarchy. From 1898 when
he sought to reform the Qing, into the 1910s and 1920s when he sought to
restore the Qing, Kang believed that China needed a symbolic head of state
to hold things together while the polity was opened up below. A Confucian
Church, however, would have meant a totally new set of relationships
between the court, the gentry (a new priesthood?), and the common people.

We can thus say that Kang's purposes went beyond politics to an effort to
make Confucianism the basis of China's national culture. In the 1890s,
however, Kang's immediate interest lay in using New Text ideas to promote
institutional innovation, which he made even more explicit with the publication
of *Confucius as a Reformer* in 1897.[18] Kang's Confucius believed in steamships
and railroads and Kang's Confucianism sanctioned institutional change. It
called on the government to call on "good men" (as had the Donglin movement) and furthermore to institutionalize this in a parliament. However, if
Confucius as an "uncrowned king" was still shocking to Kang's more conservative colleagues, a Confucius dedicated to political transformation seemed even

further beyond the pale. In putting reformist notions in a Confucian ideological framework, Kang took some of the sting out of their foreign associations. But he began with a religious view of Confucius. A passage in the introduction to *Confucius as a Reformer* links some of these issues:

> Heaven, having pity for the many afflictions suffered by the men who live on this great earth, caused the Black Emperor to send down his semen so as to create a being who would rescue the people from their troubles – a being of divine intelligence, who would be a sage-king, a teacher for his age, a bulwark for all men, and a religious leader for the whole world. Born as he was in the Age of Chaos, he proceeded on the basis of this disorder, to establish the pattern of the Three Ages, basing himself initially on those of his native state [of Lu], but stressing the idea of the one Great Community that would ultimately bind together all parts of the great earth, far and near, large and small.[19]

Politics and even culture were subsumed ultimately in Kang's larger cosmological framework. His scholarship was sloppy and his logic arbitrary, but his charismatic vision had great appeal for the generation coming of age in the late 1890s. He believed that humankind was progressing in linear fashion toward a utopian age he called the "great community." As early as the late 1880s Kang began to work out some of his ideas about the stages of human progress, though he continued to work on *The Great Community* for forty years.[20] He proclaimed that eventually a cosmopolitan world would emerge without nations, families or clans, or private property. The family would be replaced by alliances freely agreed to on an annual basis, between homosexuals as well as heterosexuals, while children were raised in public nurseries. This fantasy has struck many as the most un-Confucian notion ever espoused by this Confucian sage, but it represented a final state of human evolution when "family" was not so much abolished as extended to all humankind. World government would be based on republican and federal principles.

Kang's utopian scheme revolved around the Confucian value of *ren* (love, benevolence), which he extended by combining it with the basic goal of Mahayana Buddhism – to eliminate suffering – and the notion of universal love. His goal was to eliminate the differences between people, or to abolish institutions that supported the individual ego. It was ultimately the nature of the cosmos, according to Kang's metaphysics, that everything shares the same primal energy. He denied that gender, racial, and cultural differences in the end possessed any significance. Yet, at the same time, Kang accepted the racial analysis of the day, treating the "brown" and "black" races as genetically inferior to the "yellow" and "white" – in contrast to his unambiguous condemnation of discriminatory treatment of women. Kang led efforts to stamp out footbinding, and he educated his own daughters. But racial equality, he thought, would only come about by moving peoples of the equator to cooler, more salubrious climates and promoting miscegenation.

Still, utopia was one thing; present-day reality another. Kang refused to publish *The Great Community* in his lifetime, and the two levels of Kang's thought had little to do with each other. His ideas about institutional reform *now* and his ideas about a utopian *future* could have been written by two separate people. While Kang himself no doubt derived a good deal of comfort from reflecting that the world of the "Lesser Peace" he lived in was transitional between primitive chaos and the Great Community, he adamantly insisted that to attempt to build the institutions of the Great Community prematurely was to invite disaster. The institutional reforms he favored for China were eminently suitable to Lesser Peace: a constitutional order between the evils of autocratic despotism and the utopia of absolute democracy. His persistent opposition to republicanism stemmed from his commitment to his particular version of linear progress.

In sum, radical Confucianism failed to reform the Qing state. In fact, it acted to delegitimate the dynasty. Of course, outside pressures and the court's own incompetence also did much to destroy the Qing. The Qing's "New Policy" reforms came too little too late. It has been argued that in the long run they contributed to the rebuilding of the Chinese state, but the point here is that whatever the success of the Qing's reforms in their own terms, they tore at the delicate net that held the traditional system of politics and culture together. The Qing's abolition of the exam system in 1905, for example, immediately distressed the huge constituency of exam hopefuls. An ambitious village schoolteacher reacted to the news bitterly: "I woke at first light with my heart like dead ashes. I saw that all was vanity and there was nothing eternal ... no one knows what will become of customs and morals ..."[21]

Suddenly, culture was separated from politics; the classics were torn out of the bureaucratic system; and the court abandoned its role of providing political education. The questions asked in the exams had been a weapon of cultural control, and no new institutions were ready to provide this function. The traditional curriculum had reached down to village schools. The more expensive Western-style schools were only built in county seats. Thus one of the strands that bound elites to ordinary villagers was also broken. What had been a whole world of learning and truth was suddenly reduced to a minor subfield of a particular history.

The political and military powers of the court, the prestige and status of the gentry, the values and learning of the literati – these had once been three strong pillars supporting an apparently immovable system. The New Text school's reformism uprooted all three pillars. It criticised imperial despotism and traditional versions of classical learning. Yet it could not come to terms with the new nationalist and utilitarian values of the twentieth century.[22] The Qing and Confucianism were doomed together. Radical Confucianism might, possibly, have saved a more dynamic set of political leaders, but in the political reality of the late Qing it was too radical for the conservatives and not radical enough for the revolutionaries.

# 2   1911: History and historiography

The Revolution of 1911 remains curiously difficult to categorize. Three distinct schools of interpretation contended with each other over the rest of the century: that 1911 represented (1) the revolutionaries' revolution; (2) the rising bourgeoisie's revolution; and (3) the urban gentry's revolution (which might not be a "revolution" at all).[1] The events of 1911 and 1912 do not seem to belong in the same league as the great English Revolution of the seventeenth century, the American and French Revolutions of the eighteenth century, the Russian Revolution of 1917, or, for that matter, the Chinese Communist Revolution of 1949. Yet the 1911 Revolution not only overthrew the Qing dynasty after nearly 270 years of continuous rule but it also brought the imperial-dynastic system of some 2,100 years to an end. Of course, people at the time could not be sure the revolution did not represent just another turn of the dynastic cycle: the fall of the old and the rise of a new imperial family. Indeed, most peasants, if they heard about it at all, thought exactly that. Most educated Chinese, however, had a sense that something unprecedented had occurred.

The real reason why 1911 does not seem to fit into our notions of what a revolution should be is that in many ways it did not result in a future clearly different from the past. The new "Republic of China" was not republican; many of the old Qing bureaucrats simply stayed in their jobs. Nor did culture, society, and the economy appear to change, even with the collapse of the imperial political structure. They *were* changing, but not as a direct result of the 1911 Revolution.

Yet even if the Revolution failed to produce a new, effective political system, its effects were profound. The gentry class could not survive the loss of their special relationship with the emperor that the civil service examinations had ratified. The exams had been abolished in 1905; the last chance of basing some kind of new relationship on the old was destroyed in 1911. Other changes: China's cities emerged from the 1911 Revolution looking outward to the rest of the world, less and less concerned with the political machinations of Beijing. Even the national and provincial bureaucracies that survived the immediate aftermath of 1911 disintegrated within the decade. Without some link to the imperial center, rural elites lost their legitimacy. If the 1911 Revolution cannot be isolated as the prime cause of all these changes, since it was partly their reflection, it did stimulate further change. "Revolution" itself became a common way of thinking about change.

It is important to understand what really went on in 1911 because the revolution was later mythologized. The two major contenders for power in China in the twentieth century were intent on fitting 1911 into a national myth – rather like the way the legitimacy of the sitting American president can be linked to 1776. The government of Taiwan today (still calling itself the "Republic of China") traces its origins to Sun Yat-sen (1866–1925) and the Three People's Principles; the government of the People's Republic of China dates its creation to the Communist Revolution (1949), but also takes the 1911 Revolution as a pivotal moment in its prehistory. The PRC's official historiography treats 1911 as the beginning of the bourgeois phase of a longer revolutionary – anti-feudal and anti-imperialist – struggle.

The two governments, both with their actual roots in the 1920s, have created what might be called, respectively, the heroic and the Marxist interpretations of 1911. Western historians and social scientists comprise the third school; they look to long-term explanations that examine the key role played by relatively conservative social forces in the overthrow of the Qing. The first school (Taiwan), emphasizing the revolutionary heroism of a few leaders, in effect proposes that China advanced through the efforts of specially far-sighted and capable men and women. The teleology of the second school is Marxist (PRC), suggesting that a modern revolution would move inevitably through a bourgeois phase leading finally to the victory of the proletariat. The third school (Western) sees 1911 less as the product of deliberate, creative action, and more the result of the decay and final collapse of an old, malfunctioning system. Of course, in practice, the schools tend to overlap more than this description implies. This chapter will look at what is useful and what is mythological in each school, examine what they have in common, and pinpoint some of the issues they neglect.

## The 1911 Revolution as prologue

The first interpretation of the 1911 Revolution derives largely from the men who made the revolution, lost access to power after 1912, but began to fight their way into power in the 1920s. In this version of history, the year 1895, so important for gentry activists like Kang Youwei, was also the year Sun Yat-sen, a son of peasants from near Guangzhou, organized his first uprising to overthrow the Qing. Sun had left home to be educated in an Anglican school in Hawaii, later completing medical studies in Hong Kong. He initially tried to interest top officials in schemes for reforms, but, being ignored, then turned to revolution. His unsuccessful revolts continued, with shifting strategies, allies, and goals, until the Wuchang Uprising of 1911, which sparked the Revolution itself.

When the Qing put a price on his head, Sun fled abroad. One of his early centers of activity was Japan, where he found a ready audience among the increasing numbers of young Chinese studying there. Sympathetic Japanese were also an important source of support for the Chinese revolutionaries. Some five to seven thousand Chinese students were studying in Tokyo in the first decade of the twentieth century, and the atmosphere among them was both tense and exciting. Especially after the exams were abolished in 1905, ambitious young Chinese turned to all kinds of new schools and new careers from soldiers and police to accountants and doctors. As study in Japan was considerably cheaper than in the United States or Europe, and because Japan was culturally less alien and the language easier to read, young Chinese began to congregate in Tokyo. They were largely free to discuss anything and found the Japanese had already translated into classical Chinese exciting Western thinkers from Rousseau to Marx.[2]

Most students, including the revolutionaries, had government scholarships; most were of gentry family background but not wealthy; most took very short courses designed to equip them for a military or bureaucratic career, simply wanting to get their credentials and return home. Still, even conservative students could not help but be amazed by the sights of Tokyo and the other cities of Japan. There were big glass shop windows, streetcars, and dozens of newspapers. The cities were massive but orderly; railways were rapidly connecting the whole nation, and a constitutional government seemed to recognize the rights of the people.

Anti-Qing student revolutionaries from various provinces came together in 1905 to form the National Alliance (Tongmenghui). This umbrella group of about 400 members elected Sun Yat-sen to be its head. By this time, Sun, although never a leading intellectual, had studied Western political theory and earned some laurels as a revolutionary – a new social category. Sun had never trained in the Confucian classics and so initially lacked prestige among the traditionally better-educated students (and older radical intellectuals) in Japan; none the less, his commitment to the anti-Manchu cause gained him respect. Sun's "Three People's Principles" of nationalism, republicanism, and land nationalization (later "people's livelihood" – a vague sort of socialism) spelled out a revolutionary program.

Sun's great talent was raising money from overseas Chinese merchant communities, especially the thousands of sojourners from Guangdong and Fujian who had businesses all around Southeast Asia, and to a lesser extent the Americas and Europe. Having long been ignored and despised by the Qing, they too were concerned with China's fate and perhaps calculated that a little support now might pay big dividends after the revolution. In fact both Kang Youwei, who was plotting to replace Cixi with the Guangxu emperor, and revolutionary organizations promised contributors big benefits in the future. Sun bought arms abroad and got them to secret societies in China. So-called secret societies were usually not so secret, gang-like mutual-aid organizations in rural market towns, cities, and among overseas

Chinese communities. Although some secret societies professed a primitive ideology calling for the overthrow of the Qing and restoration of the Ming, this was little more than a mythical memory of southern China's old anti-Manchuism. The real business of secret societies was gambling, extortion (protection rackets), prostitution, opium smuggling, theft – and offering support to members in need. In the disturbed conditions of the late Qing, they were sometimes ready for rebellion.

Meanwhile, the National Alliance grew, claiming a membership of nearly 10,000 by 1911. It specifically targeted the "New Armies" of the modernizing Qing military for propaganda and organizational efforts. One of the Qing's late-nineteenth-century reforms, the New Armies were meant to replace the dynasty's hidebound Manchu and lower-class Chinese armies with a better-trained, literate, and effective fighting force. Yuan Shikai was one of their chief organizers. The Qing tried to centralize the New Armies and reassert Manchu control, especially after 1908, with partial success. But the National Alliance could also claim some success in appealing to the better-educated, more nationalistic troops. Finally, on 10 October 1911, a New Army mutiny in the central Yangzi city of Wuchang broke out. Police had discovered the membership lists of a revolutionary organization after a bomb went off by accident, and they made some arrests. The remaining revolutionaries moved fast. They seized the main arsenal; the Manchu governor-general of the area fled; and, after two days of intense persuasion, the commanding colonel, Li Yuanhong, joined their movement. Although Li had to be convinced at gunpoint to head the revolutionaries, he proved a good choice, for he was acceptable to the local gentry and could communicate with Yuan Shikai. Yuan was the leader of the Qing forces (he had been forced out of power after Cixi's death, but now the royals discovered they needed him).

By the end of October, seven provinces established revolutionary (often military) governments and seceded from the Qing Empire; in another month, seven more had seceded; and in January 1912, Sun Yat-sen returned to China to be proclaimed provisional president of the Republic of China by a rump parliament meeting in Nanjing.

A massive civil war was avoided, although the southern capital of Nanjing saw heavy fighting, and the Manchus in some towns were massacred or turned into refugees.[3] In February 1912, the Qing abdicated. Of China proper, only three provinces close to Beijing (along with Manchuria and the Western desert provinces) remained loyal to the Qing. Yuan Shikai arranged the peace deal, negotiating with the Qing royal house on the one hand and Sun Yat-sen on the other. The Qing abdicated in return for guarantees of safety and a generous allowance, and a much-reduced court continued to function into the 1920s, strictly inside the Forbidden City. More critical were the negotiations between Yuan and the revolutionaries, but with better-disciplined troops and foreign backing, Yuan held the advantage. Sun turned the presidency over to Yuan in return for promises that Yuan would move the

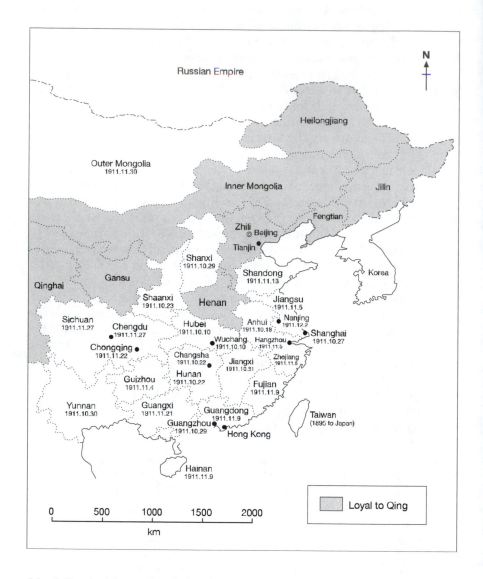

*Map 2* Provincial secession during the 1911 Revolution

The 1911 Revolution took the form of separate secession movements from the Qing Empire from October 1911 to February 1912 (dates are given "year.month.day"). Often, a combination of youthful revolutionaries, local military men, and leading gentry took control of the provincial capital or some other city and declared the province independent from the Qing. Their powers often did not extend much beyond the city limits, and their goal was not independence (except for Mongolia) but a new kind of national government The Qing never recovered from the psychological shock of widespread revolutionary action.

*Source*: Courtesy of Geospatial Information Science Team, Computing Center, Academia Sinica.

capital to Nanjing, where the revolutionaries were stronger, and establish constitutional government. In fact, Yuan was to do neither.

This, then, is the story of a revolution. As an explanation, it is fairly simple: revolutionaries made the revolution. In this case, they made the revolution because they saw that the era of empire was over and did not believe the Manchus were fit to rule over the Chinese. It is a heroic story of sacrifice, struggle, and victory against the odds. Tragically, Yuan Shikai betrayed the revolution, established a dictatorship, and suppressed the revolutionaries. The story continues to the 1920s, when the revolutionaries regrouped under Sun Yat-sen to fight for national unification. In this sense, the 1911 Revolution was a prologue to the "national revolution" of the 1920s.

However, there are some problems with this version of history. The Qing actually had very little trouble suppressing most of the uprisings Sun and other revolutionaries instigated. The uprisings from the 1890s on suffered from faulty intelligence, poor logistics, and minimal local support in most cases, and seldom lasted more than a couple of days. The revolutionaries lacked capable leaders. This is not to say that there was no revolutionary potential. Bandits were on the move; peasant disturbances were growing, especially as the Qing officials and local elites raised taxes to support reform programs. But most peasant disturbances tended to focus on specific, local grievances. Most intellectuals were attached to abstract slogans and unconvinced of the readiness of the lower classes to undertake revolution. Radical students occasionally linked up with peasants or rural workers such as miners through secret societies, but the two groups had different reasons for fighting the Qing, and divergent goals. Peasants still revolted in the name of restoring a "Han" emperor and creating a new world where all the brave rebels would become princes. The soldiers who started the Wuchang uprising had only the most tenuous links with the National Alliance, though they were certainly deeply disaffected from the Qing. In the final analysis, the Qing fell because its own army commanders were unwilling to support it and because the Chinese elites – gentry and wealthy merchants – saw no reason to prefer the Qing over the revolutionaries, and not because of the military prowess of the revolutionaries. The true face of the 1911 Revolution belonged to Yuan Shikai, not Sun Yat-sen.

## The 1911 Revolution as phase

The Chinese Marxist understanding of the revolution accepts most of the story as recounted by the first school but puts the events in a larger social framework. In this view, the 1911 Revolution represented a "bourgeois" phase of rebellion against a backward and "feudal" monarchical despotism – like the French Revolution – and was a progressive step toward the next phase of socialist revolution. The revolutionaries of 1911 thus acted not as individual patriots but as members of their social class. What bound the revolutionaries together and gave them their strength was their status as representatives of a rising bourgeoisie. The massive and sophisticated late-imperial economy had produced a thriving merchant class; the growth of the imperialist economic presence greatly furthered capitalist activity in the treaty port cities, especially Guangzhou, Shanghai, and Tianjin, even while suppressing national development on the whole. A true working class – proletariat – was also being created, but it remained embryonic at this stage of small-scale manufacturing. Modern China was beginning to create more powerful classes of factory-owners, bankers, mid-level merchants, and shop-keepers, as well as professionals like teachers, journalists, engineers, and doctors, all of whom might be called bourgeoisie and petty bourgeoisie.

In this view, China was a society in transition. The development of capitalism had been under way for several centuries, stimulated by the commercialization of the economy as peasants learned to produce for markets and as these urban markets sent cash into the countryside. However, this natural evolution was thwarted by the sudden intrusion of Western imperialism fueled by the Industrial Revolution. Opium imports sucked silver out of China, and manufactured goods from Britain and other Western nations undercut Chinese products. In the Chinese Marxist view, this created unemployment problems and thwarted the development of capitalism. This had political implications: China's bourgeoisie was not rising as strongly as it should. Therefore, the 1911 Revolution was only a partial success, undermined by the weaknesses of the bourgeoisie who initiated it.

The Marxist formula used to sum up this situation described China as a "semi-feudal, semi-colonial" society. China was *feudal* in so far as the traditional landed gentry ran local affairs and dominated the central bureaucracy; this is not "feudal" in the European sense of a decentralized aristocracy, but describes an agrarian civilization resting on powerless peasants. At the same time, China was rapidly developing a capitalist system where merchant wealth challenged gentry authority, and hence society could not be described as wholly feudal. Meanwhile, China was a *colony* in the sense that foreign powers dominated many spheres of political and economic life, but since most of this rule was indirect and divided, China was in fact a *semi-colony* under the control of a condominium of imperialists who left a shadow Chinese government in place. The notion of semi-colonialism also captured the sense of the Chinese people as being second-class in their own land. Patriots abhorred the spectacle of rickshaw drivers being berated by British soldiers, or American warships on the Yangzi River. Mao Zedong, leader of the Chinese Communist Party, spelled out his views of the 1911 Revolution in 1940:

> Since the invasion of foreign capitalism and the gradual growth of capitalist elements in Chinese society, the country has changed by degrees into a colonial, semi-colonial and semi-feudal society.... In the course of its history the Chinese revolution must go through two stages, first, the democratic [i.e., bourgeois] revolution, and second, the socialist [i.e.,

proletarian] revolution, and by their very nature they are two different revolutionary processes.... The Revolution of 1911 was in a fuller sense the beginning of that revolution [against feudal and colonial forces].[4]

Mao's true interest was not history but the politics of the day – yet he did understand those politics as the outcome of historical processes. Cautiously noting that "the Chinese national bourgeoisie retains a certain revolutionary quality at certain periods and to a certain degree," Mao was trying to offer businessmen a place in the Communist revolution of the 1940s. Mao claimed that China would skip the stage of capitalism under "bourgeois dictatorship," but elements of capitalism and bourgeois culture would be retained through a transition period before socialism was achieved. Mao thus situated the Communist revolution as heir to the 1911 Revolution. Communist political propaganda was intimately bound up with a certain view of modern history, and, regardless of changes in tactics, 1911 was always seen as one phase in a larger revolutionary progression.

Li Dazhao, one of the founders of the Chinese Communist Party in the 1920s, had earlier expressed a more optimistic vision of the role of 1911 in China's ongoing revolution. Li believed that democracy was the essential spirit of the times. Communism then became a kind of logical extension of the growth of democracy that 1911 had also reflected. Writing in the wake of the Allied victory in the First World War and the Bolshevik victory in Russia, both of which he celebrated, Li said that democracy had been born in Europe, emigrated to America, and awakened an Asia asleep in despotism through the use of machine guns, steamships, and the media.[5] China's 1911 Revolution thus represented the victory of democracy over monarchism. As long as China's new rulers followed democratic ways, they were victorious. But when, like Yuan Shikai, they turned against democracy, they would fall.[6]

The ultimate source of these views was Karl Marx. The *Communist Manifesto* (1848) proclaims: "The history of all hitherto existing society is the history of class struggles." And as Marx and Engels described Europe's past, they offered Chinese Communists a blueprint for China's future:

> The bourgeoisie, wherever it has got the upper hand, has put an end to all feudal, patriarchal, idyllic relations. It has pitilessly torn asunder the motley feudal ties that bound man to his "natural superiors," and has left remaining no other bond between man and man than naked self-interest and callous "cash payment."[7]

But if the appointed task of the Chinese "bourgeoisie" was to put an end to "feudalism," could it in fact do so? Chinese historians recognized that the Chinese bourgeoisie at the dawn of the twentieth century was far weaker than its European counterpart at the end of the eighteenth century. It faced not only an entrenched system of rural landlordism, with which it was inter-twined – in contrast to northern Europe with its hereditary nobility and its tradition of urban independence from feudalism. But the Chinese bourgeoisie also faced an imperialism that simultaneously weakened the independent ("national") bourgeoisie and co-opted elements of the bourgeoisie into its own ranks (as "compradors"). Marxists thus tried to distinguish between capitalists who produced goods in China in competition with the foreigners on the one hand (good) and "comprador bourgeoisie" who worked for foreign companies and so were allied with the imperialists on the other (evil). Chinese historians labeled both the reformism of Kang Youwei and the revolutionary ideas of Sun Yat-sen as bourgeois in one way or another. Constitutional government, parliaments, national schooling, abolition of internal transit taxes, and construction of railways, telegraphs, shipping lines, and other projects were of use to business interests.

However, the Chinese bourgeoisie, alone and divided as it was, was in no position to overthrow all the forces of feudalism and imperialism. The overthrow of the Qing was a significant but limited accomplishment. In the Marxist view, 1911's greatest weakness was its failure to attack feudal forces in the countryside. The bourgeois ideology of nationalism was, however, a useful program that went beyond anti-monarchism. Nationalist goals included two features of special concern for the bourgeoisie: strong government, necessary to encourage domestic trade, secure property rights, and limit foreign economic impact; and unity, necessary to prevent the kind of class struggle seen to be occurring in the West. Nationalist consciousness encouraged the coalitions that would eventually defeat imperialism. Indeed, from the early 1900s on, anti-imperialist boycotts of foreign goods helped Chinese factory-owners. A major boycott of American goods, supported by students, workers, and merchants alike, lasted for most of 1906 after the United States passed anti-immigration laws aimed at Asians. Different sectors of Chinese society were thus united; the failure of the Qing to support movements like this one helped create the grounds for the revolution.

Social Darwinism naturally made sense to the bourgeoisie. Traditional gentry, with their twin loyalties to Confucianism and locality, had trouble thinking in terms of national competition. But an emerging urban-based, more broadly educated class of entrepreneurs and managers naturally applied the principles of free market competition to international relations. Laissez-faire may not have been nationalistic in theory, but in practice the paradigm of contending nation-states fitted into this social Darwinian world. As only the fittest survived in business, only the fittest states and peoples ultimately survived in the world.

In spite of their ostensibly social analysis – using categories like bourgeoisie and feudal forces – Chinese Marxist historians tended to exaggerate the virtues of Sun Yat-sen and the evils of Yuan Shikai just like the historians of the first school. In this view, the revolution was necessary to overthrow a hopelessly corrupt regime – corrupt because it was rooted in feudal rural social relations and because of its cooptation by imperialist forces. Sun represented new social forces, which were not yet strong enough to fill the coming leadership vacuum, while Yuan represented feudalism. In this way, however, some historians confuse an individual's attitude toward revolution with class position. In fact, finding any kind of bourgeoisie in pre-1911 China is difficult.[8] It is true that Yuan was a landlord as well as a powerful official, but it is hard to show that the revolutionaries came from capitalist families. Real capitalists tended to support reformist elements in the court. For example, Zhang Jian (1853–1926), as a classical scholar and *jinshi* who had achieved this high rank by the age of forty-two, used his prestige and official contacts to help him raise investment funds and manage his factories. If a bourgeois program can be found at all, it is in the Qing reforms, designed to promote transportation and communications infrastructure, provide a clearer framework of commercial law, and encourage investment in key industries.

At the same time, Marxist historians are right to point to areas of conflict between the government and local elites. For example, modernizers of all political shades agreed railroads were a good thing. Perhaps, as the Qing said, they should be under central government control. But not, most nationalists felt, if the Qing had to allow foreigners to build them. Several provinces saw elite-led "railway rights recovery" movements, which often raised large sums from low-priced, immensely popular share offerings, to buy back railroads from foreign syndicates. (National interest and self-interest could coincide.) In early 1911 the Qing lost control of the great western province of Sichuan when protests against its plans to buy locally-built trunk lines with foreign loans escalated to attacks on the government. Anti-Qing provincial leaders, hardly a pure bourgeoisie, represented the interests of local capital. The arrests of the leaders led to militia action against the governor; by the summer, angry peasants were on the march as well. The tradition of peasant uprisings was maintained: warehouses were looted for food, and police and tax offices were destroyed. A mix of secret society, bandit, gentry, and revolutionary leaders added to the confusion. The Qing had just begun to restore order when the Wuchang uprising broke out.

In fact, the class structure during the late Qing was extraordinarily fluid. The lines between modern bourgeoisie and traditional merchant were hazy, and there was a gradation from rural gentry to urban businessman. Most major business activities after the 1870s were hybrid official–merchant ventures. And if "bourgeois" refers to owners of the means of production, in 1911 there were only about 600 Chinese-owned mechanized factories and mines. The non-agricultural sectors were dwarfed by farming. Industry and railroads (a mere 5,600 miles in a country of continental proportions) together represented $80 million of capital investment (in US currency), only 6–7 percent of agricultural investment.[9] In so far as the Marxist historiography represents an attempt to apply European categories, it can mis-state the nature of Chinese society. Neither birth nor hereditary title nor landownership defined the Chinese gentry, and there were no social or political bars to their entering any business activity. Over the course of the Qing, many of the richer gentry had moved out of the countryside to the cities, and although they might have retained ownership of considerable amounts of land, their main sources of income were urban-based.

This is a more complex picture of the revolutionary situation than the traditional and PRC schools of historiography acknowledged. With the collapse of Marxism as a living ideology in the 1990s, and the maturation of Taiwan as a political society, these two schools have disappeared. A number of Chinese historians have even suggested that the revolution may have been a mistake from the beginning: if the new social forces of the period had not yet matured enough to carry through a revolution, then the revolution was premature and therefore a mistake. Some historians also emphasize that, given China's nature as a multi-ethnic society, the race-mongering of Han Chinese versus Manchu was a false issue reflecting Han chauvinism. Even more controversially, it is now claimed that the Qing's own reform efforts *were* bearing fruit and would have eventually modernized the nation.[10] This might be seen as wishful revisionism, but it resonated with the acute political crisis of the 1990s, as the language of "revolution" metamorphosed into that of "reform."

## Political revolution as conservative social change

The third school, dominated by Western social historians, rejects many of the conclusions of the first two schools. In his pioneering study of the revolution in Hunan and Hubei provinces, Joseph Esherick noted, "though exiled revolutionary conspirators may capitalize on revolutionary situations, they do not fundamentally cause revolutions."[11] How, then, are they brought about? When new social forces cannot find a space for themselves in the political process, they may fight to create such a space. In the Chinese case it is important to note the conservative as well as the radical tendencies among the new professionals, students, businessmen, and, above all, local leaders including old gentry families. The social history of 1911 also gives more attention to the long-term devolution of central power to the provinces and counties. This school is less teleological, or at least less optimistic; the revolution appears not to be a step toward making China stronger so much as part of an ongoing collapse. The revolution resulted in the further militarization of Chinese society, culminating in the warlord era between 1916 and 1927.

In this view, local elites in China, especially those from the wealthier provinces along the Yangzi Valley, determined the outcome of the revolution. Once civil war broke out they abandoned the Qing for local and provincial power. Perhaps they understood events in traditional terms: the Qing had lost the mandate. But they also understood that "revolution" was an entirely new phenomenon and that they could influence the creation of new political configurations. Although the Qing survived the great mid-nineteenth-century rebellions – civil wars that left 20 to 30 million persons dead – the government was never again able to fully reassert central control. Local leaders performed a number of state functions, and a new kind of alliance between successful gentry and merchants began to dominate in at least the richer provinces.[12] Hence an exclusive focus on either a bourgeois or a gentry class is misleading. The power of local elites rested on a combination of commercial wealth, landholding, military power, and patronage, as well as the education and examination success of the full-fledged gentry.

This new kind of elite was considerably more urbanized than the traditional gentry. During the civil wars of the 1850s, cities proved safer than the countryside. Elites began to find more of their identity as managers of private and quasi-public organizations, such as guilds, water control associations, famine relief organizations, schools, and the like. In the words of the historian Mary Backus Rankin, "Commercialization encouraged the fusion of merchants and gentry into a vigorous, numerically expanding elite whose power rested on varying combinations of landownership, trade, usury, and degree holding."[13] Above all, the urban reformist elites were creating a public sphere: through discussions in places like teahouses and even brothels and through the new journals and newspapers they could talk about the kind of China they wanted to create.[14] The new elite inherited the Confucian mandate for paternalistic rule. This provided them with an ideology of political participation that now combined with their new social roles: management of religious and educational institutions, guilds and native-place associations (organizations for sojourners, particularly elite merchants, from the same district or province), and welfare and public services. Urban elites began to untie themselves from the state.

True, there were precedents for such activities. Officials had sometimes left firefighting for merchant guilds, with their obvious stake in keeping China's wood-built cities from burning down, to manage. Gentry had long administered temples, local welfare (orphanages, support for widows, burial of paupers), and schools with little official interference. In times of trouble, the state even authorized local gentry to recruit militia. And except for the largest projects, like keeping the Yellow River diked or managing the Grand Canal, rural waterways were administered locally. Such activities did not emerge in conflict with the state but to compensate for what the central government would not or could not do.

Still, something had changed by the late Qing. Even if they needed official approval, local elites often took charge of the post-Boxer reforms. The public sphere they thus created was neither free from the interference of officials nor necessarily in opposition to them. Indeed, if elites saw themselves as representatives of "society," they still saw themselves as contributing to a stronger state.[15] Local flood control advanced the national interest; provincial railways would make China stronger. The dynasty retained its hold over men's minds: merchant leaders of self-government associations still bought Qing official titles. During the decade leading up to 1911, most of the men who took charge of the revolution once it began had remained loyal to the

Qing. None the less, non-official elite organizations provided locations for political discussion, affected public policy, and pressured local officials. In this way they created a new force for social and political change. From the beginning, they had the *potential* to oppose the Qing, especially if they thought local officials corrupt or national policy mistaken.

Late Qing elites were not, then, revolutionaries, but they were shifting to a new kind of critical, conditional loyalty. They pressed the dynasty with demands for limited local autonomy, for more rapid progress toward a constitutional monarchy, and for resistance against imperialism. It was sometimes their own children who were student revolutionaries, and ties such as friendship, local origin, and common teachers often worked to unite local reformers, radical intellectuals, and even sympathetic officials. Progressive Chinese of a variety of political dispositions shared common objectives, assumptions, and worldviews. Politically, after the Qing turned to reforms in the wake of the Boxer debacle, those very reforms created forces demanding further change. Elections for provincial assemblies in 1908, for example, only increased demands for a constitution.

It is worth noting that, although 90 percent of the new assemblymen were gentry who had received a traditional Confucian education, 30 percent of them had chosen to re-educate themselves in a more Western curriculum, either in a Chinese new-style school or abroad.[16] Such men were older and more traditional than the revolutionaries, but they can no longer be called ignorant of the world.

This is not to say that the new elites were disinterestedly seeking the national good. The "railway rights recovery" movement described above, for example, was designed to make money for its leaders. Public moneys paid for the new schools, but their fees were too high for ordinary folk. But the point here is simply that public institutions expanded faster than the Qing could control them. From a mixture of motives, urban-based gentry demanded a degree of local autonomy within a constitutional framework. If the Qing were unwilling or unable to provide this, the dynasty's natural constituency could turn against it.

Once revolutionary violence began to spread in 1911, the new elites, cooperating with military allies, moved in to lead the revolution with few apparent regrets. In the view of this third school of 1911 historiography, local elites feared popular violence. They wanted to make sure the radicals who had fomented the revolution did not claim power. They opposed land reform and unions. The provincial leaders who emerged in 1912 were usually of the new elite; it was no accident that the 1911 Revolution took the form of provincial secession from the Qing Empire.

The third school's emphasis on fundamental social factors minimizes the implied teleology of the events described. Since the forces that finally tipped the balance to revolution were committed primarily to reform, events could have had a different outcome. Nor does 1911 lead in a straight line to the Communist Revolution. In the words of Joseph Esherick, "Nineteen eleven was a victory for the increasingly Westernized urban reformist elite. As a major step in the alienation of the Chinese elite from the masses, it was more a precondition than a model for Mao Zedong's peasant revolution."[17] Yet the attention social historians have paid to the new elites has its own teleology. It is not one of revolution, but it remains closely tied to the thesis of modernization – though in China's case a blocked modernization.

Western social scientists have argued that, as China's ties to the world economy increased, society required more bureaucratic and professional specialization. A traditional sacred or quasi-religious worldview had to be replaced by scientific and technological progressivism. However, this produced a growing gap between a "Westernized" elite to whom national unity had become critical and a populace slower to change. Ultimately, the very reforms necessary to modernize China seemed to fracture its social unity. Traditionally, Confucianism and the institutions of the imperial state had carefully distinguished the classes while linking them together in a system of shared values. By the beginning of the twentieth century, however, urban elites were creating a modern culture increasingly distant from that of the countryside.

This view, however, seems to me to overstate the economic dynamism of the "urban reformist elite," while neglecting their commitment to political change. Certainly, they were conservative in their concern with their property rights, and disliked "chaos," but they already knew 1911 was not simply a new twist in the dynastic cycle: it was a revolution leading to a new form of government based on new principles of legitimacy. As we will see in the next chapter, the Chinese of the day understood the events of 1911 and 1912 as a story of a national political uprising designed to replace an autocratic monarchy with a republic. This was the clear "public script" read by all the political actors and most of the urban audience.

## Structural breakdown during the Qing

All three schools have contributed enormously to our knowledge of 1911. Yet without detracting from the accomplishments of revolutionaries, of reformist elites, and of conservative gentry (and the strange combinations they produced), we also need to note that the Qing dynastic system basically broke down on its own. One sort of pressure, of course, came from outside. Imperialism created paradoxes in China. The first paradox was that Britain thrust the Western legalistic notion of "sovereignty" upon China while crushing it through imposed treaties. The very idea of a "treaty" was foreign to the way the Chinese thought about foreign relations. The second paradox is that China was denied sovereignty – it could not establish tariffs or even collect its own customs dues, it paid huge indemnities to various foreign nations, foreign police forces operated in most cities, and foreign gunboats patrolled the major rivers – yet it was officially regarded as a sovereign nation (for only such entities can sign treaties) and was never colonized.

How long could such anomalous conditions persist? In 1898, Lord Salisbury, the British Prime Minister, warned: "For one reason or another – from the necessities of politics or under the pretext of philanthropy – the living nations will gradually encroach upon the territory of the dying."[18] The operating assumption was that the world consisted of two kinds of nations. Through the 1700s, before the effects of the Industrial Revolution had created a large gap between the world's rich and poor, most Westerners respected China's culture and might. By the 1800s, both were regarded with contempt. Extraterritoriality – the right of foreigners to be tried by their own consuls according to their own laws – guaranteed what Westerners saw as their rights in China. For the Chinese, it was to become the greatest symbol of the perfidy of foreigners in the absence of full-scale colonialism.

The foreign presence in Chinese "treaty ports" grew dramatically after the first Opium War. Through the "most favored nation" clauses in every treaty, all the Powers made sure that any concession China made to one, went to all. As well, by the 1890s bits of Chinese territory had been colonized: Hong Kong was ceded "in perpetuity" to the British and Taiwan to the Japanese; several outlying frontier areas populated by non-Han peoples were detached: Tibet by the British and the Ryukyu Islands by the Japanese; sections of most major cities were "leased" to the Powers, including the new business center of Shanghai. Such leaseholds in effect became miniature colonies, run by local foreigners with final decisions made in London, Washington, Tokyo, or Paris. Japan's defeat of China in 1895 brought fears of partition – of China being "sliced like a melon" – much closer. A "scramble for concessions" brought Russia into Manchuria, Germany into Shandong, and increased British and French presence into central and southern China. Rivalries among the Powers threatened the old informal agreement to leave China largely unoccupied but open to trade and missionaries, as the American "open door" proposals piously hoped. Yet the open door itself had been less a guarantee of Chinese independence than it was loosely cooperative imperialism.

Under this system the Qing could survive, but nationalist anger intensified. The foreign presence was inherently disruptive. Missionaries became a new locus of power in country towns. Merchants assiduously pursued the myth of the China market. China was the "sick man of Asia," and Western attitudes were informed by a deep racism buttressed by science. Leading biologists pronounced the skin color and brain size of Asians to be inferior. Leading philosophers pronounced history to have stopped in Asia at a primitive stage; university history departments did not teach Asian history because Asians did not possess history. Visions of an international hierarchy dominated by race and nation prevailed at the turn of the century.

At the same time, the imperial system was stressed from within. Ironically, the strains on the Qing had much to do with its successes. The economy had benefited from international trade in the eighteenth century, and the long years of peace produced a large rise in population. Rough figures indicate growth from 150 million in the late 1600s to over 300 million by 1800 and 430 million in 1850. This left millions without enough land to support themselves. Into the eighteenth century, food production and general economic activity more or less kept up with the population increases; more labor, especially useful in wet rice agriculture, increased harvests. The final bits of hilly and frontier lands absorbed migrants, and new-world food crops such as maize (corn), sweet potatoes, and peanuts were planted in marginal areas. But by the nineteenth century, the pressure on land was beginning to mount: accounts of violent struggles – between long-established villagers and outsiders, aboriginal peoples and settlers, and different groups of migrants – multiplied alarmingly, culminating in the massive Taiping Rebellion, which combined ethnic antagonisms and anti-landlord actions across great swathes of central China.

The structure of government, however, was not fundamentally altered when the Qing, with some foreign help, was finally able to reassert its control. In the uneasy peace that followed, the natural increase in men seeking exam degrees and official careers ran up against unchanged quotas. Thus both elites and the populace as a whole faced declining chances of social mobility. It is true that new career options emerged in the wake of the Taiping Rebellion; aside from commerce, informal government careers emerged as provincial officials collected their own secretariats. Many of the intellectuals discussed in Chapter 3 came from such families, and reformist institutions such as "new schools" eventually employed many teachers. However, the numbers of over-educated men continued to press against the avenues of success.

Another problem for the entire system was endemic structural corruption. Corruption was nothing new, but in the eighteenth century, as the costs of government rose (with the increasing complexity of Chinese society), the official budget did not change. A large part of county-level government had long been "off the books." The magistrate's numerous support staff – from tax collectors and file clerks to policemen, wardens, and soldiers – had never been satisfactorily provided for and thus depended on customary fees or bribes. From a county magistrate's point of view in the 1800s, his allowances from the central government stayed the same, the tax quota he was supposed to hand over to the central government stayed the same or increased, but his staff and his expenses were up. The fiscal demands and inefficiency of local government contributed to a tax squeeze on the commoners – even though officially taxes were not supposed to go up. The result was an effective, if technically illegal, system of tax farming in many parts of the Empire. Unlike the French or Indian versions, where rulers awarded licenses to merchants to collect taxes, Chinese tax farming was more a bottom-up phenomenon. The strictly unofficial tax farmers, usually lower-level gentry, did not bid for the right to collect taxes; rather, taking advantage of their legal privileges and social contacts, they paid a household's taxes for a fee, and in return they protected that household from further government predation. Whole villages might cooperate in this way.

As the Qing faltered, fiscal problems worsened. Tax protests, which increased dramatically after the 1890s, reflected the opposition of local communities to the demands of the central state. It was often these same lower-level gentry who led tax protests. At the same time, however, in the richer regions of the central and lower Yangzi valley, the situation was exacerbated by landlords who collected both rent and taxes from their tenants, to the detriment of tenant and government alike. As the central state faced severe fiscal restraints by the nineteenth century, the military fell into disarray, and officials neglected maintenance of the infrastructure of dams, dikes, canals, and the granary system. These problems contributed to the rebellions of mid-century, and remained unchecked even after the central government recovered power.

Some historians have traced a "devolution" in power from the center to the regions, but this was not a zero-sum game. The Beijing government was trying to increase its powers and sometimes succeeded. In general, however, China saw a growth of political power that benefited a variety of local elites more than it did the state. The *functions* of government were being extended deeper into society than before, but not necessarily under the auspices or control of the imperial state. Merchants in some cities raised funds, for example, to fight fires. To a degree, this was a long-term secular trend.[19] In the wake of the Taiping Rebellion when the Qing granted provincial and local authorities unprecedented rights to collect taxes for their own military purposes, as well as the right to serve in their own districts, the central government was never fully able to recover those rights. As the bureaucracy was restored to functioning order, parallel institutions dominated by local elites also grew. Society was more militarized than before, and families with mixed commercial–landed interests made sure they dominated local militias. Occasionally, ambitious families could parlay power on the county level into provincial influence during the Qing, and even provincial domination after 1911.[20] Militarization was particularly marked in peripheral and frontier areas; in economic core areas another innovation gave certain elites new powers. When tax and rent collection were combined, landlords were given direct access to the police powers of the imperial state. It may be that in some areas, after the Taiping Rebellion was finally crushed, the state limited landlord exactions in order to forestall peasant disturbances.[21] China's elites were not completely oblivious to the lessons of the rebellion, and rural crisis was stayed for a generation. But only until the turn of the century.

Local elites derived their power and influence from a variety of sources in the late Qing.[22] For centuries elite power had revolved around displaying a particular lifestyle, maintaining critical social networks (marriage and friendship patterns), and other behavior having nothing *directly* to do with degree status. Even nationally prominent families did not rely on the examination route, at least not in every generation, but rather on private economic enterprises (including, but not limited to, landholding) and local public functions (such as coordinating the building and maintenance of irrigation works or, in times of trouble, leading local militia). Examination success depended on economic and social success, for Chinese elites lacked many of the strengths of elites in other agrarian kingdoms, such as inheritable titles, entailed property, or positions at court. They none the less depended on the state for their legitimation, just as the ruling dynasty depended on the gentry. The Taiping Rebellion had permanently weakened the Qing by battering the prestige of the imperial house, by raising the long-suppressed issue of legitimacy of Manchu rulers, by fostering militarization, and by forcing local elites to adopt new strategies of survival.

This is not to say the revolution was inevitable. The gentry and provincial officialdom remained loyal, and the reforms from the 1860s did much to restore the integrity of the Qing's administration. It was by no means apparent that the Qing would inevitably fail to suppress, adapt, or reach accommodation with such new social forces as challenged it. The military decentralization of the Taiping period set a precedent for the military reforms eventually led by Yuan Shikai, which allowed him to finally push over the tottering Qing, but the court remained in control almost until the end.

Still, if the revolution was not inevitable, the court was constantly thwarted, and its "control" reflected the weakness of the opposition – or the failure, until the end, to imagine an alternative to the Qing. The government found that any effort to make itself more efficient created dissatisfaction among some constituency. In broad historical perspective, the New Policies look like a significant chapter in modern Chinese state-building. Bureaucratic restructuring to create ministries of industry and commerce, finance, interior, and education shaped later Republican and Communist governments. But the immediate impact of the Qing's New Policies was to weaken the state. For they tried to put the dynasty and the imperial system on a new foundation while they simultaneously legitimated elite oppositional politics. The symbolic and emotional power of the emperor over Chinese elites was thus enfeebled. What might have worked in the 1890s was too late by the 1900s. Traditional moral texts in schools began to be replaced by a Westernized curriculum. Local "constitution offices" and provincial assemblies legitimated the kind of gentry politics previously condemned as "factions." A national assembly even began to meet in 1910. And again, the practical *and symbolic* lynchpin of the monarchy–gentry relationship, the exam system, was abolished in 1905.

The Qing did not simply fall; it was also pushed. Manchu aristocrats and traditional Confucians confronted a new dream of national unity. Revolutionaries were willing to kill and to die for this dream. A crescendo of uprisings and assassinations, from rice riots to revolts staged with foreign weapons, marked dynastic decline. The agenda of the revolution was established in a surprisingly widespread consensus that began with the radical Confucians of the 1890s and extended to the revolutionaries of the 1900s. Historian Michael Gasster sums up their contribution to 1911 as follows: "The [Qing] regime was found wanting primarily because of its own errors, but the verdict was pronounced according to principles that the revolutionaries had done most to establish. The principles were not entirely clear or consistent, and some who defended them [and] paid them lip service were prepared themselves to violate them, but they were the closest thing China had to a national consensus in 1911."[23] We examine those principles in the next chapter, but first we must examine how the mood created by this structural breakdown further contributed to the push for revolution.

## Revolutionary atmosphere

Over the course of the 1880s and 1890s telegraph wires had been installed between China's major cities, and ports like Shanghai were directly connected to the rest of the world even earlier. Postal services also spread, even to small towns, for private and commercial correspondence, and disseminated newspapers and magazines. Although not all printed matter was revolutionary or even political, post office figures indicate the importance of the new press. Some 36 million copies of journals and books were mailed in 1908; this does not include locally sold issues, nor does it indicate how many people shared the same copy.[24]

In the wake of the Boxer Uprising, a classically educated teacher of previously conservative disposition, Wu Zhihui (1864–1953), announced his new principles: always support the people against the monarchy, students against teachers, and the younger generation against the older generation. Wu was neither arrested nor fired from his job but simply encouraged to pursue further education in Japan. An even more telling incident occurred in 1903. The "*Subao* case" is worth outlining because it entails one of the first nationwide instances of full-blown anti-Qing feeling: not simple criticism of the government but the desire to replace the dynasty entirely. A group of radicals including Zhang Binglin, Cai Yuanpei, and Wu Zhihui (back from Tokyo) founded the Patriotic School and the Patriotic Girls' School in Shanghai to appeal to nationalistic students. The schools organized public meetings, discussions of Western political theory, and student militia training. At this time, Russian troops originally involved in the efforts to suppress the Boxers were refusing to leave Manchuria, and students demanded that the Qing do more to defend the northeast. A fourth, younger man, Zou Rong, came to study at the Patriotic School.

These men also wrote for the *Subao* daily newspaper, which openly called for revolution in 1903. Zhang Binglin had also called the emperor a "little clown" and used *Subao* to carry on a polemic against Kang Youwei's reformism. The Qing understandably wanted to execute such men, but the radicals were, ironically enough, protected in the International Settlement by British jurisprudence. The Qing tried to entice Wu and Cai outside the Settlement by inviting them to address a meeting. That did not work, but finally the British-dominated Municipal Council agreed that the *Subao* had at the least committed *lèse-majesté*, and issued arrest warrants.

Interestingly, the radicals were warned ahead of time by sympathetic Chinese officials. There were personal ties between radicals and elements of officialdom – the literati world that spawned them both was not all that large. And, at least as important, there were political ties: reformers in officialdom might think the radicals' proposals were extreme and their anti-Manchuism overblown, but many still felt that their job was to help the government move forward, not engage in repression. In the end, Wu and Cai fled to enroll in universities in Europe, but Zhang Binglin and Zou Rong gave themselves up to the Shanghai authorities – once they had made sure they would be in the custody of the British, not the Qing.

At that point, the Qing authorities demanded custody of the prisoners or at least that the Shanghai court execute them. This resulted in long legal maneuvering with the British authorities, who saw their own legal position and principles at stake. After lengthy (and public) negotiations, the two men were tried in the Shanghai Mixed Court. Zhang and Zou were given brief prison terms, though the Chinese judges urged life imprisonment. The whole incident served to augment the scope of imperialism in China, forming a chapter in the Shanghai International Settlement's rise to de facto autonomy and its long role as incubator and safe haven for Chinese radicals. Of greater immediate importance was the turn of Chinese public opinion against the Qing. Even if the radicals appeared extreme, the Qing had made itself look vindictive, incompetent, and ridiculous. It appeared the Qing was prosecuting sincere if naïve people not for treason but for their opinions on Russian aggression. In the court of public opinion, the Qing was convicted of weakness on two fronts, both in the northeast and in Shanghai. Zou got sick and died in prison, thus becoming a martyr, while Zhang emerged a hero in 1906.

The *Subao* case was more than an incident that hurt the Qing. It was symptomatic of collusion between officials, who no doubt thought of themselves as loyal to the true interests of the government, and radicals, many of whom were themselves vague about the exact line between protest and revolution. Part of 1911 is the story of generational tensions and cooperation: the struggle between conservative fathers and radical sons, and also, of course, their ultimate loyalty to each other. The local magistrate illegally protected the family of Song Jiaoren from persecution when that young man openly rebelled against the government. Such phenomena were not simply the result of particularistic ties or the weakness of the central government. They reflected the growing revolutionary atmosphere. The revolutionary atmosphere affects even elites, especially elite youth who understand that they cannot simply inherit their fathers' positions and attitudes. Elite youth form the key to revolutionary ideals, endeavor, and organization. They naturally use their personal ties to protect themselves and the movement. Meanwhile, even conservative elites lose much of their faith in the status quo and some of their nerve; without this, indeed, the revolution cannot get off the ground. Marxist historians have tried to tie Chinese revolutionaries to an emerging bourgeois class; this simply does not work. Some came from well-off traditional gentry families; many came from families that had produced officials in the past but were not in decline. Either way, they inherited a Confucian obligation to save society.

These features produced by a general revolutionary atmosphere were not unique to China. The equally agonizing death-throes of the Czarist Empire in Russia gave rise to a similar mood. In the Russian case, this was captured, if critically, by Fyodor Dostoyevsky in *The Possessed*. The notion of a revolutionary atmosphere encompasses not just the confusion of conservatives and middle men, but also the extreme millenarian hopes that suddenly seem realistic, or at least possible. Kang Youwei's utopian fantasy of a world without families, governments, nations, and other such limitations on human potential became ever more popular even though he himself tried to keep it under wraps. Revolutionaries frequently posited that, as soon as the Manchus were gotten rid of, the Han Chinese would soon have their house in order and all would be well. For the handful of Chinese anarchists, "evolution" was less a matter of blind struggle for group survival than the cosmic path heading toward true civilization.[25] Struggle was to be directed only toward universal goals, to allow humankind to exist with liberty and equality. One of the Chinese anarchists' greatest successes was to spread Kropotkin's notion of "mutual aid": the idea that both biological evolution and cultural progress were primarily achieved through mechanisms of cooperation, that groups (species) advanced as a whole rather than through intramural competition.

The belief in anarcho-communism was predicated on the assumption that the age of economic abundance was around the corner. In the years after the *Subao* incident and from very different perspectives, Liu Shipei and Wu Zhihui agreed that the old order had to be replaced with a stateless system based on natural justice. Liu thought that much in the Chinese tradition was compatible with anarchism, such as Daoism and the "laissez-faire" attitude toward government found in Confucianism, whereas Wu believed only in a scientific future. But they both favored a revolution that would begin with the overthrow of the Manchus and then go on to abolish the state apparatus entirely. The anti-Manchu revolution thus would not result in a new government but in voluntary associations. The Chinese people acting together would then throw off Western imperialism. Liu, indeed, was the first Chinese to work out a theory of revolution in which the peasantry was to play a major role. He foreshadowed the Communists' later insights, teaching a simple populist message: the oppressed will rise up. Liu also anticipated the Leninist thesis on imperialism, positing that colonial struggles for independence would lead to such stress in the home countries that the West would face domestic revolution, and he called on the victims of Western imperialism to unite.

Aside from such political tracts, a key expression of the new revolutionary atmosphere came in the form of fiction.

Modern Chinese nationalism, Han identity, newspapers and other new forms of public expression, and indeed the "people" itself, all emerged in the last years of the Qing. Traditional Chinese literature had produced much wonderful prose fiction, but the genre was regarded as inferior to poetry or philosophical commentary, both of which were tested in the exams. It cannot be a coincidence that late Qing intellectuals suddenly discovered the aesthetic and social value of prose fiction at this time. The political scientist Benedict Anderson has suggested a link between the novel and the nation. Both depended on imagined connections, linear homogeneous time, and bounded space. Novels deal with characters who may not know of each other's existence but share the same social world and move through the same time periods. As novels illustrate a "sociological organism moving calendrically through homogeneous, empty time," so are nations conceived as communities moving through history.[26] Novels also offered a way to reach larger audiences than more erudite forms of literature. Print vernacular could come closer to spoken Chinese than the classical language yet avoid regional and dialectical chaos, thus creating an important basis for national unity.

In the wake of the 1898 reform movement, progressive intellectuals called for a "poetry revolution" and a "fiction revolution." But poetry inevitably became marginalized, especially after it no longer offered useful training for the examinations. It was the novel that seemed to offer boundless possibilities: new forms of self-expression and better ways to comprehend the world, promote moral values, and advocate social change.[27] Liang Qichao, for one, thought that the novel was the ideal instrument for remaking the Chinese people. In a sense, the didacticism of the Confucian approach toward literature lived on. Lin Shu (1852–1924), a great translator who produced works in elegant literary Chinese, praised Charles Dickens's exposures of Britain's social ills. "Without Dickens describing the situation, how would people know about this nest of thieves persisting in their midst? ... I regret only that we have no Dickens capable of revealing accumulated social wrongs by writing a novel and thus reporting these wrongs to the authorities ..."[28]

In fact, Chinese writers were trying to do this. Liu E (Tieyun, 1857–1909) wrote the semi-autobiographical *The Travels of Lao Can* between 1904 and 1907. The novel opens with a dream allegory about Lao Can and two friends traveling on a ship – the Chinese ship of state. Heavily loaded, "six masts with old sails and two new masts," it is foundering in rough seas. As the water pours in, the sailors rob the passengers. One passenger tries to rouse his fellow travelers, cursing them as slaves, reminding them that the ship is their "own inherited property," and urging them to seize it back from the crew. He then collects funds from the passengers and promptly retreats when trouble breaks out. Lao Can tries to offer the crew better navigation instruments, but he is accused of peddling foreign products. He too flees.[29]

Liu E thus targeted his sharpest criticism not at foreign invaders or merchants – nor yet at the Chinese people as a whole, though the dream allegory hardly flattered them – but at the rapacity and stupidity of officialdom.

And the revolutionaries were shown as beneath contempt, both rapacious and cowardly. As the reclusive Yellow Dragon put it, "Do you think that heavenly justice, national law, and social custom will only be destroyed at the time of the southern revolution? They were overthrown long ago!"[30]

The events that historians now emphasize as central to the making of modern China, late-Qing novelists digested as the background to stories about more or less ordinary people. In *The Sea of Regret* Wu Jianren (Woyao, 1866–1910) describes the turmoil of the Boxer Uprising. The main characters are neither particularly pro- nor anti-Boxers, but simply want to avoid trouble. Some get caught in the crossfire, however. One goes into hiding, eventually emerging to find "devastation as far as the eye could see. All the buildings had burned down, and what remained was a sea of rubble. Numerous bodies still lay in the streets, shapeless masses of blood-caked flesh, strewn in all directions."[31] This brief novelistic description of Tianjin, which was indeed devastated by Boxer occupation and cruel foreign reprisals, perhaps allowed Wu's readers to absorb some of the unimaginable events of the recent past.

Fiction also provided women with their own voice. The revolutionary Qiu Jin's (1875–1907) "Stones of the Jingwei Bird" relates how some remarkable young women managed to escape their families to pursue education and independence in Japan.[32] The author herself sold her dowry jewelry in 1904, leaving her husband and two children in Beijing to enroll in a school in Tokyo. "Stones of the Jingwei Bird" emphasizes the oppression of families, especially daughters. Qiu Jin said that women would be oppressed as long as they had no way to earn their own living – and she linked the status of women to the fate of the Chinese nation. In the words of one of her characters, "The mother is essential in family education and in giving birth to the new citizens of the nation; therefore, in civilized nations, men value the relation between men and women and recognize that women's rights are equal."[33] The nation is not the property of men alone.

In sum, novels helped give rise to new expressions of feeling and ideas. The revolutionary atmosphere not only contributed to the revolution but helped people to interpret it when it arrived. When the Wuchang Uprising of October 1911 led to a series of provincial secessions, the Chinese knew what to make of these events. Revolution. But what, exactly, was revolution for?

# 3   Ideas and ideals in the fall of the Qing

Leading up to the Revolution of 1911, the reformers who favored a constitutional monarchy and the revolutionaries who favored a republic engaged in debate, often vituperative. This debate was philosophical and emotional, abstract and personal, and dominated by communities of exiles facing dangerous and precarious conditions. Both groups can be labeled "nationalist": this does not get us very far, but it is important. Both groups tended to favor a strong, modernizing state, though not the existing government; both envisioned parliamentary democracy of some sort. Differences arose on the question of political forms, but perhaps more importantly on how to define the "nation." Did "Chinese" refer to Han ethnicity or to a kind of civic participation? The revolutionaries emphasized that theirs was, among other things, a "racial revolution" and they demanded "racial revenge" for the ongoing crimes of the Manchus against the Han. For the revolutionaries, state-building depended on nation-building. They also began to think about social justice, signs of an embryonic concern for peasants and workers. The reformers tended to downplay ethnic differences, citing the assimilation of the Manchus to Han ways. They thus defined nationality in terms of the state and emphasized that true citizenship depended on education. Finally, the two groups differed on means: the gradualism of reform versus the sharp break of revolution.

Regardless of the exact terms of the debate, the radical Confucians of the 1890s had created a new conceptual space. A new language articulated ideas about nation, citizen, public opinion, freedom, authority, competition, and progress: new forms of human association. The single most powerful political image of the past – the emperor as Son of Heaven and its panoply of symbolic reaffirmations of the unity of the empire and the cosmos – was collapsing. It was not easy to escape the power of this image. Attempting to replace it with the New Text image of Confucius never really got off the ground, perhaps because Chinese culture had all along consisted of much greater complexity. Beginning in fits and starts, the image of a united people backed by a theory of the "Han race" would replace the emperor as the symbolic core of the political culture. This was the nationalist project, done under the most difficult of circumstances: the occupation of parts of China by foreign armies, the unstoppable spread of opium addiction among all classes, the slow but seemingly inescapable breakdown of central and local governments, moral failure, and deracination. Yet it was also a time of great hope – leaps of faith in the future.

And who would carry out the nationalist project? There was a bit of romance in the self-image of young men who were willing to sacrifice their lives for their countrymen. As Tan Sitong (1865–98) put it, "in an age bound by autocracy, knights-errant alone can help us to arouse ourselves and prevent the people from becoming more and more benighted, weak, and degenerate."[1] Some committed suicide to wake up their countrymen. Some attempted to assassinate government leaders. Others led armed uprisings. Tan himself died a martyr, refusing to flee Beijing and executed by the Empress Dowager in the wake of the 1898 reform movement. His death formed an unacknowledged link between the radical Confucians and the later revolutionaries. Qiu Jin became the first female martyr to the revolution when the Qing executed her for plotting an uprising in 1907. She was not only an anti-Manchu revolutionary, but also a firm supporter of women's rights – another theme of the 1911 Revolution.

## Empire and nation

To understand the ideas of the new intelligentsia, we must understand what it was they were arguing about. What was "China"? Let us begin with the problem of the historical subject. We have mentioned the importance of dating above. Time (or at least history) was divided by dynasties from their founding through their various emperor's reigns. Kang Youwei had instead wanted to date all history from the birth of Confucius (like the West's Anno Domini) – not surprising given his views on Confucius. Soon, the revolutionaries had their own dating system: from the Yellow Emperor, supposedly some 4,000 years previously. Confucius was just one thinker, but the Yellow Emperor was the progenitor of the Han race. With the success of the revolution, time started anew, and 1912 became Republic Year One, 1913 Republic Year Two, and so forth.

The question of dating captures the difference between empire and nation. Historians of China have long drawn two sets of distinctions. First, between imperial China – the multi-national empires of the various dynasties, comparable to the Roman empire, the Persian empire and, coming down into more modern times, the Ottoman and Habsburg empires – and China as a nation-state like modern France. Second, between Chinese identity as marked by culture and as marked by ethnicity or "blood." Modern nations have generally used "culture" to define the commonalities shared by the people (like language and religion), but in China cultural identity was associated with the empire. This is because ethnically diverse peoples could share Confucianism and Buddhism. Even the "barbarians" who invaded China and formed "conquest dynasties" were themselves incorporated into the Chinese way of life: the Mandate of Heaven was rewarded on the basis of virtue, not bloodlines. During the Chinese imperial era, to adopt orthodox (Confucian) culture was to become a member of the empire. But in the late Qing the modern Chinese nation was conceived ethnically, so that Chinese identity or what came to be called "Han" identity was related to a mythology of shared ancestry (bloodlines). In other words, one was either born Chinese or not, if ethnicity rather than culture is the key.

Yet the distinction between tradition/empire/culture versus modern/ nation/ethnicity can be exaggerated.[2] Recently, historians have pointed to an ethnic awareness in Confucianism itself. From their earliest contacts with the northern nomads, Chinese saw "barbarians" as culturally backward, congenitally rude, uncouth, stinking, bestial, and immoral. As well, the distinction between culture and ethnicity can be a fine one indeed – if you act in orthodox ways long enough, you can claim Han ancestry. Furthermore, the Qing had deliberately created a distinct Manchu identity for itself: the imperial line, the court aristocracy, and its military.[3] The Qing used the traditional Chinese bureaucratic system and supported the gentry class in China proper, but it ruled, sometimes only very indirectly, over the outlying areas of the empire in ways that treated the Mongols, the Tibetans, and the Uighurs as separate peoples. It tried to prevent Han Chinese migration to the outlying areas and even sometimes tried to protect the indigenous tribal groups of the southwest. Its goal, needless to say, was not to respect the rights of minorities but to preserve order across the huge empire and to acquire the benefits of imperialism, such as the fighting prowess of Mongol allies and the spiritual ministration of Tibetan lamas. The emperor sought glory in the loyalty of distinct subject groups. So, to the degree that the Qing did *not* simply assimilate into Chinese ways, it marked both ethnic awareness and imperial rather than national thinking. And it had no cultural policies designed to unite the various peoples.

From the viewpoint of most Chinese, however, the Qing did look assimilated because – within China proper, or the old Ming boundaries – it adopted the traditional bureaucratic system, promoted the Confucian classics, and generally presented itself in orthodox moral terms. Many Manchus were, over time, essentially sinified, speaking and writing only Chinese, forgetting their military roots. Yet the imperial family and other important Manchus continued to conduct strange (to the Chinese) shamanistic rituals; intermarriage was prohibited; Manchus were given stipends; and top government posts were reserved for Manchus. Ethnic and political issues were thus linked together in the minds of many Chinese radicals: the government's incompetence and corruption, Manchu privileges, republicanism, and conflicting loyalties: to dynasty or to nation? Perhaps, if a "Han" dynasty instead of the Manchu Qing was ruling when the crises struck, a constitutional monarchy could have emerged instead of the racial revolution of 1911.

Let us clarify the distinction between the nation and the nation-state. A Chinese identity existed long before the twentieth century, so we might

speak of an ancient Chinese nation, but there was never a Chinese nation-
state, and the sense of national identity was not strong. As carriers of the
dominant culture in all of East Asia, the Chinese – unlike the Japanese,
Vietnamese, Koreans, and others of their neighbors – did not have to worry
about their identity until the twentieth century. Chinese-ness thus became a

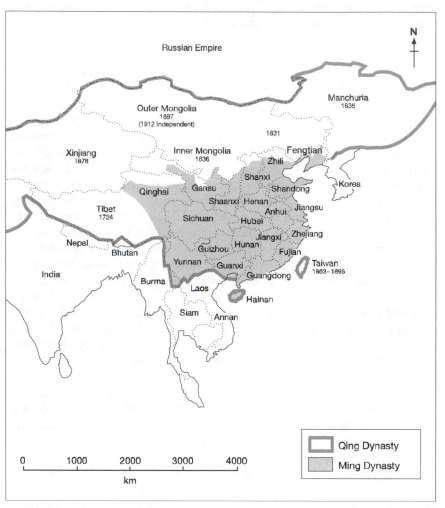

*Map 3*  The Ming and Qing empires

The territories of the Qing empire (1644–1912) were much larger than those of the
Ming (1368–1644). The Ming essentially comprised the agricultural lands of what we
now call "China proper." The Manchu conquest encompassed the Ming but also
created a new Asian empire. In addition to Manchuria and Mongolia, the new empire
also came to include much of sparsely-populated central Asia. Often, the Qing kept
local leaders in command, the emperor in Beijing acting as a distant overlord, and
Qing policy was generally to discourage assimilation to Han Chinese ways.

*Source*:  Courtesy of Geospatial Information Science Team, Computing Center, Academia Sinica.

kind of default value, seldom invoked because it could be taken for granted. At the beginning of the twentieth century, the Chinese nation-state had to be created: the people had to be convinced to identify themselves with "their" nation and to sacrifice themselves for it. And, so it was said, a strong government to oversee the nation had to be built. State-building and nation-building were thus twinned, but distinct, programs. Both were ideological processes, since different social groups promoted different versions of the nation and of the state.

The "nation-state" was a nineteenth-century European ideal. Ideally, a government should rule over one "people" and each people, if sufficiently advanced, deserved its own government. In fact, given that there are thousands of nations or potential nations ("peoples"), that different groups tend to scatter over large areas, and that ethnic identities change over time, the nation-state seems an impossible ideal. But it was a powerful concept that many, from Irish to Italians, from Germans to Hungarians, understood as offering them liberation against imperial overlords. Benedict Anderson has posited that a nation is an "imagined political community" in the sense that its members have to imagine each other since it is too large for them to actually know one another, but still a community whose members are connected to one another in "deep, horizontal comradeship."[4] Contrast the village, where everybody really does know one another. And contrast the empire, in which the citizens of a nation are completely different from the subjects of an emperor (a vertical relationship) in their expression of solidarity with one another. Though new, nation-states imagined themselves as old, a people traveling through all of time to fulfill their destiny in the form of political sovereignty: as when Kang Youwei stretched back to Confucius for a founding moment or the revolutionaries traced "Han people" genealogically back to the Yellow Emperor.

So, was a "nation" of China already hidden in the dynastic empires before the nineteenth century? Perhaps we can find it in "ritual" (*li*). Taking the family as the core of Chinese values, *li* prescribed a common emphasis on similar *behavior patterns* rather than on common beliefs, among various classes and regions.[5] Families were organized as economic units tracing descent through the father's line and giving the eldest male great authority. Property was divided equally among all surviving male heirs, and something close to the nuclear family was the basic household unit in an economy marked by the free sale of land and agricultural products. Wealthy families might avoid the splitting of property, and wealthy lineages maintained some communal property, but the nuclear family was the norm. Filial piety was a central mode of behavior, marked by required rituals of respect for parents while they were alive and mourning for them after their deaths. Daughters were "married out," thus belonging to their husband's family. Of course, there were exceptions – but the social norms were clear. Peoples who did not acknowledge these norms certainly were not Chinese.

Religious beliefs and gods took an astonishing variety of forms, but the popular religion roughly mirrored the bureaucratic structure of the state, as the gods themselves were organized into a hierarchy linked together by avenues of communication upward and downward. The local city god was analogous to the country magistrate, the lowest level of the official bureaucracy: both made periodic reports up to their superiors, and both were responsible for the well-being of their communities. The imperial state was thus not entirely a foreign, distant abstraction, but domesticated; indeed, every household contained a kitchen god, the lowliest of the gods but ultimately reporting up to the Jade Emperor. In this way the heavenly bureaucracy penetrated the village rather more successfully than the imperial bureaucracy. This was not Confucianism, but it was compatible with the state's ideology, which officially recognized many gods while proscribing (not always successfully) others. Social integration was furthered by the gentry and examination candidates who lived in most rural areas, while marketing networks brought ordinary peasants into spheres larger than their villages.

In other words, the Chinese nation in the traditional empire was defined by patrilineal and patriarchal families in a commercialized economy whose religious system gave ordinary people a domestic image of an otherwise unimaginably powerful and distant state. The vast empire was marked by regional, ethnic, and linguistic variations, as well as by distinct classes. Yet during the Qing, all males shaved their foreheads and wore queues in the Manchu fashion, further demonstrating the reach of the state as an integrative – and coercive – force. Unlike, say, the Habsburg or Ottoman empires, the empire of the Qing did not consist *primarily* of different peoples but rather *primarily* of this Chinese nation. Mongols and Uighurs occupied large territories but constituted tiny percentages of the total population, living in the literally marginal lands of Inner Asia. In China proper, the lands of settled agriculture, many layers of village, town, regional, and urban elites saw themselves as part of a larger secular world that stretched up to the emperor. Gentry learned Mandarin, the northern language that was naturally spoken in one dialect or another by some two-thirds of the population, as the lingua franca of the entire empire; the writing system of characters also worked independently of local languages. And below the level of gentry, local elites – even semi-literate village elders – knew they were part of an unimaginably large political system. Not only did they know this, but they could also use official state rituals: as county magistrates prayed for rain, so could they; as officials maintained government temples, so they maintained local temples; and as provincial gentry might found Confucian academies or charitable orphanages, so village landlords might pay for a school teacher or physician.[6]

Chinese identity in late imperial times thus stemmed from a ritual polity. Yet when all is said and done, if Qing China possessed a shared cultural consciousness, whether or not it produced a *national* identity is another question. Probably most Chinese felt a sense of centrality and civilization. However, it is difficult to find an articulated sense of nationalism ("I am Chinese and loyal to China") before the last years of the nineteenth century. Traditionally, kinship and local identities were of more immediate importance, since to be, say, a Shaoxing man in Beijing (from the city of Shaoxing in Zhejiang Province) gave one a set of contacts and a means for being known. Nor was "loyalty" – a much-prized virtue – oriented toward the nation. Below the nation, so to speak, loyalties were particularistic, given to kin, comrades, and community, and above the nation loyalty was given to the emperor or dynasty. There was no national flag or, significantly, any other particular symbol of the state. Instead, the state was embodied in the living emperor and his official servants. And these men did most of their business in private.

Overall, the imperial state encouraged local identities as a model of community cohesion and a building block of empire. The Sacred Edicts, which officials, gentry, and local elders were charged with reading to the commoners, emphasized domestic virtues: "filial piety and brotherly submission," hard work, "generosity toward your kindred," and devotion to neighborhood.[7] The classical Confucian idea was that virtuous family members would be virtuous imperial subjects. Or as a nineteenth-century merchant document, explaining the establishment of a Guangdong native-place association in Shanghai put it: "China is made up of prefectures and counties and these are made up of native villages, [and the people of each] make a concerted effort to cooperate, providing mutual help and protection. This gives solidarity to village, prefecture and province, and orders the country."[8] Native-place ties thus did not contradict other loyalties and could evolve into modern nationalism under the pressures of imperialism. As historian Bryna Goodman points out, "native-place identity incorporated feelings for territory, ancestors, cultural, and linguistic ties, all of which have tended to play important roles in the formation of modern nationalisms."[9] Yet the existence of the building blocks of nationalism in the Qing was not the same thing as full-scale nationalism itself.

The philosopher Wang Fuzhi (1619–92), living through the collapse of the Ming and the conquest of the Qing, articulated the clearest assertion of nationalism before the nineteenth century. Other gentry of his generation often proclaimed their personal loyalty to the Ming royal house, but Wang stated a principled objection to the Qing: the Manchus could never become legitimate rulers because they were a different people as defined in terms of land, language, customs, and blood, and different peoples could not mix together. However, Wang's ethnic nationalism was forgotten, his dangerous writings unpublished. During the pax Qing, the state had little trouble suppressing the relatively few eruptions of anti-barbarian sentiment, and there was no speculation about "Chinese identity" as such. The rediscovery of Wang and the secret publication of his dangerous works fed the revolutionary fervor of the late Qing.

## Nationalism and state-building: Liang Qichao

The central question of the first decade of the twentieth century was revolution. The so-called "constitutionalists" wanted the Qing to pursue reforms more wholeheartedly and to turn China into a constitutional monarchy. Their main concern was not the fate of the Qing royal house but the fate of China. They feared the disruptions that revolution would inevitably bring. Their models were Britain, Germany, and especially Meiji Japan. The revolutionaries, by contrast, wanted to overthrow the Qing entirely and create a republic. Their models were the United States and France. Both sides had convincing arguments: the constitutionalists warned that the chaos of revolution would encourage imperialists to make further incursions into China, and that the Chinese people were not ready for republicanism. The revolutionaries argued that the Qing was simply not committed to reform and that the Manchus were irredeemably evil. The constitutionalists envisioned a multi-ethnic state that would eventually be managed by an elected parliament; the monarch would serve as a symbol of national unity. The revolutionaries envisioned a Han Chinese state without hereditary privileges and a functioning democracy; some revolutionaries were socialists.

Yet it is important to note what both groups shared: a faith in the gradual development of democratic-constitutional procedures, a sense of the Chinese nation as distinct from the dynasty, a commitment to making this China wealthy and powerful, and a belief in progress. Neither group really thought the common people were ready for democracy; strong leadership and a strong state were required. Constitutionalists and revolutionaries shared another basic premise: that social Darwinism accurately described a world where "the strong eat the weak." Read optimistically, social Darwinism in China constituted an early-twentieth-century version of a "modernization" program. In the hands of Yan Fu (1854–1921), evolution became a program of institutional change. Yan's translations – really, annotated abridgements the most important of which were of the biologist T.H. Huxley in 1898 and the sociologist Herbert Spencer in 1903 – shook a still-Confucian world of cosmic harmony to its roots. In its place, Yan Fu introduced a world of the struggle for survival and selection of the fittest – a fearsome place where the unfit perished. Such a picture corresponded to the international world China had been discovering since the 1840s, and by the end of the nineteenth century, as the Chinese learned of the contrasting fates of Poland and Japan, the Darwinian version of reality seemed confirmed. Turning Spencer on his head, they replaced determinism with a new rationalization for planned change. Whether change was to be revolutionary or reformist, progress was valued in itself.[10]

The obverse side of social Darwinism was simply that China might be left behind to perish like Poland or India. Darwinism found quick appreciation in China because, in spite of the numerous ways it differed from Confucianism, it made intuitive sense. As Richard Hofstadter has observed in the American context, scientific studies may "command so much interest and acquire so much prestige within the literate community that almost everyone feels obliged at the very least to bring his world-outlook into harmony with their findings ..."[11] In the United States, conservatives welcomed the new gospel from Britain as confirmation of laissez-faire economic competition. Social Darwinism "defended the status quo and gave strength to attacks on reformers and on almost all efforts at the conscious and directed change of society."[12] Its effects in China were almost the precise opposite, while still giving the same scientific imprimatur to the new nationalism. Social Darwinism supported thinking in terms of the group; it attacked the status quo (a complacent political and social hierarchy); it strengthened the hands of reformers; and it justified planning rather than laissez faire. In China, believers in human rights and egalitarianism, as well as those who promoted a more exclusive nationalism, seized on social Darwinism as the ultimate proof of their arguments.

One reason for this was simply that social Darwinism came to China a generation later, when in Europe and even the United States individualism was waning. Around the world, by the end of the nineteenth century, Darwinian struggle was seen in collectivist terms, in the struggle among nations (or, sometimes, races) for world domination. The British bard of imperialism Rudyard Kipling was urging the United States to "take up the white man's burden" by seizing the Philippines from Spain, and "imperialism" itself was a new word that still seemed to represent good and bold intentions, without the pejorative sense it later acquired.[13]

Darwinism could be used to justify either imperialist expansion or the struggle against imperialism as the "fittest" was determined. A belief in progress had been foreign to the Confucian tradition, while social Darwinism was highly teleological. It was used to justify both cautious, gradualist reform, and outright, wild millenarianism. "Truth and justice progress everyday; education does not rest for a second and also the revolution never stops," wrote a confident revolutionary.[14] Kang Youwei's interpretation of the "three ages" of the New Text school had firmly placed Chinese history on a linear path toward the future. Whether progress was seen as slow and steady or fast and jerky; whether the process, or the end, was seen as ethical or amoral; and whether utopia or endless flux would result – all were matters of intellectual taste. The one thing Darwinism in China could not justify was the status quo, an evolutionary process gone wrong. Again, constitutionalists and revolutionaries alike tended to blame imperial "tyrants" and "despots" of the past who had turned the Chinese people into slaves. For constitutionalists, the problem lay with the monarchy itself; for revolutionaries the evils of monarchism were compounded by foreign (Manchu) control.

Both Western nationalism and anti-colonial struggles – the Philippines against the US, the Boers against the British – provided models for the Chinese. The emancipatory nature of peoples seeking liberation from shackles imposed from without and within was not lost on the Chinese.

"Young Italy" was an inspiration. Liang Qichao wrote admiringly of Mazzini as well as of George Washington. He praised the reforms of the 1868 Meiji Restoration for successfully modernizing Japan and equipping it to resist Western imperialism.

Liang was the leading spokesman for the constitutionalists between 1898 and 1911, wading into battle against the revolutionaries from their mutual exile in Japan and trying to influence events in China. His intellectual influence cannot be exaggerated; his audience included students (like Mao Zedong), the urban reformist elite, and even reform-minded officials. Even those who disagreed with Liang's specific political program, learned from him about the major categories of modern social and political organization. What he taught, essentially, was a civic version of nationalism that emphasized the role of citizens in building a strong state. He understood that national solidarity had to be created somehow, but sought a broad definition of Chinese-ness primarily as a political identity.

Liang, like his teacher Kang Youwei, was born near Guangzhou to an educated family, though in his case a rather poor farmer-scholar family with only two books. He passed the first two examinations at very young ages, becoming a *juren* at 16. He failed to become a *jinshi*, which soon became irrelevant to his real interests anyway. Meeting Kang at 17, he immediately became this charismatic sage's disciple and an adherent of the New Text school. Later, however, Liang noted more coolly that since his teacher "was so anxious to be erudite and different, he often went so far as to suppress or distort evidence, thereby committing a serious crime for the scientist.... As a man, Kang was totally subjective in myriads of things."[15] After 1898, they were usually separated and, gradually, Liang became independent of Kang: "I love Confucius, but I love the truth more."[16] If the intellectual world is divided between foxes (who "know many things") and hedgehogs (who "know one big thing"),[17] Liang was the ultimate fox, rushing from enthusiasm to enthusiasm, happy to contradict what he had said yesterday with what he believed today – as he himself admitted.

From 1898 to 1912 Liang lived in Japan, learning to read Japanese, though never learning to speak it well nor succeeding in several attempts to learn English. He made a number of acquaintances among the Japanese intelligentsia and political classes. The great majority of Liang's numerous essays from this period – on everything from the French Revolution and Russian nihilism to German theories of statism and American voting practices – were taken from Japanese sources. What Liang taught young Chinese about the West thus came through the mediation of Meiji Japan. By this time, late Meiji culture was changing.[18] Japanese who had supported radical liberalism and organized the "people's rights" movement in the 1880s had become more conservative by the end of the 1890s. In particular, they supported a stronger state – a view Liang found attractive in spite of his contempt for the Qing's rulers. Perhaps even more important for both Liang and the Chinese revolutionaries was Japanese sympathy for their cause. Pan-Asianism was in the air. Anti-imperialism appealed to both the left and the right of the late Meiji political spectrum.

In the wake of the 1898 debacle, Liang had a brief romance with democracy and revolution. However, Japanese statism, Kang Youwei's firm adherence to reform, and his personal trips to the West, brought him back to more moderate positions. Liang traveled to Hawaii and Australia in 1899–1900 and to Canada and the United States in 1903. The observant Liang saw corruption, slums, and class struggle. Western societies did not have all the answers, for all their wealth and power. Liang was also disillusioned by the Chinese communities in America, which he condemned as closed, parochial, and old-fashioned. In spite of their relative freedom and wealth, as Liang saw it, they remained devoted to private gain with no sense of the public good. He thus concluded that even under the best of circumstances democracy was a highly flawed system, and even the best Chinese were incapable of making it work. This brought Liang back to an elitist belief in top-down reform under the stabilizing influence of a wise and strong emperor.

Liang conceived of the nation as a community bound together by common political purpose. He blended notions of the "group," nation, and democracy into a potent new combination.[19] Liang's views were worked out in "The New Citizen" (1902–3), where he stressed the need for civic solidarity, a clear sense of the nation, popular sovereignty, and loosely democratic institutions. Political participation, although based on individual responsibility, still basically served to legitimate the state while also acting to unify it. Liang used the term "*xinmin*" (literally, new-people) to mean renewing the people so they could become citizens. The renewal of the people, meaning essentially their moral rectification, was a central Confucian value, explicitly expressed in the *Great Learning*, an ancient text made a basic part of the educational curriculum by Zhu Xi (1130–1200). Liang self-consciously drew on this tradition as he tried to reconceptualize the role of the people, but he also went considerably beyond it. One sign of the emergence of new ways of thinking was a new vocabulary. Liang's use of the term *guomin* to describe a participating "citizenry" represented a logical evolution of a term that had previously simply referred to the "people of the kingdom" or the "commoners." That Liang did indeed mean to refer to a citizenry and not merely the commoners is clear from his support for popular participation. Liang defined a citizenry not through individual rights but through their political membership: "The state is an aggregation of the people as a whole. If it is the people of a state who govern, legislate, and plan for the interest of the whole state and stave off the troubles that might afflict the state, the people then cannot be bullied and the state cannot be overthrown. This means citizenry."[20]

All of Liang's efforts after 1900 were bent toward the preservation and progress of China as a nation-state. "Public morality," or something like civic virtue, he defined in terms of its ability to strengthen group cohesion, while "private morality" was to shape individuals of use to the group.[21] "Among our people," Liang complained, "there is not one who looks on national affairs as if they were his own affairs. The significance of public morality has not dawned on us."[22] A state was dependent on its people; both arose out of a process of social evolution – from barbarism to civilization, from clans, to tribes, to the nation-state. Note that the state was therefore no less natural than the nation itself. At his most rhetorically exuberant, Liang showed how a state emerges out of national unity:

> It is not merely to have rulers, officials, students, farmers, laborers, merchants, and soldiers, but to have ten thousand eyes with one sight, ten thousand hands and feet with only one mind, ten thousand ears with one hearing, ten thousand powers with only one purpose of life: then the state is established ten-thousand fold strong.... When mind touches mind, when power is linked to power, cog-to-cog, strand around strand, and then a thousand roads meet in one center, this will be a state.[23]

Liang thus condemned the tendency toward fragmentation in Chinese society; the Chinese needed to find a basis of social and political unity previously lacking. These were common themes of the period, scarcely limited to Liang (Sun Yat-sen and others liked to compare the Chinese to scattered sand). If education, state intervention, and downright hectoring could produce stronger bonds, then there was hope. Liang believed that since grouping was natural to humanity, "public morality" revolved around group interests. A nation was not a chance collection of individuals, families, or tribes, but consisted of a people that, in modern times, had to become a citizenry. "In an age of struggle among nations for the survival of the fittest while the weak perish, if the qualities of citizens are wanting, then the nation cannot stand up independently between Heaven and Earth."[24]

This summarizes the political essence of Liang's nationalism: basically a civic nationalism, though with some ethnic notes. Liang fully accepted the social Darwinian vision of ruthless competition, which he saw as operating primarily at the level of nations. Like most Western theorists of nationalism and imperialism, Liang also understood "races" to be units of Darwinian competition. He once spoke of the imminent extinction of the "red" and "black" races at the hands of the "white" race, hoping that the "yellow" race would survive. Like other Chinese of the day, he understood the "Han" as a kind of race, though Liang insisted they were closely related to the Manchus. But the point here is that the language of race was really a way to talk about nationalism. With Russia threatening to the north, Japan in the process of subjugating Korea, Britain and Russia contending for influence in Central Asia, and the various Western powers dominating the Yangzi region, "racial extinction" of the Chinese was a valid fear. Liang's contribution to Chinese understanding of this fearsome world was to point out that modern imperialism did not stem from traditional state powers like the Roman or Ottoman empires but from nationalistic expansions of whole peoples, exemplified by British control over a quarter of the earth. This "national imperialism" was rooted in popular support for economic expansionism. The only way victims of this imperialism (like China) could resist was through mobilizing their populations just as their enemies had. This was the point of popular sovereignty. "Everyone who has even the slightest understanding of the concept of nationhood knows that the nation is not the private property of the imperial family but that it belongs to all," in the words of Shanghai's *Shibao* ("The Times"), a reformist paper Liang had helped found. "A nation goes into decline when its people do not know the difference between the nation and the dynasty."[25]

The "new people" were to display courage and zeal. They were to possess liberties and rights, though only in the context of loyalty to the nation. A civic identity and well-functioning political institutions would create unity without infringing on the individual's rights.[26] In other words, Liang's goal was dynamic unity; the means was citizens' rights. Individual and state are inextricably linked for Liang. This did not make Liang a republican in terms of late Qing political discourse. In Japan he learned to think of the state as something more than a collection of individual wills, or merely the sum of its parts. Following the German school of public law that dominated in the late Meiji, Liang treated the state as a concrete entity: neither as a mere abstraction nor as the traditional, despotic, dynastic state. None the less, if Liang did not promote individual rights for their own sake – that is, liberalism's faith in the dignity and worth of the individual – he generally favored the limited government of constitutionalism and the role of elected legislatures as the best means of fostering political participation. In sum, the meaning of democracy for Liang rested on the right of political participation, while his individualism was less defined in terms of legally guaranteed civil liberties than in terms of precisely that autonomy and freedom necessary to equip the citizen to participate. The point is not that Liang aimed at liberalism and failed to achieve it, but that he aimed at creating for the first time in China the notion of citizenship, and succeeded.

## Han nationalism: race and revolution

> To sweep away the despotism of these thousands of years, to cast off the servile nature bred in us over these thousands of years, to exterminate the five million and more hairy and horned Manchus, to expunge the pain and anguish of our humiliation of 260 years, to cleanse the great land of China.... This most exalted and incomparable aim is Revolution! How imposing a thing is revolution! How magnificent a thing is revolution![27]

Thus did Zou Rong, a young man originally from distant Sichuan but at the time studying in cosmopolitan Shanghai, sum up the main issues before the nation in 1903: the evil of the Manchus, the decadence of the Chinese, the inescapable opposition between the two, the sheer weight of the past (a problem greater than the Manchus alone), and the fiery powers of revolution. The term for "revolution" (*geming*) was a classical phrase referring to a change in the Mandate of Heaven given to a worthy imperial line. Japanese scholars in the nineteenth century decided "geming" was the most logical term to translate the Western notion of "revolution" (a term used in English to describe recurring cycles until the seventeenth century when it began to acquire its modern sense). Chinese intellectuals looked at French and American history to interpret revolution as the path from monarchies to republics. Still, the line between reform and revolution was hard to clarify, if only because the Qing put a price on the heads of both its critics like Liang and its enemies like Sun Yat-sen.

Zhang Binglin, Zou Rong's elder comrade in the *Subao* case, was the first Chinese to articulate a full-scale anti-Manchu ideology. He had been one of the first men in China to publicly cut off his queue. This, too, was a specifically revolutionary gesture, though so far what Zhang opposed was much clearer than what he supported. He opposed alien Manchu rule over native Han Chinese. The Manchus were trying to exterminate a vibrant native culture by a rude (but militarily stronger) barbarian one. Zhang was, to a degree, a relativist. He had no objection to barbarians being barbarians back in their own territories. He just did not think they could turn themselves into civilized Chinese. As a scholar, he claimed that the Qing had distorted the true Chinese culture and proven they were not fit to rule China. Many other revolutionaries felt Manchu rule had turned China into a "slave nation" – in fact, since the Qing was controlled by Western imperialists, the Chinese had been turned into "slaves of slaves."

Stories of the bloody battles, massacres, and rapes of the 1640s were told and retold. Anti-Manchu writings of the seventeenth century were rediscovered and reprinted. Interestingly, this was not solely the work of revolutionaries. Liang Qichao himself had revived Huang Zongxi's critique of the monarchy, and he wrote biographies of "Ming loyalists." Ming loyalists, as the term suggests, had refused to accept the legitimacy of Qing rule and gone into exile. Once seen as paragons of loyalty to the emperor under whom they had grown up – even respected by the new Manchu rulers – they were now seen as precursors of nationalist consciousness. For the revolutionaries, any form of anti-Manchuism represented a kind of spiritual ancestry. The stories of virtuous Han women jumping to their deaths rather than facing Manchu soldiers were vividly retold. If most of the Qing's soldiers were actually Chinese, the revolutionaries' point was still that the Manchus were bloodthirsty by nature. Their original crime had to be avenged. And their current crimes – suppressing the Han and cooperating with the imperialist powers – had to be dealt with. "Reform" was futile if only because the Manchu rulers would never sincerely support it. That left only revolution.

Much modern scholarship has basically accepted this position. Both the Guomindang and the Communist Party aligned themselves with revolution. However, many Western and not a few Chinese scholars have felt that the Manchus were being made a scapegoat for deeper problems. Liang Qichao said as much at the time. Anti-Manchuism may have distracted some of China's best minds from more important issues. Some scholars have even questioned the depth of anti-Manchu feeling and argue that it was simply revolutionary propaganda, effective but shallow. This is shown, they argue, by the rapid disappearance of anti-Manchuism after the revolution; indeed, it is true that the new Republic officially became a multi-national state that recognized the rights of all its peoples.

Still, the fact of anti-Manchuism cannot be denied. Republican forces in 1911 slaughtered several Manchu garrisons – including women and children. The Manchus, revolutionaries proclaimed, "have seized our lands and taken away our rights. Now in order to seek our revenge, we rightly ought to exterminate them."[28] Manchus in the south were turned into refugees, expelled from their homes and deprived of their property. (In the north, they were left alone if only because of the peace terms arranged by Yuan Shikai.) The court's own refusal to end legal privileges and governmental preferences for Manchus had added fuel to the revolutionary fire. A follower of Sun Yat-sen wrote: "The Manchu government is evil because it is the evil race which usurped our government, and their evils are not confined to a few political measures but are rooted in the nature of the race and can neither be eliminated nor reformed."[29] Others were less restrained, and Manchus were called everything from "stinking sheep" to "dogfuckers."

Revolutionary students and intellectuals adopted the language of race and imperialism that had become global by the end of the nineteenth century. It may be that racial categories as such were not new to China: typing and denigrating foreigners by skin color and other physical features can be traced to ancient times.[30] However, racism in the sense of a belief in the congenital and immutable inferiority or evil of a particular group or of other societies was not part of mainstream Confucianism. Modern Chinese nationalism also depended on a new kind of history – not the traditional history of the state but the history of the Chinese *people*. Again, Liang Qichao led the way, explicitly calling for a *national* history in 1902. But it was the revolutionaries who understood that a history of the Chinese nation meant reading ethnic differences back into the past – and into the future. Zhang Binglin and other members of the "National Essence" school looked at both biological and cultural factors to show how the "Han race" evolved historically. By biology, they were primarily thinking about ancestry and tracing lines of descent (as Chinese clans had long done). By culture, they were primarily thinking about the philosophers of the classical period of the Western Zhou (seventh through third centuries BC). One of their charges against the Qing was that the court, through the examination system, had suppressed the non-Confucian "hundred schools" of the Western Zhou, thus denying intellectual freedom to the Chinese. In historical fact, the Qing was following an orthodoxy created by the Chinese, but the rediscovery of the non-Confucian philosophers contributed to the intellectual ferment of the late Qing.

Zhang Binglin became one of the century's foremost scholars of the historical and philological research of Han Learning, specifically supporting the "Old Text" school opposed to Kang Youwei's New Text position.[31] He took such late Ming thinkers as Wang Fuzhi as his intellectual ancestors. Zhang affirmed that cultural identity rested on racial identity. Assimilation was thus a chimera: the Manchus could never become civilized. At the same time, culture was not simply determined by biology: it was built up and maintained only by the efforts of the particular people in question. Zhang believed that the Han people must understand that their historical role was to continue their common culture, lest it and thereby the Chinese people themselves be lost. Historically, he acknowledged that the Han was not a "pure" race, but in so far as other races had mingled with the Chinese over the centuries, they were not the racial enemies of the Chinese.

These propositions existed in some tension with each other. If Chinese could lose their identity and become barbarian, why couldn't Manchus become civilized? Above all, if a people is defined by cultural consciousness inherited from the past, where does change come from? Zhang saw culture as simultaneously rooted and growing. He even acknowledged that culture was learned, not genetically inherited – but he had a fallback position. He emphasized that if the Manchus *were* to become civilized, they would still have to relinquish their control over China, since civilized peoples did not oppress others. Zhang also believed that a conscious cultural identity required self-rule. This made the Manchus, defined as non-Han, automatically illegitimate rulers, though it also implied that the Manchus also deserved their own homeland. Unlike some revolutionaries, Zhang was not a committed democrat, though he was not necessarily opposed to democracy. Self-rule to him meant the self-rule of the ethnic nation.

*But who were the "Han"?* To answer this question – and in fact to pose it in the first place – Zhang and other revolutionaries turned away from cultural and moral categories to the notions of kinship and lineage. These were among the most basic tools of Chinese social organization and provided the vocabulary for separating the in-group from out-groups. The Qing had long distinguished "Man" (Manchu) from "Han," as well as the other peoples and tribes of the Empire to the west.[32] "Han" here was one of several terms used to describe the people(s) of a geographic area south of the Great Wall, east of Central Asia's mountains and deserts, west of the Pacific Ocean, and somewhat vaguely north of Southeast Asia's jungles. But the Qing was trying to classify loosely defined political groups, not genetically determined races. Zhang Binglin and the other revolutionaries, instead, spoke quite specifically of the Han people or Han race as those people who were descended from the Yellow Emperor. The Yellow Emperor myth was rewritten as a story of Han conquest of the Chinese plains some five thousand years earlier. This genealogical-racial project rested on a long-established definition of the Chinese "as a giant patrilineal descent group made up of intermarrying surname groups," as historian Patricia Ebrey has put it.[33] Unlike most peoples before modern times, the Chinese had long used surnames (passed through the father's line) as a primary mark of identity. Identity thus worked vertically back to ancestors, and horizontally: even people with no known relationship would assume they shared a common ancestor if they had the same surname. Some clans kept genealogies listing thousands of members over a dozen or more generations. One way to tell if a person were Chinese (as opposed to, say, Mongol or Turk) was to see if they had one of the relatively few Chinese surnames. In fact, many peoples adopted Chinese surnames – but this simply affirms the importance of establishing a Chinese identity.

A modern sense of "racial" identity was thus grafted onto notions of kinship and ancestry. Families had long used the principle of descent to trace their ancestral origins back to a few mythical culture-founders. To turn this into Han nationalism only took a shift to the Yellow Emperor as the only ancestor, through his twenty-five sons, of the various surname groups, all of whom then became biologically related. The Yellow Emperor became a kind of super-lineage founder and all living Chinese became brothers or at least cousins. The historian Don Price suggests that risking one's life for China thus became a matter of sacrificing for one's family, even fulfilling one's duties to the ancestors.[34]

In a demented tour de force of scholarship Zhang Binglin examined hundreds of genealogies to find China's pure descent groups. The revolutionaries' notions of identity were not refuted by the reformers but were widely seen as natural. Han identity did *not*, therefore, depend on physical appearance, language, or even birthplace, but on descent – or more precisely, on a myth of common descent. Modern Han nationalism was influenced by Western notions of racial categories (crudely: white, yellow, brown, red, black), which many Chinese, from Liang to Zhang, took as one basis of social Darwinian struggle. And Western racial subdivisions such as "Teutonic" and "Anglo-Saxon" were seen as parallel to distinctions between Manchus, Mongols, Koreans, and so forth. And "Han." Today the vast majority of Chinese accept the government's official ethnography: over 90 percent of the Chinese people are "Han," with the rest of the population being defined as of one or another minority ethnic groups (including Manchu).

*And what was the culture or "national essence" of China?* The political inheritance of the imperial state remained critical: under the Ming and Qing dynasties many people, not only elites, identified themselves both in terms of locality and in terms of larger, imperial bureaucratic structures and symbols. As noted above, a kind of ritual polity allowed ordinary commoners to understand themselves to be members of a larger, unseen community. In trying to transform this somewhat vague identity into something more modern, Kang Youwei used the New Text interpretation of Confucius as a charismatic founder of a religious tradition comparable to Jesus Christ. Yet the New Text school still respected the universal "Confucian" claims of Chinese kingship: regardless of his ethnicity, the emperor represented cosmic forces and the hopes of humankind, not a specific nation.[35]

Zhang Binglin naturally hated this approach and took a different tack. He wanted to rescue hidden parts of the past from the hegemony of Confucianism, which he associated with the bureaucratic despotism that was holding China back. Zhang attacked the New Text school's scholarship, not merely on grounds of specific textual issues but in terms of its romanticization of the Classics. Zhang felt that most of the Classics predated Confucius, who was their transmitter, not their author. To Zhang, the classics represented history, not scripture, revelation, or prophecy. This placed Zhang in the Old Text tradition of Han Learning. And the Old Text emphasis on history provided a basis for tracing the Chinese people *as* a people through time. This was the very project shared by the entire group of "National Essence" scholars, a project that lasted, in various forms, into the 1920s.[36] The term "national essence" was originally coined by Japanese concerned about the erosion of traditional Japanese culture in the 1880s, but its Chinese form grew naturally from Old Text textual and historical preoccupations. The English translation we use implies an unchanging core. This is not what the Chinese scholars meant at all, and they said so explicitly. They did not object to cultural change, but they felt it important to properly understand the past and maintain continuities with it. The national essence scholars of the late Qing were politically revolutionary, justifying revolution on the basis of Chinese history and culture. They defined identity as racial, ethnic, and genealogical, but it was also cultural. They feared that if Chinese civilization were lost, the Chinese people could not survive either. But they separated what they valued in the tradition from the institutions of the monarchy and Confucianism. Literature, painting and calligraphy, and the non-Confucian schools of thought were important to the national essence school, as well as China's legal and institutional development, heroes and loyalists, lords and great deeds, and the Chinese language itself. Scholars had a special role to play in keeping the nation strong by maintaining its cultural vigor.

The revolutionary situation also forced intellectuals to re-examine their assumptions about the nature of society. Did democratic ideals refer only to political participation or did they imply a deeper equality? How exactly would "the people" run its new government? The revolutionaries tended to be relatively optimistic. Hu Hanmin (1879–1936), one of Sun Yat-sen's closest followers, wrote in 1906:

> That absolute monarchy is unsuitable to the present age requires no argument.... The greatest difficulty in establishing a constitutional government, as experienced by other countries, is the struggle of the

common people against both the monarch and the aristocracy. The establishment of constitutional rule and the extension of democratic government were uniquely easy in America because at the time of independence there were only the common people. And this is precisely one of the great features of Chinese politics, since the aristocracy disappeared in the Qin and Han dynasties.... We can overthrow the Manchus and establish our state because Chinese nationalism and democratic thought are well developed.[37]

Hu Hanmin thus insists not on China's unique qualities but rather on China's readiness to join the trends of modern history. Revolutionaries such as Hu understood democracy as the only alternative to the monarchy they wished to destroy. Their critics accused the revolutionaries of a failure to thoroughly consider how democratic institutions could be rooted in China's monarchical soil. But it is not clear how useful detailed musings about

*Figure 3.1* A cartoon of workers and peasants carrying the burden of China's progress: a peasant pulling and a worker pushing a cart full of happy-looking gentry, officials, traders, and brokers. Merchants have the whip hand. In other words, China's better classes depended on exploitation.

*Source*: From the *Beijing Baihua huatu ribuo*, 17 May 1908, no. 241

婚姻自由

本邑周浦教民龔菜將及笄之女許字年已四十餘之同教丁姓女堅執不願與毌力爭數次龔夫婦置不理前日丁登門謁岳俗所謂通脚橋者龔擬與女與婿覿面女即奔至周猛橋教堂訴之神父並自陳不願之意神父遣人名龔夫婦至堂責令退婚且應回家後仍有雙通留龔女在堂讀書以絕其念。

*Figure 3.2* "Free Marriage" – a girl who doesn't want to marry the man of her parents' choice has brought in a (rather hairy) foreign missionary to plead her case and convince her parents to allow her to study at the missionary school for girls.

*Source*: From *Tuhua xinwen yulun shishibao*, 22 June 1909

bicameral versus unicameral legislatures or presidential versus parliamentary systems would have been. Of course the revolutionaries were naïve. But so were their critics, whose reformism was no more realistic given the obduracy of the Qing court.

And what of Hu's claim that China lacked classes? It may be that Hu was thinking more of a caste system or – as he remarks – the existence of a nobility. Gentry status could not be inherited like a dukedom. Hu regarded the destruction of the distinction between the rulers (Manchus) and the ruled as the key that would unlock all Chinese politics. But in contrasting China's situation to the economic classes of the West, he seems to be denying an obvious reality. This was the period when a few intellectuals first became aware that "society" could be mapped in terms of "classes." What the revolutionaries saw when they looked at Chinese society was not the total absence of group distinctions based on status or wealth but the relative absence of the class struggles that marked the rise of the working classes in Europe and America. Most Chinese intellectuals believed that the gap between rich and poor was not as large in China as in the West. They followed a vague kind of socialism for two reasons. First, given the backwardness of Chinese capitalism, they assumed that the state would have to play a large role in modernizing the economy – as, again, Meiji Japan demonstrated. And second, socialism promised precisely to forestall (not foster) disruptive and divisive class struggle. Chinese intellectuals agreed that the radical Western critique of capitalism was simply not very relevant to China. A few of Marx's shorter works began to be translated at this time, but there were no Chinese Marxists.

Still, the revolutionaries were dedicated to social justice. They certainly understood at least some of the hardships faced by the peasantry, and some called for nationalization of the land. Hu Hanmin condemned the status quo, whose "evil consequences" were "that the landlord can acquire absolute power in society and thereby absorb and annex more land, that the farmers can be driven out of work, that people may be short of food and thus have to depend on outside supply, and that the entire country may be made poorer while capital and wealth all go to the landlords."[38] The revolutionaries cited ancient precedents for land reform – for the problem of landlordism was hardly new to Chinese history. The populist strand of the revolutionaries was reflected in their appeals to secret societies, though in fact they shared little more than anti-Manchuism.[39] Semi-literate secret society leaders spoke in the language of popular Confucianism ("righteousness," "loyalty") whereas the revolutionaries spoke of social Darwinism and political modernity. None the less, the revolutionaries sometimes looked at the secret societies not merely as cannon fodder but as repositories of genuine Chinese identity. This romantic image did not survive 1911, by which time even the most radical of intellectuals regarded the secret societies as backward and superstitious. Only the small group of anarchists called for "social revolution" in the name of the workers and peasants, and even they as often spoke of the "whole people."

In sum, the revolutionaries clarified the concept of revolution and began to define a new national identity. "Revolution" was to clear the ground of old debris and start over. To replace one entire system with another. And one way or another, revolution in fact became one of the defining features of China's entire twentieth century. As for national identity, late Qing intellectuals constructed a vocabulary of ethnic, ancestral, racial, and "blood" terms *in addition to* cultural concepts centering around history, language, religion, and thought. What impelled political activism and a passionate kind of commitment on the part of thousands was Han nationalism. These views, in less compelling forms, influenced millions. The future republican political community would, it was thought, create a society of citizens working together to build China. The Revolution of 1911 certainly did not live up to the ideals of the revolutionaries nor, in the final analysis, was it made by them. But if – looking at the rapid disintegration of the Republic – we condemn the revolution as a failure, we are measuring by the revolutionaries' own standards.

# 4  From the military dictator to the warlords

Yuan Shikai assumed the presidency in February of 1912. He had the support of his own Beiyang Army – China's strongest – in the north and a deal with the National Alliance in the south. He was to rule China, more or less, until his death in 1916. The constitutional basis for Yuan's rule came from his selection as premier by the Qing's recently founded National Assembly and the official abdication of the Qing. The government of the southern revolutionaries also recognized Yuan, anticipating a republican political system in which they could lay claims to power as well. The new Republic adopted a five-color flag, representing the Han, Manchu, Mongol, Tibetan, and Hui (Muslim) nationalities, and it used the Western solar calendar. Time was reset. The years were to be counted not in reign periods, nor from the birth of Confucius or the Yellow Emperor, nor yet from the birth of Christ – but from the founding of the Republic itself. Year One had begun.

The new Republic claimed the mantles of both modernity and nationalism. Men cut their queues (or had them cut forcibly); more slowly, women unbound their feet. For city residents, handshaking began to replace – or supplement – bowing. Yet republican political institutions did not take root.

The revolution certainly overthrew the Qing and the entire monarchical system. Yet it is worth noting that the Qing court itself was not literally destroyed; the imperial family was not executed. When the Dowager Empress (Guangxu's widow), speaking on behalf of the infant emperor Puyi, signed the abdication agreement recognizing Yuan as premier, this was part of a deal allowing the court temporarily to remain in the Forbidden City and receive an allowance from the new government. Yuan took up official residence in the old imperial offices next to the Forbidden City – from where the Communist Party still runs the country today. Not until 1924 was the imperial family expelled from the Forbidden City, though the Republic was never able to regularly pay the agreed allowance and the old court officials sold off many imperial treasures, which are today scattered over the globe. More immediately, the ongoing practice of court rituals in the heart of Beijing into the 1920s – the young emperor receiving courtiers and even government envoys – might symbolize the magnanimity of the revolution.

Or it might symbolize the limits of the revolution and the compromises it had to make with the past.

Yuan Shikai essentially ruled as a military dictator: not only was his power derived *directly* from his support from leading army officers, but he also made plain the military nature of his rule by generally appearing in uniform. Yuan had personally established the most efficient divisions of the army when he was working for the Qing in the 1890s and early 1900s. The leading generals and other officers were thus his protégés, and he was an efficient civil administrator as well. Yuan built a successful career under the Qing in foreign affairs and administrative reform. His career demonstrates the shifting nature of power in modern China: mutating from imperial-bureaucratic forms to more militarized forms of rule. Military men had become more politicized during the late Qing and civilian politicians and bureaucrats had been building more ties to military forces. After Yuan's death in 1916, these trends resulted in outright warlordism.

One could count the bodies Yuan left behind on his rise to power. He betrayed the 1898 reformers, who had asked for his help at a crucial juncture that summer; he betrayed the Qing court, which had asked for his help in 1911; and he finally betrayed the Republic, in his monarchical campaign of 1915. Of course, each of these so-called betrayals could have been a pragmatic personal response to circumstance. The heart of any critique of Yuan goes not to his character but to his understanding of the new China that was then emerging. The state-building reforms he pursued had long been sought by the educated classes, but Yuan insisted on purely top-down administration. He stamped out elite democracy, stifled local initiative, and in the end destroyed his own regime.

## The politics of the early Republic

The politics of the early Republic was marked by a struggle between the local forces that had emerged in the late Qing on the one hand, and the bureaucratic state – which Yuan left largely unchanged from the time of the Qing – on the other. He made no attempt to harness local energies, which he no doubt considered undisciplined and dangerous. He failed to understand the potential of elite mobilization, much less popular mobilization. Yuan did attempt to reform the judiciary and financial organs of the government, employ men who had received a modern education, encourage industry, build schools (for boys), establish a modernized civil service exam system, suppress opium, and restore the infrastructure. He thus sought to continue and extend the late Qing's New Policies. Precisely because Yuan was a militarist, his government looks modern in a special sense of the word: if the army could serve as a model of disciplined popular mobilization, then the nation would advance in step. The military model later infused both Guomindang (Nationalist) and Communist notions of social mobilization. But in so far as Yuan ruled through a top-heavy bureaucracy, his government was conservative, corrupt, and inefficient.

Yuan's rule was marked – and marred – by the following actions: taking loans from the foreign banks and governments (instead of reforming the tax system), crushing parliamentary politics, repressing the so-called Second Revolution, ruling by decree, yielding to most of Japan's "Twenty-one Demands," and finally attempting to found a new dynasty in his own right. No wonder many Chinese judged the 1911 Revolution a failure. That Yuan's rule ended in disgrace and disaster, and established an escalating pattern of political crisis, violence, and fragmentation, however, was not entirely his fault.

Yuan Shikai inherited a government that was bankrupt, bleeding a deficit of 13 million yuan every month. The bulwark of the imperial tax system, the land tax, had been lost as the powers of the central government weakened. Yuan collected virtually none of the land tax, which remained in local and provincial hands. For all of Yuan's tools of repression, the new government's powers simply did not stretch as far down into local administration as even the Qing's. With customs revenues already in foreign hands, the Chinese government had to live off internal transit taxes and miscellaneous goods taxes such as the tax on tea: funds which could not possibly provide for the ordinary expenses of central administration, much less for reforms.

Yuan had no choice but to recognize all the foreign obligations of the Qing Empire. The foreign powers continued to keep virtually all of the customs tariffs and salt taxes, which they collected themselves under old treaty agreements, to repay indemnities and earlier loans. Moreover, these funds were now deposited in foreign banks during the period between collection and payment. Previously, the Qing government had handled moneys destined to repay foreign obligations, thus receiving the benefits from short-term deposits and exchange rate manipulations. But during the revolution the foreign powers took over the entire process. When Yuan's new government tried to raise tariffs, the Powers vetoed the proposal, and the effective rate remained under 4 percent. Many foreigners also pressed demands for payments for alleged property damage that occurred during the revolution.

China was actually falling deeper under imperialist control. Although World War I provided a brief respite from European pressures between 1914 and 1918, Japanese interest in China was growing dramatically. No Chinese government could have resisted the forces of imperialism at this point. In the wake of the war, the European Powers returned to China. In the historian Ernest Young's incisive phrasing, "The most vivid aspect of Western and Japanese imperialism in China in the first two decades of the twentieth century was its autonomous growth. It had struck roots in Chinese soil, as it were, and no longer needed special nourishment from London, Paris, Washington, St. Petersburg, Berlin, or Tokyo."[1] This is true so long as it is remembered that the big money came from precisely the foreign capitals. As with the International Monetary Fund today, loans to China came with many strings attached. As the political scientist Edward Friedman put it, imperialism in China created an "umbilical connection of loans, banks, debts, currency, trade, and investment with power."[2]

The first of the Republic's many political dramas opened with new elections scheduled for late 1912. Suffrage was limited by gender, wealth, and education, but some 40 million men, about 10 percent of the population, were given the vote. Political energies that had been mobilized during the last few years of the Qing carried over into the Republic. Democratic models were enthusiastically adopted by progressive social elements. In Shanghai, for example, new-style native-place associations produced constitutions, elected their officers to limited terms, and held open meetings – all in contrast to the more elitist ways of the older guild-like organizations.[3] At the national level, Song Jiaoren (1882–1913), a National Alliance member who had worked with Sun Yat-sen, organized the Nationalist Party (Guomindang) and campaigned on the promise that they would keep Yuan under control. The National Alliance was still fairly strong in the lower Yangzi Valley, and in the southeast Hu Hanmin served as military governor of Guangdong.

Liang Qichao and others organized more conservative parties. Zhang Binglin also organized a small party that attracted a few dissidents from the Nationalist Party, and a number of provincial military leaders also had their own parties. None the less, the Nationalist Party won the elections. As the new Parliament was getting under way in the spring of 1913, it was expected that Song would be elected premier, but he was assassinated in March under orders from Yuan Shikai. In October, after three ballots, and after a few arrests of MPs, many bribes, even more threats, the parliament finally elected Yuan president.

Meanwhile, after intense and difficult negotiations, Yuan put together a huge £25 million "Reorganization Loan" in April 1913. The terms of the loan to China were dictated by foreign banking interests and backed by their diplomats. A banking consortium was established so that Yuan would not be able to play off one bank against another. When Yuan concluded the deal with the consortium, foreigners were made officials in the Chinese government to oversee disbursement. The salt administration was also placed under foreign control.[4] When the Reorganization Loan was used up, Yuan granted foreigners further railroad and mining concessions. Without this money, Yuan would not have been able to pay his troops, and it is difficult to see how his government would have survived. For their money, the foreigners bought peace and continued trade – as well as advantageous interest rates. This was a new face of imperialism, of the pound sterling, the yen, and the dollar, supplementing the old traders, soldiers, and missionaries.

The Nationalist Party was not the only group that denounced Yuan, but it was the largest and most vociferous. Liang Qichao, by way of contrast, continued to give Yuan cautious support. He still feared the National Alliance – now, the Nationalist Party – as disruptive, and saw Yuan as China's best chance to maintain unity. And he hoped to be taken into the government. Liang tried to make himself a trusted adviser to Yuan; Yuan did not particularly value Liang's political acumen, but he certainly valued the legitimacy Liang's support might give him. Yuan appointed Liang to be

Minister of Justice and then as a financial adviser. Both areas needed reform, but Yuan would certainly not countenance the kind of independent judiciary Liang eventually wanted, while Liang could do little about the welter of different foreign and domestic banknotes and coinages. To survive, civilian politicians and bureaucrats had to make themselves subservient to militarists. A young radical denounced one to his face: "Now you've become Yuan Shikai's concubine. Adult men, when they've slept half the night, develop an erection. They pull the concubine who's sleeping on the floor in front of the bed in beside them like a coverlet into which they can ejaculate. Once they've ejaculated, they kick the concubine out of the bed. Be careful! Pretty soon a day will come when you will be kicked out of bed."[5]

If his treatment of Liang showed Yuan's velvet glove, his treatment of the Nationalist Party showed the fist. Although in disarray after the assassination of Song, the Nationalist Party's power to obstruct Yuan in Parliament and its deep roots in the south made it a threat. In May of 1913 Yuan dismissed the Nationalist Party's provincial governors. The so-called "Second Revolution" broke out during the summer when the former revolutionaries in the south, calling Yuan a dictator, took up arms. But the revolutionary governors were divided, and most of the urban elites were either neutral or supported Yuan as the best hope for stability. Merchants had grown to resent the National Alliance's taxes in the south, fearing they were being expected to pay for revolution as much as for local government. Yuan thus had little trouble putting down the revolt. Sun Yat-sen and others had to flee back to Japan. Yuan, officially elected president in October, proscribed the Nationalist Party and dissolved Parliament – even though the Nationalist Party's own MPs had condemned the Second Revolution. Yuan also disbanded all local and provincial assemblies. Suspected revolutionaries were tortured and killed, and even prominent gentry were executed. Zhang Xun, one of Yuan's generals, pillaged Nanjing, and martial law was declared in much of the country.

Yuan thus brought an end to the Qing experiment with local self-government. To all intents and purposes Yuan thenceforth ruled by decree. Yuan did not simply eliminate political opposition. He also instituted new censorship laws, and the post office searched out seditious materials. The heady freedoms of 1912 and the rise of political participation over the last few years were suddenly shown to be vulnerable. But fundamental trends that had been opening the public sphere could be obstructed only temporarily. When Yuan moved to make himself emperor of a new dynasty in 1915, he did so in the name of the "people." No matter how hypocritical Yuan's lip service to the principles of constitutionality, he was still forced to acknowledge the existence of a new kind of politics.

## Foreign affairs and monarchism

When World War I broke out, China initially remained neutral. British and German embassy staffs could thus still mingle at official functions. Japan, a

British ally since 1902, urged that China support the Allies, and China sent over 100,000 workers to fill the vacancies left in British and French factories as the Europeans slaughtered each other on the battlefields. The Chinese also worked as general laborers, construction workers, and porters. Many of these workers and a few students returned to China after the war as committed labor activists and Communists. At the time, the Chinese simply hoped that supporting the winning side would benefit them. Such was not to be the case. Left with a clear field, Japan took over Shandong, the German concession, in November 1914, just three months after the outbreak of the war.

Then in January 1915, Japan presented Yuan with the "Twenty-one Demands." Aside from control over Shandong, these stipulated recognition of Japanese interests in Manchuria and Mongolia, including mining rights; new business rights in Fujian Province (opposite Japan's colony of Taiwan); a Japanese interest in the huge Han-Ye-Ping iron and coal enterprise in central China – and a final set of demands that would have led to extensive Japanese participation at all levels of the Chinese government. Although Yuan had long made use of foreign advisers, who offered an extra-diplomatic avenue of communication back to their own countries, he certainly did not want Japanese police and administrators in his government. The Chinese were horrified, although, given the imperialist trends of the twentieth century, Japan's demands were hardly startling. As we have seen, foreigners already ran much of the tax system. For once in his political career, Yuan tried to make use of popular sentiment by deliberately leaking the contents of the Twenty-one Demands, hoping that protests would force the Japanese to back off. Japanese goods were indeed boycotted, but to no effect. Finally facing an ultimatum, Yuan agreed to all but the last set of demands in May. Thenceforth, 25 May became National Humiliation Day.

At this point, Yuan made his fateful decision to try to found a new dynasty. One could argue that the idea did make a lot of sense. After all, Liang Qichao and others (even revolutionaries) had long asked how a backward people could understand republican institutions. Furthermore, Yuan would be a progressive, twentieth-century emperor like those of Europe and Japan. Even his reign name sounded modern: Hongxian, or Grand Constitutional era. More immediately, the emperorship might give Yuan the standing to resist further Japanese and Western encroachment. He may even have thought his monarchy would create a kind of popular nationalism, although he made no attempt to mobilize mass support.[6] Yuan also calculated that compromise on Japan's Twenty-one Demands would assure him of the support of Japan, which after all was itself a constitutional monarchy. But these were vain dreams. Some Japanese leaders did signal their support for a new dynasty but then turned against the plan. Japan even sold arms to the opposition, including its old friend, Sun Yat-sen.

Japanese ambitions in China were of long standing. Japanese imperialism was a product of the successful development of the Meiji state against some, though not all, of the same pressures that the Qing and Yuan faced. Japan clearly saw itself playing catch-up against great odds: the European empires were already established; Western merchants were everywhere; and America and Russia had expanded across their continents over the course of the nineteenth century to the point that they were both facing Japan. And America and Australia instituted strict anti-Asian immigration laws just when the Japanese population was expanding. By the late Meiji, Japan saw itself as a civilized nation engaged in the same enterprise as the Western nations but unfairly discriminated against by them. Thus did Japan become a "Western" power; "pan-Asianism" emerged as a powerful idea that appeared to offer something to those who wanted to help China modernize and also to those who wanted to feast on its corpse. In other words, Japanese attitudes about China at this time were still mixed. To some, a strong and stable China offered the prospect of a united front against Western imperialism. Japan had welcomed thousands of Chinese students to its schools, and Japanese liberals and radicals had worked closely with Chinese reformers since the late Qing. Government policies alternated between relatively benign and more aggressive steps designed to secure Japan a place at the table of Western imperialism in China.

Meanwhile, Yuan faced the problem of how to legitimate his rule in both Chinese and foreign eyes. Already on 25 September 1914 Yuan had announced his plans to worship Confucius. In November, as if heeding Kang Youwei's old hopes, he began to turn Confucianism into a kind of state religion (though, typically, denying that he was doing so). Yuan also rededicated a Beijing temple to Guandi, Yuefei, and other military hero-gods. He seemed to refurbish the imperial prerogative of defining orthodoxy. He dealt with the gods much as the emperors had, adding yet another layer of meaning: Guandi and Yuefei represented the patriotic military, becoming gods suitable for a twentieth-century Republic. Yuan's actions did not necessarily prove he was planning to name himself emperor. A man can worship Confucius, after all, for many reasons. None the less, the clues mounted. On 23 December, President Yuan Shikai put on his field marshal's uniform, got into an armored car, drove south on a road covered with yellow sand to the Temple of Heaven. There he entered the temple in a vermilion coach, changed into sacrificial clothing (a purple robe with dragon designs and imperial-style headgear), and prayed to Heaven: "I, Yuan Shikai, representing the Republic of China," and so forth.

Though Yuan led his nation in the worship of Heaven, he invited all the people to participate in such worship. This was a distinctly modern and democratic touch since previous emperors would have executed anyone presuming to interfere with their religious monopoly of Heaven. But in late 1915 a new national assembly sent Yuan two memorials addressed to "your sacred majesty" and demanded that Yuan accept the Mandate of Heaven. The nation was renamed with the change of a single character: from Republic of China (*Zhonghua minguo*) to Empire of China (*Zhonghua diguo*), befitting a modern national monarchy as opposed to the Great Qing, which referred just to a family.[7]

The new assembly appointed by Yuan elected him emperor with remarkable unanimity (1,993 to zero). Yuan started his reign on 1 January, in line with the new rather than the old calendar. Many Chinese were understandably cynical about this process – and Yuan's attempts to combine new rituals (constitutions, elections) with the old appealed neither to traditionalists nor to progressives. The new dynasty rapidly fell apart. Yuan faced determined opposition from political groups he had previously defeated and even from some that had generally supported him as president. Liang Qichao, having failed to warn Yuan away from his monarchical ambitions, led the political opposition, and General Cai E, who had been Liang's disciple since 1898, led the military opposition from Yunnan Province in the southwest. Former members of the National Alliance and the Nationalist Party naturally opposed Yuan. Most importantly, a mild but evidently debilitating disease of mysterious origins affected many men in the upper levels of the civilian and military bureaucracies. In other words, Yuan's best and strongest military protégés, seeing that the monarchy might pass power on to Yuan's widely despised son, instead of themselves, sat out the coming civil war. The southwestern provinces, under de facto warlords, declared their independence and called Yuan a traitor to the Republic. As civil war approached, Yuan could find no reliable generals who were not on the sick list, and so the southern militarists, in spite of long odds against them, achieved some victories. In February 1916 Yuan retreated: he announced an indefinite delay of his enthronement. In March, after another month of inconclusive fighting, he announced the end of the Hongxian Era. Peace broke out: the "eighty-three days dream" was over. There followed a period in which there was no effective central government. By June the man who would be emperor was dead of uremia.

In terms of Yuan's personal psychology, he demonstrated deep ambivalence – and uncustomary indecision – about becoming emperor. Clearly, he did not seek the job with the same attitude as previous dynastic founders. He may well have wanted to be emperor, but he also sensed that the emperorship represented a flawed strategy for popular appeal or legitimacy. As a modern man, Yuan probably believed what many of his advisers, including the prominent American political scientist Frank Goodnow, felt: the people were too ignorant, the country's conditions too backward for republicanism. Monarchy offered more of a chance for China to follow the path of development blazed by the West. Indeed, did not the great majority of the people want an emperor? Did they not in fact assume in their ignorance that there already was one? But Yuan should have realized that conservative elites who still took monarchy seriously would oppose him as the man who betrayed the Qing, while the liberal elites firmly believed that monarchy was retrogressive. These groups might accept Yuan as a military dictator but not as an emperor. The masses themselves remained politically inert: if they were ignorant of republicanism, they also remained ignorant of Yuan's hybrid ceremonials.

With historical hindsight, we can see that the monarchy was truly dead, and its charisma or the awe it inspired had died with it. This was indeed Liang Qichao's main argument against Yuan's monarchy. Liang admitted he had opposed the republican revolution, but once it occurred, the clock could not be turned back. But – again with hindsight – we can see that the larger dilemma facing China's post-1911 political elites was that, while legitimacy could not exist without real, coercive powers, the requirements of power seemed to militate against legitimacy. If Yuan was inspired by the example of the Meiji's reinvention of traditions, he might have remembered that the Japanese emperor reigned without ruling.

## Militarism and the warlord era (1916–27)

Upon Yuan's death his vice president, Li Yuanhong, became acting president. Li had turned his leadership of the Wuhan revolutionaries in 1911 into a central China power base, and originally he had tried to operate as a third force between Yuan and the Nationalist Party. He was never able to establish independent authority, however, and soon disappeared from the political stage. More significant was that upon Yuan's death Feng Guozhang and Duan Qirui – his top lieutenants, though they had sat out the monarchical movement – became vice president and premier. They recalled parliament, but the entire central government quickly broke down in a welter of factional power struggles that broke out in riots and military maneuvering. Another of Yuan's commanders, Zhang Xun, moved his Anhui troops into Beijing at Li Yuanhong's invitation in June 1917 – only to disband the government and restore the child emperor Puyi to the Throne! Zhang's forces were defeated within two weeks.

The central government did not completely collapse. Japan strengthened its position in China by loaning Yuan's successors some 145 million yen in 1917 and 1918. These "Nishihara loans," like the Reorganization Loan of 1913, had strong political overtones and went to support a specific government. In return the Beijing government secretly promised Japan the right to maintain troops in Manchuria and Mongolia and even that it would not protest against Japan's presence in Shandong. Beijing continued to exchange ambassadors with London, Tokyo, Washington, and so forth. Most importantly, Beijing continued to have access through the foreigners to salt and customs revenue, though these were mostly used to pay off debts. Partly because of this, the Ministry of Foreign Affairs retained much of its importance, as well as a continuity of personnel and goals.[8] Indeed, the government could point to certain successes in education, the legal system, and foreign affairs. Although no major changes in the unequal treaty system were achieved, the government began to chip away at it, getting the Powers to agree to raise tariffs to 5 percent and, in principle, eventually to grant tariff autonomy and abolish extraterritoriality. These were achievements future governments were able to build on.

Yet this national administration was not a true central government; rather, it is better to understand Beijing as one of the prizes for which independent warlords struggled. Beijing could give a regional warlord a valuable fig leaf of legitimacy, and his followers could receive regular titles as governors and commanders. It is worth remembering that few warlords fought for provincial independence; instead, the most powerful militarists sought to control the national government while even weaker ones tried to retain ties to it. The Beijing government – the state as such – lacked its own military power, even though some ministries continued to function.

Thus did the forces of disintegration accelerate after Yuan's death; the ties that had more or less bound the Chinese polity together continued to disintegrate. The period from Yuan's death in 1916 to the political reunification of China in 1928 saw the rise of provinces and even smaller districts under independent military control. Different military commanders of different origins commanding different types of armies of various sizes at different times in a variety of factional formations managed to divide China up between them, none able to seize control of the whole country. Even with a scorecard the players are difficult to tell apart, but we will attempt to make some overall sense of the period.

"Feudalism" sums it up in some respects. Feudalism highlights the continuing militarization of society and the lack of central authority. Army commanders were both exploiters and protectors of their districts. Like the feudalism of the European and Japanese Middle Ages, Chinese warlordism linked the leadership of personal armies to a territorial base below and shifting military alliances above. In the absence of an organized state, local authority was maintained. However, there are at least two senses in which feudalism does *not* apply to the warlord era. If the institutional heart of feudalism is the fief, as it dominated parts of the European countryside during the Middle Ages – China had no fiefs. A "fief" refers primarily to a piece of territory or estate controlled with minimal outside interference by the fief-holder in return for services to a superior. Twentieth-century China's highly commercial nature of agriculture militated against the closed economies of feudalism. And if "feudalism" refers to the moral and legal relation between lord and retainer, then the Chinese warlords, who seldom if ever swore fealty to superiors, are not comparable to knights and samurai.

The "dynastic cycle" also describes aspects of the period. As a dictum of Chinese historiography, the dynastic cycle simply observed that various dynasties had risen, flourished, and fallen, to be superseded by new dynasties. It noted repeating patterns, that a confluence of events marked the end of a dynasty: official malfeasance and incompetence; imperial weakness; national disintegration; and the rise of banditry, rebellion, and regional power blocs. And following the fall of a strong dynasty, there might be several generations of "chaos" before a new dynasty could restore order, as in the centuries between the fall of the Han and the rise of the Sui dynasty (from AD 220 to 589), a period which saw only relatively short-lived and local regimes, or the fifty years between the Tang and the Song dynasties (907–60). As historical description, then, the dynastic cycle is remarkably suggestive. The chaos that came with the fall of the Qing did not surprise many Chinese with a sense of history. They expected an interregnum period, and they expected it eventually to produce a new unifier. If Yuan Shikai was not a unifier, he could still be understood as an evil last minister. However, the "dynastic cycle" does not fit the 1920s. Most obviously, there would be no new dynasty. Imperial Confucianism, the bedrock of major and minor dynasties alike, was dead. And China was facing a new kind of imperialism that provoked a new sense of national sovereignty.

One can call the warlord period an "interregnum" between the Qing and Yuan on the one hand and either the Nationalist period of unification under Chiang Kai-shek or the Communist unification of 1949 on the other: but this is only a metaphor. Neither Chiang nor the Communists created a new imperial order. Restorationism continued (as when the last Qing boy-emperor was briefly restored to the throne in 1917), but the warlords contended for power on their own terms without assuming imperial pretensions. This, too, was known to traditional Chinese historiography. But some intellectuals, at least, understood the modern "warlords" as a new phenomenon.[9] They were thrown up by national and international forces, not merely symptoms of decay.

The real heirs of the dynastic cycle would be the Nationalists and the Communists, and they broke the cycle by forging an entirely new basis of legitimacy. From the warlords' own point of view, they were less would-be emperors than the kind of hero celebrated in story and opera. This popular model judged a man by larger-than-life personal traits rather than political standards. The line between bandit leader and warlord could be thin. According to Pearl Buck:

> Without exception, the warlords I have known have been men of unusual native ability, gifted with peculiar personal charm, with imagination and strength, and often with a rude poetic quality.... The warlord sees himself great – and great in the traditional manner of heroes of ancient fiction and history who are so inextricably mingled in the old Chinese novels.[10]

Not all warlords were so charming: some were known for their harems, wealth, and extreme cruelty. What mattered was the institution of the army. This refers not to a national network of commanders and divisions, but to a congeries of forces each loyal to an essentially independent commander. These commanders relied on personal ties. The result was a system of factionalism and shifting alliances resting on top of a reality of fragmentation and regional autonomy.

The most important commanders in the late 1910s were Yuan's generals, made independent by his death. The military attracted a wide variety of men. Lower-level officers and, by the 1920s, even commanders, sometimes came from the ranks of the impoverished peasantry or bandits. Such origins help explain the warlords' curious mix of orthodox Confucianism and the popular heroic image. The army offered a kind of social mobility. Zhang Zongchang, for one, had begun as a petty thief and, as commander of Shandong, essentially continued his thievery on a larger scale. Zhang Zuolin, who rose to rule all of Manchuria and, at times, northern China, also began as a bandit. Other warlords were reformist, such as Feng Yuxiang, a Christian, in the north or Chen Jiongming, who was something of a socialist, in the south. In all cases, their soldiers were largely of peasant stock. Even if the army scarcely offered a good life, population pressure and economic dislocation drove boys from the farm. Some were conscripted. Men under arms totaled 500,000 in 1916; this doubled to 1 million by 1918 and reached about 1.5 million by 1924.

A warlord without stable control over a base area could not keep his army for long. Warlords collected taxes to provide something of a regional government. Though ordinary government functions suffered, even poorly paid armies were expensive. The land tax was often supplemented with monopolies and taxes on salt and the like. Gambling, prostitution, and especially opium provided large revenues: opium growing revived rapidly from Yuan Shikai's relatively successful attempts to eradicate it. Money was printed: a sure sign of putative government. And often businessmen were extorted: "invited" to buy bonds, licenses, and revenue stamps.

Was "warlordism" a system? Certainly, warlordism was part and parcel of China's involvement in the global economic system. The imperialist Powers, with the partial exception of Japan, would have preferred to deal with a unified (but weak) government. Instead, the warlords gave them all kinds of problems. The infrastructure was disrupted as railroads, for example, were bombed or seized for troop transport. Chinese business partners were blackmailed. No warlord would willingly offend one of the Powers, but accidents did happen. On the other hand, the Powers tended to reach accommodation with particular warlords – or perhaps the warlords did the accommodating. These relationships grew out of earlier spheres of influence. Thus Japan played a hegemonic role in Manchuria while England, to a great extent, dominated the Yangzi Valley. Both Powers attempted to make friends in Beijing and influence what little there was of a national government, and all the Powers sold arms to whoever could pay for them. China's warlordism of the 1920s was thus a "system" that can be compared to warlordism in other places and times. Yet the "tribalism" scholars often find at the roots of warlordism in late-twentieth-century Africa or early-twenty-first-century Afghanistan clearly had no counterpart in China. China's warlordism was rooted in concrete political circumstances, as we will see below.

The fundamental law of the warlord system was that if any one warlord appeared to be achieving national authority, the others would gang up on him. Warlords were constantly shifting their alliances to prevent any one of their numbers from achieving national domination, and in a search for short-term advantage. Militarism mandated that no social group could survive without its own military or reliable military connections. Would-be reformers could only operate when and where warlords permitted. No warlord, whatever his inclinations, could afford extensive reforms because he needed most of the revenue for his army. Taxes were onerous, poverty was widespread, and no group could be spared. The unusual warlord, sure of his local powers, might pursue minor reforms, building infrastructure and schools, and encouraging commerce. Yan Xishan in Shanxi Province, for example, supported charitable institutions like orphanages, bathhouses, and clinics for the poor. However, such efforts tended to be fleeting, at best like applying a bandage to a gaping wound.

There were other predictable qualities to warlordism. Territories tended to be strategically defensible and to make geo-economic sense. Sometimes a province formed a warlord territory, sometimes two or more provinces, sometimes, as in mountainous Sichuan to the west, no major warlord emerged. And the border areas between major warlord territories became the lands of minor warlords and bandit chieftains.

Still, even in its instability, the warlord system was scarcely static. In 1924 the warlord Wu Peifu, with his base in the rich central China region, nearly succeeded in defeating his major enemies. Though the Powers were officially neutral, Britain and the US were favorably inclined toward Wu's efforts to unify China militarily, in spite of his reputation as a nationalist. Japan, however, feared for its special position in Manchuria and Mongolia and sent funds to Wu's rivals. Wu had troops in a good position to retake Manchuria, which would have left only peripheral regions outside the control of his Beijing government. But one of his subordinates betrayed him to seize Beijing, others blocked his transportation lines, and the Japanese Army – going well beyond their rights under the treaties – prevented Wu from rein-forcing his northern troops.[11] The fate of Wu Peifu confirms the law of the warlord system: no single unifier could emerge due to the ambitions and jealousy of the others and due to the forces of imperialism.

Yet warlordism barely lasted a generation. In the long cycles of Chinese history interregnums had often lasted several generations. The limits of warlordism were many. In the political realm, only a claim to defend the nation as a whole could confer legitimacy. The inability of the warlords to convince urban elites that they could resist the forces of imperialism and make China great again doomed them. The drive to build a strong and unified China would fuel new social forces and be fueled by them.

## The causes and effects of militarism

The political disintegration of the late nineteenth century was not a mere repeat of the dynastic cycle. Rather, a new, Western-imported military tech-nology had changed the nature of internal state controls and given the

*Map 4* Warlord China, 1920

After Yuan Shikai's death in 1916, China collapsed into militarism. By 1920, loose congeries of "warlords" controlled particular regions as follows: the bandit-turned-general Zhang Zuolin was based in Manchuria, forming the "Fengtian clique." Yuan's former subordinate Feng Guozhang controlled the "Zhili clique" until his death in 1919, after which Cao Kun and Wu Peifu took over. Another former Yuan subordinate, Duan Qirui, controlled the "Anhui clique", which was defeated by Zhili in 1920. The southeast (Fujian, Guangdong, Guangxi) and especially the southwest (Sichuan, Guizhou, Yunnan) were divided among competing smaller warlords.

*Source*: Courtesy of Geospatial Information Science Team, Computing Center, Academia Sinica.

*Map 5* Warlord China, 1924

By 1924, the Zhili clique under Wu Peifu dominated most of central and northern China. Betrayed by his subordinate Feng Yuxiang, however, Wu was then defeated by Zhang Zuolin's Fengtian forces, which took over Beijing and much of northern China at year's end. Southwestern China remained fragmented, but the Guomindang under Sun Yat-sen was building support in Guangdong. The well-protected province of Shanxi remained politically stable throughout the period under the cautious reformism of Yan Xishan. Both Yan and Feng Yuxiang became supporters of the Guomindang in the late 1920s, though Yan was able to maintain his independence.

*Source*: Courtesy of Geospatial Information Science Team, Computing Center, Academia Sinica.

military new power. As important was the quality of the troops. In the late imperial era, Chinese troops were usually underpaid, undereducated, and underemployed. Once the Qing was consolidated after about 1680, its basic strategy – domestically as well as on the frontier – was defensive and preventive. If trouble did break out, a policy of meeting it with overwhelming numbers and compromise was generally followed. Thus the military, though essential, was politically unimportant. However, as foreign and domestic pressures increased in the late nineteenth century, the Qing began to reform the military. Training, discipline, loyalty, and morale were emphasized, and wages improved. Finally, under Yuan Shikai's guidance, the New Armies sought an officer corps from the gentry to raise the status of a military career. The new importance of the military can also be seen in the praise of anti-Qing revolutionaries for "militarism." They blamed the lack of a militaristic tradition for leaving China vulnerable to foreign attacks.

There was no direct line from the growing militarism of the nineteenth century to the full-fledged warlordism of the 1920s.[12] Warlordism arose in a complex dance between the breakdown of the central state and the rise of local needs across China. The provincial armies of the mid-nineteenth century did not prefigure the warlordism of the twentieth, because their gentry leaders were loyal to the Qing. These armies were disbanded after the war. Their existence confirmed the Qing's weakness, but militarism by itself was not a disintegrative force till the very end of the dynasty. Still, developments of the late Qing made warlordism possible if not inevitable.

First, the late Qing reforms designed to modernize and professionalize the military resulted in a more politicized officer corps. The Qing deliberately did not create a single national army, instead maintaining the old-style forces and dividing command to prevent threats to its rule. But still many officers and their men were sympathetic to revolutionary goals; they were more loyal to their commanders and an abstract notion of the Chinese nation than to the Qing. Second, the new respectability of the military in the late Qing legitimated military careers, attracting idealistic, ambitious, and capable men who could assert themselves as the Qing collapsed. Writing for Liang Qichao's *New Citizen* journal in 1902, Cai E supported military education on the grounds that "to train a good soldier is actually to train a good citizen."[13] The failure of the 1911 Revolution to create a stable government resulted not only in a power vacuum but also in an ongoing legitimacy crisis. Military men took this opportunity to "arbitrate" when civilian politicians failed to reach agreement.

Third, the form of the 1911 Revolution – provincial secession instead of a massive civil war of revolution versus conservatism – brought provincial armies to the forefront of local politics. Army commanders were often at the center of provincial political struggles. And fourth, local elites were too weak to run their communities on a civil basis once the Qing collapsed: they turned to outside military backing as all levels of society became militarized. Villages formed crop-watching militia to protect against banditry, and counties formed professional militia. The dispossessed formed bandit gangs. This all created a bottom-up militarization that would eventually combine with the top-down armies.

As long as Yuan was president, he was able to keep his officer corps loyal. He was usually able to move them around, preventing them from acquiring a power base, but not often able to fire them – or separate them from their own junior officers. The "second revolution" gave Yuan the chance to replace some local power holders. Yuan enticed Cai E, then military governor of Yunnan in the southwest, to Beijing partly by allowing him to choose his own successor. So it was in 1915 that Cai could return to Yunnan to lead the opposition to Yuan's monarchical movement. Key central and provincial government posts were held by men personally loyal to Yuan, but their obedience was conditional. By crushing republican political institutions, eliminating elite opposition, squandering his chance for nationalist legitimation, and insisting on strictly top-down rule, Yuan opened the gate for the subsequent militarism. The revolutionary uprising of 1913 and the anti-monarchical uprising of 1916 also contributed to the continued militarization of Chinese society.

The warlord system strongly affected political development. The Republic was delegitimized. Many of the ideals that had fueled the 1911 Revolution were discredited. As parliamentarians were shown to be venal and debauched, the very idea of representative democracy was set back. As constitutions were torn up and rewritten at an ever-increasing pace, the ideal of constitutional government was discredited. In the words of political scientist Andrew Nathan, "with each cycle of factional conflict after 1916 there was a perceptible increase in the mendacity of the politicians' constitutional maneuvers and a corresponding decline in public support for the republican regime."[14] Political enemies were invariably denigrated as subversive. When Yuan abolished the assemblies in 1914, he characterized their members as selfish individuals unconcerned with China's fate. The leading warlords called each other traitors, while the revolutionaries called the warlords thieves.

Every member of the political elites was tarnished. On the one hand, warlordism was hated. On the other, what we might call military values had a life of their own. "Power stems from the barrel of the gun," Mao Zedong famously stated in 1927. That statement represented a major shift of consciousness over the course of just a generation. Until it was abolished in 1905, the civil service exam system ratified the notion that power stemmed from cultural mastery of sacred texts; if this was never completely true, it still represented a basic social norm. Educated civilians were meant to rule. But the political systems that emerged with the Nationalist Party in the late 1920s and the Communist Party a generation later owed a great deal to the lessons learned from the warlord era. Military men played an essential role in all the governments that followed. Furthermore, the military provided an important model of good citizenship: discipline, faith, zeal, self-sacrifice, and a broader sense of modernity. Militaristic ideals contributed to the formation of the new political parties.

In terms of its social effects, militarism was disastrous, particularly aggravating difficulties in the countryside. Not only did warlords press taxes and conscription beyond bearable levels, but the unpredictability of passing armies made life more precarious. Rural communities needed military protectors, but local militia, bandit gangs, and outside armies all intermingled with each other. None were reliable friends of the farmers. The lack of local tax revenues, rural credit, and community leadership meant that critical infrastructure – such as dams and dikes for irrigation and water control – continued to deteriorate.

Human costs were also high. Battles could turn into routs. Triumphant armies, often filled with soldiers invading "foreign" provinces, would turn their wrath on civilians. Soldiers – mistreated by their officers, underpaid, and even hungry – would simply take what they wanted from peasants and merchants. The historian Edward McCord describes one type of pillage: "In a common tactic, a few soldiers would be sent through a village firing their guns. As the villagers tried to flee, they would run right into the hands of the main body of troops, who would then tie up and rob all the men and rape the women."[15] Mutilation of corpses was also practiced – bodies were found with eyes gouged out, genitals cut off, and hearts ripped out. A very small number of warlords won reputations for trying to maintain discipline over their troops and even punishing such acts; more won reputations as terrifying beasts. Soldiers had to live off the countryside; terror tactics were a way to ensure the passivity of captured populations. As warlords tried to increase the size of their armies, peasant boys were conscripted and bandits recruited.

Some historians have suggested that the evils of warlordism have been exaggerated. First, many areas remained unaffected: warlord rampages were often a highly local and temporary phenomenon. Second, warlords generally tried to limit actual fighting, preferring to keep their armies intact. And third, their overall impact on society and the economy was dwarfed by normal activities. Recent work by economic historians suggests that the 1910s and 1920s saw positive growth rates.[16] There was rapid industrial expansion during the decade from the mid-1910s to the mid-1920s: average annual growth rates were from 9 percent to 13 percent for most of the period, and higher during the World War I when the Powers were otherwise engaged. Agricultural output was also impressive under the circumstances, managing to keep up with a population that increased from 430 million in 1912 to 500 million in 1930. Although most arms were purchased from the West, Chinese arsenals also contributed, iron mines were developed, steel mills built, and road and railway connections improved. The historian Arthur Waldron has argued that the increasing tempo of fighting necessitated an arms race which in turn contributed to industrialization, though he also points out that the wars contributed to economic uncertainty, financial panics, ad hoc taxation, and the destruction of transportation, communication, and property.[17]

Local government also demonstrates some continuity during this period. Intellectual and cultural life – at least in the cities protected by the Powers – flourished. In other words, not all aspects of Chinese life descended into chaos. It is true that many parts of rural China escaped the fighting and most warlords preferred posturing to fighting. But although large-scale battles were rare, the intensity of warfare was increasing. 1924 saw extensive fighting across eastern China for control of Beijing. If not everybody suffered directly from warlordism, few escaped its indirect effects, especially in rural areas. Even if the precise consequences of warlordism cannot be measured in economic terms, we can assume economic growth would have been higher and more sustainable without it.

In fact, even cities were affected. Defeated and demobilized soldiers were a threat to urban areas. And when the fighting intensified, warlords squeezed merchants for the money they needed. Urban residents – and their horses, rickshaws, carts, and automobiles – were no more immune to conscription than peasants. Runaways were shot. When soldiers were stationed in or near a town, it was like an invasion. They would visit all the shops, refusing to pay for merchandise or forcing shopkeepers to take worthless script. A Western reporter described soldiers in Suzhou in 1924 on the eve of being shipped out: They "had very little money and first went to pawnshops to raise cash on their rather worthless effects. For an article worth possibly a dollar, they would demand $10 and the pawnbrokers pretty generally paid what was asked of them. One who refused had most of his teeth knocked out by a mob of soldiers and was almost beaten to death."[18] The upper and middle classes were also affected. Silver inflation hurt everyone, while investors in government bonds lost fortunes. Credit was squeezed, and business bankruptcies followed.

General histories of modern China sometimes skip over Yuan Shikai and the warlords. Certainly, they make for depressing reading. But in order to understand the more dynamic changes of the period, it is necessary to grasp the strengths of Yuan and the warlords as well as their ultimate weaknesses. They did much to determine the future course of politics. As we will see in later chapters, Mao's dictum that power stems from the barrel of a gun, though it sounds like a truism, was in fact a reluctant – and still partial – recognition of the new political realities. The fear of "chaos" that warlordism corroborated would be used to justify strong central governments into the twenty-first century. The fate of the Revolution of 1911 also remained a central feature of the political culture for a long time: all political and social criticism had to deal with it one way or another.

The expansion of the "public sphere" of newspapers and political rallies, of political parties and social movements, of merchant and professional associations, of schools and student protests, and generally of the actions of citizens concerned for their country, was slowed down but not stopped by Yuan Shikai and the later warlords. Of course, student associations, workers' unions, and even merchant groups were suspect. Journalists could be shot. Yet the administrative weaknesses of the warlords left a certain space open for social groups to organize. Local elites often stepped in to provide quasi-public services such as soup kitchens. Chambers of Commerce made sure that police were paid during the hiatuses between different warlord regimes. To a degree, freedom of speech was protected in some of the foreign concessions, especially Shanghai's International Settlement. Universities, often under foreign protection, sometimes provided havens for student dissent. The 1920s saw intellectual and cultural innovation, including strands of conservative thought, not seen again in China until the 1980s. But none of this applied to the countryside, which we examine in the next chapter.

# 5 Social conditions in the countryside

The Revolution of 1911 had mobilized new social groups that were beginning to find their voices: students, professionals (journalists, doctors, lawyers, nurses), the merchant-bourgeoisie, the intelligentsia, and women. Attempts to suppress these voices, though often harsh, were only partly successful. Warlords might monopolize coercive power, but they could not claim legitimacy and barely tried to monopolize political discourse. People felt disenfranchised as their expectations of access to power were rising while reality denied it to them, but few were silenced. New social groups were locally influential if not nationally powerful. In the cities, a public sphere of nonofficial consensual activities grew, institutionalized in the worlds of education, publishing, and professional and business organizations, and emerging in the guilds and unions of the nascent working class.

Warlordism increased pressures on Chinese society, especially in the countryside, as we have seen. But we must also take into account long-term demographic and economic developments. The early twentieth century did not mark a break in China's *economic history*, however radical were political and cultural developments.[1] The question then arises: if economic structure was not much changed, what of social structure? In regard to agriculture, researchers differ considerably on whether output fell behind, exceeded, or merely kept up with population growth. They also disagree about whether inequality was increasing or if income distribution remained about the same. Reliable data are hard to come by – neither the late Qing nor the Republican governments were in any position to keep track of these things – and China is vast and diverse. Western and Japanese surveys were decidedly limited in terms of geographic extent and the time periods they covered. These questions are also highly politicized. But some judgements about social conditions can be reached, even if the exact economic picture remains a bit hazy. We can also see how people at the time understood the situation.

The Communist narrative of modern history holds that peasant revolution was necessary for China to break out of "feudal bonds" – that landlords and warlords were increasingly oppressing the peasantry while the bourgeoisie (who might otherwise have promoted more radical change) was held in thrall by the forces of imperialism. But neoclassical economics suggests that, if inequality was *not* growing and the peasantry was actually holding its own, at least in the aggregate, then the basic problem was the lack of modern agrarian inputs (technology), not class inequalities. In other words, in the first case, exploitation is a villain who can be slain by eliminating the landlords and imperialists and redistributing economic resources. In the second case, primitive technology and overpopulation are villains to be defeated by improving farming techniques and rationalizing farm practices, and eventually taking farmers off the land into industry. Both parties agree, however, that the institutional framework for directing resources where they were most needed was lacking. And there is more basic agreement about nonagricultural sectors.

This chapter will first discuss the fundamental conditions of agriculture, and then the relationship between the state and rural communities. It is less concerned with economic history than an attempt to recapture and analyse the social aspects of rural life in the early 1900s.

## The basic patterns of rural life

The steady commercialization of agriculture continued and perhaps accelerated during the late Qing and early Republican periods. Already by the sixteenth century villages were linked horizontally and vertically through marketing networks.[2] Generally speaking, a group of villages would each be only a couple hours' walk to a central market that opened perhaps half a day once a week (a "week" being a 10-day cycle). Within this group of villages, people might intermarry, practice the same sets of religious and daily life rituals, speak the same dialect, and seldom leave. Goods, services, and even ideas traveled up and down the system through the marketing network. Peddlers, barbers, opera troupes, midwives, and ritual specialists like Daoist priests covered a circuit of day markets, returning to a central town with a permanent market perhaps once a week. Merchants bought farm produce at these periodic markets to sell to townspeople and to other merchants, who in turn transported produce to even higher level towns and cities – and took urban products down to the market towns. This was a "nested hierarchy" of networks each reproduced at a higher level: sets of villages focused on a periodic day market, sets of day markets focused on a market town, sets of market towns focused on a regional center, and so forth. Ultimately, this is how the Chinese countryside was tied to international markets. Thus might tea leaves make their way from remote mountain communities through several layers of increasingly specialized merchants and processors until large exporters in Guangzhou or Shanghai put them on ships bound for London. And so might copper pots make their way from Manchester or Boston to remote Chinese villages.

Rural markets were also sites of labor exchange and credit. Peasants with no land or without enough land of their own might hire themselves out to larger landholders by the day or for longer periods. Farmers might also take out loans, which could be usurious but also saw many families through to the harvest. Land would be put up as collateral; Yuan Shikai among many others became a major landlord through repossessing land when his mortgages were not repaid. Most farmers still grew most of their own food – up to 90 percent of basic grains – while 20 to 30 percent of all agricultural output was sold in markets.[3] All farmers had to sell at least some of their produce, for they lived in a commercialized and monetarized world. They had to pay their taxes in silver but used copper currency for most transactions. Copper coins bought tools like plowshares, fertilizers like night soil or fishcakes, and even clothes.

Tenant farmers – prevalent in the south, rarer in the north – often rented land on a sharecropping basis, but even then would be expected to pay a deposit and perhaps part of the rent in cash. Landowners and tenant farmers alike were thus oriented, to a degree, to the market. The family remained the fundamental economic unit. A "typical" household might grow most of its own rice and, for special occasions, poultry, and sell anything from mulberry leaves or silkworm cocoons to tong oil or soybeans in order to buy tools, charcoal, lamp oil, vegetables, or bean cakes. Or in some cases a family might specialize in cotton or ducks or opium and buy all of its food and other needs. In addition, "household industry" was crucial to the survival of most families. This ranged from women's work of spinning and weaving to several family members specializing in sandals, bricks, rope, or other household products.

The Chinese case was thus sharply different from, say, the pattern in Central American nations where coffee was king. Coffee estate owners virtually owned hundreds and thousands of serfs. Little industrialization or commercial agriculture (outside of coffee) was allowed. There were few opportunities for social mobility; little land changed hands; and the elite families themselves, running their estates as corporations, remained beholden only to larger, foreign business interests. Some estates existed in China (say, cotton in Shandong), but in general elite families depended on a mix of land ownership (which seems not to have brought high returns), official position, and business concerns.

The basic mode of Qing agriculture consisted of households farming small plots of land. These plots were scattered about the village, adding up to, on average, a little over five acres in the north and a little less than three acres in the more fertile south. This describes both owner-cultivators and tenant-cultivators (as well as those who mixed the two). A peasant household consisted of husband and wife, children, and perhaps a brother or sister and a parent or two. Flexibility was enhanced by using child labor in the fields, and successful farmers might hire temporary laborers as well. Sons in excess of family labor requirements could, with luck, be hired out as laborers, or perhaps apprenticed, or they might even, in the twentieth century, become soldiers. Daughters were married "out" – they became members of their husband's families; or, in bad times, they could be sold to become servants, concubines, or prostitutes. Infanticide was widespread in bad times, and female infanticide skewed the sex ratios. A stratum of the poorest men could never afford wives. All other sons divided their father's land upon his death, if not before. This universal custom of partible inheritance obviously shrank the size of the farms of each generation until the younger farmers sold out entirely or bought new land. The buying and selling of land by legal contract was widespread: another sign of how highly commercialized Chinese agriculture had become over the centuries, though at any given time few fields were available for purchase. Ownership patterns varied widely, and the categories of sharecropper, tenant, owner-farmer, and landlord often overlapped. In other words, it was possible for a single household to simultaneously farm some of its own land, rent out some of its land, and rent additional land.

Dry grains (barley, wheat, millet, sorghum) in the north and wet rice (grown in flooded paddies) in the south dominated; the chief commercial crops by the twentieth century were cotton, peanuts, tobacco, silk cocoons, and opium. Very little land was left in pasture; animal husbandry consisted largely of fowl and pigs. Soil fertility was maintained by the use of night soil and, to an extent, animal manure. The agricultural infrastructure, especially in the south, consisted of extensive canals, polders (reclaimed and diked lakes, marshes, and sea), irrigation ditches and leveled fields and terraces, and took a good deal of the farmers' time to maintain. Families and villages competed over limited resources like water or hillside brush (for household fires), but they also cooperated on building and maintaining the infrastructure, village defense, crop watching. Kin or neighbors might share tools and labor. Large-scale and inter-village projects involved gentry or even official management.

In south China even tenancies could be bought and sold, or rented, and the original landowner (holder of the "subsoil rights") might be shoved out of the picture entirely. Some villages were entirely populated by tenants while the landlord(s) lived somewhere else. Landlords seldom "rationalized" their holdings but rather rented them to tenants with no changes in the mode of agriculture. In other words, landlords seldom built "managerial farms" by putting together contiguous plots and hiring wage labor. Tenants might or might not own their own tools, pay a deposit, rent their fields with cash, a fixed share of the crop, or a percentage of the harvest. Some villages, especially in the north, were largely populated by owner-farmers, with few landlords, tenants, or laborers. The position of major landlords, with urban economic interests, might be unassailable, but in many villages a good deal of downward and some upward social mobility was common. There was a vast social distance between a small village landlord and a wealthy urban family with farms in several villages that dwarfed the gaps within the village.

Families lived by frugality and hard work; these were internalized values, not merely Confucian preachments. Mao Zedong's father provides an example of how diligence and luck could produce enough upward mobility so that if he did not become a full-time landlord (he continued to work physically himself), he was still able to build a business and send his son to school. A hundred years earlier Mao might have completed the cycle by becoming a merchant or even, possibly, passing the exams and achieving official position. Then, his sons in turn might have built up the mix of education and economic activities necessary to maintain gentry status.

Overall national estimates suggest that by the 1930s about 42 percent of farmland was rented, while 32 percent of peasant households owned no land whatsoever. Rents ranged from roughly 50 percent to 70 percent of the main harvest.[4] While custom might keep landlords from simply charging whatever the market would bear, population pressures were pushing rents higher. Tenancy rates were higher in the south where the land was more fertile and farming more commercialized, and lower in the north, where the tendency was for richer farmers to use hired labor. The point is that during the Qing this system was intensifying but not fundamentally altered. As the countryside grew ever more populated, more villages opened their own markets, weekly half-day markets became bi-weekly day markets, day markets became permanent market towns, and market towns became regional economic centers. It is true that villages could be more or less closed, and during times of troubles tended to form militia to protect their crops from predators and keep out "foreigners." But by the twentieth century, marketing patterns and outside forces made it impossible for any village to completely close itself off from outside society.

The Chinese mode of agriculture was highly responsive to labor inputs: higher yields could be achieved as more hours were devoted to the fields, and rural handicrafts also contributed to peasant incomes. But there was a limit to this process of labor intensification. The series of massive peasant rebellions of the mid-nineteenth century may have acted to relieve the pressures on the system temporarily, but by 1900 China simply could not support many more people without a new mode of agriculture. In economic terms, returns on labor eventually begin to diminish: the more hours the peasants put into farming and handicrafts, the less they were actually profiting per hour.

Growth of markets led to further specialization; perhaps half of production was grown for market by 1920, more near urban areas and efficient transportation, less in remote areas. Railroads brought some new regions into the market economy. Yet obviously other areas were bypassed in the process; economic differences between regions probably increased in the twentieth century. Opportunities for success and failure increased simultaneously. Chinese agriculture found expanding markets abroad and in the growing cities. Food crop exports increased 26 percent by value and industrial crop exports 38 percent between 1876 and 1890, and 300 percent and 600 percent respectively between 1890 and 1905.[5] To meet the growing demand, peasants further specialized in what they could grow best: for greatest profit, as determined by the markets. A peasant household might decide that growing cotton, say, would pay more than growing rice. But a bad harvest or a drop in prices could leave a family with nothing to eat, worse off than had they made the safer decision to grow rice. In this sense, the peasantry became more rather than less vulnerable as the twentieth century proceeded. Chinese producers of porcelain, silk, and tea, all major exports in the nineteenth century, faced competition in international markets from new sources of overseas production.

Early in the twentieth century, the Qing's New Policies foreshadowed the Republic's attempts to increase the reach of government. State-building, supported by urban elites, implied a closer relationship between villages and provincial and national governments than had previously been the case. State-building meant that the government would try to reach down into the villages in a way the imperial system had never attempted. For all the national integration provided by the marketing system of "nested hierarchies" noted above, peasants were only imperfectly incorporated into the state. Their world remained partly autonomous. Most peasants did not even know that the 1911 Revolution had taken place for some time, or if they did, they assumed that Yuan Shikai had already founded a new dynasty. Yet many would have known something of the events in nearby cities, if only in distorted form, through local secret societies, leaders with revolutionary contacts, demobilized soldiers returning home, queue-cutting campaigns, new officials – or old officials with new titles – touring the countryside.

Villagers tended to meet outside agents halfway. Under the Qing, taxes were theoretically assessed according to the amount and quality of land held, but in fact the surveys necessary to maintain such a system were never kept up. The result was that taxes became both customary and ad hoc; groups of villagers or whole villages often took collective responsibility to make sure they were paid. Local gentry, landlords, and village elders would pay off the "runners" and "prompters" from the county magistrate's office before they had the chance to research the exact situation. Yuan Shikai intended, however, to re-survey all of China's farms, making the rich pay their share, putting reclaimed marsh and mountain land on the tax roles. That Yuan conceived of this plan shows the extent of his administrative ambitions, but that the plan never got off the ground symbolizes the real weakness of his government.

Still, agents of the modernizing government had a major impact on villages. Warlordism, for example, brought forced requisitions of money, boys, crops, and equipment, especially draft animals and carts, which not only put an immediate strain on peasants but also forced agriculture into a downward spiral. In places, then, farmers lost even their traditional inputs of labor, capital investment, and the simple equipment to get crops to market. Or take the case of turning old temples into modern schools, mandated by the state and supported by modernizing elites. Peasants saw such a change to be to their disadvantage. It was not clear that the new schools taught peasant children what they needed to know better than the old schoolmaster, namely a little reading and writing. The new schools certainly cost more, in both taxes and tuition fees; in fact, usually peasants could not afford them at all. And of course the desecration of a temple risked the anger of the gods.

Even before warlordism, late Qing political devolution was affecting the villages: put simply, the weakness of the central government led to local gentry strength. The strength of local leaders also came at the expense of ordinary peasants. There is a good deal of evidence to suggest that relations among villagers worsened dramatically in the early twentieth century. The precise historical process, however, was not one of a zero-sum game of political power (more central power equals less local autonomy). Rather, different kinds of power were being claimed by new and old political actors.[6] The central state could grow in some respects, along with provincial and local organs. After the 1911 Revolution, villages were given legal "rights" to establish budgets and collect taxes. The newly formalized village leaders, like the old, were the richer members of the village. They were local men, and they cannot be considered state agents as yet, but they faced new pressures by the 1920s.

## The disintegration of rural society

The Republican era was marked by a paradox: as the state weakened in many respects, state and quasi-state intrusion on the village increased. The reforms that many thought would eventually make the Chinese "wealthy and strong" cost money. In turn, then, the fiscal demands of the modernizing state – *increasing local taxes wherever possible* – put enormous pressures on the communal life of the village. The state did indeed manage to increase tax revenues, but it crushed village autonomy without being able to protect villagers from predators. The state's legitimacy was weakened as its intrusive demands decimated the traditional rural elites that were its natural supporters. The historian Prasenjit Duara, looking at rural data from north China, has called this a process of "state involution," wherein the state did not precisely weaken, but state-building backfired as it extended its reach. Rural unrest contributed the lack of stability of three forms of government: the Qing in its late reform phase, Yuan Shikai's regime, and the Nationalist government of the 1930s.

In late imperial times, the limitations on the imperial bureaucracy meant that villages were left on their own to a great extent. Most Chinese officials saw the weak point of the system to be the runners and clerks of the informal county bureaucracy. These were a despised category, not allowed to take the civil service exams and unrestrained by Confucian moral education, bureaucratic sanctions (including salary, since their incomes came largely from customary fees and bribes), or by their boss, the county magistrate, who depended on them yet might not even know what they were doing. Kang Youwei, among many others in a long line of critics, wanted to do away with them, and instead institute gentry involvement from the top and village "self-government" from the bottom. Under the Qing, villages were supposed to be run by the heads of neighborhood groups. The heads were responsible to the county government for tax payments and local peace and order. These could be coveted jobs, a sign of local prestige or an avenue toward personal enrichment. Village leaders were expected to protect the community from the worst depredations of outsiders, whether these were bandit gangs or tax collectors. The powers of such local elites were essentially informal: if they were ultimately backed by the imperial state's fearsome forces, the magistrate was still far away. Village equilibrium was normally maintained by a set of moral norms, feelings of reciprocity, common practices, religious rituals and beliefs, family and market networks – what Duara calls the "cultural nexus of power."

But, beginning in the late Qing, state-building projects broke the cultural nexus of power by putting unbearable pressures on local elites. Village heads could neither satisfy the state's insatiable demands nor protect their communities by resisting those demands. The change can be seen in the fact that villagers began avoiding the job of head. Above all, irregular tax levies placed a new burden on the village as a whole (not on individual households like the land tax). The village had to figure out how to raise the money. Not only did this place great pressure on the village heads, but obviously village solidarity could suffer as well. Different kinds of villages responded in different ways. In north China, villages composed mainly of roughly equal smallholders sometimes tightened their internal ties, formed defense militia, and shared the tax burden. Other villages, already more stratified or with much of their land held by absentee landlords, tended to break apart, becoming all the more vulnerable to outside pressures. Village leaders fled their posts, and as new people – new *kinds* of people – moved into village leadership positions, their character changed. The new leaders ruled by coercion alone.

This is the structural origin of the "local bullies" of twentieth-century China. These men could come from any class background; what they had in common was the physical strength necessary to beat people. In effect they became tax farmers, though not recognized as such by the government – and as far as villagers were concerned, they were extortionists. The "local bullies" might arrange tax payments but usually cheated the state and opposed its efforts to rationalize fiscal administration. Allied with landlords, they did not represent the villagers either. Unlike traditional gentry or real village leaders, they had no legitimacy – which reflected back on the state. In other words, the delegitimation of the national government and of village power arrangements went hand in hand. This is not to say that village life was idyllic under the traditional order, but villagers operated in a reciprocal if hierarchical moral system and the state at least attempted to limit the prerogatives of local power-holders – if only to avoid provoking peasant uprisings.

The collapse of the imperial state in 1911 marked a pivotal moment not only in China's high politics but in rural society as well, for the traditional elites owed some of their legitimacy to their "relationship" with the emperor. When a man passed the examinations, his family could raise a pennant outside their home to show off their new status. The line running downward from the Incarnate Dragon in Beijing to the literate landlord in a rural county might not have run straight but it was known to exist. However, the lines of legitimation from the revolutionary militarists or Yuan Shikai's generals barely reached beyond provincial capitals. If we recognize that disintegrative processes were already under way during the late Qing, they accelerated after 1911. This is, again, not to say that 1911 itself marked a revolution in rural society: but the key class of the gentry could not survive the collapse of the monarchy, and the already-battered social order of the countryside could not survive the collapse of the gentry.

No wonder rural banditry increased dramatically.[7] Bandits were a traditional part of the social ecology, of course, as in all agrarian societies. When the harvest failed, young men might turn to banditry as women, children, and the elderly turned to begging. In some areas, banditry was a traditional off-season occupation. Yet the number and size of bandit gangs dramatically increased in the early Republic. Banditry was not only a source of income. Although dangerous and criminal, it was legitimated in two ways: the Chinese Robin Hood tradition of larger-than-life social bandits and the general prevalence of militarism. Many a warlord, with or without official title, started as a bandit chief, and many more peasants moved back and forth between soldiering and bandit life. Kidnapping for ransom as well as thievery was common. Some bandit gangs numbered in the thousands and controlled large territories. Although there were no true Robin Hoods or "social bandits" devoted to taking from the rich and giving to the poor, many gangs at least respected their local communities ("a rabbit does not eat from around its own nest").

Warlord armies were of little use against bandits. Common practice was for the armies to fire blanks to warn bandits of their approach. This had the dual advantage of avoiding the risks of fighting while, by keeping banditry alive, reminding officials that they needed to maintain the army. In all, bandits were no worse than government agents from the point of view of most peasants. Even from the official point of view, bandits were often seen as less of an evil than bringing in outside soldiers. Most gangs were ephemeral and local, but between 1911 and 1914 the famous Bai Lang (White Wolf) led thousands of men through five provinces across northern China. To move from banditry to military life was easy; to move from banditry to rebellion was barely even a conscious possibility.[8] Indeed, bandits often forged connections with elites who could protect and profit from them. Bandits were a constant reminder of the failure of the state. They also provide evidence of the decline of rural China.

In addition to banditry, there was much violence between neighboring villages. Disputes over water or woodlots could lead to pitched battles. There were many instances of riots and uprisings: impossible to count since difficult to define and because records are scattered, but noted in domestic and foreign official reports and newspapers.[9] Events like these have a traditional feel, but it is worth asking whether the rise in banditry and collective violence represented purely economic frustrations, or if popular disappointment in the results of the revolution also contributed to rural protests. By far the largest number of riots and uprisings were provoked by taxes and administrative abuses, not landlords. The point is not that class antagonisms were irrelevant to rural China but that community–state conflicts were a major facet of late Qing and early Republican politics.

The Huang Lian uprising in Xianyou county in Fujian between 1912 and 1914 is a case in point. It combined an energetic effort to protect local opium-growers against state prohibitions with anti-tax feeling, an anti-Christian movement, and general opposition to the new Republic.[10] Huang Lian had originally supported the 1911 Revolution, and by the summer of 1912 he had emerged as head of a loosely organized group of local farmers, landowners, and even a few members of the elite (gentry and urban-based community leaders), perhaps motivated to oppose the Yuan Shikai Republic for reasons having to do with local political factions. The main demands of the uprising were an end to the prohibition on opium cultivation and an end to the land tax. Yuan's troops in Xianyou sparked further opposition by their brutality and cupidity.

Meanwhile, the Second Revolution embroiled Fujian in the summer of 1913. As Yuan cemented his control over southeastern China, government troops were finally able to isolate the rebels and execute several of their leaders, including a few gentry sympathizers (Huang Lian was never found). Yuan had been able to use the uprising to crush elite opposition, and he was able to resume his anti-opium campaign. After his death, however, the area quickly reverted to the lucrative cash crop. The incident, scarcely of national importance, demonstrates the capacity of rural society to resist outside pressure. Yuan could send his troops in once the rebellion was under way, but the government in Beijing could hardly prevent such uprisings in the first place. Peasants could not yet mount the political stage, demanding to speak with their own voice. But let us examine precisely how they could still express grievances.

## Peasants: Resistance, rebellion, and revolution

To look ahead for a moment: peasants emerged as major political actors in the 1930s and 1940s. It is they who made the Chinese revolution. They had "always" been prone to resistance, riot, and rebellion, but a self-conscious peasant movement emerged only in the late 1920s. Then, peasants shaped the revolution to the point of defining it: they determined its limits, its ferocity, its direction. As we will see, the peasantry was in turn shaped by – but also shaped – the Chinese Communists. The fundamental questions regarding the peasants in the twentieth century are: (1) What problems did they face and what were the causes of these problems? (2) Why did they rebel and how did they come to support the Communists? (3) How did they perceive the state and what did they want it to do for them? Indeed, these questions are fundamental to our understanding of China. The first two questions have received the greatest scholarly interest, and we will examine the second in some detail in later chapters, but more attention should be paid to the third question.

Historically, all the great agrarian civilizations had to deal with rural unrest, but Chinese peasant revolts seem especially frequent. The state's need for agricultural surplus placed it at odds with peasants and with local elites, and the fact that per capita surplus was low meant that at times of natural disaster and bad harvests the state's demands could threaten a community. The Qing gentry were nothing like the great aristocrats of the previous millennium; they were relatively weak vis-à-vis the state. At the same time they might identify with community rather than state when struggle broke out. Peasant revolts therefore had both a class character when ordinary farmers attacked landlords, and a more explicitly political character when rural elites joined peasant movements attacking the state, or at least its local representatives. Although elites were tightly bound to the state – through Confucian education, the exam system, and the state's promise to protect property rights – gentry status was not inheritable, and family wealth was divided each generation. In other words, local elites felt downward social pressures. They might join with ordinary peasants to made demands of the state or resist taxes, or they might join with the state to suppress local disturbances. The state tried to preserve a balance between the peasantry, local elites, and the central government. Rural elites were necessary and natural allies in the business of government, but also potential rivals for resources. A smallholding peasant economy prevented the emergence of great houses that might challenge the court. But if this balance failed, the state could itself become a target of popular wrath.

### Definitions

Let us take "revolution" in the sense of "social revolution" or a fundamental reshaping of class structure and social relations. Fundamental political change – reshaping the basis of the polity – will be part of a social revolution, as will rapid cultural change. "Rebellion," on the other hand, refers primarily to illegal, organized protest; at its outer limits rebellion seeks to replace the existing government with a new one while demanding minor modifications of the class structure and political institutions.[11] Revolution, at least as a self-conscious act, is entirely modern. There are no historical examples of peasants acting on their own to make a revolution. From the point of view of the "state" – the institutions of governance – rebellion is of little consequence. The structures of power and class will be restored. From the point of view of the "government" (the court and its officials) rebellion is as serious a matter as revolution, and of course rebels are treated as traitors. From the point of view of peasants, they emerge as political actors as much in rebellion as in revolution.

It should be noted that I categorize the "peasantry" quite loosely, to refer to non-elite rural residents. Whereas peasants are sometimes defined more strictly as actual tillers or members of farming households, and sometimes even exclude non-landowning tenant farmers and laborers, my looser definition has the advantage of associating people who shared a culture, spoke the same dialects, were prey to the same economic shifts, and whose families might intermarry.[12] Not only might the purely "peasant" daughter be married to a peddler but the peasant son might be apprenticed to a barber or apothecary who in turn might buy land for his son to till. Even the professional bandit often kept village ties.

But the question remains, how do peasants decide whether to acquiesce in their fates or to revolt? The decision is not made solely on the basis of hard times and exploitation. Indeed, one school of scholarship rejects such considerations explicitly. Theda Skocpol posits that peasants are always exploited (by definition, as it were) and emphasizes the relation between class and institutional arrangements, especially the state, as the key factor in explaining peasant uprisings.[13] Yet do peasants perceive themselves as being equally exploited at all times? Peasant *perceptions* of injustice will change according to circumstances. It may be very difficult for scholars to discover the subjective moral universe of a peasantry, but to dismiss it as irrelevant is no solution.[14]

"Exploitation" here refers not simply to expropriation of surpluses, but, as Barrington Moore has put it, *coercive* demands *without reciprocity*.[15] Legitimate authority requires reciprocity, administrative competence, and a shared sense of the goals of the community. It is the notion of reciprocity, I believe, that is particularly useful in thinking about the issue of exploitation in China. Many social scientists have abjured the notion of exploitation because it is highly subjective and emotive. Yet it is precisely a subjective sense of exploitation and injustice that explains peasant anger in twentieth-century China. Not only did rural elites lose their traditional social functions; as well, the state's role was key in so far as it failed to curb the landed interests (including usurers), it imposed very disruptive "special taxes," and it allowed roads, canals, and dikes to deteriorate. Political disorder, though winding down during the Nationalist decade (1928–37), continued to disturb markets and other institutions of the commercialized economy, and the currency remained unstable. Industry, both native and foreign-owned, grew but not fast enough to absorb population increases. Even if, "objectively," peasants were not, overall, worse off than before, they still had every reason to feel that the implied social contract was fraying.

In looking at the agrarian crisis, some scholars emphasize the inadequate distribution of China's wealth while others are chiefly concerned with the lack of economic development aggravated by population growth and lack of technology. Much ink has been expended on the question of land ownership patterns. How many peasants were tenants? How many landlords? But what is a tenant? What about a family that rented only some of the land it farmed? What about a family that rented some land, farmed some of its own land, worked for wages part-time in nearby towns, and whose womenfolk made cloth at home? What about a family that on top of all that also rented out some land to others? Regional variations and even village-to-village patterns differed remarkably. Tenancy, but probably also per capita income, was higher in the south. Landlordism was a problem when it turned small-holders into landless peasants, but Chinese landlords who rented fields to scattered tenants did not wield their power over every aspect of life like the lord of a manor.

Responding to disturbances across rural China in the nineteenth century, the wealthy had moved to the cities to become absentee landlords and invest in more profitable urban enterprises. The remaining rural elites, the "local bullies and evil gentry" of the early twentieth century, were not very elite from the point of view of the cities. Urban working poor might actually have a better lifestyle – better food, clothing, and leisure activities – than a village landlord. Immediate pressures on the peasant included bad harvests, usually a result of natural disaster, and a range of state-mediated problems: conscription, infrastructure deterioration, rent, interest, and tax payments. Although rent and interest may in theory be regarded as a private, contractual affair, such contracts were ultimately enforced by state agents. At the same time, Chinese peasants often expected the state (and elites) to play a role in mitigating the effects of bad harvests. The Qing attempted to maintain a system of grain-storage depots, whose contents could then be distributed at low cost or free to hungry peasants. Or the state would contract to import grain to a region. These policies were designed to prevent suffering, riots, banditry, and price gouging. Though never perfect, the system played a role in preventing rebellions till the end of the eighteenth century, when it began to break down. The state also encouraged the voluntary cooperation of rural elites in providing charity.

Normally, of course, peasants did not risk their homes and lives to make a political point. It took urgent need to drive them to violence. Short of revolt, peasant actions included complaints and lawsuits, petitions, and riots. In a less obviously political sense, "survival strategies" included banditry, soldiery, begging, migration to cities, sale of children and wives, infanticide – and a mix of these could be expected over a lifetime. But if peasants were driven into open rebellion by despair, they might treat elites and the state with a variety of "resistance" strategies.[16] Chinese popular culture contained egalitarian and millenarian elements at odds with official ideology. As well, Confucian paternalism contained the seeds of its own critique. When officials and elites failed to treat the people with "benevolence," they were vulnerable to accusations of hypocrisy – this is the theme of reciprocity. The ordinary daily resistance of tax evasion, banditry, and disrespect, as well as folktales of virtuous officials (in contrast to the real, corrupt ones), was a kind of mirror reflection of gentry attitudes toward the peasantry as dumb oxen and dangerous brutes. Resistance and obedience, oppression and reciprocity established the fundamental moral rhythm of rural life.

Rebellions emerged under unusual circumstances out of the usual patterns of daily life.[17] Normally, the line between resistance and illegal activities on the one hand, and subversive organizations and openly political challenges on the other, remains clear. Even tax riots scarcely threatened the foundations of government. However, the kinds of organization that gave rise to tax riots and other illegal activities could, under the right circumstances, cross the line to full-scale rebellion. If the government began pressing a bandit group unbearably, they could flee, disband, or fight back: rebel. If bandits fought government troops, the conflict might draw in local villages. If the bandits could appeal to the interests and grievances of villagers, whole districts would erupt into rebellion. The social geography of China encouraged this in so far as Chinese villages were relatively open and integrated into the larger society. Would-be rebel leaders could easily slip onto a circuit that enabled them to reach many villages with no official the wiser, and so rebellion could spread as the state was caught sleeping. Rebel leaders – like the Boxer organizers – could follow the same circuits between villages and market towns as barbers, peddlers, martial arts experts.

Similarly, many peasants belonged to "secret societies" – which were, in fact, fairly open mutual aid groups. Such organizations were loosely linked in regional hierarchies, but they were scarcely centralized. In other words, secret societies were local organizations, though members from what were essentially different secret societies did learn a common set of rituals and could use these to recognize each other and form new relations when necessary – when smuggling salt or selling stolen goods, for instance. Many of these groups seemed to have had a vague restorationist ideology ("Down with the Qing, restore the Ming"), but they had little real potential for rebellion. Both bandits and secret societies might be turned into tools of the elite; they could become private landlord militia, for example, or sometimes elites served as middlemen, disposing of stolen goods.

Even more conservative were community protection organizations. Groups ranging from permanent militia to temporary crop-watching societies mushroomed in the social chaos of the nineteenth and twentieth centuries. As banditry and warlordism increased, communities had to defend their crops. Regardless of whether dominated by landlords or in some sense representative of the community as a whole, such groups sought to preserve what wealth they possessed. They fought off bandits and sometimes became involved in inter-community disputes: over water rights, say, or in the clan fighting endemic in the southeast. Above all, they resisted outsiders.

And the government could easily become one such outsider – in which case local militia became a focal point of rebellion. However, as long as protective organizations remained parochial, their rebellious potential was small: government troops could easily isolate and defeat such resistance, as in the case of Huang Lian. In contrast to bandits, who could flee, and secret society members, who might count on finding friends in distant places, communal protection groups lost their raison d'être away from home. Bargaining between local groups and the government was thus common. Yet sometimes a combination of peasant desperation, obtuse officials, and ambitious local leaders could cause community organizations to unite in a large-scale rebellion. After all, various villages had a shared interest in resisting what they regarded as unjust tax demands. Literally thousands of small-scale yet still bloody uprisings were provoked throughout the early twentieth century by the land tax, the salt tax, opium taxes, and taxes on various livestock and produce.

In one particularly drawn-out rebellion in the 1920s the "Red Spears" of the north China plain, defending their villages, attacked bandits and warlord armies alike. According to some accounts, they were descended from the Boxers, offering their magical protective skills to local militia defending villages from marauding bandits. At any rate, the plains of Henan, Shandong, and Jiangsu provinces were dotted with their fortresses. The same defensive strategies used against bandits were then used against warlord armies. Indeed, the first campaign against the Red Spears in 1923 was prompted by their very effectiveness against bandits, which threatened the livelihood of the official soldiers, who either cooperated actively with the bandits or at least needed the bandits in order to preserve their bandit-fighting jobs. The armies, with their surtaxes and labor demands, shifted the focus of the Red Spears to tax resistance. A Red Spears proclamation to the residents of Kaifeng denounced government troops:

> Here a surcharge, there a surtax. Today it is requested, tomorrow it is demanded. Sell your grain and pawn your clothing – still you haven't enough to pay his cursed taxes. See how his army is even more vicious than bandits.... Seizing one month of rent, imposing taxes on cooking oil, auctioning off the public lands, issuing five million bank notes, imposing interest bonds – all these are conscious efforts to deprive you of your very lives.[18]

Tax riots were also part of the ongoing accommodation between the state and society from the late imperial era forward. The one form of peasant resistance that did not seek accommodation was the millenarian religious sect. Millenarian movements offered a truly radical vision of a new society. Religious sectarians had what amounted to a revolutionary ideology, although an unworldly one, and when the circumstances were right they could erupt in violent mass action. In general, popular religion comprised a synthetic mélange of Buddhist, Confucian, Daoist, and shamanist features. The government proscribed but seldom interfered with non-official cults. The White Lotus cult was a Manichean-influenced form of Buddhism holding that the "eternal and venerable mother" would give birth to the Maitreya (Buddha of the future), marking the beginning of the third age ("kalpa"). Forces of light would then triumph over the darkness amidst great calamities and destruction, which only the faithful would survive – to emerge into a time of peace, plenty, leisure, and equality. Because of official proscriptions during the Ming and Qing, there was no White Lotus church nor even a coherent literary tradition. Rather, teachers (often hereditary) and disciples transmitted a loose set of doctrines to widely scattered congregations that had little contact with one another, and women often played a prominent role. As long as the third kalpa was considered to be far away, worshipers were quiescent and the government mostly ignored them. Congregations might consist of an entire village or one segment of a village.

If hunger or war came, however, they could be interpreted as the calamities marking the imminent arrival of the third kalpa. And if a charismatic leadership with organizational skills arose, then normally scattered congregations could be meshed into a movement. The imperial government, the emperor himself, was associated with the forces of darkness; rebellion became godly. Thousands of normally cautious peasants would join such a movement. Most would be newly converted, responding to the movement in the hope that they too might be saved in the coming cataclysm about them, or simply in order to get what they could in the destruction around them.

Government policy in dealing with rebellion was to exterminate the leadership while assuming that the mass of followers was "deluded" and therefore essentially innocent. The Taiping Rebellion, where government troops slaughtered all the Taipings, was an exception; usually ordinary rebels were demobilized and sent back to their villages. Such mercy was pragmatic. It also reflected a Confucian understanding of the relationship between social and cosmic force. A rebellion, like any kind of protest, was on one level a sign: a portent or omen. The people were not so much thinking beings with political opinions as they were a force of nature. Like an earthquake, a rebellion might be a sign that Heaven was displeased with the emperor. Spiritually, rectification of the imperial person was called for; socially, this should include reforms that would ameliorate the mundane causes of popular dissatisfaction. Thus the effect of rebellions was, overall, to support the basic institutions of Chinese society by fostering periodic reform. For if a rebellion reached the point where rebels had wished to build their own political institutions, they had nowhere to turn except the norms of imperial Confucianism.

Millenarian rebels could not – quite – imagine revolution. "Revolution" refers to fundamental change *in this world*; it is a mundane matter. Religious sectarians offered a critique of the existing state and a vision of an alternative order in ways that bandits, say, could not. Yet such religious visions proved, on the rare occasions they were put into practice, not to be the stuff of revolution but of rebellion. And rebellions were simply transmuted into a new Confucian regime.

None the less, millenarianism foreshadowed the revolutions of the twentieth century. It offered an alternative to Confucian assumptions about the social order and its cosmic foundations. The egalitarianism implicit in the notion of a group of people saved together went a long way toward reducing divisions of region, dialect, class, clan, family, and gender. The community-based protection organizations and the more narrowly focused loyalties of bandit gangs had greater difficulty in transcending such divisions. That transcending them was possible at all is an indication of the cultural and commercial integration of China. Peasants were thus not a force of nature but political actors all along.

# 6   Urban social change

One can almost say the Chinese city was everything the countryside was not: a place where cultures mixed and matched, growing and developing new ways of life, teeming with people: carters and rickshaw-pullers in worker's pants, bankers and professors in Western suits or traditional scholar's gowns, and entertainers, artisans, prostitutes, students, monks and nuns, foreign businessmen and missionaries of both sexes, restaurant workers, sidewalk hawkers, shopkeepers of all descriptions, con men, beggars, soldiers, waves of refugees from the troubles of the countryside, and, in sum, the followers of every kind of profession and fashion. In the case of Shanghai, immigrants included refugees from around the world – in the 1920s White Russians fleeing Lenin and in the 1930s Jews fleeing Hitler.

In a short walk the urban dweller could move from an elegant bookstore to an icehouse, a teahouse, a brothel, or a public park – numerous parks were built between 1900 and 1930 for residents to enjoy for a small fee. Beijing was particularly lucky, since after 1912 most of the old imperial temples and gardens could be turned into parks.[1] Park building symbolized the transition from empire to republic. Parks were also a mark of progress, showing that China, like the West and Japan, would build spaces for its citizens' health, recreation, and relaxation, even though working-class families could seldom afford the admission fee. Parks also became sites of political protest where demonstrators could gather and hear speeches, as well as for leisure activities.

By 1900, China's urban population was growing at nearly 2 percent a year. Shanghai dominated not merely the central Chinese interior, but East Asian trade and banking. The major Chinese cities became sites of political and cultural contestation as well as commercial competition. Political movements were organized in the cities. Urbanites learned to think of themselves as citizens. The Republican state sponsored new civic rituals like the "Double Ten" (10 October) National Day, a holiday of parades and flag drills, military reviews and rifle exercises, student sports competitions, political speeches, "new opera" performances, and official and private banquets. The new citizens marked themselves by short hair, as men cut off their queues; natural feet, as women no longer bound theirs;

bows and handshakes, as the kowtow was replaced; and Westernized clothing.[2] The new body of the citizen – a bit stiffer, straighter, and stronger than the old, and sometimes in uniform – was exemplified by the soldier, the official, and the student.

Some historians have traced the origins of Chinese civil society to such urban spaces as restaurants, native-place association halls, public parks and squares, and even bath-houses, which were used to plot demonstrations, make political deals, and hold rallies. Daily newspapers, weekly journals, monthly magazines, and books were published in great profusion. Gossip columns and other middlebrow fare were popular with clerks, shopkeepers, and housewives; serious political discussions were read by elites – but these were not mutually exclusive patterns of social communication: the various groups shared a sense of national and local political consciousness. In the case of Beijing, for example, whatever warlord had seized the city, he could not ignore urban public opinion, which increasingly was defined in opposition to the state.[3]

The "carriers" of this emerging civil society were the citizens – potentially, all Chinese, but in practice only those few who marked themselves as modern. The new Republican government mandated formal Western-style suits for its employees on official occasions. But it was the "Sun Yat-sen" (zhongshan) suit that became popular male attire: a vaguely military combination of trousers and a jacket with four pockets and a high collar. This attire lasted through the twentieth century, becoming known in the West as the "Mao suit." Modern women will be discussed in greater detail below, but they too had ways of distinguishing themselves: in addition to natural feet or bobbed hair, they might wear a jacket and skirt instead of long, loose trousers, or by the 1920s wear the long *qipao* (cheongsam) gown; and perhaps above all they felt free to leave their homes and walk about in public. Of course, in real life, different styles of etiquette could be used in different situations. A student might still kowtow to her parents while going to school in uniform and practicing sports and military drill. But overall, modern citizens recognized each other through dress, etiquette, and body language. Their new community thus excluded peasants and workers, though it included soldiers. Individuals who could afford the modern attire and learn the new etiquette but chose not to, thereby marked themselves as old-fashioned opponents of the republican spirit.

At the same time, civil society did not develop as completely independent of the state or opposed to state-building. On the contrary, various formal and informal associations – like chambers of commerce, the bar, student groups, women's organizations – and the state interpenetrated one another. Native-place associations were glad to have officials as members, but they could still represent merchant interests vis-à-vis the state. Student groups might find their actions severely restricted and might disappear after a particular confrontation, only to emerge again when circumstances changed. Urban civil society was not so much a sphere where autonomous individuals pursued their self-interest and their public concerns as it was an arena of group representation, rivalry, and negotiation. The weakness of the state and the strength of local society produced a dynamic amalgam. Society could not – and did not desire to – replace the state; indeed, the weaknesses of the state were widely seen as a serious hindrance to general progress.[4] The self-image of civil society was entirely patriotic.

Social groups remained splintered even in the cities, since the state was not strong enough to force the various classes and parochial groups to combine to defend their collective rights. In thinking about their society, what contemporaries noticed was not "classes" – a terminology not yet in general use – but "circles": particularly the circles of officials, merchants, students, gentry-merchants, the military, educators, journalists, workers, and police. These were, then, the named groups who dominated the public life of the cities. These groups were developing autonomous organizations at least partly free of state control. As such, urban society was marked by powerful new social forces. It was also changing physically. Over the first few decades of the twentieth century, the look of China's cities was transformed. Wide boulevards supplemented the small lanes; horsedrawn carriages, rickshaws, and automobiles joined the streams of human traffic and mule carts; colorful advertisements appeared everywhere; and bright electric lights illuminated the streets and shops. The city was where people read the newspaper on the day it was published, instead of waiting weeks for a batch of papers to arrive. The city was where life was more open: illicit lovers met in teahouses, political agitators spoke in parks, individuals could remake themselves by deciding to cut their hair, wear Western clothing, or drink cow's milk.

China's major cities were protected from the worst of warlord depredations. As treaty ports, they relied on the Powers, which would not tolerate a breakdown of order. By 1917 some 92 cities were officially open to foreign trade. Though filled with crime, prostitution, corrupt officials, and rapacious gangs, the major cities of China in the early twentieth century were probably considerably better places to live than London or Paris during their acute phases of industrialization a century and a half earlier. Basic sanitation was maintained by the ancient practice of selling night soil to the farmers. Some social services were provided by merchant guilds, which organized militia, fire-fighting units, street cleaning, soup kitchens, and free burials for the indigent, just as they had during the Qing.

Cities had been the first sites of the new schools, including missionary schools, and Western hospitals. Revolutionaries congregated in the cities; foreigners were of course concentrated there. And they became the locations for new industry: the armaments factories built by the state and the first factories built by foreigners and Chinese. Heavy industry (iron and steel) helped make cities in the northeast and central China. And light industry (textiles, tobacco) helped make Shanghai and Guangzhou what they are today.

## Urban development: Civil society and the bourgeoisie

As China was increasingly drawn into the world economy, merchants who exported tea and silk for silver and opium evolved into a bourgeoisie engaged in a mix of manufacturing and trade. Many of the bourgeoisie worked directly for Western companies (such "compradors" numbered 20,000 in 1900); many found profit in cooperation with Western business interests, and others directly competed with them. By 1912 "the richest and most respected section of the merchant class (including family members) must have been about 1.5 to 2 million strong, comprising 0.5 percent of the population."[5] A petty bourgeoisie of office clerks and assistants, in addition to more humble shopkeepers, independent street hawkers, and service workers like barbers and prostitutes, also grew in the cities. In 1912 Chambers of Commerce counted 200,000 members, tiny compared with China's overall population but strategically located to exert economic and political pressure. As we noted in Chapter 4, the Chinese economy benefited from World War I. In fact, this new bourgeoisie made enormous profits from the Western demand for raw materials and agricultural produce. With peace in 1918 and the revival of trade, exports to a decimated Europe rose even higher, and China's balance of trade deficit declined.

Until recently, Western historians tended to dismiss the Chinese bourgeoisie as too small and weak to fulfill the function it had performed in Western Europe of promoting democratic institutions. Chinese Marxist historians also faulted the bourgeoisie for failing to defeat the forces of feudalism (rural landlordism) and imperialism. Whether these views rest on an adequate description of European development in the nineteenth century need not detain us here. It may be that the institutions we associate with democracy today – universal adult suffrage, mass-based political parties, and populist rhetoric – owed more to the pressures of the workers' and socialist movements than to the classical liberalism of the true bourgeoisie. In any case, it is clear that the Chinese bourgeoisie did not shape China's national politics in the way that, say, the French bourgeoisie shaped nineteenth-century France. But more recent research has asked less about what the bourgeoisie was "supposed to do" and more about what it was actually like. A good deal of scholarly interest has focused on Shanghai in particular, and although Shanghai's international importance means that it cannot be regarded as a typical Chinese city, it does suggest new ways to look at the cities in general.[6] The putative historical role of the bourgeoisie is replaced by its cultural role as mediator between China and the West, tradition and modernity, and consumption and production. If the bourgeoisie did not directly lead a revolution, it did lead in changing everyday practices and attitudes.

Another approach is to ask what dilemmas the bourgeoisie faced. Leading merchants generally sought accommodation with outside powers: warlords, foreigners, revolutionaries, or bandits as the case might be. But at the same time they displayed a new political awareness and began to participate in popular movements and even informal governance. Though the bourgeoisie supported Sun Yat-sen's Nanjing government in early 1912, they also welcomed the presidency of Yuan Shikai. Yuan promised to recognize the obligations of the Nanjing government, reimburse some of the losses incurred during the revolution, reduce export taxes, unify the currency, and abolish the annoying transit taxes. Above all, Yuan promised peace and order. As the warlord era ensued, the bourgeoisie became more sympathetic to radical nationalism, though it still feared social chaos. Temporary alliances between radical nationalist students and urban business communities were rooted in a partially shared political agenda. Both groups resented foreign imperialism and were prepared to support boycotts that might pressurize the government. Though some businessmen had close relationships with the Japanese, most felt the competition of Japan during the 1910s and 1920s. British and American interests were also irksome, and the Powers tended to unify around support for the unequal treaties, low import tariffs, and other such matters of "principle." The Chinese bourgeoisie also resented the social exclusivity of the whites. Boycotts of foreign goods were encouraged, and a general "buy Chinese" feeling emerged in the late 1910s. Indeed, entire advertising campaigns were built around the importance of buying domestic products: for example, the Nanyang Brothers' cigarette ads linked beautiful women and patriotism.

None the less, the bourgeoisie supported internationalism as well, recognizing its interests in free trade, foreign capital, and imported technology. The result of the separate tugs of nationalism and internationalism was a steady desire for reform. Chinese businessmen, who were sometimes Western-educated, adopted something of an American-style faith in progress, free enterprise, competition – and union busting. If traditional Chinese merchants dedicated their lives to permanent monopolies and occasional charity (a stereotype), the modern bourgeoisie was interested in improving businesses, upgrading technologies, and influencing state policies concerning taxation, money supply, and customs dues.

Bourgeois ideology was an amorphous thing. As nationalism and internationalism tugged in different directions, so the bourgeoisie felt disgust with the disruptions, tax outrages, and market distortions caused by marauding warlord armies – while discretion dictated negotiation and compromise with de facto political power. More positively, the bourgeoisie saw itself as staunchly progressive. What did China need? As was said since the late nineteenth century: national salvation through industry! In the end, the bourgeoisie longed for a government of competent consensus. Many businessmen took their position as mediators and their social responsibilities very seriously.[7] However, the limited paternalism of the bourgeoisie was inadequate to meet the real needs of the urban populace. Nor could nationalist impulses permanently bind together the disparate interests of the bourgeoisie and the workers.

The bourgeoisie remained a fragile class. That the bourgeoisie was interested in national power is shown in its involvement in the post-revolutionary politics of 1912. Success in influencing new governments, however, came only at the local level. They were not represented by any political party; indeed, the disagreements that quickly emerged between the bourgeoisie and the supporters of Sun Yat-sen weakened both groups in their relations with Yuan Shikai. Yuan had little appreciation for what independent industrialists and financiers might do for China's economy, and he tended to favor "bureaucratic capitalism" in line with his top-down approach to governing. Throughout the Republican period, even at the provincial level the bourgeoisie remained subordinate to military and bureaucratic authority. Furthermore, foreign capital dominated the modern sector – shipping, banking, textiles and other manufacturing, even mining – though foreign investment constituted only 10 percent of the overall economy, where agriculture was still paramount.

Yet the bourgeoisie none the less continued to expand and was often able to compete successfully with foreign companies. In low-tech areas where foreign access to capital and resources was not critical, like cigarette manufacturing, Chinese companies did well. Shanghai's printing machine industry grew to dominate not just the Chinese market but all of East and Southeast Asia, including Japan.[8] Without political power, however, the bourgeoisie did not translate its wealth into political power except on the purely local level. It could do little to improve the physical or commercial infrastructure, much less counter warlord depredations. It had neither the ability nor the interest to modernize agricultural practices and thus meet the consumer needs of millions of peasants. As long as the countryside stagnated, the modern sector was moving forward with brakes applied. None the less, the bourgeoisie contributed to the structural changes of the period: the rise of the intelligentsia and radical student movements, growing urban wealth and middle-class culture, and the spread of modern educational and publishing institutions.

## New social forces: Workers

As modern industry grew, Chinese came to the cities for work. Slowly, a proletariat formed. Workers had long provided China with manufactured and crafted goods: "artisan" was a respected Confucian social category. But such craft workers had different skills and attitudes than modern factory workers. In the 1910s workers in the modern sector of shipping, railroads, electric- and coal-powered factories, machine tools, and the like, grew to over 1.5 million. Again, like the bourgeoisie, though their numbers were small when compared to China's overall size, workers were pivotally located. Yet factory workers in the 1910s and 1920s were seldom committed to a lifetime in the factory. They were overwhelmingly of peasant origin, and often returned home to help with harvests or join the weddings and funerals of kin. As in the early phases of industrialization in other societies, hours were long, working conditions horrible, and pay low, though high enough to attract workers from an agricultural system in decline. Women and children were hired extensively. Most workers were subject to the predations of labor contractors – men who recruited workers for a company and who maintained authority over them during their employment. Even so, Chinese workers were capable of persistent and effective organizing.

Workers were neither the tools of the anarchists, communists, or professional politicians who would attempt to organize them in the 1920s, nor were they an isolated, apolitical mob. Long before political organizers arrived on the scene, Chinese workers had developed traditions of collective action: work stoppages, walkouts, slowdowns, and strikes.

Immigrants from the countryside used native-place ties – as well as ethnic and sub-ethnic identities – to ease their way in unfamiliar cities. In the case of Shanghai, workers came from every part of China, using native-place associations to find jobs, some welfare and insurance provisions, and a sense of community. To a great extent, occupational specialties accorded with native place, ranging from skilled carpenters from Guangzhou and weavers from around Shanghai to unskilled rickshaw pullers and porters from the poor hinterland just north of Shanghai. Family members frequently followed kin to the cities.

Fellow provincials – employers and employees alike – tended to live and work in the same urban neighborhood enclaves. Labor contractors naturally recruited from their native regions, making promises to parents and girls (factories often recruited young women) about the beautiful future that awaited them in Shanghai, a process sometimes called "plucking mulberry leaves." In the city they formed patron–client ties with their workers, often pocketing their wages from the factory, and providing food and living quarters that might amount to prison conditions. Fights between competing labor gangs, wanting to expand their own labor opportunities, were not unusual. Yet divisions among the working class did not prevent collective action. On the contrary, as the political scientist Elizabeth Perry shows in an important study, native-place solidarity formed the basic social units through which militancy was expressed.[9] Under the right circumstances, ethnic divisions fostered opportunities for alliances based on mutual benefit, a paternalistic concern of skilled laborers for the unskilled, and even, ultimately, class-consciousness.

Class conflict was unavoidable. Electric- and coal-powered factories created a distinctly new setting, a world away from the small, cramped, family workshops that persisted alongside the massive new factors. However, proletarianization – the process whereby workers developed class-consciousness or an identity as workers – took several generations to be completed. Still, over time, workers began to identify home not with ancestral origins but with Shanghai, Guangzhou, Wuhan, and, to a lesser extent, northern cities like Tianjin. Workers gradually lost their ties to the countryside, organized in their factories, and built ties with other workers. Class-consciousness was not limited to organized labor protest. Various strategies that workers used to cope with their powerlessness in the new urban world contributed to a sense of the common condition. Work slowdowns could be effective when strikes would simply result in being fired. Sometimes foremen were attacked and beaten by groups of workers or workers with ties to organized criminal gangs. Increasingly, workers worked full-time, for a lifetime. On the other hand, they tended to keep local identities expressed in dialect, dress, cuisine, and customs that distinguished them from fellow workers from different regions. Still, even though these sub-ethnic divisions – often antagonisms – persist even today, localism did not prevent the emergence of broader identities. Working-class consciousness did not trump other forms of solidarity, but rather it emerged with them.

As early as the 1910s a distinct rhetoric of class conflict is evident. Skilled workers at the Jiangnan Arsenal (a government-run munitions factory) wanted to distinguish themselves as skilled workers from the unskilled, but the contrast between workers and capitalists was even stronger. In 1912 they stated: "craftsmen are like [mere] laborers and the arsenal is like a capitalist."[10] Modern industrial unions were slow in coming, but traditional guilds controlled skilled factory jobs from the beginning. Slowdowns, walkouts, and strikes over wages and working conditions were working-class weapons from the late nineteenth century on. At the same time anti-imperialist sentiment also provoked collective action even before 1911. As early as 1831 textile workers near Guangzhou led a boycott against British yarn. Or take the famous case of the Ningbo graveyard in Shanghai, which is often cited by historians as China's first patriotic strike. In 1874 French authorities decided to build a road through a cemetery operated by the Ningbo native-place association, next to the French Concession in Shanghai. The French abandoned their plans after protests and riots, but in 1878 they tried again. This time Ningbo workers struck all French employers and Ningbo natives boycotted all Western goods and merchants. Facing this intense defense of a sacred site by a group of people operating in terms of community and class, the French backed down again. Success to the workers and merchants of Ningbo. By 1920, about half of China's modern workers worked in foreign-owned mills.

Strikes and even unions were illegal, but guilds, which included shop owners and master craftsmen as well as ordinary workers, increasingly acted like unions and represented workers vis-à-vis owners. The Revolution of 1911 acted to politicize many workers, teaching them that their interests could be framed in terms of the fate of the nation. The general expansion of civil society led to the inclusion of workers, or at least of educated and skilled workers. The revolution also erased the Qing's anti-strike laws, though the governments of the Republic were seldom sympathetic to workers. By the late 1910s, when artisans did not agree with their more conservative and better-off guild directors, they simply met on their own or settled the matter by majority vote. They formed branch guilds that excluded bosses.

If skilled workers and craftsmen came to the cities by choice and saw themselves as modern citizens, unskilled laborers were often driven by the threat of starvation at home. During the 1910s, nearly 100,000 "coolies" migrated overseas each year, but more sought urban jobs in China. Unskilled laborers lacked guilds, earned much less than artisans, and could easily be replaced. It was they who most readily returned to their home villages. Perhaps because they had so little to lose, they could be quick to strike. Unskilled women in the textile mills accounted for 70 percent of the 50 strikes recorded in Shanghai between 1895 and 1913.

Unskilled workers depended on gang affiliations. Shanghai's criminal gangs had expanded from opium distribution into other criminal activities in the late nineteenth century. Having supported revolutionary forces in 1911, the Green Gang emerged as central to the Shanghai economy, including its labor markets.[11] Gang bosses ran commercial institutions ranging from brothels and rickshaw rental agencies to wharves and factories. Much depended on the gang-affiliated labor contractors. Though they themselves exploited the workers, if unhappy with their employers, they would lead their workers out on strike. Unskilled labor strikes were generally defensive in nature – reacting to wage cuts, for example, rather than demanding improvements. But thousands of Shanghai cotton workers joined the Green Gang – they might not get a job otherwise – and over time they could claim some successes in improving wages and conditions.

The sociologist Mark Selden has pointed out that, over the entire period from the late Qing through the Republic, strike activity peaked with nationalist movements: 1898–9 (the reform movement), 1904–6 (the anti-American boycott), 1909–13 (the 1911 Revolution), 1917–19 ("May Fourth" nationalism), and 1925–7 (the National Revolution).[12] At the same time, however, grievances remained "local," concerned with inflation and the problems in individual factories. Working conditions were harsh and grievances many. The twelve-hour day was the norm, and fourteen- and sixteen-hour days with no formal breaks common; child labor was widespread; and women and children were paid half or less than half than were the men. Gang members and foremen threatened women workers with rape. Workers labored a minimum of 340 days a year. Wage increases were often eaten away by inflation or currency fluctuations. Labor recruiters and bosses took a percentage of workers' wages – up to 50 percent – in what was essentially a protection racket; foremen arbitrarily fined, beat, humiliated, and fired workers.

What little labor legislation there was, was seldom enforced. Cotton mills and tobacco factories were full of dust, and cotton-spinning workshops and silk filatures were steamy as well: silkworm cocoons were boiled and high humidity protected the yarn. Tuberculosis was a major scourge, though not as common as heat stroke. Workers suffering from heat stroke would be dragged to a doorway and left there till they recovered enough to go back to work. Grievances were not purely economic, and often focused on what the labor historian Jean Chesneaux calls "dignity issues": the right to be called by one's name, the right to use the toilet, the right to a break for meals.[13] The apprentice system was maintained in some industries whereby new workers were effectively paid nothing for three years or more. In the printing-machine industry, apprentices worked eighteen or nineteen hours a day, waited on the masters, and slept beneath their machines as oil dripped down on them.[14] They were paid twelve copper cash per month, one of them recalled with a note of irony:

> At that time, you only needed six coppers to get a haircut. [Because of] daily work, [your] whole body would be greasy. To wash your hands and face, you needed to buy one bar of soap, and that took four coppers. In this way, you only had two coppers left.... At that time, the cheapest bathhouse was twelve coppers.... You only needed to save for six months, and you had [just] enough to save for one bath. So for the whole year we had no way to take a bath; sometimes if we had two coppers we would buy a bowl of wontons and figure this was [at least a way to] "end our meatless diet."

Living conditions in factory dormitories or the slums and shantytowns surrounding them were brutal. Commutes could be long, workers walking up to two hours to arrive at their factories by 6 a.m. One water tap sufficed for several families, toilets did not exist, and space was very limited. In Tianjin a reporter described workers' housing as so dilapidated that "pieces of mud fall down from the ceiling, and the reeds and wood frame threaten to collapse. It leaks when it rains, stinks when it is hot, and is freezing in winter."[15] Workers usually got by on cheap grains, boiled water, and vegetable scraps. Meat was for festival days.

It is therefore interesting that it was skilled workers who engaged in the most radical forms of labor activities. Adult male workers such as seamen, mechanics, and those who came out of artisan traditions were the first to form modern industrial unions. They worked closely with professional anarchist and communist organizers in the 1920s. Chen Yun, a future leader in the Chinese Communist Party, had been apprenticed at the Commercial Press, Shanghai's largest publisher. The radical union he helped form there was rooted in an earlier printers' guild. In other parts of the world as well, it was not unusual for the "labor aristocracy" to take the lead in organizing workers. They are the first to commit to urban residence, and their relative prosperity and education gives them the time, resources, and connections to place their interests in a broader socioeconomic and political context. Of course, the threat to withhold skilled labor is more effective than the threat to withhold unskilled labor.

In the case of Shanghai, artisans like carpenters and weavers tended to come from south China and build contacts with the Communist Party and radicalism generally, while unskilled workers tended to come from northern

China and become affiliated with the Green Gang and later the Nationalist Party. Another important division was a gender hierarchy in which women almost invariably took less-skilled and lower-wage jobs, giving them less commitment to the city and to industrial unions. But all groups tended to unify around protests that also involved workplace issues. Other identities – of craft, native-place, ethnic group, and nation, for example – naturally mingled with working-class "consciousness," but did not prevent proletarianization.

### New social forces: Students, women

In the early twentieth century, educated youth found its voice. Like the higher intellectuals, students – women as well as men – literally speaking were not a new social group. Traditional Confucian texts had worried about the proper place for women and the education of youth. Nor were they "classes" like the bourgeoisie or proletariat in the sociological sense. Still, gender and generation became important markers of the self. Students were almost invariably of the privileged classes, though a few worked themselves up from the wealthier segments of the peasantry – Mao Zedong was one. Yet in these turbulent times, even students from "good" families lacked the assurance of a true elite. No one knew what skills would be needed in the new China. Students were the main audience for radical critiques of Chinese society, especially iconoclastic attacks on traditional social structure, the family, and Confucianism, and they were attracted to liberalism, anarchism, and Marxism.

Students provided the shock troops of the "Second Revolution" and various anti-imperialist boycotts, demonstrations, and movements, for although they had little power, they possessed moral authority. Under the right circumstances they could prompt the bourgeoisie and workers into massive protests. They preserved the moral obligation of the traditional literati to take responsibility for the community as a whole even when they turned against the Confucian heritage. "A scholar should be the first to become concerned with the world's troubles and the last to rejoice at its happiness," said a Song dynasty statesman.[16] An entire educational system was built in the first two decades of the twentieth century. By one estimate, 4,222 public and private academies existed in 1905, when the exam system was abolished. By 1911 the number of schools had leapt to 52,348.[17] There were nearly forty national and provincial universities by the 1920s. As well, there were missionary colleges and universities, provincial tertiary schools emphasizing agriculture or engineering, military academies, and teacher-training schools. Elite students often studied abroad in Japan and Europe. Though more expensive for Chinese students, the United States replaced Japan as a destination for higher education as anti-Japanese feelings grew after the 1911 Revolution and as American missionaries and scholarships steered students there.

Universities, colleges, and middle schools became natural centers of radicalism. It may be that most students were more interested in law or engineering than revolution; university life was marked by diversity of student interests, academic pursuits, and administrative approaches toward education.[18] Students were also cut off from rural China. In contrast to the traditional gentry, which shared a symbolic universe with ordinary villagers, urban youth was increasingly cosmopolitan and "foreign." And provincial youth was being drawn to the cities by higher education: three-quarters of university graduates were produced by the three cities of Shanghai, Beijing, and Nanjing. Students knew more about the theory of social Darwinism than the brutality of life in the countryside, more about Euclidean geometry and English than the old gods. Their worldviews and interests were increasingly remote from those of rural society. Yet a "revolutionary atmosphere" persisted in middle schools and universities in spite of the efforts of some officials and schools administrators.

As for the growth of the women's movement in the early decades of the century, this was rooted in long-term social changes such as the spread of education. Women's education did not begin to become widely accepted among the elite until the end of the Qing. Of course, many elite families had educated their daughters – by the mid-Qing, women poets were flourishing. Literacy was ranked with embroidery and needlework as an important female skill, and some families would not consider marrying their sons to uneducated women. Mothers were widely regarded as the first teachers of their sons, responsible not just for good manners but for basic reading and writing as well. However, elite families would have been horrified at the thought of sending their daughters to schools; education was in the hands of private tutors in the home. By the late Qing, however, to radicalized youth, this approach seemed hopelessly old-fashioned. That Qiu Jin, for example, had acquired some literary education was not unusual; that she wanted to acquire a modern education was less common – and she had to go to Japan to escape family pressures. The tutorial–literary model was inadequate. Girls seeking modern learning identified with their brothers, not the model of the "talented woman" of earlier generations. Indeed, women writers of the late Qing tended to dismiss their Ming and Qing foremothers as mere poets who had accepted their inferior place in a corrupt society.[19]

In the first decade of the twentieth century, urban women began to add their voices to the political discourse shaped around themes of nationalism. The politics of feminism will be examined further in later chapters; here the emergence of women into the public sphere will be highlighted. As a self-conscious movement, modern Chinese feminism arose out of the reformist and revolutionary trends of the late Qing. Kang Youwei had spearheaded anti-footbinding societies whose members pledged that their sons would only marry women with "natural feet." Liang Qichao and others argued that China needed healthy, strong, intelligent, and educated women in a time of national crisis. In Liang's well-known 1896–7 "A General Discussion of Reform," he explicitly attacked the old canard that "only untalented women are virtuous."[20] Women's education had two functions, both

designed to strengthen the nation. Liang wanted women to become economically productive and better mothers.

The idea of making women economically productive was also related to
reformers' concern for national "wealth and power." As Liang Qichao put it
(wrongly): "Out of 200 million women, every one is a consumer, not one is a
producer. Because they cannot support themselves, but depend on others for
their support, men keep them like dogs and horses or slaves." He thus advocated vocational education that would prepare women for the world of work
and allow them to become contributors to the nation. "How can the nation
be strengthened? If the people are enriched, the country will be strengthened. How can the people be enriched? By making everyone self-sufficient
and by not relying on one person to support many." Of course, in reality
nearly all women were economically productive but this was invisible since
they labored in the household and family fields.

Women's education was even more critical for producing good mothers.
Ignorant mothers, the reformers felt, produced weak citizens. Since mothers
were the first formative influence on future generations, girls' education was
thus key to the very survival of the nation. Indeed, fear of decline led to a
kind of biological myth which held that if China's parents were not healthy
and strong, then the race would degenerate. Footbinding in this perspective
was less an injustice perpetuated on women than a threat to the biological
strength of the nation. This was not necessarily the view taken by women.
After the turn of the century, radical women began to unbind their feet – a
painful process made bearable by the literal liberation it promised.

Nationalism thus enabled the growth of feminism, while at the same time
attempting to restrain it within paternalistic limits. Radical women themselves emphasized that their duties to the nation were not to be confined to
serving the nation passively (as workers and mothers) but necessarily
included personal empowerment. Whether women were to be full citizens
was still in doubt. In spite of women's involvement in the 1911 Revolution,
they were not allowed the vote. Women's rights remained a radical issue, but
at least it emerged as a topic in the late Qing and early Republic.

In the last decade of the Qing, as women's education spread, independent
publishers quickly met the new need for women's textbooks and guides.[21]
The lessons they propagated ranged from the strictest Confucian orthodoxy
to the exemplary lives of Western women lawyers, scientists, and revolutionaries. Perhaps most importantly, even when women were not considered
full-fledged citizens, they were being shown how to enter the public life of
the community. Even as simply "good wives and wise mothers" – as the
phrase of the day had it – in taking care of the household and raising children properly, women were to learn about the latest scientific findings in
regard to hygiene and nutrition. Therefore, they could no longer be confined
to the family even if the family was supposed to remain their main concern.
For, again, their responsibility to the nation was grave: to make sure that the
next generation received a good start in life. Beyond this, new writings for

women showed them how to be heroic. Countless historical tales from China and the West displayed women warriors, saviors of their nations such as the sixth-century Hua Mulan or France's Joan of Arc, both of whom dressed as men to fight in battles.

Indeed, women were to physically resemble men: relinquish footbinding, forswear makeup, sell their jewelry, simplify their hairstyles, and abjure flirting. In fact, gentry women did sell their jewelry to help buy railroad shares in the patriotic "rights recovery" movement of the late Qing or to pay for further schooling. Short fingernails, like natural feet, represented modern thinking and nationalism. However, there was a limit to the similarities allowed between men and women. It may be that as men's bodies were trained to be stronger, so women could become less languorous, but not as athletic as men. Republican laws forbade women from wearing their hair too short, just as men were not supposed to let their hair grow too long. Still, girls' schools as well as boys' schools started exercise classes, and the need to shed the image of the Chinese as weaklings in Western eyes was widely felt. Bathing and cleanliness – new standards of hygiene – affected both sexes, though keeping a clean house remained the responsibility of the modern woman. Public bath-houses, running water, and sewage systems came to the cities.

The emergence of women into the public eye was as much due to revolutionary political movements as to the changing standards of the urban middle class. If the involvement of women in the 1911 Revolution failed to win them political benefits, it still brought them out of the home. Pioneers of the women's movement included the revolutionary Qiu Jin – and also Chen Xiefen, the daughter of the editor of the radical Shanghai journal *Subao*. Like Qiu, Chen linked the cause of women to the rise of the Chinese nation. In 1904 she wrote:

> The inhabitants of China number about four hundred million all together. Men and women each constitute half of this. Our nation is held in common, our territory is held in common, our assets are held in common, our rights are held in common – and our misfortunes too are held in common. Therefore, since we women have a common responsibility ... how can we let men fulfill their duties to the utmost, while we women remain silent?[22]

Chen feared that Chinese women would become the "slaves of slaves," that is, continue as the slaves of Chinese men, who had themselves become the slaves of the foreigners. The elite women who wrote in this vein did not, of course, literally see themselves as slaves condemned to labor but rather as slaves of the patriarchal family system.[23] Chen Xiefen emphasized that Chinese women had lost their rights and their sense of duty together: so as duty compelled them to fight for the nation they would regain their rights. Key was the need for women to fight *for themselves*, not waiting for equality to be handed to them. China's independence thus depended on Chinese women's independence.

Whereas Liang Qichao had emphasized the general contribution that independent women could make to the nation's economy, radical women activists emphasized the personal independence that women could achieve through the ability to earn their own livings. Many elite women sought to improve their status within the family and used their role in the family to justify their right to participate in civil society. Their critique of patriarchal relations deserves to be called radical. It is not that elite women, even radicals, despised their own class privileges, but rather that they sought to position feminism so that nationalism could not trump it. That is to say, if women deserved rights because it would make China stronger, there was the possibility that the needs of the nation (as defined by men, at least) might require their subservience, not their independence. We will see this emerge as an explicit problem in later decades.

The woman anarchist He Zhen pointed out in 1907 that women's liberation depended on complete social equality. Women were doubly denied their rights, in He's analysis. First, as workers they were bound to their capitalist-owners just like men workers (though their jobs were inevitably inferior). And second, they were bound to their husbands and fathers in what He Zhen regarded as precisely the same sort of dependent relationship. The inferior position of women thus derived from the unequal distribution of wealth as well as male oppression. "You women, do not hate the man: hate that you don't have food to eat. Why don't you have food to eat? Because you can't buy food without money. Why don't you have money? Because the rich have stolen our property and oppress the majority of the people." True gender equality depended on smashing all sources of exploitation, which capitalism and the nation-state inevitably produced. He Zhen wrote: "What we mean by equality between the sexes is not just that men will no longer oppress women. We also want men no longer to be oppressed by other men and women no longer to be oppressed by other women."[24] He Zhen, too, emphasized that women would have to free themselves, and she specifically sought to reach beyond the circle of elite women, reminding her readers of the hardships endured by servants, factory workers, and prostitutes. Thus the anarchists not only broke the link between nationalism and feminism, but their thoroughgoing attacks on traditional morality and the family foreshadowed the radical turn of the 1920s.

Women in the countryside, however, were not affected by the social changes of urban China. For all the successes of the women's movement, the position of most women only deteriorated as the old order collapsed. Demographic reality may have further cheapened the value of daughters. Sons alone were regarded as capable of carrying on the family line, a central cultural value, and sons alone provided a form of old age insurance for most parents when they could no longer work themselves. Rural women were a luxury: daughters were "married out" before they had repaid their natal families the cost of raising them. Poor farm daughters might be sold as concubines or prostitutes. Footbinding, illiteracy, and arranged marriages declined in the cities while they continued in the countryside. It would be much later before urban women took their emancipatory message to the countryside, usually under Communist auspices.

The growing chasm between urban and rural China can be seen in the lives of many social groups. As university students practiced accounting and English, peasants remained tied to the traditional gods and customs. And as urban women laid claim to rights and responsibilities, peasant women remained tied to patriarchal structures. The emergence of women out of private family quarters into public spaces had to happen in the cities. It is true that this process, even in the cities, soon ran up against restraints. Even when legal protections for women – like the right to refuse marriages or the right to divorce – were passed in the 1930s, they were difficult to enforce. Economic opportunities for middle-class women remained limited. Biological myths about women's inferiority continued to be widespread. Women's rights were thus a progressive cause. They were seen as part of China's path to modernity, but the model citizen remained the male, even as social realities continued to evolve.

# 7 Intellectuals, the Republic, and a new culture

The political chaos of the Republic drove Chinese intellectuals to explore "what went wrong" and what they might do to build democratic institutions. Most intellectuals – along with the bourgeoisie generally – chose the fairly conservative route of trying to work with Yuan Shikai. It was not until Yuan's decision to openly found a new dynasty in 1915 that the intellectuals in general turned against him.[1]

The old revolutionary movement had split in 1913 when a minority, including Sun Yat-sen, raised armed rebellion against Yuan. But most of the former revolutionaries joined with moderates like Liang Qichao to mobilize public opinion for gradual reform. In 1914 Huang Xing, Sun's former colleague, helped raise money for a loosely organized group of men dedicated to finding a national consensus in support of constitutionalism and resisting imperialism. The group included Zhang Shizhao (1881–1973), Chen Duxiu (1879–1942), Chen Jiongming (1878–1933), and Cai Yuanpei (1868–1940). They concluded that the revolution had only produced dictatorship and chaos. But what could be done now? Their answer lay in a kind of renunciation of politics. Many believed that for all the evils of the old Manchu regime, the new government's corruption and tyranny was merely a symptom of a deeper morbidity: Chinese culture. Chinese culture and society were fundamentally repressive. Mere political change would only scratch the surface of China's problems as long as these were not attacked at the root. From the classical disdain for science to the patriarchal family's contempt for the individual happiness of its members – *Confucianism* seemed to sum up everything that obstructed progress. So: first intellectual and social change, then political change could follow.

This was a rather optimistic view. Time itself seemed to be on China's side. A faith in evolution reassured intellectuals that China too could join the modern era and catch the tide of progress. Yet this faith by itself could not answer the question, what was to replace Confucianism? By the 1920s, the notion that political change should wait for cultural change had lost much of its appeal, but for a critical moment in the late 1910s it represented a general intellectual commitment. At the same time, the turn to "culture" (*wenhua* – a classical term meaning something like "transformation by civilized patterns" used by Meiji-period Japanese to translate the Western concept) was not entirely new. The man who was to found Nankai University in Tianjin in 1919, Zhang Boling (1876–1951), had originally trained as a naval officer. But in 1898 when he witnessed the lowering of the Qing flag after the British leased the naval base of Weihaiwei in Shandong, he resigned his commission to devote himself to education. "The Nankai schools were born from China's calamity," Zhang recalled. "Therefore their purpose was to reform old habits of life and to train youth for the salvation of the country."[2] By 1915 mainstream intellectual opinion came to the same conclusion: that the path to real reform lay through changing young minds.

The result was the "New Culture" movement, a vague label for intellectual changes lasting from the mid-1910s into the 1920s. "New Culture" was in fact a rallying cry for efforts to abolish everything associated with subservience, hierarchy, patriarchy, and decadence. Historians often join the New Culture and May Fourth (1919) movements as if they were a single phenomenon: as if the student demonstrations, workers' strikes, and anti-imperialist boycotts of 1919 were the logical political outcome of the earlier new thought. However, the May Fourth movement, to be discussed in Chapters 8 and 9, should be kept distinct from the New Culture movement, if only because it represented a more direct return to politics. But it is true that the New Culture movement forged the tools intellectuals would later use to justify the politics of the May Fourth movement. The whole point was that a new culture would form the basis of a new kind of egalitarian and libertarian politics.

The generation that came of age in the late 1910s and the 1920s was the first to have extensive first-hand foreign experience. Japan continued to attract Chinese students, though the numbers decreased from about five thousand in the mid-1910s to a thousand or so in the 1920s. Meanwhile, Chinese studying at American universities increased to a thousand by the mid-1910s and stayed at that level through the 1920s. English was the dominant foreign language in China, and European nations attracted only a relative handful of Chinese students. Many students avoided Britain on the same grounds they began to reject Japan: they were seen as the primary imperialists in China. The United States, in addition to offering special scholarships, also dominated the missionary education system in China. The New Culture movement was led by men who had studied in Japan, the US, Germany, Britain, and France. Many became teachers in China's rapidly expanding educational system. The number of tertiary institutions in Beijing grew from ten in 1909 to forty in 1922, while the number of students increased from 2,115 to 15,440.[3]

## Constitutionalism, federalism, reform

When Yuan Shikai decided to found a new dynasty in 1915, his public relations team presented three arguments. One might be called the traditionalist case; one the modernization case; and finally a particular rewriting of history that acted to combine the two. The traditionalist approach spoke of Yuan's sacred and sagelike qualities, his meritorious deeds and virtue, and his "transformative powers." Yuan's wisdom was a gift from Heaven, his understanding was endless, his embrace encompassed the vastness of Heaven and Earth. "Your military prowess is holy and your civil abilities sage. Your thought has long been linked to the minds and hearts of the people."[4] As emperor, Yuan would control the cosmos and execute Heaven's grace and charisma. As if events were out of his individual control, Yuan's duty was to "submit to" Heaven's will and "follow" the "clear orders" of the people. The "people"? The traditionalist view did not say that the people should be ignored. But their will was not a matter of public opinion, the consensus of thinking individuals. Rather, it was like a force of nature in its own right. "The masses unanimously and respectfully hope for order," wrote one monarchist.[5] "Your majesty knows only to take the nation as his premise and the will of the people as his goal," wrote yet another.[6]

However, there was no longer an audience for this kind of traditionalism. If we say that peasants were a conservative force, these events were played out beyond their horizon. The conservative elites for whom such classical rhetoric had the most appeal remained loyal to the Qing. Ironically, they could tolerate a Republic precisely because it did not threaten the sacrality of the Qing, which remained cornered and shrunken but alive in the Forbidden City. To true conservatives, a President Yuan was acceptable as a de facto power-holder, but they could not betray the Qing by giving their loyalty to a new dynasty and an Emperor Yuan. This kind of loyalty lay at the heart of Chinese conservatism and all those to whom Confucianism still possessed political (as opposed to merely cultural) meaning. At the same time, politically conservative Qing loyalism was a weak, tenuous force. In the traditional dynastic cycle, the fall of a dynasty resulted in a series of suicides as the ultimate expression of loyalty. In fact, no high Qing officials or Manchu aristocrats committed suicide.

The modernization argument for Yuan's becoming emperor was considerably stronger. It was not original, having been staked out by Liang Qichao a decade earlier, but perhaps it seemed even more compelling in the political confusion of the Republic. Yang Du (1875–1931) wrote an eloquent defense of constitutional monarchy in April 1915, and Frank Goodnow, Yuan's American constitutional adviser, wrote a critique of the Republic in August. They essentially argued that republicanism had failed in China because it was not suitable to Chinese conditions. China had a tradition of autocratic rule, the masses were ignorant and had little experience of participation in government, and so a constitutional monarchy was needed precisely to prepare China for republicanism. This argument was rooted in a modern political discourse. It used the same terms of reference as the anti-monarchists, and on one level a reasonable debate ensued in mid-1915 over what form of government was most suitable to China's conditions and needs, part of a discourse which had begun with the reform movement of the 1890s.

Yang Du wrote that the people were neither morally nor intellectually ready for democratic institutions, since they knew only about emperors.[7] His point was not that republicanism was wrong but merely that it was premature. Indeed, the entire reason for what he insisted would be a *constitutional monarchy* was to prepare China for *true democracy*. At this point, Liang Qichao again stepped into the political arena. For Liang, the argument of his old friend Yang Du, though fundamentally correct, missed the one crucial point. That is, even if the 1911 Revolution had been premature, it had none the less wrecked the very notion of imperial "charisma" beyond repair. Liang thus preferred to defend the admittedly flawed institutions of the Republic. He did not call for substantive participation of the masses but rather for a balance between populism and the authority of the state, between laws and morality, institutions and men, and civil rights and elite domination. Liang hoped that civility and restraint might sustain a sphere for political action that lay somewhere between the potentially dangerous powers of the state on the one hand and the selfish interests of society on the other.[8]

Unfortunately, the political reality of the early Republic left very little room for civility. The state was too weak to guarantee that the pursuit of power would be clothed in the respectable veils of formal democratic procedures. It was not Liang, however, but the supporters of Yuan who best captured the problem. They created a new historical narrative around Yuan: as the Qing lost Heaven's Mandate and the Republic declined into chaos, the nation had always supported Yuan, but the Qing had declined to follow his reform proposals and republican forms were simply not suited to China's conditions.[9]

> Recently, republics in Central and South America ... have had civil wars arising from party conflicts. Portugal adopted republicanism, which was the cause of her recent crises. The worst example is Mexico, where since the resignation of Diaz, there has not been a single day of peace. Mexican party leaders all have their own troops to fight against one another. The victorious ones occupy parts of the country, and the vanquished loot, slaughter the people, and set fire to houses before they retreat. Now the country has been ruled by five presidents and is in a lamentable state of anarchy. Ours is also a new republic, although it is in the East. Is Mexico to set an example for us?[10]

The comparisons are interesting. Unlike Mexico, China had not been colonized, nor was a new racial society created there. Unlike China, Mexico lacked a long tradition of imperial bureaucratic government and – ignoring indigenous traditions – traced the origins of its polity to Europe. Finally free of Spanish control, the regime of Porfirio Diaz (1830–1915) was considerably more stable right to the end than was the late Qing; moreover, the hacienda system, which dominated the better land, reduced the peasantry to serfdom in a way no longer known in China. None the less, the nineteenth century left both nations vulnerable while they were drawn into world trade. Both nations attempted to pursue autocratic modernization while the intelligentsia argued for a more progressive liberalism and the peasants became increasingly impoverished.

These parallels remind us that the dislocation experienced by China was not unique. Indeed, it was one of a number of revolutionary societies in the early twentieth century. By the 1890s, most late-developing nations were experiencing tremendous disruptions as they were drawn, under varying degrees of imperialist pressure, into the world economy. This process accelerated or at least coincided with the emiseration of large segments of the population, especially the peasantry. It also brought about a new relationship between the state and emerging economic actors. Neither the business community nor the intelligentsia found the old form of the state satisfactory. Hence, not just China and Mexico; witness also the 1905 revolution in Russia, the 1908 victory of the Young Turks in the Ottoman Empire, and the Portuguese Republic of 1910. It was a great era of liberal illusion, and many of these societies would see either semi-fascist dictatorship or large-scale agrarian revolution in the wake of the failure of liberal constitutionalism.

Meanwhile, as China fell into warlordism in the late 1910s, reform-minded Chinese intellectuals continued to try to work within the system. This was possible thanks to the relative stability of urban life and the growth of education, journalism, and other spheres of professional life. Provincial identities and interests gained a new legitimacy, and some intellectuals even proposed federalism as a way of holding China together. The lawyer and warlord Chen Jiongming proposed that Guangdong voters choose their own leaders in 1921 and actually began to implement elections, though Sun Yat-sen's mercenaries soon chased him out of the province. "Zhejiang [Province] is the Zhejiang of the people of Zhejiang," proclaimed the radical assemblyman Shen Dingyi in 1917 when the province faced the appointment of outside civil and military governors by Beijing. "If the Zhejiangese are not self-governing, then one by one they will appoint outsiders, and will those outsiders not rule by pulling in more outsiders?" Yet at the same time Shen linked province and nation: "If Zhejiangese cannot protect Zhejiang, then the people of the nation cannot protect the nation.... The whole country's affairs, not only Zhejiang's affairs, are the responsibility of the people of Zhejiang."[11] In essence, Shen was advocating a kind of federalism whereby the independent strength of each province would contribute to the strength of the nation.

From the late Qing, disillusionment with the failures of the central government had led to calls for provincial autonomy.[12] Urban politics could easily support federalism. Students, intellectuals, and even, sometimes, commercial elites defined themselves through protests against what passed for national and militarist government. The federalist movement perhaps was most successful in Hunan, where a young Mao Zedong went so far as to call for a "Republic of Hunan" that would "implement the new ideals and create a new life." Long before his rise to power in the Communist Party, Mao was a local activist. Hunan is also instructive, because the province's military leaders repressed the movement's democratic potential.

Calls for "self-government" thus sometimes masked the most rapacious of warlord agendas. If "local self-government" sounded progressive, "feudalism" became a term of execration by the 1920s. Its critics associated federalism with warlord separatism and the evils of imperialism.[13] In an age of strong nationalist sentiment, it was not entirely possible to justify provincialism even vis-à-vis corrupt central governments, which is one reason why the urban reformist elites who controlled the 1911 Revolution were ultimately unable to assert their legitimacy. Since the cause of the Chinese nation remained paramount, state-building projects remained righteous. The historian Prasenjit Duara points to the centrality of a "global discourse on modernity and state power" in terms of "how a new world order emerged toward the latter third of the nineteenth century, in which the only recognized actors on the world scene were sovereign nation-states.... The ideological force behind the imperative of state-building was none other than this system of nation states."[14] More concretely, many intellectuals feared that federalism could not meet the warlord challenge. Some intellectuals felt that only a new kind of military might could unify China, and in the end they were right.

### The New Culture movement

> Among the Chinese, it is a compliment to say: "Despite his youth, he carries himself with the gravity of age." On the other hand, "keep young while growing old" is a bit of advice Englishmen or Americans are likely to offer. This expression of the racial difference between East and West has far-reaching implications. "Youth is like the coming of spring, the first light of dawn.... If society follows the natural way of new replacing old, then it will flourish. But if old and decaying elements predominate, then society must perish."

Chen Duxiu wrote this "Appeal to Youth" to launch his new magazine, *New Youth*, in 1915.[15] *New Youth* expressed a widespread mood. Chen told China's youth to avoid party politics and concentrate on consciousness and "citizens' movements." Chen's anti-traditionalism was uncompromising; he pounded home the message that Chinese civilization represented decay, conservatism, and formalism. China was falling *further* behind the West, which was successful because of its dynamism, science, and high ethical principles of democracy and socialism. Chen promoted Western values in the names of "Mr. Democracy" and "Mr. Science," but criticised Western nationalism and elitist social systems as well. Chen urged his young readers to be independent, progressive, aggressive, cosmopolitan, utilitarian, and scientific – and not servile, conservative, retiring, isolationist, formalistic, or introverted. "All persons are equal. Each has his right to be independent, but absolutely no right to enslave others nor any obligation to make himself servile."[16]

Born in 1879, Chen Duxiu had passed the first level of the civil service exams before he was 20, but he soon abandoned Confucian studies for the reform movement. He later claimed his examination essay had been a deliberate mishmash of classical quotations designed to fool pretentious examiners. He was to become a Marxist, a founder and leader of the Chinese Communist Party, and later a Trotskyite drummed out of the Party and jailed by the Nationalists. But it was with *New Youth* that Chen emerged as the chief spokesman of a movement. With a monthly circulation of some 16,000, *New Youth* was a significant addition to the serious journalism of the day. But it should also be noted that urban youth everywhere across China was finding its voice. Some 700 new journals, mostly short-lived, emerged between 1915 and 1923.

Serving as a dean at Beijing University from 1917, Chen took a stand for human rights, science, and democracy – as opposed to Confucianism, traditionalism, and the dictatorship. Chen and his supporters linked Confucianism to despotism and "feudalism," and they not only called the Confucian virtues of filial piety and propriety immoral but blamed China's backwardness on them. *New Youth* was to avoid politics, at least in the sense of the arts practiced by professional politicians and military men. In the event, Chen himself would soon return to politics, though of a populist rather than party nature. He was more than ready when the May Fourth movement turned culture into street demonstrations in 1919. But for four years *New Youth* taught that better government would follow only after deeper changes were effected. "The revolution of earlier years [1911] was a revolution in forms; now the revolution must be one of spirit," wrote the Japanese-educated political scientist Gao Yihan (1884–1968). "Our people already know full well how to carry out a revolution in political institutions; they do not yet know how to carry out a revolution in political spirit and educational principles."[17]

Social Darwinism remained the dominant approach to understanding the world. Hence the reference above to "racial difference" and Chen's comment, "The contribution of the rise of science to the means by which modern Europe surpassed other races was no less than that of the theory of human rights, just as a cart has two wheels." Chen Duxiu and the other *New Youth* publicists thus accepted that China had to adapt to a world of ruthless competition, but they also thought that the world was progressing from autocratic and hierarchical societies to a more democratic and egalitarian order. Science, democracy, and individual autonomy were linked not only because they were desirable but also because they were seen as the essence of Western modernity. The notion of autonomy linked the personal to the public: autonomy was the opposite of slavery and dependence, not isolation but self-awareness. Individuals were to be free in marriage, the nuclear family emancipating both men and women. Private property was a guarantee of individual rights while individualism would free up productive forces. Darwinism even sanctioned the people's struggle to seize their rights.

Democracy, for Chen, ultimately depended on individualism, which he felt was the basis of law and liberty alike. Simplistically, Chen claimed that in Western nations the law acted to protect and regulate individualism, which did not conflict with state or society since these served the individual. In China, on the other hand, clan patriarchs ruled their families, feudal morality constrained individuals with "loyalty" and "filial piety," and ritual substituted for the law.[18] Chen took "democracy" to refer to more than a political system; it was a virtual philosophy of life. Following the 1919 lecture tour of John Dewey, the famous philosopher and reformer from the United States, Chen synthesized his version of democracy in terms of civil rights, political participation, social and economic egalitarianism, and the general improvement of social life. Chen never meant his individualism to come at the expense of national unity. But nationalism for Chen had to be democratic. A state that failed to protect the people did not deserve their loyalty or support.

> I give absolute support to nationalism not because I exalt it – today [1915] the evils of nations are appearing in Europe and the destruction of nationalism is expected – but because, looking at conditions in China, our people are still in the age of scattered sand. We have to follow the times, and nationalism has truly become the best means by which the Chinese can save themselves. To use this doctrine, the Chinese must first understand what it means.... contemporary nationalism refers to democratic nations, not nations of enslaved people.[19]

But no-one possessed a more optimistic or complete view of democracy than Li Dazhao (1889–1927). Li – who grew up in the countryside, studied in Japan, and would later co-found the Chinese Communist Party with Chen – understood the very spirit of the age as democratic. He began a 1919 article on labor education: "Every aspect of contemporary life is colored by democracy and follows the path of democracy.... To put it in a word: democracy is the only power operating in the world today, and the present era is the era of democracy." The problem of labor since the end of the war was also a manifestation of democracy, as was the women's movement.[20] What was this spirit of democracy? It was the "equal opportunity" for all individuals, regardless of race, sex, class, or locality to "develop their individual natures and enjoy their rights."[21] Li Dazhao interpreted democracy in a utopian fashion. Writing at the close of World War I, he understood the war in teleological terms. "Everyone relied on the spirit of mutual aid and upheld the truths of equality and liberty to resist this kind of violent evil. Manifested in the political realm, this kind of reason is called democracy.... The victory of democracy is the victory of the common people."[22]

In social terms, Li saw the war as a defeat for capitalism and a victory for labor. In time, everyone would become a commoner – that is to say, a worker. Though not an immediate convert to Marxism, Li was impressed by the Russian revolution. The defeat of Germany, Li wrote, was not a victory of the Allies over the German people, but the defeat of militarism and imperialism at the hands of humanism, peace, justice, liberty, democracy, socialism, Bolshevism, and the laboring classes of the world – all of which constituted "the historical tide of the twentieth century."[23]

But even among self-styled progressives, Li Dazhao's optimism was extreme. More typical was the great critic of Chinese tradition, Hu Shi (1891–1962). Optimistic by temperament, Hu none the less did not expect progress to be easy. Hu was a student of John Dewey and had studied at Cornell and Columbia Universities.[24] Of all the New Culture leaders, he maintained his skepticism about politics and his faith in long-term, slow-but-steady cultural change. At the same time, Hu was deeply committed to the most thoroughgoing reconstruction of China, calling at one point for "complete Westernization," though he explained this was only a target he knew well could never be reached, and he led a movement to "reorganize the national heritage." Like so many of the intellectual and political leaders of the late Qing and Republic, Hu came from a declining gentry family. Like Mao Zedong, born two years later in Hunan, Hu fell under the spell of Liang Qichao and the revolutionaries. In 1910 he won a Boxer Indemnity Scholarship and spent the next six years in the United States. He was a brilliant student (winning prizes in English as well as philosophy), and already he was committed to the notion that China needed less shortsighted political movements and more long-term education in citizenship.

Hu Shi returned to China in 1917 with a call for the "improvement of literature." This meant several things. Hu's was the first well-thought-out proposal for a vernacular written language – though the actual practice had flourished since the turn of the century. The classical style, copied through the generations from the earliest texts and increasingly layered with allusion and erudition, was distant from ordinary speech, like the high European culture encoded in Latin. For Hu, the vernacular offered not simply a way to reach the people, but a way for writers themselves to think more clearly. So he urged writers to be unambiguous, direct, and unpretentious. It is worth noting that Hu's proposal was written in classical Chinese, for fear that the people he wanted to reach would not have taken a vernacular essay seriously.

The "vernacular movement" grew to form the core of a new Chinese culture, replacing classical Chinese the way the national languages of the European Renaissance replaced Latin as living embodiments of literature, philosophy, and social concerns. In practice, however, a vernacular style that was clear and concise proved quite difficult to produce and the movement generated a good deal of stilted and awkward prose. Left-wing critics later pointed out that modern writing, with its numerous neologisms and imports of Western grammatical forms, was as difficult for ordinary people as the classical language, which at least they knew through popular opera and the numerous classical idioms of spoken Chinese. But the political implications of the vernacular movement for a society where literacy and power had been linked since the theocratic origins of the civilization were startling. Vernacular advocates argued that the power of the written word would filter downward into society through simple schooling instead of years of mastering the sacred texts. If the peasants could learn to read and write, they would become modern citizens; the age-old and crippling distinction between mental and physical labor, ruler and ruled, would be breached.

Hu Shi himself went on to champion China's despised traditional vernacular literature, particularly the great novels, with their roots in the cycles of professional storytellers. Although conservatives criticised Hu for threatening the classical heritage, Hu's position was relatively moderate. It was Chen Duxiu who brought out the political implications of the "army of the literary revolution" to insist "we *must* reform the literature that shapes the spirit of those who dominate public affairs." The old anarchist Wu Zhihui cried that all the classical texts should be thrown down the toilet. And the cultural radical Qian Xuantong (1887–1939) declared that "the destruction of Confucian learning and Daoist religion is the fundamental solution if China is not to perish and if the Chinese people are to become a civilized people of the twentieth century; and the eradication of the Chinese language, which has been the repository of Confucian theories and Daoist superstitions, is the necessary means to this end."[25] For a classically-trained intellectual (a student of Zhang Binglin, no less) to call for the abolition of his own language highlights a despair that was, in fact, widely felt.

Beyond literary questions, Hu Shi sought to reinvigorate Chinese civilization with the pragmatism of his teacher at Columbia, James Dewey. What worked? Or, in Hu's more elegant phrasing, "Do the institutions and customs inherited from the past retain in the present any value to justify their existence?" At the same time, he understood full well that cultural continuity was a fact. "How can we best assimilate modern civilization in such a manner as to make it congenial, congruous, and continuous with the civilization of our own making?" Tellingly, Hu preferred civilization-building to state- or nation-building. He claimed that progress would come "bit by bit and drop by drop," and that specific reforms of political and social institutions had to be pursued one by one.[26]

## The fate of Confucianism in modern China

During the first years of the Republic, a group of intellectuals trying to understand Yuan Shikai's monarchical movement indicted the "slave mentality" of the Chinese people. But blaming the people was only partly satisfying. The radical turn the intellectuals took next brought them face to face with the high cultural and social practices of Chinese tradition. They labeled these evils Confucianism. They defined Confucianism not only as a textual tradition but also as a way of life, a set of values revolving around hierarchy and respect, doctrines that were taught in the family, the village, and the guild, as well as in schools. In this sense, Confucianism survived the fall of the dynasty and was being transmitted in nearly every family. All the millions of men (and women) who had received some classical education were tainted, and even illiterates had been contaminated by the Confucianism in the air.

Yuan Shikai's death in 1916 meant that intellectuals could suddenly speak with fewer restraints. The New Culture movement came to be centered at Beijing University (Beida), where many of its leaders soon joined the faculty. Cai Yuanpei was appointed president of the university in 1916. He had long been involved in educational issues, and at Beida he tried to reform a somewhat decadent student life. Beijing residents called students the "brothel brigade," but Cai encouraged them to engage with both scholarship and social issues. He encouraged faculty independence and appointed men like Chen Duxiu, Li Dazhao, Zhang Shizhao, Qian Xuantong, and Hu Shi – as well as conservatives such as Liu Shipei and Gu Hongming.

The radicals agreed on the baneful effects of Confucianism. "Confucianism and the Chinese monarchical system possess an inextricable relationship," proclaimed Chen Duxiu.[27] And, "To urge that a Republic worship Confucius is like an autocracy worshiping Washington or Rousseau." Chen blamed Confucianism's traditional "three bonds" – the hierarchical relationships of parents–children, rulers–subjects, and husbands–wives – for preventing the evolution of autonomous individuals. Chen blamed Confucianism for China's perverted notions of morality, repeatedly condemning "loyalty," "filial piety," and the subordination of women. Confucius and Mencius had taught a "one-sided" morality which rested on distinguishing between the superior and inferior in any relationship.[28] And so Confucianism's emphasis on unequal relations resulted in suppressing individuality.[29] The point here was not what the historical Confucius thought but how the present-day Chinese social system operated. Even after Yuan's death, Chen noted in mid-1917 that he was pessimistic about the future of the Republic:

> Because at this time although the majority of the Chinese people say they are not opposed to the Republic, their minds are in fact stuffed full of the old thought of the imperial age. There is not even a shadow of the civilized systems of Western societies and nations.... To firmly secure the Republic today, we must totally wash clean the old anti-republicanism from the minds of the Chinese people.[30]

Not everyone agreed that individualism was necessarily opposed to the Chinese tradition. Casting a wide net, Du Yaquan, the editor of the popular magazine *Eastern Miscellany*, wrote in 1914 that individualism was compatible with both socialism and Confucianism.[31] Du agreed with the New Culture movement that reform originated at the level of the individual, but he tied this to the Confucian mandate for moral introspection – as had

Liang Qichao a decade earlier. He held that society was integrated through the moral rectification of its individual members; in turn, socialism represented the interests of its members collectively. In other words, socialism could be the macro-social result of micro-individual self-cultivation. But Du's opinions looked old-fashioned by the end of the decade. When individualism became the epitome of anti-Confucianism, Confucianism represented repression in every sense of the word: political, social, moral, and personal.

The New Culture movement was not the first modern attack on Confucianism. Zhang Binglin had bitterly attacked Confucianism for monopolizing Chinese learning in the decade leading up to the 1911 Revolution. Some of the anarchists, like Wu Zhihui, demanded that modern science replace traditional religion. Tan Sitong had gone so far as to condemn both the monarchy and the "three bonds," though defending Confucius himself. Even Liang Qichao had criticized the Confucian emphasis on benevolence (*ren*) as antithetical to justice (*yi*) and rights.[32] But the New Culture attack on Confucianism was devastating. Ultimately, New Culture intellectuals and their students rewrote Chinese history in a way that removed much of the glory from the traditional high culture.

But why was a long, complex, and multifaceted tradition packaged as this single thing, "Confucianism"? Partly, the recasting of tradition and Confucianism was an element of the larger effort to define national identity.[33] Of course, scholars knew very well that Confucius, Confucianism, and the Chinese past were not the same thing. Indeed, Hu Shi devoted a good part of his academic career to recovering non-Confucian aspects of the Chinese past. His ultimate purpose was not to bury Confucius and praise the rest but to contribute to a new world culture that would not be exclusively Western. Regardless, Hu Shi consigned Confucianism to the dead part of history. One generation earlier, the Confucian radicals of the late nineteenth century had wanted to reform Confucianism and the imperial state, and they rooted themselves in a mystical vision of a prophetic and utopian Confucius. Their attempt to root national identity in this cultural vision failed in 1898. Chen Duxiu inherited their totalizing view of Confucianism, but he tried to root a *modern* kind of Chinese identity in its antithesis.

The New Culture iconoclasts seemed to carry the day. Their views long dominated interpretations of Chinese history in both China and the West. Even scholars who respected Confucianism have seen it as irrelevant to the making of a modern China. Yet, by the end of the twentieth century, the situation looked somewhat different. Confucianism never completely lacked defenders, and the possibility of a Confucian contribution to Chinese modernity has recently received a more respectful hearing. Furthermore, the iconoclasts may not have left Confucianism as far behind as they thought. Just as Marxism grew out of liberalism in the nineteenth century, so the radical Chinese critique of Confucianism owed some of its impulse and premises to elements of Confucianism, inheriting some of its traits: a sense of social responsibility; a disposition toward universality; the dialectic between morality and education – that is, a dialectic of social change rooted in individual relationships; cultural self-criticism; and individual self-cultivation. Although Confucianism tended to abjure utopianism as such, it certainly possessed a notion of the good society. The Confucian discourse on social justice was neither socialistic nor egalitarian, but it gave Sun Yat-sen's call for "minsheng" (the people's livelihood), for example, great resonance. In attacking tradition Chinese iconoclasts idealized the West, about which they still knew relatively little. But objective knowledge was not the point.

## Anarchism and socialism in the early Republic

An important part of the intellectual ferment of the early period was the younger generation's great interest in anarchism and socialism, which replaced liberalism as the dominant mode of radical reform in the 1920s. Marxist historians in China and liberal historians in the West have both tended to neglect the central role of anarchism in the shaping of Chinese radicalism more generally. Both have emphasized a historical narrative that exaggerates the early appeal of Marxism and fails to show the numerous connections between liberalism and anarchism on the one hand and Marxism and anarchism on the other. The notion of individual autonomy; the importance of combining theory and practice; the core belief in revolutionary education; the thoroughgoing critique of tradition; the absolute condemnation of imperialism; the esteem given science, progress, and civilization; the emphasis placed on "mutual aid" and communal solidarity; the desire to abolish "boundaries" between mental and manual labor, between city and countryside, and between industry and agriculture; and even the language of class struggle – all represent, in part, anarchist contributions to modern Chinese political thought. Many of Mao Zedong's most radical notions reveal anarchist influence.

From the turn of the century through the 1920s anarchism came close to being the defining core of radicalism. It is not that a majority of political activists declared themselves to be anarchists; indeed, few supported the anarchists' total rejection of all state structures. Yet as the historian Arif Dirlik has noted: "At a time when a revolutionary discourse was taking shape, anarchist ideas played a crucial part in injecting into it concerns that would leave a lasting imprint on the Chinese revolution, reaching beyond the relatively small group of anarchists into the ideologies of other revolutionaries."[34] Anarchism was the only Western radical philosophy translated into Chinese in any detail until the 1920s. The major anarchist texts were translated by the two groups of exiled Chinese anarchists in Tokyo and Paris in the years leading up to 1911. That Marxism-Leninism "defeated" anarchism in the 1920s is indisputable; that Chinese communism largely emerged out of anarchism, which left a permanent impact on it, should be equally clear. Committed anarchists probably never numbered more than a few thousand, and their organizations were often ephemeral, but they seemed to be everywhere with their publications, lectures, and efforts to organize workers and peasants.

The emergence into the public sphere of students, women, and workers encouraged radical organization. Self-identified as oppressed, individual members of these groups saw theoretical reflection and political action as a personal commitment. Two themes stand out: the notion of "mutual aid" and the idealization of labor. One of the first programs established by anarchists after the 1911 Revolution sent students to France in work–study arrangements. In their Beijing preparatory school, the students were expected to do the maintenance and cleaning jobs themselves, while in France students were expected to work as well as attend classes. Before it broke down in 1920, the program had educated thousands of Chinese laborers who had been sent to France during the war. Its students became some of China's most prominent socialists, including future leaders of the Communist Party such as Deng Xiaoping.[35]

The anarchists also founded a variety of voluntary associations in China designed to promote social morality. Members were ranked according to the vices they would relinquish. People forswore concubines, official careers, electoral politics, eating meat, and other social evils, but one could swear never to become a politician, for example, but keep eating meat. Upon becoming president of Beida, Cai Yuanpei founded such an organization and immediately recruited over a thousand students. Indeed, Cai himself was something of a philosophical anarchist, and had invited many of the "Paris" group of Chinese anarchists to teach at Beida, which emerged as a center of anarchist activity.

During the early Republic, the most famous, even charismatic, anarchist was Liu Sifu (Shifu, 1884–1915). Liu established the Conscience Society in 1912 with a few comrades. He had supported the 1911 Revolution and joined the National Alliance, blowing off his hand in a bomb-making attempt and spending the next two years in prison. But by 1912 he was pointing to the flaw of the revolution: in trying to establish a new government, it naturally produced a Yuan Shikai. Liu's effort to create a new social morality began with individual self-reform, even to the point of forsaking rickshaws because they oppressed fellow humans. Liu believed the state and capitalism would collapse together. "Through the true spirit of liberty, equality, and fraternity we will attain our ideals: a society without the institutions of landlords, capitalists, leaders, officials, representatives, family heads, soldiers, jails, police, courts, laws, religion, or marriage. Then society will consist only of liberty, only of mutual aid, and only of the joy of labor."[36] Liu thus projected an anarcho-communist utopia without government and where not just production but also consumption would take place on a communal basis. Money would be abolished. Science and technology would free people from the necessity of unpleasant labor. Once governments and oppressive economic systems were abolished, the sources of human cooperation would no longer be blocked and a decent society would emerge.

Chinese anarchists did not follow a libertarian doctrine of extreme individualism. With very few exceptions, they followed the mutual aid doctrines of the Russian anarchist Pyotr Kropotkin and fervently promoted all kinds and forms of social organization. Organization was fine – in fact, it was natural to humanity – but coercive organizations like governments were immoral and counter-productive. The liberation of the individual, they optimistically thought, was precisely what would make a society based on freedom possible. They were thus precursors and fellow travelers of the New Culture movement. They were also anti-capitalist. Indeed, the most common understanding of "communism" at this time referred to anarcho-communism. Anarchists formed the first groups to reach out to peasants and workers, with some local successes. Their goal was not to "lead" the masses but to teach and help them.

Liu Shifu's Conscience Society in effect became a commune – a miniature seed of cooperative living, learning, and laboring. Not everyone could live up to Liu's ideals: some of his supporters recall visiting him by rickshaw but being sure to get out a few blocks away to walk the last bit. By the late 1910s the idea of communal experiments suddenly achieved great popularity. The "New Village" movement whereby students and peasants would together found whole new agrarian communes remained more theoretical than practical. But although the necessary funds were generally lacking, some attempts were made to reform village schools. Critics like Hu Shi condemned the movement as escapist, but Mao Zedong and other students of the day found its ideas appealing. If the movement's ultimate inspiration included the Christian agrarian pacifism of Tolstoy, there was also a nearer example in Japanese communal experiments of the day. But the key notion remained that social reform had to begin with the creation of a new kind of human being.

Communal experiments culminated in the Labor-Learning movement in 1920–1. Influenced by the French work–study program and the New Village movement, small groups of students lived together and took factory jobs or worked in restaurants and laundries. They pooled their resources, some committing themselves to sharing all property, even to the point of pooling clothes. "At the time it was our ideal that everything that should be done in the ideal society would, if possible, be tried out by us," one communalist later recalled. "We should be a model of the ideal society and our policy should be to reform [the present] society."[37]

"Laborism" and mutual aid spread beyond the anarchist communes. In a 1918 speech, Cai Yuanpei called labor "sacred" since it could overcome both the ancient Confucian distinction between rulers and ruled and the economic exploitation of capitalists and landlords. The notions of workers' rights bound together radicals of all stripes. During the mid-1910s a free-ranging, three-way debate took place among Liu Shifu's Conscience Society,

Jiang Kanghu's Chinese Socialist Party, and the followers of Sun Yat-sen, who tended to favor state and guild socialism. Liu and Jiang (1883–1945) shared a faith in the coming age of international revolution, abolition of the family, equal education, and a variety of other egalitarian social institutions. Sun did not go so far. But Jiang and Sun shared a belief that had been common in the years before 1911: that since capitalism had not advanced very far in China, socialism could be used to forestall the intense and violent class struggle that marked Western societies. The anarchists, though, believed that China too needed revolutionary struggle.

During the last decade of the Qing, Jiang had worked on educational reforms under Yuan Shikai. After studying in Europe he returned to China in 1911 a socialist; after Yuan Shikai's 1913 crackdown he traveled to the United States, becoming a professor of Chinese at the University of California at Berkeley. But between 1911 and 1913 Jiang organized a series of socialist clubs on which he based his political party. Exaggerating some-what, he claimed a membership of 400,000 for his party. Jiang did not deny his socialism was fairly moderate, and he sought to harness individual initia-tive. Jiang argued that socialism could best be realized under a republic and so, unlike Liu Shifu, accepted basic governmental institutions. As for Sun Yat-sen, he, too, continued to claim to be a socialist. But Sun clearly empha-sized nationalism over socialism. He attacked the notion of redistributing wealth and opposed "social revolution." Sun's socialism at this point amounted to little more than taxing property and using the state to build major indus-tries and infrastructure. These early debates over anarchism and socialism foreshadowed the triumph of Communism just a generation later. They established ways of thinking to which Marxism would, at least at first, have to conform. More broadly, socialist ideas about the state's role in economic development, fair relations among the classes, and society's responsibility to take care of its members, came to seem common sense to most Chinese intellectuals, even those far from radical circles.

# Part II

# Nationalism and revolution, 1919–37

From the May Fourth movement in 1919 to Japan's seizure of Manchuria in 1931 and full-scale invasion of China in 1937, the Chinese state was dramatically reconstituted. The 1920s saw the birth of ideologically charged and militant political parties. The Guomindang or Nationalist Party (GMD) and the Chinese Communist Party were not "parties" in the sense of organizations that contested elections, but political organizations building popular, military, and territorial bases of support. Both the GMD and the CCP were Leninist parties, organized from the top down, trying to capture but also empowering urban and rural groups. They worked together to mobilize popular support until the GMD moved to violently suppress the Communists in 1927. Popular social movements spread ideas of citizenship and public participation. A critical press, educational institutions, workers' organizations, and, finally, a peasants' movement, all built on the foundations of late Qing developments.

The 1920s saw warlord rampaging, ongoing imperialist pressures, and economic distress. Yet the period was also marked by broad-based social movements. The drive for labor rights in the cities and the rise of peasant movements in the countryside coincided with the social and political claims of women and students. These created a democratic tradition, though not democratic institutions. There was widespread discussion of such notions as the rights of individuals, the autonomy of groups vis-à-vis the state, legal limits on the state, and the principles of majoritarianism, "national salvation," and economic justice – discussions taking place in tandem with deep-seated social change. Institutionally, the era saw repressive but weak governments that relied on local elites to perform numerous public tasks, including the preservation of order and the collection of taxes.[1] Chambers of Commerce and bankers' associations were scarcely hotbeds of radicalism, but they were often bitterly critical of the government – sometimes for interfering with them, sometimes for failing to protect them, and sometimes for "selling out" China's rights. Merchants made alliances with student groups at times to support specific causes, especially anti-imperialist movements. Anti-imperialism was not simply a call for national unity but involved a critique of Chinese leaders and classes who cooperated with the foreigners. In the complete absence of constitutional protections, dissenters were vulnerable to arrest and assassination, but the relatively weak and very divided states of the 1920s had great difficulty in suppressing entire movements. Sometimes the goal was suppression; other times cooptation and control.

Some social groups tried to cooperate with governments to the extent possible. New professionals like lawyers, accountants, and even teachers and professors seldom sought directly to challenge the state. And merchants largely worked around the state to build a modern market system. These groups wanted both to better themselves and, through their skills and economic activities, to contribute to China's future. The 1920s were also marked by popular mobilization and the rise of street politics in China's cities and, in some parts of the countryside, Party-organized peasant protest as well. Intellectuals subjected Chinese tradition and Western imperialism to ever more searching criticisms in the "New Culture" and "May Fourth" movements, deepening the new, oppositionist social groups' understanding of the nature of their enemies. Public opinion, legitimated since the turn of the century, was able to spread in public spaces "ranging from temple grounds and brothels to public parks and theaters.… Old conventions guiding public behavior, like meeting in teahouses to mediate or conspire, combined with new ideologies and organization, like unionism and political clubs and parties, to underpin a radical  expansion of political participation."[2] The early Republic saw not only the expansion of journalism and education, but also new public parks and open spaces. These became the focal points of demonstrations, assemblies, and speech-making. Marchers were quick to seize the opportunities provided by newly widened and paved streets. Chinese governments inefficiently censored the post; the telephone and telegraph were even harder to control.

A new kind of politics arose that brought the warlord era to an end in 1928. Or at least, the rules of warlordism were changed as it was incorporated within the framework of the new Nationalist government. In 1928 the Guomindang under Chiang Kai-shek claimed to have unified the nation through the Northern Expedition. If it was not able to defeat all the warlords – instead inviting many into the GMD and giving them local autonomy – it did destroy the warlord *system* just twenty years after it began. The GMD, having broken with the Communist Party, also smashed the Communist-led labor and peasant movements. The Guomindang had originated in the revolutionary vision of Sun Yat-sen, who hoped to lead a second, "nationalist" revolution to unify a progressive China against warlords and imperialists. This was not quite to be. In spite of the considerable gains made by the GMD, especially in central China and in the cities, it was unable to penetrate much of the countryside. Rural elites and non-elites generally shared an interest in resisting the government's attempts to extract wealth from the countryside. The "local bullies and evil gentry" stood guard over villages and kept out government agents, and the Nationalist government lacked the resources and the will to reform worsening conditions in the countryside after about 1930.

In retrospect, it is clear that rural China was a site of vast revolutionary potential – not a backwater waiting to be acted upon and shaped by progressive cities but an active agent in its own history. Chinese peasants marched onto the historical stage in this period. They were by no means passive recipients of CCP largesse but actively sought to determine their own fates. The stolid "man with the hoe" image of peasant resignation never fitted Chinese peasants, who were not slow to join bandit gangs, riot against officials, threaten landlords, or simply disappear at tax collection time. After being virtually destroyed in 1927–8, the Chinese Communist Party was reborn in remote hill country. It was during this exile in the "wilderness" that the CCP learned how to mobilize peasant anger and energy through social revolution, how to organize armies and local administration, and how to maintain centralized control over centrifugal tendencies. Mao Zedong's rise to power began in the rural phase of the CCP's evolution. More than any other Chinese political leader, he seemed to understand that the promise of land and social justice was not merely a propaganda technique to win peasant support but lay at the root of the Chinese revolution.

In the realm of foreign policy, the Guomindang government was able to make some progress in revising the unequal treaties. Furthermore, the Western powers came close to conceding, at least in principle, that when China met certain conditions they would relinquish their special privileges. The early 1920s saw a respite of at least the most direct sorts of imperialist pressures, as a new world order emerged from the ashes of World War I. As Japanese hegemony in East Asia grew, however, it increasingly regarded political disorder and nationalism in China as equal threats. Japanese leaders did not believe that warlordism had ended in 1928 – proof that China was incapable of managing its own affairs. The Nationalist Decade (1928–37) was ended by Japan's invasion, but from the beginning of the decade Japan's growing presence in Manchuria and north China left the Nationalists very little room for maneuver and eroded their legitimacy.

Both the failures and the successes of the regime contributed to the growth of the political sphere. To the degree that the Nationalists were able to maintain stability, improve the educational system, and foster commerce, the Nationalist Decade was a success. Businessmen tried to work with the regime in the cities, but students and intellectuals were increasingly critical of the regime's failure to pursue social reform and – especially – to offer greater resistance to Japan. Above all, rural pressures continued to grow, and, though militarily defeated in the mid-1930s, the Communists continued to challenge the GMD for nationalist leadership while pressing for a more vigorous response to Japanese inroads in China.

In the cities, the protests of intellectuals and students suggested a vision of political and social revolution. However, in the face of intensifying Japanese pressure, Chiang Kai-shek's Guomindang moved steadily to the right as it concentrated its resources on exterminating the Communists. Politics was polarized between the right and the left, and between those who called for militant resistance against the Japanese and those who favored accommodating Japanese demands until China was in a stronger position to resist.

# 8 Politics and culture in the May Fourth movement

"May Fourth" refers to the student demonstrations of that date in 1919, in protest against China's signing of the Versailles Treaty. The Treaty marked the end of World War I and mostly dealt with the disposition of Germany and Austria in Europe, but it also transferred Germany's rights in Shandong to Japan. Most Chinese had expected them to be returned to China. In the wake of the demonstrations, which Beijing's military government tried to suppress, protests spread from the capital to other cities and from the students to other classes, particularly the workers and businessmen of coastal cities. In this sense, the May Fourth *incident* refers to the original student demonstrations. The May Fourth *movement* refers to the strikes and boycotts that followed over the next few months. And the May Fourth *era* refers to the revitalization of the public sphere in China in the early 1920s. The movement represents an entirely new type of grassroots politics based largely on nationalist feelings. But "May Fourth" has come to mean much more even than this.

Indeed, "May Fourth" has become an extremely important but ambiguous notion in all discussions of modern Chinese history. The Communists have (sometimes) gone so far as to trace the origins of their Party to May Fourth. At least, in so far as they saw May Fourth as representing progressive, patriotic elements, as marking the emergence of the working class, and as leading to "cultural revolution" – then they treated May Fourth as the necessary condition for the appearance of the CCP. In the words of Mao Zedong, the "whole of the Chinese revolutionary movement found its origin in the action of young students and intellectuals who had been awakened" by May Fourth.[1] The Nationalists held ambivalent feelings about May Fourth, but the more reformist elements of the GMD identified with its "enlightenment" themes. The May Fourth movement is inextricably associated with political, social, and cultural liberation. Heir to the New Culture movement, it has stood for such conflicting zeitgeists as the rise of communism, the heyday of liberalism, rationality and modernity, science and democracy, national unity, the awakening of young China, labor, and the rejection of tradition. Patriotism, individualism, egalitarianism, and feminism were its watchwords.

The New Culture movement, treated separately in Chapter 7, should be understood in its own terms as the reaction of a relatively small number of influential intellectuals to circumstances surrounding the presidency of Yuan Shikai. For all the important continuities, the May Fourth movement was led by a slightly younger and more activist generation. Indeed, the May Fourth movement represented a return to politics that New Culture intellectuals had earlier renounced. Of those intellectuals, Hu Shi might be emblematic of the group that remained essentially unsympathetic to the student demonstrators. At least, Hu thought they would do China more good in the long run if they returned to classes. Emblematic of intellectuals who supported the students, and indeed emerged as new political leaders, was Chen Duxiu.

We can thus conclude that May Fourth was important as an evolution of New Culture intellectual trends and especially as the beginning of a more activist political movement that deliberately sought to appeal to different social groups. However, the tendency to treat May Fourth as the origin of Chinese modernity is a fiction. This fiction is important in its own right as a powerful teleology: history moves from the benighted, shameful past toward a brighter, enlightened future – or from feudalism to the modern world. In the more or less official historiography of Communist periodization, May Fourth marks the beginning of "contemporary history" as the Opium Wars mark the beginning of "modern history." Clearly, as we have seen, the roots of Chinese modernity should be traced at least back to the late Qing, if not earlier.

Still, the May Fourth movement did mark a new scale of public action. May Fourth somehow concentrated the despair that had been growing for decades over the impotence of the Chinese government, any Chinese government, to provide efficient, honest, legitimate administration capable of resisting imperialist pressures. At this time optimism and pessimism, great hopes and great despair vied. In the autobiographical preface to his first book of stories, Lu Xun (1881–1936) declared his sense of futility and conveyed his weariness. He recounted his attempt to "deaden my senses," not with drugs or sex but by pursuing a scholarly antiquarianism: copying ancient inscriptions. Asked by a *New Youth* editor, Qian Xuantong, for an article, Lu recalls his response:

> "Imagine an iron house having not a single window and virtually indestructible, with all its inmates sound asleep and about to die of suffocation. Dying in their sleep, they won't feel the pain of death. Now if you raise a shout to wake a few of the lighter sleepers, making these unfortunate few suffer the agony of irrevocable death, do you really think you are doing them a good turn?" "But if a few wake up, you can't say there is no hope of destroying the iron house." True, in spite of my own conviction, I could not blot out hope, for hope belongs to the future.[2]

The iron house was of course China. It is an ironic comment on the Chinese revolution that Lu Xun became one of its most famous heroes. Though Lu *did* possess heroic ambitions – he hoped to change Chinese consciousness through literature – his pessimism and detachment were antithetical to the revolutionary stance. Yet he suggested that hope, no matter how feeble, impels action, and logic demands hope.[3] The iron house must be smashed.

In 1919 Lu Xun published a short story about a madman who imagined that the old society and the old morality were entirely based on cannibalism. The classics spoke of "filial piety" but, reading between the lines, he could see they really said, "eat people." The enemy was clear. In the May Fourth year, the idea of revolution, briefly discredited by the failures of the 1911 Revolution, re-emerged both broadened (to target all the old customs and habits meant by "culture") and more focused (to target warlordism and imperialism).

## The May Fourth movement, 1919–21

On 4 May 1919, some 3,000 students confounded the police by assembling at Beijing's Gate of Heavenly Peace (Tiananmen) and taking to the streets. The demonstration was well organized. Its targets were both the Powers that still seemed bent on carving up China and the Chinese politicians who cooperated with them. Students from thirteen local universities demanded that Chinese negotiators at Versailles repudiate any treaty that failed to restore Chinese sovereignty over Shandong. They also resolved that they would encourage Chinese in Paris to join their protests; that they would try to awaken the Chinese masses and hold a mass meeting in Beijing; and that a permanent Beijing students' association would be established. The students distributed leaflets to bystanders and carried flags with slogans in English and French as well as Chinese. Only a small number of student representatives were allowed into the Legation Quarter, heavily protected since the Boxer uprising, but even so they found the American, British, French, and Italian ambassadors all out. Letters were left. Several hours had passed in the meantime, and relations worsened between Chinese police and the demonstrators. After a debate, some students decided to march "on to the house of the traitor!" – that is, Cao Rulin.[4]

Smaller student groups had from the beginning evidently planned to turn the demonstration into a more pointed affair. Their goal was to directly attack the pro-Japanese officials in the Chinese government. Though the details remain surprisingly murky even after numerous memoirs (partly because of conflicting accounts), it was perhaps student anarchists who targeted Cao Rulin (1876–1966), a cabinet member who had been a Qing official and an aide to Yuan Shikai. Cao had conducted most of the negotiations with Japan over the Twenty-one Demands, worked on the Nishihara loans, and was reputed to be a Japanese agent. At Cao's house, a small riot broke out and five students broke into the house, taking Cao's bodyguard by

*Figure 8.1* On 4 May 1919, Beijing University students led demonstrations in protest to the Chinese government's willingness to sign the Versailles Treaty, demonstrations which grew over the next few weeks, spread to other cities, and led as well to boycotts of Japanese goods and strikes at Japanese factories.

surprise. Fu Sinian, a Beida student of Hu Shi and a future historian who served as a marshal for the demonstration, tried to prevent the march on Cao's house, but his own brother was one of the students who led the attack. Students poured into the house, smashing furniture and ultimately setting the house on fire. They found Zhang Zongxiang, China's ambassador to Japan, whom they beat severely. Cao, however, escaped through a window. Meanwhile, small skirmishes broke out between students and police in other parts of the city, though most of the demonstrators soon dispersed. By evening thirty-two students were under arrest; one other was hospitalized and died three days later. Martial law was declared around the Legation Quarter.

As Kuang Husheng (1891–1933), an anarchist and one of the students to break into Cao's house, recalled, "I saw that a number of my schoolmates were completely resolved to adopt a passionate commitment to resisting authority, to resisting the human bloodsuckers, and to sacrifice themselves. And I felt only the joy of self-sacrifice in going forward together." It would take blood to build "the ideal society and true liberty."[5] The demonstration started with just 3,000 marchers, but they represented China's future intellectual elite. Police on the whole were restrained; it may be that high-level police authorities had no fondness for Cao and it is even more likely that ordinary police, like nearly all Beijing citizens, agreed with the students' demands. The demonstration had been orderly, even on the way to Cao's house. However, the arrests of students also turned May Fourth into a spark. The arrested students attracted support from a wide range of Beijing's citizens, and protests spread to all major cities.

The following two weeks saw numerous student meetings, demonstrations, petition drives, and street speeches. The students raised contributions, publicized the cases of the students who had been arrested, and began organizing high school students. A student union was established in Beijing, including women members. The students bested the government's attempts to censor the news of the demonstrations by using couriers and foreign telegraph services. In Shanghai, radical teachers and students began organizing when the news from Beijing reached the city on 6 May; a Citizens Assembly, which was followed by a protest march, was held on 7 May, and on 8 May the Shanghai Student Union was formed. The anti-Japanese cause proved extremely popular, as it would throughout the twentieth century. Students garnered immediate support from the educational establishment, including most of their own principals and university presidents – as well as chambers of commerce, lawyers' associations, and other professional groups around China. Workers soon followed, becoming especially important in Shanghai. Demonstrations and strikes spread to yet more cities throughout May.

Direct antigovernment activity was temporarily quieted as the movement shifted to anti-Japanese actions. The student union publicly burned Japanese goods. Across the country, new protest organizations sprouted, and Japanese goods were boycotted. However, government attempts to restrict the protest movement continued. The trial of the thirty-two arrested students opened on 10 May; they refused to plead and demanded that Cao Rulin and the other "traitors" be put on trial instead. Public opinion tended to agree. Since the government lacked legitimacy, its appeals to the law rang hollow. A national student strike began on 19 May. Students took to the streets and also began sending liaisons to merchant and worker associations.

Further demonstrations and arrests at the beginning of June brought merchants and workers fully into the struggle. The Beijing government, like most warlord regimes, did not want to go out of its way to persecute popular students, but neither could it cave in to student demands and prosecute its own officials for treason. Diplomatic pressure from Japan was strong; its formal protests demanded the suppression of anti-Japanese activities. However, neither threats nor persuasion could placate the students. After a month of dithering, the Beijing government moved in early June to stamp out student street-lecturing; many students and bystanders were beaten and arrested. By 4 June, temporary jails were overflowing with more than 1,000 detainees. The Beijing students put 5,000 more speakers onto the streets. The news was soon telegraphed to Shanghai.

From the beginning of the movement, Shanghai's educated elites, notably including the president of Fudan University, had numbered among the leaders of the protests. Student organizing and petition drives marked much of May, and a vast student strike involving up to 20,000 students ensued on May 26. The students, deliberately and with considerable success, made a patriotic appeal to the entire city. They assembled to swear an oath to "relieve and save [China] from danger and destruction," they paraded through the city, they handed out leaflets, pasted up posters, and put on patriotic street plays. Shanghai student delegates also traveled to the major cities in central and southern China to convey their public relations knowhow to the students of those cities. Their intense seriousness – the students policed themselves quite strictly to make sure none of their number turned to "anarchy" or took advantage of the school closures to, say, go to the movies – impressed the citizens of Shanghai. By June, Shanghai had replaced Beijing as the main focus of the May Fourth movement.[6]

Shanghai students called for a "triple strike" of classes, work, and markets for June 5 – and the city virtually shut down. Still, it took a great deal of organization and persistence to maintain the strike for a week. Students pressured shopkeepers to remain shut. Boy Scouts patrolled the streets to keep order – and to discourage physical attacks on Japanese. The Shanghai General Chamber of Commerce had opposed the students throughout May, but merchants in the less prestigious Shanghai Commercial Federation simply went ahead in June, closing their shops and rebuking the Chamber. The Chamber then bent to popular pressure, and the success of various anti-Japanese boycotts from 1919 to 1923 throughout urban China was due to the support of the bourgeoisie. In fact, Shanghai's merchant-dominated native-place associations had been participating in patriotic activities since February, when several petitioned the Beijing government to resist Japan's demands at Versailles. Some merchants, at least, had already begun boycotting Japanese goods in early May. (Students organized groups to check on shopkeepers.) Those proclaimed guilty of the "traitorous behavior" of conducting business with Japanese were expelled from their native-place associations and might well have found it difficult to remain solvent. Though a seemingly more traditional organization than student unions, the native-place associations played a key role in disseminating nationalist ideas and mobilizing support for the movement.[7]

At the same time, workers' strikes finally shut down trade with Japan. In Shanghai, some 60,000 workers went on strike in June. Dockhands refused to load or unload Japanese ships. Japanese-owned textile factories were struck, and then the strikes spread to create a near-total five-day shutdown. The guilds of craftsmen and skilled workers moved to strike, and unskilled workers organized in gangs struck as well. Indeed, the gangs in Shanghai went so far as to order the beggars and pickpockets under their control to desist work. Prostitutes sang patriotic songs instead of their usual come-ons.[8] The strike finally ended on June 12, when the Beijing government dismissed the "three traitorous officials" whom students blamed for giving in to Japan.

In France, under intense pressure from Chinese students and workers there, the Chinese delegation to the peace conference ended by deciding, against instructions from Beijing, *not* to sign the treaty. The Versailles Treaty was thus concluded on June 28 without official Chinese endorsement. The students had won a great victory. A student–merchant–worker alliance had been created, if only tenuously. However, Japan still got to keep Shandong. And warlordism was just entering its most virulent phase. Given these events, why did Chinese citizens decide that, out of thousands of imperialist provocations, the Versailles Treaty was especially horrendous?

## Imperialism and liberalism

The Versailles Treaty marked a turning point in Chinese attitudes toward the West. In spite of all the humiliations of imperialism and even the perceived threat of racial extinction, leading Chinese had continued to look to Western nations as a model. But now, in the words of one Beida student, "We at once awoke to the fact that foreign nations were still selfish and militaristic and they were all great liars."[9]

May Fourth marked a moment of disillusionment. From the point of view of the Powers, Shandong was a small question, but Versailles provided a test which Wilsonian liberalism flunked. The international context was key to the radicalization of Chinese politics. The idea of national self-determination preached by President Woodrow Wilson of the United States had been designed to compete with the appeal of Lenin's anti-colonialism. The October Revolution of the Bolsheviks in Russia had been noted and praised in China by 1918, but Wilson's Fourteen Points were probably better known. Both Wilson and Lenin presented critiques of colonialism, one ameliorative and the other revolutionary. Since during World War I as many as 200,000 Chinese had participated in the war effort as replacement labor in Europe, the Allied victory in November 1918 had been greeted with enthusiasm. It was, in part, China's victory, and not Wilsonian rhetoric alone but also moral debts seemed to augur good treatment of China at Versailles. Indeed, Liang Qichao had originally argued, against great neutralist sentiment, that China should enter the war on the side of the Allies precisely to obtain favorable treatment after the war.

From Wilson's point of view, however, the case of China was but one of a number of difficult issues facing the Peace Conference and clearly of less importance than the arrangements for the former Austro-Hungarian Empire or the League of Nations. The spread of Bolshevism alarmed Wilson as much as it did the other Allied leaders; indeed, with the destruction of the Habsburg, Hohenzollern, and Romanov empires, a new world order was emerging. But while the conference concentrated on Europe, nations under imperialist domination were protesting about their status – not only China, but also Egypt, India, Turkey, and Southeast Asia. In so far as even imperialism required a degree of legitimacy, the War seriously damaged the West's posturing as the font of civilization. The West's own self-confidence was damaged as well. If the finest flowers of European civilization were dedicated to their mutual destruction, by what logic could the imperialists claim to rule "backward people" for their own good?

One of the Powers' more important tasks in 1918 was to find a place for Japan, which both criticized the old European order and was eager to join it. Japan's role in the war had been relatively minor, but its military presence in the western Pacific was major. Its diplomacy had been instrumental in convincing the Beijing regime to declare war on Germany. And it intended to inherit not just Shandong but also the German islands scattered over the Pacific. Following Allied distress over the Bolshevik Revolution and Russia's withdrawal from the war, Japan joined the invasion of Siberia, sending, like the United States, 7,000 troops in July 1918, but soon expanding these tenfold. Although the British, French, and US contingents retreated from Russia in 1920, Japanese troops remained until 1922. Unscathed by much actual warfare, Japan's economy and military had benefited enormously from World War I. It became a creditor nation; it sold munitions to the Allies and expanded in the civilian markets throughout Asia that Europe could no longer supply; its international trade, manufacturing, and high-tech industries grew; and, most dramatically, its shipbuilding rose from 85,000 tons in 1914 to 650,000 tons in 1919. Britain, France, and Italy had signed secret treaties with Japan in 1917 promising to support Japan's claims to Shandong. Japan made these treaties public as the Peace Conference opened in 1919; they came as a shock to the Chinese people, and put additional pressure on the United States not to upset what had already been agreed.

President Wilson had recognized the government of Yuan Shikai in 1913, and hence the successor Beijing regimes, as the Republic of China. Wilson's vision of the post-war era was a kind of continuation of the Open Door policy, which had been designed with British support to maintain Chinese territorial integrity at the turn of the century. Naked colonialism would be replaced by free trade, with American businessmen spreading throughout the world on the same basis as those of other countries. Backward nations would not be allowed to keep their raw materials and would be brought into the world economy. But they were to retain political independence and presumably would benefit in the long run. Chinese in 1918 therefore logically looked to Wilson for support in their struggle against Japan's more colonial brand of imperialism.

Early in 1918 Wilson made his famous Fourteen Points speech, responding to the Bolshevik critique of imperialism. The Leninist call for national independence was matched by action. As Japan had secret treaties with the European Powers, so it had with Czarist Russia. But in February 1918 the Bolsheviks revealed and renounced Japanese–Russian agreements from 1907 to 1917 that had been designed to carve up Manchuria and Mongolia. Chinese public opinion was enormously heartened by this gesture, though in fact the Soviet Union kept some rights in Manchuria through secret treaties (unknown to the Chinese people). Wilson's response was more nuanced, but his calls for open diplomacy and respect for the wishes of national peoples were clear enough. Chinese especially looked to his fifth point:

A free, open-minded, and absolutely impartial adjustment of all colonial claims, based upon a strict observance of the principle that in determining all such questions of sovereignty the interests of the populations concerned must have equal weight with the equitable claims of the government whose title is to be determined.[10]

This was cautiously phrased, but the Chinese had no difficulty interpreting nineteenth-century treaty provisions as inequitable. In any case, Wilson added, "An evident principle runs through the whole program I have outlined. It is the principle of justice to all peoples and nationalities, and their right to live on equal terms of liberty and safety with one another, whether they be strong or weak."[11] However, Wilsonian liberalism was anathema to nations with colonial empires to refurbish in the post-war period, and the United States was not prepared to press these principles. National sovereignty coexisted with a belief in economic expansion that was to be peaceful if possible but coercive if necessary. Hence Wilson's second and third points of 1918: freedom of navigation, and "The removal, so far as possible, of all economic barriers and the establishment of an equality of trade conditions...."[12] Imperialism, to Wilson, meant colonies and spheres of influence; economic relations could not, by definition, constitute imperialism. Loans and foreign ownership of China's railroads, mines, factories, and the like were, as opposed to imperialism, in the open door tradition. But on the ground in China, foreign ownership of mines and railroads and the stationing of foreign troops around the mines and along the railroads came as a single package.

In any case, Chinese indebtedness to Japan compromised its position at Versailles. In 1917 Japan's policy was to influence the government of Duan Qirui through financial aid. Duan received the Nishihara loans, eventually totaling 145 million yen, of which only 5 million yen was ever repaid, in return for important concessions. Japan was granted the right to station troops in northern Manchuria and Mongolia, provisions were made for military cooperation (targeted against Bolshevik Russia), and Japanese began to train the Chinese army and navy. The deal helped Duan consolidate his control of the parliament and governmental administration, and beef up his military resistance to the southern warlords and Sun Yat-sen. As well, Shandong railroads had been mortgaged in return for Japanese loans, and Ambassador Zhang Zongxiang (later beaten by students on 4 May, 1919) wrote in September 1918 that the Chinese government "gladly agreed" to Japanese demands to station troops in the Shandong cities of Qingdao and Jinan and along the province's railroads. These were among the documents Japan made public at Versailles.

Wilson, however sympathetic to the Chinese case, faced skeptical allies and a Japan that was still feeling its way into the world of Great Powers. Japan's efforts to get the conference to endorse the concept of racial equality were rebuffed. This might have been a harmless declaration with no legal force, but Australia and the US feared it would encourage immigration from Asia. Shandong might be regarded as a way to mollify the Japanese. Wilson also desperately wanted Japan to join the League of Nations. It might finally be noted that US–Japan trade was far larger than US–China trade, while for Japan – but not for the United States – China was strategically as well as economically important. Ironically, Japan formally returned Shandong to China just three years later in 1922, though the Japanese retained an interest as holders of Chinese bonds to pay for the Shandong railway and other improvements.

Thus in the 1920s the "open door" was more or less honored, and the situation remained fairly stable with no major grabs for territory until the end of the decade. Japan's leaders were, for a time, in agreement with the American vision of a world capitalist economy. This is also to say, however, that Chinese nationalist demands were continually thwarted. "Wilsonian liberalism" thus indicates the real power of democratic ideas but also the crippling hypocrisy of Western imperialism. World War I damaged the reputation of the West in China as intellectuals like Liang Qichao, never more a traditionalist than at this moment, questioned Western values and urged a return to older Confucian norms. Chinese judged the West by its own standards and condemned it. The dilemma of Wilsonian liberalism was that it could neither sanction the status quo nor end imperialism.

At the turn of the century, Chinese intellectuals had feared dismemberment of China. Chinese still feared the demise of their nation in the 1920s. The May Fourth movement reflected a sophisticated analysis of the situation: imperialism was not simply a threat from foreigners. A large part of China's problem was domestic, both structurally and in terms of leadership. Thus the students chanted, "Externally, resist the Powers; internally, throw out the traitors." The 1911 revolutionaries had blamed the Manchus but in 1919 it was clear the traitors were Chinese. At the same time, foreigners who came not as imperialists but as friends could be treated as friends. The philosophers John Dewey of the United States and Bertrand Russell of Britain, for example, conducted wildly popular lecture tours between 1919 and 1921. That both men were politically progressive added to their allure. The May Fourth analysis benefited from the failures of 1911; politics alone did not hold the answer. And within the political realm, if organizational breakthroughs took some further time to work out, radicals none the less realized that they had to bring the masses into politics, to carry politics to the streets.

## The political significance of the May Fourth movement

Less than 30 years separated May Fourth radicalism from late Qing radicalism. If the older generation had received a thoroughly Confucian education, the younger generation that took to the streets in 1919 were attending high schools and universities with largely Westernized curriculums.

The two generations did not necessarily speak the same political language.[13] Whereas some of the older generation had reacted strongly against their Confucian upbringing, some of the younger generation were more relaxed about the burdens of tradition. (When we speak of "generations" here, we are speaking of people sometimes just a few years apart in age. This sense of generational identity reflected the rapidity of cultural change.) Moreover, important continuities marked not just the ideas, but also the organizing strategies of the May Fourth protestors. Much of the shift from late Qing to May Fourth consciousness reflected what teachers passed on to their students. By 1919 Beida was staffed with many men who had been anti-Qing revolutionaries – including its president, Cai Yuanpei.

Western historians have sometimes found Chinese nationalism, like all nationalisms, prone to xenophobia – a matter of ignorance and reaction rather than the pride of a people in itself. In this view, imperialism, no matter how brutal, is cosmopolitan in that it inevitably links and influences different civilizations. However, in the 1920s it is Chinese nationalism that looks cosmopolitan. The student and merchant nationalists were educated, reasonable, knowledgeable about the world, interested in universal values and ideals, and spoke the language of progress and enlightenment. It is Western and Japanese imperialism that appears narrow-minded, ignorant, and racist, and still relying on the gunboat, not on reason. It is important to remember that imperialism was not merely a set of abstract questions about the economic impact of cotton imports or the British–American Tobacco Company. Rather, it was a lived experience.

In the countryside, missionaries had become notorious for interfering in lawsuits and other disputes between neighbors – especially if one party was Christian and the other not. Many ordinary Chinese would have been familiar with numerous stories such as the following.[14] In 1902 two British missionaries settled in Chenzhou, in western Hunan, and established a church and a hospital. A cholera epidemic spread and people said the missionaries' housekeeper had put white powder in the town well. A crowd of two thousand assembled to accuse her and the missionaries of poisoning the well, and events escalated to the point the two missionaries were beaten to death. The British consulate in Hankou then demanded that the community and local officials be punished. They even demanded that a fourteen-year-old waiter be executed after he was seen kicking one of the corpses. The Qing dismissed its officials and arrested three hundred people. Ten were executed, and others died in jail.

In the cities, the ubiquitous presence of foreign soldiers and sailors, often out for a good time, led to numerous disputes. If Chinese were killed in a drunken brawl, the foreign perpetrators would be punished but lightly and a bit of compensation given to the deceased's family. In Shanghai in 1904, for example, two drunken Russian sailors hired rickshaws to take them back to their boats. When one of the rickshaw pullers demanded his fare, one of the sailors lost his temper, grabbed an adze from a nearby carpenter and, instead of killing the rickshaw puller, crushed the skull of a passing pedestrian.[15] The Russian authorities, insisting on their extraterritorial rights, tried the case themselves. Remarkably, they found the sailor guilty of "quite accidental" negligent homicide, since he killed someone other than the intended victim, and he was sentenced to four years' hard labor.

Such incidents only multiplied as the years went on, and all sorts of different political groups found common cause in anti-imperialism. No Shanghai park really boasted a sign saying "No dogs or Chinese," but that most Chinese had no trouble believing that such a sign existed shows their understanding of imperialism as a lived experience. (Some parks however did prohibit Chinese, except for servants accompanying their employers.) The point here is that the popularity of the May Fourth movement and the respect given students had everything to do with imperialism. The movement brought political and policy questions once reserved for elite discussion into popular urban discourse. The students managed not only to shake the government, but also to introduce China to a new kind of politics. Street politics also expanded the old political world dominated by literati, warlords, administrators, and professional politicians. The May Fourth movement might be compared to the petition drive organized by Kang Youwei in 1895. Simply by moving political considerations into wider view, both acted as radicalizing forces. Kang turned to fellow literati. The May Fourth self-consciously turned to "the people." In 1919, even Kang – by now generally conservative – praised the students, noting that "No real public opinion or real people's rights have been seen in China in the eight years since the establishment of the Republic in 1912; if they exist today, it is due to the students' actions in this incident."[16] The excitement and danger in 1919 were far greater than in the relatively sedate protest of 1895; rumors variously had soldiers mowing down students on the streets and moving to overthrow the government with their student allies. But as young literati demanded to be heard in 1895, so the idea of citizenship was seized in 1919. Fifteen-year-old girls claimed the right to discuss policy and to speak in the name of the nation. Public speech was a right, not a privilege.

The students were not always in harmony, of course, and continued militancy through June lost them the support of teachers who wanted classes to resume. None the less, in China's major cities, students took to street preaching; this was a highly organized movement of reaching out to the urban populace. Groups of students were assigned to exhort merchants and shoppers to boycott Japanese goods. Students spoke with the authority of those who were willing to sacrifice themselves for the sake of the community. They also inherited some of the traditional prestige of the scholar. In Shanghai, at least, students moved to enforce the boycott of Japanese goods. Not all Chinese businessmen benefited from the boycott; many shopkeepers lost sales and had to be convinced not to cheat. Students feared violence since it would bring a sharp reaction from the foreign police forces, and they tried very hard to maintain order. Having preached hatred for the Japanese, students then had to dissuade crowds from attacking Japanese nationals, as sometimes occurred.

Overall the movement was peaceful and disciplined, even solemn. Student demonstrations were dedicated to the memory of martyrs killed by the police, and students swore to save the nation. The appeal of the students lay in their message and also in their conduct. Their claims to be acting selflessly were critical to their legitimacy. This was thus a politics of purity as well as a new kind of street politics. The great difference between the multi-class student movement and the machinations of warlords and politicians was thus clear. Students wrote slogans in their own blood. Students reinforced their sense of purpose by taking oaths creating rules for themselves. Even Chinese who disagreed with some of the students' demands and tactics might admire their sincerity.

This sort of politics did have a precedent. The racist immigration policies of the United States had been the target of a brief but effective student–merchant boycott in 1905. And in 1915 Yuan Shikai's government had briefly attempted to use popular protest as a tool for resisting the Twenty-one Demands. Student strikes, demonstrations, and mass meetings were rooted in the anti-Manchu movement from the beginning of the century. More fundamentally, the students' sense of their own righteousness stemmed from the same tradition of literati dissent and responsibility for governance that had motivated Kang Youwei. If we compare the role of students in 1911 and their role in 1919, it may thus seem that little had changed. But quantitatively the May Fourth movement involved unprecedented numbers: tens of thousands of students and workers and thousands of merchants across China's major cities. And "qualitatively" the May Fourth movement led to a new basis for political activity. Perhaps this reflected the changes in Chinese society in the first two decades of the century more than it did a growing maturity of political understanding, though this, too, played a role. For if the 1911 Revolution saw a temporary alliance between radical intellectuals and students, provincial leaders, and military bosses, the May Fourth movement created a multi-class political agenda based on anti-imperialism and opposition to venal Chinese administrations.

And May Fourth set the pattern for future protests as it trained future leaders. Strikes continued periodically through the next three decades; student mobilization was permanent, and huge reservoirs of sympathy for the students were maintained. The May Fourth movement brought thousands of people to treat policy questions as personally important. Some of them doubtlessly did not stay politicized, but many did. They had to move away from pure protest movements, which by their very nature are of the moment. A variety of long-term approaches was thus formed. Of particular importance was the independent political party, not attached to a warlord faction but dedicated to overthrowing the entire system of militarism. The Nationalist and the Communist Parties will be discussed in Chapter 10, but the point here is that they could not have emerged without the May Fourth movement. The 1920s saw a process not just of politicization but of political professionalization. Professional politicians – the old parliamentarians – were to the May Fourth movement nearly as despicable as the warlords. But a new kind of politician was emerging, one devoted to a cause and representing the expansion of politics. He (or, in increasing numbers, she) was not a revolutionary conspirator in the 1911 model; rather, the new Party member, even if he or she worked underground, was dedicated to the long-term quest for principled power.

The May Fourth movement represents a politically unfinished project, for it left unresolved several questions. Street demonstrations were a potent but ultimately limited technique. One might influence the government, but only to shift its stance on a specific policy or to implement specific, minor reforms. One might conceivably join a government, but would one then simply become embroiled in the machinations of the warlord system? One might want to overthrow the whole system, but how? And would the chaos of revolution only make things worse, as 1911 seemed to show?

The purely political approach of the 1911 Revolution had failed to reform China fundamentally; the purely cultural approach of the 1915 New Culture movement had failed or was too slow. May Fourth merged cultural and political issues and strategies. By the early 1920s the nascent Nationalist and Communist Parties had captured a good part of the enthusiasm kindled by the May Fourth explosion. Before these ideologically-charged political parties can be examined, however, we must first look at the intellectual and cultural changes of the period.

## Cultural revolution and social change

One of the dominant themes of the May Fourth era was women's rights. The attempt to turn women into active citizens can be traced back to the late Qing, of course, but only in the wake of the spread of educational and employment opportunities did women begin to emerge as a major social force in their own right. Conservatives who wished to limit women to the private sphere of the home opposed the women's movement. Deep-seated attitudes toward gender differences also prevented the desire for "complete equality" from reaching its potential. Legal reforms were slow to come and social change even slower. But the 1920s saw women's issues – from free marriages to career opportunities – become central to May Fourth discourse.

Much of this discourse remained dominated by men's voices. Mao Zedong, in an early (non-Marxist) essay of 1919 calling for the unity of the Chinese people, spoke for the main groups he wished to see mobilized: students, workers, and peasants. And for women, he spoke in this way:

> We are women. We are even more deeply immersed in an ocean of suffering! We are also human beings, so why won't they let us take part in

politics?... in social intercourse?... The shameless men, the villainous men, make us into their playthings, and force us to prostitute ourselves to them indefinitely. The devils, who destroy the freedom to love!... so-called "chastity" is confined to us women.... All day long they talk about something called being "a worthy mother and a good wife." What is this but teaching us to prostitute ourselves indefinitely to the same man?[17]

Mao also drew national attention to a local Hunan woman's suicide in 1919. Mao wrote a series of articles claiming that Miss Zhao had been forced into committing suicide by parents who insisted she marry against her will. She had hidden a razor in her foot bindings, and while she was being carried in the bridal sedan to her husband's house for the formal wedding, she slit her throat. Mao blamed an immoral marriage system, concluding: "Because the causes of Miss Zhao's suicide lie in society itself, such a society is dangerous."[18] In this way Miss Zhao became a revolutionary martyr for women's rights.

We may not know exactly what the real Miss Zhao thought or how despair and power were combined in her suicide, but some women did possess voices of their own. In the wake of the 1911 Revolution, the refusal of so-called revolutionaries to support women's suffrage led a number of women to call the liberation of women "unfinished business." Some educated women found that writing could be liberating. Chen Xuezhao (1906–91) recalled that, by sending her first essay to a Shanghai newspaper, she was not only challenging the authority of her strict family but also discovering the possibility of making an independent living through her writing.[19] Chen was able to finance her Ph.D. studies in France and resist her parents' pressures to get married. Perhaps the most famous woman author of the May Fourth period was Ding Ling (1904–86), who daringly wrote about women's sexuality, but she was by no means alone in exploring the dilemmas facing liberated and unliberated women alike.[20] Male authors tended to write realist fiction while much women's writing was autobiographical and intensively introspective. But women writers in the May Fourth period had no choice but to consider the problem of how to be a modern woman.

What is particularly striking about the works written by women – although of course they differed widely in tone and political commitment – is that, in contrast to male feminists, they presented women neither as completely powerless nor as satisfied with the freedoms of the new society. Ding Ling's *Miss Sophie's Diary* tells the story of a woman, not entirely unlike Ding Ling herself, who was free of the traditional patriarchal family – and yet still restless and unhappy. A number of women wrote full-scale autobiographies or semi-autobiographies about growing up and escaping from traditional families. Xiao Hong (1911–42), for example, had been sent away to school but ran away from home when her father demanded she marry the man of his choice. When she moved in with a teacher from her school, they were both expelled and forced to move to Beijing – where he abandoned her. Her fiction seemingly deals with issues that had occurred in her life, such as the story "Abandoned Child" about a woman forced to give up her child. "What will I do? I have no home, no friends. Where can I go? There's only that man I've just met and he's homeless too!"[21] In the story "Separation," written as a letter from a young woman to her lover, we see the woman literally locked up by her mother until her arranged marriage to another man can take place. The story was written by the younger sister of the philosopher and historian Feng Youlan, whose mother was actually more supportive of her children.[22] Her story was considered shocking upon its publication in 1923 due to its portrayal of romance between unmarried persons. Today it is the story's feverish expressions of love and political consciousness that seem more striking. "I have discovered that humans are selfish; although they make material sacrifices for others, they have no spiritual regard for them because they are so trapped in their historical circumstances."[23] Perhaps few women accepted the utopian visions of male radicals unquestioningly. What fates would most young women face without the support of their families?

Lu Xun's stories offered more nuanced portrayals of the dilemmas facing young men and women who wanted to be the New Man and, especially, the New Woman. One of Lu's stories tells of a man who would like to teach science and other modern subjects but can only get a job teaching the old Confucian morality – a quiet tragedy for a man who once dreamed of changing the world.

During the May Fourth era the dramas of Henrik Ibsen, the Norwegian playwright, had an influential vogue. *A Doll's House* was translated in 1918, and the play about Nora walking out of her comfortable but confining family – leaving behind husband and children – provoked admiring discussions about free love, contraception, and divorce. Few women could survive without family support, but some like Ding Ling did have the support of their mothers (Ding Ling's mother also unbound her own feet) and others had the support of friends and colleagues. But the prospect of hundreds of naïve girls launching themselves ill-prepared into Beijing, Shanghai, and other cities prompted Lu Xun to give a talk at a women's college: "What happens after Nora leaves home?"

That was a hard question to answer, but it was not just young women students who were seeing their personal problems in political terms. The "Women's Question" that dominated so much of May Fourth discourse was part of a larger attack on the traditional family. Essentially, the family was charged with suppressing individual rights and the dynamic energies needed to revitalize China. The family represented everything that was the opposite of modern, scientific, and democratic. Companionate marriage, as the historian John Fitzgerald points out, not only subverted the patriarchal lineage but also demanded that lovers make a consciously chosen commitment to stick to one another through thick and thin to build an "affective community" – rather like the relationship between citizen and nation.[24] In sum, what happened in the May Fourth period is that these abstractions became painfully concrete for the younger generation of educated students. And older intellectuals like Hu Shi, Chen Duxiu, and Li Dazhao, who had all contracted arranged marriages with relatively uneducated, even footbound women, had to decide what to do about their first wives. Divorce? Affairs? Fidelity? Among the students many a bombastic attack on patriarchy was penned anonymously so the author's father would not be angry or hurt.

Qu Qiubai (1899–1935), a literary critic and early Communist leader, recalled that his irresponsible father had frittered away the family patrimony and left his mother to raise six children. Taunted by relatives, she committed suicide and the family was dispersed. For Lu Xun, the family was society's agent of cannibalism, devouring its own children. In one of Fu Sinian's first published essays he wrote that the family was "the source of all evil." Fu had himself been married when he was fifteen.

> The enormous burden of the family makes it totally impossible for a Chinese person to pursue his own vocation. It pushes him, bit by bit, toward immorality…. Alas! Such is the benefit of the Chinese family system: it forces you to become a provider, it makes you muddle-headed, it forces you to submit yourself to others and lose your identity.[25]

May Fourth also brought the entire New Culture movement to the provinces – to young provincials like Mao Zedong in Hunan or the boys of Hangzhou. Students enrolled in the Zhejiang Provincial First Normal School in Hangzhou fervently joined the May Fourth demonstrators.[26] While Hangzhou itself was no backwater, the most radical students tended to come from rural counties far from the modernizing reach of Shanghai. From a poor peasant family, Shi Cuntong (1899–1970), for example, became an enthusiastic iconoclast. On Confucius' birthday in the autumn of 1919, First Normal students refused to worship at the Confucian temple but made a pilgrimage to the tomb of the anarchist Liu Shifu instead, and toppled the statue of Confucius on campus. Shi wrote an article "Against filial piety!" to attack the most central value of the Confucian tradition.

Like Qu Qiubai, Shi created an intellectual position out of an existential dilemma. Visiting home back in the countryside in the fall of 1919, he discovered that his mother appeared to be dying, though the family had sought help from an herbalist and from the gods. His father – whom he mostly remembered as beating him as a child – demanded that the family's resources be saved for her funeral, in accordance with Confucian ritual propriety. Shi suggested they seek further medical advice; his dilemma was that his filial duties to his mother included providing her with care while his filial duties to his father demanded obedience. His reaction was to flee back to Hangzhou, later claiming: "It was too late to try saving my mother. I thereupon resolved to save all other women who in the future might find themselves in similar circumstances."[27]

Previously, though exposed to the ardent attacks on Confucianism by the likes of Chen Duxiu, Shi had rejected them. But over the course of the May Fourth movement he was convinced of the evil of Confucianism by intellectual argument, by his reading of China's predicaments, and by existential pain. Shi attacked filial piety as the ethics of slaves and directly denounced his own father. At the same time, he noted that both his parents had been trapped in a society and a cultural system imposed on them without their consent. Instead, Shi proposed, an anarchist system without private property to divide people from one another would suppress patriarchy and other evils. The historian Wen-hsin Yeh notes that, in contrast to the more political concerns of Beijing and Shanghai intellectuals with the influence of Confucianism on state ideology, "provincials" like Shi focused on the family and society. "Although the metropolitan articulation paved the way and revealed the patterns of connection between ideology and various aspects of social reality, Hangzhou iconoclasm, charged by a rage and a fervor emanating from middle-county *traditional rural* society, selectively displayed intensity in certain areas over others and was no pale reflection of metropolitan input."[28]

In sum, attacks on the family were fueled by the desire on the parts of thousands of young and sometimes not-so-young educated men and women to build their own lives, be granted a chance at self-fulfillment, and reform China. Many saw themselves as heroes. For some, this led to an extreme romanticism and subjectivism. The literary scholar Leo Ou-fan Lee cites young writers who threw off Confucian rationalism and classical standards in search of an aesthetics that linked human sentiment and dynamism to love, truth, beauty, and freedom.[29] These romantics glorified emotionalism, and their touching agonies filled many a literary journal. Calling for "art for art's sake" and sometimes glorifying "decadence," the romantic movement was often criticised as escapist and had largely dissipated by the end of the decade. Perhaps the new political commitments of the 1930s left little room for the extreme individualism of the romantics, but the writer Yu Dafu showed how romantic and political impulses could be mixed: "Since last winter my emotional frame of mind has been a continuous series of depressions. I have harbored the idea of going to Russia in order to become a worker there, but I was stopped by my brother in Beijing.... Living in this world, one has to do something. But for such a superfluous man like me, castrated by advanced education, what can I do?"[30]

The "superfluous man" may seem to take us far from the desire to participate in the making of a new China, but the romantics' criticism of the status quo was as harsh as that of the political activists. We should probably think less of classifying May Fourth trends into distinct activist, romantic, culturalist schools, and more in terms of a shared set of possibilities and pressures. Indeed, Marxists of the 1920s such as Li Dazhao, Qu Qiubai – and the historian and literary figure Guo Moruo (1892–1978) – shared a belief in reality as organismic and vital. Such views were popular in the wake of

World War I, associated with the popular philosopher Henri Bergson. Along with Daoism and Buddhism, this resulted in a faith in the empathic commonality of life into which individuals must surrender themselves. Before his conversion to Marxism, Guo wrote in 1922:

> Pantheism is atheism. If all natural phenomena are manifestations of God, and I also am a manifestation of God, then I am God, and all natural phenomena are manifestations of me. When a man has lost his Self and become one with God, he transcends time and space and sees life and death as one. But when a man becomes aware of his Self, he sees only the alternation and inconstancy of the external appearance of the myriad phenomena of the universe and of his own external appearance, and a feeling of sorrow about life and death, being and non-being is born within him.

From this empathy with the universe – so like Kang Youwei's youthful awakening forty years earlier – Guo drew activist conclusions: "With the same energy with which a lion strikes its prey, with the whole body and the whole soul, one must seek self-realization in the fulfillment of every moment."[31] This might be called mystical activism rather than mystical escapism.

## The modern nation and limits of change

What remained of May Fourth ideals once the demonstrations petered out? Warlords and – often standing behind them in the shadows – the foreign Powers dominated politics. Urban society was illiberal and increasingly consumerist, while rural society seemed not to change at all. Nationalist trends – with their tendency toward self-glorification of the group, silencing of dissent, anti-cosmopolitanism, and demands for unity – could repress movements for democracy and cultural criticism.[32] This was not a dilemma unique to China, of course. However, the anti-traditionalism of the leaders of the New Culture movement was especially strong, which left them vulnerable to charges of "cultural treason." When competing and complementary needs for national unity, social justice, and democracy and individualism are openly debated, a balance may be struck. But the issues may not be openly debated. Something of this kind of subliminal discourse affected the "Women's Question" in May Fourth China.

For just as radicals proposed the equality of women, they could not escape a larger discourse in which femininity was associated with weakness and national disgrace, while masculine qualities of aggressiveness and bravery were associated with national salvation. Women were increasingly expected to act like men – up to a point. Moreover, Chen Duxiu, Lu Xun, and other radicals directly attacked the effeminate "pale-faced scholar." China was criticized as decadent and degenerate. The "race" itself had been degenerating for hundreds, perhaps thousands of years.[33] Attacks on polygamy and concubinage might be made in terms of individual rights, but they were also said to weaken the race. The double standard whereby men were allowed multiple partners, it was said, spread syphilis. Eugenics became a popular cause. "Race betterment" would be achieved through monogamous marriage between healthy partners. Castration and emasculation became metaphors for the fate of the nation.

Prostitution and also homosexuality became symbols of China's ills. Both were outside of legal marriage and neither contributed to procreation and the advancement of the nation. The International Settlement of Shanghai alone was estimated to provide employment for 70,000 prostitutes, servicing the increasing numbers of unattached male workers. In the hygienic version of Chinese nationalism, both female lust and male excess weakened the individual and therefore the nation. This was not entirely a new idea. Female sexuality had been tightly regulated by law and custom during the Ming and Qing dynasties. Male sexuality, on the other hand, was given some scope outside of the needs of the patriline. Traditional elites tended not to distinguish "homosexual" and "heterosexual" categories of behavior, individual preference, or personality types. Rather, the more fundamental sexual categories were the active penetrant and the passive penetrated, who could be either women or men (boys).[34] The penetrated male was analogized to a female, as younger and lower in the hierarchy. Thus society made room for a master sodomizing a servant, a military officer a soldier, and an older man a youth. No special shame attached to the active partner, though by the Qing even consensual homosexual acts were illegal. There was also something of a tradition of adolescent male lovers (less is known about lesbianism), though boys of good families would certainly be expected to take wives and eventually become family heads in their own right.

Such attitudes changed radically in the twentieth century. Following the Western medicalization of homosexuality, progressive Chinese associated it with the decadence of the old culture. Homosexuality was for the first time medicalized as an aberration or mental illness. It became the modern, healthy view to require the rehabilitation of prostitutes and homosexuals. As prostitution could spread syphilis literally, so homosexuality was conceived as spreading "like syphilis" from its unnatural haunts in armies, monasteries, and the male brothels.

The new "scientific" sexual discourse ended the Qing's obsession with female chastity, creating in its stead a basic norm of legitimate sex within the nuclear family. The husband was expected to penetrate his wife; both were expected to behave with fidelity. But this norm remained far from the equality and liberation sought by some women. For women remained tied to their role in the family as wife and mother, while the role of father and husband included the public realm as well. Both traditional cosmology and modern biology treated men as inherently active and women as passive.

Political activists proclaimed that a strong, modern nation needed healthy, modern sexual attitudes. Yet did sexual practices really change?

That is impossible to say, but the family system certainly changed for the urban middle classes: urban youth had unprecedented opportunities for meeting one another outside of their parents' arrangements. They worked and studied together, saw each other in restaurants and at films, and so "love marriages" based on monogamous intentions became the norm in China's cities. The openly polygamous gentry "big family" gradually disappeared. These were trends that, to a degree, also influenced urban working-class behavior and rural elites. Birth-control literature and devices were widely available in cities by the 1920s. But whether rates of adultery, cohabitation, premarital sex, gay sex, and visits to prostitutes actually changed before the Communists established a strict family regime after 1949 is hard to say. What can be concluded is that sexuality and family structure are inherently political issues. In a sense, female sexuality emerged into public consciousness over the course of the May Fourth movement; it was inseparable from the issues of individual emancipation and the future of China.

# 9 National identity, Marxism, and social justice

By the 1920s the relationship between intellectuals and society had been transformed. "Scholars" were no longer a status group marked by their mastery of sacred or classical texts and eligibility for official posts. Instead, a new term for intellectuals, "knowledgeable elements," signaled that they had become a specialized professional group. They no longer claimed a special relationship with the imperial center, but they did identify themselves with the modern nation. Their self-appointed task was to create new narratives of the nation, of the Chinese people moving through time, of the cultural essence, of Chinese historical destiny. Indeed, many possessed a heroic self-image appropriate for those who would awake the sleeping masses, revive what had become moribund and decadent, and help create a new world. But exactly what could intellectuals contribute to a society in violent flux, facing rapacious forces within and without, and populated by farmers whose ways had not fundamentally changed in centuries?

The burden of the past lay heavily on the new intellectuals. The New Culture movement had, of course, largely rejected the past, particularly everything that could be labeled "Confucian," as dead weight, authoritarian, anti-scientific, anti-democratic, and inherently and unreflectively conservative. This view led into the Chinese Marxist critique of the class nature of Confucianism in the 1920s and 1930s. Marxists condemned Confucianism as the ideology of the feudal landlord class, an ideology that justified exploitation of the peasantry under a false disguise of paternalism and a hegemonic ideology that promoted "false consciousness" by trying to convince peasants and workers that they deserved their cruel fate.

What was the role of Confucianism in the twentieth century? It is sometimes said that China's intellectuals were in search of a new orthodoxy to replace the lost certainties of their ancestors. As Confucianism had provided an orthodoxy that seemed to answer all questions, so, finally, Marxism came to the fore as a similarly complete ideology. The content was different but the social functions were similar. In its crudest form, this theory argues continuity in content as well: from the "oriental despotism" of the imperial age to the communist despotism of the Maoist years. Obviously, this assumes that Marxism is somehow better fitted to become orthodoxy than anarchism, liberalism, or other worldviews that attracted many intellectuals – a proposition that needs proving. A more fundamental problem is that no examination of China's twentieth century can accept the idea that there was any kind of simple route away from the imperial age. Even the briefest glance at Chinese intellectuals shows a complex search for truth, not a willful seeking for new orthodoxies. None the less, as historian Joseph Levenson pointed out, "the appearance of survivals [of tradition in Communist China] is by no means just a trick of the eye." However, "many bricks of the old structure are still around – but not the structure."[1]

Intellectuals were searching for living truths relevant to social reality. This perhaps reflected the major part of the Confucian tradition that emphasized practice, not the metaphysical, eternal truth of the Platonic tradition. It explains the enormous appeal of liberalism in the form of Deweyan pragmatism as well as Marxism. Indeed, another problem with the view that Marxism represented little more than new wine in the old bottles of orthodoxy is that Confucianism demanded relatively little in the way of ideological commitment. And whatever the appeal of orthodoxies under certain circumstances, the rapid unraveling of Chinese Marxism at the close of the twentieth century demonstrated that there is no special Chinese affinity for orthodoxy.

None the less, if the Confucian heritage little affected the content of the new thought, it may have shaped the ways intellectuals conceived their task. The historian Lin Yü-sheng has pointed out that the very totalism of the New Culture attack on Confucianism (that there was nothing of value whatsoever, that it had to be eradicated completely) reflected a traditional approach to cultural questions.[2] In particular, the faith that correct intellectual formations will lead to correct actions reflected Confucian epistemology, in Lin's view. The May Fourth generation, too, believed that it was necessary and possible to formulate correct ideas, which would meet all needs. The idea that even the most iconoclastic critics of tradition were still affected by that tradition on some level is at once ironic and unsurprising. Yet it is not clear that iconoclasm really describes mainstream thought. Iconoclasts like Chen Duxiu, Lu Xun, and Hu Shi certainly constructed powerful critiques of tradition, critiques that dominated the New Culture movement and continued to influence ideologies through the May Fourth movement and into the 1930s and beyond – but also critiques that were challenged in many ways. Quite a few intellectuals were roughly "Confucian" in their emphasis on personal morality and their faith that good individuals could serve as models for the community.

For all their eloquence, the iconoclasts cannot command all our attention. Given the variety of intellectual responses to China's problems, including efforts to reshape Confucianism, the roles of tradition should be sought fortuitously and in unexpected places. Given the existential dilemmas facing intellectuals, their spiritual quests should not be neglected. It is also important to remember that, although Marxism came eventually to dominate intellectual life, only a small minority of intellectuals actually converted to Marxism between 1920 and 1949. Therefore, the intellectual history of the May Fourth era should not be devoted *entirely* to explaining the triumph of Marxism.

Finally, another approach to the problem of tradition suggests that new ideas from the West were attractive because they offered solutions to old problems. In other words, Confucianism had set the terms in which the new thought would be placed. The historian Thomas Metzger posits that the Neo-Confucian tradition stemming back to the eleventh century had reached a kind of impasse by the eighteenth century. Individuals were supposed to pursue sagehood, but in practice they could neither perfect themselves nor lead society to its proper state. This led to intense anxieties, so "the developing Chinese decision at the turn of our century to modernize was not simply based on the discovery that certain Western methods were superior to native ones. Rather, these Western methods proved enormously appealing just because they seemed useful for solving agonizing problems and realizing social ideals with which Confucians had long been preoccupied." That is, the West's science and technology, its economic growth, and its ability to turn subjects into citizens seemed to meet traditional Chinese goals. Thus, "to a large extent, it was the indigenous, intense, centuries-old desire to escape from a metaphysical, psychological, political, and economic predicament which led many Chinese enthusiastically to devote their lives to the overthrow of traditionally revered institutions and the adoption of strange and foreign ways."[3]

This view contrasts with that of the early German sociologist Max Weber, who postulated that Confucianism had reduced the tension between ideal and reality to a minimum, and so lacked the transformative impulse and capacity that he saw in Protestantism. However, Metzger's interpretation supports the basic Weberian view of a China unable to change; both views make Western thought into an instrumentality. The problem is that this account remains reductionist: persons trying to think through problems merely fill out a schema beyond their design. Confucians were neither in such a predicament as Metzger suggests, nor was there such continuity in goals as he suggests. By no means did the Confucian essence emerge unchanged from the encounter with Western categories of thought. Nor, obviously, did the new intellectuals mean it to. Like the literati of old, the modern Chinese intelligentsia sought order, but it was a very different order. Nationalism, citizenship (political participation of the masses), progress and evolutionism, egalitarianism, the glorification of struggle: such goals represent major discontinuity with the past. We must take them seriously.

None the less, these attempts to make sense of Chinese intellectuals trying to make sense of their world offer insights that this chapter will attempt to assess. Overall, the May Fourth intellectuals may be divided into the usual suspects: liberals (or moderates), conservatives, and radicals. This division is somewhat anachronistic but certainly heuristically justified. We cannot give absolute definitions of what, say, a "conservative" is, but the three tendencies can be seen in relation to one another. Of course, there were debates and deep internal divisions within the groups as well as the overlapping contacts and themes between them. It is useful to distinguish between politics and culture – a given intellectual might be culturally conservative but politically reformist (Liang Shuming). Others were fairly conservative politically but wanted radical cultural change (Hu Shi). And by no means did "conservatism" imply opposition to all change. But such labels provide a convenient introduction to the range of intellectual possibilities. To sort out the intellectual trends of the May Fourth period, this chapter will examine three debates. First, the "problems versus isms" debate, beginning in 1919, which did much to distinguish political liberalism and radicalism, and in a sense marks the emergence of Marxism. Second, the "science versus metaphysics" debate of 1923 that did much to establish the conservative critique of Westernization. And third, the debate between anarchists and Marxists in the late 1920s, marking the demise of what had previously been highly idealistic forms of radicalism and the victory of Marxism-Leninism as the dominant form of radicalism.

## "Problems versus isms" and liberalism versus Marxism-Leninism

The success of the Russian Revolution of 1917, coupled with the disillusionment with Wilsonian liberalism in the wake of the Versailles Treaty, produced preliminary interest in Marxism. Leninism gave Marxism a practical expression it had hitherto lacked in the eyes of Chinese radicals, and the Russian Revolution seemed to prove that it was a workable formula. Conversion to Marxism was slow to develop, and commitment to the *discipline* of the Marxist-Leninist party even slower, but there was much interest in what appeared to be a successful plan for revolution. Hu Shi, for one, was disturbed by the appeal of Marxism. For all the radicalism of Hu's attacks on Confucianism, he favored working within the political status quo as much as possible. He continued to believe that the cultural regeneration of the Chinese people had to precede political activism.

Hu Shi therefore tried to discredit Marxism with a plea for pragmatism, or what he preferred to call "experimentalism." Instead of talking about general theories, abstract propositions – "isms" – people should deal with concrete problems amenable to specific solutions. Factory conditions and women's rights should be approached separately, for example, and not treated as symptoms of some common, underlying problem. Hu thus wanted to find specific and gradual, even partial, solutions to China's problems. Reforms, not revolution. He advocated his mentor John Dewey's approach of using calm, scientific inquiry to solve social problems. Even democracy was simply a matter of practice. "The only way to have democracy is to have democracy," Hu wrote as early as 1915.[4] Many historians have pointed out the fragility of Hu's hopes and the weaknesses of liberalism in the Chinese setting. Reformism implied the existence of a social consensus that in fact still needed to be built. Indeed, by the 1930s Hu's was a marginal view. Calls for gradualism seemed pusillanimous and calls for calm seemed simply ignorant. Marxism, meanwhile, claimed to be entirely scientific, but not gradualist. Justifiably or not, Hu's calls for patient optimism seemed to lack a certain sympathy for the horrendous conditions in which so many Chinese found themselves.

None the less, Yan Yangchu (1893–1990) illustrates liberalism's potential for social reform. Known as Jimmy Yen in the United States, where he received graduate training and maintained sources of support and fund-raising, he began his career with the YMCA.[5] Yan was part of the "social gospel" movement in the 1920s, whereby Christian missionaries began spending more time providing social services than worrying about conversions. Spearheaded by the American Protestants who dominated the Chinese missionary scene by this time, effort went into such programs as hospitals, schools, orphanages, career-training for beggars and prostitutes, and sanitation campaigns. Yan worked on literacy programs, vastly enlarging adult education with networks of schools, volunteer teachers, student-teachers, and what can only be called savvy marketing to attract students after their long day's work. New night school classes might be advertised with marching bands, for example.

Yan's attention was soon directed toward rural issues, and his organization founded an experimental project in Dingxian, Hebei. There Yan built schools, an agricultural extension program, a health-care system, and farmers' cooperatives. The Dingxian project did not bring in outside money and experts so much as it mobilized local resources, including the enthusiasm of ordinary villagers. Agricultural reforms, for example, resulted from working closely with local farmers to find appropriate and practical technology; they did not depend on importing costly scientific machines that did not fit local conditions anyway. Yan's cadres worked closely with farmers to find usable hybrids, fertilizers, breeding techniques, pumps, and insecticides to raise productivity. Cooperatives both to provide credit and to aid marketing were important tools where peasants were often in debt to middlemen. Yan's dream was to move from educational reforms to economic improvement and local mobilization, to cooperatives to free the farmers from the problems of price manipulation and credit squeeze, to light industrialization, and finally to true village democracy. Indeed, Yan wanted to turn the peasants into full citizens. But local and national political leaders put limits on reform – land distribution was *not* on the agenda. The new political operas that Yan's cadres wrote, dealing with such village problems as indebtedness, had to draw back from revolutionary implications lest officials shut them down. So, while audiences might be chanting "kill the usurer," actors on stage resolved the plot by organizing themselves to hold the usurer for official arrest.

In the eyes of more radical intellectuals, the reformism of Hu and Yan was doomed. Li Dazhao replied to Hu's critique of "isms." Li agreed about the need to be concrete, but called for collective action. He abandoned his earlier faith that managers or technicians could solve problems; rather, Li now emphasized a kind of democratic populism. A majority should determine that a problem existed and what course of action to take. And the majority could only do so in the context of its general ideals, out of its "collective sense of dissatisfaction."[6] Li implied that Hu's ideas might be suitable for a more advanced society, but in China – subject to warlord misrule and imperialist incursion, fragmented, disorganized, and decaying – a piecemeal approach could not work. Instead, the economic infrastructure presented an opportunity for a fundamental solution. He confessed, "I recognize that my recent discussions have mostly been empty talk [existing only] on paper with little involvement in practical problems. From now on I vow to go out and work in the practical movement."[7] But Li's version of pragmatism tied concrete problems to fundamental social reform rather than trying, like Hu, to isolate them. Li believed that once China experienced a social revolution, the remaining, particular problems would by and large solve themselves. Li and other radicals were increasingly looking to Leninist Russia as a model of political revolution and nation-building.

Several important issues underlay the debate. One was the question of means versus ends. Hu Shi did not want to get his hands dirty with the compromises and betrayals inherent to political movements. His was a self-avowedly elitist approach where experts would make decisions. Li had vowed to take action, though his vision of political process had more to do with awakening a sleeping nation than the deal-making and saber-rattling of warlordism. Hu did not trust "the people" as Li did; on the other hand, Li was turning away from constitutionalism and parliamentary democracy and adopting something closer to the "general will" – Li imbued the people with something like a mystical single consciousness. Hu's instrumentalist understanding of democracy would trust educated people to make the correct decision after informed discussion. However, Hu recognized the ignorance and backwardness of the majority of the populace and put his trust in professionalization and administrative expertise. Hu thus held that the exact nature of the regime (warlord or democratic) mattered less for the time being than trying to place competent managers and honest administrators in the civil service. But Hu did not confront the problem of how to assure administration remained responsible to the people. More urgently, he failed to confront the reality of warlord regimes that had neither the interest nor the capability to institute competent administration.

Li Dazhao at least had an answer for the second problem: revolution. Li's populism – his faith in the people – was extremely important in his turn to Marxism, and continued to shape his understanding of Marxism. After 1919 he saw the Bolshevik world Lenin was creating in Russia as a "workers' government" that would turn all citizens into workers. Li thought the Russian Revolution would be to the twentieth century what the French Revolution had been to the nineteenth. He rationalized the "dictatorship of the proletariat" as a brief, transitional phase necessary for the elimination of the bourgeoisie. In a society without classes, government would become a matter of good administration of the popular will rather than an arena of competing interests. Li paid little attention to Lenin's notion of the vanguard role of the Party, and his basic frame of reference remained more generally socialist or even anarchist.[8] Humanitarianism, mutual aid, community, and equality remained his watchwords. He even hoped, like most radicals, that China could avoid the revolutionary violence of class struggle – or if this was not possible, then class struggle was an unfortunately necessary means to good ends. How could a man with these views consider himself a Marxist?

At first, Li was more of a commentator than a believer. Working as head librarian at Beida, Li published his views on Russia and his growing knowledge of Marxism, and discussed them with colleagues and students. Mao Zedong, a young graduate from a provincial teachers' college, worked at the Beida library and came into contact with Li in late 1918. Most of the founders of the Chinese Communist Party in 1921 and 1922 came out of this environment.[9] They first appreciated its political effectiveness: more Russian Leninism than German Marxism. They also appreciated its analytical powers: how Chinese history and the intrusion of Western imperialism could be understood through the workings of economic forces and class struggle. Actually, China's early communists remained highly critical of Marxism for what they perceived as its lack of an ethical or humanist dimension. But they drew strength from the Marxist doctrine of "historical materialism" in so far as it placed humans in their society and tried to understand them as social beings. Li Dazhao reconceptualized history as a story of progress fueled by struggle. And he consistently favored a voluntarist approach to Marxism, emphasizing not the economic forces that shape individual destinies but rather focusing on how humans were largely free to determine their own history. As a philosophy, voluntarism emphasizes the role of the will.

At the same time, the intellectuals were often baffled by Marxism's complexities. Li quoted a German scholar who denied that anyone could understand Marxism before he or she reached 50. Above all, then, Marxism-Leninism's appeal lay in its promise to guide to practice, not in its abstract philosophy. Chen Duxiu seized upon Party organization and popular mobilization as the keys to revolutionary action. With his usual lack of reserve, by 1920 Chen was attacking individualism – for which he previously served as China's foremost spokesman – on the grounds it was anti-social, bourgeois, and even nihilist.

Another feature of Li Dazhao's thought was his identification of the collectivity with its poorest members. In this, Li anticipated much of Mao Zedong's thinking.[10] It was peasants, said Li, who constituted most of China's working class. Unlike Marx, who relegated peasants, with their ownership of small farms or at least their desire to own land, to the petty bourgeoisie, Li saw in peasants both revolutionary potential and a kind of natural goodness. Li, himself the offspring of relatively well-off farmers, might be presumed to understand village society better than many of the urban-raised intellectuals around him (or Marx). He denied that class divisions within the village were as destructive as outside forces on China's villages. Moreover, he saw China itself as a "proletarian nation" surrounded by harmful powers. That is, all Chinese were at least potentially members of the revolutionary working class.

Most important, he gave a new role to the intelligentsia and especially to students. They were to go to the villages, work with the peasants, improve the lives of the peasantry, and in the process give meaning to their own lives. Li's was not the first voice to call for "going to the people," but he emphasized that both parties would benefit from the exchange.

> My young friends drifting about the cities! You should know that the cities are full of crime, and that great contentment is to be found in the villages; that life in the city is more or less the life of a ghost, but that the work going on in the villages is the work of people; that the air in the city is foul and the air in the country is pure ... do something to develop the village or to improve the livelihood of the peasants.[11]

Once awakened, the people would be able to cast aside the intellectuals and act on their own. Intellectuals and students were not permanently to be teachers, paternalistically dispensing higher wisdom; they were to be catalysts, provoking an independent reaction. Li's populism was widespread in the 1920s. In an essay written in the summer of 1919, for example, Mao Zedong called for a vast social and political movement. There is no hint of Marxism in the essay and not much sense of an intellectual or political vanguard that would lead the revolution. Rather, Mao called for a highly inclusive mass politics – a "great union of the popular masses" to undertake thorough reform.

> Why is the great union of the popular masses so terribly effective? Because the popular masses in any country are necessarily more numerous than the aristocracy, the capitalists and the other powerful people in a single country.... If we truly want to achieve a great union ... we must necessarily have all sorts of small unions to serve as its foundation. The human race has an innate talent for uniting together ... peasants, workers, students, women, primary-school teachers, rickshaw boys and others of all sorts....
> The more profound the oppression, the greater its resistance; that which has accumulated for a long time will surely burst forth quickly.[12]

Perhaps the germs of class struggle are here, but so is a conviction in the fundamental unity of the Chinese people and, indeed, of international brotherhood. In this, Mao was echoing Kang Youwei's cosmopolitan utopianism.

The cautious and piecemeal liberalism of Hu Shi, resting on a more pessimistic if not cynical view of human nature, had little patience for writings like Mao's. In fact, Mao would later complain that the major figures at Beida, like Hu, snubbed him. We will return to Mao. Nor was this the last of Hu Shi. Yet some of the weaknesses of liberalism faced in China should already be clear. Above all, liberals, with their abhorrence of violence and militarism, had no way to suggest how the reformist programs they favored could be executed. As long as warlords and foreign powers controlled China, they wielded veto-power over any attempts to ameliorate the situation. As well, liberalism lacked a social base. A liberal political system depends on a liberal society based on procedural consensus. Political losers have to be prepared to wait and make their case again, and political winners have to be prepared to give them that chance. As many observers noted, China's bourgeoisie or middle class was small and weak. Perhaps political consensus might have emerged from a stable rural society, but the Chinese countryside was far from stable. Endemic violence made liberalism irrelevant. For although liberalism, with its emphasis on individualism and property rights, seems to negate the state, it actually depends on a strong civil society coinciding with a strong state able to monopolize violence.

Still, Chinese liberalism should not be underestimated either. Prominent liberals and their followers basically dominated the worlds of education, journalism, publishing, and perhaps even commerce. Not only were a few warlords sympathetic to reform, but also the limitations of warlord power often presented interstices within which the liberals could work. Thus could a Cai Yuanpei become president of Beida. Forced to compromise with the powers-that-be, whether of the right or, later, the left, liberals acknowledged the righteousness of nationalist concerns, at least parts of Confucian morality, and peasant uprisings, without losing their essential respect for the individual or limited government.

### "Science versus metaphysics" and modern Chinese conservatism

If many of China's students became disillusioned with Wilsonian liberalism in the wake of World War I, turning to the left, others were disillusioned by the war itself and rediscovered Confucianism. Liang Qichao, for one, found his faith in progress challenged. If the West represented a better future, then how had it collapsed into insane warfare? Visiting Europe in 1919, he met the anti-positivist, intuitionist philosopher Henri Bergson, and concluded that Europeans "have dreamt the dream of the omnipotence of science, but today they are declaring the bankruptcy of science."[13] Bergson, who also appealed to Li Dazhao, emphasized the limitations of rational thought. Rationality was a useful tool, he said, but insufficient to grasp the ceaseless flux of the universe. Only intuition or the unconscious and disinterested mind can do that and also allow the self to attain freedom. For Liang,

Bergson and other critics of Enlightenment rationalism confirmed his sense that the Chinese tradition had something to offer China and the world. Chinese thought did not have all the answers, but its humanism could complement the technological successes of the West. Liang particularly focused on the Confucian–Mencian ideal of *ren*, compassion. In contrast to Western competitiveness, he said, *ren* taught harmony and compromise. Liang's ultimate vision was an amalgamated universal culture to which various civilizations would contribute. It is worth noting that Bertrand Russell, no friend of intuitionism, shared this composite view of a new world civilization. After his successful May Fourth speaking tour of China, Russell wrote: "The distinctive merit of our civilization, I should say, is the scientific method; the distinctive merit of the Chinese is a just conception of the ends of life."[14]

In 1923 certain Chinese thinkers mounted a direct attack on science's inability to answer the important questions. Science was analytical, objective, and useful for solving practical problems. But ultimately more important was "philosophy of life": understanding the human experience. Philosophy of life was the opposite of science: synthetic, subjective, and with moral concerns. Zhang Junmai (1886–1969) frankly laid out the heart of the issue in East-versus-West terms. "The controversy throughout our country in recent times over the New Culture, and the direction of cultural change, is not extraneous to the philosophy of life. We have our culture. The West has western culture. How are we to select what is beneficial from the West and get rid of what is harmful?" For all of science's advances in understanding nature, it had little to say about the good or just life. For that, Zhang turned to Confucianism.

Zhang was a disciple of Liang Qichao and had traveled with him in 1919 to Europe, where he stayed to study with Rudolph Eucken and read Henri Bergson and Hans Driesch. Ding Wenjiang (1888–1936), a professional geologist, led the defense of science, soon joined by Hu Shi, Chen Duxiu, and others. Ding's was not a crude positivism; he emphasized that the methodology of science guaranteed not an absolute grasp of reality but one of truth, defined as verifiable sense-data. But he insisted that scientific methodology was applicable to all questions. Moreover, the defenders of science remained loyal to evolutionism and progress. Solutions to human drudgery and disease would only come through science, the precondition for true social and moral improvement.

Clearly a variety of issues, albeit linked, was being raised – not so much science versus metaphysics but how to define roles for the scientific and the spiritual or intuitive; not so much West versus East but how to selectively adapt; not so much determinism versus free will but how to balance inner and outer freedom. In the temper of the times, the "scientists" were acknowledged the winners of the debate. But Confucianism continued to produce articulate defenders. It is worth noting that Zhang Junmai himself was no obscurantist. He offered respect for science in its proper place; he was also a believer in constitutionalism and social democracy. Both the "scientists" and the "Confucians" basically supported democratic socialism.

A more radical challenge to accepted May Fourth verities came from Liang Shuming (1893–1988).[15] Liang explicitly denied that Chinese tradition should be junked, and he even repudiated the idea of "taking the best of East and West." For syncretism still negated the *essence* of Chinese civilization. It thus denied the Chinese their identity. Liang Shuming accepted modern technology, but he was deliberately trying to save the remnants of a specifically Confucian essence. Liang was not alone in this endeavor. Philosophers like Xiong Shili emphasized the role of empathy and intuition in creating the good person. Generally accepting science (not just technology) and scientific values like rationality and empiricism, they denied that science could solve all human problems or provide a basis for morality. The point is that in making this critique of science, they turned to the Confucian tradition for answers.[16] In doing so, they marginalized themselves from the New Culture–May Fourth "mainstream" and did not seem responsive to China's urgent needs. At the level of high philosophy, Xiong's somewhat religious ontology was not meant to speak directly to politicized students or ordinary workers. But his attempt to relate traditional philosophical ideas to existential problems facing the Chinese of his day did attract a few followers. These men arguably had an influence on Chinese thought that emerged more prominently in the post-war years, after 1950.

Liang Shuming, however, did connect his philosophy to immediate social problems. He argued that human progress resulted from dealing with the environment: the first stage is the subjugation of nature, the second stage is the betterment of the community – the social ethic – and the third stage is one of spirituality. The stages can also be represented synchronically: as seen in the West, China, and India, respectively. This at least had the advantage of turning Orientalist teleologies around, for here it is not "the East" which appears as the undifferentiated Other but the West. Not a West that represents final perfection, but just the opposite. Liang ascribed the evident superiority of the West not to its being more advanced but its being more primitive. Western technology represented an earlier stage of human evolution. China, he admitted, had made the mistake of turning away from the way of aggression, vitality, and nature-subduing too early. But now the West was moving into the second stage, as seen by the rebellion of contemporary Western philosophers such as Bergson against positivism and by the new humanitarian interest in socialism there. Liang's conclusion? China must "accept Western culture as a whole but make some fundamental changes." So in the end Liang had to turn to syncretism after all. But he strongly believed that Chinese culture would mark the *next* stage of world evolution. And what was this Chinese culture? Liang's answer was that "The fundamental spirit of Chinese culture is the harmony and moderation of ideas and desires."[17]

In particular, Liang believed that democracy, individualism (personal freedoms and rights), and, up to a point, science, were of value to the group and the individual. The West's economic growth was ultimately an expression of its decision to grapple with nature directly and aggressively. However, the environment had been conquered but humanity was left unsatisfied and spiritually cramped. Their selfishness had alienated Westerners from humanity and cut them off from the cosmos. Liang was not simply turning the West's critique of the East back on itself. For not only did he accept the virtues of the West, but he was echoing a feeling of self-doubt widely felt in Europe in the years after World War I. Yet unlike, say, Zhang Zhidong, Liang had to struggle for cultural confidence. The Chinese spirit he wanted to promote in fact needed promotion; he could not take it for granted. Indeed, raised by a progressive Confucian father, his education had been considerably less classics-oriented than Chen Duxiu's or Hu Shi's. He had attended modern schools with Western curricula. Liang was politicized by the events leading up to the Revolution of 1911, and then became a Buddhist, before he turned to Confucianism. One senses in Liang's life a personal spiritual quest. And if Liang had thoroughly absorbed certain Western notions, he still insisted that certain other basic values were uniquely Chinese: that humanity was good, for example. The Confucianism of his mature years was thus re-forged and hardened.

What exactly, then, did China have to offer the world? For Liang, the Confucian notion of *ren* was the true spirit of Chinese culture. However, without the material resources to carry out this ideal, Chinese culture had ossified and society had become oppressive. Now that the world was ready for a more harmonizing approach, the Chinese conception of the universal human feelings that sprang from the parent–child relationship would fill the void left by crass materialism.

Liang was no mere cultural patriot. His scheme of epochal progress did not stop with Chinese harmony but continued to the final stage of human evolution in Indian nirvana. Liang's 1921 book, *Eastern and Western Cultures and their Philosophies*, was quite popular, though it was unkindly remarked that Liang was most respected among high school teachers (rather than the *haut* intelligentsia). Liang's criticism of the West's "excesses" was widely shared, and not just by conservatives. But Hu Shi's reply was uncompromising. Hu found spiritual qualities not in China's poverty and backwardness but in the West's search for material improvement, which he said rested on its quest for truth. In the "race course" of human evolution, China had simply fallen behind. Even more pointedly, Lu Xun satirized "Eastern spirituality" and its promoters in his short stories. In "Kong Yiji" the main character Kong (Confucius's surname) is a failed scholar in ragged clothes, a poverty-stricken thief, and a drunkard unable to pay his bar bill, who still sees himself as a highly civilized, superior, and cultured gentleman. In "The True Story of Ah Q" Ah Q is not only a petty thief, lecher, and bum, but whenever he is beaten up he regards his defeat as a spiritual victory. "Then Ah Q, clutching at the root of his queue, his head on one side, would say, 'Beating an insect – how about that? I am an insect – now will you let me go?' … In less than ten seconds, however, Ah Q would walk away also satisfied that he had won, thinking that he was the 'Number One self-belittler,' and that after subtracting 'self-belittler' what remained was 'Number One'."[18]

Liang Shuming is especially interesting because he pursued his Confucian ideals in a utopian experiment of rural social reforms. Inspired by the Communists' example of successful peasant organizing in the late 1920s, he recognized the problems of poverty, low productivity, and peasant alienation from the sources of power. He too criticised ameliorative reforms and charity projects, and he found that even well-intentioned government bureaucracies were too heavy handed. In the 1930s in a small area in Shandong he and his disciples were able to help peasants adopt new technologies and improve productivity. But he failed to achieve social mobilization of the peasants, simply because he did not intend for them to have direct political power. His disciples did not evolve into a new class of local leaders. Liang's efforts remained limited in scope; he failed to revitalize the countryside that he himself took to be the locus of Chinese identity.

The effort to find something strong and living in the Chinese tradition was not limited to self-proclaimed Confucians. Buddhism experienced something of a revival in the early decades of the twentieth century as well. Under the leadership of the reformist monk Taixu (1890–1947) some Buddhist institutions such as schools and lay societies, as well as monasteries, moved in a more this-worldly direction, not unlike the "social gospel" of the progressive wing of Christian missionaries.[19] Taixu thus emphasized the need for monks and lay believers to work together to provide *systematic* charity to poor families, medical clinics, and free, modern schools. Taixu tried to form a loose synthesis of the various schools of Chinese Buddhism – from Chan (Zen) and Pure Land to the more esoteric Huayan and Tantric traditions – claiming that none possessed the complete truth but all were legitimately based on the Buddha's teachings. And he tried to reshape traditional Mahayana beliefs so they would be compatible with modern science, though he too noted the failure of science to provide moral or spiritual grounding. Buddhism transcended the limitations of science, offering "inward illumination" and intuitive understanding. Clearly, the ideas of Taixu, Liang Shuming, Zhang Junmai, and the late Liang Qichao overlapped in important respects, not the least of which was their faith in social progress.

Taixu foresaw the conversion of the entire world to Buddhist principles. Though his reforms did not, in his own lifetime, affect the majority of Buddhist institutions and believers, who continued traditional practices, Taixu's self-appointed task to make the Buddhist dharma useful and meaningful to conservatives and progressives, and to Chinese and foreigners, in the end inspired many and was thus a significant element of intellectual life in the Republic. Liang Shuming's attraction to Buddhism was in fact a quite widespread phenomenon. Still, the attempt to make creative use of tradition while pursuing modernity could never be easy, either intellectually or psychologically.

## Anarchists versus communists: Defining Marxism

The tendency of historians to define "May Fourth" in terms of "radicalism" and "iconoclasm" seems overdrawn. The May Fourth thinkers were not all radicals, either culturally or politically. But it seems no exaggeration to say that belief in socialism of one kind or another was widely shared across the spectrum. Zhang Junmai and Liang Shuming counted themselves as socialists. At the other end of the political spectrum, anarchists were almost all supporters of communism, though a few exponents of extreme individualism and followers of Nietzsche and Max Stirner existed. Sun Yat-sen advocated a kind of state socialism, as we have seen, and his followers were among China's first serious students of Marxism. Guild socialism, syndicalism, labor-learning, and the New Village movement, were all variations on the theme of social radicalism. Marxist ideas thus had to compete, first, not with conservative or liberal ideas but with other forms of socialism. Chinese radicalism in the May Fourth era had a basically anarchist flavor.[20] Witness the words of the philosophy polymath and one of the founders of the CCP, Zhang Shenfu (1893–1986), who explained his conversion to Marxism in 1920: "My basic opinion is simply this: destroy the state, burn down class barriers and marriage. Having realized the evil that is capitalism … I have an absolute faith in socialism. Communism is the essence of socialism, so naturally I have an absolute faith in communism."[21]

Hundreds of anarchist groups were formed in the wake of May Fourth. Shenfu's disciples founded newspapers and established propaganda bureaus. Most of these efforts were ephemeral, but they illustrate the appeal of anarchist ideas – wide if not always deep. Radicals wanted to see the fundamental restructuring of society along more egalitarian and democratic lines. Social revolution was expected to be inclusive, and hence minimally violent (coercion might only been needed against warlords and the small number of comprador bourgeoisie). Mutual aid, adapted from Kropotkin, was the keystone of Chinese anarchism, designed to complement and complete the picture of social struggle and competition presented in Darwinism. What we might call "mutual aid thinking" was widespread in the May Fourth era. It could even be seen as an extension of the Confucian emphasis on social harmony, though without Confucianism's hierarchical thinking. And mutual aid offered another way to think about organized political action outside of the boundaries imposed by militarism.

To begin with, anarchists and Marxists shared a great deal. The CCP itself was organized in the early 1920s with many anarchist members; it took several years for the anarchists to leave or be expelled. Ideologically, the two shared a belief in social revolution. The early Marxists also tended to start with a fairly inclusive notion of revolution, with an emphasis on voluntarism: the ability of people to make changes in society according to their will. The strain of Marxism that emphasized economic determinism was never popular in China. Li Dazhao, for one, kept the ethico-spiritual transformation of humanity through "mutual aid" constantly in mind.

Furthermore, both groups believed in democracy of a participatory and radical kind. They combined individual liberation and community solidarity. On the one hand, many communists were nearly as critical of the state as anarchists, and on the other, many anarchists increasingly accepted class struggle and even a special role for the proletariat. The very term "communism" in Chinese was at this time largely associated with the compound "anarcho-communism."

Both anarchism and communism, as modern political ideologies, were Western imports. They represented a new language to talk about social questions, and Chinese thinkers had to adopt neologisms to label such imported intellectual systems. Anarchism literally refers to something like the "doctrine of no-government," while communism might be called the "doctrine of shared-property." Translation into Chinese did not significantly affect the meaning of the terms, though the range of connotations differed. The Marxist notion of "proletariat" or industrial working class was translated as the "property-less class" (which is faithful to the root meaning of proletariat), but the Chinese were more inclusive than Marx. Foreign loan words, precisely because of their obvious origins, were understood to need defining and could not be taken at face value. The process of defining terms was part of the modernization of political discourse. Such terms were often derived from the Japanese, who dealt with many of the same problems a generation earlier.

One result of the extensive use of neologisms and new concepts was to make political discussions rather strange for everyone. Political concepts were defamiliarized. Theorists could find Chinese precedents for democracy and socialism, even anarchism, but these precedents were used to explain and define what still remained new concepts. Ideologies were seen as modern, whether or not they were entirely Western. And none seemed intrinsically less strange or more idealistic than any other.

Anarchists and communists initially did not disagree much about democracy or the role of the state. Chinese had to educate themselves on the finer points of correct Marxist-Leninist ideology. Their debates with the anarchists were part of this education. The first major disagreement was over revolutionary strategy. Anarchists distrusted the communist (or Bolshevik) emphasis on Party organization, the discipline required of Party members, and the whole notion of a leading vanguard. While most anarchists appreciated the power of class struggle, they would not make it the keystone of the revolution. They proposed turning power over to the "whole people" as rapidly as possible. And they grew increasingly dubious of events unfolding in the Soviet Union under Lenin.

In 1921 Chen Duxiu and Ou Shengbai (1893–1973), a young anarchist student at Beida, debated their differences. Reprinting the debate in *New Youth*, Chen ridiculed Ou's vision of a society without any state structures to compel obedience to social norms.[22] What about reactionaries and criminals? For his part, Ou essentially denied that a conflict existed between the individual and the group. He pointed out that he was not advocating the extreme individualism associated with some anarchists, and he thought the interests of society and those of the individual could be reconciled. Proper education would eliminate a-social behavior, and people would find their individual freedom *in* the group. In present-day society, it was the state and laws that prevented individuals from building a natural society where they could associate freely and cooperatively. Chen, however, in a complete turnabout from his New Culture position, explicitly demanded that the individual must give way to the group. He saw societies as complex entities requiring coercive laws.

The two men also differed on the nature of revolution. Chen denounced distant utopias and advocated revolution in the immediate, far-from-perfect present. But he did not spell out what this might mean for democracy. It is true, of course, that the anarchists had weak organizations. Their study groups, communes, publishing enterprises, and labor groups, all operated entirely on a voluntary basis. They saw themselves as educating and promoting rather than as leading other classes to revolution. Chen said that communism would come to China when it won 100,000 converts – regardless of the wishes of the majority. This implied that the "dictatorship of the proletariat" would oppress society itself, including the proletariat.

The anarchists saw this potential for authoritarianism and explicitly criticized it. They pointed out that the communist experience in Russia was demonstrating that the dictatorship of the proletariat actually referred to the "vanguard party." Whatever necessity might justify proletarian dictatorship, nothing could justify dictatorship by a handful of intellectuals or professional revolutionaries. Anarchists worried that Communists, in spite of worthy goals, were in fact heading down a road that would raise up the Party, strengthen the state, and actually lead away from a classless society. The vanguard party signified minority rule; this minority could not be trusted to rule well or to give up power. Rather, it would inevitably be drawn to defend its narrow interests and re-establish classes.

For anarchists, the problem was rooted in the state, and so "regardless of whether you have a democratic government or a government of the workers and peasants, in fact they all exploit the blood of the workers for the benefit of the minority who have special privileges."[23] (By "democracy" was meant *bourgeois* democracy – tricking ordinary people to think they were freely electing representatives while in fact big money was making all the political decisions.) The anarchists believed that coercion was evil whatever its origins. In effect, anarchists criticized the communist dichotomy between revolutionary means and utopian ends. To the anarchists, the revolutionary process itself had to encompass the values they fought for. Cooperatives, for example, were a perfectly legitimate goal: they would be a feature of the new society, and they also could be a means of promoting revolution in a particular place by freeing the people of the exploitation of a middleman and teaching them about what we might today call participatory democracy.

There might be leaders for specific tasks, but privileges would be allowed in neither revolutionary organization nor future society.

But to the communists, the anarchists' ideals were simply unrealistic. Communists argued that the proletariat was uniquely positioned, due to its oppression, to lead the liberation of all of society. Furthermore, the state would be necessary for a long, long time. Like all forms of authority, the communists argued, government was a tool that could be used for good or for evil. Without coercion, how could the oppressed ever succeed in demanding their rights? Through violent class struggle, class consciousness would be produced. Even after revolutionary victory, the bourgeoisie, skilled in the ways of manipulation, would need to be controlled. Finally – and here the communists certainly seemed more realistic than the anarchists – human nature was not all good. As such, it would take generations of social education to produce individuals truly capable of group life. Meanwhile, the dictatorship of the proletariat could evolve into the democracy of the whole people, uncorrupted by capitalism but still needing vigilance against evil forces.

Thus the main appeal of Marxism in the 1920s was its promise to guide effective revolutionary action. In this sense, Leninism or Bolshevism might be said to have been more important than "Marxism" as an abstract theory. By the mid-1920s disillusionment with the mass movements of the May Fourth period had set in. All those marches, student unions, and merchant–worker alliances had produced no long-term results. Nor did the ephemeral anarchist publications and communal experiments actually create the germs of a new society. Leninism, on the other hand, offered a technology of revolution. And at the same time, Marxism-Leninism offered a powerful tool to analyse Chinese society in terms of class structure. The gentry was linked to "feudalism" and the bourgeoisie was linked to imperialism and capitalist exploitation: these classes did not represent the true China of workers and peasants. Yet Marxism-Leninism did not promise easy solutions. Years of hard, disciplined work would be necessary – perhaps that appealed to a certain type of person. The Chinese Communist Party slowly built up a cadre of dedicated converts: communism was a full-time job. Communists were expected to make sacrifices – communism appealed to people both idealistic and ambitious.

Representatives of the Communist International (Comintern) first arrived in China from Moscow in March of 1920. Their activities will be examined further in the next chapter, but it is sufficient here to note that their meetings with radical Chinese intellectuals and students produced study groups that would form the basis of the Chinese Communist Party. It is important to remember, too, that this entire process occurred "underground." Aside from temporary pockets of tolerance, anarchists and communists could not organize legally. For some time, the CCP remained tiny.

We should not imagine Marxism-Leninism sweeping all before it and converting an entire generation. Few intellectuals could accept Party discipline, which would basically turn them into professional revolutionaries.

Organization-building and ideological purification went hand in hand. The second Congress of the CCP in 1922 saw the expulsion of heterodox elements such as anarchists. The self-image of the intellectual as hero – enlightening the benighted masses – gave way to the image of the self-abnegating servant of the people. As the "oppressed" learned to speak for themselves during the 1920s, the intellectuals had even less of a role to play. Where the Confucian gentleman had been expected to fulfill his humanity through leading society and government, the modern intellectual was expected to awaken and enlighten. Marxist intellectuals were expected to understand Marxist-Leninist dogma, but the only claim to power came through successful revolutionary practice. None the less, the first CCP members were nearly all intellectuals and students; then workers and finally peasants were admitted into the Party.

## Common themes in May Fourth discourse

Liberals, radicals, traditionalists: Chinese faced a range of questions associated with China's incorporation into a larger world. This went beyond the problem of imperialism. Doctrines widely regarded as self-evidently true just a generation before now appeared to be handicaps, irrelevant, or at best needing fundamental rethinking. Strikingly different doctrines and ideas needed to be understood if not followed. Some kind of relativism was inevitable; norms and values could no longer be regarded as universal. Such were the challenges of modernity, made especially painful for Chinese intellectuals since so much of the process seemed to be driven from outside. The problem of becoming modern, then, unavoidably involved the question of national identity. Who were the Chinese? How were they to survive these evil times? If they were inadequate – unable to "adapt" in the Darwinist language still in use – how could they be made better? The conservative impulse to safeguard Chinese culture was closely tied to questions of national identity and national pride. Even in anarchist discourse, there is a certain national pride in the possibility that it might be the Chinese who would lead the world to the anarchist paradise. For Marxists, a new answer focused on the common Chinese people: the "masses."

The changing reputation of the Boxers illustrates some of the intellectual transitions of the May Fourth period. The leaders of the New Culture movement, dedicated to rationalism, modernity, and the twinned "science and democracy," had little use for the Boxers. Hu Shi attacked their superstitiousness. Chen Duxiu impartially blamed Daoism, Confucianism, Buddhism, popular opera, and conservatism for causing the Boxers in the first place. He worried about a revival of Boxerism, arguing in 1918 that

> ... the ideas of the Boxers and the reality of the Boxers are everywhere throughout China and are in the ascendant. Can we be sure that the Boxers will not re-emerge in the future?... There are at present two

paths open to us: one is the path of light that leads toward republicanism, science, and atheism; the other is the path of darkness leading toward autocracy, superstition, and theism.[24]

But such elitism was to come under challenge. By 1924 Chen Duxiu himself, then secretary-general of the CCP, had completely reversed his position. The anti-foreignism of the Boxers, no matter how extreme, was justified by the "bloody oppression suffered by the whole of China" at the hands of the foreign imperialists. The Boxers' superstitiousness only reflected the social conditions of the age, and at least they contributed to the movement for national resistance. "Instead of loathing the barbarism of the antiforeign Boxers of those years, we should loathe the civilization of the warlords, bureaucrats, unscrupulous merchants, university professors, and newspapermen who at present curry favor with the foreigners!"[25] In this view of modern China, the Boxers deserved to be grouped with the reform movement of 1898, the 1911 Revolution, and the May Fourth movement itself. Non-communists too began to re-evaluate the Boxers. Even Hu Shi acknowledged that the Boxers might be seen as an example of national resistance to barbaric Western aggression, though he remained horrified by their indiscriminate killing.

Professional historians played a key role in redefining what it meant to be Chinese. That their voices were influential was perhaps due to the traditional respect granted to history in the Confucian view.[26] A school of May Fourth historians, often students of Hu Shi, called themselves "doubters of antiquity" and demonstrated that myths about ancient Chinese emperors and dynasties were, indeed, only myths. Fu Sinian (1896–1950) emphasized that history was a universal process toward rationality and science.[27] At the same time, Hu and Fu found important precursors of scientific thought in the pre-Qin classical period from about the fifth to the third centuries BC, thus maintaining *a*, if not *the*, central position in world history for China. Other historians emphasized unique qualities of Chinese history and culture which contributed over time to its unique national spirit. More conservative historians found Confucian social ethics to be at the core of the national identity, but they also acknowledged that "China" was built by many different peoples and classes over thousands of years of invasions, population shifts, and a mixed process of assimilation and change. In the case of invasions, for example, outside conquerors both assimilated to Chinese ways, to a degree, and also contributed new features to the ongoing growth of the civilization. The notion that China always and completely assimilated foreign conquerors remained popular, obviously fitting into the antiforeignism shared across the political spectrum; however, professional historians, both the "doubters of antiquity" and those of a more conservative bent, were moving away from this comforting view to a more complex vision of amalgamation.

Beyond the work of historians using traditional written sources lay a broader intellectual movement to learn more about popular culture. For all the disdain felt by intellectuals for the crudities of the popular imagination, folk literature became a way to redefine Chinese culture.[28] Studies of folk songs, puppet theater, popular legends, fairy tales, and countless other expressions of the collective imagination multiplied in the 1920s and 1930s. This was another avenue intellectuals could follow to the countryside. Folklorists were often attacked for vulgarity and even obscenity, or for insulting particular religions or groups (by publishing, for example, non-Muslim folk versions of why Muslims do not eat pork), and encouraging superstition. However, the folklore movement originated out of the iconoclasm of the age, finding "national spirit" in the hitherto little-known world of popular tales and songs. Folklorists certainly did not turn away from "democracy and science" to embrace village culture unquestioningly, but they found in that culture building blocks that could be used to construct the new culture they hoped for. As opposed to the rotten edifice of Confucianism and – significantly – the equally perverted modernity, as they saw it, of the dance halls and new mass consumerism of cities like Shanghai, traditional folk culture displayed the intelligence and independence of the people.

In sum, the end result of these researches was to expand and broaden possible definitions of Chinese culture and national identity. Only by including the people in the story of Chinese culture would it be possible to democratize the society. Back at the turn of the century Liang Qichao had called for a "new history" that would trace the development of the nation, not the trivial policies of emperors. A generation later, this task was well under way. The new historians might grant the old literati a special historical role as the carriers of a valuable high culture, but the folk became culture-carriers as well. Recognition of the changes Chinese culture underwent over time and of its multifaceted qualities created a broader sense of national identity.

# 10 The rise of political parties

Karl Marx looked at imperialism from the viewpoint of bourgeois capitalism and so praised the breaking down of Chinese walls. Lenin's view was for once more subtle. Lenin's analysis began with the expansive tendencies of the European powers, which he traced to the stage of "monopoly capitalism." This had produced a crisis of overproduction, since exploited workers could not afford the products being churned out by ever-more-efficient factories. The concentration of production and ownership into fewer and fewer hands, and the corresponding concentration of finance capital, would have led European workers into revolution if capitalists had not found a solution. Their solution, Lenin saw, was to force excess production into captive colonial markets and exploit those colonies for their resources and cheap labor. This, in combination with what might be called the politico-military strengths of the Powers, resulted in a division of the world among the Powers. But monopoly capitalism was unstable or "parasitic," since creditor states became economically unproductive.[1]

Today, few economists, if any, agree with Lenin's analysis. It may be doubted that creditor states remain unproductive instead of switching to higher technologies as the global division of labor evolves, though the "problem" of excess capital was widely noticed in the early twentieth century. But the point is not that Lenin's understanding of imperialism was partial. The point is that it had political consequences. Lenin believed that, since capitalism now depended on imperialism, anti-imperialist movements threatened the entire world capitalist order. World revolution would begin in the colonies, not the advanced nations (as Marx had posited). In the wake of the Russian Revolution, Lenin founded the Comintern (Third Communist International) in 1919 to help the national struggles of the "oppressed nations." By striking the capitalist Powers where it hurt – their colonial enterprises, sources of raw materials, cheap labor, and markets – colonized peoples would be allying themselves with the industrial proletariats.

What this meant for the oppressed nations themselves was that local revolutions should not be limited to their own proletariats. According to Lenin's analysis, in societies still dominated by the peasantry and crafts production, proletariats were tiny. The Comintern thus sought to aid "bourgeois nationalists" as much as local communist parties. Indeed, Lenin fully expected the struggle in Asia to be mainly waged by the bourgeoisie and the peasantry.

Lenin's theory of imperialism made sense to Chinese radicals. Indeed, important elements of it were anticipated by a number of Chinese writers, as early as Liu Shipei in 1908. Liu, who as an anarchist favored a revolution of the "whole people" anyway, said that if all the world's oppressed people rose up in revolution, they would deprive the Powers of their ill-gotten gains and encourage Western peoples to overthrow their own governments. Unlike Lenin, Liu had understood imperialism as a combination of racism and state power as well as capitalism. In this, he was closer to the views of scholars today.

Chinese were consumed with the problem of foreign imperialism from the turn of the century, fully aware that unlike some of its neighbors China did not – fully – become a part of any particular Empire. No Chinese government from the late Qing until the founding of the People's Republic in 1949 could claim genuine sovereignty over the whole of the country. They were constrained, no doubt, by internal weaknesses, but they were also constrained by the unequal treaties; the presence of foreign military forces in the cities and on the rivers and railroads; and the domination of foreign ownership of the key elements of modern industry: banking, utilities, mining, shipping, and railroads. By many measures the foreign presence was dwarfed by the size of China; the Chinese governments would not or could not do everything that the foreigners wanted; the foreign powers were themselves divided; and to a degree the Chinese did continue to govern themselves. But the dynamics of imperialist expansion operated in China just as they did in full-fledged colonies. Though Western capital looks small against China's overall economy, it bought a lot of government. Furthermore, it was directed at the key points of the Chinese economy, especially transportation and manufacturing. And China's debtor status severely limited the scope of action available to any Chinese government after the huge Boxer indemnities of 1901. Politically active Chinese of all ideological persuasions and attitudes toward the West were well aware of the realities of imperialism.

In the wake of the May Fourth movement, initial patriotic energies dissipated. Students were eventually ready to go back to classes, workers could not strike indefinitely, and merchants needed to reopen their shops. Yet, while anti-imperialist actions disappeared from the front pages, anti-imperialism became more focused in two small political parties. The Guomindang (Nationalist Party) and the Chinese Communist Party were to lead a new, more disciplined "National Revolution" in the 1920s. These "parties" were not political parties in the Western sense of the term: primarily devoted to waging elections based on a fairly loose set of interests and ideologies. Rather, both became Leninist parties, tightly structured, centralized (within limits imposed by contending leaders and factions), and ideologically committed organizations. They restricted membership – would-be members had to demonstrate their commitment and loyalty – while they strove to mobilize mass support. The GMD quickly built up its own army and schools, prelude to the military reunification of the country. The GMD and the CCP both emphasized correct ideology and loyalty to leaders.

What most distinguished them from Western political parties, however, was not their organization but the political context in which they had to operate. The political realm is an arena of contestation over power and resources: who gets what, when, and how. "Politics" in the West generally refers to an arena of policy-making ostensibly demarcated from society by its rules of the game, and to a loose but broad consensus on values that lies behind them. Secondarily, "politics" refers to an arena of unscrupulous struggle for power and wealth. In this view, politics is dirty and politicians corrupt. In the early twentieth century in China the latter view predominated. "Politics" referred to the obvious machinations of the various camps of the warlords. Politicians were widely seen as unprincipled minions. The various constitutions promulgated in Beijing were each more hopeless than the last. Each parliament seemed more venal than the last.

## Guangzhou and the early Guomindang

The revolutionary government that had come to power in Guangzhou in the 1911 Revolution was dedicated to the radical restructuring of local society. Sun Yat-sen's old comrade in arms, Hu Hanmin (1879–1936), and the local activist Chen Jiongming (1877–1933) supported universal schooling, equality for women, compulsory military service, and popular mobilization. But as they increased taxes, confiscated the property of guilds and native-place associations, and attacked traditional but popular institutions like temples, the Cantonese elites turned against them.

The government collapsed in the defeat of the so-called second revolution. Hu Hanmin and other leaders were forced to flee with Sun to Japan in July of 1913. Local elites across China sought accommodation with Yuan Shikai. Sun's new Chinese Revolutionary Party was not a success, though it allowed Sun to strengthen his contacts with some powerful men, including leaders of the criminal gangs, in Shanghai. Sun also accepted money from the Japanese and, apparently, the Germans, and so in the rise of warlordism after Yuan's death Sun was able to buy military support to force his way back into Guangzhou.[2]

Before we turn to the rise of the Guomindang under Sun's leadership, the controversial issue of his foreign contacts should be aired. If he was such a nationalist, how could he beg and take so much from the Powers? In fact, throughout his political life, Sun was frequently willing to promise benefits to foreign nations in return for their support. From a nationalist point of view, this has proved embarrassing, diminishing Sun's right to be called a patriotic leader. Sun was well aware of the problem, often seeking to keep such agreements secret. Particularly embarrassing was Sun's support for concessions to Japan in the 1910s, which did in fact damage his reputation. However, it should also be pointed out that Sun was a natural cosmopolitan. Born in the Guangzhou area, the region of China most open to international trade from early times, Sun was also educated in Hawaii and Hong Kong, and spent considerable time abroad, with Japanese, British, and American friends. Perhaps naïvely, he thought that the world would welcome a stronger China. Though possibly an opportunist, Sun's ultimate patriotism cannot be doubted. Indeed, he seems to have had no intention of keeping many of the promises he made to foreigners. He probably received as much as two million Chinese dollars from Germany in early 1917, for example – and his Guangzhou government declared war on Germany in September.

Meanwhile, back in Guangzhou in the late 1910s, Sun tried to establish a new government that did not recognize the legitimacy of the warlord regimes in Beijing. In fact, he claimed to be the legitimate government of the Republic of China. More practically, he hoped Guangzhou would become a model of good government and a base for the military reunification of China. Sun recognized the need for military support. "To re-establish a true Republic, we need to have at our disposal two forces: the army and the navy," he declared. "It is impossible to re-establish a true Republic ... without recourse to the armed forces."[3] He had some support from Chen Jiongming's troops, but this was dwarfed by the opposition of the larger warlords of Guangdong, Guangxi, and Yunnan, all of whom took an interest in the commercial wealth of the Guangzhou–Hong Kong axis. By the spring of 1918 Sun was again forced to abandon Guangzhou. He was able to make a brief return in 1921, but when Chen Jiongming turned against him in 1922 Sun had to flee again.

These confusing machinations not only reflect the militarism of the period, but also the contradiction between the two goals of treating greater Guangzhou as a model and as a military base. In Nationalist historiography, Chen Jiongming is condemned as a traitor to Sun. But Chen was dedicated – along with much of the Guangzhou elite – to a federalist vision of local development. In control of much of Fujian Province to the north, Chen pursued social reform and offered a haven for anarchist and Communist organizers. Sun, on the other hand, remained a centralist who wanted to use the resources of the southeast to conquer the rest of China.

Finally, in 1923 Sun's supporters, including mercenaries from Yunnan, were able to push Chen out of Guangzhou, and Sun named himself generalissimo of a small military government in the city. This was to form the basis of a reorganized Guomindang. Was Sun, then, simply a minor warlord? Public opinion generally regarded him more as a troublemaker than a potential leader of the nation. He made deals with the major warlords, trying to play one off against the other, or what Sun called "the customary expedient strategy of allying with someone in order to expel someone else." Although he spoke in the name of the Republic, Sun's small Guangzhou-based government was simply not politically significant in national terms. Although Sun's idealism might seem to have set him apart from the other warlords, ideals by themselves, especially without the means to carry them out, may be dismissed as mere propaganda.

Sun's insistence on the legitimacy of his government and his idealism did distinguish him from the other warlords to a degree. But the significant break with warlordism came in his organization of a new Party – the Guomindang. No warlord had a political party as extensive or as well organized. The Guomindang soon developed an ideology designed to appeal to progressive patriots; the means to promote social mobilization, especially of workers and students in Guangzhou and Shanghai; newspapers and schools; and its own military wing. It was ideally positioned to ride the crest of the nationalist upsurge of the 1920s.

The Guomindang was born on 10 October 1919 – the eighth anniversary of the 1911 Revolution amidst the tumult of the May Fourth movement. It might be seen as simply a new form of the associations Sun had been organizing since the 1890s. The Revive China Society, the National Alliance, the Chinese Revolutionary Party; one after another Sun had built insurrectionary organizations around himself. His lack of leadership skills had been one factor behind their repeated failures. Organizationally, the GMD stood between the loose structure of the National Alliance (founded in 1905 out of various revolutionary organizations) and the cultist Chinese Revolutionary Party (1913, where members vowed personal fealty to Sun). The GMD was to develop an elaborate, if elastic, ideology, and its own military wing. For Sun and his supporters came to realize that the student movement had created new political possibilities. Sun was not personally sympathetic to the cultural iconoclasm of the New Thought movement, but he appreciated the democratic and nationalist thrust of May Fourth.[4] After all, Sun's Three People's Principles encompassed nationalism, democracy, and people's livelihood. The calls of the younger generation for science and democracy were compatible with Sun's views, which included a faith in technological modernization, and the ideal of "people's livelihood" was congruous with the popularity of socialism.

Sun and his followers used their forced retirement from politics between 1918 and 1920 to develop the Guomindang's ideology. This ideology will be examined in the next chapter; here, we simply need to note that the Three People's Principles (Sunism) were elaborated into a political platform that targeted warlordism and imperialism. Sun also developed the notion that, once the GMD seized power, a "revolutionary period" would follow. This would be a time of "political tutelage" as the people were prepared for constitutional government. This time, the mistakes of 1911 would not be repeated, and the revolutionaries would not lay down their arms.

Sunism did not provide the new Guomindang with immediate appeal. For several years the Party remained small and ineffective. At first, it was not clear that the GMD would be different from the parliamentary parties of the early Republic. Yet by 1923 it was attracting students who had participated in May Fourth organizations. Hundreds moved south to become part of the "national revolution." Why? What had changed?

In February 1923 Sun was able to resume his title as generalissimo of a Guangzhou-based government. It remained at the mercy of larger warlord armies, and relied on the support or neutrality of rival militarists from the southeast, southwest, and central China – who preferred that a relatively powerless Guomindang control the important port of Guangzhou rather than one of their more serious rivals. At the same time, in spite of Sun's claims to ideological certainty, the GMD was paralyzed by factional rivalries. But the Comintern was coming to save Sun. He seems to have initially accepted Russian assistance and an alliance with the Chinese Communist Party reluctantly. But he drove the Guomindang to the left after being rebuffed in other quarters. No doubt the "May Fourth spirit" of revolutionary optimism helped radicalize the GMD; however, the specific alliance with the Soviet Union depended on Sun's reading of the needs of the GMD. He had rejected Russian overtures in 1920 and 1921, but by 1923 he had nowhere else to turn.

It is important to understand the international situation of the 1920s in order to make sense out of political developments in China itself. At the end of World War I the world was dominated by a kind of British–US axis. Some room was being made for Japan in East Asia, but the "Washington system" did not recognize Russian or Chinese interests. It was, in essence, devoted to preserving a post-war capitalist world order. The Washington Conference of 1921–2 brought together the European powers, the US, and Japan in an effort to avoid both another world war and nationalist revolutions. The US, Britain, and Japan agreed to restrict the size of their battle fleets. In regard to East Asia, the treaties theoretically recognized China's "sovereignty" but in reality they were designed to bolster the status quo. The Washington system thus in effect ratified imperialism in China. For Sun, Britain's attitudes were made clear in the autumn of 1923. He formally requested that a share of the revenues from China's customs tariffs be given to his Guangzhou government instead of all being sent to Beijing. The Maritime Customs Service had been under foreign control since the nineteenth century in order to make first claim on revenues to repay indemnities. Although there was some support in the West for Sun's claim, London rebuffed him. When Sun threatened to take the revenues by force, a large display of British naval power in Guangzhou Harbor followed. Gunboat diplomacy was alive and well. Not until this point did Sun abandon his hopes of international cooperation under the Washington system and begin to speak the language of anti-imperialism.[5]

The new Soviet Union, on the other hand, denounced imperialism without qualifications. In March 1920 it publicly renounced all the unequal treaties signed between the Czarist government and the Qing. All Chinese patriots, leftist or not, were impressed. This move also paved the way for Comintern agents to sneak over the border into China. Anti-imperialism was not only a major tenet of Leninist theory; Lenin also devoted hard resources to the Comintern. Lenin was happy to support Asian communist parties but, as we have seen, he was even more eager to support stronger "bourgeois" movements as long as they were anti-imperialist. Indeed, Leninism held that China was *not* ready for a revolution of the proletariat which, defined as the urban industrial working class, was of course too small. Instead, given its backward economy, China was ready for a kind of popular, multi-class revolution.

In actual fact, the Soviet Union did not abandon all the special privileges of the old Czarist treaties. In particular, it wanted to ensure the security of its Pacific railroad routes. But the Comintern none the less found common cause with Chinese anti-imperialists. Its first efforts to find support among the northern warlords failed. Efforts to turn May Fourth Marxists into Communists were more successful, but proceeded slowly. That left Sun Yat-sen. The Comintern agents Grigori Voitinsky (who spoke fluent English and so could communicate with Sun directly) and Hans Maring held extensive discussions with Sun during his Shanghai "exile" in 1920 and 1921. As always, Sun was interested in whatever aid could help him put together a military force to unify the country. He also seems to have had a genuine interest in the modernization policies of the Soviet Union, though he never accepted Marxist-Leninist ideas about revolution. Unable to find any northern warlords interested in an alliance with the Soviet Union, and with no real communist movement to speak of, Sun increasingly looked like the Comintern's only hope.

## The Chinese Communist Party and the First United Front

With the encouragement of Comintern advisers, a small group of intellectuals founded the Chinese Communist Party (CCP) in 1921. Its growth over the next two decades was extremely rocky and uneven. The CCP, important as it was in certain spheres, remained a relatively minor political actor in China as a whole. It did, however, play a key role in turning another relatively minor party, the GMD, into a powerful and dynamic force.

It was the Chinese who built the CCP, but the role of Comintern advisers was essential.[6] Aside from meeting with Sun Yat-sen, Voitinsky also held frequent meetings with Chen Duxiu and other radicals in the summer of 1920. He presented the Russian Revolution as a model for the Chinese to follow. Voitinsky seems to have been well chosen for his job. He treated the leading Chinese radicals with great respect; he presented himself as a guide and teacher, not a commander. The Chinese radicals already had formed Marxist study groups; by late 1920 some of these were being converted into underground cells. At Beida, in Shanghai, and in other cities like Guangzhou, Wuhan, and Changsha, as well as among overseas students in Japan and

France, the members of these cells devoted themselves to the study of Marxism and the Russian Revolution, to translation of Marxist works, and, where possible, to public discussions of socialism.[7] The next step, under Voitinsky's guidance, was to form these cells into a party that would be committed to political action.

The formation of a disciplined party over the course of 1921 and 1922 was a process of winnowing, even of purging, not growth. Anarchists, guild socialists, and even Marxists who did not want to accept Party discipline, either left voluntarily or were purged from membership. New members were recruited: from among workers, especially leaders in the Shanghai union movement, and also women and youth. But the ideological and personal requirements for membership in the CCP were strict. Only a few of the May Fourth generation were initially interested. One who was, was Mao Zedong. Over the course of 1920 he seems to have abandoned anarchism as impractical and turned to Marxism-Leninism in its stead. Mao attended the first Party Congress that established the CCP in July 1921. This secret meeting in Shanghai, of some twenty men representing local cells, adopted an official platform. Ironically, neither of the "founders" of the Party, Chen Duxiu or Li Dazhao, were able to attend, and about half of the representatives at the first congress had dropped out within a year. Chen Duxiu was elected general secretary in absentia, but it is clear that neither he nor many of the other original CCP members regarded Party work as their primary responsibility or source of identity – yet.

The CCP was a secret organization some of whose activities, like schools and bookstores, could be conducted in the open. Its leaders, though openly radical, were tolerated by the police in the French concession in Shanghai. A certain amount of free speech was allowed; socialism could certainly be discussed, though *New Youth* was banned at one point. Heavy police pressure against radicals in Beijing tended to push them to Shanghai, where, ironically, they were partially protected by Western legal culture. By the second Party congress in 1922 the winnowing process was producing a more cohesive, if smaller, organization. Twelve delegates represented some 195 members across China. They committed themselves to working closely with the Comintern, including sending members for further training in Moscow.

Where did China's first Communists come from? Many came from provincial China. Chen Duxiu, Li Dazhao, and Zhang Shenfu stand out as the only major intellectuals involved in the early CCP. Nor did many of the other members come from powerful families or have brilliant university careers. Rather, many came from areas somewhat outside the rapidly modernizing and Westernizing metropolitan areas (though not the truly remote parts of the countryside). Mao himself is a good example. So was his friend, Cai Hesen (1895–1931), who played a pivotal role in first interesting Mao in Marxism. Cai was a high-school classmate of Mao, from a fairly distinguished lineage but brought up by his mother in a poor household. He was not able to start elementary school until he was sixteen, though, self-taught, he made rapid progress. At the end of 1919 he sailed to France as part of the Work–Study program established by anarchists. But in France he became a convert to Marxism, quickly establishing himself as one of China's best Marxist theoreticians and describing the advantages of Marxism in letters to Mao back in Hunan. Cai worked to build a Chinese Marxist Party in Europe in 1920–1, and he was elected to the CCP's Central Committee in 1922.

Friendships and provincial connections were a major part of the recruitment process. Take Shen Dingyi (1882?–1928), son of a landlord in Zhejiang Province.[8] He had worked with the 1911 revolutionaries and built a political career in Zhejiang Province, though a career interrupted by the crackdowns of Yuan Shikai and warlords. Working as a journalist in Shanghai during the May Fourth movement, in 1920 Shen became a member of the Marxist Study Society, a group of ten men in their twenties and thirties (plus Chen Duxiu, then 41). Some of their meetings produced quarrels so caustic that they had to break up for the evening. But soon they formed a Communist cell, and Shen went on to help found the CCP. Another Zhejiang Communist, Shi Cuntong, an iconoclastic young anarchist who had denounced his own father in the May Fourth movement, moved to Shanghai after his work–study commune in Beijing fell apart.[9] There Shen Dingyi and others guided him toward Marxism, and sponsored him to study Marxism in Tokyo. Shi continued to work as a Communist organizer until 1927, when, though breaking with the Party, he remained an independent Marxist intellectual.

The debates between communists and anarchists and other socialists served to define Chinese Marxism, as noted in the previous chapter. It was not that the CCP's leaders wanted to purge their membership so much as the process of defining a coherent Marxist identity inevitably did so. Li Dazhao, at least, had hoped all Chinese socialists would remain united. Ideological purity, however, could not be fudged. Communists may have been a minority among radicals – themselves a minority – but they already possessed a notable presence due to their organizational coherence. Some among the anarchists and socialists found their promise of more effective revolution-building appealing. Moreover, if anarchists and other socialists found it natural to mix politics and interrupt their political activities with their careers as students, educators, or journalists, Communists committed themselves to whatever it took to build the revolution. As the historian Arif Dirlik put it, "The appearance of an exclusive Communist identity that brooked no ideological 'confusion' does not imply that the identity of every participant in the early Communist movement was therefore transformed, and purged of the legacy of the past. What is at issue here is not the identity of every individual Communist, but the emergence of an organizational and ideological identity that clearly demarcated the boundary between Communist and non-Communist, and brooked no eclecticism or pluralism."[10] Of course, disagreements within the CCP continued along ideological, personal, and factional lines, and local branches operated with some autonomy.[11] But basically you decided you were either a Communist or not. If you were, then you recognized a chain of authority that went through your local branch up to CCP headquarters in Shanghai and ultimately to Moscow.

The Comintern, following the Leninist theory of imperialism, demanded that Communists support all Asian nationalists, even if they were bourgeois. The smaller CCP therefore should form an alliance with the larger GMD, sacrificing its own revolutionary plans (for the time being). Neither the GMD nor the CCP was enthusiastic about an alliance. Many in the GMD feared that the obviously different goals of the CCP would divide their movement or even highjack it, while many in the CCP feared the loss of their autonomy. None the less, the Comintern insisted. In ideological terms, the Comintern's representatives in China decided that the GMD was not purely a bourgeois party, but rather a blend of the intelligentsia, overseas Chinese, workers, and soldiers. Already, then, ideology was being shaped to meet organizational needs rather than the other way around – though the GMD was indeed much more a blend of various forces than the "bourgeois party" that Communists later claimed it to be. The CCP went on record as favoring a United Front in 1922. Sun Yat-sen took more convincing, but since he could find no other allies, he accepted the United Front the following year.

The GMD's alliance with the Soviet Union specified that Russia would not try to convert China to communism and that it continued to renounce the Czarist treaties. In return, Sun accepted that the Chinese Eastern Railway would continue to be managed by the Russians and that Soviet troops could remain in Outer Mongolia. More importantly, Sun agreed to allow Chinese Communist Party members to join the GMD as individuals. He would not accept a formal alliance between the CCP and the GMD as between two equal entities but, in effect, this is what happened. Communists joined the GMD "as individuals" but secretly continued to work together as communists.

This was the origins of the First United Front between the GMD and the CCP. Though the details were largely kept secret at the time, something like 3 million rubles (2.7 million yuan) was given to the GMD between 1923 and 1927, and the Comintern sent well over a hundred advisers. Aid included the gift of some arms and the sale of more. No wonder the British and Americans considered Sun – and later Chiang Kai-shek – to be "Red Bolsheviks." From Sun's point of view, the price the GMD had to pay was not great. Chinese communists agreed to abide by GMD rules and policies. The Comintern expected the GMD to strengthen itself organizationally, to pursue anti-imperialist policies, to prepare for agrarian revolt, and to support the workers' movement. All of this Sun wanted as well. Moreover, the Comintern and Sun reorganized the GMD along Leninist lines: with more centralized and stronger leadership. With Comintern help, then, Sun came to control an efficient political machine for the first time in his life.

Fortunately for the United Front, the Comintern's chief representative was now Mikhail Borodin (1884–1953), an experienced revolutionary, a highly capable organizer, and "a subtle psychologist."[12] Borodin was descended from a family of rabbis in Belorussia. Arrested after the revolution of 1905, he fled to the United States for twelve years. He could thus communicate directly with Sun in English. His first job was to convince Sun to delay plans for launching a military expedition against the northern warlords. Borodin heaped praise on Sun in public, though in his confidential reports to Moscow he called Sun "very backward" and egotistical. But if Borodin gained Sun's trust, he did so on the basis of his competent advice, not trickery.

At a time when the GMD was hard-pressed to survive even in Guangzhou, Soviet aid was of immediate significance. On the Communists' side, Li Dazhao was the CCP leader most in favor of the United Front, promising that the CCP would help the GMD promote revolution as far as their aims coincided. Though some of Sun's most trusted aides were hostile to the Communists, Sun was genuinely committed to the United Front, confident that he could ultimately manipulate the Comintern and the CCP to his own ends. "We merely yoke up the Soviet Union and mount it," Sun promised.[13] However, who was riding whom would prove to be a difficult question.

The role of the Comintern in the Chinese revolution has been controversial in the West and China. Some Western historians argued, particularly at the height of the Cold War in the 1950s, that the entire Chinese revolution was directed from Moscow. This seems vastly exaggerated. Over time, Chinese leaders emerged who made decisions according to local conditions. Communism was "sinified" not only through practice but through the creative input of Chinese ideas. There were continual tensions between the Comintern and the CCP – Chinese Communists were not passive agents of Moscow. At the same time, the Comintern itself understood that the Chinese would have to develop their own policies rather than imitating the Russian Revolution. Comintern agents were always at least one step removed from Chinese realities: they depended on the very Chinese they were trying to influence to tell them what was going on in the first place. Sun Yat-sen persistently refuted Marxism, and he rejected Comintern tactics that he did not agree with.

The Chinese Communists, on the other hand, had to follow Comintern orders. This contributed to disaster, as we will see, in 1927, but thereafter the Chinese kept Moscow at a distance. It is misleading, overall, to conclude that the Chinese revolution was "directed" by the Comintern. In a word, the Comintern made it possible for strong revolutionary parties in China to be formed – that is, both the CCP and the GMD – but it could not determine the priorities of the Chinese revolution. In the 1911 Revolution students and intellectuals had focused their attention on assassinations and mercenary armies rather than trying to reach out to large groups or classes. But in the Nationalist Revolution of the 1920s, the new professional revolutionaries repudiated the individual as the key agent of meaningful social change. Rather, the disciplined Party organization emerged in theory and practice as the key to systematic political change. The new revolutionaries did not look inward to questions of culture or the family but outward to the whole economic and social structure.

What Borodin taught the GMD was the need to reach out to "the masses" – first the workers of Guangzhou and the peasants of Guangdong Province – and the need to restructure the Party. A Reorganization Congress took place in January of 1924. Pushed hard by Sun, the congress voted to make Party discipline absolute. For example, GMD members of a labor union or some other extra-Party body were to act as a unit, always voting together. Organizationally, each membership level elected representatives to the next higher level in congresses; between elections members were to obey orders that came to them from higher levels. Many saw these provisions as democratic assurances that new "emperors" would not be able to emerge. In practice, however, the GMD was built as a Leninist party: the reorganization actually ensured top-down decision-making. The reorganization and the GMD's commitment to "national revolution" gave the Party an unprecedented sense of organizational purpose and cohesion. Members were re-registered to emphasize the significance of the reorganization.

Still, the GMD remained highly factionalized. Many of its oldest members distrusted the Communists. They would go along with Sun, but they did not like it. Hu Hanmin, for example, opposed the GMD's apparent turn to the left and saw the Communists more as rivals than allies. Even though Sun brought all his prestige and authority to the United Front, GMD opposition to the Communists bubbled up frequently before and after Sun's death in March 1925, until the alliance collapsed in a bloodbath in 1927. Sun himself, at the January 1924 Party Congress, resisted Borodin's efforts to get the GMD to declare a public anti-imperialist alliance with the Soviet Union, and to confiscate land across Guangdong and redistribute it to the peasants. A formal alliance with the Soviet Union would only heighten the Powers' distrust. And land distribution was tricky, because the GMD still depended on overseas supporters, many of whom owned land in rural Guangdong. But the manifesto did call for land redistribution, a clear step to the left, although without specifying where such land was to come from. The Guomindang claimed some 30,000 members in Guangdong in late 1923, but barely 3,000 had renewed their membership when the Congress met. By 1926 it had some 200,000 members.

GMD control of even Guangzhou was at first tenuous. Still, taxes were reorganized, which proved profitable since the city was an important port. Sun simply seized control of the foreign-managed salt monopoly, but the foreign-managed customs revenue continued to go to Beijing. Guangzhou received fairly good government by most accounts, and Sun was able to support a growing army. GMD tax revenues increased from 8 million yuan in 1924 to 15 million yuan in the first 6 months of 1926.[14]

Growing revenues allowed Sun to plan for a northern expedition to conquer Beijing, which dismayed the Communists (and others) who thought it premature. More immediately, the GMD was able to spread its control of Guangzhou into much of Guangdong Province. Military skirmishes with neighboring warlords continued throughout the period. Originally, the loyalty of many of Sun's generals was highly suspect, and, as in any part of China, they were given a great deal of financial autonomy. Quickly, however, Sun and his Comintern advisers were able to create a more unified command. The key to its long-term maintenance lay in the Huangpu Military Academy.

Sun, the Comintern, and also the CCP, staffed the Academy with some of their best men to train a new GMD officer corps. Both military and ideological education was intensive. Cadets studied political economy, theories of imperialism, Chinese history, and the history of revolutions in the West. Sun's aide, Chiang Kai-shek (Jiang Jieshi, 1887–1975), was named head and the Communist Zhou Enlai (1898–1976) was in charge of ideology. The purpose of the Huangpu Military Academy was to create a professional Party army. Some cadets were recruited from existing armies, but most came from the students and young intellectuals moving south to become part of the nationalist revolution. They were idealistic. One said he wanted to join "to seek military knowledge in order to bring prosperity to my country and people." Another: "Because society is in a bad way I wish to receive mental training in an ideology for saving the country."[15]

Chiang Kai-shek not only emphasized the politics of revolution along with his otherwise fairly standard military training, but he fought against allowing any other academy to offer Party training.[16] Huangpu thus became the primary source of reliable GMD officers – most of whom, not coincidently, were loyal to Chiang himself. The Huangpu Corps grew rapidly, from 3,500 at the beginning of 1925 to 10,000 by mid-year. But they still constituted only a minority of the roughly 65,000 troops Sun could count on.

In later histories, only Huangpu is remembered, though the academy had rivals – and imitators. Other army commanders sought to instill their armies with Party discipline and political education. Rival GMD armies called the Huangpu cadets the "Doll's Army" and Chiang the "Doll's commander." Finally, however, officer training was centralized at the beginning of 1926 under Chiang Kai-shek. He won a great victory over his GMD rivals at a Party conference dealing with organizational problems in the wake of Sun Yat-sen's death. The new GMD armies were distinguished from the usual warlord armies by their loyalty and discipline: the inner and outer forces of any effective organization. Dead soldiers were buried – with memorial services – instead of being left to rot on the field; wounded men and their families were given special payments; formal battlefield reports determined promotions and demotions. "Collective responsibility" encouraged central control; for example, if a squad retreated without orders, all its members might be executed.

Rationalization of GMD armies remained imperfect but was *relatively* good. Above all, the army was thoroughly politicized. Called the "National Revolutionary Army," it was frankly a division of the GMD, though

Communists often acted as the most effective political commissars. The political bureaus and Party representatives of the armies had various functions. They were to make sure officers followed GMD directives, instill discipline in the troops, and oversee army–civilian relations. They were to punish military abuses of civilians but also, more importantly, to convince civilians of the desirability of cooperating with the army. They issued propaganda to the troops and to the civilians in areas where the army was based or traveling. Finally, they represented soldiers who had grievances against officers, providing an important safety valve and a way for generals to learn which officers were incompetent or sadistic. The GMD armies totaled about 100,000 troops by mid-1926 and could defeat armies several times their size.

Much of the great success of the GMD and the CCP – or the United Front – in the mid-1920s cannot be attributed to superior organization, military strength, or the Comintern's advisers and cash. Rather, the political force generated by the United Front meshed with ongoing social change to produce a synergistic effect. Radical demands for change among urban workers, peasants, women, and youth were not *caused* by GMD and CCP "mobilization of the masses" but were vastly strengthened when they could combine with these outside political organizers. Communist work with the peasantry will be discussed in more detail in Chapters 11 and 14, but let us look at the radicalization of workers here.

### The "May Thirtieth" movement (1925)

In January 1922 a massive strike broke out in Guangzhou and Hong Kong. Some 30,000 seamen and dock workers refused to sail ships or move cargo, immobilizing over 150 ships and directly challenging the authority of Great Britain. Over the next two months their strike was joined by an estimated 120,000 sympathetic workers, from street stall vendors to the advanced electrical plants' workers. The ship owners thereupon capitulated. The seamen won the right to a union and wage increases from 15 to 30 percent. This demonstrates what workers could achieve largely on their own, before the GMD and CCP became involved in workers' issues. It also impressed the Comintern agents in China. However, the political context was still crucial. The 1922 seamen's strike resulted from organizational energies that in many ways stemmed from the May Fourth movement. Moreover, the political sympathies of Sun Yat-sen and Chen Jiongming in the southeast had at least indirectly fostered the union movement over several years. And the British authorities in Hong Kong were relatively restrained.

Without detracting from the energies and skills of the Guangzhou seamen themselves, the importance of political context is made clear when we consider what happened to railway workers who went on strike in northern China the following year. In that case the workers, who had formed a union under Communist guidance, were directly attacked by the armies of Wu Peifu – a major warlord with a reputation of being somewhat sympathetic to social reform. However, his soldiers killed thirty-five recalcitrant workers and wounded many more. Then one of the union leaders who refused to give a back-to-work order was beheaded and his head hung on a telephone pole by way of example. The workers went back to work.

As workers organized in the course of the May Fourth movement, disciplined unions grew – able to conduct lengthy negotiations, to adopt a variety of tactics, and to prepare for strikes.[17] Shanghai and the Guangzhou Delta saw the most labor activity, often against foreign firms, while northern China had a less developed economy and harsher anti-union policies. Strike waves occurred during the broad anti-imperialist movements of 1919–22 and 1925–7, with a lull during the recession of 1923–4 and after the suppression of the left in 1927. Wages and working conditions prompted the great majority of strikes, which often achieved at least partial gains. In other words, strikes were not "caused" by anger at imperialism, and strikes against Chinese owners were as common as against foreign owners. Yet workers certainly were motivated by patriotic sentiment, as were other groups. As a cotton worker from Shanghai recalled the May Thirtieth movement of 1925 (discussed below, pp. 206–209):

> At the time anti-imperialist sentiments were not only prevalent among workers. Any Chinese who lived in Shanghai shared such feelings. During the strike even the police, the night-soil carriers, the servants at foreign residences, and the cooks all joined.... Certainly the Communist Party could never have been powerful enough to generate these sentiments. When people heard that the foreigners had killed one of us Chinese they were furious and felt that we must resist.[18]

Many actions were limited to a single factory, but over time workers were able to cooperate across the boundaries of status, occupation, and place of origin. The workers' movement was eye-opening to radical students. Thinking of the workers' involvement in the May Fourth movement of 1919, one such student later recalled:

> The gentlemen of the upper stratum had so far not bothered to take note of laborers. With this movement, laborers demonstrated their power to bourgeois intellectuals, who could not but be impressed with its magnitude.... Some student leaders of the May Fourth Movement henceforth launched their "down to the people" movement and organized laborers' schools and trade unions. This group of petty bourgeois students was naturally close to the proletariat; they gradually became Communists and joined the Communist Party.[19]

So spoke Deng Zhongxia (1894–1933), who was describing himself among others. Not that the workers became the pliant tools of Communists or the GMD. They maintained their own traditions of protests and their own goals, as political scientist and labor historian Elizabeth Perry stresses. Shanghai was China's premier center of modern industry, with both foreign-owned and Chinese-owned factories producing everything from cloth and machinery to cigarettes, paper, and matches. Shanghai's factories were the largest and most modern in the country, yet most were still little more than small dark workshops. Aside from factories, Shanghai found employment for thousands of service workers in transportation, the post office, the barbershops, night-soil removal, and construction. We have seen how these workers were organized to strike with remarkable speed in the May Fourth movement through guilds, native-place associations, and gangs. The strongest workers' organizations were neither modern industry-wide unions nor work-place associations. Rather, they were guilds combining workshop bosses with ordinary craftsmen; native-place associations with their merchant leadership; and the gangs heavily involved in drugs, smuggling, extortion, robbery, and labor recruitment could mobilize the most workers.

Yet a new kind of labor movement began to emerge out of the May Fourth movement. As the initial burst of enthusiasm died down in June, a core of activist workers from disparate industries met to plan for a permanent workers' organization. Such organizations were often modeled on foreign workers' movements – news of which was spread by China's early anarchists, by the May Fourth radicals, and by the thousands of Chinese workers who were returning from Europe after World War I. From this time onward, May Day – the international labor day – became an important occasion for demonstrations and protests, at least in Shanghai and Guangzhou.

Hundreds of young GMD and CCP organizers joined the workers in the wake of the creation of the United Front. By 1924, there were over 120 CCP cells in greater Shanghai, though not all of them were involved in the labor movement. The Communists were the first to try to influence Shanghai's workers, though the Nationalists later won control of the postal union. Initially, Communist organizers faced many problems. Students could infiltrate the guilds of skilled artisans and help turn them into unions such as those of the mechanics and printers. But the world of unskilled labor was much more amorphous to begin with, and the influence of Shanghai's criminal gangs was hard to dent. The Communists discovered they would have to infiltrate the gangs, especially the large and powerful Green Gang, in order to make an impact on Shanghai's unskilled workers. Even so, they found it particularly difficult to unionize Shanghai's tens of thousands of *women* workers. Perhaps as a male-dominated organization, the CCP was not very well equipped for this task. Certainly, the CCP often dismissed women workers as "backward," although they struck their factories as frequently as did men workers. But they often did so for different reasons and on the basis of traditional mutual aid "sisterhoods" rather than unions.[20] Still, during the major strike waves of 1919 and 1925, women and men workers cooperated in a common cause.

The Communists preached the gospel of class conflict – but real, breathing workers did not necessarily think of themselves as a united proletariat. Rather, they were divided horizontally by job, native-place, and status, and they frequently made use of vertical ties to factory foremen, gang bosses, and wealthy merchants from their home provinces. Conversely, the Nationalists preached the gospel of class harmony – economic development through cooperation between labor and capital – but the workers had genuine grievances against their bosses, both foreign and Chinese. The United Front did not end the rivalry between the GMD and the CCP, but formal cooperation at least led to more effective mobilization of Shanghai's working class. Communist organizers were mostly students or former students – but an increasing number of workers were admitted to the Party in the mid-1920s. Both students and workers came to understand that effective organization had to be built on existing structures. This meant, for example, trying to make alliances between workers who had emigrated to Shanghai from different provinces rather than erasing provincial boundaries in a super-union. In other words, it was futile to replace gangs and guilds based on native-place ties; Communists had to appeal to their leaders and members on their own terms. Brotherhoods were cemented by swearing oaths in dark temples and drinking wine with chicken blood and other "feudal" practices.

The "May Thirtieth movement" of 1925 led to a nationwide wave of radicalization. Early 1925 was a time of increased tension in Shanghai. The Chinese bourgeoisie was disturbed over the desire of the Powers to raise wharfage fees; workers were hurt by a fall in the currency and a rise in rice prices. When forty adult male workers in a Japanese-owned cotton mill were fired and replaced by young female workers, workers struck twenty-two Japanese factories. That strike petered out, but a new strike was called in May. A Japanese foreman killed a Chinese worker in a scuffle on 15 May. A large public memorial service was held for the Chinese worker on 24 May; strikes spread. On 30 May, under Communist auspices, a demonstration was held. It resulted in the British Sikh police firing into the crowd, killing thirteen and injuring over fifty, mostly workers. This provoked wide-scale reaction and indeed garnered sympathy for China from around the world. Shanghai and Guangzhou were shut down by a general strike: merchants, workers, and students joined the struggle. Demonstrations and anti-foreign boycotts spread to other cities as well.

In Shanghai, more than 200,000 workers from 200 businesses joined the strikes. The Chinese Chamber of Commerce contributed heavily to strike funds. After about a month, Chinese-owned businesses opened, and they did rather well as the boycotts continued. However, when the foreign-owned electricity companies shut off services to the Chinese portions of Shanghai, Chinese businessmen turned against the general strike. A number of workers, too, grew disgruntled with meager strike pay or the difficulty in getting any financial support at all. Warlord suppression began to tighten.

The strike was finally called off in September. Workers won a few economic gains, but none of their political demands were granted. These had ranged from the recognition of trade unions, the right to organize, and freedom of speech and assembly, to the withdrawal of foreign troops and the abolition of extraterritoriality.

Still, Shanghai's working class – and its Communist supporters – had shown their muscle. The Communists formed the Shanghai General Labor Union in June, just after the strike wave got under way. This was theoretically part of the United Front, but the GMD was in disarray after Sun Yat-sen's death in March and played little role in the Shanghai labor scene. By this time a significant number of Communists had become the "brothers" and "disciples" of Green Gang bosses. The support of the Green Gang was critical for any widespread strike since factory foremen and labor bosses were almost invariably members. The May Thirtieth strikes in Shanghai can be seen as an alliance between workers, Communists, and the Green Gang that won general support in the name of Chinese nationalism. Its enemies included the GMD right, conservative workers associated with GMD politicians, some gang leaders, and of course foreign officials and merchants.

The May Thirtieth movement was not simply an acute example of labor strife, however. Like the May Fourth movement of 1919 it rapidly turned into a national set of workers' strikes, student demonstrations, and boycotts against foreign goods. It was essentially a political movement, with political consequences. It is important to note that it was not the death of the worker in the 15 May scuffle that caused national reaction. It was the deaths of unarmed students on 30 May that provoked shock and horror across China.[21] One poet wrote in proud mourning:

> The British police have killed and wounded countless numbers of students.
> We honor all you have served as a sacrificial vanguard!
> Oh, the dead,
> Oh, the dead,
> Glorify these dead!…
> Your blood will irrigate the soil and bring forth bright red flowers.[22]

For several months, then, student associations and merchant guilds joined workers' groups to organize street lectures, rallies, pamphleteering, and, of course, memorial services. Youths performed street skits to teach Shanghai's citizens what had happened. "Wailing corps" cried in unison during memorial services. Blood was smeared on flags to symbolize the martyrs. Photographs and woodblock prints served as constant reminders of the dead. From Shanghai, waves of strikes and demonstrations spread to other cities, spurring unionization in places like Tianjin, where factory workers and sailors virtually brought the city to a halt. In Beijing, 30,000 students left their classes to demonstrate on 3 June. In Manchuria, British–American

Tobacco Company workers in Shenyang went on strike on 5 June. Up the Yangzi River, British machineguns killed eight Chinese demonstrators in Hankou on 11 June. Strikes began in Hong Kong and Guangzhou on 19 June. These were brilliantly led by Deng Zhongxia with the cooperation of the Guomindang's left wing. By July, a Tianjin General Labor Union was established. On 23 July some 60,000 demonstrators attempted to cross into the Shamian concession in Guangzhou. The demonstrators included armed cadets from Huangpu Military Academy and firing broke out. No one knows who started the firing, but when it was over British troops had killed at least 52 demonstrators and wounded 117. A national general strike followed. From Hong Kong, some 250,000 Chinese, about 45 percent of the Chinese population, left for Guangzhou or their native villages around Guangdong, where they would stay for the next sixteen months of strikes and boycotts. Deng made sure that labor organizers did not neglect the countryside.

Throughout the summer of 1925, then, students and workers periodically threatened to take over the streets of China's cities. In Shanghai and Guangzhou they marched to such slogans as "Help the workers," "Support the arrested students," "Down with imperialism," and "Take back the concessions." However, at the national level the movement was suppressed by the end of the summer. Chinese troops with British and Japanese support began to detain demonstrators in August. In Tianjin, 8,000 troops killed dozens of workers and arrested 500, suppressing student and worker unions. Chinese business interests were ambivalent after the first wave of patriotic emotion passed. Merchants were susceptible to patriotic appeals, as in the earlier May Fourth movement, but they were no friends to radical unionism and many ultimately depended on foreign trade. Across northern and central China the movement was halted in its tracks. In Shanghai, the General Labor Union was soon forced underground, its leaders executed.

In one sense, it is difficult to say that the May Thirtieth movement accomplished anything. Unlike the protestors in the May Fourth movement, who held victory parades when the "three traitors" were dismissed from government, the May Thirtieth protestors could point to few specific accomplishments. The addition of a few Chinese to the Shanghai Municipal Council (governing the International Settlement) was obviously tokenism. Perhaps the defenders of foreign privilege felt satisfied with the situation as autumn began. If so, they did not remain complacent for long. The May Thirtieth movement fueled the rapid growth and expansion of both the GMD and the CCP. The prestige and authority of the United Front was enormously increased by its leadership of the movement. The tide of radical anti-imperialism was not in fact turned but continued to flow out of the southeast. It is significant that even anti-student warlords were forced to tolerate some demonstrations at the peak of the movement. Though Hunan's governor threatened to shoot anyone who "preached Bolshevism" or "disturbed the peace," the political balance of power had shifted.

The May Thirtieth movement occurred against a background of the intensification of warlordism, the growing prestige of Sun Yat-sen, and the illegitimacy of the Beijing governments, which were failing to deal with new refugee problems, financial crises, and the unequal treaties. However, for all its obvious importance, it might be better to see the May Thirtieth movement as neither a beginning nor a culmination, but as part of a longer, painful process in which demands for social justice and the desire for collective identity meshed to bring increasing numbers of people into the political process. More sectors of society became radicalized – workers, obviously, and in some areas peasants as well. Above all, the Guomindang and the Chinese Communist Party emerged from the movement as newly legitimate *national* representatives of China's future.

# 11 Ideology and power in the National Revolution

Between 1926 and 1928 the Guomindang brought the warlord era to an end and, to a great extent, unified China. These years marked the rise of Chiang Kai-shek to national power, though this was by no means an unrestricted power, even within the GMD itself. Was this a revolutionary era? A counter-revolutionary era? As a new national government was being formed, how did Chinese society continue to change? What problems did this present for the new government? To answer these questions, it will be necessary to review some events from the early 1920s. Thus this chapter overlaps chrono-logically with the last and will focus on the Nationalists (GMD) and the Communists (CCP). These two parties provided China with enormous polit-ical dynamism; however, until 1928 the vast majority of Chinese continued to live under various warlord regimes.

A clear evolution of Chinese attitudes toward the outside world had occurred since the nineteenth century. To younger intellectuals and students the outside world represented both threat and opportunity, with lessons to be learned. This trend produced Liang Qichao, Chen Duxiu, and Mao Zedong. At the same time tens of thousands of less-educated Chinese, particularly from the southeast, emigrated to Southeast Asia, Australia, Europe, and the Americas to sell their labor and find opportunities in trade. There they learned much about the West firsthand. This trend produced Sun Yat-sen. The commingling of these two trends gave rise to a strongly anti-imperialist form of nationalism that was at the same time cosmopolitan. This was a nation-alism born less of pride than of humiliation and less of isolationism than of a desire for dignity. Chinese nationalists of the 1920s, had they achieved power, might well have raised protective tariffs to limit foreign competition and allow Chinese manufacturers to get off the ground. And they might well have spon-sored state enterprises, especially in transportation, mining, and infrastructure, such as railroads and electric plants. But they would not have sought to close China off from the world. The May Thirtieth movement of 1925 demon-strated the committed nationalism of the various classes of the urban sectors of China. Nothing like the Boxer Uprising re-emerged, however. Foreign companies were boycotted, foreign factories struck, foreign consulates pick-eted, but foreigners themselves were generally safe.

Neither the GMD nor the CCP could yet be called a national political party. But they both aimed at converting popular energies into political power. And they both fostered a revolutionary image. This marked China's first experiment with the mobilization of social groups by disciplined revolutionary parties. In historical fact, however, the results of the "National Revolution" were less than revolutionary. Although the GMD gained power, it pursued state-building policies designed to strengthen the Party, the military, and the government's financial organs. Many Nationalists had roots in the parliaments of the 1910s, and others in the warlord bureaucracies. In power, the GMD sought to cool off revolutionary anti-imperialism and basically followed the gradualist policies of the old Beijing governments.

Sun Yat-sen's attempt to turn the Guomindang into an ideologically-charged, revolutionary, Leninist party was not a success, but "Sunism," or the Three People's Principles, was to have a permanent effect on China. Sun Yat-sen has been dismissed by some Western historians as neither profound nor consistent. It is true that Sun's thinking was unsystematic and self-contradictory. His ideas were ambiguous and might change from one moment to the next as his political opportunities changed. However, he was often extraordinarily insightful. Sun and his followers used their forced retirement from politics between 1918 and 1920 to develop the Guomindang's ideology. Their critique of imperialism, their revolutionary strategies, and their developmental programs have influenced Third World politics across the globe. Sun's ideas in many respects foreshadowed and contributed to Chinese Marxism and Maoism.

Criticism of Sunism often misses the point of political rhetoric in modern Chinese politics. From Sun Yat-sen to Mao Zedong, political rhetoric was not designed primarily to sway intellectuals (or win popular votes) but was above all intended to provide guidance to followers. In the West the platforms of political parties are studies in vagueness, and no one expects politicians to relate their ideas about policy to a serious political philosophy. In this kind of "normal" politics, nowhere more than in the US, politicians try to please as many groups as possible with vague promises, and to avoid offending anyone. But in a revolutionary situation politicians do attempt to root their policies in a political philosophy. From Thomas Paine's *Common Sense* to the *Quotations of Chairman Mao* such projects include elements of public relations but they also turn out to be quite frank statements of intention.

Above all, revolutionary politicians do not hesitate to offend and to call for sacrifices. The question is not whether their philosophies are profound but what they show about leadership style and direction. The Three People's Principles were taken seriously by the GMD, and Sunism survived Sun's death to help shape a new kind of government in the late 1920s. To the extent that the GMD was an ideological regime, the Three People's Principles provided that ideology and limited the capacity of the regime to pursue other kinds of policies. In a way never seen before in China, the Nationalist government (1928–37) would be controlled by a political machine that defined itself as the major vanguard element in society. It hoped to mobilize mass support but deeply distrusted genuine mass organizations. It was anti-imperialist but hoped to cooperate with the forces of international capitalism. It gave China not a new emperor but a new kind of dictatorship.

## Ideology and the Guomindang

"To know is difficult" while "to act is easy." Sun Yat-sen made this epistemological formula the basis of his faith in the vanguard party. He thus also added his views to one of the classic questions of Chinese philosophy. The problem of the relationship between knowledge and action was as perennial in China as the question "What is truth?" has been in the West. Sun considered that the traditional Chinese belief was "to know is easy and to practice is difficult," and that this was the root of political error. He concluded that the Chinese had been conditioned to seek understanding before acting on a problem. "Then finding that this cannot be accomplished, they feel helpless and give up all thoughts of attempting."[1] In other words, Sun blamed disillusionment with revolution on a fundamental Chinese cultural predisposition. The other side of the epistemological coin was the Chinese tendency to rush to action before thoroughly thinking it through. No wonder the 1911 Revolution had failed – "old corrupt practices had still not been abolished."[2]

Sun claimed to be following Confucius and Mencius. It was typical of Sun to root his ideas in the Chinese past as much as in Western ideologies. The historian Ying-shih Yü has suggested that Sun's position agreed with Neo-Confucian orthodoxy on the knowledge–practice question.[3] Sun, however, explicitly attacked the doctrine of the Neo-Confucian Wang Yangming (1472–1529), who denied any real distinction between knowledge and practice. Wang's writings had inspired a generation of Japanese and Chinese radicals in the late nineteenth century through his emphasis on intuition. To know – really to know – *was* to act, as to act was to know. Wang explained, "There have never been people who know but do not act. Those who are supposed to know but do not act simply do not yet know... knowledge is the direction for action and action the effort of knowledge ... knowledge is the beginning of action and action the completion of knowledge."[4] For example, it made no sense to speak of a man "knowing" filial piety unless he practiced it. Furthermore, Wang's notion of "intuitive knowledge" implied not that knowledge was easy but that every person had the potential of achieving knowledge, or in Neo-Confucian terms becoming a sage. Wang's ideas would continue to have resonance – for example in the sinified Marxism of Mao Zedong.

For Sun, however, knowledge had to be separated from practice precisely to justify a vanguard party. Sun divided the world into three kinds of people: 1) the "foreknowers" or inventors, those equipped to rule because of their intellectual ability to understand the world; 2) the imitators, who are capable of understanding once they are taught and so may become administrators under the rulers; and 3) the masses of ignorant and not particularly competent people who can only follow. Did this theory leave any room for republicanism? Sun still believed in democracy, as long as it was understood in the sense of representative institutions that would not threaten the efficiency of the executive. By 1924 Sun seemed to have come to the conclusion that for the foreseeable future a vanguard party was not only necessary to lead the revolution but actually to create the state. This was a Leninist view of revolution shared by the CCP, but Sun did not need Lenin to lead him to this view. He had already come to the conclusion that the revolutionaries' failures after 1911 were not due to larger socioeconomic forces, imperialism, or Chinese conservatism, but to their own fear of action.

Sun's thoughts about the "period of political tutelage" became the theoretical blueprint of the Nationalist government two years after his death. In this scheme, a stable legal system would define the relationship between state and society; citizens would have duties and rights. Beginning locally and then spreading, self-government would train the new citizens in democracy. Sun pointed out that Americans had practiced self-government before their revolution, but in China the revolution would have to come first, before the people were ready for self-government. Tutelage was more than education. Sun also suggested that the Party could control, even create, the state, which implied that power must stem from the "foreknowers" (like Sun). Tutelage might therefore become part of the very structure of government.

Chinese liberals criticized "tutelage" on the grounds that it provided a rationalization for dictatorship instead of a transitional period to democracy. This criticism is just, yet misses the main point, for, after all, given Sun's premises about the capacities of the Chinese masses, democracy was not an immediate option. In practice, the real problem was not that tutelage denied people the vote but that it repressed civil society. Aside from discrediting the institutions of representative government, tutelage also promised to suppress dissent. The GMD (and the CCP) would support the mobilization of workers and peasants only on their own terms. For Sun Yat-sen the need for Party unity was analogous to the need for national unity, and "European and American" ideals of liberty and equality were outmoded. For "if the revolution is to succeed then it is the institution that must have the freedom and not the individual."

> Political organizations such as states and political parties ... should all enjoy freedom and equality in their dealings, whether in struggles between one country and another or struggles between one party and another. But this is not to say that in our party or our state everyone should have freedom and equality.[5]

Sun's proposed constitution placed limits on the powers of the state, and much of his rhetoric spoke of the people as rulers. However, Sun's vision was undoubtedly a statist view of the people turned into a unified and loyal citizenry. He emphasized the powers of the state over the individual and ultimately the power of the disciplined, revolutionary Party over the state. In one formulation Sun granted "sovereignty" to the citizens but still insisted on the state's tutelary role in guiding and educating those citizens – just as ancient emperors, he said, were sovereign but were guided by their tutors. One reason Sun doubted the present capacities of the Chinese people and feared "individualism" was his sense that the imperial government, far from being too autocratic, had been too lax. The Chinese people had been spoiled by excessive liberties. He famously proclaimed: "Foreign observers say that the Chinese are like a loose sheet of sand. Why? Simply because our people have shown loyalty to family and clan but not to the nation – there has been no nationalism."[6] Therefore, discipline was needed to consolidate this sand into hard cement. Since Sun distrusted the political process of parliamentary debate and compromise, discipline could only come from a party that was itself disciplined.

Sun's historical importance lies in his turning the loosely-organized GMD into a Leninist party. The notion of the supremacy of the Party in China did not stem from the Communists but from Sun. But he was not alone in his sense that China needed revolution, that revolution needed a disciplined party, and that post-revolutionary construction would still need that party's leadership. The GMD became an organization intolerant of dissent, from within the Party even more than from the outside. Members were supposed to transcend their local attachments, and the notions of local self-government or provincial autonomy seemed to strike at the very root of Nationalist principles. These ideas, too, were largely inherited by the Communists. But the Communists also inherited the New Culture movement's harsh critique of traditional morality, while Sun thought that Confucian virtues such as loyalty, faithfulness, and filial piety could contribute to a sense of national identity and unity.

As for the "three people's principles," in the 1920s Sun completely revamped "nationalism" from the anti-Manchuism of 1911 to a broader anti-imperialism. He focused on the outside threat. Sun complained, "Our people keep thinking that China is only a 'semi-colony' – a term by which they seek to comfort themselves. Yet in reality the economic oppression we have endured is not just that of a 'semi-colony' but greater even than that of a full colony." For China

> ... is the colony of every nation with which it has concluded treaties; each of them is China's master. Therefore China is not just the colony of one country; it is the colony of many countries. We are not just the slaves of one country, but the slaves of many countries.[7]

One might disagree with the economic argument Sun made, but psychologically he captured the sense of powerlessness felt by politically aware Chinese.

The trope of slavery had been widespread since the 1890s, and Sun's claim that China was even worse off than a colony had great force. He argued that colonizers took some responsibility for their colonies, while the Powers simply ignored China's problems. As for China's ethnic divisions, Sun thought minorities would basically be transcended by assimilation to Han culture. "The Chinese people totals four hundred million people; for the most part, the Chinese people are of the Han or Chinese race with common blood, common language, common religion, and common customs ..."[8] The Chinese were a strong people with traditions to be proud of, Sun taught. But he also informed them of their faults, especially as seen through foreign eyes. He complained about Chinese table manners, spitting, long fingernails, and dirty teeth. The point was that these were the indicators foreigners used to judge the Chinese.

> Once, in Shanghai, a big Chinese merchant invited some foreigners to a feast and passed gas right at the table until the foreigners' faces were red with embarrassment. He not only did not check himself but even stood up and slapped his clothes, loudly saying, "ee-s-ko-s-me." Such behavior is uncivilized and vulgar in the extreme, yet even scholars and students are constantly guilty of it and reform is certainly difficult.[9]

The issue of personal habits and appearance became central to the revolutions of both the Nationalists and the Communists. As historian John Fitzgerald points out, remaking the person and remaking the state were twinned projects. True citizens wore modern but modest clothes, short hair, took a daily bath, and brought the same discipline to every aspect of their lives. Some of these grooming points we have already seen in the birth of the Republic in 1912; in the 1920s they became Party policy and in the 1930s government doctrine.

The second principle, "democracy," may have been battered by the idea of tutelage, but Sun did propose a constitutional order that would try to balance popular power and the government's needs. Sun sought a powerful government that would still be responsive to the will of the people. He thought he found the solution in distinguishing between the executive powers to carry out administration and ultimate sovereignty. He compared a republic to a business: the people are the shareholders and the president the manager. In other words, the people set basic goals that the government figures out how to meet; the actual administration is removed from the people. Sun proposed a constitution of five branches, deliberately mixing Western and Chinese traditions: executive, legislative, judiciary, examination (to select the civil service), and censorate (to prosecute official misconduct). The people were to have rights of suffrage, recall, initiative, and referendum. However, none of these principles – and that is all they were – detracted from Sun's essential statism.

Sun's ideas about the "people's livelihood" were at least as vague as his ideas about democracy. Sun saw considerable overlap between this principle and Western socialism. In the future, everybody would share in the profits of capital. The "equalization of land rights" was sometimes talked about, as it had been since the early 1900s, but the GMD devoted relatively little attention to rural problems. Sun never rejected capitalism or glorified class struggle. "People's livelihood" thus came to refer to "control of capital" or a regulatory regime. In 1924 the GMD asserted that the state would control finance, the infrastructure, and other large-scale enterprises, and promised land reform for farmers (though without calling for the appropriation of landlords). The GMD favored workers' rights to decent wages and working conditions, but Sun, for one, was skeptical of the right to strike, which might harm the national economy. Private enterprise might be trusted to develop farming and commerce; foreign investment and Chinese business were to be encouraged. In a word, a moderate state socialism devoted to development.

Above all, for Sun, China's deepest problem was its general poverty. He consistently hoped that economic modernization would allow China to avoid the class struggle and labor strife that had appeared in the West. And for all of his attacks on warlords and imperialists, Sun remained attached to an ultimately internationalist vision of foreign investment that would gradually turn China into an advanced producer and market. As Sun's biographer Marie-Claire Bergère points out, such views seem better to represent the late twentieth century than Sun's own times. But Sunism was nothing if not elastic. After his death, the GMD declared Sun's writings were never to be contradicted; Communists could continue to join the GMD as long as they accepted Sun's views. But like the Bible, Sun's legacy could be used for highly disparate purposes by selecting the appropriate passage. If Sun therefore seems a sloppy thinker, his ideas nevertheless formed the flexible basis of an influential ideology. This influence ultimately rested, not on Sun's powers of persuasion nor even the political successes of the Nationalists, but on the fact that so many could agree with Sun. He had encapsulated the essence of Chinese political thought going back at least to Liang Qichao: that China needed stronger government; that the goals of that government would be to develop and modernize the nation; that Chinese society was anarchic; that civil society and individual rights themselves depended on a strong state; and that a constitutional political order would reconcile conflicting interests.

## Social radicalism in the 1920s: The peasantry

We have seen how workers emerged as a stronger social force, especially in Shanghai and the Guangzhou delta. Other groups also demanded social and political change, including peasants and women. The Communists would eventually come to power on the basis of rural revolution and large peasant-based armies. No one could have foreseen that in the 1920s. The Communists did not foresee it. Peasant associations and peasant uprisings in the 1920s were suppressed, but the lessons they learned were to aid the Communists in later years. We can also learn a good deal about the Chinese countryside from the peasant movements of the 1920s.[10]

In spite of the urban bias shared by both the Nationalists and the Communists, a few GMD activists saw the peasantry as a useful source of support for the Guangzhou government. They saw a power vacuum in the rural counties of Guangdong Province that might aid the GMD. Disciplined peasant associations under the authority of the GMD could become agents keeping rural order and collecting taxes. As we have seen, Sun Yat-sen promised land to the peasants, though he could not say where it was going to come from: this at least offered ideological justification for working with peasants. Communists sometimes saw in the peasantry a source of support for the workers' revolution. At the same time, peasant politicians saw in the United Front outside contacts that could help them in local struggles.

For educated men to penetrate the world of the village was not easy. Even if they were from the countryside, they had to communicate with people who had every reason to distrust them. One who tried was Shen Dingyi. Whether because he was disillusioned with the hothouse of the personalized politics of Shanghai or because he saw the possibilities of local organizing, Shen returned to his hometown, Yaqian in Zhejiang Province, in the fall of 1920.[11] He insisted that the family servants call him by his personal name instead of "Third Gentleman" (meaning the third son of the master of the household). He taught that the peasants and workers were victims of the capitalist system and therefore natural allies against the exploitation of landlords and merchants. He wore farmers' clothes, sometimes gave money to tenants in difficulty, and established a free village school, recruiting teachers from the Zhejiang Provincial First Normal School – the same radical institution that had produced Shi Cuntong. Out of these tentative beginnings – not so much different from the paternalism of the old gentry – came the Yaqian farmers' movement. Severe inflation in 1921 prompted farmers to attack the stores of merchants who raised their prices. This apparently occurred without Shen's direct participation, though no doubt the propaganda he and the young teachers were spreading played a role. In any case, Shen then called on farmers to form an anti-landlord association, predicting that "one day the great landlords will surrender to you."

The Yaqian Farmers' Association that was formed in September called for a 30 percent reduction in rents, the abolition of prepayments of rent before harvest, and other improvements to the position of tenant farmers. The association also stood for a more general progressive agenda: giving women equality, abolishing superstition, teaching literacy, forbidding footbinding, and so on. The words on an old Yaqian memorial arch, "Respect chaste women and filial sons," were replaced with "Long live women's liberation," and this echo of Lu Xun was added: "Beyond doubt in the Twenty-four Histories [of the imperial dynasties] are written the ethical teachings of those who eat people." Shen may be considered the Association's patron, but – elected to the provincial assembly – he left local farmers to manage its day-to-day business. Within weeks, farmers from the entire southern Hangzhou Bay region were coming to Yaqian to join the association and learn more about organizing themselves.

Within a couple of months farmers' associations were formed in 82 villages, with a total of 100,000 members. Landlords who tried to collect full rents were beaten or chased away. Responding to their pleas, the provincial military moved in to break up the associations and arrest their leaders, a number of whom were tortured and executed. The provincial governor frankly announced that the rent reduction movement was illegal because it threatened tax collection. The government did not, however, hold Shen responsible, and he returned home literally to bury the dead.

The farmers' demands fell short of land distribution; their aims were more reformist than revolutionary, though the associations were certainly coercive. Perhaps Shen and the young men from First Normal who joined him thought that the farmers' movement would be able to survive in the interstices of warlordism. Or perhaps they were simply naïve about the land-lords' powers. But in any case they represent an early case of the "discovery" of the peasants – not as an abstraction but as real victims of a particular economic system; yet also as potential political actors in their own right. Even those who grew up in the countryside may not have been able to "see" how poor farmers lived until they were ready to. Now, visiting peasants in their homes, young scholars saw that the "floors were covered with chicken shit; and people walked through it with their bare feet." They discovered that bad weather meant whole villages could go hungry.

A peasants' movement on the northern Guangdong coast was tied more closely to the United Front and lasted much longer. In Haifeng and Lufeng Counties, Peng Pai (1896–1929), an educated scion of a wealthy Hakka family in the area, led a political movement that turned into a potent revolu-tionary force. Like Shen, Peng was a generic radical, influenced by anarchism, and he joined the CCP only after he already had begun orga-nizing peasants. Chen Jiongming financed his studies in Japan in 1917, where he became acquainted with Marxist ideas and with Japanese agrarian reformers. In 1921 he became chief of the education bureau in Haifeng but he soon came to doubt that schooling could effect social change. Peng turned to more direct action. He recounted that the peasants rebuffed his first attempts to explain to them how they were being exploited. They assumed he was a tax collector or, if they gathered anything of what he was saying, that he must be insane – a rumor encouraged by his family.

Peng learned to attract villagers with magic tricks in the evening after work, before beginning his lectures. Though they listened, the peasants still did not necessarily believe or trust him. Yet, finally, Peng made a few young converts. When their parents objected to their unremunerated waste of time, Peng loaned first one then the others the same three dollars to show their parents. This ruse symbolizes the shoestring innovativeness of Peng's opera-tion. The young peasants also advised Peng to treat the villagers' gods with respect and work within traditional frameworks as much as possible. As the peasants concluded, "We do not want our Buddhas destroyed. Our gods are revolutionary and look with favor on the Soviet."[12] The Hai-Lu-feng peasant association began as an organ by which village youth protected the village from outside attack – a perfectly orthodox front. But under Peng's guidance its mutual aid and union functions quickly grew. If a landlord tried to raise rents, no one would pay at all. If a landlord removed his tenants, association members could not farm those fields. Furthermore, the ex-tenants qualified for aid. The association also offered medical and prescription services. Equally important, Peng was able to negotiate prices with merchants and was soon involved in both civil and criminal cases.

Peng and the peasant organizations in Guangdong in the 1920s were filling roles left vacant by the state and the failure of local gentry to provide traditional social services. For a time provincial authorities, caught up in their own power struggles, failed to react. Not only did Peng's family background help him, but he deliberately suppressed any moves toward class struggle. Unlike Shen Dingyi's experiment, the Guangdong farmers' associations avoided demands for rent reduction at first. Peng's actions, at least on the surface, were largely traditional in scope. Village schools, for example, were ancient institutions; now, however, students were taught useful skills and radical ideas, along with basic literacy. Landlords and merchants would find it harder to cheat peasants who knew arithmetic.

But Peng's enemies were growing impatient and, when landlord–tenant disputes erupted in 1923, the association was disbanded and Peng exiled from the area. Peng took his organizational talents to other parts of Guangdong Province while work in Haifeng and Lufeng continued underground. Peng also tried to bring peasant women into the associations, some of whom became community leaders. However, male peasants remained the backbone of the associations, and Peng was not willing to encourage notions of gender equality that would divide the poor peasants. Poor peasant males worried about finding enough money to arrange a marriage; Communist organizers swallowed their criticisms of the "feudal family system" because the struggle against landlords had to come first.

Peng Pai's experiences demonstrate the strengths and weaknesses of peasant-based revolution. On the one hand, without sufficient military strength the peasant association could not protect itself when the authorities cracked down. Its growth was dependent on regional political conditions over which it had no control. Chen Jiongming had been sympathetic to reform and originally supported Peng Pai. But a resurgent GMD would not ignore the area as it consolidated its power in the 1920s. On the other hand, what choice did Peng Pai have but to take advantage of circumstances, including his connections to Chen Jiongming? Self-imposed restraint – the early focus on education, health, and intra-community conciliation – was wise. It allowed for rapid growth with minimal opposition, but more radical steps provoked immediate opposition. For under conditions of intense rivalry for land whereby landlords were often able to increase rents by setting tenant against tenant in a bidding war, even a moderate peasant union was bound to lead to confrontation. Although Peng evidently tried to keep demands reasonable (rent reduction, not abolition; tenants to be as bound to contractual obligations as landlords), this still represented a *political* attack on the traditional balance of powers and rights. Significantly, disputes not only arose when peasants asked for rent reductions due to bad harvests (a traditional enough request), but also when landlords tried to raise the rents of tenants who considered themselves to possess lifetime tenure – taking advantage of basic demographic conditions which worked against the peasants.

If vulnerability to military attack was the most obvious weakness of the organization, it faced other obstacles as well. First, of course, peasants had to be convinced to join it: and to remain in it. They had to be persuaded that it offered them benefits and that they would not be punished for joining. Furthermore, not joining should have a price. Non-members had to be denied medical services at the clinic and loans for family emergencies. Once they joined, they had to abide by the rules and pay their dues. The point was to build community solidarity. But this very solidarity could lead to new traps. Parochialism was a constant constraint on Communist organizers. To set one community against another, in the traditional fashion of clan organizations and protection gangs, was easier than uniting peasants on the basis of class. Inter-community disputes were often deeply embedded in local culture. And having built up some kind of trans-village solidarity, organizers then had to prevent themselves from being co-opted by the peasants. The CCP certainly did not want to become a peasants' party; it saw itself as representing transcendental national and (ultimately) international proletarian interests. Peasants might rest content with a few economic gains, but Communists wanted to eliminate landlordism or "feudalism" entirely.

None the less, the Communists declared their support for "land to the tiller" and peasants' associations in October 1925. Based in no small part on Peng's experiences, the Party's "Proclamation for the Peasantry" eloquently stated:

> The peasants suffer oppression from four sources: the landlords, through rent, usury, etc.; the foreign capitalists because of their goods and industry had destroyed traditional handicraft work and because of their control of such things as the salt tax; the warlords with the indirect taxes and extortion of moneys needed to wage their wars; corrupt officials and evil gentry who collect in bribe money at least twice as much as the state levies.... The peasants have an important job growing food and account for the majority of the population, but now they are so miserable that they have to wander about the country.[13]

The GMD–CCP United Front founded a Peasant Movement Institute in 1924 to train rural organizers. This might be compared to the Huangpu Military Academy, though it was a much smaller enterprise, graduating only

1,700 men who were given just three months' training. Its teachers included Peng Pai, Zhou Enlai, Qu Qiubai, and Mao Zedong. The trainees were not poor peasants but young men who had received at least a few years of formal education. Training included extensive military drill, which probably reflected Sun Yat-sen's desires to field larger armies as much as the need to raise village self-defense militia. The greatest problem of the institute was that it was too small to produce enough skilled organizers. Even in Guangdong, there was at most one trained organizer for every thousand farmers in the peasant associations. The peasant associations themselves were of varied quality, frequently isolated, prone to extremism, and unarmed. Still, even if Communist national estimates of nine million members at their height were exaggerated, a wave of rural organizing swept across large parts of southern China between 1924 and 1927 before it was violently suppressed.

## Social radicalism in the 1920s: Women

In Chinese histories of feminism, a distinction is often made between women's rights as such – the right to an education, a career, voting, choosing one's own husband – on the one hand, and women's liberation as part of a larger revolutionary process on the other. The first have been called the "bourgeois rights" of women who otherwise accepted an unjust system, thinking they could gain rights in isolation from other oppressed groups. But in the words of Song Qingling, Sun Yat-sen's wife, "From the very start, our women fought not under the banner of a barren feminism but as part and parcel of the democratic movement as a whole."[14] The note of disdain regarding "feminism" is not accidental but is itself a product of the larger Chinese revolution. Although women had their own journals ranging from the sternly political to fashion magazines, although women had their own issues ranging from suffrage and educational opportunity to marriage and divorce rights, and although women sometimes publicly explored their own sexuality – politically they tended to act in tandem with other groups. Many women turned in the 1920s to the Nationalists and the Communists. Chinese women would not be free as long as imperialists, warlords, and perhaps capitalists enslaved all Chinese. Some women thus became professional revolutionaries and politicians dedicated to a larger struggle, of which women's rights was one part.

Chinese feminists (that is, women's rights activists, whether or not they used the terminology of feminism), mostly women, had been sharply disillusioned by the failure of the revolutionaries to support female suffrage in 1912. Still, they continued to use the language of citizenship and nationalism to justify their demands for gender equality. China could be neither a strong nation nor a just nation without the full and unfettered participation of women in its civic life. By the early 1920s, the new Guomindang seemed the only major party willing to acknowledge the justice of women's claims. But women also organized their own groups. The United Women's Associations represented networks of largely middle-class women in China's cities. They pursued women's issues within the existing political framework. The UWA could put hundreds and even thousands of women on the streets to demonstrate for the vote. Success was achieved in Hunan when women were elected to the provincial assembly and several country assemblies. Like other groups, the UWA was in a constant process of defining itself; it faced internal conflict over decisions such as whether to admit concubines, for example. Given its appeal, the GMD saw the benefits of an alliance with the UWA. Even the Communists pulled back on their criticisms of "bourgeois" women to attract their support.

The United Front was thus committed to women's equality, inheriting the New Culture movement's attack on the traditional patriarchy that vested authority in the senior males of the family line. This was quite a direct "inheritance" – many of the early Party leaders, especially in the CCP, had developed the very language of liberation and rights that applied to women. As we have seen, the "women's question" was central to intellectual concerns of the period. Men such as Chen Duxiu and Zhang Shenfu, and for that matter Mao Zedong, did not abandon their feminism when they became Communists. They and their colleagues proposed changes in the legal and social status of women that would have amounted to a cultural revolution. Many tried to change themselves: to live personal lives that recognized the equality of the sexes. At the same time, we may note that the price of such decisions could be high. Chen, Zhang, and Mao all abandoned their first wives as the unwanted products of arranged marriages. They found new lovers and wives among the minority of educated, activist women. Abandonment at least gave the first wife the option of staying at home in the countryside as the official first wife. Divorce, though seeming more modern to Communist men, was still a disgrace that led in at least one case to a first wife's suicide. But to modern, freethinking urban women, companionate marriage – or even partnerships bypassing formal marriage altogether – was a critical mark of their own liberation.

At the same time, many women pursued their liberation entirely outside of Party structures. On the one hand were practical questions: the search for an independent career with or without marriage. Teaching in one of the growing number of girls' schools was probably the most popular option, but women became lawyers, writers, publishers, nurses, and doctors as well. On the other hand was a change in consciousness. The historian Wang Zheng has described this as a "liberal feminist discourse" to distinguish it from a more politicized view of women as (merely) one part of a larger revolutionary process.[15] She emphasizes that women used May Fourth ideals of human rights to argue for an essential same-ness between men and women. In this way, in their own minds, they were able to break old gender boundaries. It is true that the "human" was modeled in male form; liberal women, then, did not demand equality *as women* who were essentially different but still equal to men, but rather as human beings who were as intelligent, as strong, as patriotic, and generally as capable as men.

Yet, again, this describes a relatively small proportion of women who lived in cities and had access to education. Women workers – factory hands, servants, prostitutes, and coolies, as well as farmwives who struggled to survive on a daily basis – were in no position to challenge gender boundaries in this way. And numerous middle-class and upper-class women were content to be "good wives and wise mothers" without directly challenging the patriarchal system. There is little reason to think that men, even supporters of feminist points of view like the liberal Hu Shi, the Communist Chen Duxiu, or the cultural radical Lu Xun, made the equality of the sexes a core element of their consciousness. But the emergence of women as a completely new social category was a consciousness-altering experience for women, beginning in the late Qing and achieving a kind of universality in the 1920s. In this sense, we cannot assume that either women workers or middle-class "good wives" were unaffected by the radical changes of the period. Indeed, the "good wife, wise mother" ideal justified many breaks with patriarchal tradition. However, some elements of gender hierarchy proved indelible. The GMD and the CCP themselves remained largely patriarchal organizations. We have already seen how the latter placed greater stress on organizing male workers than female workers. Few women were to reach top positions in either party, and prominent women politicians tended to be the wives or girlfriends of even more prominent men politicians.

The Guomindang created a Central Women's Bureau as part of its reorganization at the beginning of 1924. Much effort was spent on propaganda, including the performance of dramas for largely illiterate audiences in the countryside around Guangzhou. There was no problem in fitting women's issues into the anti-warlord and anti-imperialist framework of Sunism. Nor did international proletarian solidarity experience any tensions with feminism at the level of official symbolism. A Russian woman recalled dressing up as a Chinese for the 1926 Women's Day celebrations in Guangzhou: "I portrayed awakened China and stretched out my hands toward Soviet Russia. No matter how surprising it may seem, the Chinese recognized themselves in me and applauded deafeningly."[16] As John Fitzgerald points out, the symbol of the awakening female captured the hopes of a captive nation. Symbolically, the oppressed woman could represent women's issues or the suffering of the entire nation.[17] Thus was the Chinese nation itself gendered.

To show their revolutionary modernity, progressive Chinese women bobbed their hair in a more boyish style. This was virtually a declaration of radicalism, like men cutting off their queues before the 1911 Revolution. In Guangzhou in the mid-1920s, women called for equal wages and educational opportunities, free marriage and divorce, and the abolition of concubinage, prostitution, and child brides. With Guangzhou finally in Sun Yat-sen's hands, organizers made their way into the countryside. They often found rural towns and villages "backward," but once they gained a foothold they

*Figure 11.1* Women of the new urban middle classes were expected to be "good wives and wise mothers" – understanding hygiene – and good consumers who knew how, in the words of this soap advertisement, to "SAVE TIME, SAVE LABOR, SAVE MONEY."

*Source*: From *Lanyan ribao*, 20 May 1920

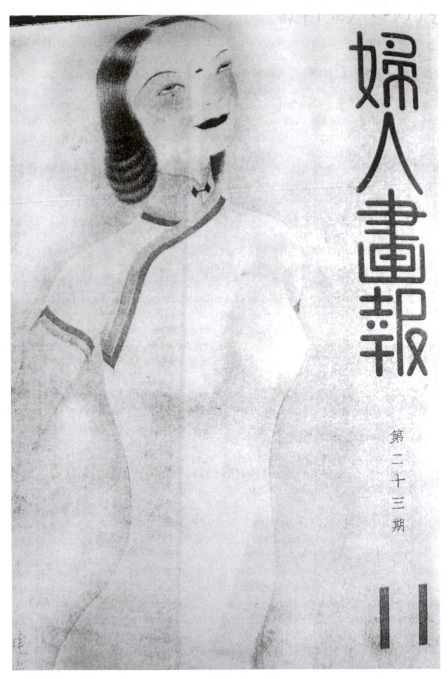

*Figure 11.2* Women continued to achieve a new public presence through the 1920s, at least in the cities. Wearing an elegant *qipao*, this beauty adorned the "Women's Pictorial."

*Source*: From *Funü huabao* no. 23, November 1935

could alter local conditions and recruit activists. Hakka communities tended to be relatively responsive. Rather than discussing anti-imperialism, the key seemed to be focusing on specific women's issues: education, job training, prostitutes, bond servants, and above all marriage rights. Women's associations at the village level could pursue the issues most important to rural women, such as wife-beating. Some began granting divorces on their own, but it was the indissolubility of marriage that peasant men often felt most strongly about. Divorced women sometimes had to be helped to leave their villages – and where could they go?

The CCP's Women's Bureau had been formed in 1923. More explicitly than European Marxists, the Chinese Communists recognized class and gender as a double form of oppression. Some Communists even compared the status of women as such to the proletariat. Partial translations of Friedrich Engels's *Origins of the Family, Private Property, and the State*, which linked the oppression of women to private property, exerted great influence. Engels seemed to justify the New Culture movement's attack on patriarchy in Marxist terms. The family-clan that was the bulwark of the feudal property system was also the source of such evils as footbinding, concubinage, the cruel isolation of women, and the treatment of women as mere property. The goals of the revolution included not only the liberation of workers but also ensuring that women learned the skills necessary to become workers in the first place. In the words of the CCP's 1922 "Resolution on the Women's Movement":

> The women of the entire nation are still imprisoned in the yoke of the feudal ethical code and lead lives similar to prostitutes. Women of every class in China are unable to obtain political, economic, and education rights. Therefore the Chinese Communist Party in addition to ardently protecting and struggling for the interests of women workers – like striving for equal wages and drafting laws for women and children – also should struggle for the interests of all oppressed women.[18]

Of course, the theme of women's economic independence was not new and it did not take a Marxist to highlight it. Marriage was more controversial. Some male feminists considered marriage to be a form of prostitution – powerless women selling their bodies in return for material sustenance – though radical females took sharp exception to this insult. Either way, family issues were not to be dismissed as irrelevant to the class struggle. One female Communist stressed the need for birth control to free women from their role as unpaid child-minders.[19]

As leader of the CCP, Chen Duxiu was personally inclined to emphasize the feminist cause, and, seeking allies for the CCP, he encouraged contacts with such "bourgeois" groups as the UWA that could agree on a minimum program of equal legal rights and suffrage for women. He also encouraged Communist women to take the lead in organizing women for the Party. The first woman to emerge as a Communist leader was Wang Huiwu (1898–1993), wife of the Communist intellectual Li Da. One of the most important women leaders was Deng Yingchao (1904–92), wife of Zhou Enlai. And the woman who led the movement through the United Front period was Xiang Jingyu (1895–1928), wife of Cai Hesen, Mao Zedong's friend.

These women were impressive writers and organizers. Mere nepotism did not get them leadership positions, but it seems to have been a necessary qualification. Nor were women comrades given major responsibilities outside of organizing women workers. Wang Huiwu started the Shanghai Commoners' Girls' School in 1922 to offer a more "modern" education than was available in upper-class schools that concentrated on preparing "good wives and wise mothers." The school offered a range of science and language courses as well as a work–study program designed to prepare women for a vocation. The notion of work–study as a way to change the individual's selfishness and create a communitarian society was rooted in anarchist traditions. The training in sock-knitting, tailoring, and weaving, however, looks fairly close to traditional "women's work." Some of the thirty students were the illiterate wives of Communist men who wanted them to have an education. Others were escapees from families trying to marry them against their will.

Male Communists were divided on the usefulness of this kind of women's schooling. With his commitment to education and enlightenment as a tool for changing society, Chen Duxiu was an enthusiastic backer. Shi Cuntong, on the contrary, wanted the school to focus on training activists rather than providing basic education. With her emphasis on economic liberation and work–study, it is not surprising that Wang Huiwu was accused of anarchist tendencies at a time when the CCP was trying to purify itself. When Li Da, who had clashed with Chen Duxiu, failed to be re-elected to the Central Committee, Wang's school and a women's journal she edited were both closed down. Cai Hesen was instead elected to the Central Committee and his wife, Xiang Jingyu, became the head of the new Women's Bureau. As historian Christina Gilmartin suggests, the treatment of Wang and the Commoners' Girls' School suggests that "certain unarticulated traditional assumptions" inhibited the acceptance of women as full-fledged members of the CCP and led to skepticism regarding programs that would empower women.[20] The notion that women could wield power in the public sphere was still very new, easier to welcome in theory than in practice. Li Da had been the figurehead principal of the school that Wang had actually organized and run. Of the CCP's 195 members in July 1922, only four were women.

Xiang Jingyu struggled to combine Marxism and feminism under these difficult circumstances. Born to a prosperous merchant in western Hunan, she attended a girl's school in Changsha and was clearly influenced by the radical trends of the time, especially the nationalism of Liang Qichao. With six classmates she formed a group that swore to study hard in order to achieve women's equality and save the nation. When she was just twenty-one, she founded a girls' primary school in her hometown. Defying her father, she insisted on arranging her own marriage with the Changsha radical Cai Hesen. In 1919 Xiang traveled to France with Cai as part of the Diligent-Work Frugal-Study Association's program there. They converted to Marxism together, and their wedding picture shows them reading *Das Kapital*.

Returning to China in 1922, Xiang initially ignored women's issues. However, named head of the Women's Bureau, she dedicated herself to trying to organize women workers and influence the "general women's movement." Xiang was one of the first CCP women members to join the GMD, and she became a dominant force on women's issues in the United Front. Interestingly, Xiang supported the CCP–GMD alliance while Cai Hesen opposed it. However, she remained wary of "bourgeois" women's issues. If equal rights, suffrage, and social reform seemed too tame, Xiang's solution was to drive women into the larger revolutionary struggle. She frankly condemned the suffrage movement as self-deceiving, at least while political institutions ultimately remained under warlord control. "Their efforts will result in the whole bunch of them entering the pigsties in the capital and the provinces where, together with the male pigs, they will preside over the country's catastrophes and the people's calamities."[21] Yet Xiang was anything but dogmatic, revising her earlier criticism of the YWCA (Young Women's Christian Association) to acknowledge its commitment to social activism.

Xiang particularly emphasized solidarity with women workers. Shanghai's silk workers worked under especially harsh conditions and had a strong tradition of striking. However, the CCP was not able to make many inroads among these workers, partly because their union was anti-Communist. Furthermore, though organizing women workers was theoretically a central goal of the CCP, they were actually a secondary concern. In the lead-up to the May Thirtieth movement, it was the firing of male workers to make way for female replacements that provoked violence. Even when women workers were explicitly targeted, organizing them was more difficult than in the case of men workers. They often lived in company dormitories and, if married, their husbands expected them to devote all their non-factory time to house-hold chores. Most were illiterate, so propaganda pamphlets and newspapers could not reach them. Xiang, with her Hunan accent, could barely communi-cate with the Shanghainese. And male Communist organizers could be insensitive to women's concerns. One young woman worker remembers being shocked when the organizer Deng Zhongxia entered her bedroom. "At that time women were not supposed to talk to men."[22]

Workers' schools were ineffective in reaching women since it was improper for women to participate in shared activities with unrelated men, especially in the evenings. Xiang Jingyu condemned the "leftist error" of not taking tradi-tional attitudes into account and sensibly suggested establishing separate women's schools. But perhaps because the male-dominated CCP was simply not willing to take the special needs of women into account, it never recruited among women workers the way it did men. It was left for the more reformist YWCA to establish separate schools for women workers in the late 1920s.

As the CCP entered its great period of growth during 1925, more women joined the Party and Xiang gained greater power. Women students and workers joined all the street demonstrations of 1925. Some were permanently radicalized by the experience, and Communist-sponsored women's associations spread across many of China's cities. Yet women Communists were largely ghettoized with positions in the Women's Bureau, and Xiang's authority was not formalized. For example, although she participated in Central Committee meetings, she does not appear to have been a member of the Central Committee. And like many women members, her status remained ultimately dependent on her husband's. As long as women's power within the CCP remained informal, it could not become fully legitimate. In their personal lives, male Communists were comfortable with traditional household arrangements (wife doing housework and raising children, husband in the outer world) and some seemed to have visited brothels. Nor are cases of women directly protesting against these arrangements known. While representative of a gap between theory and practice, none of this should be surprising.

At the height of the May Thirtieth movement, Xiang Jingyu was suddenly removed as head of the Women's Bureau. The CCP was apparently upset by the deterioration of her marriage with Cai and her becoming close to another Communist leader. Without Cai's backing, she could not maintain her Party position, no matter how successful she had been. Her replacement was capable – but Yang Zhihua was also the wife of Qu Qiubai, the intellectual who would replace Chen Duxiu as leader of the entire CCP in 1927. Even in theory, male Communists expressed reservations about the women's movement. The simple equation between female gender and proletarian status did not hold up. Communist men feared that the goal of "equality" might refer to equality with capitalists instead of with workers. Similarly, women's "rights" might refer to bourgeois individualism. Some seem to have feared that the movement encompassed man-hating, and they emphasized that the desire to keep women as chattels stemmed from feudal socioeconomic structures, not from any essential male qualities. They attacked the birth control movement as a distraction, arguing that the fundamental problem was unequal distribution of wealth, not overpopulation. Communists excluded a range of issues from what counted as women's liberation by condemning them as counter-revolutionary.[23] Thus were parameters established that narrowed women's discourse and even deprived women of their own voices.

This latent antifeminism stemmed from two sources. First, an intellectual analysis that gave more importance to class revolution than to gender revolution (or, in the case of Nationalists, to the anti-imperialist, anti-warlord movement than to women's issues). And second, a deeply-rooted aversion to seeing powerful women in public life. Probably the majority of men, even in radical movements, could not help but feel this way given their upbringing. However, whatever limitations fettered Chinese radicals from today's perspective, they encouraged forces that favored liberation of all kinds.

# 12 The Northern Expedition and the rise of Chiang Kai-shek

By the end of 1928 the Guomindang had defeated the forces of the major Chinese warlords and more or less controlled the provinces of Hunan, Hubei, Jiangxi, and Fujian, as well as Guangdong and Guangxi. Nationalist forces under the command of Chiang Kai-shek had brought the warlord era to an end in just over two years. This was the Northern Expedition – GMD troops marching out of Guangdong to unify the country. Success begat success as the GMD armies grew by accepting surrendering armies into the command structure. There was neither time to indoctrinate them politically nor easy access to funds to pay them, but these were not fatal weaknesses.

What explains the GMD's success? Chiang Kai-shek could claim a number of assets. A corps of soldiers who believed in what they were fighting for. A reliable financial base resting on modern-sector banking and taxation. Popular support, which meant that workers and peasants in enemy territories aided the Northern Expedition. Professional Russian military advice and aid. Severe disunity among the enemy, and the willingness of many of them to join the GMD. This chapter examines the process that, within limits, unified China.

That process included the beginning of a social revolution. With the direction and aid of Nationalists and Communists, workers in Shanghai and in the southeast continued to make significant strides in union organization and were able to claim major victories against foreign and Chinese-owned industries in 1926 and early 1927. Also, at the height of the movement, in Guangdong, Jiangxi, Hunan, and Hubei provinces peasant associations were able to bargain with landlords over rents and sometimes even to arm themselves. Communist organizers in the countryside seemed to be starting a chain reaction. Throughout the country, social groups looked to the United Front, willing to sacrifice for the national cause, in the anticipation that those sacrifices would benefit them later. Workers, women, peasants, students, and merchants mobilized in the course of the National Revolution. They linked their rights to the nation's rights.

The alliance between the Nationalists and the Communists broke down under the strains of success, and the Communists became hunted criminals,

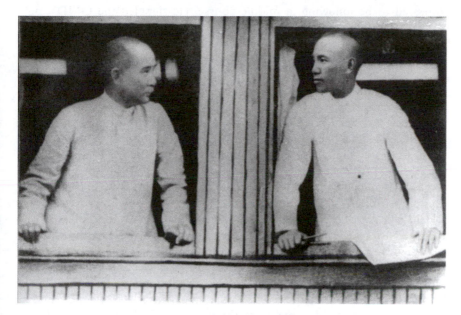

*Figure 12.1* Sun Yat-sen (left) and Chiang Kai-shek (right), aboard a train.
*Source*: Courtesy of Academia Historica, Taipei

their political capacities reduced to virtually nothing after 1928. The Guomindang under Chiang Kai-shek faced the task of building a national government virtually from scratch. State-building involved disarming warlord enemies and local elites, maintaining social order and ending banditry, regularizing a bureaucracy and tax-collection, and strengthening China's military and industrial capacity. Yet the National Revolution that had led to the success of 1928 also contained the seeds of its own inability to fulfill its goals.

## The Northern Expedition

Sun Yat-sen died in March 1925 of stomach cancer while attempting to broker a peace with the warlords in Beijing. He was never so popular as in death, and the Nationalists were able to use his memory to garner new national support. At the same time, intra-GMD disputes became more visible. Chiang Kai-shek began his rise to power. His greatest tactical advantage was his position as head of the Huangpu Military Academy and the GMD's main forces. But he was also a capable organizational politician; that is, he knew how to make advantageous alliances and thwart his enemies. Initially, he did not seem to be angling for power because he was not one of the GMD's senior politicians; no one considered him a threat. In the months immediately after Sun's death, Chiang followed, or at least appeared to be following, a middle course. He signaled the GMD's right wing that he understood their suspicions of the Communists and their fears of social revolution, but he also said that the United Front must continue, that he was committed to Communist participation and the Russian alliance. Chiang's allies ranged from some of the richest members of the merchant community to leaders of Shanghai's largest criminal gangs. How had he become so strong?

Chiang was born in 1887 to a family that had long worked in the salt trade in Ningbo, Zhejiang. Like many of his class and generation, he went to Japan to study military science in the last years of the Qing, and he joined the National Alliance there. He saw action during the 1911 Revolution and worked with Chen Qimei, a fellow Zhejiangese who was close to Sun Yat-sen and served briefly as governor of Shanghai. Although unproven, it was widely believed that Chiang assassinated a member of the Alliance who belonged to a faction opposed to Chen. At any rate, Chen was Chiang's mentor in revolutionary politics until Yuan Shikai had him assassinated in 1916. Chiang soon acquired a new mentor: the wealthy Shanghai businessman Zhang Jingjiang. Zhang had old revolutionary ties with both the anarchists and Sun. Chiang worked as a stockbroker for several years; he also made underworld contacts at this time, particularly with the Green Gang. Not much is known about the details of Chiang's life in Shanghai, but Sun sent him to Russia in 1923, and it was upon his return to Guangdong that he became head of the Huangpu Military Academy. Military leadership was Chiang's key to power; and he kept his Shanghai contacts, which repeatedly proved useful.

Still, no one would have tapped him for leadership of the Guomindang in 1925. There seemed to be many better candidates, especially the well-educated, eloquent men who had worked closely with Sun since the early days of the anti-Manchu struggle. However, none of them was able entirely to fill Sun's shoes, either. Hu Hanmin, who had been moving away from socialism to the right, was accused of involvement in the assassination of a leader of the GMD left. Wang Jingwei, another old associate of Sun, possessed a long-standing reputation for intelligence and heroism and so started with a number of advantages, but he was increasingly vacillating and vague. Though their struggle took several years to finally work itself out, Chiang's position as at least one of the leaders of the GMD was cemented by military victories in 1925. It was further reinforced by the decision to pursue a Northern Expedition to reunify China militarily. This decision inevitably strengthened the military wing of the Guomindang, and in that sense Chiang might be regarded as the logical successor of Yuan Shikai rather than of Sun Yat-sen.

Still, it was undoubtedly Sun's goal to lead a Northern Expedition, so Chiang could claim to be carrying out the sainted leader's wishes. Chiang needed Russian aid for such an expensive task, but the Comintern and the CCP were dubious about his plans (and about him). Revolutionary politics was subject to thrust and counter-thrust. In March 1926 – as the high tide of radical movements continued – Chiang staged a mini-coup, suddenly arresting a number of Communists and Russians and declaring martial law in Guangzhou. His motivation is far from clear. A gunboat under the command of a Communist may have been part of a plot to kidnap Chiang, as he later charged, or he may have decided to take pre-emptive action to consolidate his military authority in Guangzhou. In any case, if it was a gamble, it was successful. Negotiations with Borodin to end the brouhaha resulted in agreement to curb the role of the Communists in the GMD and promises of Russian support, finally, for the Northern Expedition.

Why would Borodin and the Communists agree to these terms? It is true that Chiang reiterated his support for the United Front and the GMD's alliance with the Soviet Union, but internal Russian politics were also involved.[1] Stalin was still trying to consolidate his power in the wake of Lenin's death in 1924 and hoped that he could point to success in China. Chiang had essentially threatened to break off the alliance, even at the price of losing Comintern and CCP support, unless he got his way. Stalin was prepared to compromise rather than risk that Chiang would carry out his threat. Most Chinese Communists would probably have preferred to leave the GMD than support the Northern Expedition; at the least, their policy was to focus on workers and peasants rather than military unification. However, Stalin demanded that the CCP sacrifice its interests to the United Front, or in other words to the Soviet–GMD alliance.

China thus became an important element in the power struggle between Stalin and Trotsky in Moscow. While Stalin argued, in basic accord with Lenin's ideas, that China's "national revolution" under the command of the bourgeoisie (that is, the GMD) would strike a blow against the Powers, Trotsky argued that the Chinese bourgeoisie was too weak, compromised, and treacherous to carry out this task. He wanted the CCP to take a more militant line, moving ahead with an outright worker–peasant revolution even if this meant defying Chiang Kai-shek. Trotsky pointed out that China's bourgeoisie had close ties with foreign capital. Stalin pointed out that China's workers were a minuscule class and its peasants hardly revolutionary. To the extent that both men were right, Chinese conditions hardly appeared to be revolutionary. Yet revolutionary actions were occurring.

Chiang was ready to move his troops northward by July 1926. One prong moved up the east coast through Fujian and Zhejiang to Hangzhou. One moved straight north through Jiangxi and Anhui to Nanjing. The third moved northwest through Hunan and Hubei to Wuhan. Chiang's strategy ultimately depended on four factors. First, money, which he obtained from Russia and from the increased revenues available from Guangzhou by the second half of 1925. Guangzhou was left, in the words of one observer, looking "like a squeezed lemon," for "all the juice and flavor was gone."[2] The GMD also began to sell bonds. Second, manpower, including the key element of over 7,000 officers who had graduated from Huangpu by this time. Well over 100,000 troops, many loyal, motivated, and well trained, were available to Chiang.

The third factor was popular mobilization, which was largely in the hands of the Communists. Peasant associations in warlord-dominated territory cooperated with the Nationalists, and, perhaps most important, workers were made available to carry military supplies. Unlike warlord armies that simply press-ganged the locals to carry their supplies, Nationalist officers renounced the use of force in recruiting porters. But with thousands of striking workers from Shanghai having made their way to Guangzhou and with thousands of Guangzhou strikers also available, the strike committees released their men for porter duties with Chiang's armies. If Communist leaders were unhappy at doing this, they had no choice, as Chiang's mini-coup of the preceding year had made clear. But from the military point of view, the Nationalist armies now had the advantage of willing volunteer porters and did not have to terrorize local populations to find men to carry supplies, dig trenches, build paths, and so forth. Workers and volunteers from the peasant associations were also assigned to sabotage infrastructure – for example, preventing warlord armies from using railroads. Peasants offered information on the movements of warlord troops and helped Nationalist armies set traps. Thus the Nationalist troops were under strict orders not to occupy civilian homes or seize provisions without fair payment.

And fourth, warlords themselves. Chiang depended on the major warlords' inability to unite against him. He also depended on the willingness of a number of warlords to surrender to him. This is not to negate the importance of military strategy. The Nationalist troops fought and won several key battles. Better trained and better motivated troops defeated larger armies. Casualties were in the thousands, and by the end of 1926 Chiang controlled the central Yangzi region. But the rapid advance north was also aided by critical defections of several warlords, who were then incorporated with their armies into the Nationalist army. Such forces could not be fully integrated in the heat of war, but they were valuable allies. Some warlord armies cooperated fully, some were just sidelined. The reputation of the Nationalists for providing even common soldiers with reliable wages and decent treatment was an important aid in recruiting. The big loser of this first phase of the Northern Expedition was Wu Peifu, whose control over central China had been badly dented, though he was not entirely defeated yet.

Zhang Zuolin, the master of Manchuria, was waiting, having taken over the Beijing government. Zhang ordered the execution of Li Dazhao and other Communists in Beijing. He signaled his desire to become emperor by personally offering sacrifices to Confucius and by sprinkling yellow dust on the roads he traveled. The fact that he countermanded an order for a large army to march south in November of 1926 has convinced many that he and Chiang Kai-shek came to a deal of some sort. Certainly, Zhang was pleased to see his old rival Wu Peifu defeated. For its part, the Nationalist army paused for the winter, and the decision was made that, instead of marching further north, they would take the great prize of Shanghai (that is, the Chinese city; of course, they would not threaten the International Settlement).

The Nationalists' victories had sparked even wider social mobilization in China's central and southern provinces. Unlike the 1911 Revolution, women did very little actual fighting in the Northern Expedition, but hundreds served as nurses, propagandists, spies, and porters. Perhaps a majority of these were Hakka women, since they had natural (unbound) feet. One won fame for dragging a wounded soldier off the battlefield while dodging

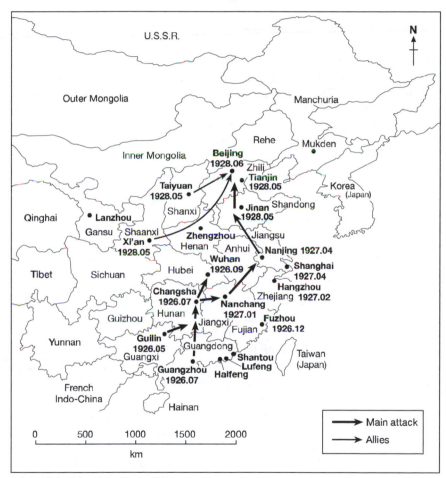

*Map 6* The Northern Expedition

The Nationalists under Chiang Kai-shek launched the Northern Expedition in July 1926, fulfilling Sun Yat-sen's dream a year after his death. Two years later they had conquered Beijing. Along the way, they took major cities including Shanghai (dates are marked "year.month"). They were joined by several warlords, including Feng Yuxiang from Shaanxi and Yan Xishan out of Shanxi.

*Source*: Courtesy of Geospatial Information Science Team, Computing Center, Academia Sinica.

bullets. As the armies marched northward, counties and towns in their wake formed women's associations to support the revolution – and fight for women's rights. Both Nationalist and Communist women spread out into the countryside encouraging women to unbind their feet, wear short hair, divorce bad husbands, seek education, and try to end the evils of prostitution and concubinage. Warlords were associated with all the depravities of the old order including military rapes. Women who had not heard the gospel of modernity before were now suddenly exposed to it. At the top levels of the GMD, Sun Yat-sen's widow, Song Qingling, emerged as a firm supporter of women's rights and the leftist GMD faction generally.

Conservative warlords defended the patriarchal order and attacked women's rights – and activist women. Few women protestors had been attacked by police and soldiers during the May Fourth or the May Thirtieth movements, though they numbered prominently among the demonstrators. But in the radicalized atmosphere of 1926 this changed. One example occurred in Beijing in March 1926. Six thousand demonstrators took to the streets demanding that the government resist Japanese demands. Six women were among forty-seven protestors simply shot dead. Lu Xun, one of whose female students was killed, bitterly remarked, "I am always ready to think the worst of my fellow-countrymen, but I could neither conceive nor believe that we could stoop to such despicable barbarism."[3] He added: "I hear that she – Liu Hezheng – went forward gaily. It was only a petition, and no one with any conscience could imagine such a trap... she was shot before Government House, shot from behind, and the bullet pierced her lung and heart.... But Chinese and foreign murderers are still holding their heads high, unaware of the bloodstains on their faces." As the Northern Expedition proceeded, female activists often became victims of warlord executions, their heads joining those of male activists hanging from city walls.

The sweep of the Nationalist armies through southern China also encouraged peasant activists. In Guangdong, the associations started by Peng Pai revived in the face of landlord opposition and were even able to form militia. Such areas saw a virtual exodus of old gentry and merchant families. In other areas, like central Hunan, peasants simply seized land for themselves and formed "poor peasant associations" to threaten landlords. Although unsystematic, such actions had the effect of weakening warlord control of the countryside and aiding the Nationalists' cause.

In Shanghai, the General Labor Union also revived. As Nationalist control of the Yangzi valley was established, pressures against the warlord regime of the Chinese city in Shanghai grew. Zhou Enlai headed a series of massive strikes in February and March 1927 that weakened the regime and finally brought it down. On 21 March some 800,000 workers struck the entire city, and thousands of armed workers began patrolling key institutions. Police stations, military depots, and railway stations were seized. Although many warlord troops simply abandoned their posts, there was some fierce street fighting, resulting in at least 200 workers killed. The revolutionaries took care not to harm foreigners, however. By way of contrast, in Hankou, Chinese crowds "invaded" the foreign concession, resulting in property damage and the evacuation of the foreigners to Shanghai. In Nanjing, Nationalist troops looted foreign consulates and killed several foreigners; in response, British and American naval vessels shelled the city.

But in Shanghai, the "Shanghai Insurrection" was better controlled through the cooperative efforts of the CCP, the GMD, merchants, and the Green Gang, which donated money, spied on warlords, and protected activists trying to operate in the foreign concessions. At the end of March a new municipal government composed of representatives of these organizations took over the Chinese city. Shanghai had been won for Chiang Kai-shek without the Nationalist Army firing a shot. Chiang Kai-shek entered Shanghai at the end of March. This marked the beginning of the end of the United Front. Within two weeks Chiang had begun a massive "White Terror" with the goal of exterminating all "Reds" or Communists.

## The breakdown of the first United Front

At first glance the incompatibility between the Nationalists and the Communists seems too obvious to require explanation. The GMD was essentially devoted to national unification, the CCP to worker–peasant revolution. It is the United Front that needs explanation. Indeed, without the insistence of the Comintern serving as marriage broker the relationship would never have been consummated. The differences in each group's ultimate aims could not but influence their tactics, strategies, and attitudes.[4] The Nationalists did not want to target entire social groups – such as "landlords" – even if they opposed the Nationalists' mass movements. Class struggle remained anathema to Nationalists. Merchants were to be disciplined and brought into the fold, but it was impossible for Nationalists to admit that major social interests could be opposed to the national interest. No class, no social group could possibly be unpatriotic. Only a few utterly corrupt individuals like warlords and the old bureaucrats were enemies of the revolution, as Sun Yatsen himself said. Communist ideology, on the other hand, stigmatized landlords as inherently feudal, the social force behind warlordism, and frankly said that the bourgeoisie was today's ally but tomorrow's enemy.

Still, the United Front was enormously successful, benefiting both parties. It is hard to imagine the Northern Expedition would have conquered southern China without it. Yet if it kindled the sincere enthusiasm of many Communists, including Li Dazhao, Mao Zedong, Peng Pai, Xiang Jingyu, and Deng Zhongxia, many Communists remained skeptical about the alliance. And it provoked bitter factional struggles within the GMD. In late November 1925 a group of GMD members met in the Western Hills outside Beijing and called for the expulsion of Communists from the Party. This "Western Hills faction" was condemned at the time but was brought back into power after 1927.

For the Communists to justify their participation in the United Front, the concept of class had to be reinterpreted so that political rather than economic position determined one's "class status." Warlords were classified with feudal aristocracies, successfully mixing a class that in Europe had depended on land-ownership and military status with the motley commands of coercive forces that had arisen in the breakdown of central government in China. As mandated by Leninism, this created a link between the Chinese class structure and foreign imperialism, the enemy of the moment. But conversely, at its most flexible, Chinese Communism was willing to count ordinary landlords as friends as long as they did not oppose the National Revolution. Ultimately, this was in line with the notion that the National Revolution had to precede a true Communist revolution. In class terms, Communists should ally themselves with the bourgeoisie to defeat feudal forces. In pragmatic terms, we can say that the Nationalists and the Communists faced common enemies. The Communists agreed to define those enemies narrowly:

> We should understand that the Chinese revolution now is undoubtedly a bourgeois national democratic revolution. Therefore, when estimating the social forces in the revolutionary movement, it is not a question of whether we desire the participation of the bourgeoisie, but rather a question of whether the bourgeoisie wants to participate in it and to participate to the end.[5]

The official Communist analysis was that GMD factions represented different social groups or classes. Of these, the bourgeoisie might be the most powerful but would also tend *not* to pursue the revolution "to the end." Satisfied with small gains, it might become counter-revolutionary "probably within one to three years." Chinese business interests that worked with foreign companies were dismissed as an extreme right-wing "comprador class" opposed to a "national bourgeoisie" in competition with foreign interests. Mao Zedong, for one, equated the GMD right with compradors who were neither anti-imperialist nor anti-feudal. As John Fitzgerald describes Mao's approach, it "offers a crude but effective analysis of the relationship between the interests ascribed to various social classes on the one hand and the interests ascribed to warlords and imperialists on the other, and attempts to link both sets of interests to emerging political divisions within the revolutionary movement."[6] The question was whether the compradors would command the GMD or whether the national bourgeoisie would continue to do so. Mao was eager to confront the "contradictions" – or enemies – within the alliance and bring them out into the open. Even Chen Duxiu, though he and the Comintern insisted that the CCP was dedicated to the "united front of all classes," seemed to anticipate the breakdown of the alliance. Unfortunately for the Communists, they did not prepare for the breakdown in any practical way.

The Communists' relative frankness about their skepticism of the strength and determination of the Chinese "bourgeoisie" only contributed to the doubts of the Guomindang rightists about the loyalty of the Communists. The real issue was political control, not class representation. Chiang Kai-shek used the Northern Expedition to assert his control over the GMD; this necessitated the elimination of the Communists. Over the course of 1926 rural disturbances increased in southern and central China in tandem with the Northern Expedition. Peasants confiscated grain stores, renegotiated land contracts by force, prevented merchants from shipping grain out of their districts, and murdered "local tyrants and evil gentry." Rice shortages in the cities followed, as peasants refused to let grain circulate freely precisely when upper class refugees were fleeing to cities. Warlord armies and local "gentry militia" acted to suppress peasant associations. GMD army officers complained that their families were being expropriated. The situation threatened to spiral out of control; at the same time, the analysis of political activists grew more radical. For the Communists and left-wing Nationalists, it became easier to define landlords as a "class" with "feudal" interests that drove them in a counter-revolutionary direction. By these new, more Marxist definitions, warlords became representatives of the larger landlord class. Fighting landlords thus meant advancing the Northern Expedition.

Meanwhile, in the cities, workers' unions grew increasingly factionalized by their very successes. Clashes between Nationalist-dominated unions and Communist-dominated unions broke out, and political murders occurred. CCP leaders and the Comintern continued to hope they could isolate the right wing of the GMD by cooperating with its leftists and with a supposedly centrist Chiang Kai-shek. They staked the whole future of the Party on this hope.

Chiang Kai-shek spent the first three months of 1927 in negotiations with leading Shanghai businessmen, the Green Gang, and representatives of foreign businesses. He was fighting the GMD left for control of the Party while trying to allay the suspicions of the Powers, get financial support from Chinese merchants, and prepare for the next phase of the march north. In order to maintain the United Front, the CCP itself disarmed Shanghai's workers after their successful takeover of the Chinese city. When the Nationalists entered Shanghai at the end of March, they encountered no resistance. Then, on 12 April, at 4 am, armed members of the Green Gang and Nationalist troops attacked the General Labor Union, killing and arresting workers. The troops killed almost 100 protestors at demonstrations the next day, and over the next few weeks Communists and suspected Communists were hunted down across Shanghai. To gain the Green Gang's critical support, Chiang offered to allow the lucrative Yangzi valley opium trade to continue. And Shanghai capitalists, fearful of the unions, "loaned" Chiang 10 million yuan that he desperately needed to pay his soldiers. Foreign authorities donated 5,000 rifles and ammunition and guaranteed safe passage to gangsters through the International Settlement. It seemed a small price to pay for the promise of labor peace. Blacklists circulated with the names of known and suspected radicals. Women with bobbed hair – a sure sign of radical tendencies – were arrested. Women activists were invariably accused of sexual immorality rather than political crimes, and the bodies of executed women were sometimes mutilated and exhibited as warnings.

The purge of the Communists, if not necessarily the bloody terror, was supported by a significant element of the GMD's leadership. Cai Yuanpei, the 1911 radical and former president of Beida, and Wu Zhihui, the anarchist friend of Sun Yat-sen, both supported the purge. Except for a minority of left-wing Nationalists, the United Front was already a hollow shell: it was a matter of them or us. Shanghai was not the only city where the workers' movement was brutally crushed. And in the countryside, as agrarian radicals were hunted down, the peasant associations either fell apart or were put down by military force. To make the situation even more confusing, left-wing Nationalists tried to make their own stand against Chiang. A new Guomindang government had been established in Wuhan on 10 October 1926. The Wuhan government, under Sun Yat-sen's long-time disciple Wang Jingwei, tried to continue the "National Revolution" in central China, disregarding the White Terror – until, that is, the Comintern's representative in Wuhan made the mistake of showing Wang Jingwei a telegram from Stalin ordering uprisings of peasants and workers. This scared Wang, who then turned against the Communists.

Why would Stalin, who was resolutely supporting the United Front and skeptical of the capacities of the workers and peasants, suddenly risk alienating even the left-wing Nationalists? For one thing, his policies in China were clearly collapsing. This was occurring just as the Russian Communists were meeting in the Kremlin to choose a new leader. If Stalin could prompt wide-scale rebellion, no matter how outgunned and futile, his China policy might look successful just long enough to assure his own power. Stalin's instructions to this effect were probably meant to be kept secret. The immediate result of making them known to Wang Jingwei was to make the Communists look untrustworthy. The GMD left was sympathetic to orderly peasant associations; they certainly did not favor armed insurrection against landlords. Wang ordered the expulsion of all Communists from the GMD.

Communist uprisings kept alive the myth of revolution in late 1927 and early 1928, but in each case were swiftly, brutally, and totally suppressed. Stalin was able to claim the movement was still alive as the Russian Communist Party's fifteenth congress met in December. But in reality the CCP was already decimated; Russian policy was in ruins. Leon Trotsky had been urging the CCP to abandon the clearly disintegrating United Front before this happened. But Stalin resisted. Trotsky's suggestion to start a Communist-led armed uprising earlier would almost certainly have failed, but at least it would have left the CCP organizationally intact. Stalin disarmed it just as it faced its greatest threat.

By the end of 1927, when the magnitude of the CCP's defeat was plain, Stalin simply blamed naïve Chinese Communists. CCP histories have tended to make a scapegoat of Chen Duxiu, who was expelled from the Party. In fact, Stalin himself deserves most of the blame for exacerbating the Communists' problems just as fatal events began unfolding. But it is not clear what choices the CCP faced back in March, or that the Communists could have predicted Chiang's turnabout. The eventual breakdown of the United Front seems inevitable given the conflicting interests of the two parties. Yet the Communists would never have experienced the growth they did had they worked entirely underground and in isolation. From 1,000 members at the beginning of 1925, the CCP had grown to 58,000 by April 1927, mostly workers in Shanghai and Guangzhou. Those very numbers, as well as the efficiency of Communist organizers, perhaps doomed the Party in Chiang's eyes.

When Chiang staged his quasi-coup in 1926 it proved to be only a dress rehearsal for the real purges a year later. The militarily weak Wuhan government sought compromise with Chiang, and Wang Jingwei decided to leave for France. Chiang's attack on the Communists simultaneously eliminated a major rival and demonstrated how much the GMD needed him personally. And the elimination of the left was key to neutralizing foreign opposition to the GMD. It bought valuable financial support from China's leading bankers and industrialists, who naturally despised the CCP. And it showed rural power-holders that the GMD would support them. It also eased fears in the GMD's own ranks about the costs of social revolution to their families. Thousands were killed in the White Terror, and Communists remained subject to execution for a decade. Here is a very incomplete list:

Li Dazhao: seized in 1927 by Zhang Zuolin and executed;
Xiang Jingyu: arrested in 1928 by the GMD and executed;
Peng Pai: arrested in 1929 by the GMD and executed;
Cai Hesen: arrested in 1931 by the GMD and executed;
Deng Zhongxia: arrested in 1933 by the GMD and executed;
Qu Qiubai: arrested in 1935 by the GMD and executed;
Chen Duxiu: arrested in 1932 by the GMD (released in 1937).

## The National Revolution and consolidation of power

In 1923 Lu Xun commented: "Unfortunately China is very hard to change. Just to move a table or overhaul a stove probably involves shedding blood; and even so, the change may not get made. Unless some great whip lashes her on the back, China will never budge. Such a whip is bound to come, I think."[7] He might have been predicting the fate of the National Revolution and the coming Sino-Japanese war. But what a historian must ask is: was the White Terror a counter-revolutionary blow or was it the logical culmination of the National Revolution, forestalling further divisive social struggle? Certainly, Chiang Kai-shek claimed to be carrying out the revolution as envisioned by Sun Yat-sen. The Northern Expedition resumed in the summer of 1927 – and was immediately checked. At one point, the lower Yangzi warlord Sun Chuanfang, in spite of the loss of Shanghai, even threatened to take Nanjing. Internecine struggles continued between the Wang Jingwei and Chiang Kai-shek factions of the GMD, and in August Chiang abruptly resigned as commander-in-chief.

With China in turmoil, Chiang traveled to Japan to marry Song Qingling's younger sister, Song Meiling. Chiang's new family, politely ignoring his first wife and son, gave him valuable new connections. The Songs were a wealthy Christian family. Qingling's marriage to Sun Yat-sen had caused a major scandal at the time. Both Qingling and her elder sister Ailing had worked for Sun as his secretaries, and Sun had originally fallen in love with Ailing. Since the Songs and Sun were Christians, the match might have seemed suitable except for the fact that Sun had not divorced his first wife. A few years later, in 1915, however, Qingling eloped with Sun. Over time the scandal subsided, Sun repeatedly insisting that he regarded himself as divorced from his first wife, and Qingling began to appear in public with him. Ailing went on to marry a wealthy Chinese financier, and by the time Meiling was willing to marry Chiang first wives were a minor issue. Now Chiang could claim a family connection to Sun, had access to his brother-in-law's financial acumen, and enjoyed a wife who had been educated in America, spoke perfect English, and could serve as his representative to the foreign community.

Even if Chiang never returned to politics, he could live a comfortable life as a wealthy socialite. But Chiang did not really leave politics. His resignation was a ploy to highlight his indispensability. His absence left the GMD starved of funds and unable to find new leaders. So Chiang was called back to screw more money out of Shanghai's businessmen and resume the Northern Expedition in early March 1928. As early as the end of April of 1927 Chiang's alliance with Shanghai's capitalists had collapsed. To raise money, Chiang had leading businessmen and bankers arrested or simply kidnapped by his Green Gang allies. He issued bonds that they were required to buy. This was not the White Terror of street executions but it was, according to the American consul, "a veritable reign of terror among the money classes."[8] Perhaps 50 million yuan was raised in this way for the Northern Expedition.

The Nationalist army's final drive to Beijing was coordinated with the support of two major northern Chinese warlords, Feng Yuxiang (who had defeated Wu Peifu), and Yan Xishan (who had long established his dominion over Shanxi Province). Zhang Zuolin was thus pushed out of Beijing and forced to retreat to his base of Manchuria. However, the train carrying him out of Beijing was bombed and Zhang was killed. Zhang's executioners were his erstwhile supporters in the Japanese army. Although

Japanese influence in Manchuria was already growing quickly, some army officers hoped that Zhang's murder would produce a general conflagration in north China and that this in turn would induce the Japanese government to support a full-scale invasion of China. They were not to succeed in 1928, but their wishes came true in less than a decade. Meanwhile, Zhang's son, Zhang Xueliang, took over his father's troops and reached a deal with Chiang, recognizing the new Nationalist government while maintaining, at Japan's insistence, an independent Manchuria.

We will return to Japan's role in China in later chapters. Here, suffice it to say that the GMD's success was magnificent but not absolute: "Nationalist China" or the "Nanjing decade" was about to begin. The new capital was not placed in Beijing, vulnerable to northern invaders and seen as decadent, imperial, and bureaucratic, but in Nanjing, the old Ming capital in central China. The Northern Expedition created a new government but it also left a number of warlords in effective control of specific regions. Not all tax revenues flowed to Nanjing, and – most tellingly – even in provinces where the Nationalists had real control the land taxes mostly remained in local hands. The new government gained foreign recognition, the maritime customs revenue that Sun had failed to procure in 1925, and even regained the right to set its own tariffs in 1928. The Powers thus recognized the new national government in a way they had never recognized the Beijing regimes in the 1910s and 1920s. Even more important, GMD control over the central and southern provinces, China's richest region, was firmly established.

The biggest threat to the triumphant Nationalists came neither from warlords on the periphery nor, immediately, from imperialist pressures, but from what might be called the warlordization of the GMD itself. Chiang's own chief of staff complained: "Party headquarters at all levels are concerned only about the quantity, and pay no attention to the quality [of new members]. The spirit of the Party therefore becomes more rotten by the day."[9] In effect, the GMD was left a hybrid organization. It had ridden to power on three horses: revolutionary momentum, a professionalized military, and a tax-rich modern economic sector. In the wake of achieving power, the first was purged, the second weakened by the infusion of warlord armies, and the third threatened by the conservatism and fiscal demands of the second. Although several supporters of the GMD's left wing, including Song Qingling, left China in protest, the termination of social revolution probably did not weaken the GMD in the short run. "Public opinion," that growing but still largely urban and educated phenomenon, remained positive. The GMD offered a major improvement over warlord rivalries, incompetence, and corruption. A modern administration promised social reform. Leftists were silenced, and liberals who demanded immediate democracy were a small minority. The Nationalists could claim, with some justification, to speak for the nation.

They were thus committed to remaking the nation in their own image. Chiang Kai-shek inherited Sun's notion that the Party would lead the nation to democracy through a period of tutelage, or in other words dictatorship. Yet authoritarian government did not mean that social and political interests could be suppressed. The very process of state-building required that interest groups be brought into the public arena. And the legitimacy of the Nationalist government depended on the myth of popular sovereignty. For all the Sunist rhetoric about the backwardness of the people and the need for tutelage, not all of the political developments of the 1920s could be reversed. Demands for wider political participation and the growth of elite participation through professional associations and other interest groups were already rooted in the modern political culture. Education was necessarily tied to political questions, and even mass mobilization that was supposed to be under GMD control inevitably escaped control at times. By the same token, however, the GMD – and the new Nanjing government – operated independently of any particular social group. As we will explore in the next chapter, in theory – and to a great extent in practice – the GMD was autonomous.

Whether we see the new government as marking a National Revolution, a counter-revolution, or something in between, it finally confirmed the 1911 Revolution. Warlordism proved to be a brief transition from one centralized administration to another. The new Nanjing government also killed off the old myths of the imperial state. Chiang Kai-shek confirmed the beliefs of educated Chinese: not the cosmic powers of the emperor, but rulers who represented the Chinese people and a state that rested on a disciplined and well-ordered citizenry. The Nationalists thus tried to create a top-down model of gradual enlightenment radiating from the state itself to elites and ultimately to the common people. However, demands for democracy ran counter to the Nationalist program in key ways. For all the general belief in a strong state, popular sovereignty remained the most widely accepted replacement for the cosmocratic emperor. It was not necessarily that urban groups favored egalitarian enfranchisement of the masses, but they demanded to represent themselves, thus challenging the GMD's claims to represent them. In other words, Chiang Kai-shek tried to convert the GMD into a routinized agent of social control before the basis of that control had been accepted by society. He tried to convert a Leninist party dedicated to ideological indoctrination, discipline, and revolutionary mobilization into a bureaucracy that institutionalized controls over society. But this conversion was only partial. The GMD government remained part revolutionary party, part rationalized bureaucracy, and part warlordized military. This was an awkward amalgam.

Chiang did not want to share power with social groups like industrialists or landlords (much less workers or peasants) because they might deflect energies from the task of state-building. But precisely because social groups were ignored, the new government had to invest more effort into raising tax revenues and fighting its rivals – which led to greater distrust of social groups. Ironically, the process led to the greater politicization of Chinese society as repression ultimately backfired.

The goal of Chiang Kai-shek, following Sun Yat-sen, was not to create a state whose main function would be to mediate between the conflicting interests of its citizens but rather, in a very real sense, to rise above society and pursue the interests of the Chinese people as a whole.[10] Citizenship then lay in the individual's or the group's abandonment of self-interest, and outright sacrifices were necessary because the needs of state-building – especially a military strong enough to suppress localist forces, instill social order, and resist foreign encroachment – required the new state to extract the economic wealth produced by Chinese society to an unprecedented extent. The notion of legitimate opposition seemed self-contradictory in the Sunist-Leninist vision: no true Chinese could oppose this plan, and any opposition was therefore unpatriotic. In reality, of course, many groups saw their self-interest as compatible with patriotism but not necessarily with the Nationalists' version of state-building. Everywhere new Nationalist state agents were dispatched, they were regarded as outsiders.

Above all, the state penetration of rural society threatened both vested interests and community solidarity. In so far as the Nationalists wished to extract taxes from the countryside, they represented a threat to peasants and landlords alike. For the Nationalists, for example, the purpose of peasant associations was to weaken the control of local elites and so make resources available to the state, but not to empower peasants. The Nationalists' denial of class struggle arose partly from their nightmare vision of divisiveness and partly because they saw the great dividing line as existing between state and society, not between different social groups. Their legitimacy rested on the claim to represent the people as a whole; that is, a classless Han race of disinterested citizens. But this meant that they failed to see how the very process of state-building could exacerbate class tensions.

Chiang Kai-shek's power was under constant challenge. But his command of China's most modernized armies, rooted in his leadership of the Huangpu Military Academy, ensured that he would have at least a major role in an era of militarization. He formed powerful teacher–student bonds between the Academy's staff and the thousands of cadets who graduated from Huangpu, and he continued to give loyal armies the best training and equipment through the 1920s and 1930s. And Chiang was a master of the personal politics of manipulating factions: switching alliances at key points, bribing enemies, keeping opponents divided.

As for the question of whether to characterize the 1920s as revolution, counter-revolution, aborted revolution, or partial revolution, all of which have been suggested, there can be no final answer. Certainly from the Communist perspective, the events of 1927–8 were counter-revolutionary since they had eliminated the peasant and worker movements that represented anti-imperialism, anti-feudalism, and social justice. Conversely, the

Nationalists saw themselves as loyal to the revolution – whose goal it was to build a strong state – because the White Terror had saved the nation from class struggle. Yet the very process of trying to build a stronger state provoked opposition to the "revolution," however it was defined. The new government therefore dedicated itself to imposing conformity on a refractory society.

In this atmosphere the ghost of Sun Yat-sen was naturally called upon not only to enforce ideological purity but also to add charismatic magic and meaning to a rapidly graying revolution. We have already noted his popularity in death. When Sun died in Beijing in 1925, he had been given two funerals. One belonged to the family and was Christian. The other belonged to the Party and featured recordings from Sun's speeches.[11] Given Sun's sudden rise in national prestige, the northern warlords had to allow him to be buried with considerable pomp. Sun's body lay in state for three weeks while the public filed past his glass coffin. They could see Sun wearing a Western suit and partly draped in the Guomindang flag. The place chosen for this was the old imperial altar to earth and grain, a sacred symbol of state under the Ming and Qing dynasties, ironically linking the republican revolution with past emperors. Yet, judging from the brief written comments left by the mourning citizens, Sun was already being remembered as the founder of the Republic and for promoting popular sovereignty, education, and women's rights.

When the mourning period was over, Sun's body was stored in a monastery in the Western Hills outside Beijing. After the Nationalists' victory, in 1929 the coffin was moved south, as Sun's own dying wish dictated: "After I have died, bury me on Purple Mountain in Nanjing, because Nanjing is the place where the Provisional Government was established. This is so that the 1911 Revolution will not be forgotten." An open competition had been held for the design of Sun's mausoleum in 1925. The winner was a young Chinese architect trained at Qinghua and Cornell Universities, and his design reflected both Chinese and Western elements. The 1929 funeral ceremony was of course led by Chiang Kai-shek. The diplomatic corps and thousands of citizens attended as Sun was installed in his final resting place amid the wooded hills above Nanjing. The procession following Sun's coffin was deliberately chosen to symbolize the nation: Guomindang, government, and army representatives; workers, peasants, and merchants; women; students; and overseas Chinese, Chinese from the different provinces, Tibetans, and Mongols.

The cult of Sun Yat-sen struck a chord among the Chinese people. Spontaneous mourning for the man who represented so many hopes occurred across the country upon his death and again with the 1929 funeral. He was, of course, a symbol that the GMD and others deliberately manipulated. During the Nanjing decade, Sun's picture was placed in every government office, every school, and every military barracks. Every Monday government officials and schoolchildren bowed to Sun three times, listened to a reading of Sun's final "Political Testament," and observed a three-minute silence. Chiang Kai-shek continued to use Sun to legitimize his rule after the Nationalists fled to Taiwan in 1949. The Communists half-heartedly praised Sun as a "bourgeois revolutionary" and "pioneer" patriot, and Zhou Enlai visited his tomb at the end of World War II. Today it is an officially recognized "cultural relic." Sun served as a unifying symbol of his nation, as he had wished, but the Chinese still did not agree on exactly what constituted Sun's vision of the nation.

# 13 The Nanjing decade, 1928–37
## The Guomindang era

The "Nationalist decade" ended with Japan's invasion in 1937 and Chiang Kai-shek's retreat from Nanjing. But the Nationalists' defeat was not preordained. The Nanjing decade is often studied in terms of state-building. Scholars speak of the "expansion" of the state and its "penetration" of society. It sometimes seems to be assumed that a strong society means a weak state and vice versa. Certainly, autonomous local elites would limit the powers of any central government, and the Nationalists themselves believed that creating strong government depended on institutionalizing controls over social forces. However, in so far as this implies a zero-sum game, it is misleading, as examination of the actual successes and failures of state-building shows. "Social forces" from peasants to industrialists were not passively waiting to be penetrated but were active participants, sometimes favoring and sometimes resisting particular government initiatives. Still, to observers in the 1920s and 1930s, much of Chinese society looked anemic and anarchic, and a few foresaw that a stronger state and a stronger society might be compatible.

The basic patterns of the Nanjing era were determined by the compromised nature of the Northern Expedition. It was completed in the second phase, from mid-1927 through 1928, by the incorporation of regional warlords and their bureaucracies. Regional governing bodies formed by the GMD in 1928 were in the hands of major warlords, and twenty-five of the twenty-seven provincial and regional governments were headed by military commanders. Most of these men joined the GMD during the Northern Expedition but they preserved their local power-bases.[1] Zhang Xueliang in Manchuria, Yan Xishan in Shanxi, and various commanders in the southeast and southwest made their peace with Chiang, but sometimes only temporarily.

There were thus two levels to the politics of the Nanjing decade: the powers of the regime as a whole, and how policy was determined within a highly factionalized regime. While dictatorial – ruling without constitutional checks on its powers – the Nanjing regime was not an autocracy under the sole control of Chiang Kai-shek. Chiang was persistently challenged by rivals within the GMD, and he found the bureaucracies of the Party and the government difficult to deal with. The military and secret police were the real basis of his power. Chiang's authority rested on uneasy coalitions of GMD supporters (who had nowhere else to turn) and regional allies (anti-Communist warlords and local elites, who had to be placated). Chiang faced repeated "rebellion" – Guangxi generals in 1929, Generals Feng Yuxiang and Yan Xishan in 1930, a growing Communist insurgency in Jiangxi in the early 1930s, Guangzhou supporters of the conservative GMD leader Hu Hanmin in 1931, Fujian dissidents in 1933, and Guangdong and Guangxi forces again in 1936.

As he dealt with his enemies, Chiang was slowly able to increase his power. In 1928 Nanjing's rule was strong in only Jiangsu, Zhejiang, and Anhui provinces; by 1931 it had extended to Henan, Jiangxi, Hubei, and Fujian, and it continued through the 1930s to expand in southern and western China. The powers of the Nanjing regime increased in the wake of the expulsion of the Communists from the Jiangxi hinterland in 1934. Known in later Communist lore as the glorious Long March, the Communists' retreat enabled pursuing Nationalist armies to exert at least some control over Hunan, Guizhou, Yunnan, and Sichuan provinces, drawing them into Nanjing's orbit. Nanjing's currency reforms and road-building projects were deliberately designed to weaken provincial autonomy. By the mid-1930s, then, the Nationalists could claim a fair degree of control over most of China proper: the economic heartland of the rice-producing center and the industrialized eastern cities.

New institutions were designed to help the Nationalist state dominate the regions. These were only partly successful during the Nanjing decade, but they established precedents and patterns that the Communists could build on in the 1950s. In the schools, students learned the Three People's Principles as the ideological bedrock of the regime. Nationalism was taught in history, geography, and literature classes. Even science and arithmetic taught how foreigners had cheated the Chinese (working out the exact sums, for example), and the tradition of special "humiliation days" was continued to remind students of the wrongs China had suffered. Modern history became a story of defeat (beginning with the Opium War) followed eventually by Sun Yat-sen's triumphs of the 1911 Revolution and the Northern Expedition.

Chiang Kai-shek also built up control systems: mutual surveillance (*baojia*) whereby village leaders were held responsible for the crimes of any villager, police forces backed by the national military, intensive ideological discipline in the schools, and general "party-fication." These were all inherited and perfected by the Communists. Any evaluation of the Nanjing decade must therefore take into account the long-term effects of its policies as well as the accomplishments and failures of the regime while it lasted.

Historical debate over the Nationalist decade will remain forever irresolvable. Some scholars posit that the modest but definite successes in unification, political stability, and a variety of modernization projects would in the long run have produced a stable and prosperous country – had not the

Japanese invaded in 1937. That the regime had survived the pressures of imperialism up to that point, and weathered the world depression, argues that it was on the right track. By promising the foreign powers to abolish internal transit taxes and miscellaneous commercial taxes, the Nationalist government won tariff autonomy in 1928. The regime thus achieved one of the major goals long held by Chinese nationalists. Customs revenue increased enough to cover about half the government's expenses (the rest coming from industry).

However, corruption, incompetence, and authoritarianism marked the regime from the beginning. Chiang was not personally corrupt, but many around him were, and the GMD was collectively corrupt to the point that it was not only expensive but a drag on efficiency – as Chiang himself often complained. Incompetence is harder to measure, but corruption and nepotism weakened the bureaucracy. Chiang relied on military men even in positions such as economic administration, for which they were not suited, and many of Chiang's top advisers were useless. "One can only be surprised," recalled one of Chiang's more progressive aides, "to know just how unaware people at the top were of what was going on, how little they knew of actual conditions in the country, and how they were even less aware of the theoretical basis of those conditions."[2] The authoritarian instincts of Chiang and his regime gave them false answers to the problems of unrest. They barely understood the immense agrarian crisis in the first place, and to meet it with repression simply insulated the regime from reality. Even the student movement and popular discontent in the cities were only pushed underground, while the regime's weaknesses prevented it from completely exterminating such threats.

The regime squeezed money out of the modern sector too severely to be considered a representative of capitalist interests, and it borrowed heavily, about a fifth of its revenues deriving from bond sales and bank loans. By standing above society and attempting to control rather than enfranchise even its most established elements, the regime denied itself what might have been creative input. If the regime had chambers of commerce, labor unions, and student organizations, much less peasant associations, it would have been recognizing the reality of the politicization that had occurred during the 1920s.

The growing Japanese threat throughout the 1930s was disastrous to the Nanjing government. To an extent, the threat benefited Chiang Kai-shek by unifying public opinion and weakening his enemies – but Chiang's own refusal to resist the Japanese demoralized the GMD and encouraged further Japanese encroachments.[3] With some justification, Chiang argued that China was not strong enough to face Japan. His first task was therefore to unify the country and build up its military. He especially wanted to exterminate the Communists. But this approach made a mockery of the first of the Three People's Principles: nationalism. True heir of Yuan Shikai, Chiang distrusted mass movements and barely attempted to rally the nation around him.

## State-building in the Nanjing decade

The Nanjing regime under Chiang Kai-shek followed two basic strategies to maintain and increase its powers, oscillating between them.[4] The first stressed hierarchical bureaucracies, division of responsibilities, and legal routines. The second stressed indoctrination and the popular mobilization techniques of the mid-1920s. The first strategy promised to sustain the authority of the center even while it delegated powers. But this strategy suffered from several drawbacks. Finding enough trained and competent bureaucrats was a constant problem; technocrats like trained economists were not only rare but oriented toward the cities at a time when more attention needed to be paid to the countryside. And Chiang's predilection for balancing factions and appointing trusted subordinates to key positions confounded the ideal of clearly defined job descriptions necessary to smooth bureaucratic functioning. The second strategy was not only cheaper but was in accord with the traditional ideal of appointing "good men" to carry out the emperor's will. The obvious problem was how to assure that appointees were virtuous, especially when a weak bureaucracy could not guarantee that central government could curb local interests.

One of the first issues facing the new government was demobilization of soldiers. There were two million men in the dozens of armies that survived into 1920, of which Chiang Kai-shek personally commanded 240,000. The Nationalists' own armies cost more than 360 million yuan per year, while Nanjing's net revenues amounted to only 300 million yuan. But the real purpose of demobilization was to disarm Chiang's rivals. In the event, war was endemic through the 1930s, and its effects on the regime were mixed. The military continued to absorb resources that would have been better spent elsewhere – well over 40 percent of the budget – but in the wake of Chiang's victories the Nanjing bureaucracy was often able to penetrate into more regions.[5]

Similarly, although village militias seemed to symbolize the weakness of the central government, under the right circumstances they could be adapted to state-building purposes.[6] Based in particular counties and sworn to local defense, militias had generally resisted the efforts of warlords to incorporate them into larger, peripatetic armies. Militia leaders often became de facto "county kings" and were numbered among the "local bullies and evil gentry" in the National Revolution. Once the Nanjing regime was established, however, the question became whether local militia should be disbanded or brought under bureaucratic control. In many parts of China neither option was possible, and even when Nanjing appointed a county magistrate, he might have no control over the militia. Local militias might cooperate with the magistrates to chase down Communists but would not collect land taxes for a distant government. In Hunan, however, the provincial government made a point of providing training and indoctrination for local militias and was gradually able to bring them under official control.

Local militias were essentially incorporated into provincial armies under a military chain of command. Even ad hoc militia "taxes" were finally regularized at the provincial level, enabling the Hunan government to gain greater control of rural resources.

But rural reform remained outside Nanjing's purview. Sun Yat-sen had traced the rural crisis to bureaucratic corruption, the lack of modern inputs, and a backward infrastructure. Contrary to the Communist understanding, he did not blame "feudalism" – as seen in the European and Russian patterns of aristocratic landowners expropriating the labor of large numbers of serfs. Rather, the gap between small landlords and free peasants was insignificant in China, where landlords were not aristocratic and their holdings usually not very large. Chiang Kai-shek himself said very little about rural conditions one way or the other, but recently published archival materials from Russia show Chiang resisting the Communist interpretation during his visit to Moscow in 1923.[7] Chiang claimed that the ties of affection among villagers and between clan members moderated landlord–tenant tensions. As the early 1920s marked the most radical phase of Chiang's career, we may assume that he saw the government's role as restoring stability. Here, he displayed a romantic or nostalgic conservatism also at odds with Sun Yat-sen's more realistic appraisal of rural distress.

If Chiang's views seem naïve in a certain sense, the failure of Nanjing's rural policies stemmed less from the suppression of "class struggle" and more from the neglect of Nanjing's own laws. These laws would have lowered rents, regulated agrarian relations, provided credit and expertise to peasants; they even gave the government the right, under certain circumstances, to redistribute land in order gradually to implement the "land to the tiller" ideal. Had these policies been carried out, Nanjing would have truly penetrated the countryside. Many Guomindang members favored strong rural policies and urged the regime to invest in peasant cooperatives. However, Chiang did not wish to risk the social instability they might have engendered. Even the availability of outside credit, which could have enormously increased agricultural production, threatened the monopoly held over credit by rural elites.

If Nanjing's control of the vast countryside remained flimsy, what of its reach into perhaps more manageable cities? In the case of the most important of China's cities, Shanghai, the regime's record is at best mixed. The government used the city as an administrative showcase to demonstrate to foreigners how well Chinese could administer the treaty ports. The regime derived about 85 percent of its revenues from the trade and manufacturing sectors, much of which was concentrated in Shanghai.[8] Nevertheless, Shanghai proved only partially governable. With the city budget constantly in deficit, many governmental functions continued to be carried out by native-place associations.[9] Up to 200 native-place associations, the largest with memberships of over 20,000, mediated disputes, including kidnappings and labor strife, and provided philanthropy for the beleaguered city.

Gangsters were also members of these associations, as were officials, especially police. The Chinese city of Shanghai was thus run by overlapping elites of wealthy businessmen, officials, and gang bosses. In effect, they had to pay off Chiang, but while industrialists with fixed assets suffered, some gangsters and bankers did well.

The weakness of the Nanjing government can be seen in the fate of policing in Shanghai.[10] The police and the military represent state-building at its most straightforward. Police are the arm of government that reaches directly down into urban neighborhoods. The Nanjing regime wanted to make local police forces part of the national government, and the Shanghai police were used to hunt down Communists. This use of police, however, deprived the system of resources that could have been used for ordinary policing. Shanghai – both the foreign concessions and the Chinese city – was notorious for its robberies, murders, and kidnappings. Gambling, prostitutes, and narcotics were available throughout the city. Opium had grown in popularity since the Opium Wars. By the dawn of the Republic, poppy cultivation had spread to most provinces, and domestic opium rivaled the Indian imports. Opium became an important source of peasant income in many places and a mainstay of rural taxes. Opium use spread into the countryside, and it has been estimated that as many as one in ten Chinese were addicts.[11] Since opium was technically illegal, its clandestine trade provided employment opportunities for thousands of gangsters. Indeed, Shanghai's gangs alone had 100,000 members by many estimates. From the beginning, narcotics were an integral part of Shanghai's economy and politics, bribes and deals forging intimate connections between officials and gangsters. The opium trade was an important source of revenue for the Nationalist government. Chiang Kai-shek promised to stamp out the drug by taxing it – and the Nanjing regime became addicted to this revenue stream. Indeed, Sun Yat-sen had already established the precedent of the Guangzhou opium monopoly.

But government–gangster–police–business contacts were not limited to opium. One of the top leaders of the Green Gang was chief of detectives in the French Concession during the 1920s. His successor as boss of the Green Gang, the notorious Du Yuesheng, was appointed by Chiang Kai-shek to be in charge of opium suppression. Chinese and foreign officials felt they had to tolerate the Green Gang since only it could manage labor relations and keep any kind of order over Shanghai's vast underworld. In return, the Gang not only paid vast bribes that amounted to a significant portion of the revenues that kept government functioning, but it also played a role in the White Terror, which continued to hunt down Communists throughout the Nanjing decade. Through the Green Gang, the government assassinated dissenters and rival GMD faction leaders, though often to so much public outrage that the regime lost more than it gained.

Over the course of the 1930s the ties between gangsters, business leaders, and officials grew more intimate. Chiang Kai-shek was personally involved in decisions that gave the government a greater take of the narcotics business. By all accounts, Chiang personally detested drug use but saw no alternative ways to raise revenue. Attempts to reform drug policy (legalizing supplies for addicts, establishing detoxification clinics) were also sabotaged by Japan's decision to manufacture narcotics to sell in north China, both to disrupt Nanjing's finances and simply to weaken the Chinese people. The Shanghai police were part of a system where the lines between corruption and legality were blurred. The historian Frederic Wakeman has concluded that Chiang Kai-shek's efforts to nationalize the police just as the Shanghai gangsters were trying to become respectable "created a new set of circumstances in Shanghai which made it difficult to distinguish between policing and criminality, between patriotism and terrorism" and amounted to "criminalizing the government."[12]

In sum, the contradictions of state-building crippled the Nanjing regime. Chiang was unable to imagine new ways of organizing power, delegating power, and dealing with the polyphonic interests of a vast nation. He used his control of the Nationalist armies to dominate the Guomindang and the government. However, de facto independent armies remained strong in many parts of China until the Communist consolidation of power in the early 1950s. Chiang's real but limited efforts to modernize ironically destabilized the very status quo that he depended on. If the GMD was "warlordized" during the Northern Expedition, it was also "bureaucratized" with the absorption of the bureaucrats of the former warlords and the skeletal central government – men who felt no commitment to the Three People's Principles. In some cases, this mattered little. A few ministries managed to become efficient, effective, and at least partially shielded from political interference.[13] The Ministry of Foreign Affairs consistently attracted talented and highly educated men to its service, and made progress toward one of the government's most popular goals: treaty revision. The Ministry of Finance was also able to preserve its autonomy and limit corruption; having first access to tax revenues allowed it to pay good salaries, while the competence that resulted allowed it to increase revenues and so please the government.

The bureaucracy was probably weakest in terms of local government. The Nanjing regime's dilemma was that without more resources it was not able to build a strong civil administration; without a strong civil administration, it could not extract the resources it needed from Chinese society. Specifically, military expenses meant that the civil bureaucracy in the 1930s only got 8 to 13 percent of the budget. The government did not want to destroy local elites, which would leave a vacuum of social disorder. But it did want to incorporate them in ways that would diminish their autonomy. If the CCP targeted "local bullies and evil gentry" as an oppressive and exploitative class, the GMD used the same phrase with a different meaning: to denote local elites not authorized by the central government. The Guomindang never fulfilled its Sunist-Leninist role: to lead the entire society. Idealists left, leaving more room for corrupt careerists. Could appeals to spirit and mobilization fill the gap? Chiang Kai-shek's effort to reinstall discipline and spirit in Chinese society is discussed below.

## Blue Shirts and new life: Guomindang fascism?

In early 1932 a group of military officers who had studied under Chiang at Huangpu organized the "Blue Shirts" association to combat the ills of social decadence, GMD corruption, communism, and the Japanese threat. The secret core of the association, the Lixingshe (Act Vigorously Society), ultimately reached out to 500,000 members, dominated army training, and influenced the police, universities, high-school summer camps, the Boy Scouts, and the New Life movement.[14] The leaders of the new association wanted to combine what they had learned at Huangpu about military efficiency and personal discipline with the lessons Germany and Italy were teaching about building a strong state in the 1930s. China's Blue Shirts, like the Black and Brown Shirts of Italy and Germany, admired power for its own sake. They called Chiang "leader," a new title derived from "Führer." Though anti-Japanese, they were also loyal to Chiang's highly controversial decision to annihilate the Communists before trying to deal with the Japanese.

The wing of the Lixingshe most evident to the public was the Blue Shirts – thugs who attacked and even assassinated Chiang's enemies in and out of the Party – and the whole movement of fanatical ultra-nationalist Chiang loyalists is generally labeled the Blue Shirts. But the Lixingshe established a variety of front organizations, and their members formed secret cells in propaganda, intelligence, military, police, and other government bureaus. The Blue Shirts frankly wanted China to become a fascist nation. In the context of the 1930s this was not as strange as it may sound today. The world depression of the 1930s led may to conclude that liberal-democratic capitalism was doomed. Chinese travelers in Europe were often impressed by what they saw in Germany or the Soviet Union – or both countries. Germany, especially, was much admired in Nationalist China. It had recently unified under Bismarck, and it had become a historical success, even recovering from total defeat after World War I through hard work and discipline. This was not just ideological appreciation. Chiang encouraged industrial and military contacts between China and Germany at all levels.[15] German advisers quickly replaced the Guomindang's Russian advisers in the late 1920s. Fascism obviously would have a great appeal to authoritarian modernizers, and as a top-ranking Blue Shirt remarked much later, "Fascism is now thought to be backward. But then it seemed to be a very progressive means of resurrecting the nation."[16]

In one sense, fascism offered yet another foreign model that might be applied to China. As the historian William Kirby points out, "fascism" meant different things to different groups of Chinese, both inside and outside of the GMD. Some believed in the dynamic purpose of "totalitarianism" and the role of the Great Leader, while others saw in fascism the possibility of a non-authoritarian technocracy; some wanted to reconcile it with "traditional morality," while others thought it would displace tradition entirely – an iconoclasm that weakened its appeal. Chiang and the GMD right admired the promise of fascism to override a class struggle they feared would divide China, just as they saw fascist nationalism as superior to liberal individualism. The banner of fascism was a useful way to proclaim the supremacy of the state and so to criticize excessive individualism and freedom. China's fascists agreed with their mortal enemies, the liberal and radical proponents of a "New Culture" movement: that the culture itself had become decadent. Only, in their analysis, the cultural problem was less the pernicious effects of tradition and more the decadence fostered by Western liberalism. Men were dissipating their energies in brothels, while women were tarnishing themselves with cosmetics. "In the last several decades we have in vain become drunk with democracy and the advocacy of free thought." So spoke Chiang himself, and in 1933 he explained:

> The most important point of fascism is absolute trust in a sagely, able leader.... Therefore the leader will naturally be a great person and possess a revolutionary spirit, so that he serves as a model for all party members. Furthermore, each member must sacrifice everything, acting directly for the leader and the group, and indirectly for society, the nation, and the revolution.[17]

In the ideal Blue Shirt society of the future, all children would belong to the nation, not to individual families or clans, and they would be schooled in "groupism" and trained in militarism. Vocational education would be emphasized to avoid the useless study of "dead books." The more radical or ultra-nationalist Blue Shirts favored complete nationalization of the economy, views which resonated broadly with Russia's Stalinism, Japan's agrarian fascism, and Germany's national socialism. In this view, the scattered farms of China's peasants and landlords would be turned into state collectives. However, more moderate Blue Shirts simply supported the official line of modest reforms. One problem of the Lixingshe's secrecy is that it was not clear whose voice, aside from Chiang's, was authoritative. And Chiang did not speak clearly on many issues.

What fascism could not do was to override the inherent factionalism of the GMD or conclusively turn Chiang into a Führer figure. The Lixingshe and Blue Shirts were but one of three or four major factions. Chiang understood that his personal power depended on their continued struggle, for as long as no one of them became all-powerful, he could preside over all of them. Another weakness of the fascist model in China was Chiang's skepticism toward mass mobilization of any kind. The Blue Shirts were never allowed to organize a popular following like the state-controlled mass movements of Italy and Germany. Membership remained largely limited to military officers and Party officials. Finally, the anti-traditional aspect of the Blue Shirt ideology was contrary to Chiang's own instincts.

For all of Chiang's faith that military discipline provided a model for society, he also believed that traditional values could play a major role in creating such a society. The New Life Movement was inaugurated in September 1934 as a kind of ideological reconstruction of the body politic as enforced by legal measures.[18] In many respects it was compatible with the ideals of the Blue Shirts, especially in terms of the enemy: Chinese decadence and communism. The overall goal, too, was to produce a thoroughly disciplined society. But the New Life Movement was not, in the final analysis, compatible with fascism. It brought Confucianism and even Christianity back into Chinese political life. It was also a means to compensate for weaknesses of the government rather than to extend its powers. If the people were truly disciplined, then they would spontaneously serve society and sacrifice for the nation, without a strong state necessarily driving them.

The "starting point" of the Three People's Principles, Chiang declared, was *gong*, and the "moving spirit of the National Revolution" *cheng*.[19] *Gong* signified public, public-spiritedness, sharing: that which was not private and selfish; *cheng* signified sincerity, deep commitment, and obedience. These were ancient virtues that had been given prominence in the Neo-Confucian revival of the Song dynasty. They illustrate Chiang's belief in self-discipline as the basis of a rational state. Chiang's New Life Confucianism was an attack on "selfishness" both large and small. It emphasized the Neo-Confucian virtues of propriety, duty, honesty, and sense of shame. Chiang wanted to improve the customs of the Chinese people. He urged frugality and hard work: the old-time religion. Social improvement would flow naturally from this.

Chiang explained what he meant with the example of the beggar, the man who consumed without producing. If he could be morally improved, if he had a better grasp of the four key virtues, he would go out and get a job. Ultimately, social order – which Chiang premised on hierarchical relations – would be restored. But, as Li Dazhao had argued to Hu Shi nearly fifteen years earlier, didn't providing jobs for the beggars and robbers who filled China require a functioning economic system first? Chiang was sure that virtue came first. He explicitly argued that virtue had to be demanded even of the hungry; otherwise, if they became rich, they would remain unvirtuous. As Chiang's critics pointed out, even Confucius had held it unreasonable to expect virtue from people whose basic economic needs were unmet. However, Chiang explained that virtue had to come first, because if "one cannot be a man, what is the use of having abundance of food and clothing?" With virtue, then "even if food and clothing are insufficient, they can be produced by manpower ..."[20]

The New Life Movement's goals ranged from these detached heights to detailed rules about brushing teeth and washing faces (use cold water). Operating under its auspices, the police sometimes closed down dance halls, and Blue Shirt thugs ripped up dangerous journals and poured acid on people dressed immodestly. Instructions on grooming and dress were ridiculed even at the time, and the Nationalists' censorship of decadence was predictably futile. Still, the movement reflected a widespread sense that society was too chaotic. The limited fascism of the Nanjing decade would evolve into the puritanical aestheticism of Maoist China.

For Chiang, Confucian virtues were less an end in themselves and more a means to apply military standards to Chinese society. Grooming, like the old Confucian academies' emphasis on students sweeping floors, was meant to instill an inner seriousness and discipline. But New Life Confucianism also reflected a hierarchical model of society – unregulated people were dangerous. In sum, Chiang found much to admire in European fascism: its exaltation of the state, its rejection of democracy and glorification of the leader, and its vision of a new fascist man as a de-individualized member of a disciplined mass. But fascism was not fully compatible with his neo-traditionalism, the Three People's Principles, or the many forms of Westernization that marked the Nanjing decade. And in so far as fascist movements in Germany and Italy tried to mobilize the masses, they were completely irrelevant to Chiang's concerns.

## Economy, state, and society

The Chinese economy essentially stagnated through the 1930s. Agriculture produced about 65 percent of the net domestic product and employed the vast majority of Chinese. From 1934 to 1936 less than 4 percent of the government's total expenditure was devoted to economic development, and even much of that was siphoned off into private bank accounts or lost in wasted efforts. International trade and capital investment were important for major cities and contributed to small but fairly steady growth for China's economy as a whole. Real aggregate output may have risen as much as 2 percent a year between World War I and 1937, per capita output rising by one-fifth.[21] These figures pale in comparison to Meiji Japan or a number of post-World War II economies – including China's. A spirit of small-scale commercial enterprise, which can be traced back to the Ming and Qing dynasties, dominated domestic manufacture and trade.

Although from 1931 to 1936 industry grew at a healthy annual rate of 6.7 percent, this was from a very small base. Chinese industry remained but a small part of the overall economy and was vulnerable to high taxes and the difficulty of finding capital. The famous Nanyang Brothers Tobacco Company could not pay its taxes and went bankrupt. (Ironically, the tax code actually favored foreign companies, because Nanjing needed the revenue from politically weaker Chinese firms.) Businessmen were expected to make sacrifices. The world depression hit exports badly by weakening European and North American demand for silk and other products. Initially China benefited from a decline in silver prices from 1929 to 1932. While the industrialized nations were on the gold standard, China still used silver currency and so cheaper silver in effect devalued the Chinese yuan, making exports cheaper. But as the United States began buying more silver to balance its gold reserves, the price of silver increased, the metal flowed out of China, and the Chinese economy fell into a deflationary spiral. Between 1932 and 1935 wholesale prices fell by a quarter. Net exports fell from 1,417 million yuan in 1931 to 535 million yuan in 1934. Already by 1932 one-third of urban factories and 40 percent of stores had closed. Farmers were badly hurt by lower prices, as well as by devastating floods in the mid-1930s. Chiang Kai-shek refused to move military funding into flood relief. Nanjing and local governments still ran deficits – between a sixth and a quarter of Nanjing's annual expenditures were covered by borrowing, thus starving the economy of funds that might have been used for investment. Interest rates on business loans started at 18 percent per annum.

The situation improved in 1936. In the course of the 1934–5 depression, Nanjing had nationalized the banks (to the great profit of a few friends), suspended silver trading, and essentially begun printing paper money. An unintended consequence of these policies was a bout of inflation, which helped farmers by raising the prices of agricultural products. The 1936–7 agricultural season saw better weather and harvests. With the help of German advisers, the government devised a five-year plan in 1935 to develop heavy industry in the inland provinces – a policy that later became a main-stay of Maoist economics. Steel, tools, electricity, and mining made great strides in areas away from the relatively developed east coast. Nanjing nationalized private enterprises ranging from spinning mills and meat-packing factories to telecommunications and paper production. This facilitated massive corruption at all levels of the bureaucracy. The outbreak of full-scale war with Japan in 1937 curtailed economic growth, but it also encouraged the government to take an even greater role in the economy.

The Nationalists tried to remain autonomous from society, so the govern-ment would not be subject to outside pressures. Nanjing tried to include (or co-opt) potential enemies such as capitalists, warlords, gangsters, and rural elites. It recognized group interests but only in so far as they were subordi-nated to the whole. Citizenship rested on the disinterested individual's duties toward the state, which was the only organ that could speak in the name of the nation. Citizenship was seen as restricted. As early as 1929 the new Nanjing government stipulated: "During the period of political tutelage ... the Chinese people must obey and support the Guomindang and swear fealty to the Three People's Principles ... before they may exercise the rights of citizens of the Republic of China."[22] Citizenship was to be earned, not claimed. More concretely, the Nationalists sought ideological conformity from all formal voluntary groups. This applied to professionals, whose orga-nizations had their roots in the late Qing. The professional groups of lawyers, doctors, teachers, journalists, accountants, and other groups, and of course the Chambers of Commerce and native-place associations of merchants, played a major role in urban life. Professionals in particular regarded themselves as natural social leaders of critical modernization projects; they wanted the government to recognize their privileges.[23] On occasion, they opposed the government, lawyers, for example, criticizing the Nationalists' disregard for due process and human rights. They claimed to speak for the public, implicitly striking at the heart of GMD legitimacy. But only implicitly; there was no open break. Professional groups did not operate independently of the state.

The Nationalists saw the proper role of the state as much in terms of coordinating society as controlling it. They wanted the state to mediate social conflicts. This corporatist approach was immediately applied to industrial relations. Communist influence was expunged from the workers' movement in the late 1920s. In Shanghai, where Communist penetration of the union movement was broad and deep, the process was bloody and factionalized. But even here the Nationalist regime displayed a fairly positive attitude toward labor. Although workers were herded into "yellow unions" that abjured class struggle, conditions and wages were to be improved. The GMD did not deny workers the right to take collective action against employers, though activities relating to larger political questions were forbidden. In the event of a dispute between a union and an employer, the municipal government sought to mediate a compromise. During the mediation period strikes were illegal, but neither could the employer fire or lock out workers. Ideologically, the GMD continued to deploy the anti-capitalist rhetoric of late-Sunism, picturing business leaders as selfish and exploitative. However, the inefficiencies of the Nationalists' administration and the fact that most factories were in the International Settlement, outside of Chinese control, doomed reforms from the start.

During the Nanjing decade, working conditions and wages differed from industry to industry and city to city. Workers suffered in the 1930s from the Depression and factory closings. Government mediators forced factories to pay bonuses on occasion and, if closing, severance pay that might tide workers over until they could find new jobs or return to village homes. And workers were to be turned into (passive) citizens; in Tianjin, for example, they were taught such slogans as "Promote cooperation between labor and capital!" and "Stamp out the CCP!"[24]

In Shanghai, the Green Gang became critical to labor organization. Du Yuesheng formed alliances with major company unions as well as the GMD, in ways that benefited Du but that also enabled unions to win concrete benefits for their members.[25] More workers volunteered to join the Green Gang, and so Du won more supporters as well as racketeering opportunities. Du sometimes used his personal funds to bankroll strike pay and even to augment management's awards when the strike ended. Du was thus able to transform himself from opium king to civic hero. Du's political connections were visible in a strike against the British American Tobacco Company that was also tied to the Guomindang's efforts to raise taxes on the company. His gangster interests were shown in a strike against the French Tramway Company that was actually designed to discourage reformist French officials from interfering with opium and gambling. The role of the Green Gang in controlling a significant portion of Shanghai's workers – only unskilled dockworkers and the most highly-skilled craft workers remained largely independent – might be regarded as another sign of the Nanjing regime's weakness. It had to reward local power holders, in this case Du, to maintain any control over the working class at all. But from another point of view Nanjing incorporated Du into a regime that secured his cooperation. Without relinquishing control of the Green Gang, Du became a respectable banker and philanthropist.

Shanghai did possess one autonomous organization. The YWCA (the US-based Young Women's Christian Association) held a privileged position, providing popular forums for women workers outside of Guomindang control. Its foreign and Christian sponsorship protected it, while it shamed even the hard-headed businessmen of the International Settlement into reforms to improve working conditions for children. At first, the YWCA offered literacy classes and stayed away from direct involvement in labor issues. But the YWCA's education program quickly evolved into classes that gave women a sense of their position as women and as workers. Ideas about social change and even Marxism were introduced, along with writing, arithmetic, history, and other less threatening fare. Advanced classes discussed labor legislation and unionism; student projects included compiling lists of the illegal conditions in each woman's factory.

Unlike workers, women as a whole could not be incorporated into the regime through specific organizations. Furthermore, the Nanjing regime spoke in two voices on women's issues. In the New Life Movement, women were told to return to the home to be dutiful daughters, chaste wives, and good mothers. Feminists risked being branded as Communists. However, the issue of women's rights was not entirely buried by the White Terror. Middle-class urban women led campaigns devoted to gender equality that were explicitly based on notions of universal human rights – "human rights are common to all and there are no so-called special rights for women," read one manifesto.[26] Such women were less vulnerable and also less threatening to the regime than a mass-based women's movement including workers would have been. Finally, the 1936 constitution finally granted women suffrage. Indeed, within a decade they had even won a 10 percent minimum quota of legislative seats.[27] Under the Nanjing political system, this might be regarded as more a symbolic than a practical victory, but it was still a victory for a cause which extended back to the late Qing and which had seen numerous defeats.

The Nanjing decade also saw some practical reform of family law. Between 1929 and 1931 a modern civil code was adopted that explicitly granted women rights in marriage, divorce, and inheritance.[28] In terms of divorce, it was one of the most liberal of its day, granting equal access to women on ten grounds, including adultery and ill-treatment. Couples could even get "no fault" divorces by mutual consent. None the less, even at its most liberal reading, the code was intended to provide specific remedies and rights, not instigate a social revolution. It had no effect in the countryside, where traditional norms prevailed. Its effects in the cities were relatively small, though real. If we remember that husbands could traditionally take concubines against their wife's wishes, visit prostitutes, beat their wives, and demand divorce on a wide range of grounds, then the Nanjing code was a real breakthrough. While the total number of divorce suits remained small – seldom more than 100 per year in the largest cities – they were not restricted to the upper classes. Most were instigated by women who represented themselves.

The double standard did not disappear, but it was modified. For example, under the Qing code, a wife might ask for divorce if she was beaten so badly as to cause permanent injury, and even then she needed her husband's agreement. A husband could demand a divorce if his wife merely slapped him, or was rude to his parents, or failed to bear children. The 1931 code equalized the definition of physical cruelty, though judges held that beatings, if slight, did not constitute grounds for divorce. Nor would women be granted a divorce if their own bad conduct, as determined by the judge, had provoked their husband's beatings.

Concubines were not given the status of wives, but the new law gave them more rights than they had possessed before. They were regarded as legitimate members of the household, and the husband/family head could not arbitrarily expel them. Precisely because they were not actually wives, they could leave if they wanted to, unlike a legal wife. Wives, by the same token, could not expel concubines either, though *if* they could prove that they had opposed their husband taking a concubine, they could get a divorce on grounds of adultery. Of all the divorces that were granted, the large majority were by mutual consent. Perhaps more than a few couples traced their incompatibility to the weight of Chinese tradition; one couple announced in a newspaper:

> We both have suffered a loveless, unfree marriage for a long time. To express our revolutionary spirit in today's world, we should quickly liberate ourselves. It is only because there is no love or freedom that we divorce.... Divorce is definitely not a shameful affair, and we do not divorce out of enmity.[29]

With the New Life Movement the government's conservative hand sought to reclaim what its liberal hand had granted. In Shandong, for example, women with bobbed hair or short-sleeved dresses were arrested. In Changsha, hair-curling machines were removed from beauty salons. But women's appearances were not to return to Qing style in clothing, hair, or, of course, feet. One new style of dress that became common in the 1920s was the qipao (cheongsam), a long, single-piece dress.[30] It was generally a decorous gown that could be worn on the streets, shopping, to class, or on more formal occasions. It could also be turned into a sexy uniform of sorts for prostitutes and nightclub singers, by wearing it tightly fitted with high slits on the sides, but the qipao began as a way for urban students and middle-class women to dress more soberly, like men. While men were encouraged to wear the "Sun Yat-sen suit" to demonstrate their modernity, for women the qipao went with short, bobbed hair, natural feet, and less jewelry and makeup. The qipao represented a step toward androgyny – women wore sober colors and in general looked more like men. Essentially, the Nationalists-as-reformers wanted to masculinize China with the respectable but active daughter–wife–mother helping to strengthen the nation. But the Nationalists-as-conservatives wanted women to be more feminine, even as men became more masculine, so women could be the passive, home-based support for their men. Conservatives complained that men were dressing in flowing silks while women were dressing like men, and "under these circumstances, the people's sense of purpose declines and there is no elevation of the spirit."[31]

The conservatism of the New Life Movement was undercut by the outbreak of war with Japan in 1937, which gave women a greater public role.[32] Literally hundreds of patriotic women's groups emerged to do nursing, take care of orphans, practice other philanthropy, and raise public awareness of war needs. Though women also fought, particularly under Communist auspices, the majority engaged in arguably feminine tasks associated with nurturing. But they increasingly broke out of the roles of daughter, wife, and mother. The Nationalists could no more confine women to the home than they could prevent workers from asserting their rights.

## Legitimacy, nationalism, and dissent

Intellectuals were initially depressed by Chiang Kai-shek's violent destruction of the National Revolution in 1927. As the intellectual historian Vera Schwarcz has noted, "Each, for a while, experienced history as a personal defeat; each viewed his or her own fears as a sign of individual weakness exacerbated by the class foibles of the petty bourgeoisie."[33] Gradually, however, they rediscovered their public voice and, in defending the victims of the White Terror, they learned not to be terrorized themselves. Liberal intellectuals could not mobilize against the persecution of thousands of anonymous workers and Communists, but they did protest against the arrests and assassinations of particular writers, educators, and students known to them personally. Once again, the universities and human rights organizations emerged as nodes of resistance to the Nanjing regime. The 1932 arrest of Chen Duxiu was turned into a *cause célèbre* as even solid anti-Communists rushed to defend him. His defense lawyer was Zhang Shizhao, who had abjured his former radicalism of the 1911 period and become a conservative critic of the May Fourth movement. Fu Sinian, the former student leader who had now joined the GMD, associated Chen with the "spirit of freedom itself." The anti-Marxist Hu Shi continued corresponding with him in jail.

The Nanjing government tried to establish censorship, but a mass market in entertainment and ideas, which had been growing since the late Qing, could hardly be shut down and was difficult to control. Ironically, the foreign concessions in Shanghai continued to provide a base for relative

intellectual freedom. Daily newspapers carried cultural columns, and prominent figures in the arts wrote short essays for journals. Serious journals and
left-wing literature did sell. Intellectuals thus had a place in middlebrow
culture. Academic institutions also continued to grow, both public and
private, including Christian schools both reformist and conservative.
University education, as well as study abroad, remained largely for a tiny
elite, though a network of provincial secondary schools and teachers'
colleges somewhat broadened the educational base. University graduates
might find work in government ministries, teaching, journalism, business,
and so forth, but unemployment and underemployment were also problems.

The Nanjing regime asserted some control over education, and schools
were subject to what it called "partification," but students and teachers were
seldom subject to political tests as such. New censorship laws in 1930 gave
the government the power to withdraw postal privileges and close journals,
but such censorship seems to have been highly inefficient: determined voices,
at least, could get through. The GMD even resorted to assassination and
kidnapping but not thoroughly enough to be convincing. The government
suffered from the worst of both worlds. Its authoritarianism was blatant
enough to attract opposition for that reason alone, disillusioning potential
supporters and ultimately throwing its legitimacy into doubt, while its
policing was not efficient enough to smother dissent. While the GMD kept
urban workers under firm control, intellectuals and particularly the growing
student community remained relatively free. Communists remained subject
to arrest, but non-Communist criticism was often tolerated.

Nanjing was subject to criticism on two major grounds. A relatively
small group of liberal intellectuals, students, and urban professionals
accused it of delaying democracy and violating human rights. And growing
Nationalist sentiment, especially among students, accused it of failing to
offer effective resistance to Japanese encroachments. The two groups, to a
degree, overlapped. Neither was a tool of the Communists. Although
Communists did play a role in mobilizing student opposition during the
1930s, their influence was limited by a reluctance to cooperate with non-
communist groups. Both liberal intellectuals and nationalist students
represented urban public opinion. The legitimacy of the Nanjing regime
did not depend directly on plans to build democracy, though the Sunist
promise played a role in the public relations of the regime. But the promise
to make China strong and united was central to the Nationalist cause – and
also provided a yardstick against which the regime fell short. It is impossible to exaggerate the stresses that Nanjing's reluctance to confront Japan
in the 1930s placed on the regime.

The regime also feared its human rights critics and sometimes tried to
silence them.[34] Nanjing announced in 1929 that the GMD might "restrict
the freedoms of assembly, association, speech and publication within the
limits of the law." This provoked Hu Shi into writing a sharp critique, noting
that the government could not be trusted to police itself. The government

decided what the limits of the law were, he complained, and if officials violated human rights there were no institutions to check them. In fact, Hu continued, both the government and, even more dangerously, the GMD were acting as if they were above the law. Citing the arbitrary arrests during the White Terror, Hu asked if anyone was safe from being tarred with the Communist brush. In objecting, not to the Sunist notion of "political tutelage" but to lack of law, Hu favored a moderate constitutionalism very much in line with Liang Qichao's views of a generation before.

Other intellectuals elaborated a more philosophical basis for human rights in China, perhaps the most famous of these being Luo Longji (1896–1965). Luo had been a politically active student at Qinghua University in Beijing during the May Fourth movement, and he went on to study at the University of Wisconsin, the London School of Economics, and Columbia University. He became known as China's most prominent Fabian socialist, advocating expertise in government or, in a word, technocracy. He was to be disappointed in the Nanjing regime for both its inefficiency and its ideological fervor. Luo strongly favored a liberal rather than an authoritarian technocracy, stressing the importance of civil rights for a well-functioning community as much as for the individual. "It is considered 'rebellious' to discuss a constitution," he complained, "and 'a cover for nefarious plotting' to discuss human rights. We are labeled 'petty-minded' if we vent our dissatisfactions."[35] Luo traced the incompetence and corruption of the regime to its repression of democracy. He was briefly imprisoned in 1930, and the liberals' journal was shut down.

Liberals like Hu and Luo – products of the New Culture tide – criticized the Nanjing regime for what they saw as retrogressive tendencies. It was not simply that Sun Yat-sen's notion of tutelage betrayed authoritarian desires, but the entire neo-traditional approach was (naturally) being used to impose autocratic measures. Hu Shi argued that the ideological training the regime tried to impose on the Chinese smacked of the old emperors' support for Confucianism. "One may still denounce the emperor [Chiang Kai-shek], it's true," Hu noted, "but one cannot criticise Sun Yat-sen. One is not yet forced to worship Confucius, although his birthday has become sacred again." Hu traced the root of the problem to the Guomindang's "extremist nationalism," a conservative ideology that "has continued to engender conservative theories."[36]

In an explicit debate over democracy versus dictatorship, defenders of the Nanjing regime argued that Japanese incursions had created a national emergency that required authoritarian measures. Yet even supporters of Nanjing's autocracy often wished the regime were more open to criticism and reform. In spite of the appeal of fascism, and although many argued that dictatorship was a necessary stage in building a stronger nation, few thought autocracy was an ideal political system. Democratic-minded critics, including some within the GMD itself, went much farther. They now rejected the old argument that the Chinese people were not ready for democracy. They asked: even if the Chinese people were not ready for democracy, could dictatorship offer the "tutelage" they needed? Didn't one-party rule create vested interests that would never share power? Where would democratic models come from? And, more pointedly, was a GMD dominated by old-style bureaucrats and militarists even capable of fostering democracy? Luo Longji argued in 1932:

> It is time to return politics to the people. Three years ago, opposition to one-party rule might have been a little too radical or emotional. Three years on, the achievements of one-party rule and the state of affairs in the Nanjing government are all before our eyes. On what justification can one-party rule continue?[37]

More fundamentally, however, democrats argued that the way to have democracy was to have democracy. In other words, constitutional procedures had to be instituted immediately. Democracy was not about the dictatorship admitting elite intellectuals into its counsels but about letting people vote. Hu Shi went so far as to argue that democracy was "kindergarten government" – a system suitable to less developed nations. Dictatorships, on the contrary, needed highly trained expertise and so represented a more advanced form of government. Hu argued that democracy did not need great talents but would train the mediocre for political participation. Critics were quick to point to the flaws of this argument. Democrats felt it was perverse to consider dictatorship "more advanced." Hu's argument also ignored the fact that working democratic systems had deep historical roots; it neglected the need of any political system for expertise; and it was remarkably sanguine about the ability of ignorant, illiterate people to elect wise representatives.

Still, Hu's argument rested on a number of very powerful premises. First, that "common knowledge" was possessed even by people ignorant of the finer points of political theory, and that common knowledge provided a useful basis for local democracy. Everyone, not just elites, possessed the right to order their lives in ways that made sense to them. Second, that political participation was the only way to train the populace for further political participation. Third, that in so doing, the "base of political authority" would be enlarged. Hu promised that this would actually increase rather than detract from the powers of government, since the government would be acting in accord with the wishes of the majority of people. Fourth, that a democratic system would unite the nation more reliably than could an authoritarian system, because it would create ties between localities and the center, between the masses at the bottom and the elites at the top, and between the different regions. The argument from unity had been made in the first calls for a parliament in the nineteenth century, but Hu was not proclaiming that the emperor should simply *listen* to the masses. He was insisting that the masses had the right to say "yes" or "no" to the government at the ballot box. And fifth, democrats argued that only electoral accountability could force any government to curb corruption, perform more efficiently, and initiate reform.

In the end, such arguments had little effect on the Nanjing regime. The intellectual historian Jerome Grieder has pointed to the "liberals' dilemma" in their inability to gain access to China's political and social resources. Translating liberal ideals into daily behavior needs a consensus of social expectations and shared confidence. "Such a consensus cannot be imposed, nor can it evolve out of lives too distantly situated, in terms of day-to-day experience, to share a language of aspiration and determination." China's democrats did not know how to reach out to the masses or create a space where democratic politics could justify liberal values.[38]

Of greater immediate concern to the Nanjing regime was patriotic criticism. When Japanese army officers in Manchuria assassinated the warlord Zhang Zuolin in June 1928, hoping to plunge Manchuria into a chaos from which Japanese troops could then rescue it, Tokyo was not supportive. Indeed, the ironic effect of Zhang's assassination may have been to help Chiang Kai-shek in his efforts to dominate the northern warlords. Zhang Xueliang was able to assume control over his father's troops, and in December he allied himself with the GMD – but tensions with the Japanese Kantō Army in Manchuria could not be contained. In September 1931 Japanese officers blew up part of a railway line near some Chinese barracks outside of Mukden (present-day Shenyang), provoking skirmishes that they then used to justify the takeover of all Manchuria. The "Mukden incident" provoked international condemnation of Japan, but no action. Again, the civilian leaders in Tokyo had not supported the action, but Chinese troops offered no resistance to the Kantō Army. Kantō officers were thus able to set up a puppet government and proclaimed "Manchukuo" an independent nation in 1932. Probably, Zhang's 200,000-plus troops would not have been able to defeat the modernized Kantō Army, even though it had only 11,000 troops (plus reservists).

But Japan's actions naturally inflamed Chinese nationalism, and in Shanghai anti-Japanese boycotts and strikes led to student demonstrations, the reappearance of Communists, and anti-GMD riots.[39] Chinese were shocked not by defeat but by the utter failure to offer any resistance. Chiang Kai-shek too supported non-resistance. Chiang pointed out that China was much weaker than Japan, and he called for complete unification first. The Communists were a "disease of the heart" while the Japanese were but a "disease of the skin." Chiang's decision was also motivated by the strategic realities of domestic military politics. He had dispatched Zhang Xueliang to put down a rebellion headed by Feng Yuxiang and Yan Xishan. Half of Zhang's troops were south of the Great Wall. If he let those forces return to Manchuria, he risked a revival of the rebellion – and Chiang was not necessarily unhappy to see Zhang lose his base in Manchuria. The Communists gained great propaganda advantage from criticizing Chiang's pusillanimity and offered to form a second United Front to resist Japan. Chiang was surely right to fear a wider war with Japan, though such "appeasement" severely weakened the legitimacy of the Nanjing regime. Furthermore, if the Japanese were but a superficial disease, the loss of Manchuria none the less cost the Nationalist government 15 percent of its tariff revenues. Stronger resistance to Japanese aggression might have made Japan's victories more expensive. The Tokyo government might then have been able to restrain the Kantō Army, though some kind of blow-up over Manchuria was probably inevitable.

*Map 7* Japanese incursions, 1931–6

Japan had cemented its control over Manchuria by 1932, and throughout the 1930s continued probing into northern China. Japanese military incursions to the northwest and even Mongolia were not as politically sensitive as its moves south of the Great Wall, including the bombing of Chinese Shanghai in 1932. The Tangu Truce Line of 1933 was meant to stabilize the situation, as Chiang Kai-shek was willing to offer unofficial acknowledgement not only of Japanese control of Manchuria but also of Japanese interests (including military bases) in Rehe and Chahar. But the Line proved ephemeral.

*Source*: Courtesy of Geospatial Information Science Team, Computing Center, Academia Sinica.

The White Terror had left the student movement considerably less militant and highly factionalized. None the less, students remained a reservoir of dissent. The Nanjing regime tried to offer the students military training and generally give the impression that war was imminent. Such was not the case, and once again students led the way in organizing boycotts of Japanese goods, strikes against Japanese-owned factories, and street demonstrations and assemblies – some of which attracted over 100,000 citizens. Some 30,000 Japanese now lived in Shanghai, and the effects of the boycott and strikes on Japanese business in the entire lower Yangzi region were drastic. By October 1931 Japan was issuing threats to Nanjing and Japanese plans to invade Shanghai were rumored. As the Japanese occupation of Manchuria continued to the north, student demonstrations spread from Shanghai to Nanjing, and students began to confront their own government. Shanghai's native-place associations and some unions sided with the students. In Nanjing, students marched on the house of the foreign minister, who was rumored to be pro-Japanese, and severely beat him, much as May Fourth students had beaten "traitorous officials" in 1919.

By December GMD hoodlums were attacking student activists, and students were attacking police. The mayor of Shanghai resigned, and by the end of the month Chiang Kai-shek himself resigned briefly. GMD offices were smashed. Government-controlled labor unions threatened students. Anti-Japanese agitation continued, but without leading to a general strike of the kind associated with the movements of 1919 and 1925. By January the student movement was petering out. But on 18 January 1932, five Japanese Buddhist monks were attacked by a Chinese mob and one was killed. In fact, the attack had been instigated by the Japanese military itself, anxious to divert attention from Manchuria and angry at anti-Japanese boycotts. The Japanese consul-general then issued an ultimatum demanding that the Shanghai government bring the entire anti-Japanese movement to a halt. The mayor agreed to Japan's terms, but the Japanese were already on the move. Fighting broke out at the end of the month, with Japanese planes from nearby aircraft carriers bombing the city. Chinese troops managed to hold the northern part of Chinese Shanghai – Zhabei, just north of the International Settlement – until the Japanese brought in reinforcements in February. Air bombing completely destroyed Zhabei, and 230,000 refugees fled to the International Settlement. Not until the beginning of March did the Chinese troops retreat and Japan declare a unilateral truce.

The Japanese had suffered 4,000 casualties, the Chinese 14,000, but they had proved they could fight. Public opinion was electrified. Yet Nanjing did not alter its policies. And Japanese incursions into northern China continued from their new base of Manchukuo. Students took to the streets again in massive numbers at the end of 1935, when Japanese plans to turn large regions across north China into "autonomous zones" (really, small puppet regimes) became known. In November, eastern Hebei was put under an "Anti-Communist and Self-Government Council," and on 9 December thousands of students took to the streets of Beiping (formerly Beijing and still a center of higher education). Police, in freezing weather, turned fire hoses on them, beat them, and arrested a number of the demonstrators. This provoked the "December Ninth movement" and within a couple of weeks students were marching in Shanghai, Guangzhou, Nanjing, Wuhan, and other cities. From the beginning the movement had an antigovernment cast, although students appealed for support from all citizens, even the police, in the name of patriotism. In some cities, Blue Shirt activists managed to take control of the demonstrations and turn them into unity rituals of support for the GMD leadership. But Beiping, Tianjin, and Shanghai saw real confrontations.

If the 1931 student movement, for all its furious clashes, had failed to change Nanjing's policy, the December Ninth movement of 1935–6 fed into a growing national impatience with "appeasement." By the end of 1936, plans were being put into place for a second United Front and for military resistance to further Japanese demands. At the same time, student protestors and intellectual critics had created a new political space in between the Nationalist and Communist Parties. This would never be a broad or comfortable space, but it offered refuge to those dissatisfied with both Marxism and the Three People's Principles. This democratic anti-Japanese center evolved into the "Third Force" of Chinese politics in the 1940s. Some of its representative figures were men like the philosopher Zhang Junmai, who had never trusted the National Revolution. Others were activists like Shi Cuntong, who had converted to Communism and joined the United Front, but become disillusioned with both the CCP and Chiang Kai-shek's betrayal of socialism.[40] Both men narrowly escaped arrest. Zhang remained committed to democratic socialism. Shi turned himself into a Marxist intellectual but abandoned all ties with the CCP. Such men were to contribute to building the political culture of the war years, before they were silenced in the 1950s. In the 1930s, however, they represented the voice of dissent.

# 14  Peasants and Communists

From the Philippines to Guatemala, the twentieth century was marked by massive peasant uprisings and revolutionary actions. No peasant revolution was greater than the Chinese, which was still studied at the end of the century by revolutionaries in Peru, Mexico, Sri Lanka, Nepal, and beyond. For many Chinese peasants in the 1930s, struggles for concrete resources like water, land, and firewood, or for access to markets and credit, were life-and-death concerns. Violence remained endemic. Above all, the Nanjing regime proved unable to assert real control over local government. This was the result of a historical devolution or loosening of power that began in the mid-Qing and was fundamentally related to the failure of the court to respond to the great population growth of the eighteenth century.[1] As the official bureaucracy failed to keep up with the growing size and sophistication of Chinese society, imperial officials increasingly were forced to rely on local elites to maintain order – and to collect taxes. The entire relationship between state and society was thereby changed. By the twentieth century, neither the GMD's use of force nor its attempts to inspire ideological fervor significantly weakened local elites vis-à-vis Nanjing.

There is an intriguing gap between the recent findings of economic historians based on quantitative estimates and the picture social historians draw based on impressionistic evidence. Some economic interpretations date the agrarian crisis to the 1920s at the earliest and conclude that in many respects the peasantry was relatively well off until then.[2] Agricultural growth may have averaged as much as 1.5 percent per year – about 0.5 percent above population growth. But journalists' and travelers' accounts suggests strongly that conditions were deteriorating long before then. The large number of anti-tax petitions, anti-rent movements, and rural riots suggest that something was going badly wrong.[3] Of course, the most optimistic of economic historians do not argue that the peasantry became suddenly immune from bad harvests, market fluctuations, or misgovernment: only that in the aggregate rural incomes might well have been improving, if only slightly, into the twentieth century.

Signs of endemic agrarian crisis marked the 1920s. The economic historian Ramon Myers has concluded: "This was not just a temporary crisis of subsistence for rural people but a series of dislocating effects taking place on a sustained basis," resulting in rural misery.[4] Other historians see the peasantry holding its own until the Great Depression hit in the 1930s.[5] The loss of agricultural exports as the industrialized nations closed their markets pushed segments of rural China (already facing difficulties) over the edge. One must also note the great Yangzi floods of 1931 and the 1934–5 drought in central China.

Given the lack of precise quantitative records, we will never know exactly how the rural economy was developing year by year and region by region; statistical analysis and inference can be easily skewed along the lines of the old Chinese colloquialism "off by an inch in the beginning, off by a thousand miles at the end."[6] Regional downturns occurred periodically in Chinese history, but a national depression when there was no slack left in the economy, on top of demographic explosion, on top of a broke government, on top of China's vulnerability to international financial shifts – this was unprecedented. Unemployment rates were catastrophic, not to mention underemployment. And this was the legacy inherited by the Nationalists. As a Japanese traveler succinctly noted in 1911: "The peasantry cannot escape from their bare subsistence level as they cannot accumulate any savings. And if there is one bad harvest, they are reduced to starvation."[7] Twenty years later a British observer noted: "There are districts in which the position of the rural population is that of a man standing permanently up to the neck in water, so that even a ripple is sufficient to drown him."[8] The socialist economist R.H. Tawney was particularly struck by the systemic nature of the crisis: "The individual cannot be rescued by his neighbours, since whole districts together are in the same position. The district cannot be rescued by the nation because means of communication do not permit of food being moved in sufficient quantities." The rural economy had, in significant ways, slid back from the days the Qing maintained relatively efficient famine-prevention systems.[9]

The chief division in Chinese society as a whole was the rural–urban split. Rural areas were defined by what they were not: they lacked radio, cinema, department stores, paved roads, newspapers, electricity, modern schools, and any of the features that made cities a virtually different world. At the same time, industrialization depended on the rural economy: cotton, silk, tobacco, foodstuffs, all produced by extremely cheap farm labor. The migration of the wealthy to urban areas was a long-term trend related to the rise of merchant culture from the sixteenth century, but it was exacerbated by the political instability of the late Qing. The result was that "rural elites" were not all that elite and their wealth was not very secure. Such families were often not much better off than their poor peasant neighbors – whom they feared and whom they feared becoming. Thus the Chinese countryside turned on itself in an extremely harsh way.

The engine producing the disintegration of rural society was perhaps more political than economic. The institutions that had held imperial China together had failed. Yet, in the final analysis, the politics and the economics of decline are tightly related. Longterm economic and demographic pressures created strains the political system could not cope with, while the collapse of political order in 1911 made balanced economic development impossible. The historian Philip Huang thus emphasizes the deep roots of the modern agrarian crisis.[10] Neither the vigorous commercialization of agriculture in the sixteenth century – something like a modern market economy with sophisticated trading techniques and the use of wage labor – nor China's incorporation into the world economy in the nineteenth century – transformed the basic shape of the ancient small-peasant economy. The family farm continued to rely on its members' labor and consumed most of its own production. The peasant economy revolved around minimizing risks rather than maximizing profits like a capitalist enterprise. Furthermore, peasant family farms often made use of labor in ways that were rational from their point of view but inefficient from a capitalist point of view. For "a capitalist farm will stop putting in labor when its marginal returns drop below the market wage, for that would mean a negative return. A peasant family farm, on the other hand, will continue to put in labor so long as household consumption needs are not met, even if the marginal returns to that labor sink well below prevailing market wages."[11]

In other words, some members of the household worked for returns that were below what they needed to survive, because they were still contributing to the income of the household as a whole. This kind of "self-exploitation" arises since peasants do not "pay" for their labor; they cannot freely acquire and get rid of members and so have a rational motive to use some of their labor inefficiently or for "diminishing returns" rather than not at all. China's population growth – to 500 million by the 1930s – has led some economists to argue that the system must have remained basically healthy, but in fact it was producing "surplus labor" that could not find outside employment or settle new land. The last frontiers had been developed; all arable land was being intensively farmed. Double and even triple cropping was the norm. The traditional mode of farming had reached its limits.

This brings us to technological issues, such as chemical fertilizers, improved seeds, farm machinery, and the like. Modern, scientific inputs could, in theory, have improved yields in the 1920s as they did in the 1950s, though it remains unclear to what degree and at what cost. In any case, as long as peasants engaged in self-exploitation on tiny family farms in an unstable political system, the potential for technological reforms remained virtually nil.

Chinese agriculture became more and more intensified over the late imperial era, as increased labor raised production, and then faced "involution" by the twentieth century as production *per labor input* fell (though total production increased). Philip Huang posits that agricultural involution in China was not felt as a particular crisis but marked a long-term trend. In contrast to Western Europe, where both absolute output and output per labor unit grew in the early stages of industrialization, albeit at huge social cost, China saw growth in the first category but not the second. Basic standards of living, relations of production, and modes of production did not change in the countryside. As population and commercialization increased in a linked fashion, peasants planted more commercial crops, such as cotton, peanuts, and opium poppies, which were also more labor-intensive. But eventually peasant incomes stagnated and fell. Long before this point, whenever it occurred exactly, Chinese peasants subjectively experienced immiseration, due to the objective experiences of economic disruptions, a high degree of expropriation (taxes, rent, and interest), and the constant threat of violence and natural disasters. Here is where the Communists tried to make revolution in the 1930s.

## The survival of the CCP

The Chinese Communist Party was decimated in the course of the GMD crackdown in 1927 and 1928, and it took another three to four years of intra-Party fighting for the CCP to come up with a coherent set of policies. Eventually the Party adopted three interrelated strategies: appealing to peasant anger; creating an army that followed guerrilla tactics; and building protected base areas ("soviets"). Mao Zedong headed the most successful soviet, though he was not one of the CCP's top leaders, and he developed these strategies in the teeth of the Nationalist White Terror and critics within the CCP alike. Even after the United Front had irretrievably collapsed, Communist leaders had difficulty understanding that their days of organizing urban workers were over.

The leadership of the CCP responded ineffectually to the White Terror – which is understandable. Men with very imperfect knowledge of the facts had to improvise quickly. In the end, the key to the survival of the Party turned out to be in the field, not at Party headquarters. Under conditions of the White Terror the wisest strategy was for Communists to go underground and retreat to areas beyond Nationalist control. But, as we have noted, Stalin still needed to claim victories in China to demonstrate his leadership of the international movement, and so the Comintern ordered uprisings. Some Chinese Communists also hoped that seemingly futile uprisings would spark a wider revolution. In fact, they simply resulted in the further slaughter of Communists and workers. In the end Chen Duxiu was expelled from the Party as a supposed "Trotskyite," though he had carried out the very alliance with the GMD that Trotksy had argued against. Opposing Stalin, Trotsky had criticized attempts to limit the actions being taken by workers and peasants as the National Revolution reached its peak in 1926. He suggested that the Communists should encourage the most radical movements among workers and peasants even if the GMD opposed them. In another ironic twist, it might seem that this was exactly what Stalin decided to do in the summer and fall of 1927. But by then it was too late.

The literary critic Qu Qiubai was named the new head of the CCP in 1927. Wildly, he predicted imminent success over the GMD. One of the largest uprisings was staged in Guangzhou at the end of the year. Communist soldiers and workers managed to seize the city, declare a "soviet," and retreat, all within 60 hours. Guangzhou's White Terror then lasted the next five days, resulting in the slaughter of about 6,000 people. The mop-up arrests, torture, and executions of anyone connected with the soviet lasted for the next two years.[12] The uprising was timed to coincide with critical Party meetings in Moscow; it was also an explosion of local revolutionary energies that had been building for some time. Perhaps 20,000 workers fought for the soviet: only a small percentage of Guangzhou's population, but in Deng Zhongxia's words, "one might say that the numbers were too few, but not that there were no masses."[13]

Yet this was not to prove the end of Communism in China. As for Trotskyism, in opposition and exile himself after 1928, Trotsky began to favor more democratic approaches to revolution. Efforts to combine democracy and Communism also appealed to Chen Duxiu, so he did finally become a Trotskyite. Small groups of Chinese Trotskyites offered a critique of the CCP's "bureaucratic corruption" into the 1950s.[14]

Meanwhile, in the wake of the White Terror, about a dozen small soviets emerged as rural base areas in the interstices between feuding warlords, usually in the traditional no-man's-lands of mountainous provincial border regions. These were the most remote areas in the most difficult terrain – areas where bandits had long fled beyond the reach of imperial armies. Some 300 counties (out of 1,800) fell under some degree of Communist influence, though the bulk of the population remained "white." The CCP leadership feared, with some justification, that rural soviets threatened the proletarian (or urban working class) nature of the Communist movement. Perhaps they would degenerate into mere banditry. But with nowhere else to turn, the Party encouraged rural activism – at least as a temporary expedient until contact with workers could be re-established.

If the Party was to rebuild, it had to find a new basis in Chinese society. It had to shift from the cities and urban workers to the countryside and peasants. Haltingly, this was done. The Communists were fortunate that Chiang Kai-shek had more formidable opponents who required his attention into the 1930s. Even after consolidating his Nanjing regime, Chiang failed to use his best troops against the soviets. Instead, he tried to use warlords nominally under his command, hoping that both warlord armies and Communists would be weakened. But such armies were not the most efficient fighters, and this strategy gave the CCP some breathing space.

After the initial onslaught of the White Terror, membership increased slowly, and the CCP began to recruit peasants and soldiers. Under the leadership of Mao Zedong, a large soviet was created in Jiangxi Province. CCP membership would ebb and flow over the next two decades as circumstances shifted. The following approximate figures (Table 14.1) show the cycles of CCP growth:

*Table 14.1* CCP membership

| Year | Number |
| --- | --- |
| April 1927 | 60,000 |
| December 1927 | 10,000 |
| 1928 | 40,000 |
| 1930 | 122,000 |
| 1933 | 300,000 |
| 1936 | 30,000 |
| 1937 | 40,000 |
| 1940 | 800,000 |
| 1941 | 760,000 |
| 1942 | 735,000 |
| 1944 | 853,000 |
| 1945 | 1.2 million |

Though the United Front had not given rural organizing high priority, the rural organs it did have were dominated by Communists. Mao Zedong himself briefly worked in this area under the United Front. It was on the basis of this experience, then, that the CCP was able to look for peasant support in the midst of the White Terror.

China's first "soviets" were established on the Guangdong coast in 1927; they were based on the old peasant associations in Haifeng and Lufeng counties that had been established in 1922 by Peng Pai.[15] But they remained isolated: surrounded by "white" counties, outnumbered, and outgunned. Communist leaders wanted to retreat, but locals wanted their revolutionary gains to be defended. Naturally peasants, tied to their fields and now committed to revolution, did not want their only protectors to leave. Throughout the remainder of 1927, the soviets retained control of the countryside, although the county seats were garrisoned with anti-Communist armies. Neither side felt strong enough to uproot the other (and suffered severe casualties when they tried), and so the stalemate continued. According to Peng Pai's later analysis, peasants were attached to their associations and very good at defending their native villages, but they felt little abstract loyalty to the CCP and were ineffective in offense. In September, the Communists, helped by a mutiny among the government's forces, were able to occupy and plunder several larger towns.

But Peng Pai's hopes for outside assistance never materialized. After the Guangzhou uprising was defeated in December, Guangdong's Nationalist-allied leaders were ready to move against the soviets. By late February 10,000 well-armed troops simply invaded the "red" counties, occupied market towns, and gradually strangled centers of Communist support in the countryside. In retrospect, it can be seen that Haifeng and Lufeng were less than strategically ideal. They were too close to urban centers, not mountainous enough to provide hideouts for guerrilla troops, and vulnerable to foreign pressure as well.

Already in early 1927 (when the National Revolution still seemed strongly committed to the United Front) Mao had conducted an inspection of peasant associations in his home province of Hunan. His report broke from official policy, and the CCP suppressed it. Rather than criticizing peasant "excesses" for fear they might alienate the GMD, Mao glorified them. And he went so far as to virtually ignore the proletariat, finding instead that peasants – especially *"poor peasants"* – were the vanguard of China's revolution.

> In a very short time, several hundred million peasants in China's central, southern and northern provinces will rise like a tornado or tempest – a force so extraordinarily swift and violent that no power, however great, will be able to suppress it.... All revolutionary parties and all revolutionary comrades will stand before them to be tested, to be accepted or rejected by them. To march at their head and lead them? To follow in the rear, gesticulating at them and criticising them? To face them as opponents? ... circumstances demand that a quick choice be made.[16]

Mao's enthusiasm was unwarranted. The rising storm was more like a small tornado touching down here and there than a typhoon blowing down all before it. He was also to discover poor peasants could not make a revolution by themselves. Yet Mao's instincts were accurate. Peasants were more than shock troops. If they could be persuaded to demand land, they would overthrow the entire "feudal" system of unequal rural wealth and power.

Mao was born in 1891 in an upwardly mobile peasant family. His father had begun poor but eventually owned about 22 *mou* (3–4 acres) to become what would later be called a "rich peasant" dealing in grain transport and hiring a full-time laborer.[17] Mao was sent to the village school and he personally saw local food shortages and peasant uprisings. "These incidents, occurring close together, made lasting impressions on my young mind, already rebellious."[18] At 16, Mao left home to attend a "modern school," where he was one of the poorest students. There he encountered the works of Kang Youwei and Liang Qichao. He was soon admitted to the Middle School in Changsha, the capital of Hunan, protesting against but absorbing much of its classical curriculum. In 1911 Mao left school briefly to join the revolutionary forces, and at this time first read about socialism in the newspapers. He then embarked on a brief but intense period of self-study.

> I read many books, studied world geography and world history. There for the first time I saw and studied with great interest a map of the world. I read Adam Smith's *The Wealth of Nations*, and Darwin's *Origin of Species*, and a book on ethics by John Stuart Mill. I read the works of Rousseau, Spencer's *Logic*, and a book on law written by Montesquieu. I mixed poetry and romances, and the tales of ancient Greece, with serious study of the history and geography of Russia, America, England, France and other countries.[19]

Mao became intellectually and politically alive as an adolescent. Pressured by his family, he abandoned self-education for the Hunan Provincial First Normal School, graduating in 1918 with a solid background in the Westernized curriculum and alert to the New Culture movement emanating from Beijing. Mao also began exercising his enormous organizational talents with student associations and study societies dedicated to New Culture principles. Mao remembered: "At this time my mind was a curious mixture of ideas of liberalism, democratic reformism, and Utopian Socialism. I had somewhat vague passions about 'nineteenth-century democracy,' utopianism and old-fashioned liberalism, and I was definitely anti-militarist and anti-imperialist."[20] As a typical "new youth," then, Mao traveled to Beijing, where Li Dazhao gave him a job in the Beida library. Here Mao was ignored by many of the leaders of the New Culture movement, which obviously rankled at the time and perhaps played a role in his later anti-intellectualism. But he was also able to pursue systematic investigation of anarchism and socialism, and during the May Fourth movement he turned toward Marxism with his friend Cai Hesen. By this time he was back in Hunan, well known in radical circles. He became principal of the Normal School's elementary school, a position of some prestige. Several of his articles were published in the May Fourth press.

According to Mao, his conversion to Marxism came in 1920 out of his experiences organizing workers in Changsha, his further reading of Marxist works, and his interest in the ongoing Russian revolution. As a delegate from Hunan, Mao joined the first organizational meetings of the infant Chinese Communist Party in 1921 – and in 1923 he moved to Shanghai to work for the United Front full-time. What did Marxism and Communism mean to Mao? He accepted the United Front principle of an interclass union of the Chinese people to oppose militarism and imperialism, as well as the Communist emphasis on organizing peasants and workers for class struggle. In spite of his special interest in politics, in many ways Mao was a typical educated but provincial young man.

In the course of the White Terror in 1927, Mao – and other Communists – came to the realization that "power comes out of the barrel of the gun" and that mass movements alone could not guarantee victory. At an "emergency conference" held in August, Mao also took advantage of official Comintern blame of the CCP to add his own self-justifying critique: why had his Hunan report been ignored? "I cannot help wondering if the leadership of our party was counter-revolutionary because, while the broad masses both in and out of the party wanted to make revolution, the leaders did not. The peasantry caused me to draw this conclusion."[21] Mao was ordered to lead Hunanese peasants in an attack on Changsha. If successful, worker and peasant troops could then link up with the Guangdong soviet that Peng Pai was putting together. However, the situation in Hunan, like elsewhere, had already turned against the Communists, and the futile effort to capture Changsha only lost more men and support. Mao was to resist all future initiatives that came from the urban-based CCP leadership as best he could.

Like others in his position, in late 1927 Mao simply fled from GMD forces. First he went to Jinggangshan, an isolated mountain about 200 km south of Changsha on the Hunan–Jiangxi border. There, Mao was joined by a military man, Zhu De, with a handful of troops, and by a renegade GMD officer, Peng Dehuai, with his detachment. Recruiting local bandits, they established a new "Red Army" and began to try to convert the peasants. But their first task was simply to survive in the remote countryside. Bandit lairs were common in remote areas where the government was weak, and the Communists found refuge among them. But geography was hardly the basis for a sound marriage. Many bandits resisted discipline, and the Communists executed them once the military situation was stable. Still, if bandits could be "remolded" to accept discipline they made fine soldiers, brave and used to hardship. After all, they had come from the peasantry, not the landlord class.

Chiang Kai-shek was to persist in calling the Communists "bandits" as a generic insult to the end of his days. The Jinggangshan base area had some successes, and some peasants came to believe that a certain "Zhu-Mao" who gave them land was destined to possess the Mandate of Heaven. Again, Mao was not the only Communist to make contacts with bandits, and CCP leaders had reason to fear that bandits might convert Communists instead of the other way around. After all, both groups used armed gangs of poor people to swoop down on wealthy families and towns. Bandits, however, moved around to flee pursuit and find new victims. What rural Communists needed was a stable base area.

Mao thus led the Red Army east to the hill country of the Jiangxi–Fujian border region around the town of Ruijin. This area was slightly more hospitable, though still remote. This became the Jiangxi Soviet: not a lair but a functioning government. It was in the Jiangxi Soviet that the CCP "experimented" with a mix of policies that allowed it to survive: peasant-based guerrilla war; land reform to create popular support; professional army troops; and a willingness to abandon the cities indefinitely to "counter-revolutionary" forces.

## The Jiangxi Soviet

Mao Zedong was not yet a member of the top echelons of the CCP, but he commanded the Jiangxi Soviet – at least most of the time.[22] From late 1929 to late 1934 Mao built a "revolutionary base area" eventually covering over thirty counties and perhaps two million people in southwestern Jiangxi and western Fujian. The soviet faced continuous attacks from Nationalist armies, and from within the soviet Mao faced opposition both from the CCP's top leadership and from local cadres. But, through victories and defeats, the Communists learned a great deal about peasant revolution. The main lessons can be summarized in four points. First, an army as well trained and equipped as possible was necessary, though ultimately political rather than military factors were decisive. Second, a safe base area was necessary to convince peasants to take the risk of supporting the Communists and to provide resources for the army. "Base area" thus refers not to a military camp but to farming country, though in remote or inaccessible terrain. Third, poor peasants alone provided an insufficient base of support; since stable and long-term administration rested on the middle peasants as well, radical land redistribution policies were self-defeating. And fourth, peasant support and the economic success of the soviet therefore depended on *moderate* land reform that in turn rested on astute social analysis. The revolution of the base area was at heart a land revolution that dispossessed what the Party defined as an exploiting class of landlords. It released energies sufficient to fend off attacks for five years and built up military and civilian bureaucracies.

The region encompassed by the future Jiangxi Soviet had already experienced mobilization during the National Revolution and the Northern Expedition. It is worth emphasizing that Mao did not bring Communist ideas to the area – that task had been accomplished by radicalized educated youth of the region in the 1920s. We have already seen how Communists such as Shi Cuntong, Shen Dingyi, and Peng Pai emerged from small towns to join the Party; it was also common for local youth who studied perhaps at the provincial capital – like Mao Zedong – to return home and teach. Newly founded Westernized schools were a major source of employment for the educated youth of the period. In the wake of the White Terror, radical youth also returned home to escape from persecution in the cities. Young schoolteacher radicals spread ideas about nationalism, communism, and modernity. In the case of the Jiangxi Soviet, local radicals were protected by the arrival of Mao's forces, but they did not necessarily agree with all of Mao's policies.

Mao maintained a precarious personal dominance in the region until 1933. His Red Army combined guerrilla tactics with a base strategy. This was tricky, requiring that the army try to avoid positional warfare on the one hand without degenerating into wandering bands on the other. The base area provided the financial resources necessary for the army, first through confiscation of the property of the rich and later through regularized taxes. Meanwhile, assured of Communist protection against GMD and landlord reprisals, peasants joined the war on rural elites and in the process received something of a political education along with their new fields. Long-pent-up hatreds were released. Once peasants committed themselves, there was no turning back; even passively receiving a plot of land meant punishment if the old regime returned. Recruitment of peasant boys into the army followed, and the base's territory expanded. Four GMD "annihilation campaigns" were successfully repulsed.

Certainly, the above summary became part of later Communist mythology, and there is much truth to this story. The reality was, however, more complex, and the fifth annihilation campaign destroyed a soviet that had not been able to expand much over the preceding few years. One problem was divided leadership. Mao was given political responsibility for the Jiangxi Soviet itself, but when the Central Committee moved to Ruijin after its underground existence in Shanghai proved untenable, Mao had to cooperate with CCP superiors, themselves under pressures from the Comintern and Stalin. No one has ever accused Mao of being inept at the game of bureaucratic politics, but his position was far from secure. Though the Party recognized his usefulness as an administrator, Mao lost his military positions, and his authority had shrunk by the time of the Long March retreat in 1934. The top echelons of the CCP remained in the hands of urban intellectuals, many of whom were slow to understand the nuances of rural life.

The lower levels of the CCP included rough-and-ready types capable of fighting but not necessarily of leading by persuasion. Problems of guerrilla commanders who insisted on fighting on their own ("adventurism") and of CCP cadres who bullied peasants ("commandism") plagued the soviet. Many new CCP members were illiterate activists who might fall prey to commandism or graft. None the less, it says something about the quality of Maoist organization that these problems were discussed and not, in GMD-style, simply ignored. Education in both basic skills and Marxist precepts was stressed wherever possible. Mao's faith in education and the ability of individuals to reform became a key to his thinking about revolution itself. *Voluntarism* – an emphasis on the individual's will – became a key element of Maoism, explaining how intellectuals and peasants might become good Communists, in spite of their non-proletarian backgrounds. It also suggested how the Communists might overcome great odds.

Yet perhaps the most critical problem was land policies that kept changing. Policies had to be based on an understanding of rural classes, which the Communists defined as:

- Landlords: wealthy enough to avoid physical labor, renting out fields on a sharecropping and/or cash basis.
- Rich peasants: wealthy enough to need to hire additional labor, loan out money, or rent out a small portion of land, but physically engaged in farming themselves.
- Middle peasants: owner-farmers with enough land for the household to survive on but no more.
- Poor peasants: owning a little land but needing to rent land or hire themselves out to continue farming. "A poor peasant also does not have enough to eat and is chronically in debt."[23]
- Farm laborers: owning no land, possibly possessing tools, hiring themselves out by the day or for longer periods.

Mao described the process of investigating landownership and other forms of "exploitation" in ways that influenced subsequent rural investigations through the 1950s.[24] The first village investigations revealed that landlords and rich peasants owned about 50 percent of the land though they comprised only 10 percent of the population. With another 20 percent of the land in "public fields" (like temple lands, often controlled by land-lords), poor and middle peasants – 90 percent of the population – owned just 30 percent of the land. In some counties peasants owned just 15 percent of the land while sharecropping rents as high as 60 percent of the grain harvest were common. The first land reform, which began as part of the National Revolution preceding Mao's arrival, essentially consisted of counting the fields and the people in a township and giving every person an equal amount. Landlords and rich peasants were thus dispossessed, an often violent process, although if they did not run away they then received some land back. Landlords and "local tyrants" were also dispossessed of their savings and stored grain. But class analysis was not important in the actual process since all fields were thrown together for redistribution on a strictly per capita basis. Approximately 60,000 people received land in this way.[25] Such policies were effectively summarized as "take from those who have more to help those who have less" and "take from the fat to compen-sate the lean." Land reform could not, of course, be implemented over the entire region at one stroke, but followed peasant uprisings and the appearance of the Red Army in a district. By the summer of 1931 land redistribution was complete.

This kind of radical land reform won the CCP much support, but it created problems as well. According to later CCP analysis of "leftist mistakes," equal redistribution hurt middle peasants, thus alienating a crit-ical segment of rural society – one with more skills like literacy than poor peasants but with a greater stake in the revolution than rich peasants. Middle peasants did not like losing their ancestral fields, even if they received back about the same amount of land. Another problem was *lack* of thoroughness: many rich peasants reportedly obtained more than their fair share of land by claiming to have larger families, especially in the early days of weak CCP penetration into villages. Investigations were conducted by outsiders and depended on households self-reporting their landholdings. Even with neighbors checking on each other, this was a recipe for ineffi-ciency and mistakes. Perhaps most disruptive of all, the principle of egalitarianism inspired dissatisfied peasants to demand repeated redistribu-tion of land, creating more and more bad feeling and literally making farming difficult. If a peasant invested in seeds and fertilizer but lost his land before the crops could be harvested, he soon learned not to work hard or make further investments.

Mao Zedong thus took the lead in moderating these early policies. Rich peasants would lose some of their land, but instead of being reassigned new plots, they were to retain a portion of their original fields. They were also allowed to keep all of their businesses except usury and pawn-broking. Middle peasants were allowed to keep all their land, land they had already invested time and resources in. Poor peasants and the landless were to be given only land specifically confiscated from landlords and rich peasants and the fields belonging to schools, temples, and lineage estates. Poor peasants who lacked labor power (whether because they were too old or had too many small children) were even allowed to rent out some of their land. Mao also emphasized that the goal was "to let the broad masses of the peasants obtain through revolution the one thing that they strongly desired, the right to ownership of the land" – in other words, the CCP was *not* to encourage "public ownership of the land."

After 1931 the CCP's top leadership moved to the left again, and against Mao's advice returned to radical land redistribution, denying landlords the right to any land whatsoever, giving rich peasants only poor land, and affirming the goal of public ownership. This rekindled the problems fostered by the first land revolution and even exacerbated them as peasants struggled to be put in a favorable class category. The CCP shifted back to Mao's more moderate policies in the summer of 1933, but in some ways it was already too late. A certain amount of enthusiasm and productivity was lost forever. Overly strict or simplistic class analysis classified households that were basically "rich peasant" as "landlord" only because they rented out a few fields. Middle peasants who were doing well, perhaps because several strong sons were just entering their most productive years, were classified as rich peasants if they had made the mistake of making small loans to their neighbors. Only through making these blunders did the Party eventually learn not to confuse mere wealth with patterns of exploitation. Mao emphasized that cadres should conduct class analysis on the basis of whether families *basically* lived off the rents or *generally* hired long-term labor. The process of listening to appeals and correcting mistaken classifications was time-consuming and probably confusing to most peasants – but it was central to the revolutionary process.

## The lessons of the Futian Incident and guerrilla war

Another factor in the complex politics of the Jiangxi Soviet was that the region's "vertical" conflicts between villages cut across the "horizontal" class struggle that the CCP talked about. In spite of its successes, the CCP could not create a solid community. Instead, social revolutionary policies and pre-existing local conflicts tended to mesh together. Before the establishment of the Soviet, Communist organizers in Jiangxi in the 1920s were mostly from relatively well-off families returning from city schools. They might become schoolteacher activists, as we noted above, and they often led resistance to the country government on issues such as taxes that affected the whole community. But they were less inclined to represent the interests of the poorer hill people. In the nineteenth century, well-established clan-based villages farmed in irrigated valleys while newer Hakka ("guest people") villages, perhaps renting lands from the clan villages below, made their livings on the less fertile hillsides, occasionally growing rich off commercial crops or timber but usually surviving more precariously.

It was thus easy for "class struggle" to lead to inter-community and ethnic feuding. Though the evidence is far from clear, after the GMD purges of 1927–8 the more developed valleys became "white," and it would have been natural for Mao's Red Army to turn to the hill folk for support. Certainly, Mao made clan structures, which were more prominent in the fertile valleys, one of his chief targets. These social tensions lay behind the Futian Incident, which reflected the resistance of the native Jiangxi Communists to Mao's policies. Mao began purging local cadres in the summer of 1930, and a local Red Army battalion rebelled against him.[26] The rebels were massacred at Futian in December. It may well be that one key element of the struggle was a conflict between Mao and radical activists (Hakka hill folk?) on the one hand and parochial and moderate local elites (valley clans?) on the other. Mao's search for disloyalty soon led to false accusations that prolonged the divisions. The historian Yung-fa Ch'en has pointed out that Mao later forbade killing so that future campaigns to ferret out disloyalty would not become so bloody.

The Futian Incident can be read in several ways. From the longer perspective of CCP history, it was a fairly minor, if bloody, purge that occurred at a precarious and disturbed time. It involved mistakes that the Party learned from. But it also reveals what was to become a pattern. The incident was surrounded by accusations and counteraccusations, and Mao claimed with no foundation that his opponents were counter-revolutionaries. Ambitious cadres would have learned they had little to fear from excesses of prosecutorial enthusiasm: that is, it was better to err on the side of persecution than leniency. On the other hand, it is important to remember that an atmosphere of paranoia and violence reflected the fact that enemies really were all around.[27] It is hardly surprising that Mao wanted to build a secret shadow party. By 1934 Kang Sheng had established a secret police apparatus. Trusted CCP members were to report on local activities and keep an eye out for traitors. The slightest violation of Party discipline was a serious offense for Party members.

Still, for all the complexity of the task and for all the mistakes, the Jiangxi Soviet succeeded in eliminating landlordism, satisfied much of the land hunger of ordinary peasants, and improved the local economy by encouraging handicraft manufacturing. No attempts were made to interfere with markets. Most debts were wiped out, and the multifarious old taxes were replaced by a unified, progressive tax system. The Southwest Jiangxi Work Report of October 1931 claimed: "The peasants enthusiastically remitted taxes, knowing that they are being applied toward such things as expansion of the Red Army, building the soviet government, and for official and medical expenses that are for their own protection and benefit."[28] Families of Red Army soldiers were exempt from taxes. The soviet government took responsibility for a whole range of agricultural needs: obtaining seeds and fertilizer, maintaining irrigation works, convincing the peasants to share scarce draft animals and even to pool labor. "The question of soviet or collective agriculture," Mao reported, "of course, cannot as yet be raised, but with the objective of promoting progress in agriculture, it is urgently necessary to set up small experimental farms, agricultural research schools, and exhibitions of farm produce in every district."[29] These extension services were designed to improve peasant life while transferring resources to the war effort. The export of rice was prohibited while attempts were made to smuggle in necessities like salt through the GMD blockade. "As regards the private sector of the economy," Mao added, "the soviets shall not hamper it but rather shall promote and encourage it.... For the development of private enterprise is essential to the interests of the soviets at the present stage."

Equally important, a realm of popular political participation was created that gave rise to new local leadership. Elections held in 1931 reserved a disproportionate place for "workers" and poor and middle peasants. Another important "target group" of CCP cadres was village women. The 1931 marriage laws codified the right to choose one's spouse and the right to divorce, and prohibited polygamy, the sale of women into marriage, and child marriages. Many village women had been married against their will and detested their brutal husbands. The problem for the CCP then became one of balance. Most marriages had to be held together or else peasant men would become disaffected. Many women, too, regarded "free marriage" as little more than a euphemism for licentiousness. The new laws were therefore only partly implemented, the Party dedicated to mediating marital disputes rather than promoting individual freedom. None the less, women's associations were established, and these brought more women into political participation even while often acting as marriage counselors. A quarter or more of city and township government delegates were often women.[30] The energies of women, once freed, improved economic production. Women's plowing and planting brigades were formed, and the talent pool grew for administrative tasks, nursing, and propaganda work. Some women even joined the army. Even when women unbound their feet, it remained difficult for them to get around (except for Hakka women, who had never bound their feet). None the less, activist women organized parties for Red Army soldiers, held farewell ceremonies for departing battalions, and made straw sandals for the troops. Such public ceremonies – and not only those involving women – helped surround the Communists with an aura of power and legitimacy.

The Red Army was perhaps the Chinese Communists' greatest single innovation within the traditions of communism. Lenin had foreshadowed the role of intellectuals in the Party and even the legitimacy of peasant participation, but revolutionary armies had been created in Russia only after the seizure of power in the eastern cities. Nor did the French Revolution of 1789 (which served as a historical model for Marx), the European revolutions of 1848, or the Paris Commune of 1870 rely on armies. The revolutions had come first. However, the European experience was urban; in China, an army was necessary to any base area strategy because local populations had to be guaranteed security before they would participate in the revolution. Organized armed forces were necessary to defeat local militia under the control of elites as well as to defend core areas within which the revolution – land reform – could proceed. The Red Army performed several other key functions as well: integrating disconnected base areas and spreading information and propaganda about the revolution; providing military training and advice to local activists; and socializing volunteers from among the peasantry, GMD armies, and bandit gangs. As the following chart (Table 14.2) shows, the Red Army, based in the Jiangxi Soviet, grew rapidly in the 1930s before shrinking again in the course of the Long March, and then expanding again.

In proclaiming that "political power grows out of the barrel of a gun," Mao Zedong was *not* conflating violence and power. He understood that violence was necessary but far from sufficient to the exercise of power. Mao had quickly grasped that the White Terror meant that mass movements had to be supplemented by an organized military. He dismissed as "pedantic" orthodox Marxist-Leninists who held that a revolution comprised the rise of a class, not the organization of armed forces. Mao did not deny the importance of class; on the contrary, he criticized the "purely military viewpoint." Still, it is clear that without the Red Army the CCP would not have survived. Unlike the previous revolutions of modern history, the Chinese revolution was built with the army as a key element from the beginning. Mao's insight was to synthesize separate political and military considerations into a unified concept of "revolutionary war." In 1936 he noted: "The Red Army, though small, has great fighting capacity, because its men have sprung from the agrarian revolution and are fighting for their own interests, and because officers and men are politically united."[31]

Above all, Mao believed that the CCP, not the Red Army, must remain in charge of the gun. In so far as the CCP was creating a state, with cadres, schools, mass movements, and a new culture, then the army would form one

*Table 14.2* Red Army soldiers

| Year | Number | Year | Number |
|------|--------|------|--------|
| 1928 | 10,000? | 1937 | 90,000 |
| 1929 | 60,000 | 1938 | 180,000 |
| 1930 | 70,000 | 1939 | 300,000 |
| 1931 | 100,000 | 1940 | 500,000 |
| 1932 | 200,000 | 1941 | 440,000 |
| 1933 | 500,000? | 1942 | 450,000 |
| 1934 | 150,000 | 1943 | 465,000 |
| ... | | 1944 | 475,000 |
| ... | | 1945 | 860,000 |

component of the state. If all war is the continuation of politics by other means, only revolutionary war, in Mao's view, possessed the strengths of revolutionary politics. As imagined by Marx, a communist revolution against a bourgeoisie might be relatively peaceful – marked in its early stages by strikes and protests, to be followed by seizure of the cities. China, however, given its "semi-colonial and semi-feudal" condition, faced enemies that gave no quarter and so Mao imagined almost precisely the opposite course: that through armed struggles the CCP would seize control of the countryside and only then move to occupy the cities. In 1936 Mao explicitly said that neither previous Western experience nor the Russian Revolution offered models that could be followed by China (in his officially published works, this was later revised to give greater credit to the "Soviet experience"). China's revolution would be an armed one, and its revolutionary war was rooted in the land revolution. In political terms, Mao was saying that he should not be subservient to the Comintern or Russian-trained Chinese Communists.

Mao designed political training to give soldiers – increasingly peasant volunteers – both an understanding of the reasons they were fighting and a sense of discipline. The commissar system (pioneered in the early GMD armies) was used not only to place trusted cadres among the troops, but to provide the Party representatives required to countersign all military orders. There was no question that the army would be subservient to the Party. It was this discipline that distinguished the Red Army from warlord and GMD troops. The abolition of corporal punishment served further to stress the difference from other armies. Mao noted:

> Apart from the role played by the Party, the reason why the Red Army can sustain itself without being exhausted ... is the thoroughness of its democratic practice. The officers do not beat the soldiers; officers and soldiers have the same food and clothing and receive equal treatment; soldiers enjoy freedom of assembly and speech; cumbersome formalities and ceremonies are abolished; the financial administration is absolutely open to all.[32]

Most of Mao's writings from the 1930s discuss the tactics and strategy of guerrilla war. Many of the men who were to become leaders of China after 1949 were Mao's military colleagues in this period: not only Zhu De and Peng Dehuai, but also Lin Biao and Chen Yi. Deng Xiaoping served as a commissar; another future national leader, Liu Shaoqi, was unusual in that he spent the period working underground in the cities. Mao systematized some of the "rules" of guerrilla fighting, though many of these simply reflected the traditions of rural resistance of bandit gangs and secret societies. In sum, soldiers needed flexibility, patience, and a long-term perspective. They were to wait for enemy mistakes, retreat when the enemy was strong and attack when it was weak, concentrate their numbers to surprise smaller enemy divisions, and take advantage of the cooperation of local people and superior knowledge of the terrain. Then, "when the enemy comes into the red areas, he will be like a shrimp washed up on the beach."[33]

The fundamental problem, never entirely solved, was that guerrilla tactics required giving up territory when superior forces attacked, or even giving up territory as part of a "luring deep" strategy. Inevitably, then, local peasants and cadres were left vulnerable to the enemy, and the Party lost prestige. There was a contradiction between the notion of a secure base area and guerrilla tactics. The end came in 1934. Chiang Kai-shek personally led 750,000 troops to surround the Jiangxi Soviet in a blockhouse strategy. Formulated with his German advisers, this strategy involved keeping GMD troops behind fortifications and within sight of one another so that Communist guerrillas could neither pick them off nor escape.[34] Chiang built 1,500 miles of roads and 14,000 blockhouses. The circle tightened. The CCP tried regular, positional warfare. Its troops lost battles. The circle tightened; the economic blockade worsened. Rural elites around the Soviet sided with the Nationalists. Chiang reintroduced the *baojia* mutual surveillance system. In October 1934 Communist forces broke out of a weak point in the GMD circle. Thus began the Long March, which eventually led China's decimated Communist forces to a new refuge in the northwest. Although the Jiangxi Soviet was lost, the CCP learned an important lesson: even this relatively large and successful base area could not support an army capable of positional warfare. A bigger economic base was needed to resist the onslaught of a government capable of mobilizing resources from almost the entire nation. But there were more positive lessons as well. The Communists had learned how to mobilize the peasantry, promote revolutionary land reform, and integrate an effective military machine with the revolution.

## Intellectuals and their discovery of the masses

The discovery of the countryside by educated Chinese only seems obvious in retrospect. It was a discovery not of beautiful landscapes but of human ruin. Concern with the welfare of the people was, of course, central to Confucianism, and this concern undoubtedly eased the transition of the modern intelligentsia from faith in the urb as the source of progress to passion for the condition of the peasantry. What was new was that – slowly – peasants became not faceless and passive but rather, first, victims of specific social wrongs and finally moral agents in their own right. Since the early 1900s anarchists had been calling for a social revolution that would include the peasantry. Marxism tended to focus attention away from the village, yet concern for the countryside was never entirely lost. Li Dazhao urged university students to return to the villages to teach the peasants – and also to learn from their less frenetic rural lifestyle. If Mao was unorthodox in Marxist terms, his rural turn was hardly anomalous. The debacle of 1927–8 may have literally forced the CCP into rural areas, but it is also true that peasants were invading the consciousness of educated Chinese.

Peasants – living, breathing, and thinking – began appearing in fiction as distinct characters with distinct personalities. Writers like Mao Dun (1896–1981), Shen Congwen (1902–88), and Luo Shu (1903–38) used realistic and naturalistic techniques to write of the hardships of the countryside. In their stories, country people have their virtues and also their vices. There is even a note of nostalgia for the stability of better days that creeps into such supposedly anti-feudal stories. (Women writers tended to be more critical.) Since femininity tended to be associated with both virtue and weakness, it was a small step in the 1930s to turn women into a literary symbol of Japan's rape of the nation.[35] Women writers, though, sometimes insisted that rape had significance for women, not for China. In Xiao Hong's *Field of Life and Death*, dealing with the anti-Japanese struggles of Manchurian peasants, the one rape scene in the novel is a Chinese man raping a Chinese woman. Xiao Hong feared that nationalism would perpetuate the patriarchy.

What prevented all these stories from sentimentality was the matter-of-fact diction employed in them. In the popular Mandarin Ducks and Butterflies fiction, on the other hand, the countryside seems a more ambiguous place.[36] On the surface, it was idyllic. Peasants were honest, the scenery beautiful, life itself in closer touch with the eternal verities. Trapped in stressful cities like Shanghai, urban Chinese enjoyed thinking of the country as a place where the traditional virtues remained untarnished. Yet a note of contempt for the rural lay beneath the surface. The consumers of popular fiction, after all, were largely urbanites, and many had fled the countryside not long before. The city remained the place for new ambitions to be realized; and even if the city should reject such hopes, urbanites were well aware of the misery of the countryside.

Even in academic settings the countryside intruded. The 1920s and 1930s saw the birth of sociology and anthropology in China, and so we have some remarkable studies of village mores and class structures.[37] Under the direction of Chen Hansheng (1897–2004), the sociology section of Academia Sinica, the national research institute headed by Cai Yuanpei, began a systematic empirical survey of rural life. Chen was a Jiangsu native who did university work in the West, graduating from Pomona College, earning an MA from the University of Chicago, and evidently a Ph.D. from the University of Berlin. He conducted fieldwork in his home county in the economically advanced Yangzi region, and moved on to less advanced areas. But regardless of the exact circumstances of each district, Chen found peasant immiseration, rising rents, falling wages, and excessive taxes and usury. He also found that, while economic conditions might be reported, political corruption was a sensitive issue. One of his assistants was arrested as a Communist and a colleague was assassinated.

As a Marxist, Chen asked whether Chinese agriculture was moving from feudalism to capitalism. His answer was that it was not. Neither growing inequality nor the strains put on poor peasants, who increasingly were driven to non-agricultural employment, were creating surplus capital that could be used to create more efficient – capitalistic – farms. This was because the *rich peasants* who might have invested in agriculture were being squeezed out by *landlords* who were taking their rents entirely out of the agricultural community. This, then, described the dead end of semi-feudalism. In other words, the problems facing Chinese farmers were not poverty and backwardness but, at a deeper level, "the direct and indirect dominance of China's agrarian sector by imperialist capital, the intensification of the feudal nature of Chinese society, the differentiation of the peasantry [into distinct classes], and the predominance of the small scale peasant economy."[38]

Aside from sociological interest in rural life, humanistic interest in non-elite traditions and folklore blossomed. Hu Shi himself opened the way to serious literary and historical analysis of China's great novels, formerly despised in high culture. His students and colleagues moved on to recover and study ballads, popular opera, proverbs, legends, and even nursery rhymes. If not exclusively rural, such sources none the less illuminated forgotten corners of Chinese life. Thus did a Chinese "folk" emerge into Chinese consciousness and feed into Communist populism.

From Christian liberals like Jimmy Yen to Confucian conservatives like Liang Shuming, from Communists to unaffiliated professors, Chinese intellectuals were increasingly concerned with the peasantry. The discovery of the people also led to a new way of thinking about the role of the *intellectual* in society. Intellectuals had already learned through painful lessons that they were not part of the military and political ruling elite. Many sought to be teachers and so leaders of the people, but increasingly they discovered that they also had much to learn from the people. A sense of humility and self-abnegation marked intellectuals who attributed all virtue to the people.

Marxism was thus both a political phenomenon and a cultural one. If its initial appeal to radicals in the 1920s was based on the promise of more effective action through organizing the working class, its intellectual appeal to intellectuals and artists grew in the 1930s, even in the face of the White Terror. Increasingly, intellectuals began to put their faith not in their own powers of ratiocination but in the masses. Criticism of the "petit bourgeoisie" became a form of self-criticism; in a sense, intellectuals no longer trusted themselves (not that the notorious intellectual disease of arrogance was entirely wiped out). This was something of a paradox. If wisdom lay with the masses, what was the role of intellectuals? To submit entirely to Party discipline? To speak for the masses – or merely to listen to the masses? But an intellectual following Party discipline or only listening was hardly an intellectual.

Guo Moruo, the romantic "pantheist" who linked his ego to the dynamism of the universe, converted to Marxism in the late 1920s. He criticized Chinese intellectuals as lazy, uninvolved, and cowardly. Marxism satisfied some of Guo's romantic desire to tilt against the status quo and to save the world; at the same time, he at least claimed that it disciplined his egoism. He found one thread of hope in China's despair:

… we must go to the soldiers!
We must go to the masses!
My friends, it is useless to deplore the situation,
Words are no longer of any use![39]

If Guo Moruo wanted to go to the soldiers and the masses in the ardor of the National Revolution, Yin Fu (a young Communist executed in 1931) spoke even more plainly of the transformation of intellectuals in a Brechtian poem:

Gone is the era of the Romantic
Together with its Byron,
Its noble ladies and nightingales as well …
Now we'd like to sing a new song,
Perhaps it is "A New Spring since January,"
Who cares, as long as
It suits our voices.
The factories all abound with life:
Yesterday we rioted in the office,
Today the children's squadron went on strike and demonstrated,
Leaflets line up with leaflets.[40]

Pictorial art, too, was to become a tool of reform. "All art not compatible with the masses' demands definitely must fall into decay. Contemporary painting proceeds from this. It first must have lively truth adequate to move a general audience's hearts, minds, and spirit."[41] So stated Gao Jianfu, an innovative and creative painter – and no iconoclast and certainly not a Marxist (in fact, he was a supporter of the GMD). The literary historian Leo Ou-fan Lee has summarized the tenets of the revolutionary writers of the 1930s: "1) all literature is based on and determined by class; 2) all literature is a weapon for propaganda …; 3) literary criticism must be derived from materialism (it must be interpreted from the point of view of Marxist economics); 4) revolutionary literature should be proletarian literature; that is, it should be written for and by the working class. For the time being, however, it could only be written by the petty-bourgeois intellectuals. The crucial determinant was the 'standpoint' or 'outlook': if a writer adopted the class standpoint and outlook of the proletariat, he could, in fact, still produce proletarian literature."[42]

There was one solution to the dilemma of how the dispossessed could speak. That was, to present their situation through the eyes of a middle-class, educated narrator. In Lu Xun's stories from the 1920s, it is clear that the narrators only partially understand the masses they empathize with. For example, in "New Year's Sacrifice" the tragic story of the nameless servant "Xianglin's wife" is not only told second- and third-hand, but the narrator finds himself literally unable to communicate with her. Similarly, in Luo Shu's story of the servant Aunty Liu she is seen only through the eyes of the daughter of the household. Such characters could bear witness and might also represent a kind self-criticism (representing self-consciously bourgeois authors), but this writing strategy still left the masses without their own voice. Could the masses even read such accounts? Qu Qiubai charged that proletarian literature was a mere intellectual fad that, if anything, separated intellectuals from the masses rather than drawing them together.

Even the famous turn to the vernacular of the original New Culture movement came under attack as a "half-dead language" that had smuggled in pretentious Western grammatical structures to create a written language as far from actual spoken Chinese as the original enemy, classical Chinese. On the right, the Guomindang picked up this criticism to call the written vernacular "un-Chinese" and propose returning classical Chinese to the school curriculum. But on the left, efforts were devoted to listening to the common people in order to create a "mass-language." Wu Zhihui – now politically to the right as an anti-Communist but still a cultural radical – proclaimed that "the common language spoken by the masses themselves" could form the basis of a new common Chinese language. Lu Xun's contribution to this debate was more nuanced. While criticizing conservative contempt for the masses, he noted their limitations: illiteracy, narrowmindedness, ignorance of the outside world. The role of intellectuals, then, was to extend their knowledge to the masses but remember their own limitations as intellectuals. Language was not a goal in itself but a means to enlightenment. Enlightenment always began with a few, but those few had the duty to bring it to the masses. There is no doubt about Lu Xun's elitism, though it was combined with a strong sense of the shortcomings of intellectuals. Radicals proposed that intellectuals transform themselves into the masses' own "flesh and blood" – but even they spent so much time in literary disputes that little proletarian literature was actually produced.

Neither the left nor the right had much use for "individualism." Well into the 1930s, it is true, few students saw any contradiction between devotion to the nation and devotion to a search for their own happiness. A "subservient mentality" – which Chen Duxiu had roundly condemned in 1915 – was still associated with obedience to family and political authorities. Ba Jin, who was probably China's most popular writer in the early 1930s, captured this mood. Much of his writing dealt with the coming of age of young men. *Family*, for example, told of three brothers, the eldest of whom was trapped by his despotic grandfather into a loveless marriage and ultimately a meaningless life. The middle brother did somewhat better, but it was the youngest who openly rebelled, defying the tenets of filial piety and finally leaving to make his own life in Shanghai. If sentimental and psychologically one-dimensional, such tales of the scions of old gentry families were wildly popular – among the scions of old gentry families seeking to free themselves from the old culture. As an anarchist, Ba Jin sought to attack the Confucian pretensions of people who wanted to avert their eyes from the social and political crises afflicting China. Ba Jin offered not only a romantic image of individual protest but, perhaps of even greater appeal, a sense of the progressive movement stemming from May Fourth activism. First serialized in a Shanghai newspaper, *Family* went through ten editions between 1933 and 1937, and thirty-three more between 1937 and 1951.

Yet the iconoclasm of the May Fourth era could not survive the need for national pride. Zhang Shenfu, the philosopher and a cofounder of the European CCP (among Chinese students in France and Germany), wrote a defense of Confucius in 1934.[43] It is true that Zhang was still critical of the Chinese tradition, his new slogan being "Down with Confucianism! Save Confucius!" He was trying to rebut Chiang Kai-shek's New Life Movement and Japan's justification of its invasion of Manchuria in terms of preserving traditional Confucian culture. Zhang sought to discredit the GMD and the Japanese by defining a true, critical Confucianism based on a respectful yet skeptical appreciation of Confucius as a great man but not a source of absolute norms. Zhang was none the less stepping back from the iconoclasm of his youth. Like Tan Sitong, Zhang separated the master from the later doctrines, finding in Confucians' philosophy of benevolence or humaneness (*ren*) the key to something of great use in the present. Like Kang Youwei, Zhang claimed Confucius as a social activist. Zhang, one of China's foremost experts on Western philosophy, found in Confucian humanism not the answer to all questions, but a way to make up for some of the deficiencies of Western philosophy. Yet more broadly speaking, his turning away from iconoclastic radicalism represented a new reaction to the national crisis of the 1930s.

# Part III

# War and revolution, 1937–49

Between 1937 and 1938, Japanese armies swept over eastern China, bringing under their control virtually all of China's major cities, its industry and international trade, and most of its productive farmland. However, instead of becoming a pacified region of the expansive Japanese Empire and a source of goods and revenue, China was never successfully assimilated, and the protracted resistance consumed large amounts of Japan's military resources. For all their control of China's key economic and coastal areas, Japan's powerful armies were never able to quell the Chinese resistance. The Nationalists retreated to the southwest and the Communists to the northwest, and these regions became the bases from which to launch challenges to Japanese power. Chiang Kai-shek's troops resisted the Japanese onslaught in a number of extremely bloody battles, but by 1939 they had retreated to Sichuan, thousands of miles up the Yangzi River. There, Chiang attempted to wait out the war, preserving his military strength until the United States should enter the war and defeat Japan. Isolated from its traditional sources of support and revenue, the GMD became increasingly arbitrary, dictatorial, factionalized, and corrupt, and, after 1942, dependent on US aid. But the Communists continued to organize peasants behind the Japanese lines and staged persistent guerrilla attacks to keep Japanese forces off balance. Local elites who had previously benefited from their ties to the GMD were forced to cooperate with the CCP or flee as the Communists established base area governments across large areas of North and Central China.

Twelve years of war and revolution created popular nationalism, encouraged popular participation and the disintegration of the existing government, and finally defined a new nation through class-based revolution. The Communists became stronger during the war, exercising leadership in the resistance and gaining experience in both rural mobilization and local government.

In the 1930s, Chinese political leaders had to maneuver in a regional and global context that threatened to overwhelm their every effort. Sino-Japanese relations explain much of the dynamics of East Asia's twentieth century. In 1972, when the first Japanese delegation visited China since the war, Prime Minister Tanaka apologized for Japan's invasion of China. Mao is said to have responded that the CCP would never have come to power without the invasion. Or so the story goes.[1] Certainly, the Japanese gravely weakened the GMD, decimating conservative forces and fostering popular nationalism, which the CCP was able to tap. Even before the outbreak of war, the Japanese military presence in North China led to the Second United Front, thereby saving the CCP from obliteration (conversely, though, the United Front heightened Japanese fears of the Chinese and intensified Japanese militarism).

Indeed, Mao might also have pointed out that not merely the future of the CCP was shaped by Japan. Throughout the 1920s, Japanese imperialism in China drove both Chinese and Japanese domestic politics, eventually resulting in the devastation of both countries that was the product of Japan's aggressive military expansion across China and then Asia. As we have seen, Chiang Kai-shek's inability to come to grips with the expanding Japanese domination of the northeast left him open to criticism throughout the Nanjing decade and made the task of creating a strong and legitimate state nearly impossible. To understand the 1930s and 1940s in China, it is thus necessary to come to grips with the sources of Japanese imperialism. The invasion is a clear example of several broader issues. It is a good example of factors "contingent" to China's domestic politics, yet the larger international context was ultimately inseparable from internal events. If the Japanese invasion ultimately assisted the Communist Revolution, so too the fear of communism had contributed to the decisions made in Tokyo and Xinjing (Changchun), the capital of Japan's Manchukuo.[2] Although the Japanese justified their militant imperialism in terms of the Communist threat, Japan's actions in the 1930s were also a product of global economic and political trends, including the world depression and the rise of the Axis powers in Europe, and American isolationism. Japan defeated many of Chiang's best forces and the Nationalist regime decayed under wartime circumstances. After attacking Pearl Harbor, British Malaya, Hong Kong (and Shanghai's previously protected International Settlement) in December 1941, Japan humiliated Western forces throughout East and Southeast Asia, creating a vast but short-lived empire, and ultimately contributing to post-war national independence struggles.

During the war, the CCP grew to 1.2 million members and the Communist armies grew to almost a million soldiers. China, including both GMD and Communist forces, lost every major battle against Japan in the course of the war. If Japan was ultimately defeated by the United States, China's contributions – and sacrifices – were large. China, which to some degree had been fighting Japan for fifteen years from the time of the Manchurian Incident of 1931, tied down two-fifths of Japan's forces. And while Japan enjoyed a high degree of success in pacifying the areas that it conquered all across East and Southeast Asia, continued Chinese resistance sapped Japanese strength. Following Japan's defeat in 1945, Chiang Kai-shek rebuilt his dictatorship; the revivified Nanjing government could finally claim real national sovereignty. Extraterritoriality was abolished in 1943; Chiang used the war to push Soviet forces out of Xinjiang (though China recognized Outer Mongolian independence under Soviet auspices); China recovered Taiwan and Manchuria from Japan, and the United States continued to back the GMD government. China became a founding member of the United Nations with its own Security Council seat in 1945, though it was still a desperately poor nation with little international influence.

Yet if China – and the Nationalist government – won the war, the Nationalists also seem in a sense to have lost it, so quickly did the subsequent civil war turn against them. They faced a Communist movement far stronger than it had been at the start of the war. The Nationalists emerged from the war with a number of apparent advantages: military strength, control of the cities and China's industrial resources, a real degree of legitimacy, and the political and military support of the United States. The CCP, headquartered in Yan'an far to the northwest, was isolated, but in the early years of the war the Communists organized a vast military apparatus ranging from small guerrilla bands operating well behind Japanese lines to large armies capable of positional warfare. By 1941, GMD and CCP armies had clashed on a number of occasions. After 1942, the CCP, too, ceased large-scale conventional operations against the Japanese, as they too waited for Japan to collapse under US pressure. However, the CCP military organization was in the long run less important than the reorganization of local society on which it rested.

At war's end, Communists ruled over 90 million people, mostly peasants in "liberated base areas" – islands in a sea of Japanese occupation. The Party learned how to govern in those years, following policies of economic self-sufficiency, administrative discipline, and mass mobilization (but not radical land reform). Land reform would have scared off educated persons most capable of assuming administrative responsibilities, but Communist policies did include tax reform, interest reduction on loans, and rent reduction. Tax reform and interest reduction were particularly important in improving the position of poorer peasants. Honest collection of taxes and the imposition of progressive tax systems acted, modestly, to transfer wealth from the wealthier segments of rural society. Rural China had long suffered from lack of credit, and interest rates were often exorbitant, costing many families their land; hence reductions in interest payments also helped the poorest families. The CCP also encouraged industry, i.e., non-farming enterprises we would consider handicrafts, such as brickmaking, manufacturing rope, weaving cloth, and the like. In sum, these policies benefited the poor without much punishing the rich. The number of independent owner-cultivators increased, and society became more stable.

The civil war between the CCP and the GMD followed a brief respite of uneasy concord in 1945 and 1946. The Nationalists, in retaking the vast areas of eastern China occupied by the Japanese, misgoverned them badly. Too many Nationalist officials devoted themselves to personal enrichment after the long dry years in Chongqing (Chungking). In some cases landlords who had been expropriated returned to their villages with military support and instituted a kind of White Terror. The rural crisis of the 1930s thus continued. In the cities, acute corruption on a huge scale undermined GMD attempts to institute effective government. As Chiang printed money to pay his soldiers, hyperinflation ensued, with disastrous consequences for the economy and for the urban middle classes in particular. And in his anxiety to defeat the Communists, Chiang overextended his troops.

The Communists were able to melt back into the countryside, regroup, and begin to pick off the most advanced of Chiang's armies. From long experience, the Communists knew how to build revolutionary armies on the basis of peasant support and intellectual leadership. Militarily, the Communists' strategy of "from the countryside to the cities" meant that the top priority remained focused on the annihilation of the enemy's forces, not the conquest of territory. But then, once the northern countryside was under control, Communists would move on to take the cities.[3] Thus guerrilla warfare evolved gradually into mobile maneuvers and finally large-scale positional battles. As the Communist armies swept south in 1948–9, the urban populace was resignedly hopeful. The Communists were scarcely regarded as conquering heroes, but their reputation for firm resistance against the hated Japanese and the promise they offered of honest, effective government, together with deep mistrust of the GMD, did much to counter fears of expropriation. In Communist historical memory, the civil war would be summed up as "the countryside surrounding the cities." But this is too simplistic. The CCP leadership was largely urban in origins and consistently maintained the goal of ruling China from the cities. True, the Communists were initially dependent on rural resources and peasant soldiers who did not know how to turn on an electric switch and had never seen indoor plumbing. Yet the CCP's triumph, while spelling transformation of the countryside, brought not country bumpkins but experienced, educated, and sometimes cosmopolitan administrators to national power.

# 15 The War of Resistance, 1937–45

Facing imminent defeat by Chiang Kai-shek, some 86,000 Communist troops pulled out of the Jiangxi Soviet in October 1934. Euphemistically called a "strategic transfer" at the time, this retreat later emerged into history as the Long March. The Communists initially headed west but did not know their final goal. One possibility was to double back to Jiangxi, if Chiang's armies could be led away from the Soviet. Other options included linking up with smaller soviets or Communist armies in the interior. Chiang's pursuit of the Communists closed off most of these options, until they found themselves heading to the northwest. This was an even more remote area than the Jiangxi hills, but it was to place the Communists closer to Japan's armies in the northeast. In Communist mythology, the Long March thus came to represent the determination to fight the Japanese invaders.

In January 1935 the retreating troops found a brief respite in a northern Guizhou town called Zunyi and took the opportunity to figure out what should be done next. This task inevitably involved questioning what had gone wrong in the first place. Indeed, by January, troop strength was down to 40,000. Mao Zedong began to emerge as the dominant leader of the CCP at the Zunyi Conference. He was appointed to both the Secretariat – the five-person group that headed the CCP – and the top military committee, though a few others (like Zhou Enlai) remained his superiors. The fact that Mao had pressed for a more aggressive response to Chiang's fifth encirclement campaign during the last months of the Jiangxi Soviet gave his analysis additional credibility at Zunyi.

The Chinese Communists were on their own: contact with the Comintern, which could no longer help them anyway, was lost. Yet the troops from Jiangxi were not the only Communist armies on the move. Zhang Guotao, who had been Li Dazhao's student at Beijing University, had formed a small soviet in the Sichuan–Xikang border area. After several months of continuous harassment by Chiang's pursuing armies, Mao's forces met up with Zhang's army there in June 1935. By this time, Mao had only 15,000 troops versus Zhang's 80,000, and a power struggle ensued. The immediate question was whether the armies should move further north to establish a new base area in the Sichuan–Shaanxi–Gansu border region. Against Zhang,

Mao and his supporters in the central Party organs voted for the move north. They also restated the fundamental lesson of the Jiangxi Soviet experience: that rural revolution would liberate the peasantry and lead the Communists to victory. Finally, Mao led his armies north into Shaanxi, while Zhang moved south into Sichuan.

For Mao, the Long March was virtually over. After 10,000 winding kilometers, mostly west and then north into arid hill country, the survivors – about 8,000 plus a few more who had joined the Communists en route – reached

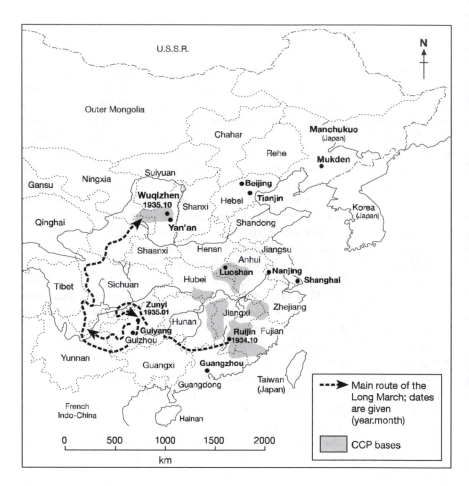

*Map 8* The Long March (and CCP base areas)

In 1934, facing imminent defeat at the hands of Chiang Kai-shek's Nationalist forces, the Communists fled the Jiangxi Soviet heading west and then north. Remaining bases were abandoned or forced underground. Although the CCP had suffered another major defeat, the safe haven of Shaanxi offered a new, strategic base from which they could rebuild.

*Source*: Courtesy of Geospatial Information Science Team, Computing Center, Academia Sinica.

a small, extremely poor base in northern Shaanxi. The fleeing forces had been under nearly constant attack, if not by GMD troops, then by local warlords and on occasion even aborigines. By historian Lucien Bianco's count, "A skirmish every day, a full-dress battle every two weeks: this is the approximate score for the 370 days of retreat."[1] The eventual significance of the Long March lay in mythology and legitimation. Those who survived it became the fathers of the Chinese Revolution. Their exploits were remembered as a victory, complete with moral dramas of individual resourcefulness, bravery, and self-sacrifice. There is, for example, the story of the suspension bridge whose deck had been removed by the enemy. In the face of heavy enemy fire Communist solders crawled across the span to put new planks on the bridge. The army again survived. The Long Marchers suffered in order to lead China to a promised land. In Mao's poetic recollection of "Loushan Pass," he wrote:

> Keen is the west wind;
> In the endless void the wild geese cry at the frosty morning moon.
> The frosty morning moon.
> The clatter of horses' hooves rings sharp,
> And the bugle's note is muted.
> They say that the strong pass is iron hard
> And yet this very day with a mighty step we shall cross its summit,
> We shall cross its summit!
> The hills are blue like the sea,
> And the dying sun like blood.[2]

Ensconced in Shaanxi, the Communists edged closer to their call for a second united front against Japanese aggression. They did not trust Chiang Kai-shek; at first they envisioned a new class alliance: peasants and workers united with the anti-Japanese bourgeoisie. This would have been a "united front from below" that was simultaneously opposed to Japan and to the Nationalists. As the CCP consolidated its rule in northern Shaanxi, it launched an expedition in the spring of 1936 across neighboring Shanxi to engage the Japanese to the east. Though the expedition ended in failure, it seemed to many to prove that the Communists had to be taken seriously. More and more Chinese outside of either part called for the GMD and the CCP to ally against Japan.

The CCP resumed contact with the Comintern in late 1935. But Comintern influence had waned during the Jiangxi Soviet and disappeared in the Long March. When the Communists finally re-emerged into world consciousness in the northwest, Stalin, for one, seems largely to have dismissed them as peasant bandits. The Comintern did encourage the CCP to think of a new united front. (The Soviet Union hoped a strong Chiang Kai-shek would discourage Japanese incursions into northern Asia.) Locally, to gain broader support, at the end of 1935 Mao moderated the

CCP's program along the lines of the Jiangxi Soviet. The fields of rich peasants were not to be confiscated, and they were to have the same civic rights as poor and middle peasants; entrepreneurs would be encouraged; and it was to be easier to join the Party.

By no means was Shaanxi the only site of Communist armies. Some 30,000 troops had been left behind in the Jiangxi Soviet when the Long March began.[3] Chiang Kai-shek's troops captured 16,000 of them by mid-1935, but, remarkably, remnant Communist forces survived and were even able to regroup over the next three years to conduct guerrilla warfare. When a new political reality unfolded in 1937 – as Chiang Kai-shek entered into a Second United Front with the Communists – they re-emerged as an organized military force in southern China. And after Zhang Guotao virtually split with the Party Center, his armies were fiercely pressed by Nationalist and local troops. In mid-1936 they decided to march north to join Mao in Shaanxi, a major political defeat for Zhang, who soon defected to the Nationalists. This gave Mao a significant force of about 30,000. The CCP hoped to develop a truce with the other northern army leaders, particularly Zhang Xueliang. Zhang was officially under the command of Chiang Kai-shek and, kicked out of Manchuria by the Japanese, was supposed to be attacking the Communists. But Zhang – and his troops – really wanted to return to Manchuria. He was thus receptive to Communist overtures.

Worried about Zhang and his other northern commanders, Chiang Kai-shek flew to Zhang's headquarters in Xi'an in December 1936. Rather than cooperating, however, Zhang held Chiang prisoner for a week in what became known as the "Xi'an Incident." This incident has been much studied. It shocked Nanjing, which was left headless for a week. It has long been seen as a turning point: before, grudging acceptance of Japanese encroachments; after, national unity against outright invasion. Much about the incident remains mysterious – a frontier kidnapping with warlords and Communists and government representatives telling each other secrets. Chiang forever denied that he agreed to terms in Xi'an, but it seems likely he made an oral promise to ease up on the Communists. Negotiations were frantic during the week of his captivity. Some in the Nanjing government wanted to attack Xi'an regardless of the risk to Chiang's life, for which Chiang never really forgave them (this spelled the end of the Blue Shirts). Most historians believe that some Communists wanted Chiang killed, but Stalin, in perhaps his last major act in China, made it clear that he felt Chiang should be left alive as the only leader capable of uniting China against Japan. Certainly, public opinion in China rallied around Chiang – but only *with* Zhang Xueliang and the Communists, not against them.

The Xi'an Incident was not so much a turning point as a part of a string of events pushing Chiang to take a more active anti-Japanese stand.[4] The Anti-Comintern Pact signed by Japan and Germany in November 1936 had already forced Chiang to think about an alliance with the Soviet Union. He basically understood that the Chinese public would accept no more concessions to Japan, and even his most loyal troops were unhappy with his policies. Chiang did not enter the Second United Front as a ransom payment for his release but as a calculated policy. After all, once released, he could have continued his refusal to confront Japan, and in fact Chiang tried to keep his options open. Unrelenting Japanese pressure on northern China, however, prevented him from launching another attack on the Communists. Once released, he promptly put Zhang Xueliang under house arrest, where he remained virtually for the rest of his long life. Zhang's armies were broken up – to the benefit of Chiang and also the Communists, who expanded their territories and occupied a larger town, Yan'an, which became their new capital. Little changed immediately on the surface of Chinese politics, but the nation knew that Chiang had implicitly agreed to be less accommodating to Japanese demands. Chiang found himself a national hero for the first time, and public opinion held him to the anti-Japanese alliance. The GMD and the CCP reached a formal agreement in August 1937, well into the full-scale Japanese invasion.

## The Japanese invasion

Japan began its all-out assault on China in the summer of 1937 as Nazi Germany was moving to conquer Europe. By 1938 most Chinese were governed by the Japanese or a collaborationist regime. Japanese efforts to make some kind of deal with Chiang Kai-shek failed, however, and the war dragged on and on. Why did Japan invade in the first place? The Japanese had been building up their interests in Manchuria, a fertile and resource-rich land, since the turn of the century. Conservative Tokyo bureaucrats simply wanted to keep China weak, but military officers deeply resented the "disarmament" imposed by the Washington system in the 1920s and hoped to see Japan become dominant in Asia. Domestically, as Japan faced the great economic and social strains of the Depression, calls for a "Showa Restoration" symbolized hopes for a renewal under the Showa Emperor (Hirohito) like the Meiji Restoration. In many ways, Japan's international position had improved dramatically in the twentieth century. Its manufacturing production had doubled from 1913 to 1923 and more than quintupled by 1938. Its chemical and shipbuilding industries (key to any war effort) were first-class. However, rural Japan looked distinctly pre-modern. Families farmed small plots, and high tenancy rates led to social tensions. Farmers were hurt by rice imports from Korea and Taiwan, outposts of the Japanese empire that were supposed to make the nation stronger. And they were hurt by the collapse of foreign markets for silk as the Western powers restricted trade in the wake of the Depression. Small landlords – a class that produced much of Japan's officer corps – were hard-pressed, and many were radicalized to the right. That is, they blamed capitalists and Jews for the economic plight of honest, diligent farmers, while they blamed socialists for stirring up tenants and workers and leading them astray from the path of loyalty. That

Japan did not have a Jewish population (the Jews blamed were connected to "Wall Street," a slightly less mythological entity) did not prevent the right-wing from imagining themselves as victims of international conspiracies of capitalists and communists. To radical military men, Japan's need to import raw materials and food rendered its strategic position inherently precarious.

There seemed to be two fundamental alternatives open to Japan: either liberalism, which is to say cooperation with the Western powers, free trade policies, and the "open door" in China; or expansionism, monopolizing the trade of Northeast Asia, especially Korea and Manchuria, and dominating East Asia. The conquest of Manchuria in 1931 was supposed to solve these problems by making Japan economically self-sufficient. As the economy slowly recovered from the Depression, Manchuria, with its vast coal and iron resources, was developed into an industrial powerhouse. Manchuria was run directly by the Japanese army. Radical officers wanted Manchuria not only to benefit Japan materially but also spiritually. They could create, they thought, a model society based on military–fascist–Confucian norms of hierarchy, obedience, and respect. While Japan itself was corrupted by capitalists and socialists, Manchuria, to be called Manchukuo (or the country of the Manchus), might become a utopia. The last boy-emperor of the Qing, Puyi, was brought in as its titular monarch. Western nations condemned the Japanese takeover of Manchuria, which provoked Japan to walk out of the League of Nations. However, no action was forthcoming, as Europe became fixated on the rise of Hitler and America on itself. The incapacity of the Powers to offer China assistance to protect Manchuria, long recognized as Chinese territory, is understandable, but it contributed to the international instability of the 1930s. Even more damaging, the League of Nations was shown to be ineffective.

Manchukuo was but one part of a much larger set of plans held by Japan's radical right. Army factions were involved in political assassinations and coup attempts in Tokyo that removed more liberal civilian leaders. If these hyperpatriotic army officers never quite succeeded in gaining control of Japan, they were able to carve out an independent base of action on the Asian mainland. Many of them sincerely thought they were creating not just a stronger Japan but a stronger Asia. The great enemy of all Asians, "Anglo-American imperialism," was to be extinguished in the name of Pan-Asianism. An economic sphere was to be built around the Japan–Korea–Manchuria core, and a political sphere was to be created by a so-called Japanese Monroe doctrine – a demand that the Western Powers keep their "hands off China," coined in 1934 to highlight American hypocrisy. But while promising to protect Asia, Japanese were often contemptuous of other Asians. In his study of Japanese attitudes toward China, historian Joshua Fogel has traced a harsher tone in Japanese writings about China after about 1930.[5] Some Japanese had begun drawing a distinction between themselves and "Asians" a generation before, and now even more Japanese thought the Chinese as incapable of running their own country. They saw Chiang Kai-shek as another incompetent warlord and the Chinese as incapable of building a real nation, at least without Japanese guidance. But, fearing Chinese nationalism, they also opposed Chinese efforts to modernize.

The chances for cooperation between the governments of China and Japan had remained high through the 1920s. Pan-Asianism was attractive to some Chinese, and many recognized that Japan, thanks to its decades of economic modernization, was in a position to lead the Asian nations in an anti-imperialist struggle against the West. More Chinese by far had studied in Japan than in any other foreign country, and throughout China there was great and widespread admiration for the Meiji Restoration. Japanese who saw themselves as returning the ancient favor of Chinese teachings had a ready audience. Nanjing and Tokyo came close to accommodation in 1934, as a series of high-level meetings essentially agreed to the status quo: China would tacitly accept the existence of Manchukuo and Japan would desist from further incursions. However, Japanese army officers interpreted China's stance as a sign of weakness – or even a plot, given China's obvious anti-Japanese feelings, as witnessed in ongoing boycotts. They wanted to incorporate north China into a larger Japanese sphere with Manchuria and Mongolia.

The Japanese preparations for war did not foresee fighting all the Powers at once, but that is exactly what happened. The navy secretly built beyond the limits imposed by the Washington Treaties. Its heavy cruisers displaced nearly 14,000 tons instead of the allowable 8,000. Japan built ten aircraft carriers, and invented the world's biggest torpedoes. The US Navy and even the British Navy, by contrast, remained below allowable strength in the 1920s in order to save money. The Japanese army was built up to a million men, with another 2 million trained reserves.

In one of a series of border incidents that marked the mid-1930s, Japanese and Chinese troops clashed at Marco Polo Bridge (Lugouqiao), about ten miles west of Beijing, during the night of 7 July 1937. There was nothing particularly unusual about the circumstances, not even that they led to a series of clashes around Beijing. Neither Nanjing nor Tokyo wanted a large-scale war, in spite of the creation of the Second United Front a few months earlier. But the Chinese were determined not to give up this impor-tant railway junction. While Japanese naval officers and diplomats feared that the Kantō Army's actions might threaten war with Russia, even the army did not foresee that they would snowball into a full-scale Japanese invasion and the beginning of World War II in Asia (known as the Anti-Japanese Resistance War in China).

How had this happened? At the beginning of July, Chinese troops around the Marco Polo Bridge decided to strengthen their defenses. On 7 July the Japanese conducted night maneuvers around the bridge, firing blank cartridges. The Chinese returned fire briefly, and no one was hurt. A missing Japanese soldier at roll call the next morning, however, prompted the Japanese to begin an attack (though the man returned after twenty minutes).

The Chinese successfully repulsed the Japanese. Over the next few days feints and counter feints on the ground produced inflammatory statements from Tokyo and Nanjing: demands for apologies, complaints about insults, and references to sacred territories. On 17 July, Chiang Kai-shek declared:

> China is a weak country, and if, unfortunately, we should reach the limit of our endurance, then there remains only one thing to do, namely, to throw the last ounce of our national energy into a struggle for the independent existence of our nation.... If we allow one more inch of our territory to be lost, then we would be committing an unpardonable offense against our race.[6]

By the end of the month, calculated feints had been replaced by continuous, fierce fighting, and the Beijing–Tianjin corridor had fallen to the Japanese. Japan's massive invasion of China in the second half of 1937 was not thoroughly planned, but it was the logical result of an unstable situation. What Japan persisted in calling the "China incident" years into the Sino-Japanese War quickly turned into a quagmire. At first, events seemed to be falling Japan's way. Japan's best hope was that quick victories might pressure the Nanjing regime into accommodation with Japan. World opinion was sympathetic to China, but China was isolated. Yet the Nationalists would not surrender.

Chiang Kai-shek's resistance to the Japanese made him a national hero, but after some initial damage inflicted on Japanese attackers, Chinese armies overall were ineffective. Chiang decided to take the war to Shanghai. Perhaps urban fighting would nullify some of Japan's great advantages in tanks and artillery. It might divert Japanese attention from the northern plains, giving Chinese armies more time to build up defenses. And it might even involve the Western powers as they witnessed Japan's invasion from the concessions. However, for all the bravery of their defense of Shanghai, the Nationalists lost many of their best troops while Japan took the north anyway. Chiang Kai-shek's attempt to slow down the Japanese by bombing the dikes on the Yellow River failed, leaving 800,000 Chinese dead in 1938. And it was Chinese bombers, missing the Japanese fleet, that hit Shanghai instead. The defense of the city persisted through October, resulting in 250,000 Chinese military casualties (almost 60 percent of Chiang's troops) and 40,000 Japanese. Much of the fighting was hand-to-hand, and one foreign account noted: "No quarter was given and no dead were buried. Fly-blown corpses lay in the August sun until the smells of death and burning were wafted over Soochow Creek into the Western area."[7]

Finally, Japanese troops, supplemented by armies landed at Hangzhou Bay, broke though Chinese lines and pursued their enemy up the Yangzi River to Nanjing. After swearing to defend his capital to the last, Chiang entrusted its defense to a former warlord who soon fled. Nanjing was then subjected to seven weeks of terror by the Japanese. Standard accounts, based on the contemporary observations of foreign observers, estimate that 200,000 Chinese civilians were murdered (not killed in battle but bayoneted, buried alive, or burned with kerosene) and 20,000 women raped. Whatever the exact numbers, the "Nanjing massacre" – still a controversial issue in Sino-Japanese relations today – represented a breakdown of Japanese military discipline. Perhaps the brutalization, anger, and anxiety of ordinary Japanese soldiers, who had faced far tougher Chinese resistance than they had been led to expect, combined with the vagueness of the goals of this still-undeclared war to produce a sense that all Chinese were the enemy and should be made to pay.

For reasons having as much to do with the role of historical memory in China and Japan today as the history of the event itself, the Nanjing massacre has been the subject of intense debate.[8] Ultra-nationalist Japanese continue to deny that anything special took place at all; on the Chinese side, estimates of over 400,000 civilians slaughtered cannot be substantiated. But there can be no doubt of a seven-week spree of killing and rape. The diary of a foreign eyewitness recorded for Friday 17 December:

> Robbery, murder, rape continued unabated. A rough estimate would be at least a thousand women raped last night and during the day. One poor woman was raped thirty-seven times. Another had her five months infant deliberately smothered by the brute to stop its crying while he raped her. Resistance means the bayonet. The hospital is rapidly filling up with the victims of Japanese cruelty and barbarity. Bob Wilson, our only surgeon, has his hands more than full and has to work into the night. Rickshaws, cattle, pigs, donkeys, often the sole means of livelihood of the people, are taken from them. Our rice kitchens and rice shop are interfered with ...[9]

The larger issue is not the details of what happened in Nanjing but the extreme brutality of the war overall. Why were civilians repeatedly subjected to terror? First, of course, war-terrorism was not unique to the China theater – modern war is "total war" and as the Allies bombed German and Japanese cities to demoralize civilians, so the Japanese sought to break the Chinese will to fight. At the time of the Nanjing massacre, Japanese themselves blamed a breakdown of discipline, as troops, exhausted and hungry, suddenly found themselves in a relatively wealthy city. Western observers, not yet involved in the war, sometimes agreed. However, that misses the point that officers did not try to stop the murder, rape, and robbery for weeks. Thus others – at the time and since – have focused on the extreme brutality of Japanese military culture, which subjected enlisted men to mistreatment and humiliation, as well as the desire of ordinary soldiers to take revenge for comrades who had died in the sieges of Shanghai and Nanjing. By this time, many Japanese soldiers and officers had been hastily recruited and were not well trained. As well, although the average Japanese

*Figure 15.1* During the Japanese invasion, numerous atrocities were documented. Sometimes Japanese soldiers had Chinese prisoners dig their own graves (holes in the ground) before killing them, as in this photograph that Guomindang sources attribute to the Nanjing massacre of 1937.

*Source*: Courtesy Guomindang Historical Materials Foundation

*Figure 15.2* Later in the war, Japanese bombed a Guangzhou neighborhood.

*Source*: Courtesy Guomindang Historical Materials Foundation

soldier was probably no more "fanatical" than any other soldier, a number of the younger officers were supporters of the radical right-wing that regarded the Chinese with contempt.

Nanjing was unique in the scale of the slaughter but not in the decisions to execute surrendered prisoners or attack civilians after a battle had been won. The Japanese army was not – is not – the only military force in human history to use terrorism, rape, and torture to cow a population. But the attention paid to Nanjing should not deflect attention from what amounted to policy. The Nanjing massacre was foreshadowed, for example, by a rampage of slaughter in Dongzhou that lasted several days, provoked by the Chinese killing of a number of Japanese civilians there. The Nanjing massacre was then followed by hundreds and thousands of atrocities and a general policy that was, at best, indifferent to civilian lives. Some areas were subject to daily bombings, others to periodic mopping up campaigns. Eighteen million Chinese civilians were killed and a hundred million displaced, becoming refugees in their own nation. (Three million Chinese soldiers were also killed.) With no medical assistance available, an injury was generally tantamount to a death sentence. In the countryside, facing guerrilla opposition, the Japanese often moved through areas killing everything that moved: man, woman, child, or livestock. It is estimated that property losses in the war totaled US$100 billion.

Japan had put 700,000 troops into China by the end of 1937, a number that was to rise to 1 million and finally 1.5 million. By way of contrast, the Chinese Nationalist army had about 1.7 million soldiers, but only 80,000 were fully equipped with modern weapons. About 300,000 had received some German-style training. Worse, Chinese forces remained divided among semi-independent and jealous commanders. At the beginning of the year the Japanese consolidated their control over the railroads, most of the north China plain, and major rivers. The navy sailed up the Yangzi to Wuhan and in 1940 to Yichang, chasing the Nationalist government far into the interior. Chiang Kai-shek was forced to relocate his capital to Chongqing, while Japan controlled the coastal regions.

Virtually all major cities were in Japanese hands by the end of 1938. Yet still the Chinese did not surrender. Japan's military strategy was to seize the cities and key lines of communication and transportation. From this network of points and lines, control would expand into the countryside, through Chinese agents. Most of the active collaborators were local elites or sometimes bandit gangs. Yet Chinese resistance continued. When the Japanese spread their network thin, guerrillas attacked weak points, such as railroad lines, and then escaped among the peasantry before reinforcements could be brought to bear. Local collaborators proved ineffective or even secretly anti-Japanese while genuine collaborators were subject to assassination by partisans.

In 1940, following a major but failed offensive by CCP troops in northern China, Japan began sweeps of entire districts known to shelter guerrillas.

This was the "three alls" policy: kill all, burn all, destroy all. In northern China entire villages were razed, crops seized or destroyed, and peasants slaughtered. The strategy succeeded in reducing an underground Communist structure to roving guerrillas and reduced the size of the Communist base areas, but it obviously was no way to make China an economically productive part of the Japanese Empire. Even if Japan could afford the loss of soldiers in battle, the financial costs were another question. The bill for the China war soon came to $5 million per *day*.[10] Japan, a

*Map 9* The Japanese invasion, 1937–45 (Japanese/GMD/CCP territory)

The Japanese Army first moved southward in the summer of 1937 (dates of conquests given "year-month"), and then, supported by the Navy, up through the rich agricultural lands along the Yangzi River into central China. The Nationalists under Chiang Kai-shek were pushed into the backward southwest, while the main CCP was maintained in the far northwest. Yet the Japanese occupation was never secure.

*Source*: Courtesy of Geospatial Information Science Team, Computing Center, Academia Sinica.

creditor nation after World War I, took on a large national debt. As the war with China stretched on with no end in sight – only further troop commitments – total mobilization at home followed. Rationing was imposed as early as 1938, and under "total war" conditions Japan's domestic politics became increasingly dictatorial.

Japan needed oil, rubber, and other raw materials, which made it dependent on the United States, Britain, and the Netherlands. If Japan could take the Western colonies in Southeast Asia, it would satisfy its immediate material needs. But war with either the United States or the Soviet Union was highly risky. The Soviet Union had put into Mongolia and Siberia twice the military power Japan had in Manchuria. If the main enemy was Russia, then war with China, much less the Western powers, was unwise. Conversely, would the United States stand by if the war were extended to Southeast Asia? The industrial capacity of the United States dwarfed Japan's, and as the China war dragged on, US reaction grew increasingly stern: in 1938 it banned the export of aeronautical materials in a "moral embargo" and in 1939 abrogated the US–Japanese trade treaty. When Japan took Indochina in July 1941, it faced a US–Dutch–British export ban on the life-blood of military operations: oil and iron ore. For Japan, paranoia about the "ABCD" encirclement was coming true. The *A*merican embargoes, with *B*ritish, *C*hinese, and *D*utch support, were going to make the China war impossible to continue.

But if China could be knocked out quickly – as some in the Japanese military still thought possible – and if it could be economically incorporated into the Japanese empire along with Korea and Manchuria, then Japan would be in a very strong position. All of this was occurring in the context of European instability. The alliance between Germany and Japan, formalized in the Anti-Comintern Pact of November 1937, was a *realpolitik* decision made in spite of Nazi Germany's official racism, which included "Asiatics" among the inferior races, and Japan's official condemnation of Western imperialism. From Japan's point of view, the treaty was simply designed to provide it with assistance in case of war with the Soviet Union. It was thus effectively broken by the Nazi–Soviet pact of 1939, which shocked the entire world and led to great confusion in Tokyo. None the less, Japan's military leaders – facing imminent shortages of vital supplies and the enormous expenses of the ongoing China campaign – decided on double or nothing.

The surprise attack on the US Navy at Pearl Harbor in Hawaii (December 1941) was a desperate gamble to knock the player with the deepest pockets out of the military game. If the US Pacific fleet were neutralized, then Japanese attacks on the Philippines, the Dutch East Indies (today's Indonesia), and the Southeast Asian mainland would face only minimal resistance. And if Japan gained the time to incorporate these territories, with their rich resources, into an empire that included China, then it might be able to build up a military machine that would keep the United States out of the Western Pacific. But Japanese leaders had miscalculated.

China was indigestible and the United States instantly declared war on the Axis powers.

## Nationalists at war

The heroic and dogged, if sometimes incompetent, resistance of Nationalist troops against the Japanese in the first year of the war literally cost Chiang Kai-shek most of his best troops. After 1938, his strategy was to retreat and wait: "trading space for time." Giving up territory for time to build up strength was the only choice, although the long years isolated in Chongqing were hard on the GMD. The Second United Front meant that the GMD would allow the CCP to build its base areas in the north unimpeded and even grant it financial support, but this remained an uneasy coalition.

Chongqing, the Nationalists' new capital, was isolated and backward compared to Nanjing; indeed, the story of China's war against Japan was a story of the most backward parts of China resisting a stronger and more advanced invader. From Chongqing, Chiang Kai-shek had to rebuild an army based in a province that had never been a Nationalist stronghold. The Nationalists also had to bring Yunnan under their control. Kunming, the capital of Yunnan, became the home of a new university designed for refugee scholars and students, who found themselves somewhat freer to criticize the Chongqing government. Since Kunming was a key military link to supplies that the Western powers might ship from Southeast Asia, Chiang could not afford to alienate its leaders. The "Burma Road" – over 700 miles of muddy, treacherous, often single-lane passage through tropical jungles – was built with great loss of life, but, opening at the end of 1938, it was a critical source of *matériel* and gasoline for Chongqing. The Nationalists also had some control over Hunan, southern Jiangxi, western Hubei and Henan, and southern Shaanxi, and pockets in Guangxi and Guangdong.

In the early years of the Sino-Japanese War the GMD received small amounts of aid from both Russia and the United States. Stalin did not hold a high opinion of the Chinese Communists and decided to support Chiang Kai-shek as the best way of keeping the Japanese too busy to mount another attack on eastern Siberia. Several thousand Soviet advisers (largely replacing Germans) helped improve China's combat ability, and Russia sent several hundred warplanes to China as well. The United States proffered a series of loans to Chongqing in the $25–$50 million dollar range. This was not much compared to the government's needs; the Chinese currency slipped and, as Chongqing printed money, inflation ensued. Chiang Kai-shek understood that more aid might be forthcoming if he could continue to hold out against the Japanese. China's heroic resistance against the Japanese drew admiration in the West. With greater calculation, the British statesman Lord Halifax commented: "China is fighting the battle of all the law-abiding States and she is incidentally fighting our own battle in the Far East, for if Japan wins, our interests there are certainly doomed to extinction."[11]

But with the outbreak of war in Europe in the summer of 1939, Russia and the United States concentrated their attention there. Russia and Japan signed a neutrality pact early in 1941, and Germany invaded Russia in June. That left the United States as Chiang's only important backer, but that country remained officially neutral. Fortunately for the Chinese, when the Japanese attacked Pearl Harbor in December, the United States responded with war – and by increasing aid to Chongqing. Chiang's trade of space for time was finally to be rewarded.

Could the Nationalists have done more to resist Japan during the initial onslaught of 1937 and 1938? For all the bravery of the Nationalist troops, especially during the Shanghai fighting, the fact remains that Chiang never consistently entrusted command to his best generals. Cai Tingkai, who had led the successful Chinese resistance to Japan in Shanghai during the 1932 fighting, was never given command again. The legendary military genius Bai Chongxi quarreled with Chiang in the wake of the Northern Expedition and did not serve under the Nationalists again until the summer of 1937. Chiang convinced Bai to become his chief of staff in August, and Bai fought his way to several victories in 1938, but it was too late to resist the Japanese onslaught by then.[12] There is no doubt of Japan's vast advantages over the Chinese in terms of *matériel*: guns and ammunition, planes, battleships, transport vehicles, and tanks. In 1935, China had only 457 pieces of artillery in its entire army.[13]

Chiang Kai-shek, trained as a military man, served as commander-in-chief and not a field commander. Yet Chiang feared rivals so much that he constantly replaced capable subordinates with mediocre and incompetent syco-phants. As well, Chiang sometimes did interfere with battles when they were in progress, with disastrous results. He was known for countermanding his own staff and telephoning detailed orders directly to commanders – who would thus receive conflicting orders in the midst of battle. Even if Chiang under-stood military strategy, no one can direct a battle from hundreds of miles away. Finally, the rapid success of the Japanese was also due to the unpreparedness of the Chinese. No plans had been made to ambush Japanese troops as they made use of China's few north–south railroad lines. Even as Chinese armies retreated south, a few attacks on vulnerable points would have dramatically slowed the Japanese advance. Although individual cities were sometimes defended with great valor, by and large Chinese troops were simply routed.

In the north, the Communists launched the "Hundred Regiments Offensive" against Japanese-held forts and railroads in 1940. Under the general command of Peng Dehuai, Communist troops inflicted considerable damage, but the Japanese responded with the even more effective "three-alls" campaign. The main Communist army lost 100,000 men to casualties and desertion; the population in areas under CCP control plummeted from 44 million to 25 million. Yet the Chinese still did not surrender.

The stalemate that then ensued was not exactly stable. Chinese cities were systematically bombed in order to shake civilian morale. Chongqing was bombed 268 times between 1939 and 1941; 4,400 people were killed in the first two days of the campaign in May 1939. Casualties subsided when the Nationalists built underground shelters, and Chinese behind the Japanese lines would radio warnings when Japanese planes took off. Fierce fighting flared on several occasions, then ebbed. Both the Nationalists and the Communists understood that guerrilla actions were an important means of harrying Japanese troops and countering their great advantages in *matériel* with minimal losses to China. Such harassment never amounted to a significant military threat to Japanese positions, but it made the war more expensive for them. More importantly, it also prevented them from advancing further into the countryside.

In 1942, then, the nature of the war changed fundamentally. It is true that little changed on the ground: the stalemate persisted. And for the Allies, the importance of the China theater lay in bleeding Japan rather than in its immediate defeat. But US aid to Chiang Kai-shek soon amounted to $630 million in supplies and a $500 million loan. China fulfilled its end of the bargain, preventing a million and a half Japanese soldiers from fighting in Southeast Asia, the South Pacific, and Australia over the next three years. At the same time, US military men in China were disappointed that more was not done to attack the Japanese front lines. What they did not understand was that Chiang needed to disperse Nationalist troops to defend territories from local rivals as well as the Japanese. With the United States in the war, he also wanted to preserve his best troops for the future struggle with the CCP. Chiang's was a defensive strategy, including an economic blockade against the CCP bases.

Japan's main goal was to conquer Southeast Asia: Hong Kong, Singapore, the Philippines, and Burma, as well as the Western Pacific islands. The Japanese conquest of Burma was completed by June 1942, thus severing Chongqing's main link with its allies and threatening it from the south. Given Britain's weakness, the defense of Burma had been largely in the hands of Chinese troops under the command of the American general Joseph Stilwell. Chiang, who had basically opposed the campaign from the beginning, was bitterly disappointed and blamed both the British and Stilwell for the defeat (with some justification, since the British, fearful of weakening their authority, initially refused to cooperate with the Chinese and then preferred to abandon Rangoon rather than risk forces that might be needed to defend India). Stilwell, in turn, formed a very low opinion of Chinese army officers up to and including Chiang. According to Stilwell, too many Chinese officers were guilty of corruption, padding their troop rolls to steal the rations and wages of non-existent soldiers, stealing directly from their soldiers, and practicing extortion on civilians, as well as gambling, cruelty, and commercial sidelines.

The relations between Stilwell and Chiang went from bad to worse, and Stilwell was eventually recalled to Washington. At the end of 1943 Stilwell's political adviser, John Paton Davies, wrote to Washington that Chiang was "probably the only Chinese who shares the popular American misconception that Chiang Kai-shek is China.... His philosophy is the unintegrated product of his limited intelligence, his Japanese military education, his former close contact with German military advisers, his alliance with the usurious banker-landlord class, and his reversion to the sterile moralisms of the Chinese classics."[14] None the less, good US–Chinese relations were key to the war effort. It was no accident that Chiang appointed his former critic, the American-educated intellectual Hu Shi, to be ambassador to Washington, and that Washington preferred to recall a capable general rather than risk Chiang's cooperation.

The Japanese poured men into China in order to prevent the allies from gaining access to airfields there – close enough to bomb Japanese cities. But the American advance was inexorable, and Japan faced steady bombardment from 1944. Although the Allies were doing well by 1944–5, Chiang had permanently lost a significant number of quality troops – which would hurt the Nationalists in the coming civil war against the Communists. Germany was defeated in June 1945. Preparations immediately began for a final assault on Japan that might involve massive numbers of Chinese troops. Instead, the atomic bombings of Hiroshima and Nagasaki in August forced Japan's sudden surrender, which took most of the world, including China's leaders, by surprise.

Even in defeat Japan had achieved, at least partially, one of its propaganda goals. Western colonialism had received a fatal blow. Attempts by the British, the Dutch, and the French to regain control of their possessions in Southeast and South Asia after 1945 met with renewed nationalist opposition. The surrender of the "impregnable" Singapore with its 130,000 troops after just one day's fighting in February 1942 was a severe blow to British prestige. The surrender of Hong Kong at the end of 1941 – the first military loss of a crown colony since Yorktown – had not been much better. Furthermore, the Japanese deliberately humiliated Westerners wherever it gained control of their colonies. Before native eyes the foreign communities were marched, carrying their own bags, to railway stations and internment camps. And in China, too, the story of imperialism was nearly over.

## Chongqing and Nanjing at war

The Tokyo and Chongqing governments, in spite of the nearly incessant and truly savage fighting that marked the stalemate around its edges, did explore the possibility of a peace settlement on various occasions between 1938 and 1941. Such a settlement would have required that China recognize the independence of Manchukuo and Inner Mongolia, agree to the demilitarization of north China, and accept Japanese economic and political privileges throughout China. How seriously Chongqing pursued these negotiations cannot be determined until the relevant archives are opened; it may be that Chiang Kai-shek would have considered peace overtures had Japan offered better terms. Yet it may also be that he used the prospect of Chinese accommodation with Japan simply to screw more support out of the United States and Russia. Chiang had tied his political career to the war of resistance. It would have been difficult for him to shift course, though an important peace faction did exist within the GMD.

Since Chongqing refused to surrender, Japan had to find other Chinese to work with. It had to consolidate the vast territories that had been won so quickly in 1937 and 1938. And it had to strangle Chongqing with an economic blockade. Japan worked to cut Chongqing's railway and other links to the world. The Communists in the northwest were already effectively isolated, though still a major annoyance. The Japanese preferred to rule eastern China with the active cooperation of recognized Chinese leaders, but it proved hard to win such men over. A North China government was established with former Beiyang government officials – but the Japanese could not convince major warlords like Wu Peifu or even the May Fourth "traitor" Cao Rulin to join it. The largest and most prestigious puppet government was eventually established in central China under Wang Jingwei. In March 1940 Wang – Sun Yat-sen's old disciple and colleague, the Guomindang's second-ranking official, and Chiang Kai-shek's longtime rival – created a new Nanjing government. Wang seems to have assumed that, since the war would inevitably be lost, some kind of Chinese government would salvage whatever degree of autonomy was possible by working with the Japanese. Relatively little scholarly work has been done on "collaboration" and puppet governments, or on what life was like for the majority of Chinese who lived in Japanese-conquered territory. Even several generations after the war, these remain sensitive issues (as they do in Europe). Historical memory focuses on resistance, but collaboration – or just getting by – was a fact of life. Collaboration came in degrees. A businessman might have no real choice but to sell shoes to the Japanese army, while another might volunteer to secretly spy on his neighbors.[15]

The Communist national story that emerged in the 1950s long ignored all but resistance to the Japanese, and even discounted the contributions of Chongqing. Life under the Japanese was reduced to a story of many victims and a few villains, while heroes took positive action. In this scheme, capitalists and landlords were natural collaborators, preordained to work with the Japanese by their long ties to imperialist forces. Ironically, the Nationalist myth was actually quite similar, condemning the majority of businesses who stayed in Tianjin or Shanghai under the Japanese and reserving praise for the minority of "patriotic capitalists" who relocated their factories to the interior. But most Chinese lived under Japanese occupation.

Why would Wang Jingwei risk his good name for the hollow power the Japanese were willing to grant him? Historians have pointed to an element of opportunism in his motives – he regarded himself, rather than Chiang, as the natural heir to Sun Yat-sen, and finally saw a chance to outshine his rival. But opportunism does not explain why this man and his followers made the specific decisions they did. Wang had been firmly anti-Communist at least since 1928, and he had been loyal to Chiang in the early days of the war. He had headed the GMD left, and it would have seemed absurd to question the nationalist credentials of a man who had risked his life to assassinate Manchu nobles and who was trusted by Sun Yat-sen. But Wang consistently urged a peace policy on Guomindang circles from 1938 to 1940, pointing to Sun's friendship with the Japanese. In a sense, he was more loyal to the principle of national unity before war than was Chiang himself. War seemed a betrayal to Wang, and he ultimately accused Chiang of betraying the Chinese people. To Wang, the main issue was that Chiang had abandoned the people to the tender mercies of the Japanese while saving his corrupt cronies. The Chongqing government thus no longer deserved allegiance. Wang died in November 1944 after medical treatment in Japan. As Wang's widow put it at her trial in April 1946: "It was after the government and its troops took to their heels that we common people came forward and took charge. Is it right that the government should neglect the life and death of its own people?"[16]

Above all, Wang misread the international situation. He foresaw a Japanese victory and so thought that resistance against Japan would be disastrous. Even if China under Chiang could scrape out some kind of victory, it would be at the expense of subservience to the Soviet Union. In this view, China would be under the heel of either Russia or Japan, and Wang preferred Japan.

Historians are in general agreement that, even if epithets like "puppet regime" and "traitor" are too much of knee-jerk reactions to characterize Wang's government completely, it none the less had very little freedom of action.[17] Japanese authorities kept a close eye on it, and the Japanese army had the final say in all decisions. The army took what resources it needed from Chinese industry and agriculture, and it directed counter-insurgency. Wang probably thought he would be given more responsibility than actually turned out to be the case. The new Nanjing regime broadcast an endless stream of propaganda for peace, pan-Asianism, and anti-communism, all the while claiming the mantle of Sun Yat-sen. It seems unlikely that this propaganda had much effect. It was constantly undercut, as pointed out in 1942 by Wang himself:

> The political and economic conditions in the peace areas [under the Wang regime's control] do not meet general expectations. It is an undeniable fact that the regime in the peace areas is not yet free, the people in the peace areas are suffering unbearably from [Japan's policy of] material control, and Sino-Japanese economic cooperation has not been actualized.[18]

With or without Wang Jingwei, the Japanese failed to mobilize central China's potentially rich economy for their war needs. By and large, Japan succeeded in integrating the poorer *northern* China into its imperial economy, capturing industry and resources, and using Japanese companies to monopolize communications, transportation, harbors, salt, coal, and iron and steel.[19] But Chinese people felt no compunction to sacrifice any more than they were actively forced to – and China's economy was never turned into a war economy.[20] In other words, we can find much passive resistance: deliberately shoddy work, slacking off whenever possible, stealing, and the like. Control policies that worked in small, industrialized Japan did not necessarily work in China. As well, Japan had not prepared for its occupation of the eastern cities. Since China was supposed to surrender and cooperate, the Japanese lacked detailed plans to take over Chinese industry. Massive corruption drained profits into private hands, both Japanese and Chinese. Competition among Japanese agencies remained as great a drag on efficiency as corruption. The vast majority of Shanghai's capitalists did *not* flee inland with the Nationalists, who offered little help in any case. Rather, they tried to keep their factories operating under the Japanese.[21] Yet few industrialists actively collaborated with the puppet authorities, if only because the Japanese offered few rewards.

Shanghai was attached to Wang Jingwei's bailiwick after Japan failed to find competent Chinese puppets to run the city. Du Yuesheng fled to Hong Kong, although other Green Gang leaders cooperated with the Japanese. Yet some of these also kept their lines of communication open to Chongqing. Students who remained in Shanghai were largely quiescent, since the slightest sign of resistance meant death. None the less, working underground, Communist and Nationalist organizers tried to infiltrate student groups set up by the Wang Jingwei regime. Many intellectuals had fled Beijing, Shanghai, and other cities with the Nationalists or to join the Communists, but of course many remained under Japanese rule as well. Resistance might be expressed indirectly – in plays about female chastity (representing national loyalty), for example – but most were fairly passive, or "collaborated" only minimally (remaining in teaching positions, for example).[22] Very few intellectuals rallied to Japan's "Pan-Asianism" or even Wang Jingwei's "Peace Movement."

Shanghai's workers also faced choices, not so much *between* collaboration and resistance as along a continuum between them. The retreat of the Guomindang weakened the hold of the gangs on labor.[23] Though they had long been forced underground, Communists still influenced segments of the workers' movement, and after eastern China was occupied the CCP was able to rebuild a strong presence in Shanghai. As many workers lost their jobs when their factories were bombed out, refugee shelters (sometimes opened with Green Gang donations) became places men and women could turn to for meals or simply to meet. These "little teahouses" could not engage in overt anti-Japanese activities, but served as recruitment grounds for CCP activists who provided mutual aid, newspaper reading, and recreational activities. Economic hard times contributed to growing radicalism. Rice riots became common as the cost of living rose dramatically. However, the Japanese secret services in alliance with some of the gangster community kept Communists in check and certainly prevented unions from threatening the war effort.

For the Chongqing government, the problem was how to find the economic resources to conduct any kind of war at all. But the roots of Chiang's difficulties lay in his own choice of policies a decade before, such as his failure to extirpate the warlord nature of the Nationalist armies. Now, if he attacked the Japanese with competent troops loyal to himself, he was weakening his own base. If he ordered regional commanders into battle, they would either refuse to go or demand more money and equipment. And if he did nothing, his government and military decayed while patriotic garlands went to the Communists. In spite of American pressure, Chiang essentially chose the latter course, carrying the waiting strategy to its logical conclusion. But the costs were high. The regime lost popularity as peasants were drafted into the army regardless of their families' needs. Taxes were also high in the areas under Chiang's control, leading to popular unrest, while intellectuals and students were particularly hurt by inflation. Critics of the regime faced arrest and assassination. Although the Communists were also pursuing a waiting strategy, they provided better government in the areas under their control and continued to put pressure on the Japanese. Morale was far higher in Yan'an than in Chongqing.

The long stalemate weakened the Nationalist armies in several ways. First, ongoing fighting eliminated many competent men, especially the junior and noncommissioned officers that form an army's backbone. Second, Chiang promoted second-rate military men, as we have seen. Senior officers were more noted for their factional infighting than their military prowess. Third, officer training, inadequate to begin with, did not keep up with wartime needs. And fourth, enlisted men faced horrifying conditions. Conscripts were sometimes deprived of their clothing at night so they could not sneak away. Food rations (stolen by senior officers) were inadequate; men sometimes had to drink from puddles in the road, producing diarrhea. Once enrolled in a unit, conditions for the men might improve somewhat, but dysentery, malaria, scabies, skin ulcers, eye infections, tuberculosis, and venereal disease were common. There was little treatment available for wounded men, and units could easily lose over half their soldiers to disease and desertion. It is generally agreed that, due to official malfeasance, over a million Nationalist troops died of disease and malnutrition during the Sino-Japanese War. Chinese leaders, including Chiang, were aware of these problems, but little could be done within the existing political structure.

Democratic criticism of Chiang Kai-shek's autocratic ways continued as before the war. Kunming's Southwest Associated University was formed out of Beijing, Qinghua, and Nankai Universities, and became a center for criticism of the regime. In all, some fifty-two educational institutions had fled into the interior, while another twenty-five uprooted themselves to Hong Kong or the foreign concessions. At the beginning of the war, Chiang tried to become head of a united Chinese war effort, encouraging minor parties to re-establish themselves and of course recognizing the CCP. In effect, the freedoms of speech, assembly, and the press briefly returned. However, Chiang never trusted popular mobilization, even in war, and Chongqing soon moved against the minor parties and dissent. Ironically, even with the de facto breakdown of the United Front in 1941, Communists in Chongqing were protected like foreign diplomats, but other critics of the Guomindang were subject to arrest and assassination. The promise of an American victory over Japan freed Chiang of the need to placate his opposition.

Intellectuals recognized their responsibility to the war effort.[24] Individualism and iconoclastic attacks on traditional culture came to seem self-indulgent and decadent. Historians like Gu Jiegang and Fu Sinian, once known for their critical methodologies, now emphasized glorified stories of national unity and patriotic struggles. Fu had once attacked the family as oppressive; now he argued, "We Chinese people ... are a real family.... Of all the races in the world, we are the largest and of all histories, ours is the longest." None the less, democratic ideals remained mainstream and, even if seen in collectivist terms, could not justify GMD dictatorship. Intellectuals continued to insist that democracy demanded constitutional political order, rule of law, and separation of Party and government. In late 1944 Luo Longji reminded his readers that "Democracy believes that people are an end in themselves.... Therefore, all institutions in society, be they political, economic, or anything, are mere means to an end."[25] Like-minded intellectuals, many of whom had become friends and acquaintances in the course of the New Culture movement, formed a "third force" deliberately placed between the Nationalists and the Communists. With no military of their own and no real popular support, these democratic activists never wielded real political influence, but they held the nation's political leaders up to demanding standards and influenced an important element of the next generation of leaders, their students.

In the economic sphere, for all its inefficiencies, the earlier Nanjing regime at least had been farsighted enough to begin building industrial enterprises deep in the interior by the mid-1930s. Thus Hunan, Jiangxi, and Sichuan were blessed with state-owned steel, heavy machinery, and electrical equipment factories.[26] Unfortunately, factories in Hunan and Jiangxi were vulnerable to Japanese bombing. The industrialization of Chongqing's territories remained backward, but in the first years of the war over 600 private factories were relocated to the southwest, and some 42,000 skilled and semi-skilled workers followed. This was less than 6 percent of Shanghai's factories, but was none the less critical to Chongqing. Tons of equipment were loaded onto junks as the bullets were flying in Shanghai in the summer of 1937. At first, the crates were unloaded in Wuhan – a sign that Chiang Kai-shek had not expected the rout to be so complete or quick – and so were reloaded to be towed further up the Yangzi. In the end, harmful as it was to the Guomindang to lose its eastern Chinese industrial base, one of the "secrets" of China's victory in the war was that it remained a preindustrial nation on the whole. The loss of urban industry thus mattered less than would otherwise have been the case.

Chongqing was able to take control over much of the southwestern economy, such as it was. In 1941 it reclaimed the land tax, long lost to provincial or lower-level governments. State monopolies were established in tobacco, sugar, salt, and matches. The state took over all mines and freely commandeered factories for war production. Grain was seized from the peasants, budget deficits were partially financed by forced bond sales, and price controls were tried to slow down inflation. Not all of these policies were successful, and many of them had disastrous long-term consequences. But they illustrate the degree to which Chongqing became involved in economic planning and management. Economic planning became one of Chongqing's largest bureaucracies, expanding as the war continued. Some of the economic bureaucrats were frankly interested in "following the socialist road" and, given the influx of US advisers after 1941, were perhaps influenced by New Deal approaches as well. The hands-on training given thousands of economic officials during the war aided the economic growth of Taiwan under the GMD in the post-war years and perhaps also contributed to Maoist development policies. The world's largest dam, the Yangzi Three Gorges project, which was only started in the last years of the twentieth century, had its roots in the Nationalists' economic planning for post-war development.

Inflation ran at 230 percent a year from 1942 to 1945 in Nationalist territories. This was a major problem, since key GMD supporters – army officers, bureaucrats, teachers – were especially vulnerable to inflation. The rate in occupied east China was even higher. In the words of historian Lloyd Eastman, "Like leukemia blood, the depreciated currency of the National government flowed through the body politic, enfeebling the entire organism – the army, government, economy, and society generally."[27] But it is not clear what choice the government had. It had to pay for the military and new infrastructure: roads, railroads, and industry. It lost its old revenues – and so 75 percent of government wartime expenditures were met by printing money. Chongqing moved to collect the land tax in kind, which might seem a reversion to the pre-monetary fiscal system of the fifteenth century but in fact had definite advantages. It gave the government instant access to food for its soldiers and lessened its need to print money. But it also kept grain from reaching the markets, which further contributed to price pressures and popular anger.

Unemployment rose as Japanese bombing destroyed mines and factories. Property losses in the war totaled US$100 billion.[28] Famines in the countryside were unchecked by any significant relief efforts. Farming suffered as something like 6 million peasant boys were conscripted – along with livestock and carts. Half of Shanghai's industries were destroyed in the first two years of the war; up to 80 percent in the Nanjing region.[29] By the end of the war 72 percent of shipping and 96 percent of railroads were damaged. Mines were flooded or looted. Industrial equipment was destroyed or stolen. As the war continued, resentment at the war profiteers only increased. A newspaper editorial (suppressed by the censors) captured this mood:

> Government officials are corrupt and laws are abused by them; the people's livelihood becomes daily more grievous and desperate. With the nation in hardship and the people in poverty, a small corrupt element is growing increasingly richer and living even more luxuriously. This rotten phenomenon, together with many other reactionary political factors, has lowered both the people's and the soldiers' morale nearly to the vanishing point.[30]

# 16 Mao, Maoism, and the Communist Party

Maoism was a critical ingredient in the making of modern China. At the end of the twentieth century Mao was often dismissed, in China as well as the West, as a murderous tyrant. But even if this is true, not merely his murders but also his ideas must be taken seriously.[1] Mao was the revolution's foremost theorist, and his writings formed a kind of sacred text that subsequent theoretical work had to follow. Mao's ideas were often original and insightful. More importantly, they shaped the cadres who shaped the Party that would shape China. They especially shaped the CCP's revolutionary strategy.

Mao Zedong's thought revolved around the problem of combining theory and practice. Raised on May Fourth liberalism, Mao had to learn most of his Marxism in the field. He developed a distrust of dogma and a contempt for intellectuals, but he learned how to use ideas in Party infighting. For Mao, class analysis was not an academic discipline but a means of making revolution. Since theory was not his strong point, in contrast to other Party leaders, his emphasis on practice was a shrewd tactical move. But to be a successful CCP leader, Mao had to possess a mastery of Marxist theory. Knowledge of peasants and military strategy was not enough. Mao's deliberate effort to become a master of theory in the late 1930s thus partly stemmed from his need to demonstrate Marxist credentials. He had to prove he was more than a peasant guerrilla leader; he needed to be an intellectual capable of following in the footsteps of Lenin and Stalin. Yet perhaps even more important was a personal need to make sense out of his experiences in revolutionary organizing; Marxism was the language Mao chose to analyze, generalize, and systematize those experiences.

For these reasons, once ensconced in Yan'an after 1937, Mao turned to philosophy. Above all, he praised "practice" as the highest truth of "theory" – which played to his strengths. Communist opposition to Mao came from a more orthodox camp worried about the divorce of the CCP from the urban proletariat. They feared the prospect of the CCP turning into a peasants' party. Lenin's revolution, after all, occurred in the cities and was then taken to the countryside. Mao's response was to emphasize voluntarist assumptions: the power of the human will. Here, the point was that an individual's commitment to revolution (political stance) was as much a matter of will (or ideological training) as of personal class background. A kind of proletarian consciousness was to be carried by the CCP into the countryside, where necessity had dictated the strategy of bases and land reform. Mao accused his opponents of dogmatism and leftist extremism. One cannot apply mechanically the "truths" of Marxism and the very different experiences of the Russian revolution to the Chinese case, he said.

Mao ultimately called for the "sinification of Marxism" – a daring approach but also obvious and inevitable. Scholars are generally in agreement that Mao succeeded in sinifying Marxism; nevertheless, there is disagreement on whether the resulting "Mao thought" should be regarded as a legitimate and orthodox species of Marxism or a kind of heterodoxy. In Mao's terms, sinification referred to applying the general truths of Marxism to China's specific circumstances. But it is not so simple; what of Marxism actually survived under Chinese circumstances? It is possible to argue that Mao burst beyond the bounds of Marx in his emphasis on the peasantry and his voluntarism. Yet the fundamental point is that Marxism provided Mao with useful tools to analyze Chinese society, find revolutionary supporters, isolate opposition, and predict the course of the revolution. It is not clear that one can isolate a particular Marxist orthodoxy in the first place, but even if one could hold up such an orthodoxy and find that Mao deviated from it, we would still have to begin with the inspiration and influence of Marxism on Mao.[2]

Mao's knowledge and his philosophy of life were gained over a lifetime of reading and experience. He was influenced by Daoist and Confucian notions, ideas about natural justice acquired from Chinese popular culture, and a thorough grounding in Western liberalism. His readings in Marxism, however, beginning in the 1920s and intensely pursued in the late 1930s, overlaid his earlier, more random ideas. Marxism allowed Mao to relate his revolutionary practice to such basic issues as how one knows something is true, how progress can occur, what constitutes human nature, and like questions. During the acute struggle of the Jiangxi Soviet to survive in the early 1930s, Mao focused on practical matters of maintaining popular support, administrative control of guerrilla armies, mass campaigns, and ground-level investigations of local conditions. In Yan'an in the late 1930s and early 1940s, however, he began to incorporate these experiences into a broader theoretical framework that would serve as a revolutionary guide for the CCP as a whole. Yet Mao's role in the revolution went deeper, recalling the epigram of the Viennese poet Hugo von Hofmannsthal: "Politics is magic. He who knows how to summon the forces from the deep, him will they follow."[3]

## Maoism to 1949

In 1937 Mao gave a series of lectures on dialectical materialism. Borrowing heavily and plagiarizing Soviet sources, Mao's conclusions were worked up and later published as the essays "On Practice" and "On Contradiction."

Mao emphasized that "contradictions" mark human reality. They are the source of all change and progress. In terms of human history, class antagonisms are perhaps the most important or basic of an infinite number of contradictions. Economic structures ("base") are ultimately determining factors in shaping history, but not the sole factors. Mao felt that the "superstructure" of cultural factors and the relations of production are also potential sources for change; indeed, base and superstructure have their own dialectical interactions. This led Mao to emphasize the importance of politics in the here and now; if the economic base ultimately determined the shape of politics, political action could also shape economic realities. Mao promised that practical questions – like whether class struggle should be intensified and rich peasants expropriated, or class struggle moderated and rich peasants and even landlords appeased – could be answered by the correct understanding of dialectical materialism, or the working out of the contradictions of natural forces. Judging which contradictions were more acute than others at a particular moment was key, and this in turn depended on concrete experience or *practice*. Practice was thus necessary to bringing action and knowledge into harmony:

> If a man wants to succeed in his work, that is, to achieve the anticipated results, he must bring his ideas into correspondence with the laws of the objective external world; if they do not correspond, he will fail in his practice. After he fails, he draws his lessons, corrects his ideas.... The dialectical-materialist theory of knowledge *places practice in the primary position*, holding that human knowledge can in no way be separated from practice....[4]

One of the things Mao meant by dialectical materialism was the mutual influence of practice and theory in an ongoing process of refinement, or, as Mao said, "deepening." Perceptions of reality had to be superseded by a conceptual understanding: a synthesizing mode of constructing the relationships between the objects perceived. If knowledge begins with mere empiricism – sense perceptions – such knowledge remains useless until deepened with the introduction of theory; yet theory remains unrooted until tested in practice. This is a process never really completed. Mao thus emphasized that theory alone was useless. Even geniuses like Marx and Lenin could formulate correct theory only through their personal involvement in the class struggle. But practice without theory was also useless, if not impossible in the first place. Humans always act out of cognition based on experience or "practice" – in fact, there can be no such thing as "pure" empiricism – while the point of formulating explicit theory is to guide action.

But what guarantees that theory and practice will produce change that is progressive rather than random? Contradiction, the key to Mao's notion of dialectics, propels meaningful change. This is a mode of thinking ultimately derived from the German philosopher G.W.F. Hegel (1770–1831), whom

Marx followed. Dialectical materialism is scarcely the "science" Marxists claim it to be, but at least Mao attempted to make it an applied technology. First, contradictions are everywhere, universal. Mao cited several fundamental examples coined by Lenin: in mechanics one finds action and reaction; in chemistry the association and repelling of atoms; and in society the class struggle. Second, contradictions are essentially internal; they may be resolved according to certain laws, as in the development of an embryo. Then, there are different kinds of contradiction and resolution:

> For instance, the contradiction between the proletariat and the bourgeoisie is resolved by the method of socialist revolution; the contradiction between the great masses of the people and the feudal system is resolved by the method of democratic revolution; the contradiction between the colonies and imperialism is resolved by the method of national revolutionary war; the contradiction between the working class and the peasant class in socialist society is resolved by the method of collectivization and mechanization in agriculture; contradiction within the Communist Party is resolved by the method of criticism and self-criticism; the contradiction between society and nature is resolved by the method of developing the productive forces.[5]

Such contradictions have an objective existence; none the less, Mao's is not at all a deterministic scheme. The role of the revolutionary is, through practice, to come to an understanding of the contradictions of the situation. This allows the will of the historical actor to be felt. Mao called upon his audience to remember Lenin's admonition: concrete analysis of concrete conditions. Mao stressed the need to recognize the "principal contradiction" and the "principal aspect of the contradiction" – by which he meant, for example, that in 1937 the principal contradiction lay between the Chinese nation and Japanese aggression. The struggle between the proletariat and the bourgeoisie remained a contradiction, but secondary. After China defeated Japan, the secondary contradiction would come to the fore. The "principal aspect" of a contradiction constituted the immediate task: the "difficulties" or point of attack. In treating the theory of contradictions as a means of refining practice, Mao was buttressing the voluntarism that in fact preceded his theorizing.

Was this any way to make a revolution? Mao referred repeatedly to the need for Chinese Communists to make Marxism their own. They had to learn how to apply it to China's immediate problems and concrete circumstances. Mao's goal remained consistent: to encourage cadres to take Marxism as an intellectual foundation, not a cookbook. He "sinified" Marxism by attacking "abstract Marxism" as unreal; only "concrete Marxism" adapted to each people's national experience could guide revolution.

Mao was not only attacking Party competitors who had a more thorough grounding in Marxism: he was also wanting to encourage a different kind of thinking as a source of support for his policies. He felt that the traditional education based on memorization and regurgitating correct answers still marked Chinese Marxism. Ironically, the post-May Fourth turn to Marxism put a premium on the same kind of textual hermeneutics as had the old classical education. Mao forthrightly noted his concern that a theoretical grasp of Marxism gave undue powers to intellectual over "proletarian" cadres. Lenin and Stalin had proposed correct policies – for Russia. These policies could be learned from – but could not be applied directly to China. Mao's was a demand for action, not intellectualizing. He stressed that Marx was able to develop his theory of capitalism only through his participation in political struggle. "If you want to know the taste of a pear, you must change the pear by eating it yourself.... If you want to know the theory and methods of revolution, you must take part in revolution."[6] This defined the kind of cadre he sought.

There is an important difference between Mao and Sun Yat-sen here. Sun declared that knowledge was difficult while action was easy, in order to reserve power for the so-called fore-knowers. In contrast, Mao refused to reify knowledge as a kind of possession. Like Wang Yangming, the Ming dynasty philosopher and statesman, Mao Zedong emphasized the indivisibility of knowing and doing.[7] This was, moreover, a collectivist vision. Mao felt that vast historical forces were propelling China and the world onto a higher stage of material existence and consciousness. At the same time, human actors struggled within contexts defined by contradiction; one of their struggles was internal: to find correct theory. This meant that ideology, like social consciousness, could then be divorced from class background. The CCP, even if dominated by the peasantry or the intelligentsia, could still embody proletarian consciousness, for once the proletariat had developed its new worldview, this became a kind of knowledge available to all. Mao's voluntarism was clearly expressed as early as 1928. In the wake of the White Terror, when the entire Communist movement faced extinction, Mao had to justify his use of bandits and beggars to create a Red Army. Defensively, he claimed that part of the army consisted of workers, but more practically he explained in a report to the Central Committee:

> The [army's] contingent of *éléments déclassés* [bandits, soldiers captured from the Guomindang, landless peasants, lumpen proletariat] should be replaced by peasants and workers, but these are not available now. On the one hand, when fighting is going on every day, the *éléments déclassés* are after all especially good fighters. Moreover, casualties are mounting high. Consequently, not only can we not diminish the *éléments déclassés* now in our ranks, but it is even difficult to find more for reinforcements. In these circumstances, *the only method* is to intensify political training, so as to effect a qualitative change in these elements.... The Red Army soldiers have generally become class conscious and acquired elementary political knowledge about land distribution, establishment of soviets, arming the workers and peasants, etc.[8]

## Rectification

In 1942 Mao Zedong wanted to instill a new "style" of leadership in the future ruling elite, the Communist cadres. Gone would be the arrogance and smugness of the old literati, gone would be pedantry and physical laziness, gone, above all, would be the selfishness and clannishness that marked the old gentry. This was an attempt to give the new ruling class a new sense of purpose. At the Yan'an Forum on Literature and Art, Mao recounted his own spiritual coming of age:

> If you want the masses to understand you, if you want to be one with the masses, you must make up your mind to undergo a long and even painful process of tempering.... I began life as a student and at school acquired the ways of a student; I then used to feel it undignified to do even a little manual labor, such as carrying my own luggage in the presence of my fellow students, who were incapable of carrying anything, either on their shoulders or in their hands. At that time I felt that intellectuals were the only clean people in the world, while in comparison workers and peasants were dirty.... But after I became a revolutionary and lived with workers and peasants and with soldiers of the revolutionary army, I gradually came to know them well, and they gradually came to know me well too. It was then, and only then, that I fundamentally changed the bourgeois and petty-bourgeois feelings implanted in me in the bourgeois schools. I came to feel that compared with the workers and peasants the unremolded intellectuals were not clean and that, in the last analysis, the workers and peasants were the cleanest people, and, even though their hands were soiled and their feet smeared with cow-dung, they were really cleaner than the bourgeois and petty-bourgeois intellectuals. That is what is meant by a change in feelings, a change from one class to another.[9]

What is going on here? Mao's personal remarks came in the context of a "party rectification" movement. The immediate issue was his demand that artists and intellectuals make their work more popularly accessible (ironically, this might involve more use of traditional techniques and less of Westernisms). Beyond this, artists were to take a "class stand" (follow Maoist orthodoxy), and ultimately remold themselves in order to serve the masses. Mao's personal remarks were preceded with the note that "If you want the masses to understand you, if you want to be one with the masses, you must make up your mind to undergo a long and even painful process of tempering." He was thus offering himself as an example of such tempering. The goal was to transcend the class one was born into and become as one with the masses: Mao specifically held out the promise of class transformation. One could *learn* – if painfully – proletarian consciousness. Thus Mao's voluntarism explained how something like religious conversion could remake committed individuals – "religious" because they were remade or reborn through painful self-examination, "self-cultivation," and revolutionary tempering.

The rectification campaign of 1942–4 was designed to achieve several broader goals. From the nadir of 1934, by 1942 CCP membership had grown to over 700,000. Students and intellectuals who had sought out the CCP in Yan'an, perhaps because they saw it as a more effective anti-Japanese force than the GMD, needed to be taught Party discipline if they were to make useful cadres. Their skills were valuable; their independence of mind and their tendency to hold the behavior of Party leaders up to the highest standards of Communist idealism were less so. And the numerous peasant activists who had emerged across the north China countryside also had to be socialized into Communist ways. Young peasant men suddenly achieving power had to be disciplined not to abuse that power, not to favor their own relatives in the traditional manner, and, above all, to follow changing Party dictates even if they did not fully understand them. Many who had emerged through brutal anti-landlord struggles found it difficult to carry out the more moderate Second United Front policies of the late 1930s. Some had to be taught basic literacy. The rectification campaign also sought out GMD and collaborationist spies. Finally, it confirmed Mao's own standing as the source of correct knowledge for the entire CCP.

In the future, Mao was often to seek to achieve several goals with one campaign, and the 1942–4 movement established this pattern. The rectification campaign cemented Mao's position as head of the CCP in at least two ways. When it began, he was still vulnerable to charges of being an effective tactician but a poor Marxist. Mao had to defend policies that essentially ignored China's cities (and therefore ignored the proletariat) and treated the Second United Front in a pro forma fashion instead of seeking real cooperation with the GMD. Mao wanted to deflect criticism from high-ranking Communists who had studied in Moscow. More broadly speaking, by creating a new orthodox version of theory, policy, and history, the CCP leaders were agreeing that what would be called "Mao Thought" would be the ideological basis of the CCP. Mao's word thus became the final ideological truth. The majority of the texts used in the study sessions of the rectification campaign were written by Mao – or at least by Mao and his close associates, including intellectuals like Zhou Yang, Chen Boda, and Ai Siqi. Such men were not for the most part high-ranking cadres in their own right, but they worked closely with Mao. Indeed, Mao Thought was from the beginning conceived as a collective enterprise, though it is convenient to speak of Mao's authorship.

According to Mao, the Party was basically on the right track: certain bad features or mistakes had to be dealt with, that was all. The Party faced not moral weaknesses but problems of attitude and behavior that could be corrected. Mao demanded flexibility and close attention to the immediate needs of the revolution:

Our comrades must understand that we do not study Marxism-Leninism because it is pleasing to the eye, nor because it has some mystical value.... Marxism-Leninism has no beauty, nor has it any mystical value. It is only extremely useful. It seems that right up to the present quite a few have regarded Marxism-Leninism as a ready-made panacea: once you have it, you can cure all your ills with little effort. This is a type of childish blindness, and we must start a movement to enlighten these people.... We must tell them openly, "Your dogma is of no use," or to use an impolite formulation, "Your dogma is less useful than shit." We see that dog shit can fertilize the fields and man's can feed the dog. And dogmas? They can't fertilize the fields, nor can they feed a dog. Of what use are they?... Marx, Engels, Lenin, and Stalin have repeatedly said, "Our doctrine is not dogma; it is a guide to action."[10]

The heart of the rectification campaign consisted of small groups of cadres participating in study sessions that were devoted to examination of Maoist documents and to self-criticism. Study sessions were part-time and on rolling schedules so as not to interfere with normal administration. The campaign gradually spread across the Yan'an base area. Practical considerations prevented it from being fully implemented in less secure base areas. But once started, sessions could go on for weeks and months; it was not clear what was to be achieved before they should be ended. From a grass-roots perspective, the campaign was not about Mao but rather a melding together of disparate men and women in a common cause, a movement with its own special language, symbols, rituals, sacred texts, ways of bonding, stories, and myths: ultimately creating a set of true believers convinced they could change the world.[11] The task was thus to take ordinary human material and make it part of a vast project, amenable to discipline but still capable of independent and creative action. It can be assumed that most cadres, students and peasants alike, were distinguished by an activist disposition. They would not have traveled to Yan'an or joined the revolution unless they were willing to make sacrifices. The main problem was undoubtedly discipline. This was particularly difficult for intellectuals. Mao insisted that the campaign was not about destroying people but that through self-criticism and repentance would come the creation of a new self. In Mao's words, to "cure the disease," not "kill the patient."

At the same time, the campaign included a hunt for spies and enemies within the Communist camp. A few people were beaten and driven to suicide. Some who confessed promptly to working for the enemies became models, virtually heroes, for others to follow. Most cadres emerged from this baptism of fire feeling strengthened. But if most cadres could be whipped into shape, one group remained especially suspect: intellectuals and artists. These people were prone to such sins as "subjectivism" and "formalism." Most of China's intellectuals, it should be noted, either stayed in the cities, trying to survive with their families as best they could under the Japanese, or else fled to Chongqing or Kunming. The ones who traveled to Yan'an were predisposed to favor the Communists, if unrealistic about their expectations. They found harsh conditions, which could be adjusted to, and a level of hypocrisy that was harder to tolerate. They initially welcomed Mao's call for rectification as an attack on bureaucratism. Ding Ling, the famous woman writer whose novels and short stories had caused a stir in the 1920s and 1930s, and Wang Shiwei, a translator, complained about the better food and housing given to upper-level cadres, the unequal treatment women faced, and the refusal of the leaders to accept criticism. Writing on Women's Day (8 March 1942), Ding Ling was particularly scathing on the double standard applied to women. Expected to be as devoted to the revolution as male cadres, Communist women were also expected to marry and raise a family. If they continued to work, they would be accused of neglecting husband and children, but if they became housewives, they would be criticized as politically backward and their activist husbands would divorce them. "It would be better if there were less empty theorizing and more talk about real problems," such as providing childcare and canteens, she said.[12]

Under attack, Ding Ling retracted her arguments. Wang Shiwei, on the other hand, refused to recant and was put on trial, accused, among other matters, of "Trotskyism." Ding Ling even joined his accusers. Wang was "struggled against" or ruthlessly criticized and subjected to public humiliation for two weeks in the early summer of 1942, then imprisoned as a "traitor" and finally executed when the CCP had to retreat from Yan'an under GMD pressure in 1947. The Party dismissed criticism of the Yan'an system for being excessively hierarchical and bureaucratic as "ultra-egalitarianism." Attitudes appropriate for the "garrets" of GMD- or Japanese-controlled cities were not appropriate for an unprecedented revolutionary society, the Party said. It was "infantile" for many artists, arriving in Yan'an from the zones under Japanese occupation or GMD control, to expect to find a paradise of absolutely egalitarian comradeship. Both Ding Ling (who was later imprisoned in 1957 as a "rightist") and Wang Shiwei are tragic figures, but it is Wang who much later became a hero to some Chinese intellectuals.

While maintaining that the CCP was China's best hope, Wang resisted incredible pressures to recant his criticisms of it. Wang said he was criticizing CCP leaders for the good of the movement. In retrospect, we can see that he exposed deep contradictions in the thought of Mao himself. Mao did oppose bureaucratism, did distrust hierarchy, and did favor egalitarianism – but he could not forgive Wang for exposing the hypocrisies of the Yan'an system, and he certainly did not think outside criticism a valid way to deal with the CCP's problems. To Communist leaders, Wang had not earned the revolutionary credentials to criticize them. He was posthumously rehabilitated in 1990.

For most cadres, the orgy of "self-criticism" was part of an ongoing process by which small groups studied approved texts, applied them to their own lives, and ended with a sense of self-transformation.[13] This did not turn them into brainwashed zombies. Rather, partly through their own efforts, they were "re-educated" to learn the story of China's rape by the foreign powers, the oppression and exploitation of the Chinese peasant by landlords, and the rise of revolutionary forces under the tutelage of the CCP and Mao. New lessons were blended with old, familiar stories in a seamless synthesis. The small study groups built bonds of comradeship that could be extended to all the individuals who voluntarily underwent re-education. A small core of common Maoist texts provided a single source of true doctrine.

Self-criticism and study groups were to become fundamental institutions of the Communist order. In time, cadres would react to them with greater cynicism; they became a means of adjusting oneself to changing signals from Party Central. In the 1940s, however, they were largely seen as a rite of passage. The trick was less to learn orthodox doctrine than to apply it to one's own life, and to think of oneself as a cog in the machine of revolution. There was a certain self-abnegation in devotion to revolution. At the same time, cadres were to learn the ruthlessness necessary to achieve the larger goal of revolution. Personal considerations were simply not very important. For a man to care for his wife or children more than the revolution, for example, was considered a feature of bourgeois (sinful) thinking. Pity for class enemies was not an admirable emotion.

Above all, Mao systematized "stories" which explained Chinese history, the inevitable rise of the CCP, and the correctness of Mao himself; these stories created a "mythology" that gave events meaning and also gave a place, a role, for every individual seeking to help the dispossessed Chinese people regain their patrimony. Not everyone could put the revolution ahead of personal considerations, especially in the long run, but in the short run, surrounded by more powerful enemies, the Communists created a movement dedicated to beating the odds through hard work, self-sacrifice, and faith. Those who were successfully "rectified" felt that they had learned how to touch their best selves, overcome their baser instincts, and act in the larger interest. Like the politically active Puritans of the seventeenth century, the Communists made themselves into *self*-disciplined, chosen men and women who would create a new world through their own actions.[14] People who waited passively to be told what was right could never make revolution, but people who found their own way to a common vision might.

## The mass line

And what were rectified cadres actually supposed to do? The goal was not to work *for* the masses but to "become one" with them – thoroughly understanding them, and yet still distinct from them. Self-reflection and self-criticism were not valued as individual morality (like the introspective "self-cultivation" of the Confucian gentleman, who was supposed to work for the common people but never, ever become one). Rather, public self-criticism and the criticism of others were linked in a process that took on definite spiritual overtones but was designed ultimately to produce a social creature. The cadre might well go through some kind of catharsis, after which he or she would at least subjectively feel transformed. The closest late-twentieth-century analogy might be to drug treatment programs. More intense than the voluntary Alcoholics Anonymous meeting and more goal-oriented than an encounter group devoted to self-discovery, CCP criticism meetings were also more this-worldly than the religious quest for spiritual awakening. The intensely self-revelatory atmosphere was marked by hints of coercion and the goal of transcending the self to improve the self. Still, parallels to religious cults and, for that matter, institutionalized religions also come to mind. Rectification was an initiation ritual that brought the believer into a new community. Mao's own chosen metaphor was medical. The goal of the group was to "save men by curing their ills." Willingness to engage in self-criticism was the key sign of redemption; the group might shout at a targeted individual but should not "cure him to death." Cures lay in exposure to the great light of day. Some of Mao's remarks may have reflected attempts to limit the campaign. We do not know how many beatings occurred; certainly, later accounts told of cynical manipulation of small group meetings for the sake of back-stabbing and revenge. But in 1942–3, facing the mixed pressures of Japanese bombardment and an expanding movement, an atmosphere of intense sincerity and something approaching religious hysteria was perhaps normal.

The rectification campaign also possessed elements of Confucian spirituality. Liu Shaoqi, whose writings made him the best-represented leader in the campaign's official curriculum after Mao, had frankly referred to the remolding of the individual with the traditional term "self-cultivation." He pronounced that "Marxist principle states that the interests of the individual are subordinate to the interests of the Party," for, after all, "… the interests of the Party are identical with the interests of the liberation of the proletariat and all mankind."[15] The instrument of social change was traditionally taken to be the virtuous leader. The Song dynasty statesman Fan Zhongyan (989–1052) had defined the literati ideal as "one who is first in worrying about the world's troubles and last in enjoying its pleasures." The Communists democratized this notion by making it a standard for all, not just for a cultural elect. Even in the midst of the viscerally nationalistic war against Japan, Liu Shaoqi relentlessly preached not only self-sacrifice but also self-abnegation: for the sake of "the world and mankind." As well, twinned warnings against "leftist extremism" and "rightist opportunism" seem eerily reminiscent of the Confucian Middle Way. It is not surprising that Confucian notions of ascetic devotion of the self to the community should prove handy to Communist leaders, even if the good cadre was not to be confused with the Confucian gentleman. Maoist voluntarism was inevitably highly moralistic, as indeed revolutionary movements tend to be.

But once made virtuous, how should a Communist deal with the ordinary people? Here, Mao's notion of the "mass line" tried to combine the Party's ultimate control with a degree of democracy. The "mass line" crystallized power relations in the revolution. The Communist Party was to direct, to guide, to lead. But its powers should not, and ultimately could not, be exercised in an arbitrary or absolutist manner. Leading meant listening; the mass line assumed that a kind of sovereignty lay in the people, but a sovereignty at some distance from the actual instruments of power. In Mao's classic 1943 formulation:

> In all the practical work of our Party, all correct leadership is necessarily "from the masses, to the masses." This means: take the ideas of the masses (scattered and unsystematic ideas) and concentrate them (through study turn them into concentrated and systematic ideas), then go to the masses and propagate and explain these ideas until the masses embrace them as their own, hold fast to them and translate them into action, and test the correctness of these ideas in such action.[16]

The ultimate goal is thus the conversion of the masses themselves. And then of course there will be new ideas, and new action, and new testing "in an endless spiral": the mass line represented Mao's application of his notion of the unity of theory and practice to political work.

The ideas behind the mass line were gradually and inchoately formed out of the National Revolution of the 1920s and the persecution of the Communists that followed. To survive, the Communists had to work closely with ordinary villagers, as we have seen. Mao then formulated the theory of the "mass line" as one part of his larger theoretical turn in Yan'an. It may be that the mass line is Mao's most original contribution to Marxist theory (it is not found in Marx or Engels or the Russian Marxists), and it is closely related to praxis: a method of leadership.

Mao also assumed that, in a given context, a group of activists – or heroes and leaders – would emerge. It was they who had the responsibility to bring the mass line into effect in order to avoid becoming dictatorial or divorced from the reality on the ground. Moreover, it may well be that those who come forward initially do not remain in the leading group; indeed, new activists are expected to emerge in the course of the movement. This leading group must remain in close contact with the masses as a source of "concrete experience" without which they cannot survive. It went without saying that the long-term desires of the populace and the policy goals of the CCP were the same. Mao also assumed that, although popular demands could act as a check on power, leadership inevitably stemmed from an elite. The mass line thus succeeded in preventing Communists in local government from getting too far ahead of the people, while rectification guaranteed organizational unity. The mass line was designed to teach cadres a particular form of mobilization. This inherently involved sharing power in a way impossible for the GMD. As their capabilities grew, for example, the Communists unhesitatingly gave arms to as many peasants as they could: an action unthinkable for the GMD.

The rectification campaign thus combined cynical power politics with an optimistic view of human capabilities. On the one hand, it was not entirely clear if all were sinners or only some. Probably, everybody had something to confess – even Mao. And nearly everybody was redeemed and, new and improved, welcomed back to the fold. In later years, self-criticism was institutionalized and so became merely pro forma. Group meetings became orgies of boredom as people read their newspapers and drank their tea while someone droned on in the front of the room. Having been institutionalized, though, the intensity of self-criticism could be turned up on occasions like the Cultural Revolution (1966–9). As well, the rectification groups of the 1940s, centered on colleagues from a particular work unit (*danwei*), foreshadowed the rise of the "danwei system" in the 1950s. Under this system, work units were not only places of employment (and criticism) but also provided housing, food, entertainment, and even the chance to travel, becoming the key social unit in urban China.

In all, the rectification campaign of 1942–4 combined coercion and redemption. On the one hand Party members (it never involved ordinary people) were told what to do, while on the other they learned a kind of Maoist map of the world so they could find where they were supposed to be for themselves. One practical problem was that, since the campaign's goals were not entirely clear, it could not be formally ended, and it finally petered out. Or, to put it another way, if the goal was individual conversion, there was no objective way to judge the sincerity of the conversion. None the less, the vast majority of young cadres survived a process that welded them into a tighter, more disciplined body, and undoubtedly made most feel that they had undergone revolutionary tempering.

The historical paradox – and tragedy – is that, while the CCP during the Yan'an decade offered local communities a real voice in their fates, drawing them into a democratizing process, organs of control over the people were also put into place. On the one hand, voluntarism in the sense of the power of humans to change things, a stress on voluntary cooperation and participation, elections, education, egalitarianism, and an unprecedented mobilization of the poor, the young, and women. A distinctively *Chinese* form of Marxism appealed to urban-derived intellectuals; they were not just following another Western doctrine but a distinct ideology based on broad claims to universal significance. On the other hand, the elitism and privileges of officials, the intolerance of dissent, the tendency to label critics as enemies of the people, ideological controls, police and secret police, and the centralization of policymaking.[17] If the new state that emerged in 1949 was singularly efficient, this was in no small part because its range of controls over society was unprecedented as well. The rectification campaign established the basis for the later cult of Mao, which would present him in world-historical terms as the successor of Marx, Lenin, and Stalin.

# 17   Revolution and civil war

Let us begin with the end – or at least with an ending that was also a beginning: the culmination of the Communist Revolution in 1949, after a
four-year civil year. In many ways the revolution continued through the
1960s, but the victory of 1949 marked the Communists' coming to national
power. The extent of the revolution can be defined by the massive social
changes put into effect between 1946 and 1952: the abolition of landlordism and the extermination of the landlord class, the mobilization of
the peasantry, and the severe limits placed on capitalists, not to mention the
takeover of government by a new Party–military machine that would soon
impose new controls over all elements of society. It can also be defined by
the ability of the new government – once again in Beijing – to command the
resources of the country and the loyalty of its citizens. The powers of
the Communist government were soon greater than Chiang Kai-shek's
Nanjing regime had been able to effect, far greater than any of the post-
1911 governments, and indeed greater than the preceding imperial
dynasties, limited as they were by small bureaucracies, little knowledge of
local conditions, and pre-modern transportation and communication. The
Communists were institution-builders.

The civil war that finally brought the Communists to power between
1946 and 1949 was hard-fought – by no means was the final outcome
preordained. In hindsight, one can see the fundamental strengths of the
Communist military machine and government-in-waiting. And the
Nationalists' weaknesses are laid bare by defeat – though they were obvious
enough at the time and provoked US doubts about its ally. (In the end, the
United States declined to commit troops to the Guomindang cause, giving
the Nationalists roughly the same aid as the Soviet Union gave the
Communists.[1]) When the Chinese civil war broke out, the United States was
not yet committed to the strong "containment" policies that were soon to
mark the Cold War. And when the Cold War first heated up, US policy-
makers devoted their attention instead to Europe. Had the Nationalists
deployed their still-considerable resources more wisely, the Communists
might have been limited to agrarian insurgencies in more or less remote
areas, rather like the 1930s.

The basis of the Chinese Communists' strength lay in the revolutionary mobilization of society. The Nationalists also lost the support of key groups. Intellectuals and students did not, for the most part, ally themselves with the Communists. But they sought democratic reforms – hoping, perhaps naïvely, that these would bring the Communists into a new political sphere, but in effect attacking the undemocratic Nationalists. By 1944, as Japan's defeat looked more and more certain, both the United States and the "third force" of Chinese intellectuals sought to mediate between the Nationalists and the Communists. But the leaders of these two military machines doubted the possibility of peaceful political struggle and were primarily concerned about who would be blamed for starting civil war.

The United States supported the Nationalists by requiring Japanese forces to surrender only to official GMD armies, except in Manchuria, where they were to surrender to the Soviet Union. Chiang Kai-shek ordered Japanese troops to continue fighting the Communists through September, a full month after Japan's official surrender, while Nationalist troops were readied to return to eastern China. Though officially neutral, the United States helped transport half a million Nationalist troops out of the southwest; the majority of Japanese arms and equipment went to Nationalist armies. Meanwhile, the Communists emerged from the war with Japan with no less than ten base areas across north China. Though they soon lost control of these bases, they maintained their military machine. They were able to take advantage of the Soviet Union's presence in Manchuria to build up a strong presence there, and to inherit Japanese arms.

In all, the Nationalists had 2.5 million troops, more than double the Communist forces, better arms and equipment, and even a rudimentary air force. They resumed control of all of the major cities and the eastern China industrial base – where they quickly gained a reputation for rapacious corruption and cruelty. The problems that had developed in Chongqing blossomed as GMD officials returning to the rice-growing plains and the cities simply grabbed whatever they could: factories, farms, buildings, automobiles, machinery, and virtually anything that could be sold or possessed. At the same time, the government's attitude toward collaborators was, at best, inconsistent. A few were prosecuted, while many who had worked as officials under the Japanese continued to do so under the re-established Nanjing government under Chiang – often to popular dismay. Yet the government also stigmatized whole populations that had simply lived under Japanese rule, especially in Manchuria (fourteen years under the Japanese) and Taiwan (fifty years). Students and teachers in all occupied areas were presumed corrupted and required to pass GMD ideological tests that were simple enough, but insulting.

Even more important were the disastrous effects of the Nationalists' economic policies. Property was seldom returned to its rightful pre-war owners, but uncertainty over legal ownership hindered the efficient use of economic resources. Factories shut down in the last moments of the war remained closed for months or even years. Yet, even during this industrial recession, the inflationary policies of the Chongqing years were continued until the prices of daily necessities doubled by the day. Money was printed to pay for the civil war; speculators and hoarders simply ignored price controls. Profiteers flaunted their wealth amid the acute suffering of the many.

## Political protest and civil war

Workers were badly hurt by the combination of industrial recession and inflation. In the wake of Japan's surrender, they flocked back to the cities, where the more skilled and better-off workers were in a position to take militant action. In the winter of 1946–7 Shanghai department store workers pretended to be too tired to wait on customers, putting up signs to explain that management's refusal to give an annual bonus had left them exhausted; others embarked on a "frowning" movement, telling customers that inflation and low wages made them too unhappy to make any sales.[2] When the Japanese withdrew from the city, Communist labor organizers were able to pick up where they had left off seven years before. The CCP quickly recruited engineers, mechanics, service and utility workers, silk weavers, and printers to protest against the deterioration of living standards. The Party still faced Guomindang suppression; the growth of the underground Shanghai CCP from 2,000 members in 1945 to 8,000 in 1949 is not all that impressive. With the help of a revived Green Gang and labor racketeers, the Nationalists attacked radicals, arrested suspected Communists, and disbanded the unions.

None the less, the Guomindang was not in control of the situation. As the civil war began to turn against the Nationalists, more labor leaders and even gangsters in Shanghai switched to the Communists. Students were caught in a similar kind of crossfire: Communists versus anti-Communists, and the various GMD factions at war with one another.[3] When the war with Japan ended, students flocked back to the educational centers of Beijing and Shanghai. Communist students (and intellectuals) were able to reach out to general discontent with the Nationalists. Student movements in the post-war years were ongoing, although there was no specific climactic incident like May Fourth 1919. Rather, protests against the civil war emerged gradually. Perhaps most students condemned both the Nationalists and the Communists, and feared the imperialism of the United States and the USSR equally. But even such "uncommitted" students followed political developments closely and wanted greater freedom. Rights issues like freedom of speech, assembly, and press, all worked against the GMD.

The civil war created a dynamic that the government, for all its police powers in the cities, could scarcely control. Blame for the foreign presence – US troops being the most obvious – fell on the government. The foreign soldiers quickly lost their mantle as liberators; stories were spread of American soldiers driving over pedestrians, beating rickshaw pullers, and even shooting at people they suspected of robbing them. A rape case involving US soldiers in Beijing in 1946 provoked Chinese students to take to the streets. Blame for the civil war, too, tended to fall on the government. Why? One factor was that most Chinese were exposed to the Nationalists' corruption and incompetence. Although little might be known about the Communists, it became hard to imagine they were worse than the Nationalists. Many wanted Chiang Kai-shek to find a way to work with the Communists rather than annihilating them – an echo of the early 1930s.

The GMD sponsored pro-government demonstrations, but the anti-civil war movement grew. Class boycotts brought out thousands of students to listen to well-known speakers like Xu Guangping, Lu Xun's widow, and the historian Wu Han. In 1947 students, who by now were suffering acutely from the effects of inflation, put together a combined Anti-Hunger, Anti-Civil War Movement, demanding an increase in student stipends among other issues. In May student representatives from Shanghai, Hangzhou, and Suzhou who traveled to petition the Nanjing government were denied the right to demonstrate. They were beaten and sprayed with fire hoses, and 50 were arrested. This provoked a nationwide movement to gain the support of merchants and workers – self-avowedly in the May Fourth tradition. Facing the prospects of a politicized urban population, the government newspapers that gave favorable publicity to the students (the official newspapers ignored them entirely), police and secret agents arrested several thousand, and pro-government thugs attacked suspected Communists.

Students did not merely risk expulsion or arrest. State-sponsored violence was a part of protest. For example, when police raided a Wuhan campus to arrest radicals, they fired several rounds of dumdum bullets into a dormitory on their way out, killing three and wounding five. The secret police were vigilant and omnipresent. In her memoirs, Jung Chang recounts her mother's experience as a schoolgirl distributing secret pamphlets. "One day a copy of one of the pamphlets my mother had been distributing, Mao's *On New Democracy*, ended up with a rather absentminded school friend of hers, who put it in her bag and forgot about it. When she went to the market she opened her bag to get some money and the pamphlet dropped out. Two intelligence men happened to be there and identified it from its flimsy yellow paper. The girl was taken off and interrogated. She died under torture."[4] Intimidation gave the government immediate success in quieting the streets, but its legitimacy continued to leak away. To blame everything on "Reds" hardly dealt with the grievances felt by the various classes in China's cities.

Intellectuals involved in "third force" politics, trying to bring about peaceful compromise between the Nationalists and the Communists and establish a democratic system of government, were also subject to government persecution.[5] Their homes were searched and ransacked, meetings disrupted, newspaper offices smashed. Several were simply assassinated – the poet Wen Yiduo, for example, became a well-publicized martyr. In 1946, still a time of relative hope, a liberal professor declared:

The present regime is monopolized by a feudal clique that is politically impotent, ignorant, stupid, reactionary, corrupt and autocratic.... If the Communists are "red bandits," then the Nationalists are "white bandits." Perhaps we may call the Nationalists "black bandits" since "white" implies purity.... This regime is a "black gang" that maintains itself in power by means of violence and guns.[6]

Intellectuals and urban populations did not turn to the Communists en masse, but inevitably, as the power-holders, the Nationalists received the lion's share of the blame. Civil war was far more demoralizing than the anti-Japan war. At the same time, the GMD's endemic corruption not only cost it popular support but allowed Communists to infiltrate its ranks by buying positions in government offices and even the secret police.

As for the civil war itself, from the moment Japan surrendered, sporadic fighting between Communist and Nationalist troops flared and for all practical purposes all attempts to find a compromise were over within a year.[7] Nationalist planes bombed Yan'an in August 1946, and within another year had captured Manchuria and the major cities of the north. Communist armies retreated and base areas were abandoned. They had been taken by surprise, but they did not surrender. Renamed the People's Liberation Army, Communist troops initially dispersed into small units to pursue guerrilla attacks on the enemy's weak points. This basic strategy, conceived at the highest levels of the CCP, required that the leadership place a great deal of trust in unit commanders. Not to gain territory but to destroy enemy units, destroy or seize equipment, and damage the infrastructure was the goal. For the Nationalists did indeed have their weak points, particularly overextended supply lines and feebly defended railroads. The Communists' strategy was enormously costly in terms of abandoned territory – which meant abandoning peasant supporters. Villages recaptured by the Nationalists suffered cruel reprisals; landlord militia following the government's troops took back the landlords' original fields, or appropriated new land, and killed thousands of peasants.

However, by putting virtually all of his troops in a nationwide offensive chasing down fast-moving Communists, Chiang Kai-shek lost his source of replacements. Nanjing's offensive had begun to seize up by mid-1947. Spread too thinly, the Nationalists could not move on beyond north China's cities and county seats to occupy the smaller towns and rural areas (though they were unchallenged south of the Yangzi). Following the long-planned second stage of their strategy, larger Communist armies then began to abandon guerrilla tactics and counterattacked in limited offensives in Manchuria and Shandong. By the end of 1947, the military balance had shifted in the Communists' favor. They built larger and larger armies by encompassing militia and recruiting defeated Nationalist troops. Under Lin Biao, Communist armies of up to 400,000 men in Manchuria pushed the Nationalists back into heavily protected cities. Though the Nationalists retained superior numbers, training, and equipment on paper, the Communists outfought them.

In the key region of Manchuria, few Nationalist soldiers were originally from the area. Manchurian troops who might have fought harder for the Nationalists were still loyal to Zhang Xueliang. Instead of releasing the man who had kidnapped him in Xi'an in 1936, Chiang kept him in prison, sending him to Taiwan for safekeeping. Meanwhile, as they built new base areas, the Communists were able to recruit local people to their cause – taking advantage of the growing resentment against the Nationalists. The

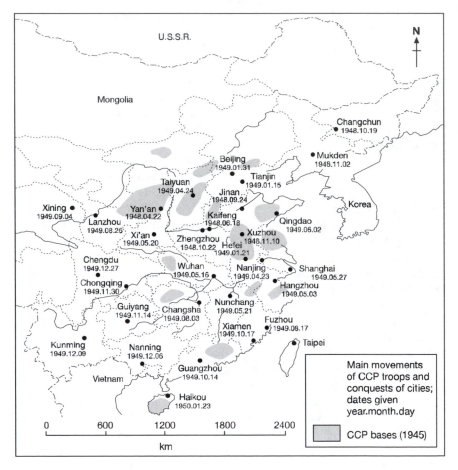

*Map 10* The civil war, 1946–9

After Japan's surrender in August 1945, Chiang Kai-shek rushed to shore up his position, retaking the eastern cities and even rearming Japanese troops to prevent the CCP from enlarging its bases. In the meantime the Communists essentially retreated to Manchuria. After the breakdown of peace talks in 1946, the CCP began to move south at the beginning of 1947, very slowly at first. Not until the beginning of 1949 did massive CCP armies move into central China, then to the southeast and southwest and finally the far west. The Nationalists had no choice but to retreat to Taiwan.

*Source*: Courtesy of Geospatial Information Science Team, Computing Center, Academia Sinica.

Communists also attacked Nationalist forces in Shandong and northern Jiangsu, thus threatening critical transportation and communication links to the lower Yangzi region. In early 1948 Communist troops under Peng Dehuai reconquered old bases in the northwest and moved into Henan. In Manchuria, even as the Communists began their final advance, Chiang refused to withdraw his armies, which were then lost. By mid-1948 the military forces of the two sides were roughly equal.

The final rout of the Nationalists occurred with astounding speed once Manchuria and the north China plains were firmly in Communist hands. Command of nearly 900,000 troops was unified under Lin Biao. Tianjin and Beijing were captured in January 1949, the Nationalists losing 500,000 troops in the process. They lost another 500,000 in subsequent fighting on the east China plains. At this point, Chiang's main forces had been destroyed, and the PLA began moving across the Yangzi in the spring of 1949. Lin Biao captured Wuhan in May and Guangzhou in October. Chiang's only recourse was to retreat to "fortress Taiwan," where the remnants of the Nationalist military and about US$300 million in hard currency were preserved. As he had foreseen the eventual defeat of Japan by US forces even in the darkest days of the Japanese occupation, so now Chiang decided to wait for a war between the United States and the Soviet Union that would allow him to retake the mainland. In order to preserve his power, he even undercut attempts to defend Nationalist territories south of the Yangzi during the first half of 1949. By December, some two million Nationalists had fled to Taiwan, leaving only mop-up operations for the Communists on the mainland.

Historians are generally agreed that the Nationalists, with a great deal of responsibility resting on Chiang personally, threw away their advantages and exacerbated their problems, while the Communists did the opposite. Having (against US advice) overextended his supply lines, Chiang next entrusted battlefield command to generals of proven incompetence. When Chiang did allow good generals in the field, he refused them needed supplies, as with Bai Chongxi's attempt to save Hunan in 1949. Most Nationalist generals – often former local warlords, it should be remembered – mastered neither mechanized warfare nor air power, thus negating two of their advantages over the Communists. The Nationalist armies repeatedly suffered from a lack of planning and coordination.

When the initiative passed to the Communists, the Nationalists' retreats turned into routs and defense became entirely passive. Many generals tried to use the ancient tactic of holing up behind city walls, as if twentieth-century artillery had not yet been invented. The Communists, on the contrary, had a battle-hardened command that was unified and flexible, quick to react to changing battlefield situations. It is almost as if they were able to graft guerrilla principles onto large-scale positional warfare, attacking the enemy's weak points, able to retreat when necessary, and making efficient use of primitive logistics like horse carts and wheelbarrows. And taking full advantage of civilian support, especially in the countryside.

## Communists and peasants, 1937–46

The key to the Communists' triumph was their mobilization of the peasantry. Due to the new availability of CCP documents and local records, as well as the possibility of conducting interviews with old peasants and cadres, scholars have begun to rewrite the history of the period. Such work necessarily remains preliminary and partial – we may learn a great deal about revolution and war in one village while we remain ignorant of the very different experiences in a village just a few miles away. Still, scholars are beginning to paint a more nuanced, accurate picture of the revolution. Earlier notions that peasants were eager to join a national struggle against landlords, Japanese, and the GMD were mistaken. Rather, though often politically active, peasants tended to retain a parochial mindset, more concerned with community grievances against the state than with class grievances. The first groups to respond to Yan'an's propaganda were elites and bandits, not farmers. Promises of land were of little use in areas where most families owned at least a little land but faced problems of raising its productivity, paying taxes, finding credit, and getting access to markets. Appeals to anti-Japanese sentiment were of little use when peasants believed, "Whatever dynasty it is, we still have to pay taxes."[8]

This makes the Communists' success in mobilizing peasants all the more remarkable, if harder to explain. The CCP "was trying to initiate a peasant movement without peasants," in the historian Lucien Bianco's words.[9] The CCP's decision to moderate its program for the sake of a Second United Front in the mid-1930s did not weaken its appeal to peasants, and in fact led to policies that strengthened it. Instead of redistributing land at gunpoint, the Communists were forced to build functioning economic systems that provided what many peasants wanted most – security – and gradually redistributed wealth in ways that seemed more just to both rich and poor than taking it by force. In fits and starts, the revolution did create a peasants' movement.

Millions of rural folk were brought into political participation for the first time by the revolution. United Front moderation largely succeeded in mobilizing the peasantry while minimally disaffecting rural elites. These were in any case weakened by the Japanese invasion. Much of the rural elite – already diminished by the lure of the cities – simply fled before the Japanese. If they stayed, and some did, and if they further collaborated with the Japanese, they became assassination targets and vulnerable to military shifts. Sometimes the sons of rural elites joined the CCP or the Red Army, if not out of reformist convictions then out of patriotism or the desire to protect their families. Whatever their motives, they brought valuable skills to the CCP. In the Chinese countryside, simple literacy was a useful skill. Though "class analysis" remained important, a place for the offspring of elites could be found in the CCP. The Communists built up peasants' associations, women's associations, and poor peasant associations, as well as army units and local militia. Indeed, simply by treating soldiers decently – and above all insisting that soldiers treat the people decently – the Red Army did much to transform peasant attitudes toward the military.

Landlordism – officially defined by the CCP as the condition of living primarily off rents – was not prominent in north China. Where there were big landlord properties, the landlords generally lived in distant cities rather than the village where their land was located. Village landlords tended to be little better off than their neighbors and were frequently no more than labor-short households, such as widows, who had to rent out their bit of land to survive. Tenants, conversely, were frequently smallholders in their own right simply leasing a little extra land. And where there were large farms, they were often "managerial" farms run with hired labor rather than through rent or sharecropping arrangements.[10] Though policy sometimes shifted, the Communists officially regarded managerial farms as progressive capitalist enterprises rather than feudal landlordism.

The main burdens placed on northern Chinese peasants were not rents but chiefly taxes and the difficulty of securing credit. By dealing specifically with these issues in individual village contexts, the Communists found supporters – first in village activists and then in the bulk of the peasantry. Communist policy was to reduce rents to 37.5 percent of harvests, down from the usual 50 percent or more. But it was equally significant that interest rates were reduced to 1.5 percent a month. Charging high interest on credit had been an important component of rural elite strategy: if the debt was repaid, one made a large profit, and if the debt was not repaid, one seized the debtor's land. Any Communist effort to abolish interest altogether would have been self-defeating. Even poor peasants and tenants saw paying interest as just – but, in bad times, to reduce rates was also just.

And taxes were hardly irrelevant to social divisions. The CCP thus worked to redistribute the tax burden, which fell disproportionately on the poor. Making taxes fairer went a long way toward meeting peasant grievances without the disruptions and divisiveness of land reform. Taxes were not reduced overall, but they were rationalized and a degree of progressivity was introduced. This ultimately encouraged a kind of indirect land reform, as wealthier villagers sold land to reduce their taxes. The Japanese occupation only increased tax demands, especially for corvée labor. Yet the Communists were able to institute a more progressive tax system even in areas within the Japanese sphere. For example, Wugong village in Raoyang County in Hebei instituted a new tax system while it was paying two sets of taxes, one to the Japanese and one to the resistance.[11] Since Wugong paid its taxes to the Japanese, it was not subject to the three-alls treatment, although many villagers were tortured and executed when the Japanese were chasing resistance fighters. But the point is that the Japanese did not care how village leaders raised the money as long as it was paid, and so they did not keep track of how the tax burden was distributed. Communist policies were instituted through a trusted underground village government with secret ties to the CCP.

Communist control over villages in the base areas was even stronger. Base areas included core regions more or less immune from Japanese attack, where Communists could operate openly, though they shaded into guerrilla areas where control was contested. Since the Japanese could not find enough collaborators to "fill in" rural areas, they relied on a few heavily fortified towns from which they could emerge to terrorize the countryside. The Communists never built up armies large enough or well enough equipped to face Japanese forces directly in conventional battles. None the less, even behind enemy lines, local partisan forces were often supported and linked together by Communist regular army troops. The Communists also cooperated with such traditional rural organizations as militia and protection societies and even bandits in anti-Japanese maneuvers. Yet if such organizations might be infiltrated or co-opted, they usually were not willing to leave their locality. The "stalemate" of the war years was thus highly unstable. At times, the Japanese were bottled up in their fortified towns; at other times, such as during the three-alls campaign, their armies marauded through the countryside. But no matter what the Japanese tried, they could not expel the Communists from the vast countryside.

The Communists' goal was to appeal both to elites, as far as possible, and to the poor, while also improving the economy. Only if the economy of the base areas was developed could the army continue to fight, would the elites, who were needed for their skills, stay, and would the poor be able to think about questions beyond sheer survival. The first tax reform in Wugong was instituted in mid-1938, before the Japanese had reached the county. Land was graded according to quality or expected yield, which was an ancient technique of Chinese tax collectors. The standard unit was said to be a plot of land able to produce 150 catties of coarse grain. The first 1.5 units per person were tax-exempt, as were the first 225 catties of grain, regardless of a household's total landholdings. A flat-rate agricultural tax was then levied above the exemptions. The flat-rate tax was obviously not progressive, but the exemptions meant that the poorest villagers paid no taxes at all. The total tax burden on the village remained roughly what it had been before, but the effects of the reforms were profound. Some 40 percent of Wugong households were exempt from taxes. Most independent farming households (middle peasants) paid about the same, while the twenty-five richest households assumed most of the new burden (previously shouldered by the poorest).

In order to encourage small-scale industry the Communists left all off-farm income untaxed. The basic structure of the village economy was unchanged: renting out fields and hiring labor certainly continued. Village elites who branched out into manufacturing (bricks, rope, clothing, etc.) could easily preserve their wealth. But the poor were no longer crushed by economic pressures, and village solidarity was fostered.

Three years later, in mid-1941, the flat tax was replaced with a genuinely progressive one: the greater a household's land (taking quality into account), the higher the tax rate, up to 40 percent. This had a real leveling effect: not just the poorest but many independent farmers found their tax burden eased, while that of the richest farm owners increased sharply. In Wugong, the richest families sold off plots of land, and the number of independent tillers increased. At the same time, manufacturing remained exempt from taxes, as did reclaimed land. All of the reforms could be publicly justified to the rest of China under the United Front rubric, and they were also good for the economy.

Similar gradualism marked rent reduction programs. In the Huaibei eastern base area, for example, rent reduction went through four phases between 1940 and 1944. Only at the end was it fully accepted by rich (reluctantly) and poor (as just), and the peasant "who did not have his rent reduced was a laughing-stock."[12] At the same time, a key feature of the Communist economy, kept secret for many years, was opium sales. Opium-smoking was illegal in Communist areas, but the Communist government sold the drug outside between 1943 and 1945 to make up for crushing deficits.[13]

Throughout the Communist base areas, reforms produced social change without disrupting the economy, and probably encouraged important non-farm investments. Beyond tax reform, a whole series of political reforms transferred power from the rural wealthy to poorer villagers. Honest tax collectors represented a major break with the past, which as we have seen had tended to degenerate into tax farming. When the rich tried to find loopholes, for example by paying poorer relatives to claim some of their land, they were eventually caught. The welter of extra taxes was eliminated. The details of ownership and tax responsibility were discussed in open meetings, so much so that many villagers adopted a new slogan: "Under the Nationalists, too many taxes; under the Communists, too many meetings."[14]

Local CCP members and government cadres (not necessarily Party members) operated in chains of command that extended back to Yan'an, but practically they also possessed much autonomy. Outside of the Yan'an base area, base areas were physically divided by Japanese troops. Recruitment to Party and army occurred amid the fighting, and new members often retained parochial concerns and local loyalties that might trump orders coming out of Yan'an. Even in the central base area, local activists initially resisted their superiors' calls for moderation in the late 1930s.[15] None the less, the top echelons of the CCP were able to coordinate administrative policies and military actions at least roughly. The Rectification Campaign of 1942 was one means to this end. Another technique was to mix experienced outsider cadres with village and county CCP leaders. The process of learning how to govern thus occurred at the various levels of the Party hierarchy.

Local conditions and administrative experience differed radically. In part of the Huaibei region of the north China plains, a base area was formed in the remote country where Hebei, Shandong, and Henan provinces met. Here, the CCP found that it could most effectively mobilize among salt-makers, and farmers were never to play a major role.[16] Where the land was too poor – too salty – to support profitable agriculture, families had learned to produce salt. And they had long fought imperial and republican government agents for the right to do so. China's Imperial governments had treated salt, which people had to buy to survive, as a lucrative monopoly. The Nanjing regime had also seen salt as a major source of tax revenue and declared war on local salt-makers, trying to close their markets. It was among these rural enemies of the state, with their long traditions of protest, that the CCP was able to put down roots. Campaigns to reduce rent and interest payments were secondary, and the first attempts to form peasant cooperatives failed utterly. After Japan surrendered in 1945, salt-producers saw the return to power of the Guomindang as a direct threat to the free salt markets the Communists had helped maintain. In turn, the Communists benefited not only from access to salt, but also from the availability of salt-peter, used to make gunpowder.

In rural communities of various types, then, Communist reform policies resulted in revolutionary changes. Progressive taxation, village elections, and limits on rent and interest payments profoundly changed village society. Wealth and power shifted from a few top families to a broader spectrum of middle and poor peasants in the course of a few years. Yet the mere redistribution of wealth still left communities – and the Communists – very poor. One solution was to try to make more efficient use of land, tools, and human resources through cooperatives. Relatives or neighbors temporarily coming together to share tools and draft animals and exchange labor was part of traditional village life, but permanently establishing groups which pooled land, tools, and labor was unheard of. In Wugong, at least, the keys to a successful program proved to be guaranteeing the rights of members to leave and stipulating that profits would be distributed based half on land and half on labor.[17] That way, neither those who contributed more land than labor nor those who contributed more labor than land would feel cheated. Indeed, labor-short and land-short households could help each other. Finally, the underground CCP government supported co-ops by providing cash and supplies when they ran into trouble.

Co-ops were not the answer to every problem, and without capable leadership they quickly faltered. In 1945, when the Communist government demanded that the Wugong cooperative award labor more and land investment less (60–40 instead of 50–50), some members chose to leave rather than get less return on their land. Both land-rich households and even land-poor households that were also labor-poor preferred to farm their own land, and the co-op declined. Yet the advantages of co-ops were clear. As long as they were voluntary – and well organized – people tended to work hard for clear material rewards. With land pooled from different areas, a hail storm or lowland flooding would not ruin the entire crop the way bad weather might ruin a single household. More land could be planted with commercial crops, such as peanuts or cotton, which could earn cash income.

The Communists never defined "classes" precisely, and economic definitions were influenced by immediate political considerations. Even without
political pressures, cadres would have had to decide what portions of a
family's income over what period of time constituted their *primary* sources
of support. None the less, class labels serve as a rough guide to economic
change in the villages. If peasants had traditionally thought more in terms
of kinship and community ties than classes, they learned class analysis over
the course of the revolution. Surveys revealed that the numbers of landlord, rich peasant, and poor peasant households declined during the war
years, while middle peasants increased. There was often simply not enough
land to eliminate the poor peasant class as such, but overall the changes
were dramatic. In the case of the Taihang region, the data suggest how new
middle peasant households were created as wealthier villagers lost their
land to poorer villagers.

David Goodman's careful study of the Taihang base area shows how
Communist organization of remote Taihang mountain villages grew into the
Shanxi–Hebei–Shandong–Henan Border Region. Although the Taihang was
hardly invulnerable to Japanese attacks, the Japanese could not maintain a
permanent military presence there, and so the Communists were able to
build village militia, guerrilla forces, and government organs capable of
mobilizing the resources (taxes and men) necessary to far-flung military
operations. Tax and rent reforms gave the CCP a new social base: middle
peasants, particularly the "new" middle peasants who had most benefited
from the reforms.

The first Communists to reach many north China villages were total
outsiders – often unfamiliar even with the local patois and shocked by rural
poverty. But as intellectuals they were convinced of the righteousness of
their mission and their fitness to save China by leading the peasants. In the
Taihang, the Party grew to 10,000 members by mid-1938 and 20,000 by the
end of the year. In general, teachers and the educated joined the Party; the
young, but few older people (over 40), joined; middle peasants and even
landlords, but relatively few poor peasants and tenants joined.

*Table 17.1* Farm holdings, Taihang region (percentage of farmland), 1936–44

| Social category | 1936 | 1941 | 1943 | 1944 |
| --- | --- | --- | --- | --- |
| Landlord | 26.3 | 16.8 | 12.9 | 5.3 |
| Rich peasant | 23.4 | 19.4 | 16.6 | 13.4 |
| Middle peasant | 31.4 | 43.1 | 47.0 | 65.0 |
| Poor peasant | 17.6 | 19.7 | 21.3 | 15.4 |
| Tenant | 0.8 | 0.4 | 0.7 | 0.1 |
| Artisan | 0.1 | 0.3 | 0.5 | – |
| Trader | 0.2 | 0.4 | 0.6 | – |

*Source*: From David Goodman, *Social and Political Change*, p. 30

*Figure 17.1* Communist propaganda. Mao Zedong (top right) is praised for two policies. First (top left and middle), satisfying the needs of the poor peasants and laborers. Easily-remembered doggerel speaks of the successes of land reform. Second (right and bottom), uniting with the middle peasants. Again, easily-remembered rhymes claim a unified poor and middle peasantry overthrows the landlords.

*Source*: The cover of *Nongmin huabao* no. 8, 11 March 1948

*Figure 17.2* Communist propaganda comparing "before" and "after." The before picture on the upper right shows a landlord who looks remarkably like Chiang Kai-shek lording it over peasants. But the after picture on the left shows the landlord overthrown "under the leadership of the Communist Party" and the peasants rejoicing. Similarly, the before picture on the lower right shows a family in deep poverty. But the after picture on the left shows that the distribution of goods gives everyone enough food to eat and clothes to wear; this picture also suggests a traditional peasant utopian ideal of household production – men farming and women weaving – that in fact the CCP did not intend to institute.

*Source*:  From *Nongmin huabao* no. 4, 7 January 1948

In fact, it seems that throughout the base areas, the most important social characteristics defining CCP recruits were not class or wealth but age, gender, and marital status. Young, unmarried men were the most likely group to volunteer in the Communist movement.[18] A majority of these were poor, but it was CCP policy to recruit "poor peasants." Still, in Taihang at least, official organs long remained dominated by intellectuals who mostly came from north China's cities. Concerned over their own capacity to absorb and socialize so many new members, the CCP tried to slow recruitment, but the Taihang base area housed over 36,000 Party members by the end of 1939.

A sense of two distinct types of members can be gained by looking at the 272 Taihang representatives to the CCP National Congress: almost half had completed university, but 38 percent were illiterate. The majority were males under 25 who had joined the Party since 1937; just 6 percent were women. After 1940, it became much harder to recruit cadres, since many people feared the political burdens involved in trying to repulse Japanese attacks, meet local needs, and satisfy CCP directives all at once. If the extreme radicalism of some of the landless and poor peasant activists seemed counterproductive, many cadres were also criticized for their conservatism and quiescence. The CCP tried to attract more middle-peasant support, but, at least in the Taihang region, recruitment of middle-peasant cadres was enormously controversial among local leaders.[19] Many thought them too conservative, interested only in their own farms even if they had originally been poor. But Party leaders valued their skills and appreciated their very moderation and ability to serve as bridges among the various groups in rural society. Middle peasants also had the economic resources to support themselves while working as cadres. As a practical matter, the relative equalization of landholdings by the end of the war created middle-peasant dominance in most villages. At the same time, Communist organizers kept track of which middle peasants had formerly been poor and thus were "redder" than their neighbors.

## Peasants and politics: Radicalization

Even relatively moderate policies, under wartime conditions, produced fundamental social change – a rural revolution – in the base areas and even beyond. And the effects were felt in terms of village power relations, not just economically. New organizations gave peasants a voice. Of course, the Communism, even revolutionary Communism, did not create a democratic utopia; coercion was part of the story. For the CCP, the key was to get peasants actively involved in local politics pursuing goals set by the top. Village-wide assemblies became common in base areas. They might be initially manipulated by traditional elites, but the tendency over time was for power to ebb away from the landed classes toward new activists. The term "democracy" in Chinese hands thus came to refer more to the idea of *participation* than representative government. Elections were held in reasonably secure areas, and the Communists even voluntarily limited their own election to a third of county and base area assembly seats. Another third were to be non-Communist leftists and a final third "petty-bourgeoisie" or landlords, even GMD members. In the Taihang base area, local governments were also required to elect at least one woman. The Communists did not win all the elections they contested; nevertheless, the reality of Communist hegemony was generally accepted.

These elections were not an attempt to create Western-style parliamentary democracy. Rather, they were part of a legitimation process. The premise was not that truth or wisdom would emerge in open contests between competing interests but that avenues of communication between government and the people would be improved. In the context of 1939–40, when the "three-thirds system" was first implemented, it was also designed to allay the fears of rural elites by guaranteeing them a formal voice. But the program did more than open lines of communication; along with the poor peasants' associations, women's associations, youth leagues, and the like, it opened a new arena of political participation to ordinary peasants. Elections represented an attempt to work out democratic ideas advocated by progressive intellectuals since the late nineteenth century. To bring the people into political processes did not mean that decision-making was turned over to them, but it meant that their voices were heard. It fostered a sense of citizenship – a sense of full membership in the community.

Naturally, the Communists faced opposition, even uprisings. Landlords covertly tried to get around land tax reforms by pretending to give land to poor relatives. Or they publicly signed leases with reduced rents but secretly threatened to find new tenants unless they were paid the old rates. Some cases of spying and sabotage for Japanese puppet armies may have been motivated by discontent with the Communists. Ordinary people, as well, were often angered by cadre misconduct. A fairer tax system may have improved impressions of the government, but taxes were still collected under duress. This was even more the case with recruitment of boys into the army. A few cadres even practiced outright extortion, and not just against wealthy families. The CCP knew well that bad cadres would inspire popular dissatisfaction and weaken the revolution, and crimes were occasionally prosecuted. For the most part, however, cadres were only subject to ideological re-education.

It may be that the CCP naturally judged its own leniently. The Party also did not want to create passive cadres. A cadre afraid of doing anything for fear of public or Party criticism was as counterproductive as a corrupt cadre. All cadres were subject to periodic review, at least after the rectification campaign of 1942–4. One county-level leader frankly noted: "Cadres do enjoy more privileges. They can raise bank loans, borrow grain from the army, and beat their wives." She added, "Cadres who engage in these kinds of behavior are mostly capable and experienced but they act this way because of social influences, poor class status, or through their own weaknesses."[20] Ordinary people might not have been so forgiving: it essentially depended on how well local cadres did in serving their communities. And on the whole cadres could rely on the help of "activists" or "progressive elements" to help them win over village doubters.

Wartime conditions were appalling. Disease and even starvation were major problems. In the Taihang region, malaria and typhus were widespread; locusts, floods, and droughts led to famines which relief efforts could limit but not eliminate. And if there could be mobilization of the peasantry, there could also be demobilization. That is, Communist organizers in north China initially benefited from the Japanese army's decision to press the war quickly on to central China, which left a power vacuum across the northern plains. But by 1939 Japan returned military resources to the north, supplementing garrisoned towns with Chinese puppet troops. In some areas, villages were made collectively responsible for maintaining roads and railroads – if sabotage occurred, the entire village might be held responsible.[21] The "three-alls" extermination campaigns after 1940 destroyed whole villages, and the Japanese built fortified roads designed to carve up base areas. Partisan activities declined, and the Communists faced desertion problems. If Communist guerrillas were forced to abandon an area, village peasant associations seldom survived. Morale plummeted, and popular hostility toward Communists grew. In effect, the peasantry was thus demobilized.

None the less, in the long run Communist-led resistance in north China kept the Japanese at bay. The political scientist Kathleen Hartford has concluded that one reason the Japanese failed to crush resistance as they had in Korea and Manchuria stemmed from their decision in 1937 to march on central China rather than consolidate control over the north.[22] Of course, in terms of defeating or cowing the main enemy – Chiang Kai-shek's Nationalists – this decision was virtually inevitable. But it gave the embryonic Communist resistance a chance to grow stronger before it faced real repression. Later extermination campaigns were less effective than they might have been, since the resistance had built underground tunnels and storage areas around thousands of villages. The Communists responded to Japanese pressure with some flexibility. Secret guerrilla cells curtailed their activities until conditions became safer. The CCP could either assassinate Chinese puppet leaders, or, often, work with them. By absorbing Japanese-approved county leaders into CCP networks, the Communists drastically weakened Japanese knowledge of local conditions. Japanese officers no longer knew whom to trust, since any Chinese could be a double agent secretly protecting guerrillas or sending grain into base areas.

If mobilization was sometimes followed by demobilization, Communists could also lead remobilization. Carefully timing their efforts, organizers would arrive in a village after a nearby military victory to reinvigorate the local Party and peasant activism. Mass meetings would conduct tax reassessments and challenge landlord rents, and eventually restore morale. It was during a period of great Japanese pressure that the rent and interest reductions, the tax reforms, and the democratic election movements were carried out. In the words of one Communist organizer:

> Among the guerrilla units we have organized, there is a saying, "victory decides everything." That is to say, no matter how difficult it has been to recruit troops, supply the army, raise the masses' anti-Japanese fervor, or win over the masses' sympathy or help, after a victory in battle the masses fall all over themselves to send us flour, steamed bread, meat, and vegetables; the masses' pessimistic and defeatist psychology is smashed, and many new guerrilla soldiers swarm in.[23]

Once the civil war was under way in 1946–7, the CCP abandoned its policies of moderation and returned to radical land reform. Raw class struggle returned to the top of the agenda. Rural elites were again expropriated, sometimes attacked, and peasants were encouraged to voice their grievances at "speak bitterness" meetings. These were emotionally charged events that local cadres carefully prepared for. But they also gave rise to spontaneous expressions of traumas and grievances that energized entire villages. Mobilization, then, depended on such "emotion work" as much as on fear of the Guomindang.[24]

Peasant egalitarianism, suppressed during the Sino-Japanese War, was allowed to come to the fore again. Landlords and usurers were often accused of murder, if only because it seemed unfair they had lived (relatively) well while poorer villagers starved. Many were beaten to death. Such "excesses" (as they were later officially designated) roused villagers to a more and more intense, shared participation. The killings often occurred during land reform when it was discovered that there was simply not enough land to go around. Even if a village's "landlords" – or simply above-averagely rich peasants – were entirely expropriated, many peasants still could not reach the middle-peasant status of self-sufficient holdings. Many of these village struggles had little to do with landlordism as the CCP had painstakingly tried to define it, and more to do with simple wealth. In the midst of the civil war, a violent struggle between haves and have-nots, regardless of their theoretical relationship to the means of production, served to intensify mobilization at the cost of increasing divisiveness and anxiety. Such explosions of peasant anger suggest long-suppressed grievances finally coming to the fore, expression of which the CCP made possible. Villages were torn apart in "struggle sessions" and "speak bitterness" meetings – though reconstructed by denying those labeled landlords, rich peasants, and pro-Japanese traitors any rights in their communities.

Given the success of the moderate policies of the war years, why would the Communists return to radical land reform? Part of the answer lay in the view that rent reduction was only a first step, inevitably to be followed by a stricter land-to-the-tiller program (which would in turn eventually be replaced by collectivization). Radicals also pointed out that in 1946 villages were still places of rich and poor. In that sense, land reform was the beginning of the revolution. But more important was the situation on the ground. After the Japanese were defeated and the civil war was under way, the CCP faced the possibility of counter-revolution. At least in some areas, in spite of all attempts to soften rural elite opposition over the preceding years, landlords greeted early discussions of coalition government and a return of the Guomindang with glee. One landlord told one of his workers, "Heh! Still pressing us to pay grain tax. Fuck you. Chee! The Guomindang armies will be here in a minute. Gonna cut your little prick off! Chee!"[25] Land reform, then, was less about economics than about political mobilization. The CCP knew that many peasants feared the return of the GMD and would have preferred not to commit themselves publicly to the CCP.

The civil war was thus a class war and a rural–urban war; the alliances of the preceding era were no longer useful. Once fully-fledged land reform was pursued again after 1946, peasants had to continue fighting for their gains: if the GMD returned, they might be killed. Radical land reform was an enormous gamble. It was designed to produce a rural society of middle peasants who, however, lost the conservatism natural to landowners by participating in revolutionary action. One did not gain land during land reform simply by being poor. One was expected to demand it in a process of class affirmation that was required as long as any chance of the GMD's returning remained. In reality, new middle peasants often wanted only to farm their fields, and cadres complained no one volunteered to join the Red Army. But villages that had undergone land reform were inevitably committed to the revolution.

In the strategically critical provinces of Manchuria, where the Japanese had successfully prevented base areas from being formed, the CCP had little time to cultivate peasant support when the civil war broke out in 1946. Land reform tended to be carried out directly by cadres under the protection of Communist armies.[26] There was no time to carefully investigate land ownership patterns and the local economies of the various villages, to recruit peasant activists, or to organize meetings that would attract mass support. This naturally gave traditional rural elites opportunities to subvert land reform, while ordinary peasants simply remained unmobilized. Landlords might lie about their holdings, bribe cadres or supply male cadres with women, or join, even lead, the peasant associations.

None the less, anti-Communist forces in the Manchurian countryside remained unorganized and leaderless in the wake of Japan's defeat. Communist-led violence across 1947 weakened traditional patterns of dominance and deference and destroyed community cohesion. Land reform did at least bring increasing numbers of peasants into the political process, finally mobilized as full members of their communities. In his careful study of the CCP in Manchuria during the civil war, Steven Levine concludes that, while many peasants benefited from redistribution, the wartime demands of the CCP did not leave them better off than before land reform; rather, what made the Communists different from previous regimes was that they "instituted an exchange relationship with the peasantry marked by reciprocity and a measure of justice."[27] Absent a revolutionary tradition in Manchuria, the CCP quickly moved to offer ordinary peasants concrete benefits, activists the right to participate in new political institutions, and cadres and soldiers a chance for social mobility outside the village. And in Manchuria, as elsewhere, although the CCP put a heavy burden on local resources, they did so in relatively equitable and predictable ways.

In other words, land reform did not wait for victory in the civil war but occurred as part of the war, making it a revolutionary war. By pitting villager against villager, in the words of the historian Yung-fa Chen, the CCP "undermined and destroyed almost all of the traditional and particularistic relationships, while it harnessed localism by linking it to larger causes."[28] The old alliances between clan members and local elites were smashed, while the avenues of individual advancement were all controlled by the CCP. The point is not that Communists justified violence in the name of class struggle, though they did, nor that peasants took the law into their own hands, though they did. Rather, the revolution on the ground – in village after village – set have-nots against haves, Communists and activists against GMD supporters or Japanese collaborators, and sometimes allowed private vendettas to assume the label of class struggle. The ongoing civil war was clearly a struggle to the death. As villagers became caught up in the revolution, new activists and military recruits emerged.[29] In northern China (outside of Manchuria), the CCP did not march into a village, determine the socioeconomic status of each household, and order a new division of resources. Its goal was to have local activists, under Party guidance, lead the people themselves in these revolutionary acts – a process designed to create these very activists.

The situation in central and southern China in the late 1940s was different. There, the CCP came in as a conquering army, and land reform was a task of government rather than popular revolutionary forces. Established procedures and class definitions tended to be followed more closely. Though the government still wanted to create a revolutionary experience, and landlords (and others) were targeted for struggle and expropriation, land reform was basically controlled from the top down. Violence was still widespread, but the revolution became ritualized.

The Chinese revolution, with its roots in the northern Chinese peasantry, defeated the materially stronger Nationalists through a combination of professional military actions and popular mobilization. At the same time, it is important to note that "the" Chinese revolution was not one revolution but hundreds, even thousands, of local revolutions. Nor was there a single "peasantry" or even a single homogeneous Communist Party. Since the 1920s thousands of students, intellectuals, professional revolutionaries, soldiers, and ultimately millions of farmers were mobilized in a process that brought them onto the political stage in villages and counties across rural China. And for the first time, in 1949, it brought them to the national stage.

# Epilog

There's Persimmon Valley Village, for instance. Well, there was a landlord named Mu Shi'an there. Did he deal justly with the people? I'll tell you. He was a member of the Guomindang. When the Jap Devils came, he drafted us for a joint defense corps. He said it was to fight the Japs and the 8th Route bandits [Communists]. But almost at once he surrendered to the Japs. Then he told the families who had men with the guerrillas to call their sons home. "I'm afraid the Japs will kill you otherwise," he said. He promised that no harm would come to anyone who came back. When an 8th Route sub county leader came back, he killed him and then held a public condolence meeting for him. Oh, he was two-faced, you know. After that no soldiers wanted to come back. So he killed the closest relative of anyone who had a son with the guerrillas. In all he killed one member of each of over one hundred families here. When he saw the Japs were winning, he rounded up thousands of us to carry stones to build Jap blockhouses. Every one of those stones had our blood on it. And this landlord settled other men's lives as if he was God …

So the American journalist Jack Belden quoted his driver in 1947.[1] So, in one case, patriotic resistance was linked to the struggle of ordinary peasants against their Chinese oppressors. The triumph of the Chinese Communist Party – unifying China after twelve years of total war, thirty-seven years of division and weak government, and over 100 years of imperialist battering – was a world-historical achievement. In reviewing how that achievement came about, we can ignore neither the historical grievances of the peasants nor the CCP's own organizational genius.

For the sociologist Theda Skocpol, the key to understanding the Chinese revolution, like other great social revolutions, lies in the process by which the CCP was gradually able to consolidate state power.[2] In outline: after the breakdown of the imperial state in 1911, heated political and class conflicts came to the fore. The class structure was in flux due to heavy population pressure on the land, urbanization, migration, sprouts of industrialization, and challenges by revolts from below. Nationalist revolutionaries had no choice but to incorporate peasant struggle into their efforts to build new state structures. The Communist movement, which was also an emerging state, responded astutely to the social, economic, and political crisis of the era, strengthened by its ability to survive in a context of contending nations, including but not limited to the Japanese invasion.[3] Skocpol also emphasizes the decay of the GMD; Japanese pressure aggravated its pre-existing weaknesses: lack of control over China's financial resources and a decentralized military structure. The CCP, meanwhile, was able to recruit peasants into its growing army and build up base areas. By the early 1940s CCP cadres were intimately involved in the economies and the reorganization of many north China villages that would form the basis of the outright land revolution of the late 1940s. (We can also emphasize that the CCP offered positive inducements to the peasantry: reasonably honest and competent village government, a fair tax system, a check on landlord power, and a modicum of economic opportunity.) Skocpol points out that redistributing land and terrorizing landlords and other exploiters developed a momentum of its own as the peasants took advantage of the new CCP order to go beyond original CCP intentions. The CCP none the less supported its radicals and was able to utilize the land reform process to further reward them and harness their activism to economic and military needs, while eliminating anti-Communist rural elites.

This is surely correct as far as it goes. Yet Skocpol makes the CCP's tasks sound almost easy. The GMD, while decaying, did not entirely self-destruct, and the CCP's success in resisting both Japanese and GMD attacks depended on a variety of factors, including Mao Zedong's farsighted leadership. CCP organizing techniques did not fortuitously "synthesize" with a peasant revolution already under way but rather depended on complex and flexible strategies to turn some peasants into revolutionaries. Class struggle there was, but societies are divided along other lines as well – kinship, regional, linguistic, gender, ethnic divisions – and class struggle does not just happen: it has to be made. A thorough grasp of the cross-cutting divisions and unities of the countryside was probably Mao's greatest strength as a revolutionary leader. Even the most chronically rebellious peasants will not engage in anti-state revolution unless they have outside leadership, as Lucien Bianco and Elizabeth Perry have both emphasized.[4] On their own, peasants remain parochial, defensive, and with little class consciousness, though possessing concepts of a just society and techniques of rebellion honed over the millennia of China's history.

Ultimately the Chinese revolution must be understood in the broadest possible context. The Japanese invasion of 1937 and the Russian revolution of 1917 both played roles, and new economic and intellectual currents drew China ever deeper into the world system both materially and culturally. But the revolution must also be understood in its particularities. In thousands of communities involving millions of people, men and women pursued transformative visions. For the revolution was really thousands of small revolutions. None the less the CCP remained devoted to a national and even international vision of progress.

Its victory symbolized the power of anti-colonial struggle harnessed to revolutionary social goals. Thus "1949" is a major turning point in Chinese and world history. For Mao Zedong, the essence of the Communists' triumph was that "the Chinese people have stood up," as he famously pronounced. This is a concise formulation of nationalism with a revolutionary cast. The Communist Party led a movement that contributed to the defeat of Japanese colonialism and united China in a stunning victory over the US-backed Guomindang in the subsequent civil war. Indeed, "1949" also marks a fundamental shift in Chinese alliances from the US to the Soviet Union.

Mao seemed to be promising that the Chinese people, particularly its oppressed classes, would now gain control over their fate, in ways already augured by the initial stages of land reform. In Mao's formulation, China belonged to the people – that is, to "the masses" – not to feudal forces nor to capitalist forces, though the latter might be harnessed. It certainly did not belong to the foreign Powers. In other words, Mao's image of standing up was based on an understanding of the nation in terms of social classes. During the years of the anti-Japanese War (1937–45), the Second United Front marked the Communists' promises to cooperate with all "patriotic classes," including the bourgeoisie. Certainly, they attracted widespread intellectual support, bourgeois students and intellectuals flocking to Yan'an and becoming a critical component of the cadre or Party bureaucracy in the war years. The United Front was less significant as an alliance between the Guomindang and the CCP, since the alliance was shaky from the start, than it was a means for Communists to work with rural elites and communicate with urban intellectuals. As the revolutionary struggle sharpened in the wake of the anti-Japanese War, the peasant-based land revolution emerged more clearly. This is not to say that relations between the CCP and its constituencies were always smooth. Coming to power, the Party was not directly responsible to either workers or peasants, but rather claimed to "represent" them on the grounds that only it understood their true interests.[5] Workers and peasants were not to mount the political stage as individuals, sovereign and autonomous. Rather, their political and social meaning emerged out of their class character as interpreted by the Party.

At the same time, limited but real forms of village and factory democracy did emerge in the course of the revolution. Peasant and poor peasant associations, women's associations, and unions gave organizational form – and above all "voice" – to many ordinary people. The CCP's concerns with social justice and "economic democracy" were expressed concretely in a readjustment of taxes, rents, and debts, along with policies designed to encourage small producers in agriculture and handicrafts. The result was to give most people a new stake in their communities.

More broadly speaking, we can see that nationalism implies democracy, or at least a certain kind of egalitarian thinking. Liah Greenfeld's comparative analysis of Western forms of nationalism suggests that, as nations develop, "sovereignty" is relocated from monarchs to the people.[6] In the classic British form, a struggle for status equality within the nation led to an emphasis on the sovereignty of the individual and a particular notion of "liberty." Chinese nationalism was more reactive or defensive in nature; we have seen the development of a state-based nationalism, where the languages of humiliation and salvation, wealth and power, and rights and duties were all mixed together. Still, the notion of popular sovereignty found clear expression among Confucian radicals as early as the 1890s; the Revolution of 1911 then discredited any other form of sovereignty. The will to overthrow the monarchy led to a further exploration of the equality of the nation, as opposed to the hierarchies of the imperium, and this energized nationalist movements into the 1920s and beyond.

Popular sovereignty and egalitarianism were not just abstract political ideas but also applied in personal life, particularly in urban areas. Relations among family members, between the sexes, and even between teacher and student began to be remodeled, from a sense of hierarchy supposedly embedded in the cosmos to a sense of equality supposedly found in nature. The handshake and the simple bow began to replace the kowtow; simple, practical clothing for both sexes began to replace elaborate gowns. Bodies were to be held erect, proudly. All this fostered a new psychological identity, a self-definition as a national. Individuals did not lose their gender, family, village, education, class, and other forms of identity, but did become "Chinese" more importantly than ever before. First as an idea, then as a political project, and then as embodied behavior – national identity required the recognition of other nationals, psychological identification and empathy with them, and hence a kind of equality.

It can be objected that, throughout the early decades of the twentieth century, Chinese political leaders were not genuinely committed to popular sovereignty but rather to the pursuit of power. But the point is not that Chinese sought to build liberal-democratic institutions and failed, but that the pursuit of power took place in an evolving political culture in which the sovereignty of the emperor had collapsed and the nation was subjected to protracted war and invasion. Critical to that evolution, China's twentieth century was marked by dramatic cultural change, social upheaval, economic dislocation, and endemic violence. From the social Darwinian perspective popular in those decades, it seems only natural that the Chinese would form a strong state or perish.

"Sovereignty" in the sense of independence and control (impervious to control by others) must always be mythical. The question is not whether the popular will is to be represented, but *how* it is to be represented. Liberal-democratic institutions are one way of connecting popular sovereignty to real power. In the 1920s and 1930s the Nationalists and then the Communists claimed to offer another way. Under the Nationalists, the nation was defined as the entire Chinese people represented by the "fore-knowers" of the Guomindang. The only identity that mattered was one's identity as Chinese. But many resisted the Party's determination to speak for them.

Few of China's first Marxists were Communists, and relatively few Communists began with a firm grasp of Marxism. Some turned to Marxism as a useful paradigm – to explain historical developments and contemporary society. But they too believed China should *avoid* class struggle; they found Marx's description of capitalism convincing but not his prescription for action. Some of the modernizers of the GMD fell into this camp. But as the Communists discovered how class struggle could be a useful way to mobilize supporters and activists, they determined to risk internal divisiveness. And many still retained their original utopian hopes, not focused on the "proletariat" and "poor peasants." Both United Fronts (1924–7, 1938–45) were temporary compromises, and the Communists defined the "nation" through class identities alongside of ethnic and political ones. A bourgeoisie that could be usefully moved into the national category could be moved out again. Core Chinese identity lay only in workers and peasants, in this view.

In fact, many of the CCP's leaders were drawn from bourgeois and intellectual, landlord, and rich peasant families. As "revolutionaries," they were embraced by the Party. They were offered a chance to transcend their original class backgrounds through devotion to the masses – and obedience to CCP dictates. The CCP's rectification campaigns of the 1940s marked the creation of a new Maoist dogmatism. This is especially clear in retrospect, as de facto sovereignty was placed in the CCP itself. Still, the campaigns were also based on the voluntarist faith that class was ultimately a product of will. Whereas Guomindang ideology imagined a nation standing above particular classes and ruled by an enlightened elite that was descended from the gentry, Maoism finally collapsed the nation into social revolution. The nation would be saved by workers and peasants, who would inherit it and who would also remake it in their image, creating an entire society of workers and peasants. The turmoil of the early twentieth century allowed workers and peasants to mount the political stage, and the CCP mobilized them as its shock troops. Having said this, though, we need to remember that countless members of China's lower classes took action on their own behalf – shaping Chinese politics, and the CCP, as much as they themselves were being shaped.

In the late 1920s, with its turn to rural base areas, the CCP began to act as a government, not merely a revolutionary party. This meant its leaders had to think in terms of satisfying the populace's needs, and its "citizens" had to think in terms of their rights and duties (or privileges and restrictions) as well as what the Party might offer them. The CCP strove to carry out modernization. As a matter of both revolutionary theory and governmental practice, irrigation was to be improved, wells built, roads constructed, commerce encouraged, taxes rationalized, and bureaucracy streamlined. In the Leninist–Maoist analysis of China's semi-feudal/semi-colonial condition, the conditions for socialism were not yet present; China still needed to develop the infrastructure and industrialization hitherto associated with capitalist economies. Thus, again, willing members of the bourgeoisie – in particular, urban intellectuals and students – were to be included in the CCP's embrace. The twinned pursuits of social revolution and modernization marked CCP policies from the 1930s, and, though scarcely ever in perfect tandem, continued to do so past 1949.

The political symbolism of the new regime captured these concerns. The flag that flew over China by the end of 1949 was the five-star red flag: four yellow stars representing workers, peasants, the petty bourgeoisie, and the national bourgeoisie, and a larger yellow star for the CCP that professed to represent and unite these classes in the Chinese nation. Red for communist revolution and yellow for China itself, blending old and new symbolism. The Communist flag's class symbolism broke from the ethnic significance of the first flag of the Republic in 1912. In that flag, five horizontal bands represented the major peoples of China: red for Han, yellow for Manchus, blue for Mongols, white for Hui, and black for Tibetans.[7] In the Communist flag, the nation is defined socially and politically. And the Party seems to stand above the classes, as it were – a remarkable echo of the Guomindang ideology.

So exactly whose nation had the revolution won? The national question was first posed in the 1890s by the Confucian radicals. They began to conflate the people and the state, seeking a new, modern nation-state. During the 1911 Revolution the "Han race" or Han people came to represent the Chinese people as opposed to the Manchu invaders, and minority groups were expected to be assimilated into Han ways. This ethnic or quasi-racial sense of nationhood included cultural components as well. It was possible for intellectuals in the first decades of the twentieth century to imagine the incorporation of neighboring tribes, peoples, and nations into a larger Han synthesis defined through common language, religion, philosophy, customs, and, above all, history.

Yet the 1911 Revolution itself created a new problem. The "Republic of China" inherited most of the territories of the old Qing Empire, which included non-Han peoples. The new myth of the "Republic of the five peoples" thus included Han, Manchu, Mongol, Hui ("Muslim"), and Tibetan as major groups not entirely assimilable to one another but all somehow "Chinese." The category of Han itself was a late Qing myth that included southerners, northerners, easterners, and westerners speaking different languages, composed of mutually antagonistic groups practicing different rituals, and following distinct economic patterns. Still, if "Han" was an invention of late-Qing intellectuals who opposed the "Manchu conquerors," it was a remarkably successful one, as some 90 percent of Chinese today regard themselves as Han.[8] Han identity was essentially based on membership in the Ming dynasty territories that the Qing conquered in the seventeenth century. Han, then, were the settled farmers and merchants who paid taxes to the emperor. In effect, this was a state identity before it became a national identity. The Han were tied to the state and its official culture through local elites trained in the Confucian classics. By and large they accepted the legitimacy of the Qing dynasty, which ruled them through the traditional exam-based bureaucratic system inherited from the Ming – along with new territories: the Qing's home base to the northeast (land of the Manchus), lands to the northwest (Mongols), west (Hui), and southwest (Tibetans). The new Republic of China also tried to absorb a number of smaller ethnic minorities, generally living in the mountainous lands of the south and southwest or the vast deserts of the northwest. The Communists took control of lands that were subject to competing national definitions. Over the course of the twentieth century, the tasks of state-building and nation-building might have been easier had the new China inherited the smaller lands of the old Ming.

Intellectuals thought about the problem of ethnicity, even obsessed about it before 1911, but they tended to focus on a "universal human" or at least a "universal Chinese" rather than thinking about particular groups. Their intense debates over how much of the past should be used in creating a new future influenced elite modernization plans. Their goal was to raise the cultural and material level of a supposedly benighted people and strengthen the state. To this end, some intellectuals and political activists began thinking about specific groups: not ethnic groups, but the new social forces being created by global capitalism and cultural transformation. Political activists did not create them but helped them emerge into the political arena.

Chinese nationalism – anti-imperialist and anti-feudal for the Guomindang as much as for the CCP – was thus a mass nationalism inextricably linked to social issues like workers' rights, women's rights, and eventually peasants' rights. Mass nationalism was ultimately based on the late Qing notion that revolution would turn a decadent empire into a unified nation-state of "wealth and power." The failure of this vision in the early decades of the twentieth century forced some elites to seek support from lower classes. In a previous century, this might have involved the recruitment of peasant armies based on chiliastic promises. But in the early twentieth century there was a rapidly growing urban population, new efforts to educate the workers, and burgeoning "print-capitalism" – media such as novels and newspapers, and then films and radio, constantly appealed to larger audiences. These fostered new conceptions of time and space that allowed people to imagine themselves in "horizontal comradeship" or fraternity as a single community.[9] People learned to feel ties to distant "ancestors" (a "people" moving through time vertically) and to perfect strangers (in a mapped, defined space horizontally). It is this horizontal aspect of nationalism that implied a kind of egalitarianism: all fellow nationals shared this particular, key status in their identity as compatriots. Social movements implied a commitment to nationalism as a shared political identity.

These ideas would seem to exclude the largely illiterate peasants, who still lived in a world of different distinctions. Not native/foreigner but villager/outsider, kin/non-kin, farmer/merchant. But, as we have seen, Chinese farmers were tied to regional and inter-regional trading networks that included cultural exchanges in religious practices, opera, and storytelling. Commoners could at least form a hazy picture of the imperial state that was the nation-state's predecessor. Older, established gentry-landlords abandoned the countryside, leaving "local bullies and evil gentry" and warlords and bandits to dominate rural politics. But part of the power vacuum they left behind was filled by progressive-minded young men who often became village schoolteachers. These men originated in better-off elements of the peasantry and the small landlord class. Returning after secondary schools and teachers' colleges to villages and rural towns, they formed nodes of radical thought and action. Educated peasant youth like Mao Zedong could be found all over China. In the 1920s many joined either the Guomindang or the CCP, and it was often through schools that the peasant associations of the day were organized. By the 1930s many intellectual youth were virulently anti-Japanese. Modern ideas of participatory nationalism – or citizenship – thus combined with pre-existing notions of the state to create a basis for peasant nationalism. The Japanese invasion occurred just as the basis of this popular nationalism was being laid, and the Japanese became its target. Just as early-twentieth-century intellectuals had formed a sense of Han nationhood in opposition to the Manchus, so popular nationalism was formed in opposition to the Japanese.[10] This is not to say that the Japanese created peasant nationalism, because the groundwork was already laid, but the Japanese served as a catalyst in its spread – as the Communist Party linked class mobilization to the anti-Japanese resistance.[11]

China was not unique in forging national identity out of a revolutionary moment. In the case of the United States, in addition to "rugged individualism," American national identity includes a complex of notions about an enterprising and innovative people, self-reliant but disciplined individuals, and the glories of freedom of commerce.[12] Whatever its colonial roots, this complex essentially emerged in the course of the American Revolution in self-conscious reaction to European decadence. Somewhat similarly, Chinese national identity was conceived in the course of revolutionary struggle in opposition to foreign imperialism and native decadence. Radical intellectuals intuitively understood the nation-building potential of the Japanese invasion from the beginning. Leftists greeted the invasion with all the hope born of angry desires to sweep away the old society and patriotic frustration at the years of compromise with Japan. Take, for example, Communist writer Guo Moruo's 1937 poem:

> When I heard the rumble of guns above Shanghai,
> I felt nothing but happiness.
> They are the auspicious cannons announcing the revival of our people.
> And our nation has determined to resist till the end.[13]

Communism – class struggle, the proletariat, the soviets in the Chinese countryside – is nowhere to be seen here. Guo uses the language of nation, recalling Liang Qichao's dream of the "new people," now through the cleansing of war.

The old society was corrupt, and the new modernizing elites that had emerged in the first decades of the twentieth century had failed as well. That left only the masses to save China. Guo brings us back to class after all.

Perhaps no one linked class to nation more clearly than Mao Zedong. He created a grand narrative of Chinese history that ultimately linked democracy or social justice and equality with "wealth and power" of the state, or modernization. Mao had the unique ability to relate the individual tragedies of tens of thousands of individuals to China's tragedy and promise.[14] The Maoist narrative began in the ancient past, when the mighty agrarian civilization of China was built on the backs of the peasantry. Idle landlords monopolized learning and land, though their claims certainly did not go unchallenged. The "revolutionary tradition" of peasant uprisings never succeeded in overthrowing the landlord system, but was no less noble for that. This noble class tradition Mao linked to the special qualities of the "Han." "The history of the Han people," Mao proclaimed in Yan'an, "demonstrates that the Chinese never submit to tyrannical rule but invariably use revolutionary means to overthrow or change it. In the thousands of years of Han history, there have been hundreds of peasant uprisings, great and small, against the dark rule of the landlords and the nobility."[15] Revolution and class and national identity: all merged into an indissoluble whole. However, this age-old story was of less interest to Mao than the intrusion of Western imperialism in the nineteenth century. The foreigners and the Chinese who worked for them – the evil class of compradors – betrayed their country, addicted the people to opium, turned China into a virtual colony, exploited Chinese labor, and displaced China's birthright to world greatness. Cheap imports threw Chinese out of work, and imperialism hindered the development of Chinese capitalism. Still, it was China's landed classes that represented the "feudal forces" of an absolutely reactionary nature. They were complacent about the loss of China's sovereignty, opposed to any kind of material or spiritual progress, and interested only in maintaining their exploitation of the peasantry.

This Maoist historical parable of defeat and loss helped make sense out of individual stories of loss and trauma. Formerly comfortable households were in decline. Perhaps grandfather became addicted to opium and began selling off land. Perhaps father became ill. The expenses of weddings and funerals could drive families, which needed to honor their ancestors and future generations properly, into bankruptcy. A remarkable number of China's leading intellectuals came from declining gentry families, including the old anarchist Wu Zhihui, the satiric writer Lu Xun, and the liberal Hu Shi, not to mention Communist leaders like Zhou Enlai and Deng Xiaoping. Perhaps this explains the general lack of sentimentality about the old society. The individual stories of millions of peasants were, of course, much harsher. Complete destitution was the result of the slightest setback. Of course, upwardly mobile peasant families like Mao's had little role in the Maoist mythology, while the nouveaux riches thrown up by urban capitalism represented only decadence. The point of the Maoist narrative was that all China had been victimized. But it had a glorious future. China was to become both a new nation (anti-imperialism) and a new society (class struggle), together the foundations upon which to build a vibrant material and spiritual civilization. Even at the height of the anti-Japanese resistance, the simple rhetoric promoted by the CCP spoke of the "new society." The "laborers" and "masses," having "suffered hardships," would "turn over" and "take charge of their own fates." These terms became common parlance.

This basic class-nationalist narrative was ritualized and spread among the people. "Speak bitterness" meetings re-enacted individual stories of suffering; subjectively, peasants relived their hardships as a precondition for joining the new society as full members. And "struggle sessions" literally and ritually punished evil and rewarded virtue, opening the door to liberation or redemption. "Redemption" was not simply for chosen individuals; it was a gift of the masses (represented by the Party) to the nation as a whole. By claiming that the nation belonged to the masses, the Communists established that the nation *was* the masses, in class terms, on the way to creating a classless society. Citizenship became a matter of both class and activism. In this way, nationalism expanded the political sphere to the nation: to encompass an entire people conceived as heroic. Politics, then, worked through the myths and rituals of mass participation. And soon, except for the "black classes" not allowed to participate, all would be *required* to participate.

The power of Communist nationalism stemmed from its ability not only to explain a social reality but to change it. To define an entire, inherited social structure as bankrupt requires a great leap of imagination; it does not stem automatically from oppression or exploitation. Chinese peasants could not have turned against the status quo without the fall of the dynastic system and the failure of its successors to form a legitimate government. Two things had to happen. First, local elites lost their own sense of self-worth. And second, the peasants were shown a new way of realizing their individual and collective ambitions. The old Confucian myth of benevolent government was destroyed by Confucian radicals in the first years of the twentieth century. The Communist Party then redefined the surviving power structures as illegitimate and taught the peasants to trust a new human agency: themselves. Village-level groups provided new bases of solidarity and ultimately increased production, the most solid manifestation of the new society in the 1940s. Peasant associations, women's associations, and poor-and-hired groups linked individual peasants to the CCP, thus incorporating peasant identity into national identity.

But not national identity into peasant identity. That is to say, the Communist Revolution was not modeled on peasant ideals. It aimed instead at modern, "rational," industrial modernization: the model of the factory, not the farm. A powerful state bureaucracy was built over the course of the revolution, capable of mobilizing humans and *matériel*. It combined Party, military, and administrative wings to reach down into every urban neighborhood and rural hamlet. In some ways, the revolution was just beginning.

# Notes

## Part I: The road to revolution, 1895–1919

1 Paul A. Cohen, *History in Three Keys: The Boxers as Event, Experience, and Myth* (New York: Columbia University Press, 1997) and Joseph W. Esherick, *The Origins of the Boxer Uprising* (Berkeley: University of California Press, 1987).
2 Boxer rhyme, cited in Joseph W. Esherick, *Origins of the Boxer Uprising*, p. 299.
3 John E. Schrecker, *Imperialism and Chinese Nationalism: Germany in Shantung* (Cambridge, MA: Harvard University Press, 1971), p. 33.
4 Cited in Paul A. Cohen, *History in Three Keys*, p. 55.
5 A tael was a Chinese ounce of silver.
6 In 1908, the U.S. Congress authorized the President to remit $10 million of the United States' share of the indemnity provided China used the money for educational purposes. This helped establish the school that became Qinghua University and funded scholarships to send students abroad. However, the total indemnities imposed on China were crushing and were not abandoned until World War II.
7 Paul A. Cohen, *History in Three Keys*, esp. pp. 211–88.
8 See the overview in Albert Feuerwerker, "The Foreign Presence in China," in *The Cambridge History of China*, vol. 12, Republican China, Part 1 (Cambridge: Cambridge University Press, 1980), pp. 128–207.
9 Succinctly described in Mary Backus Rankin, "State and Society in Early Republican Politics," *China Quarterly* 150 (June 1997), pp. 260–81.

## 1 The rise of Confucian radicalism

1 For an insightful overview, see Hao Chang, "Intellectual change and the reform movement, 1890–1898," in *The Cambridge History of China*, vol. 11, Late Ch'ing, part 2 (Cambridge: Cambridge University Press, 1980), pp. 274–338.
2 Cited in Joseph W. Esherick, *Reform and Revolution in China: The 1911 Revolution in Hunan and Hubei* (Berkeley: University of California Press, 1976), p. 12.
3 Jerome B. Grieder, *Intellectuals and the State in Modern China* (New York: The Free Press, 1981), p. 81.
4 Cited in Laurence G. Thompson, *Ta T'ung Shu: The One-World Philosophy of K'ang Yu-wei* (London: George Allen & Unwin, Ltd, 1958), p. 12.
5 "Yu Youling xiansheng shu" [Letter to Youling (Yan Fu)], *Yingbingshi heji, wenji* [Collected writings from the ice-drinker's studio, 12 vols.] (Taibei: Zhonghua Shuju, 1960), 1:108. For background, see Hao Chang, *Liang Ch'i-ch'ao and Intellectual Transition in China, 1890–1907* (Cambridge, MA: Harvard University Press, 1971).
6 Young-tsu Wong, "Revisionism Reconsidered: Kang Youwei and the Reform Movement of 1898," *Journal of Asian Studies* vol. 51, no. 3 (August 1992), p. 513.

7 Huang Zhangjian, *Wuxu bianfa shi yanjiu* [Studies on the history of the 1898 reforms] (Taibei: Zhongyang yanjiuyuan, lishi yuyanyanjiusuo, 1970), and Luke S.K. Kwong, *A Mosaic of the Hundred Days: Personalities, Politics, and Ideas of 1898* (Cambridge, MA: CEAS, Harvard University Press, 1984) are critical of Kang. For a critique of their revisionism, see Young-tsu Wong, "Revisionism Reconsidered," and Tang Zhijun and Benjamin Elman, "The 1898 Reforms Revisited," *Late Imperial China* vol. 8, no. 1 (June 1987), pp. 205–13.

8 Sue Fawn Chung, "The Much-Maligned Empress Dowager: A Revisionist Study of the Empress Dowager Tz'u-hsi in the Period 1898–1900," Ph.D. dissertation (University of California–Berkeley, 1975).

9 "Qingding lixian kaiguohui zhe" [Memorial advocating the establishment of a constitution and parliament] in Jian Bozan, *et al.*, eds, *Wuxu bianfa* [The 1898 reforms, 4 vols], vol. 2 (Shanghai: Shenzhou guoguangshe, 1953), pp. 236–7.

10 Richard John Lufrano, *Honorable Merchants: Commerce and Self-Cultivation in Late Imperial China* (Honolulu: University of Hawaii Press, 1997).

11 The examination system is described in detail by Benjamin A. Elman, *A Cultural History of Civil Examinations in Late Imperial China* (Berkeley: University of California Press, 2000).

12 Chung-li Chang, *The Chinese Gentry* (Seattle: University of Washington Press, 1955), Table 32, p. 164, figures that legal gentry (degree-holders by exam or purchase) and their families constituted about 1.3 percent of the population in the early nineteenth century and 1.9 percent later. Evelyn Sakakida Rawski, *Education and Popular Literacy in Ch'ing China* (Ann Arbor: University of Michigan Press, 1979), p. 23, concludes that functional literacy would have been much higher, 35 percent–40 percent among males and 2 percent–10 percent among females. Higher-level classical literacy could be claimed by many more than just the legal gentry, including some monks, women, government clerks, and merchants.

13 See James M. Polachek, *The Inner Opium War* (Cambridge, MA: Harvard University Press, 1992).

14 Charles O. Hucker, "The Tung-lin Movement of the Late Ming Period," pp. 132–62 in John K. Fairbank, ed., *Chinese Thought and Institutions* (Chicago: University of Chicago Press, 1963).

15 These paragraphs are indebted to Benjamin A. Elman's *From Philosophy to Philology: Intellectual and Social Aspects of Change in Late Imperial China* (Cambridge, MA: Harvard University Press, 1984) and *Classicism, Politics, and Kinship: The Ch'ang-chou School of New Text Confucianism in Late Imperial China* (Berkeley: University of California Press, 1990).

16 Elman, *Classicism, Politics, and Kinship*, p. xxv.

17 His *An Inquiry into the Classics Forged During the Xin Period (Xinxue weijing kao)* of 1891, for example.

18 Kang presented *Kongzi gaizhi kao* to the emperor in 1898.

19 Translated in Fung Yu-lan, *A History of Chinese Philosophy* (trans. Derk Bodde), vol. 2 (Princeton: Princeton University Press, 1952–3), p. 675, with minor modifications.

20 *Datong shu* was finally published in full in 1935, after Kang's death, though he claimed to have finished it in 1902 and published parts of it in the early 1910s; parts of it were circulated among his disciples in the 1890s.

21 Liu Dapeng, cited in Henrietta Harrison, *Inventing the Nation: China* (London: Arnold, 2001), p. 91.

22 See Anne Cheng, "Nationalism, Citizenship, and the Old Text/New Text Controversy in Late Nineteenth Century China" in Joshua A. Fogel and Peter Zarrow, eds, *Imagining the People: Chinese Intellectuals and the Concept of Citizenship, 1890–1920* (Armonk, NY: M.E. Sharpe, 1997), pp. 61–81.

## 2   1911: History and historiography

1   See Winston Hsieh, *Chinese Historiography on the Revolution of 1911* (Stanford: Hoover Institution Press, 1975), for the first two schools. The third school was pioneered in the essays in Mary Wright, ed., *China in Revolution: The First Phase, 1900–1913* (New Haven: Yale University Press, 1968), and worked out in Joseph W. Esherick, *Reform and Revolution in China: The 1911 Revolution in Hunan and Hubei* (Berkeley: University of California Press, 1976).

2   Classical Chinese was the language of high Japanese culture as well. A Japanese view of the Chinese revolutionaries can be found in Miyazaki Tôten, *My Thirty-three Years' Dream: The Autobiography of Miyazaki Tôten* (trans. Etô Shinkichi and Marius B. Jansen) (Princeton: Princeton University Press, 1982).

3   The fates of the different Manchu communities are clearly outlined in Edward Rhoads, *Manchus & Han: Ethnic Relations and Political Power in Late Qing and Early Republican China, 1861–1928* (Seattle: University of Washington Press, 2000), pp. 187–205.

4   Mao Zedong, "On New Democracy," *Selected Works of Mao Tse-tung* (Beijing: Foreign Languages Press, 1967), vol. 2, pp. 339–84.

5   Li Dazhao, "Pingmin zhuyi" [Democracy], *Li Dazhao wenji* [Selected writings of Li Dazhao] (Beijing: Renmin chubanshe, 1984), vol. 2, p. 588.

6   "You pingmin zhengzhi dao gongren zhengzhi" [From popular politics to workers' politics], ibid., vol. 2, p. 502.

7   Karl Marx and Friedrich Engels, *The Communist Manifesto* (New York: Washington Square Press, 1964), pp. 57, 61–2.

8   See Marie-Claire Bergère, "The Chinese Bourgeoisie, 1911–37" in *The Cambridge History of China*, vol. 12, Republican China, part 1 (Cambridge: Cambridge University Press, 1983), pp. 722–825; and *The Golden Age of the Chinese Bourgeoisie, 1911–1937* (trans. Janet Lloyd) (Cambridge: Cambridge University Press, 1989).

9   Wellington K.K. Chan, "Government, Merchants, and Industry to 1911" in *The Cambridge History of China*, vol. 11, Late Ch'ing, part 2 (Cambridge: Cambridge University Press, 1980), p. 416.

10   See for example Ma Yong, "Xinhai geming: xiandaihua de zhuguan yizu yu keguanxiaoguo" [The Revolution of 1911: The subjective will for modernization and its objective results], *Jindaishi yanjiu* 1 (1995), pp. 138–63.

11   Joseph W. Esherick, *Reform and Revolution in China*, p. 1.

12   See Mary Backus Rankin, *Elite Activism and Political Transformation in China: Zhejiang Province, 1865–1911* (Stanford: Stanford University Press, 1986); Roger Thompson, *China's Local Councils in the Age of Constitutional Reform* (Cambridge, MA: Harvard University Press, 1995).

13   Mary Backus Rankin, *Elite Activism and Political Transformation*, p. 7.

14   For discussions on how this public sphere was forming in the late Qing, see the symposium in Philip C.C. Huang, ed., "'Public Sphere'/'Civil Society' in China?" *Modern China* 19, no. 2 (April 1993), pp. 107–240, and the summary in Peter Zarrow, "The Origins of Modern Chinese Concepts of Privacy: Notes on Social Structure and Moral Discourse" in Bonnie S. McDougall and Anders Hansson, eds, *Chinese Concepts of Privacy* (Leiden: Brill, 2002), pp. 122–9.

15   Michael Tsin, "Imagining 'Society' in Early Twentieth-Century China" in Joshua A. Fogel and Peter Zarrow, eds, *Imagining the People: Chinese Intellectuals and the Concept of Citizenship, 1890–1920* (Armonk, NY: M.E. Sharpe, 1997), pp. 212–31.

16   P'eng-yuan Chang, "Political Participation and Political Elites in Early Republican China: The Parliament of 1913–1914," trans. Andrew J. Nathan, *Journal of Asian Studies* vol. 37, no. 2 (February 1978), pp. 293–313.

17   Joseph W. Esherick, *Reform and Revolution*, pp. 256–7.

18 Cited in Jerome Grieder, *Intellectuals and the State in Modern China* (New York: The Free Press, 1981), p. 137.

19 There is a large literature on the subject of state–society relations, a topic returned to often in this volume. A succinct and pointed review is Frederic Wakeman, Jr, "Models of Historical Change: The Chinese State and Society, 1839–1898" in Kenneth Lieberthal, *et al.*, eds, *Perspectives on Modern China: Four Anniversaries* (Armonk, NY: M.E. Sharpe, 1991), pp. 68–77; see also his "The Civil Society and Public Sphere Debate: Western Reflections on Chinese Political Culture," *Modern China* vol. 19, no. 2 (April 1993), pp. 108–83.

20 See Edward A. McCord, "Local Military Power and Elite Formation: The Liu Family of Xingyi Country, Guizhou" in Joseph W. Esherick and Mary Backus Rankin, eds, *Chinese Local Elites and Patterns of Dominance* (Berkeley: University of California Press, 1990), pp. 162–90.

21 Kathryn Bernhardt, *Rent, Taxes, and Peasant Resistance: The Lower Yangzi Region, 1840–1950* (Stanford: Stanford University Press, 1992).

22 See in general the essays in Joseph W. Esherick and Mary Backus Rankin, eds, *Chinese Local Elites and Patterns of Dominance* (Berkeley: University of California Press, 1990); also see Mary Backus Rankin, *Elite Activism and Political Transformation in China: Zhejiang Province, 1865–1911* (Stanford: Stanford University Press, 1986).

23 Michael Gasster, "The Republican Revolutionary Movement" in *The Cambridge History of China*, vol. 11, Late Ch'ing, part 2 (Cambridge: Cambridge University Press, 1980), p. 516.

24 Mary Backus Rankin, "State and Society in Early Republican Politics, 1912–18," *China Quarterly* 150 (June 1997), p. 273.

25 For Chinese anarchism, see Peter Zarrow, *Anarchism and Chinese Political Culture* (New York: Columbia University Press, 1990); and Arif Dirlik, *Anarchism in the Chinese Revolution* (Berkeley: University of California Press, 1991).

26 Benedict Anderson, *Imagined Communities: Reflections on the Origin and Spread of Nationalism* (London: Verso, New Left Books, 1993), p. 26.

27 David Der-wei Wang, *Fin-de-Siècle Splendor: Repressed Modernities of Late Qing Fiction, 1849–1911* (Stanford: Stanford University Press, 1997); Theodore Huters, "A New Way of Writing: The Possibilities for Literature in Late Qing China, 1895–1908," *Modern China* vol. 14, no. 3 (July 1988).

28 Cited in Theodore Huters, "A New Way of Writing", p. 253.

29 Liu T'ieh-yun (Harold Shadick, trans.), *The Travels of Lao Ts'an* (Ithaca: Cornell University Press, 1952), pp. 7, 9, 11.

30 Ibid., pp. 125, 132.

31 Wu Jianren (Patrick Hanan, trans.), *The Sea of Regret: Two Turn-of-the-Century Chinese Romantic Novels* (Honolulu: University of Hawaii Press, 1995), p. 163.

32 The *jingwei*, a mythical bird, tried to fill the ocean with pebbles; Qiu Jin reconstructs a parable about futility into one of hope. See Amy D. Dooling and Kristina M. Torgeson, *Writing Women in Modern China: An Anthology of Women's Literature From the Early Twentieth Century* (New York: Columbia University Press, 1998), pp. 43–81.

33 Quotations from ibid., pp. 55, 72.

## 3 Ideas and ideals in the fall of the Qing

1 Tan Sitong, *An Exposition of Benevolence: the Jen-hsueh of T'an Ssu-t'ung*, trans. Chan Sin-wai (Hong Kong: Chinese University Press, 1984), p. 165 (modified).

2 The problem of identity has become a major focus of academic research. See Frank Dikötter, *The Discourse of Race in Modern China* (London: Hurst &

Company, 1992); Prasenjit Duara, *Rescuing History From the Nation: Questioning Narratives of Modern China* (Chicago: University of Chicago Press, 1995); and James Townsend, "Chinese Nationalism," *The Australian Journal of Chinese Affairs* 27 (January 1992), pp. 97–130. Joseph R. Levenson, *Confucian China and Its Modern Fate* (Berkeley: University of California Press, 1965), esp. 1:95–108, highlighted the problem. More recent work tries to relate traditional forms of identity-formation to national identity – see Bryna Goodman, *Native Place, City, and Nation: Regional Networks and Identities in Shanghai, 1853–1937* (Berkeley: University of California Press, 1995); and Kenneth Pomeranz, "Ritual Imitation and Political Identity in North China: The Late Imperial Legacy and the Chinese National State Revisited," *Twentieth Century China* vol. 23, no. 1 (November 1997), pp. 1–30. The locus classicus that reopened the topic of nationalism is Benedict Anderson, *Imagined Communities: Reflections on the Origin and Spread of Nationalism* (London: Verso, New Left Books, 1983).

3  See Pamela Crossley, *Translucent Mirror: History and Identity in Qing Imperial Ideology* (Berkeley: University of California Press, 1999); and Mark C. Elliott, *The Manchu Way: The Eight Banners and Ethnic Identity in Late Imperial China* (Stanford: Stanford University Press, 2001).

4  Benedict Anderson, *Imagined Communities*, pp. 6–7.

5  See James Watson, "Standardizing the Gods: The Promotion of T'ien Hou ('Empress of Heaven')" in David Johnson, Andrew Nathan, and Evelyn Rawski, eds, *Popular Culture in Late Imperial China* (Berkeley: University of California Press, 1985), pp. 292–324; and "The Structure of Chinese Funerary Rites" in Evelyn Rawski and James Watson, eds, *Death Ritual in Late Imperial and Modern China* (Berkeley: University of California Press, 1988), pp. 3–19.

6  See Kenneth Pomeranz, "Ritual Imitation and Political Identity" in Prasenjit Duara, *Culture, Power, and the State: Rural North China, 1900–1942* (Stanford: Stanford University Press, 1988).

7  Victor H. Mair, "Language and Ideology in the Written Popularizations of the *Sacred Edict*" in David Johnson, *et al.*, eds, *Popular Culture in Late Imperial China*, pp. 325–59.

8  Cited in Bryna Goodman, *Native Place, City, and Nation: Regional Networks and Identities in Shanghai, 1853–1937* (Berkeley: University of California Press, 1995), p. 13.

9  Ibid., p. 313.

10 See Benjamin Schwartz, *In Search of Wealth and Power: Yen Fu and the West* (Cambridge, MA: Harvard University Press, 1964) for the definitive English-language study of Yan Fu; see also James Reeve Pusey, *China and Charles Darwin* (Cambridge, MA: Harvard University Press, 1983) for a broader study of the issue.

11 Richard Hofstadter, *Social Darwinism in American Thought* (Boston: Beacon Press, 1955), p. 3.

12 Ibid., p. 5.

13 "The word first entered … [British] politics in the 1870s, and was still regarded as a neologism at the end of that decade. It exploded into general use in the 1890s." Eric Hobsbawm, *The Age of Empire* (New York: Pantheon Books, 1987), p. 60.

14 Wu Zhihui, cited in Peter Zarrow, *Anarchism and Chinese Political Culture* (New York: Columbia University Press, 1990), p. 121.

15 Cited in Jerome B. Grieder, *Intellectuals and the State in Modern China* (New York: The Free Press, 1981), p. 117.

16 Cited in Tse-tsung Chow, "The Anti-Confucian Movement in Early Republican China" in A.F. Wright, ed., *The Confucian Persuasion* (Stanford: Stanford University Press, 1960), p. 292.

17 As the modern philosopher and historian Isaiah Berlin, half-jokingly, proposed.

18  See Kenneth B. Pyle, *The New Generation in Meiji Japan: Problems of Cultural Identity, 1885–1895* (Stanford: Stanford University Press, 1969).
19  Hao Chang, *Liang Ch'i-ch'ao*. Liang's ideas on citizenship are also discussed in Peter Zarrow, "Introduction: Citizenship in China and the West" in Joshua A. Fogel and Peter G. Zarrow, eds, *Imagining the People: Chinese Intellectuals and the Concept of Citizenship, 1890–1920* (Armonk, NY: M.E. Sharpe, 1997), pp. 3–38, and Andrew J. Nathan, *Chinese Democracy* (Berkeley: University of California Press, 1986), pp. 45–66.
20  Cited in Hao Chang, *Liang Ch'i-ch'ao*, p. 164.
21  Liang Qichao, *Xinmin shuo* [On the new people] (Taibei: Taiwan Zhonghua, 1959), pp. 12–16; see Hao Chang, *Liang Ch'i-ch'ao and Intellectual Transition in China, 1890–1907* (Cambridge, MA: Harvard University Press, 1971), pp. 151–2.
22  Cited in Wm. Theodore de Bary, *et al.*, eds, *Sources of Chinese Tradition*, 2 vols (New York: Columbia University Press, 1960), 2:95.
23  Cited in Hao Chang, *Liang Ch'i-ch'ao*, p. 100.
24  Liang Qichao, *Xinmin shuo*, p. 6.
25  Cited in Joan Judge, *Print and Politics: Shibao and the Culture of Reform in late Qing China* (Stanford: Stanford University Press, 1996), p. 59, modified.
26  For a somewhat different interpretation, see Stephen Angle, *Human Rights and Chinese Thought: A Cross-Cultural Inquiry* (Cambridge: Cambridge University Press, 2002), pp. 140–62.
27  Zou Rong, *Gemingjun* [Revolutionary army], trans. John Lust, *The Revolutionary Army: A Chinese Nationalist Tract of 1903* (The Hague: Mouton & Co., 1968), p. 1.
28  Cited in Edward J.M. Rhoads, *Manchus & Han: Ethnic Relations and Political Power in Late Qing and Early Republican China, 1861–1928* (Seattle: University of Washington Press, 2000), p. 189.
29  Hu Hanmin, translated in de Bary, *Sources of Chinese Tradition*, 2:101–2.
30  See Frank Dikötter, *The Discourse of Race in Modern China*.
31  Zhang has been historically controversial for a number of reasons, including the sheer difficulty of much of his prose. A recent overview is Young-tsu Wong, *Search for Modern Nationalism: Zhang Binglin and Revolutionary China, 1869–1936* (Hong Kong: Oxford University Press, 1989).
32  For Qing attitudes toward ethnicity, see Mark Elliott, *The Manchu Way*, and Pamela Crossley, "Thinking About Ethnicity in Early Modern China," *Late Imperial China* vol. 11, no. 1 (June 1990), pp. 1–35, and especially *Translucent Mirror*.
33  Patricia Ebrey, "Surnames and Han Chinese Identity" in Melissa J. Brown, ed., *Negotiating Ethnicities in China and Taiwan* (Berkeley: Center for Chinese Studies, University of California, 1996), pp. 19–36.
34  See Don C. Price, "The Ancestral Nation and China's Political Culture," Centennial Symposium on Sun Yat-sen's Founding of the Kuomingtang for Revolution (Taibei, Taiwan, 19–23 November 1994) and "Early Chinese Revolutionaries: Autonomy, Family and Nationalism" in *Family Process and Political Process in Modern Chinese History* (Taibei: Modern History Institute, Academia Sinica, 1992), pp. 1015–53.
35  See Anne Cheng, "Nationalism, Citizenship, and the Old Text/New Text Controversy in Late Nineteenth Century China" in Joshua A. Fogel and Peter Zarrow, eds, *Imagining the People*, pp. 72–8.
36  See Martin Bernal, "Liu Shih-p'ei and National Essence" in Charlotte Furth, ed., *The Limits of Change: Essays on Conservative Alternatives in Republican China* (Cambridge, MA: Harvard University Press, 1976), pp. 90–112; Laurence A. Schneider, "National Essence and the New Intelligentsia" in ibid., pp. 57–89; and Lydia Liu, *Translingual Practice: Literature, National Culture, and Translated Modernity – China, 1900–1937* (Stanford: Stanford University Press, 1995), pp. 239–56.

37  Cited in Wm. Theodore de Bary, *et al.*, eds, *Sources of Chinese Tradition*, vol. 2, pp. 102–3, modified.
38  Ibid., vol. 2, p. 104, modified.
39  See Prasenjit Duara, *Rescuing History From the Nation*, pp. 115–46.

## 4  From the military dictator to the warlords

1  Ernest P. Young, "Nationalism, Reform, and Republican Revolution: China in Early Twentieth Century" in James B. Crowley, ed., *Modern East Asia: Essays in Interpretation* (New York: Harcourt, Brace and World, 1970), p. 154.
2  Edward Friedman, *Backward Toward Revolution*, p. 188.
3  Bryna Goodman, *Native Place, City, and Nation*, pp. 217–22.
4  Jerome Chen, *Yuan Shih-k'ai* (Stanford: Stanford University Press, 1972), pp. 116–28; and Ernest P. Young, *The Presidency of Yuan Shih-k'ai* (Ann Arbor: University of Michigan Press, 1977), pp. 123–9.
5  The radical was Shen Dingyi, a sometime colleague of Sun Yat-sen. Cited in R. Keith Schoppa, *Blood Road: The Mystery of Shen Dingyi in Revolutionary China* (Berkeley: University of California Press, 1995), p. 29 (modified).
6  See Ernest P. Young, *The Presidency of Yuan Shih-k'ai*, pp. 212–14.
7  For discussions of Yuan's attempt to become emperor, see Jerome Chen, *Yuan Shih-k'ai*, pp. 162–78; Ernest P. Young, *The Presidency of Yuan Shih-k'ai*, pp. 210–40; and Peter Zarrow, "Political Ritual in the Early Republic of China" in Kai-wing Chow, Kevin Doak, and Poshek Fu, eds, *Constructing Nationhood in Modern East Asia: Narrative Schemes, Nostalgia, and Ambiguity of Identities* (Ann Arbor: University of Michigan Press, 2001), pp. 149–88.
8  See Andrew J. Nathan, "A Constitutional Republic: the Peking Government, 1916–28" in *The Cambridge History of China*, vol. 12 (Cambridge: Cambridge University Press, 1983), pp. 256–83.
9  Arthur N. Waldron, "The Warlord: Twentieth Century Chinese Understandings of Violence, Militarism, and Imperialism," *American Historical Review* vol. 96, no. 4 (October 1991), pp. 1073–100.
10  The point and the citation are from Hsi-sheng Ch'i, *Warlord Politics in China, 1916–1928* (Stanford: Stanford University Press, 1976), pp. 183–5.
11  These events are well analyzed in Arthur Waldron, *From War to Nationalism: China's Turning Point, 1924–1925* (Cambridge: Cambridge University Press, 1995), pp. 181–207.
12  Edward A. McCord, *The Power of the Gun: The Emergence of Modern Chinese Warlordism* (Berkeley: University of California Press, 1993).
13  Cited in Hans van de Ven, "The Military in the Republic," *China Quarterly* no. 150 (June 1997), p. 357.
14  Andrew J. Nathan, "A Constitutional Republic," p. 259; see also his *Peking Politics, 1918–1923: Factionalism and the Failure of Constitutionalism* (Berkeley: University of California Press, 1976).
15  Edward A. McCord, "Burn, Kill, Rape, and Rob: Military Atrocities, Warlordism, and Anti-Warlordism in Republican China" in Diana Lary and Stephen MacKinnon, eds, *Scars of War: The Impact of Warfare on Modern China* (Vancouver: University of British Columbia Press, 2001), p. 21: in the spring of 1918 the military governor of Shandong, Zhang Huaizhi, led his eastern troops into Hunan.
16  Thomas G. Rawski, *China's Republican Economy: An Introduction* (Toronto: University of Toronto–York University Joint Centre on Modern East Asia, 1978).
17  Arthur Waldron, *From War to Nationalism*.
18  Cited in Arthur Waldron, *From War to Nationalism*, p. 143.

## 5 Social conditions in the countryside

1 Loren Brandt, "Reflections on China's Late 19th and Early 20th-Century Economy," *China Quarterly* no. 150 (June 1997), p. 284.
2 See G. William Skinner, "Marketing and Social Structure in Rural China," Parts I, II, III, *Journal of Asian Studies* 26, nos 1–3 (November 1964, February 1965, May 1965), pp. 3–44, 195–228, 363–400; and "Chinese Peasants and the Closed Community: An Open and Shut Case," *Comparative Studies in Society and History* 13, no. 1 (July 1971), pp. 270–81.
3 The figures are reviewed in Madeleine Zelin, "The Structure of the Chinese Economy during the Qing Period: Some Thoughts on the 150th Anniversary of the Opium War" in Kenneth Lieberthal, *et al.*, eds, *Perspectives on Modern China: Four Anniversaries* (Armonk, NY: M.E. Sharpe, 1991), pp. 32–3.
4 Lloyd Eastman, *Family, Fields, and Ancestors: Constancy and Change in China's Social and Economic History, 1550–1949* (New York: Oxford University Press, 1988), p. 75.
5 These figures are from Ramon Myers, "The Agrarian System" in *The Cambridge History of China*, vol. 13, Republican China, part 2 (Cambridge: Cambridge University Press, 1986), pp. 250–1.
6 Prasenjit Duara, *Culture, Power, and the State: Rural North China, 1900–1942* (Stanford: Stanford University Press, 1988).
7 Phil Billingsley, *Bandits in Republican China* (Stanford: Stanford University Press, 1988).
8 In addition to ibid., see the fine descriptions in Elizabeth J. Perry, *Rebels and Revolutionaries in North China, 1845–1945* (Stanford: Stanford University Press, 1980); and Edward Friedman, *Backward Toward Revolution: The Chinese Revolution Party* (Berkeley: University of California Press, 1974).
9 The state of our knowledge is ably summarized in Lucien Bianco, "Peasant Movements" in *The Cambridge History of China*, vol. 13, pp. 270–328 and "Rural Tax Resistance in Early Republican China (1912–1937): The Variety of Tax Targets," paper delivered at the Conference on Eighty Years History of the Republic of China, 1912–1991 (Taibei, 11–15 August 1991).
10 This description is based on Joyce Madancy, "Revolution, Religion, and the Poppy: Opium and the Rebellion of the Sixteenth Emperor in Early Republican Fujian," *Republican China* vol. 21, no. 1 (November 1995), pp. 1–41.
11 See Elizabeth J. Perry, *Rebels and Revolutionaries*.
12 Henry A. Landsberger includes the landless in his definition of peasants, "Peasant Unrest: Themes and Variations" in Henry A. Landsberger, ed., *Rural Protest: Peasant Movements and Social Change* (London: Macmillan, 1973), pp. 6–18.
13 Theda Skocpol, *States and Social Revolutions: A Comparative Analysis of France, Russia, and China* (Cambridge: Cambridge University Press, 1979), esp. pp. 114–15; see also William Skinner, "What Makes Peasants Revolutionary?" in Robert P. Weller and Scott E. Guggenheim, eds, *Power and Protest in Countryside: Rural Unrest in Asia, Europe, and Latin America* (Durham, NC: Duke University Press, 1989), pp. 157–79. Complex issues are clearly discussed by Daniel Little, *Understanding Peasant China: Case Studies in the Philosophy of Social Science* (New Haven: Yale University Press, 1989).
14 The "moral economy" school has exercised great ingenuity in profiling a kind of "collective unconsciousness" of the peasantry; although somewhat exaggerated, it is clear that a sense of injustice plays a role in peasant perceptions. The locus classicus is James Scott, *The Moral Economy of the Peasant: Rebellion and Subsistence in Southeast Asia* (New Haven: Yale University Press, 1976), and see again Daniel Little, *Understanding Peasant China*.

15 Barrington Jr Moore, *Reflections on the Causes of Human Misery and Upon Certain Proposals to Eliminate Them* (Boston: Beacon Press, 1972), p. 53: "... exploitation forms part of an exchange of goods and services when 1) the goods and services exchanged are quite obviously not of equivalent value, and 2) one party to the exchange uses a substantial degree of coercion."

16 See James C. Scott's *Weapons of the Weak: Everyday Forms of Peasant Resistance* (New Haven: Yale University Press, 1985) and *Domination and the Arts of Resistance: Hidden Transcripts* (New Haven: Yale University Press, 1990).

17 This entire chapter is indebted to Elizabeth J. Perry's *Rebels and Revolutionaries in North China, 1845–1945*, which seminally treats a century of peasant activities in the Huaibei region (between the Huai and Yellow Rivers) in terms of ecological and adaptive factors.

18 Cited in Elizabeth J. Perry, *Rebels and Revolutionaries*, pp. 165–6.

## 6 Urban and social change

1 Mingzheng Shi, "From Imperial Gardens to Public Parks: The Transformation of Urban Space in Early Twentieth-Century Beijing," *Modern China* vol. 24, no. 3 (July 1998), pp. 219–54.

2 Henrietta Harrison, *The Making of the Republican Citizen: Political Ceremonies and Symbols in China, 1911–1929* (New York: Oxford University Press, 1999); citizenship is also discussed in Merle Goldman and Elizabeth J. Perry, eds, *Changing Meanings of Citizenship in Modern China* (Cambridge, MA: Harvard University Press, 2002); and Joshua A. Fogel and Peter Zarrow, eds, *Imagining the People: Chinese Intellectuals and the Concept of Citizenship, 1890–1920* (Armonk, NY: M.E. Sharpe, 1997).

3 David Strand, *Rickshaw Beijing: City People and Politics in the 1920s* (Berkeley: University of California Press, 1989).

4 Marie-Claire Bergère, *The Golden Age of the Chinese Bourgeoisie, 1911–1937*, trans. Janet Lloyd (Cambridge: Cambridge University Press, 1989).

5 Marie-Claire Bergère, "The Chinese Bourgeoisie, 1911–37" in *The Cambridge History of China*, vol. 12, Republican China, part 1 (Cambridge: Cambridge University Press, 1983), p. 730. This section is also indebted to *The Golden Age of the Chinese Bourgeoisie*.

6 For a focused and suggestive review of the literature on Shanghai as of the mid-1990s, see Wen-hsin Yeh, "Shanghai Modernity: Commerce and Culture in a Republican City," *China Quarterly* no. 150 (June 1997), pp. 376–94.

7 David Strand, "Mediation, Representation and Repression: Local Elites in 1920s Beijing" in Joseph W. Esherick and Mary Backus Rankin, eds, *Chinese Local Elites and Patterns of Domination* (Berkeley: University of California Press, 1990), pp. 216–35; and David Strand, *Rickshaw Beijing*.

8 Christopher A. Reed, "Sooty Sons of Vulcan," *Republican China* vol. 20, no. 2 (April 1995), pp. 28–34.

9 Elizabeth J. Perry, *Shanghai on Strike: The Politics of Chinese Labor* (Stanford: Stanford University Press, 1993); also her "Labor Divided: Sources of State Formation in Modern China" in Joel S. Migdal, Atul Kohli, and Vivienne Shue, eds, *State Power and Social Forces: Domination and Transformation in the Third World* (Cambridge: Cambridge University Press, 1994), pp. 143–73.

10 Cited in Elizabeth J. Perry, *Shanghai on Strike*, p. 47.

11 See Brian Martin, *The Shanghai Green Gang: Politics and Organized Crime, 1919–1937* (Berkeley: University of California Press, 1996).

12 Mark Selden, "The Proletariat, Revolutionary Change, and the State" in Immanuel Wallerstein, ed., *Labor in the World Social Structure* (London: Sage, 1982), p. 86.

13 Jean Chesneaux, *The Chinese Labor Movement, 1919–1927* (Stanford: Stanford University Press, 1968).

14 Christopher A. Reed, "Sooty Sons of Vulcan."

15 Cited in Gail Hershatter, *The Workers of Tianjin (1900–1949)* (Stanford: Stanford University Press, 1986), p. 69.

16 Fan Zhongyan (989–1052), cited in E-tu Zen Sun, "The Growth of the Academic Community, 1912–1914" in *The Cambridge History of China*, vol. 13, Republican China, part 2 (Cambridge: Cambridge University Press, 1986), p. 365.

17 Hu Fengxiang and Zhang Wenjian, *Zhongguo jindai shixue sichao yu liupai* [Intellectual trends and schools in modern Chinese historiography] (Shanghai: Huadong shifan daxue chubanshe, 1991), p. 257.

18 Wen-hsin Yeh, *Alienated Academy: Culture and Politics in Republican China, 1919–1937* (Cambridge, MA: Harvard University Press, 1990).

19 See Joan Judge, "Re-forming the Feminine: Female Literacy and the Legacy of 1898" in Rebecca E. Karl and Peter Zarrow, eds, *Rethinking the 1898 Reform Period: Political and Cultural Change in Late Qing China* (Cambridge, MA: Harvard University Asia Center, 2002), pp. 158–79.

20 Liang Qichao, *Yinbingshi heji* [Collected writing from the ice-drinker's studio, 12 vols] (Taibei: Zhonghua shuju, 1960), wenji 1:37–44.

21 Joan Judge, "Citizens or Mothers of Citizens?" in Merle Goldman and Elizabeth J. Perry, eds, *Changing Meanings of Citizenship*, pp. 23–43.

22 Chen Xiefen, "Crisis in the Women's World" in Amy D. Dooling and Kristina M. Torgeson, eds, *Writing Women in Modern China: An Anthology of Women's Literature From the Early Twentieth Century* (New York: Columbia University Press, 1998), pp. 84, 85.

23 See Rebecca E. Karl, "'Slavery,' Citizenship and Gender in Late Qing China's Global Context" in Rebecca E. Karl and Peter Zarrow, eds, *Rethinking the 1898 Reform Period*, pp. 212–44.

24 He Zhen, cited in Peter Zarrow, "He Zhen and Anarcho-Feminism in China," *Journal of Asian Studies* 47, no. 4 (November 1988), pp. 801, 810.

## 7 Intellectuals, the Republic, and a new culture

1 For general studies of the intellectual background, see Jerome B. Grieder, *Intellectuals and the State in Modern China* (New York: The Free Press, 1981), pp. 203–79 (chapter 6); Tse-tsung Chow, *The May Fourth Movement: Intellectual Revolution in Modern China* (Stanford: Stanford University Press, 1967); Vera Schwarcz, *The Chinese Enlightenment: Intellectuals and the Legacy of the May Fourth Movement of 1919* (Berkeley: University of California Press, 1985); and Yüsheng Lin, *The Crisis of Chinese Consciousness: Radical Anti-traditionalism in the May Fourth Era* (Madison: University of Wisconsin Press, 1979); Timothy B. Weston, "The Formation and Positioning of the New Culture Community, 1913–1917," *Modern China* vol. 24, no. 3 (July 1998), pp. 255–84 is especially insightful on the first years of the Republic.

2 Cited in E-tu Zen Sun, "The Growth of the Academic Community, 1912–1914" in *The Cambridge History of China*, vol. 13, Republican China, part 2 (Cambridge: Cambridge University Press, 1986), p. 373 (modified).

3 Jerome B. Grieder, *Intellectuals and the State*, pp. 210–11, 215.

4 Yang Du and Sun Yujun, *Zhengfu gongbao* (Government gazette – hereafter ZFGB) 1304 (25 December 1915), p. 990.

5  Shen Yunpei, ZFGB no. 1304 (25 December 1915), p. 987.
6  ZFGB 1293 (13 December 1915), p. 456.
7  Yang Du, "Junxian jiuguo lun" (A constitutional monarchy will save the nation), *Yang Du ji* [Collected works of Yang Du] (Changsha: Hunan renmin chubanshe, 1986), p. 568.
8  See Peter Zarrow, "Liang Qichao and the Notion of Civil Society in Republican China" in Joshua A. Fogel and Peter Zarrow, eds, *Imagining the People: Chinese Intellectuals and the Concept of Citizenship, 1890–1920* (Armonk, NY: M.E. Sharpe, 1997), pp. 232–57.
9  ZFGB 1293 (13 December 1915), pp. 471–2.
10 Statement of the Chou'an hui, cited in Jerome Chen, *Yuan Shih-k'ai* (Stanford: Stanford University Press, 1972), p. 169.
11 Cited in R. Keith Schoppa, *Blood Road: The Mystery of Shen Dingyi in Revolutionary China* (Berkeley: University of California Press, 1995), p. 44 (modified). See also R. Keith Schoppa, "Province and Nation: The Chekiang Provincial Autonomy Movement, 1917–1927," *Journal of Asian Studies* vol. 36, no. 4 (August 1977), pp. 661–74.
12 See Prasenjit Duara, "Provincial Narratives of the Nation: Centralism and Federalism in Republican China" in Harumi Befu, ed., *Cultural Nationalism in East Asia: Representation and Identity* (Berkeley: Institute of East Asian Studies, University of California Press, 1993), pp. 9–35; *Rescuing History From the Nation: Questioning Narratives of Modern China* (Chicago: University of Chicago Press, 1995), pp. 177–204 (chapter 6); Jean Chesneaux, "The Federalist Movement in China" in Jack Gray, ed., *Modern China's Search for a Political Form* (Oxford: Oxford University Press, 1969), pp. 96–137; also Leslie H. Chen, "Chen Jiongming (1878–1933) and the Chinese Federalist Movement," *Republican China* vol. 17, no. 1 (November 1991), pp. 21–37.
13 See John Fitzgerald, *Awakening China: Politics, Culture, and Class in the Nationalist Revolution* (Stanford: Stanford University Press, 1996), pp. 150–67.
14 Prasenjit Duara, *Rescuing History From the Nation*, p. 158.
15 Cited in Jerome B. Grieder, *Intellectuals and the State*, p. 223 (modified). Originally named simply "*Youth*," the journal's name was changed to "*New Youth*," by which it became universally known, in 1916.
16 Cited in Ssu-yu Teng and John K. Fairbank, *China's Response to the West: A Documentary Survey 1839–1923* (New York: Atheneum, 1970), p. 241 (modified).
17 Cited in Jerome B. Grieder, *Intellectuals and the State in Modern China*, pp. 225–6.
18 See Chen's "Dong Xi minzu genben sixiang zhi chayi" (Basic intellectual differences between the nations of the East and the West), *Duxiu wencun* [Collected works of Chen Duxiu, 4 vols] (Shanghai: Yadong tushuguan, 1924), pp. 35–40.
19 Chen Duxiu, "Jinri zhi jiaoyu fangzhen" (The direction of education today), *Duxiu wencun*, p. 23.
20 "Laodong jiaoyu wenti" (The problem of labor education), *Li Dazhao wenji* [Selected writings of Li Dazhao, 2 vols] (Beijing: Renmin chubanshe, 1984), vol. 1, p. 632.
21 "Zhanhou zhi furen wenti" (The problem of post-war women), ibid., vol. 1, p. 635.
22 "Shumin de shengli" (The victory of the common people), ibid., vol. 1, p. 594.
23 "Bolshevism de shengli" (The victory of Bolshevism), ibid., vol. 1, pp. 598–9. Li's conversion to Marxism is discussed in Chapter 10.
24 See Jerome B. Grieder, *Hu Shih and the Chinese Renaissance: Liberalism in the Chinese Revolution 1917–1937* (Cambridge, MA: Harvard University Press, 1970); and *Intellectuals and the State*, pp. 226–79ff.
25 Cited in Jerome B. Grieder, *Intellectuals and the State*, pp. 231–2 (romanization modified).

26 Hu's political views will be treated more fully in Chapter 9. Citations are from ibid., pp. 242, 239, 251.

27 Chen Duxiu, "Bo Kang Youwei zhi zongtong zongli shu" (Contra Kang Youwei's petition to the president and premier), *Duxiu wencun*, p. 100.

28 Chen Duxiu, "Xianfa yu Kongjiao" (The constitution and Confucianism), *Duxiu wencun*, pp. 107–9; also see "Fubi yu zun-Kong" (The restoration and respect for Confucius), ibid., p. 167.

29 Chen Duxiu, "Kongzi zhi dao yu xiandai shenghuo" (The Way of Confucius and contemporary life), *Duxiu wencun*, p. 117.

30 Chen Duxiu, "Jiu sixiang yu guoti wenti" (Old thought and the problem of the national polity), *Duxiu wencun*, pp. 148, 149.

31 See Lydia H. Liu, *Translingual Practice: Literature, National Culture, and Translated Modernity – China, 1900–1937* (Stanford: Stanford University Press, 1995), pp. 87–9.

32 See Marina Svensson, *The Chinese Conception of Human Rights: The Debate on Human Rights in China, 1898–1949*, Ph.D. dissertation (Lund: University of Lund, 1996), p. 146.

33 See Lionel M. Jensen, *Manufacturing Confucianism: Chinese Tradition and Universal Civilization* (Durham, NC: Duke University Press, 1997), pp. 153–265.

34 Arif Dirlik, *Anarchism in the Chinese Revolution* (Berkeley: University of California Press, 1991), p. 2. See also Dirlik, *The Origins of Chinese Communism* (New York: Oxford University Press, 1989), esp. pp. 74–94; Hung-yok Ip, "The Origins of Chinese Communism: A New Interpretation," *Modern China* vol. 20, no. 1 (January 1994), pp. 34–63; Peter Zarrow, *Anarchism and Chinese Political Culture* (New York: Columbia University Press, 1990); and Anna Gustafsson Chen, *Dreams of the Future: Communal Experiments in May Fourth China*, Ph.D. dissertation (Lund: Lund University, 1998).

35 See Marilyn A. Levine, *The Found Generation: Chinese Communism in Europe during the Twenties* (Seattle: University of Washington Press, 1993).

36 Cited in Peter Zarrow, *Anarchism and Chinese Political Culture*, p. 214. See Edward S. Krebs, *Shifu: Soul of Chinese Anarchism* (Lanham, Md.: Rowman & Littlefield, 1998).

37 Shi Cuntong, cited in Anna Gustafsson Chen, *Dreams of the Future*, pp. 51–2.

## Part II: Nationalism and revolution, 1919–37

1 David Strand, "'Civil Society' and 'Public Sphere' in Modern China: A Perspective on Popular Movements in Beijing, 1919–1989," Working Papers in Asian/Pacific Studies (Durham, NC: Duke University Press, 1990).

2 David Strand, *Rickshaw Beijing: City People and Politics in the 1920s* (Berkeley: University of California Press, 1989), p. 168.

## 8 Politics and culture in the May Fourth movement

1 Cited in John Fitzgerald, *Awakening China: Politics, Culture, and Class in the Nationalist Revolution* (Stanford: Stanford University Press, 1996), p. 93. This statement was excluded from Mao's official works, presumably for neglecting the proletariat and peasants.

2 Lu Xun, *The Complete Stories of Lu Xun*, trans. Yang Xianyi and Gladys Yang (Bloomington: Indiana University Press, 1981), p. ix.

3 In Leo Lee's reading, the parable refers as much to the intentionality of writing, which awakens the author and a few of his readers out of their dark, private

inner worlds. Leo Ou-fan Lee, *Voices from the Iron House: A Study of Lu Xun* (Bloomington: Indiana University Press, 1987), pp. 86–8.

4  For a masterly description of the events of 4 May 1919, and most of the related issues of the 1917–21 era as well, see Tse-tsung Chow, *The May Fourth Movement: Intellectual Revolution in Modern China* (Stanford: Stanford University Press, 1967), especially chapter 4.

5  Kuang Husheng, "Wusi yundong jishi" [Factual account of the May Fourth movement] *Wusi aiguo yundong* [The May Fourth patriotic movement] (Beijing: Zhongguo shehui kexue chubanshe, 1979), pp. 493–4. Kuang later became an educator in Shanghai.

6  See Joseph Chen, *The May 4th Movement in Shanghai* (Leiden: E.J. Brill, 1971); Jeffrey Wasserstrom, *Student Protests in Twentieth-Century China: The Views from Shanghai* (Stanford: Stanford University Press, 1999).

7  Bryna Goodman, *Native Place, City, and Nation: Regional Networks and Identities in Shanghai, 1853–1937* (Berkeley: University of California Press, 1995), pp. 260–77.

8  Elizabeth J. Perry, *Shanghai on Strike: The Politics of Chinese Labor* (Stanford: Stanford University Press, 1993), pp. 70–1.

9  Cited in Tse-tsung Chow, *The May Fourth Movement*, p. 93.

10 Cited in Lloyd C. Gardner, *Wilson and Revolutions, 1913–1921* (Philadelphia: J.B. Lippincott, 1976), p. 107.

11 Ibid., p. 108.

12 Ibid., p. 107.

13 See Vera Schwarcz, *The Chinese Enlightenment: Intellectuals and the Legacy of the May Fourth Movement of 1919* (Berkeley: University of California Press, 1985), esp. chapter 2.

14 Recounted in Christina Gilmartin, *Engendering the Chinese Revolution: Radical Women, Communist Politics, and Mass Movements in the 1920s* (Berkeley: University of California Press, 1995), pp. 73–4.

15 Bryna Goodman, *Native Place, City, and Nation*, pp. 179–83.

16 Cited in Tse-tsung Chow, *The May Fourth Movement*, p. 127 (modified).

17 Mao Zedong, "The Great Union of the Popular Masses," trans. Stuart R. Schram, *China Quarterly* 49 (January/March 1972), p. 81.

18 Cited in Ono Kazuko, *Chinese Women in a Century of Revolution, 1850–1950*, trans. Joshua A. Fogel (Stanford: Stanford University Press, 1989), p. 101. See also Roxane Witke, "Mao Tse-tung, Women, and Suicide" in Marilyn B. Young, ed., *Women in China: Studies in Social Change and Feminism* (Ann Arbor: Center for Chinese Studies, University of Michigan Press, 1973); and Christina Gilmartin, *Engendering the Chinese Revolution*, pp. 26–7.

19 Amy D. Dooling and Kristina M. Torgeson, *Writing Women in Modern China: An Anthology of Women's Literature From the Early Twentieth Century* (New York: Columbia University Press, 1998), pp. 14–15.

20 For Ding Ling, see Tani Barlow with Gary J. Bjorge, ed., *I Myself am a Woman: Selected Writings of Ding Ling* (Boston: Beacon Press, 1989).

21 Amy D. Dooling and Kristina M. Torgeson, *Writing Women in Modern China*, p. 348.

22 Ibid., p. 106.

23 Ibid., p. 112.

24 John Fitzgerald, *Awakening China*, pp. 94–5.

25 Cited in Vera Schwarcz, *The Chinese Enlightenment*, p. 110.

26 Wen-hsin Yeh, *Provincial Passages: Culture, Space, and the Origins of Chinese Communism* (Berkeley: University of California Press, 1996). We return to women in the 1920s in Chapter 11.

27 Cited in ibid., p. 176.

28 Ibid., p. 183.
29 Leo Ou-fan Lee, *The Romantic Generation of Modern Chinese Writers* (Cambridge, MA: Harvard University Press, 1973).
30 Cited in Leo Ou-fan Lee, "The Romantic Temper of May Fourth Writers" in Benjamin I. Schwartz, ed., *Reflections on the May Fourth Movement: A Symposium* (Cambridge, MA: East Asian Research Center, Harvard University Press, 1972), romanization modified, p. 73.
31 Cited in David Tod Roy, *Kuo Mo-jo: The Early Years* (Cambridge, MA: Harvard University Press, 1971), p. 135.
32 See Andrew J. Nathan, *Chinese Democracy* (Berkeley: University of California Press, 1986); Vera Schwarcz, *The Chinese Enlightenment*, esp. pp. 286–302. We will examine these issues in more detail in later chapters as self-avowed nationalist leaders claimed more and more power.
33 See Frank Dikötter, *Sex, Culture and Modernity in China: Medical Science and the Construction of Sexual Identities in the Early Republic Period* (London: Hurst & Company, 1992); Lung-kee Sun, "The Presence of the Fin-de-Siècle in the May Fourth Era" in Gail Hershatter, *et al.*, eds, *Remapping China: Fissures in Historical Terrain* (Stanford: Stanford University Press, 1986), pp. 194–209; and Gail Hershatter, "Sexing Modern China" in ibid., pp. 77–93.
34 Matthew Sommer, "The Penetrated Male in Late Imperial China: Judicial Constructions and Social Stigma," *Modern China* vol. 23, no. 2 (April 1997), pp. 140–80; elite traditions are discussed in Bret Hinsch, *Passions of the Cut Sleeve: The Male Homosexual Tradition in China* (Berkeley: University of California Press, 1990).

## 9 National identity, Marxism, and social justice

1 Joseph R. Levenson, *Confucian China and Its Modern Fate* (Berkeley: University of California Press, 1965), 3:113.
2 Yüsheng Lin, *The Crisis of Chinese Consciousness: Radical Anti-traditionalism in the May Fourth Era* (Madison: University of Wisconsin Press, 1979).
3 Thomas A. Metzger, *Escape from Predicament: Neo-Confucianism and China's Evolving Political Culture* (New York: Columbia University Press, 1977), p. 17. For critiques of Metzger's project, see "Review Symposium", *Journal of Asian Studies* vol. 39, no. 2 (February 1980), pp. 237–90.
4 Cited in Jerome Grieder, *Hu Shih and the Chinese Renaissance: Liberalism in the Chinese Revolution, 1917–1937* (Cambridge, MA: Harvard University Press, 1970), p. 336.
5 Charles W. Hayford, *To the People: Jimmy Yen and Village China* (New York: Columbia University Press, 1990).
6 Cited in Jerome Grieder, *Intellectuals and the State in Modern China* (New York: The Free Press, 1981), p. 329.
7 Cited in Maurice Meisner, *Li Ta-chao and the Origins of Chinese Marxism* (New York: Atheneum, 1974), p. 106.
8 Arif Dirlik, *The Origins of Chinese Communism* (New York: Oxford University Press, 1989), pp. 23–59 (chapters 2–3).
9 The organizational aspects of the Party are discussed in Chapter 11.
10 Maurice Meisner, *Li Ta-chao*.
11 Cited in John Fitzgerald, *Awakening China: Politics, Culture, and Class in the Nationalist Revolution* (Stanford: Stanford University Press, 1996), p. 136.
12 Mao Zedong, "The Great Union of the Popular Masses," trans. Stuart R. Schram, *China Quarterly* no. 49 (January/March 1972), pp. 76–87.
13 Cited in Philip C. Huang, *Liang Ch'i-ch'ao and Modern Chinese Liberalism* (Seattle: University of Washington Press, 1972), p. 146.

14 Bertrand Russell, *The Problem of China* (London: George Allen & Unwin, Ltd, 1966), p. 194.
15 Guy S. Alitto, *The Last Confucian: Liang Shuming and the Chinese Dilemma of Modernity* (Berkeley: University of California Press, 1979); see also Hung-yok Ip, "Liang Shuming and the Idea of Democracy in Modern China," *Modern China* vol. 17, no. 4 (October 1991), pp. 469–508.
16 Chang Hao, "New Confucianism and the Intellectual Crisis of Contemporary China" in Charlotte Furth, ed., *The Limits of Change: Essays on Conservative Alternatives in Republican China* (Cambridge, MA: Harvard University Press, 1976), pp. 276–302.
17 Wm. Theodore de Bary, *et al.*, eds, *Sources of Chinese Tradition* (New York: Columbia University Press, 1960), 2:190, 188.
18 Lu Xun, *The Complete Stories of Lu Xun*, trans. Yang Xianyi and Gladys Yang (Bloomington: Indiana University Press, 1981), p. 73.
19 For a thoughtful study of Taixu and Buddhism in the Republican period, see Don A. Pittman, *Toward a Modern Chinese Buddhism: Taixu's Reforms* (Honolulu: University of Hawaii Press, 2001).
20 Arif Dirlik, *The Origins of Chinese Communism* and *Anarchism in the Chinese Revolution*; see also Peter Zarrow, *Anarchism and Chinese Political Culture* (New York: Columbia University Press, 1990), pp. 217–37.
21 Cited in Vera Schwarcz, *Time for Telling Truth is Running Out: Conversations with Zhang Shenfu* (New Haven: Yale University Press, 1992), p. 99.
22 "Taolun wuzhengfu zhuyi" (Discussing anarchism), *Xin Qingnian* 9.4 (1 August 1921). For an overview of the Communist–Anarchist debates, see Arif Dirlik, *The Origins of Chinese Communism*, pp. 234–44; Dirlik also discusses the Communist–Guild Socialism debate on pp. 225–34.
23 "Zhongguo wuzhengfutuan gangling caoan" (Draft provisions for Chinese anarchist groups), reprinted in Zhang Yunhou, *et al.*, eds, *Wusi shiqi de shetuan* (Societies of the May Fourth Period), 4: 267.
24 Cited in Paul A. Cohen, *History in Three Keys: The Boxers as Event, Experience, and Myth* (New York: Columbia University Press, 1997), p. 229.
25 Ibid., p. 243.
26 See Axel Schneider, "Between Dao and History: Two Chinese Historians in Search of a Modern Identity for China," *History and Theory* 35 (October 1996), pp. 54–73 and "Conservatism in Twentieth Century China," paper delivered at "The Role of the Republican Period in Twentieth Century China: Reflections and Reconsiderations" (Venice: University Ca' Foscari di Venezia, 30 June–3 July 1999).
27 Wang Fan-sen, *Fu Ssu-nien: A Life in Chinese History and Politics* (Cambridge: Cambridge University Press, 2000).
28 Chang-tai Hung, *Going to the People: Chinese Intellectuals and Folk Literature, 1918–1937* (Cambridge, MA: CEAS, Harvard University Press, 1985).

## 10 The rise of political parties

1 V.I. Lenin, *Imperialism, the Highest Stage of Capitalism* (Beijing: Foreign Language Press, 1975).
2 See Marie-Claire Bergère, *Sun Yat-sen*, trans. Janet Lloyd (Stanford: Stanford University Press, 1998), esp. pp. 259–76. Guangzhou politics in the period after 1917 is discussed in Michael Tsin, *Nation, Governance, and Modernity in China: Canton, 1900–1927* (Stanford: Stanford University Press, 1999); Ming K. Chan, "A Turning Point in the Modern Chinese Revolution: The Historical Significance of the Canton Decade, 1917–1927" in Gail Hershatter, *et al.*, eds, *Remapping China: Fissures in Historical Terrain* (Stanford: Stanford University Press, 1986),

pp. 224–41; and Wang Ke-wen, "Sun Yatsen, Wang Jingwei, and the Guangzhou Regimes, 1917–1925," *Republican China* vol. 22, no. 1 (November 1996), pp. 1–22.

3 Cited in Marie-Claire Bergère, *Sun Yat-sen*, p. 272.

4 Marie-Claire Bergère, *Sun Yat-sen*, pp. 277–8; Lü Fang-shang, "The Intellectual Origins of Guomindang Radicalization in the Early 1920s," *Chinese Studies in History* vol. 26, no. 1 (Fall 1992), pp. 3–41.

5 See John Fitzgerald, *Awakening China: Politics, Culture, and Class in the Nationalist Revolution* (Stanford: Stanford University Press, 1996), pp. 169–70.

6 Arif Dirlik, *The Origins of Chinese Communism* (New York: Oxford University Press, 1989); Bruce Elleman, *Diplomacy and Deception: The Secret History of Sino-Soviet Diplomatic Relations, 1917–1927* (Armonk, NY: M.E. Sharpe, 1997).

7 For the Chinese converts to Communism in Europe, see Marilyn A. Levine, *The Found Generation: Chinese Communism in Europe during the Twenties* (Seattle: University of Washington Press, 1993).

8 R. Keith Schoppa, *Blood Road: The Mystery of Shen Dingyi in Revolutionary China* (Berkeley: University of California Press, 1995).

9 Wen-hsin Yeh, *Provincial Passages: Culture, Space, and the Origins of Chinese Communism* (Berkeley: University of California Press, 1996).

10 Arif Dirlik, *The Origins of Chinese Communism*, p. 244.

11 Hans van de Ven, *From Friend to Comrade: The Founding of the Chinese Communist Party, 1920–1927* (Berkeley: University of California Press, 1991).

12 Marie-Claire Bergère, *Sun Yat-sen*, p. 315.

13 Cited in ibid., p. 323.

14 C. Martin Wilbur, "Military Separatism and Reunification, 1922–1937" in Ho Ping-ti and Tang Tsou, eds, *China in Crisis* 1, no. 1 (Chicago: University of Chicago Press, 1968), p. 227. Somewhat arbitrarily we may calculate that U.S.$100 = 180 yuan.

15 Cited in Henrietta Harrison, *Inventing the Nation: China* (London: Arnold, 2001), p. 184.

16 John Fitzgerald, *Awakening China*, pp. 294–5; for an incisive discussion of the Huangpu Military Academy and the GMD's armies, see pp. 290–313.

17 See Elizabeth J. Perry, *Shanghai on Strike: The Politics of Chinese Labor* (Stanford: Stanford University Press, 1993), pp. 69–129; Daniel Y.K. Kwan, *Marxist Intellectuals and the Chinese Labor Movement: A Study of Deng Zhongxia (1884–1933)* (Seattle: University of Washington Press, 1997); Jean Chesneaux, *The Chinese Labor Movement, 1919–1927* (Stanford: Stanford University Press, 1968), esp. pp. 376–8; and Ming K. Chan, "Labor and Empire: The Chinese Labor Movement in the Canton Delta, 1895–1927," Ph.D. dissertation (Stanford: Stanford University, 1975).

18 Cited in Elizabeth J. Perry, *Shanghai on Strike*, p. 250.

19 Cited in Daniel Y.K. Kwan, *Marxist Intellectuals*, p. 18.

20 Emily Honig, *Sisters and Strangers: Women in the Shanghai Cotton Mills, 1919–1949* (Stanford: Stanford University Press, 1986), pp. 202–17; Elizabeth J. Perry, *Shanghai on Strike*, pp. 60–4.

21 See Jeffrey Wasserstrom, *Student Protests in Twentieth-Century China: The View from Shanghai* (Stanford: Stanford University Press, 1991), pp. 95–145.

22 Jiang Guangzi, cited in ibid., p. 112.

## 11 Ideology and power in the National Revolution

1 Wm. Theodore de Bary, *et al.*, eds, *Sources of Chinese Tradition* (New York: Columbia University Press, 1960), 2:123.

2 Cited in Marie-Claire Bergère, *Sun Yat-sen*, trans. Janet Lloyd (Stanford: Stanford University Press, 1998), p. 378.

3  Ying-shih Yu, "Sun Yat-sen's Doctrine and Traditional Chinese Culture" in Chu-yuan Cheng, ed., *Sun Yat-sen's Doctrine in the Modern World* (Boulder: Westview Press, 1989), p. 98.

4  Wing-tsit Chan, *A Source Book in Chinese Philosophy* (Princeton: Princeton University Press, 1973), pp. 669–70.

5  Cited in John Fitzgerald, *Awakening China: Politics, Culture, and Class in the Nationalist Revolution* (Stanford: Stanford University Press, 1996), pp. 17–18, 215.

6  Cited in ibid., p. 85.

7  Wm. Theodore de Bary, *et al.*, eds, *Sources of Chinese Tradition*, 2:107.

8  Cited in Marie-Claire Bergère, *Sun Yat-sen*, p. 358 (modified).

9  Cited in John Fitzgerald, *Awakening China*, p. 11.

10  See Roy Hofheinz, *The Broken Wave: The Chinese Communist Peasant Movement, 1922–1928* (Cambridge, MA: Harvard University Press, 1977); Fernando Galbiati, *P'eng P'ai and the Hai-lu-feng Soviet* (Stanford: Stanford University Press, 1985); and Robert Marks, *Rural Revolution in South China: Peasants and the Making of History in Haifeng County, 1570–1930* (Madison: University of Wisconsin Press, 1984). Communist–peasant relations are discussed in more detail in Chapter 14.

11  R. Keith Schoppa, *Blood Road: The Mystery of Shen Dingyi in Revolutionary China* (Berkeley: University of California Press, 1995), pp. 95–126.

12  Cited in Fernando Galbiati, *P'eng P'ai and the Hai-lu-feng Soviet*, p. 306.

13  In Tony Saich, ed., *The Rise to Power of the Chinese Communist Party: Documents and Analysis* (Armonk, NY: M.E. Sharpe, 1996), p. 163.

14  In Yu-ning Li, ed., *Chinese Women Through Chinese Eyes* (Armonk, NY: M.E. Sharpe, 1992), p. 91. I am indebted here to Christina Gilmartin, *Engendering the Chinese Revolution: Radical Women, Communist Politics, and Mass Movements in the 1920s* (Berkeley: University of California Press, 1995); and Elisabeth Croll, *Feminism and Socialism in China* (New York: Schocken Books, 1978).

15  Wang Zheng, *Women in the Chinese Enlightenment: Oral and Textual Histories* (Berkeley: University of California Press, 1999).

16  Vera Vladmirovna Vishnyakova-Akimova, a translator attached to a visiting Russian delegation, cited in Christina Gilmartin, *Engendering the Chinese Revolution*, p. 154.

17  John Fitzgerald, *Awakening China*, p. 284.

18  Cited in Christina Gilmartin, *Engendering the Chinese Revolution*, pp. 68–9.

19  Wang Jianhong, cited in Christina Gilmartin, *Engendering the Chinese Revolution*, p. 57.

20  Christina Gilmartin, *Engendering the Chinese Revolution*, pp. 69–70.

21  Cited in Christina Gilmartin, *Engendering the Chinese Revolution*, p. 91.

22  As recounted to Emily Honig, *Sisters and Strangers: Women in the Shanghai Cotton Mills, 1919–1949* (Stanford: Stanford University Press, 1986), pp. 207–8.

23  See Harriet Evans, "The Language of Liberation: Gender and Jiefang in early Chinese Communist Party Discourse," *Intersection* no. 1 (September 1998).

## 12  The Northern Expedition and the rise of Chiang Kai-shek

1  See Harold R. Isaacs's meticulous if partisan 1938 account, *The Tragedy of the Chinese Revolution* (Stanford: Stanford University Press, 1961); supplemented by Bruce Elleman, *Diplomacy and Deception* (Armonk, NY: M.E. Sharpe, 1997); and, for an overview of the Northern Expedition itself, Donald A. Jordan, *The Northern Expedition* (Honolulu: University of Hawaii Press, 1976).

2  Cited in John Fitzgerald, *Awakening China: Politics, Culture, and Class in the Nationalist Revolution* (Stanford: Stanford University Press, 1996), p. 291.

3 Lu Xun, *Lu Hsun: Writing for the Revolution: Essays by Lu Hsun and Essays on Lu Hsun* (San Francisco: Red Sun Publishers, 1976), pp. 60–1.
4 See John Fitzgerald, *Awakening China*, pp. 171–9.
5 Chen Duxiu, in Tony Saich, ed., *The Rise to Power of the Chinese Communist Party: Documents and Analysis* (Armonk, NY: M.E. Sharpe, 1996), pp. 171–2.
6 John Fitzgerald, *Awakening China*, p. 256.
7 Lu Xun, *Lu Hsun: Writing for the Revolution*, p. 105.
8 Cited in Parks M. Coble, Jr, *The Shanghai Capitalists and the Nationalist Government, 1927–1937* (Cambridge, MA: CEAS, Harvard University Press, 1980), p. 35.
9 He Yingqin, cited in Lloyd Eastman, "Nationalist China during the Nanking Decade, 1927–1937" in *The Cambridge History of China*, vol. 13, Republican China, part 2 (Cambridge: Cambridge University Press, 1986), p. 118.
10 See John Fitzgerald, "The Misconceived Revolution: State and Society in China's Nationalist Revolution, 1923–26," *Journal of Asian Studies* vol. 49, no. 2 (May 1990), pp. 323–43.
11 This and the next two paragraphs are indebted to Liping Wang, "Creating a National Symbol: The Sun Yatsen Memorial in Nanjing," *Republican China* vol. 21, no. 2 (April 1996), pp. 23–63. See also Marie-Claire Bergère, *Sun Yat-sen*, trans. Janet Lloyd (Stanford: Stanford University Press, 1998), pp. 407–14; John Fitzgerald, *Awakening China*, pp. 1–15.

## 13 The Nanjing decade, 1928–37: The Guomindang era

1 Hung-mao Tien, *Government and Politics in Kuomintang China, 1927–1937* (Stanford: Stanford University Press, 1972), appendix A, pp. 185–7.
2 He Lian (Franklin L. Ho), cited in Lloyd Eastman, "Nationalist China during the Nanking Decade, 1927–1937" in *The Cambridge History of China*, vol. 13 (Republican China, part 2) (Cambridge: Cambridge University Press), 1986. p. 165.
3 Parks M. Coble, *Facing Japan: Chinese Politics and Japanese Imperialism, 1931–1937* (Cambridge, MA: CEAS, Harvard University Press, 1991).
4 Julia Strauss, "The Evolution of Republican Government," *China Quarterly* no. 150 (June 1997), p. 344; see also Strauss, *Strong Institutions in Weak Polities: State Building in Republican China, 1927–1940* (Oxford: Clarendon Press, 1998).
5 Hans van de Ven, "The Military in the Republic," *China Quarterly* no. 150 (June 1997), pp. 369–70; Parks M. Coble, *Facing Japan*.
6 Edward McCord, "Local Militia and State Power in Nationalist China," *Modern China* vol. 25, no. 2 (April 1999), pp. 115–41.
7 A. Pisarev, "State and Peasant in Republican China: Dilemmas of the Guomindang Agrarian Policy During the 1920s–1940s," paper delivered at "The Role of the Republican Period in Twentieth Century China: Reflections and Reconsiderations" (Venice: University Ca'Foscari di Venezia, 30 June–3 July 1999), pp. 5–7.
8 Lloyd Eastman, "Nationalist China during the Nanking Decade," p. 132; see also Parks M. Coble, *The Shanghai Capitalists and the Nationalist Government, 1927–1937* (Cambridge, MA: CEAS, Harvard University Press, 1980).
9 Bryna Goodman, "Creating Civic Ground: Public Maneuverings and the State in Nanjing Decade" in Gail Hershatter, *et al.*, eds, *Remapping China: Fissures in Historical Terrain* (Stanford: Stanford University Press, 1986), pp. 164–77.
10 This and the next two paragraphs follow Frederic Wakeman, *Policing Shanghai, 1927–1937* (Berkeley: University of California Press, 1995). For gangsters, see Brian Martin, *The Shanghai Green Gang: Politics and Organized Crime, 1919–1937* (Berkeley: University of California Press, 1996); for opium, Edward

*Notes*

R. Slack, *Opium, State, and Society: China's Narco-Economy and the Guomindang, 1924–1937* (Honolulu: University of Hawaii Press, 2001).

11 Jonathan Spence, "Opium Smoking in Ch'ing China" in Frederic Wakeman, Jr and Carolyn Grant, eds, *Conflict and Control in Late Imperial China* (Berkeley: University of California Press, 1975), p. 154.

12 Frederic Wakeman, *Policing Shanghai*, pp. 244, 260.

13 Julia Strauss, *Strong Institutions in Weak Polities*.

14 See Frederic Wakeman, "A Revisionist View of the Nanjing Decade: Confucian Fascism," *China Quarterly* 150 (June 1997), pp. 395–432; Lloyd Eastman, "Fascism in Guomindang China: The Blue Shirts," *China Quarterly* no. 49 (January/March 1972), pp. 1–31, and *The Abortive Revolution: China under Nationalist Rule, 1927–1937* (Cambridge, MA: CEAS, Harvard University Press, 1990).

15 William Kirby, *Germany and Republican China* (Stanford: Stanford University Press, 1984).

16 In a 1969 interview with Lloyd Eastman, cited in "Fascism in Guomindang China," p. 3.

17 Cited in Lloyd Eastman, "Fascism in Guomindang China," pp. 5, 6.

18 In addition to the sources cited above, see Arif Dirlik, "Ideological Foundations of the New Life Movement: A Study in Counterrevolution," *Journal of Asian Studies* vol. 34, no. 4 (August 1976), pp. 945–80.

19 Chiang Kai-shek, *China's Destiny*, trans. Wang Chung-hui (Westport, CT: Greenwood Press, 1947), p. 99.

20 In Wm. Theodore de Bary, *et al.*, eds, *Sources of Chinese Tradition* (New York: Columbia University Press, 1960), vol. 1, p. 140, romanization modified.

21 This is the conclusion of Thomas G. Rawski's review of available statistics, *Economic Growth in Prewar China* (Berkeley: University of California Press, 1989); see p. xxix and, for more detail, pp. 268–343. However, even Rawski's statistics do not support his claim that economic achievements were "considerable."

22 Zhongguo guomindang zhongyang zhixing weiyuanhui xuanchuan weiyuanhui, ed., *Zhongguo guomindang yi er san ci quanguo daibiao dahui huikan* (n.p.: 1934), p. 160.

23 See Xiaoqun Xu, *Chinese Professionals and the Republican State: The Rise of Professional Associations in Shanghai, 1912–1937* (Cambridge: Cambridge University Press, 2001).

24 Cited in Gail Hershatter, *The Workers of Tianjin, 1900–1949* (Stanford: Stanford University Press, 1986), p. 222.

25 Elizabeth J. Perry, *Shanghai on Strike: The Politics of Chinese Labor* (Stanford: Stanford University Press, 1993), pp. 95–103.

26 Cited in ibid., p. 74.

27 Louise Edwards, "From Gender Equality to Gender Difference: Feminist Campaigns for Quotas for Women in Politics, 1936–1947," *Twentieth Century China* vol. 24, no. 2 (April 1999), pp. 69–105.

28 Kathryn Bernhardt, "Women and the Law: Divorce in the Republican Period" in Kathryn Bernhardt and Philip C.C. Huang, eds, *Civil Law in Qing and Republican China* (Stanford: Stanford University Press, 1994), pp. 187–214.

29 In *Shenbao*, 26 May 1935, cited in ibid., pp. 192–3.

30 Antonia Finnane, "What Should Chinese Women Wear? A National Problem," *Modern China* vol. 22, no. 2 (April 1996), pp. 99–131.

31 (1928); cited in ibid., pp. 115–16.

32 Louise Edwards, "From Gender Equality to Gender Difference," pp. 82–4.

33 Vera Schwarcz, *The Chinese Enlightenment: Intellectuals and the Legacy of the May Fourth Movement of 1919* (Berkeley: University of California Press, 1985), p. 198.

34 See Edmund S.K. Fung, *In Search of Chinese Democracy: Civil Opposition in Nationalist China, 1929–1949* (Cambridge: Cambridge University Press, 2000).

35 Cited in Jerome Grieder, *Intellectuals and the State in Modern China* (New York: The Free Press, 1981), p. 342.
36 Cited in Vera Schwarcz, *The Chinese Enlightenment: Intellectuals and the Legacy of the May Fourth Movement of 1919* (Berkeley: University of California Press, 1985), p. 203.
37 Cited in Edmund S.K. Fung, *In Search of Chinese Democracy*, p. 74.
38 Jerome Grieder, *Intellectuals and the State in Modern China*, p. 353.
39 Parks M. Coble, *Facing Japan*; John Israel, *Student Nationalism in China, 1927–1937* (Stanford: Stanford University Press, 1966); and Jeffrey Wasserstrom, *Student Protests in Twentieth-Century China: The View from Shanghai* (Stanford: Stanford University Press, 1991).
40 For Zhang Junmai, see Roger Jeans, *Democracy and Socialism in Republican China: The Politics of Zhang Junmai (Carsun Chang), 1906–1941* (Lanham, MD: Rowman & Littlefield Publishers, 1997), pp. 57–72, 97–117; for Shi Cuntong, see Wen-hsin Yeh, *Provincial Passages*, pp. 254–60.

## 14 Peasants and Communists

1 See Philip A. Kuhn, "The Development of Local Government" in *The Cambridge History of China*, vol. 13, Republican China, part 2 (Cambridge: Cambridge University Press, 1986) and "Local Self-government under the Republic: Problems of Control, Autonomy, and Mobilization" in Frederic Wakeman, Jr and Carolyn Grant, eds, *Conflict and Control in Late Imperial China* (Berkeley: University of California Press, 1975), pp. 257–98.
2 Thomas G. Rawski, *China's Republican Economy: An Introduction* (Toronto: University of Toronto–York University Joint Centre on Modern East Asia, 1978); Ramon Myers, *The Chinese Peasant Economy: Agricultural Development in Hopei and Shantung, 1890–1949* (Cambridge, MA: Harvard University Press, 1970); and Loren Brandt, *Commercialization and Agricultural Development in Central and Eastern China: 1870–1937* (New York: Cambridge University Press, 1989). For a somewhat more moderate approach, see David Faure, *Rural Economy of Pre-Liberation China: Trade Expansion and Peasant Livelihood in Jiangsu and Guangdong, 1870 to 1937* (Oxford: Oxford University Press, 1989). See also Daniel Little, *et al.*, "New Perspectives on the Chinese Rural Economy, 1885–1935: A Symposium," *Republican China* vol. 18, no. 1 (November 1992), pp. 23–176, for a critical discussion of the economic historians' debates.
3 Lucien Bianco, "Peasant Movements" in *The Cambridge History of China*, vol. 13, Republican China, part 2 (Cambridge: Cambridge University Press, 1986), pp. 270–328, and *Peasants Without the Party: Grass-roots Movements in Twentieth-Century China* (Armonk, NY: M.E. Sharpe, 2001).
4 Ramon Myers, "The Agrarian System" in *The Cambridge History of China*, vol. 13, Republican China, part 2 (Cambridge: Cambridge University Press, 1986), p. 257.
5 The latest date proposed would seem to be that of Thomas Rawski, who concludes that per capita output, income, and living standards rose through 1937. See *Economic Growth in Prewar China* (Berkeley: University of California Press, 1989), pp. 280–329.
6 For examples, see Joseph Esherick, "Number Games: A Note on Land Distribution in Prerevolutionary China," *Modern China* vol. 7, no. 1 (October 1981), pp. 387–411.
7 Masuko Teisuke, cited in Ramon Myers, "The Agrarian System," p. 231.
8 R.H. Tawney, *Land and Labour in China* (New York: Octagon Books, 1972), p. 70.
9 Pierre-Etienne Will and R. Bin Wong, *Nourish the People: The State Civilian Granary System in China, 1650–1850* (Ann Arbor: Center for Chinese Studies, University of Michigan Press, 1991).

10  Philip C.C. Huang, *The Peasant Economy and Social Change in North China* (Stanford: Stanford University Press, 1985), and *The Peasant Family and Rural Development in the Yangzi Delta, 1350–1988* (Stanford: Stanford University Press, 1990).

11  Philip C.C. Huang, *The Peasant Family and Rural Development*, p. 10, citing A.V. Chayanov.

12  Arif Dirlik, "Narrativizing Revolution: The Guangzhou Uprising (11–13 December 1927) in Workers' Perspective," *Modern China* vol. 23, no. 4 (October 1997), pp. 363–97.

13  Cited in ibid., p. 365.

14  For Trotskyism in China, see Gregor Benton, "Lu Xun, Leon Trotsky, and the Chinese Trotskyists," *East Asian History* no. 7 (June 1994), pp. 93–104; *China's Urban Revolutionaries: Explorations in the History of Chinese Trotskyism, 1921–1952* (Atlantic Highlands, NJ: Humanities Press, 1996); and the fascinating memoir *An Oppositionist for Life: Memoirs of the Chinese Revolutionary Zhang Chaolin* (Atlantic Highlands, NJ: Humanities Press, 1996).

15  Roy Hofheinz, *The Broken Wave: The Chinese Communist Peasant Movement, 1922–1928* (Cambridge, MA: Harvard University Press, 1977).

16  "Report on an Investigation of the Peasant Movement in Hunan" in Stuart Schram, ed., *Political Thought of Mao Tse-tung* (New York: Praeger Publishers, 1969), p. 250.

17  The main source for Mao's early life is an interview he gave to an American reporter in 1936. Edgar Snow, *Red Star Over China* (New York: Grove Press, 1961).

18  Ibid., p. 131.

19  Ibid., pp. 141–2.

20  Ibid., pp. 147–8.

21  In Tony Saich, ed., *The Rise to Power of the Chinese Communist Party: Documents and Analysis* (Armonk, NY: M.E. Sharpe, 1996), pp. 316–17.

22  Wen Rui, "A Study of the Land Revolution in the Central Soviet," *Chinese Economic Studies*, vol. 27, nos 5–6, and vol. 28, no. 1 (September–October 1994, November–December 1994, January–February 1995), pp. 5–96, 5–85, 6–95; Stephen Averill, "Party, Society, and Local Elites in the Jiangxi Communist Movement," *Journal of Asian Studies* vol. 46, no. 2 (May 1987), pp. 279–303; and James Polachek, "The Moral Economy of the Kiangsi Soviet," *Journal of Asian Studies* vol. 42, no. 4 (August 1982), pp. 805–29.

23  Cited in Wen Rui, "A Study of the Land Revolution" (I), p. 43.

24  Mao Zedong, *Report from Xunwu*, Roger Thompson, ed. and trans. (Stanford: Stanford University Press, 1990). Xunwu was a county seat in southern Jiangxi.

25  Wen Rui, "A Study of the Land Revolution" (I), p. 21.

26  The issues are outlined in Yung-fa Chen, "The Futian Incident and the Anti-Bolshevik League: The 'Terror' in the CCP Revolution," *Republican China* vol. 19, no. 2 (April 1994), pp. 1–51.

27  Hans van de Ven, "The Military in the Republic," *China Quarterly* no. 150 (June 1997), pp. 366–7.

28  Cited in Wen Rui, "A Study of the Land Revolution", (III), p. 56.

29  "Solemn Opening Remarks: Transcript of Chairman Mao's Remarks at the Second National Soviet Congress," *Mao's Road to Power: Revolutionary Writings, 1912–1949* (Armonk, NY: M.E. Sharpe, 1992), vol. 4, pp. 692–3. Cf. "Our Economic Policy" (1934), *Selected Works of Mao Tse-tung* (Beijing: Foreign Language Press, 1967), 1:143–4.

30  Wen Rui, "A Study of the Land Revolution" (III), p. 78.

31  In Stuart Schram, ed., *Political Thought of Mao Tse-tung* (New York: Praeger Publishers, 1969), p. 278.

32  In Stuart Schram, ed., *Political Thought*, pp. 270–1, romanization modified. Cf. "The Struggle in the Chingkang Mountains" (1928), *Selected Works of Mao Tse-tung*, 1:83.
33  In Tony Saich, ed., *Rise to Power*, p. 525.
34  William Wei, "Law and Order: The Role of Guomindang Security Forces in the Suppression of the Communist Bases during the Soviet Period" in Kathleen Hartford and Steven M. Goldstein, eds, *Single Sparks: China's Rural Revolutions* (Armonk, NY: M.E. Sharpe, 1989), pp. 34–61.
35  Lydia Liu, *Translingual Practice: Literature, National Culture, and Translated Modernity – China, 1900–1937* (Stanford: Stanford University Press, 1995), pp. 195–213.
36  See Perry Link, *Mandarin Ducks and Butterflies: Popular Fiction in Early Twentieth-Century Chinese Cities* (Berkeley: University of California Press, 1981), pp. 202ff.
37  See Yung-chen Chiang, *Social Engineering and the Social Sciences in China, 1919–1949* (Cambridge: Cambridge University Press, 2001).
38  Qian Junrui, one of Chen's researchers, cited in ibid., p. 204 (modified).
39  Written in 1923, cited in David Tod Roy, *Kuo Mo-jo: The Early Years* (Cambridge, MA: Harvard University Press, 1971), pp. 150–1. See Chapter 9 for Guo's pantheism.
40  Cited in Sun Lung-kee, "Out of the Wilderness: Chinese Intellectual Odysseys from the 'May Fourth' to the 'Thirties," Ph.D. dissertation (Stanford University, 1985), p. 25 (modified).
41  Cited in Ralph Croizier, *Art and Revolution in Modern China: The Lingnan (Cantonese) School of Painting, 1906–1951* (Berkeley: University of California Press, 1988), p. 113.
42  Leo Ou-fan Lee, "Literary Trends II: The Road to Revolution, 1927–1949" in *The Cambridge History of China*, vol. 13, Republican China, part 2 (Cambridge: Cambridge University Press, 1986), p. 424.
43  Vera Schwartz, *Time for Telling Truth is Running Out: Conversations with Zhang Shenfu* (New Haven: Yale University Press, 1992), pp. 145–9.

## Part III: War and revolution, 1937–49

1  The story is told in Li Zhisui, *The Private Life of Chairman Mao: The Inside Story of the Man Who Made Modern China* (New York: Random House, 1994), p. 568. True or not, Mao enjoyed making such "shocking" statements, and had said something similar to visiting Japanese Socialists in 1964.
2  Recent work on Manchukuo includes Louise Young, *Japan's Total Empire: Manchuria and the Culture of Wartime* (Berkeley: University of California Press, 1998); Prasenjit Duara, *Sovereignty and Authenticity: Manchukuo and the East Asian Modern* (Lanham, MD: Rowman & Littlefield, 2003), and Rana Mitter, *The Manchurian Myth: Nationalism, Resistance and Collaboration in Modern China* (Berkeley: University of California Press, 2000).
3  Tang Tsou, "Interpreting the Revolution in China: Macrohistory and Micromechanisms," *Modern China* vol. 26, no. 2 (April 2000), pp. 213–14.

## 15 The war of Resistance, 1937–45

1  Lucien Bianco, *Origins of the Chinese Revolution, 1915–1949* (Stanford: Stanford University Press, 1971), pp. 67–8.
2  In Stuart R. Schram, *The Political Thought of Mao Tse-tung* (New York: Praeger Publishers, 1969), p. 283.

3　Gregor Benton, *Mountain Fires: The Red Army's Three-year War in South China, 1934–1938* (Berkeley: University of California Press, 1992).

4　Parks M. Coble, *Facing Japan: Chinese Politics and Japanese Imperialism, 1931–1937* (Cambridge, MA: CEAS, Harvard University Press, 1991), pp. 334–74.

5　Joshua Fogel, "Japanese Travelers in Wartime China," paper delivered at the "International Symposium: Reassessing the Sino-Japanese War (1937–1945): New Sources and Interpretations," Historical Society for Twentieth Century China (Vancouver, 16–18 December 1995).

6　Cited in Frederic Wakeman, *Policing Shanghai, 1927–1937* (Berkeley: University of California Press, 1995), p. 277.

7　Cited in ibid., p. 281.

8　A recent set of more nuanced and critical essays is Joshua Fogel, ed., *The Nanjing Massacre in History and Historiography* (Berkeley: University of California Press, 2000). Also useful is Yang Daqing's thoughtful "Atrocities in Nanjing: Searching for Explanations" in Diana Lary and Stephen MacKinnon, eds, *The Scars of War: The Impact of Warfare on Modern China* (Vancouver: University of British Columbia Press, 2001). Iris Chang's *The Rape of Nanking: The Forgotten Holocaust of World War II* (New York: Basic Books, 1997) is sensationalized. There is considerable historical agreement that the death toll was somewhat over 100,000, almost certainly between 100,000 and 200,000.

9　Originally published in H.J. Timperly, *Japanese Terror in China* (New York: Modern Age Books, Inc., 1938); excerpted in Pei-kai Cheng and Michael Lestz, eds, *The Search for Modern China: A Documentary Collection* (New York: W.W. Norton, 1999), p. 327.

10　Paul Kennedy, *The Rise and Fall of the Great Powers: Economic Change and Military Conflict from 1500 to 2000* (New York: Random House, 1987), p. 302.

11　Cited in Akira Iriye, "Japanese Aggression and China's International Position, 1931–1949" in *The Cambridge History of China*, vol. 13, Republican China, part 2 (Cambridge: Cambridge University Press, 1986), p. 524.

12　Diana Lary, "Star Generals: Bai Chongxi and Cai Tingkai," paper delivered at "The Role of the Republican Period in Twentieth Century China: Reflections and Reconsiderations" (Venice: University Ca'Foscari di Venezia, 30 June–3 July 1999).

13　According to one investigation; Hsi-sheng Ch'i, "The Military Dimension, 1942–1945" in James C. Hsiung and Steven I. Levine, eds, *China's Bitter Victory: The War with Japan, 1937–1945* (Armonk, NY: M.E. Sharpe, 1992), p. 170.

14　Cited in Akira Iriye, "Japanese Aggression", p. 535.

15　Parks M. Coble, *Chinese Capitalists in Japan's New Order: The Occupied Lower Yangzi, 1937–1945* (Berkeley: University of California Press, 2003).

16　Chen Bijun, cited in Jiu-jung Lo, "Survival as Justification for Collaboration (1937–1945)," paper delivered at the "International Symposium: Reassessing the Sino-Japanese War (1937–1945): New Sources and Interpretations" (Vancouver, 16–18 December 1995), p. 3; modified.

17　David P. Barrett, "The Wang Jingwei Regime, 1940–45: Continuities and Disjunctures with Nationalist China" in David P. Barrett and Larry N. Shyu, eds, *Chinese Collaboration with Japan, 1932–1945* (Stanford: Stanford University Press, 2001); and Ke-wen Wang, "Portrait of a Puppet: The Final Years of Wang Jingwei, 1940–1944," paper delivered at "The Role of the Republican Period in Twentieth Century China: Reflections and Reconsiderations" (Venice: University Ca'Foscari di Venezia, 30 June–3 July 1999).

18　Cited in Ke-wen Wang, "Portrait of a Puppet," p. 4.

19　T'ien-wei Wu, "Contending Political Forces during the War of Resistance" in James C. Hisung and Steven I. Levine, eds, *China's Bitter Victory: The War with Japan, 1937–1945* (Armonk, NY: M.E. Sharpe, 1992), p. 70.

20 Christian Henriot, "War and Economics: The Control of Material Resources in the Lower Yangzi and Shanghai Area between 1937 and 1945," paper delivered at "The Role of the Republican Period in Twentieth Century China: Reflections and Reconsiderations" (Venice: University Ca'Foscari di Venezia, 30 June–3 July 1999).
21 Parks M. Coble, *Chinese Capitalists in Japan's New Order*.
22 Poshek Fu, *Passivity, Resistance, and Collaboration: Intellectual Choices in Occupied Shanghai, 1937–1945* (Stanford: Stanford University Press, 1993).
23 Elizabeth J. Perry, *Shanghai on Strike: The Politics of Chinese Labor* (Stanford: Stanford University Press, 1993), pp. 109–33.
24 Vera Schwarcz, *The Chinese Enlightenment: Intellectuals and the Legacy of the May Fourth Movement of 1919* (Berkeley: University of California Press, 1985), pp. 230–9.
25 Cited in Edmund S.K. Fung, *In Search of Chinese Democracy: Civil Opposition in Nationalist China, 1929–1949* (Cambridge: Cambridge University Press, 2000), p. 214.
26 William Kirby, "The Chinese War Economy" in James C. Hsiung and Steven I. Levine, eds, *China's Bitter Victory: The War with Japan, 1937–1945* (Armonk, NY: M.E. Sharpe, 1992).
27 Lloyd Eastman, "Nationalist China during the Sino-Japanese War, 1937–1945" in *The Cambridge History of China*, vol. 13, Republican China, part 2 (Cambridge: Cambridge University Press, 1986), p. 584.
28 Hsi-sheng Ch'i, "The Military Dimension," p. 179.
29 William Kirby, "The Chinese War Economy," p. 185.
30 The *Huaxi ribao* (West China Daily), 1944, cited in Lloyd Eastman, "Nationalist China during the Sino-Japanese War," p. 601.

## 16 Mao, Maoism, and the Communist Party

1 There is today a tendency to see Mao *only* as a mass murderer, and therefore to dismiss Maoism as not worth studying (or perhaps to denigrate its study as immoral). The first view is simplistic and the second illogical. For an example, see Ian Buruma, "Divine Killer," *The New York Review* vol. 47, no. 3 (24 February 2000), pp. 20–5. On the other hand, scholars have long recognized the importance of Mao's thought – some emphasizing its significance as a contribution to Marxism, others its role in shaping the Chinese revolution (monographs on Mao are listed in "Recommended Reading"). A solid brief introduction to Mao's early thought is Stuart R. Schram, "Mao Tse-tung's Thought to 1949" in *The Cambridge History of China*, vol. 13, Republican China, part 2 (Cambridge: Cambridge University Press, 1986), pp. 789–870; also interesting are Nick Knight, "*On Contradiction* and *On New Democracy*: Contrasting Perspectives on Causation and Social Change in the Thought of Mao Zedong," *Bulletin of Concerned Asian Scholars* vol. 22, no. 2 (April–June 1990), pp. 18–34, and "*On Contradiction* and *On Practice*: Pre-Liberation Texts*", *China Quarterly* no. 84 (December 1980), pp. 641–68.
2 The case for Mao's orthodoxy is argued by Nick Knight, "The Laws of Dialectical Materialism in Mao Zedong's Thought – The Question of 'Orthodoxy'" in Arlif Dirlik, Paul Healy and Nick Knight, eds, *Critical Perspectives on Mao Zedong's Thought* (Atlantic Highlands, NJ: Humanities Press, 1997), pp. 84–116; and by Paul Healy (on the post-1949 Mao), "A Paragon of Marxist Orthodoxy" in ibid., pp. 117–53.
3 Cited in Carl E. Schorske, *Fin-de-Siècle Vienna: Politics and Culture* (New York: Vintage Books, 1981), p. 134.
4 "On Practice", *Selected Works of Mao Tse-tung* (Beijing: Foreign Languages Press, 1967), 1:296–7 (my italics); see also Nick Knight, "*On Contradiction* and

*On Practice*: Pre-Liberation Texts"; and the discussion in Stuart Schram, "Mao Tse-tung's Thought," pp. 837–44.

5  "On Contradiction", *Selected Works of Mao Tse-tung*, 1:321–2.

6  "On Practice", in ibid., p. 300.

7  Frederic Wakeman, *History and Will: Philosophical Perspectives of Mao Tse-tung's Thought* (Berkeley: University of California Press, 1973), esp. pp. 238–73.

8  In Stuart R. Schram, ed., *The Political Thought of Mao Tse-tung* (emphasis added), p. 269.

9  "Talks at the Yenan Forum on Literature and Art," *Selected Works of Mao Tse-tung*, 3:73.

10  Stuart R. Schram, *Political Thought*, p. 179; from "Rectify the Party's Style of Work" – some of this passage is missing from the version in the *Selected Works*, 3:35–51.

11  This section is indebted to David E. Apter and Tony Saich, *Revolutionary Discourse in Mao's Republic* (Cambridge, MA: Harvard University Press, 1994).

12  In Gregor Benton and Alan Hunters, eds, *Wild Lily, Prairie Fire: China's Road to Democracy, Yan'an to Tian'anmen, 1942–1989* (Princeton: Princeton University Press, 1995), p. 80.

13  See David E. Apter and Tony Saich, *Revolutionary Discourse in Mao's Republic*, esp. pp. 263–93.

14  Michael Walzer, *Revolution of the Saints: A Study in the Origins of Radical Politics* (Cambridge, MA: Harvard University Press, 2000).

15  In Boyd Compton, *Mao's China: Party Reform Documents, 1942–44* (Seattle: University of Washington Press, 1952), pp. 108–9.

16  "Some Questions Concerning Methods of Leadership," *Selected Works*, 3:119.

17  Mark Selden, "Yan'an Communism Reconsidered," *Modern China* vol. 21, no. 1 (January 1995), pp. 8–44.

## 17  Revolution and civil war

1  Steven Levine, *Anvil of Victory: The Communist Revolution in Manchuria, 1945–1948* (New York: Columbia University Press, 1987), p. 8.

2  Elizabeth J. Perry, *Shanghai on Strike: The Politics of Chinese Labor* (Stanford: Stanford University Press, 1993), pp. 117–19.

3  Jeffrey Wasserstrom, *Student Protests in Twentieth-Century China: The View from Shanghai* (Stanford: Stanford University Press, 1991), pp. 168–70, 240–76, for this and the following paragraphs.

4  Jung Chang, *Wild Swans: Three Daughters of China* (New York: Anchor, Doubleday, 1991), p. 96.

5  Edmund S.K. Fung, *In Search of Chinese Democracy: Civil Opposition in Nationalist China, 1929–1949* (Cambridge: Cambridge University Press, 2000); and Young-tsu Wong, "The Fate of Liberalism in Revolutionary China," *Modern China* vol. 19, no. 4 (October 1993), pp. 457–90.

6  Zhang Xiruo, cited in Edmund S.K. Fung, *In Search of Chinese Democracy*, p. 254.

7  The standard study remains Suzanne Pepper, *Civil War in China: The Political Struggle, 1945–1949* (Berkeley: University of California Press, 1978).

8  Cited in Lucien Bianco, *Peasants Without the Party: Grass-roots Movements in Twentieth-Century China* (Armonk, NY: M.E. Sharpe, 2001), p. 233.

9  Ibid.

10  Philip C.C. Huang, "Rural Class Struggle in the Chinese Revolution," *Modern China* vol. 21, no. 1 (January 1995), pp. 114–17.

11  Wugong is the subject of the best socio-historical study of a particular Chinese village during the revolution to date. See Edward Friedman, Paul G. Pickowicz,

and Mark Selden, *Chinese Village, Socialist State* (New Haven: Yale University Press, 1991), pp. 40–4.

12 Yung-fa Chen, *Making Revolution: The Communist Movement in Eastern and Central China, 1937–1945* (Berkeley: University of California Press, 1986), p. 156.

13 In 1944 up to 27 percent of the revenues of the Shaan–Gan–Ning base area (in Shaanxi–Gansu–Ningxia provinces, centered on Yan'an) and in 1945 up to 40 percent came from opium sales. See Yung-fa Chen, "The Blooming Poppy Under the Red Sun" in Tony Saich and Han van de Ven, eds, *New Perspectives on the Chinese Communist Revolution* (New York: M.E. Sharpe, 1995), pp. 263–98.

14 Edward Friedman, *et al.*, *Chinese Village, Socialist State*, p. 41.

15 Joseph Esherick, "Revolution in a Feudal Fortress: Yangjiagou, Mizhi County, Shaanxi, 1937–1948," *Modern China* vol. 24, no. 4 (October 1998), pp. 350–3.

16 Ralf Thaxton, *Salt of the Earth: The Political Origins of Peasant Protest and Communist Revolution in China* (Berkeley: University of California Press, 1997).

17 Edward Friedman, *et al.*, *Chinese Village, Socialist State*, pp. 54–79ff.

18 Lucien Bianco, *Peasants Without the Party*, p. 237.

19 David Goodman, *Social and Political Change in Revolutionary China: The Taihang Base Area in the War of Resistance to Japan, 1937–1945* (Lanham, MD: Rowman & Littlefield, 2000), pp. 166–71, 194–200.

20 Zhai Ying, Director of the Liaoxian CCP committee Organization Department, cited in David Goodman, *Social and Political Change*, p. 99 (modified).

21 Kathleen Hartford, "Repression and Communist Success: The Case of Jin-Cha-Ji, 1938–1943" in Kathleen Hartford and Steven M. Goldstein, eds, *Single Sparks: China's Rural Revolution* (Armonk, NY: M.E. Sharpe, 1989), pp. 92–127.

22 Ibid., pp. 126–7.

23 Tie Yan, cited in ibid., p. 122 (modified).

24 Elizabeth J. Perry, "Moving the Masses: Emotion Work in the Chinese Revolution," *Mobilization: An International Journal* vol. 7, no. 2 (Fall, 2002), pp. 111–28.

25 Cited in Joseph Esherick, "Revolution in a Feudal Fortress," pp. 362–3.

26 Steven Levine, *Anvil of Victory*, esp. pp. 197–235. Joseph Esherick, "Revolution in a Feudal Fortress," also emphasizes the role of violence in land reform, especially during the civil war.

27 Ibid., p. 230.

28 Yung-fa Chen, *Making Revolution*, p. 18.

29 Philip C.C. Huang, "Rural Class Struggle," p. 120.

## Epilog

1 Jack Belden, *China Shakes the World* (New York: Monthly Review Press, 1970), p. 30 (romanization modified).

2 Theda Skocpol, *States and Social Revolutions: A Comparative Analysis of France, Russia, and China* (Cambridge: Cambridge University Press, 1979), pp. 252–81.

3 Skocpol applied this analysis to France (1789) and Russia (1917), as well as to China – see ibid., pp. 284–7.

4 Lucien Bianco, "Peasant Movements"; Elizabeth J. Perry, *Rebels and Revolutionaries in North China, 1845–1945* (Stanford: Stanford University Press, 1993).

5 John Fitzgerald, "The Republic of Sentiment – Representing the People in Modern China," paper delivered to the international conference on "The Construction of the Chinese Modern State," The Chinese Modern History Society (Nankang, Taiwan, 13–14 December 2002).

6 Liah Greenfeld, *Nationalism: Five Roads to Modernity* (Cambridge, MA: Harvard University Press, 1992).

7 The five stars of the PRC's flag are sometimes interpreted as references to the five peoples, but this was not the original intention.

8 The historian Pamela Crossley, *Translucent Mirror: History and Identity in Qing Imperial Ideology* (Berkeley: University of California Press 1999), shows how these identities, especially those of Manchu and Han, were established as a direct result of Qing policies in the eighteenth century.

9 Benedict Anderson, *Imagined Communities: Reflections on the Origin and Spread of Nationalism* (London: Verso, New Left Books, 1983).

10 Prasenjit Duara, *Rescuing History From the Nation: Questioning Narratives of Modern China* (Chicago: University of Chicago Press, 1995), p. 77, emphasizes that the common fight against imperialism began to define the nation in the 1930s and 1940s, but popular nationalism also had a class basis.

11 In this regard, see Chalmers Johnson, *Peasant Nationalism and Communist Power: The Emergence of Revolutionary China* (Stanford: Stanford University Press, 1962), which is overstated but still useful.

12 Gordon S. Wood, "Early American Get-Up-and-Go," *New York Review of Books* 47, no. 11 (29 June 2000), pp. 50–3.

13 Cited in Chang-tai Hung, *War and Popular Culture: Resistance in Modern China, 1937–1945* (Berkeley: University of California Press, 1994), p. 272.

14 David E. Apter and Tony Saich, *Revolutionary Discourse in Mao's Republic* (Cambridge, MA: Harvard University Press, 1994), esp. pp. 69–106.

15 Cited in ibid., p. 93; cf. Stuart Schram, *The Political Thought of Mao Tse-tung* (New York: Praeger Publishers, 1969), p. 65.

# Index